RED SOX NATION

The Rich and Colorful History of the Boston Red Sox

PETER GOLENBOCK

TRIUMPH
BOOKS

The Library of Congress has catalogued the previous edition as follows:

Golenbock, Peter, 1946–
    Red Sox nation : an unexpurgated history of the Boston Red Sox / Peter Golenbock.
    p. cm.
    Rev. ed. of: Fenway. New York : G.P. Putnam's Sons, c1992.
    Includes bibliographical references (p.) and index.
    ISBN 1-57243-744-8
    1. Boston Red Sox (Baseball team)—History. I. Golenbock, Peter, 1946–. Fenway. II. Title.

GV875.B62G67 2005
796.357'64'0974461—dc22

2005041746

This book is available in quantity at special discounts for your group or organization. For further information, contact:

Triumph Books LLC
814 North Franklin Street
Chicago, Illinois 60610
(312) 337-0747
www.triumphbooks.com

Printed in U.S.A.
ISBN: 978-1-62937-050-7
Page production by Patricia Frey

The author gratefully acknowledges permission from the following sources to reprint material in their control:

The Putnam Publishing Group for material from *Baseball As I Have Known It* by Fred Lieb. Copyright © 1977 by Fred Lieb.

Jonathan Schwartz for materials from "A Day of Light and Shadow," first published in *Sports Illustrated*, February 26, 1979. Copyright © 1979 by Jonathan Schwartz.

The Saturday Evening Post for material from three articles: "What's Wrong with the Red Sox?" by Harold Kaese, copyright © 1946 by *The Saturday Evening Post*; "They Called Me Crazy, and I Was" by Jimmy Piersall, copyright © 1955 by *The Saturday Evening Post*; "The Sad Case of the Red Sox" by Al Hirshberg, copyright © 1960 by *The Saturday Evening Post*.

The Trustees of the Boston Public Library for material from the Boston Tradition in Sports collection, Harold Kaese Archive.

Viking Penguin, a division of Penguin Books USA, for material from *Yaz* by Carl Yastrzemski and Al Hirshberg. Copyright © by Carl Yastrzemski and Al Hirshberg.

Dedication

This book updates the 2005 edition of *Red Sox Nation*. It adds a decade of turmoil and joyful success for Red Sox fans everywhere. And so it is with great pleasure that this book is now dedicated to Red Sox Nation, and especially my wife, Wendy Sears Grassi, a Chestnut Hill native; her sister, Heidi; her brother, Sam, and his wife, Sally; and my sister, Wendy, who lives in Roxbury; her wife, Cheryl, and their son, Max; my dear cousin, Douglas, and his wife, Chris; and my college roommate, Rich Hershenson, whose favorite player growing up was Don Buddin.

Contents

Acknowledgments

Red Sox Nation, which was first published in 1992 under the title *Fenway*, is the third in a team-history trilogy that began my publishing career in 1975 with *Dynasty: The New York Yankees 1949–1964* and continued with *Bums: An Oral History of the Brooklyn Dodgers*, published by G. P. Putnam's Sons in 1984. *Red Sox Nation*, which attempts to cover the history of the Boston Red Sox from the beginning, was particularly difficult to write economically because of the Red Sox' plethora of colorful players and remarkable events both on and off the field.

In *Red Sox Nation*, you won't find many descriptions of individual games other than the no-hitters, pivotal games at the end of seasons, and some World Series games. Given the choice between writing about the games and writing about the people who played them, I opted to concentrate on the participants and their relationships with each other. The Red Sox have been blessed with gods such as Babe Ruth, Ted Williams and Carl Yastrzemski, and subdeities such as Harry Hooper, Bobby Doerr, Johnny Pesky, Dom DiMaggio, Mel Parnell, Ellis Kinder and Dick Radatz. And then there are the men of tragedy, including Chick Stahl, Smoky Joe Wood, Big Ed Morris, Harry Agganis and Tony Conigliaro. *Red Sox Nation* is a compilation of stories of these men and many, many more. It is also about a team that is beloved by its fans, regardless of where it is in the standings. These fans, including the famous and the not-so-famous, are another element of this saga.

Dozens of Red Sox players gave their time and memories to this book. I owe each and every one of them a large debt of gratitude. Among them are Billy Rogell, Walter Shaner, Jack Russell, Milt Gaston, Bob Weiland, Doc

Cramer, Ben Chapman, Fabian Gaffke, Bobby Doerr, Dominic DiMaggio, Tony Lupien, Tex Hughson, Lefty LeFebvre, Eddie Lake, Frank "Red" Barrett, Eddie Pellagrini, Mel Parnell, Matt Batts, Walt Dropo, Frank Malzone, Gene Mauch, Pumpsie Green, Jerry Casale, Gene Conley, Eddie Bressoud, Dick Radatz, Dave Morehead, Dennis Bennett, Gary Bell, Russ Gibson, Darrell Brandon, Sparky Lyle, Gerry Moses, Ken Brett, Joe Lahoud, Bill Lee, Rick Wise, Jim Willoughby, Jerry Stephenson, Bernie Carbo, Sammy Stewart and Joe Sambito.

Among the civilians, my gratitude goes out to Glenn Stout, acting curator of the Boston Tradition in Sports collection of the Boston Public Library; the late Bernard "Dick" Casey; William Taylor and Neil Singelais of *The Boston Globe*; Dick Johnson, the head of the New England Sports Museum; Frank Gendreau Jr.; and John and Stuart Savage of The Sox Exchange. Also to John Marston, Monte Irvin, Mark Onigman, Jeffrey Lyons, Cleveland Amory, Roger Kahn, J. Anthony Lukas, David Margolick, Robert W. Parker, Roy Mumpton, Joe Cashman, Tack Burbank, Pat Jordan, Susan Turner, Julius Tygiel, Danny Frio, Dick Durrell, Richard Hershenson, John Updike and Mark Starr. And to Mike Menery—you left us too soon.

In the world of publishing, I wish to thank Charlie Hayward for signing the project initially. Also Phyllis Grann and Neil Nyren—sane, wonderful people to work with—and Jeffrey Mitchell and Glenn Stout (again) for their dedicated assiduousness.

And to Tom Bast and Mitch Rogatz of Triumph Books—you guys make my profession fun.

RED SOX NATION

CHAPTER 1

The Fans

It was late morning on a chilly October day in Boston, and the city was alive. In just a couple of hours, the hometown baseball team, once called the Pilgrims, or sometimes the Puritans or Somersets, but now called the Red Sox, would play in the seventh game of the 1912 World Series against the Giants from New York. The Red Sox led three games to two (that day's game was the seventh because there had been a tie). Everyone in Boston was confident that this would be the day of celebration.

Packed into a Boston bar called Third Base, the Royal Rooters, the most famous fans in America, were bending elbows, preparing for the game.

The Royal Rooters, three hundred strong, rabid and loyal fans of the Boston Red Sox, had been founded in the late 1890s by the owner of this Whittier Street bar, a short Irishman with a mustache named Michael "Nuf Ced" McGreevey.

McGreevey's bar was called Third Base because, McGreevey liked to say, "it was the last place you stopped before you went home." Outside, there had once been tethers to tie up the horses and carriages. By 1912, automobiles were taking over the streets. In the window was placed the daily score sheet, and a crowd of curious fans would stand around and discuss the latest results before pushing through the swinging doors and entering.

Inside, the din was continuous, as the Irishmen would argue politics and sports, women and finance, but mainly sports, second-guessing, recriminating, their strident arguments echoing through the bar, until finally, through the cacophony of voices, the florid-faced McGreevey, his mustache quivering, would holler out, "Nuf Ced," silencing the combatants long enough for them to bark orders at the bartenders for refills. That done, the clamor would begin once more.

Through the years, one customer McGreevey had trouble silencing was one of Boston's most influential, John F. (Honey Fitz) Fitzgerald, father of Rose and grandfather of John F. Kennedy. Fitzie was short and stout, loud and pugnacious, and for twenty years he had held court at Third Base, talking nonstop for hours. An active participant in the Royal Rooters, he had been voted to the state senate in 1892, and in 1910 been elected mayor of Boston.

One reason Honey Fitz was so successful was that by the turn of the century the Irish had begun to outnumber the Brahmins, Boston's Protestant aristocracy. His constituency and McGreevey's customers were the men who were Boston's waiters, house laborers, and dockworkers. They were the men who built Boston's roads, canals, railraods, and other public works, using their muscle and brawn. "Those aren't cobblestones," an Irishman once remarked, "they are Irish hearts."

The Brahmins looked down on the Irish, and the Irishmen, for their part, were equally contemptuous of the culture of Protestantism, thinking the somber, long-faced Yankees to be "narrow of soul" and gloomy in demeanor. The Irish joined together in societies and political and social clubs, and in saloons like Third Base, celebrating their fellowship and rooting for sports teams, especially the Boston Pilgrims.

Even before the turn of the century, baseball had become an Irish passion. Part of the reason for such zeal was that many of the early top professional players had been Irishmen. John McGraw, Hughie Jennings, Connie Mack, Ed Delahanty, and Roger Bresnahan, all early stars, were adored by their Irish fans. In Boston, the National League team's roster included such notables as Dan Brouthers, Tommy McCarthy, Hugh Duffy, Cozy Dolan, and Bill Dinneen.

Boston's biggest nineteenth-century baseball hero was the son of an Irish immigrant papermaker. His name was Michael J. "King" Kelly. In 1887, Chicago sold him to the Boston Beaneaters of the National League for $10,000, and immediately he became known as the "$10,000 Beauty." The song "Slide, Kelly, Slide" was written about him, and during the off-season the matinee idol appeared in a Boston theater reciting "Casey at the Bat."

In 1901, when Boston's American League team was founded, the Royal Rooters switched allegiance to the Somersets, the name of the new team before it was changed to the Pilgrims in 1903, and then the Red Sox in 1907. One reason was that the new team signed some of its best players from the old league—including Cy Young and Lou Criger of St. Louis, Chick Stahl, and Boston's favorite, Jimmy Collins, the best third baseman in baseball— and became a powerhouse. The other reason was that a Somersets ticket cost only half that of a visit to the Boston Beaneaters at the Walpole Street Grounds: a mere 25 cents against the Beaneaters' 50 cents.

The Royal Rooters made their presence felt at the very first World Series in 1903, when the Pilgrims played against the Pittsburgh Pirates. Their entrance into the park was not easily forgotten. Novelist John R. Tunis was waiting in line to buy tickets to one of the games in Boston's Huntington Avenue Grounds. In the distance, he heard the music signaling their arrival. When the Royal Rooters came into sight, they were wearing black suits with high white collars, blue rosettes pinned on their lapels.

"Each man had his ticket stuck jauntily in the hatband of his derby," said Tunis, and "at their head was the leading spirit, 'Nuf Ced' McGreevey."

The first three games were held in Boston, and the Rooters took the train to Pittsburgh for Game Four. McGreevey had wanted the Rooters to have an anthem to sing at the Series, and when he arrived in Pittsburgh, he sent Tom Burton, a piano player, to comb Pittsburgh music stores for a battle hymn. Burton found sheet music to a song called "Tessie," which had appeared in the musical comedy *Silver Slipper*. The tune was catchy and easy to sing.

> *Tessie, you make me feel so badly;*
> *Why don't you turn around?*
> *Tessie, you know I love you madly;*
> *Babe, my heart weighs about a pound.*
> *Don't blame me if I ever doubt you.*
> *You know I couldn't live without you.*
> *Tessie, you are my only, only, only.*

When the Pirates took a three-to-one lead in games, the Royal Rooters were despondent. They were looking for a key to beating the Pittsburgh team, and they were willing to try a lucky charm, an amulet, anything to change their luck.

They sang "Tessie" during Game Five, and as the sotted voices of the faithful filled the field, the Pilgrims scored. Was it perhaps the power of the song? they wondered. When the Boston team again came to bat, the Royal Rooters again broken into song. It seemed that every time they sang "Tessie" during the game, Boston scored. The Pilgrims won the game 11–2, and during the final three games, also won by Boston, the three-hundred-strong chorus again sang the tune over and over, becoming a torturous chorus for the Pittsburgh fans and their team. After the Pilgrims won the Series, the Boston players swore it was because the Royal Rooters had driven the Pirate players to distraction by incessantly singing that damned "Tessie."

The rabidness of the Royal Rooters continued to gain attention, until by 1908 McGreevey was known all over the country. His face even appears in early game programs, and he was asked to pose in the 1908 team photo. In 1909, during spring training, he presented second baseman Amby McConnell, the team's leading base stealer of the year before, with a $250 diamond ring.

That spring the athletic McGreevey was taking ground balls with the team during training when the owner of the Natchez minor-league ballclub asked Red Sox owner John I. Taylor to sell McGreevey to him.

"How much will you give me?" asked Taylor. He was offered $300.

"Done," said Taylor. The Natchez owner wrote the check. When the owner told McGreevey he had just bought him, McGreevey had to tell him he hadn't bought a ballplayer, but a fan.

By 1912, the Royal Rooters had become a Boston institution. The Red Sox, no longer the Pilgrims, were winners of Boston's second pennant that year, led by their splendid outfielders, Tris Speaker, Harry Hooper, and Duffy Lewis, and by Smoky Joe Wood, the winning pitcher in 34 ballgames. When the Red Sox returned from the road after clinching the pennant, 100,000 fans, led by the Royal Rooters, were there to greet them.

Around noon on that chilly October day of Game Seven, with the Red Sox leading three games to two and victory in the air, the Royal Rooters were in top spirits as they congregated outside Third Base for their raucous procession into the ballpark. Behind a marching band stood Mayor Fitzgerald, Michael McGreevey, and the three-hundred-strong corps. Their routine was to march to Fenway Park, enter through the center-field opening of the modern arena, and parade to their seats along the third-base line. The skies were overcast, but the Royal Rooters had spent the morning bracing themselves against the cold and were looking forward to watching their star pitcher, "Smoky" Joe Wood, lead their team to a triumphant ending in baseball's world championship.

In the Red Sox ticket offices, the treasurer of the team, Robert McRoy, was fretting. As he looked out his office window at the fans flocking into the stadium, he was guessing that this would not be a sellout. McRoy was in his first year as team treasurer. He had come aboard with James McAleer, the team's owner.

McRoy's discomfort stemmed from his not knowing what to do with the seats reserved for the Royal Rooters. The Royal Rooters had not arrived as yet, and McRoy was afraid that if the group didn't show because of the weather, he would be stuck with empty seats. McRoy made a decision. He decided that he "could not be sure that the Royal Rooters would have a large enough following to fill the section reserved for them," and so he ordered their seats sold on a first-come, first-served basis.

Joe Wood was warming up on the sidelines as the Royal Rooters, Honey Fitz at the lead, entered through the center-field gate behind their band and headed for their accustomed seats. When they arrived, there was a loud outcry and great confusion. The band music ceased when the Rooters discovered that the Red Sox management had sold their seats.

The Royal Rooters, not knowing where to go or what to do, massed on the field near the railing, refusing to move and blocking the view of the seat holders, whose mood turned ugly. Mounted police rode over, trying to force the Royal Rooters to disperse. Some of the police charged full gallop into the angry fans. Meanwhile, the spectators sitting in the third-base sections began bombarding both the cops and the Royal Rooters with peanuts, scorecards, canes, and other makeshift ammunition.

Heinie Wagner, the Red Sox shortstop, appealed to the Royal Rooters to remove themselves from the field, pleading that the Red Sox might have to forfeit if they didn't. When Wagner was told what had happened, he went and got manager Jake Stahl, who suggested that management find a spot for them in the grandstand. Nothing was done. Police had to forcibly clear the Royal Rooters off the field. They left, cursing all the way.

When the game finally began a half hour later, the Royal Rooters were sequestered in the wooden bleachers out in left field. They were still so rambunctious, they knocked down the railing separating the stands from the playing area. Meanwhile, back on the field, Joe Wood had stood around in the cold, waiting for the Royal Rooters to get off the field, and when he finally went out to pitch, his arm had tightened. He lasted one inning and was shelled for six runs.

After the game, the Royal Rooters stood outside the Red Sox offices singing "Tammany," the Giants' anthem, and booing the Red Sox management. Other Red Sox fans were in a similarly nasty mood over the treatment of the Royal Rooters. Cries were heard: "The hell with the Red Sox!" and "Who cares a damn whether they win or lose?" One newspaper compared the Boston police to Russian Cossacks working over Moscow citizens.

The next day, many Red Sox fans boycotted. Only 17,000 showed up for the game. Not a single member of the Royal Rooters attended. Nevertheless, Boston club executives acted amused in response to reporters' questions.

A Red Sox executive, probably McAleer, stated that he was certain the Royal Rooters would forget all about the snub over the winter and be as loyal as ever in the spring. "They always have," said the official.

It didn't even take that long. After the final game, won by the Red Sox when Joe Wood beat Christy Mathewson in relief, Mayor Fitzgerald got McAleer to apologize to the Royal Rooters. The apology was all that was necessary. On October 18, the city of Boston held a parade for their world champs. The Royal Rooters were at the head of the parade.

It was a lesson for Red Sox management. Whatever the indignities heaped upon their most loyal fans, team owners from then on could be sure they would be forgiven. And they were. Always.

CHAPTER 2

The New League

BAN JOHNSON GETS REVENGE

In 1893, Ban Johnson, a Cincinnati newspaper reporter, and Charles Comiskey, the player-manager of the Cincinnati baseball team, met at a local bar called the Ten-Minute Club (so called because someone at the table had to order a drink every ten minutes or else everyone at the table would be asked to leave). When they emerged, they had mapped out a plan to start a new league that eight years later would become the American League.

Ban Johnson's father was an educator, a scholar, and the editor of The World's Great Books, a massive 120-volume showcase of world literature. After going to Oberlin College, where his father taught, and then to Marietta College, Ban attended the University of Cincinnati Law School, but he quit for the money and excitement of becoming the sports editor of Cincinnati's *Commercial-Gazette*.

In 1890, the baseball players had attempted to band together to form a rival league—the Players League—but National League owners controlled who played in the big ballparks, dooming this upstart league to failure. Laced with strong satire, Johnson's columns often stung the National League owners with criticism of the National League's monopolistic practices. After one scathing column, John T. Brush, the owner of the Cincinnati team, angrily dared Johnson to "do something about it."

Challenged, Johnson sat down with Comiskey, Brush's own manager, to do just that, and out of their drinking session came what was at first called the Western League, made up of teams from the Midwest, including Grand Rapids, Sioux City, Minneapolis, Milwaukee, Kansas City, Toledo, Indianapolis, and Detroit.

Johnson became the president of the Western League, and during its six years of existence, he established himself as a man with an excellent business sense, as most of the teams made money. In 1899, Johnson changed the name of his league to the American League to give it a more national character. The league now consisted of franchises representing Cleveland, Chicago, Detroit, Minneapolis, Milwaukee, Kansas City, and Indianapolis.

In October 1900, the league was strong enough to declare itself a second major league, and it expanded eastward, adding franchises in Buffalo, Baltimore, Philadelphia, Washington, and Boston, while dropping Minneapolis, Kansas City, and Indianapolis.

A friend of Ban Johnson by the name of Charles Somers backed some of the new teams. Somers put up most of the money behind the Cleveland franchise, and he also helped start the Philadelphia and Boston teams. Comiskey backed the Chicago franchise, Connie Mack ran the team in Philadelphia, and John McGraw ran the Baltimore club. Johnson owned stock in both the Cleveland and Boston clubs (not until 1927 was ownership in more than one team prohibited).

On June 10, 1900, three delegates from each league met to form the Protective Association of Professional Baseball Players. Johnson agreed to respect all National League contracts, but he refused to be bound by the reserve clause in those contracts, which was interpreted by the National League owners to mean that when a contract expired, the team that owned the player had the right to sign the player for the following season. Johnson said it meant no such thing. The end of a contract was the end of a contract, he said. And so the American League clubs began offering the National League stars large salary increases to play in the new league. The players jumped leagues in droves. Of the 182 players in the American League in 1901, 111 were former National Leaguers.

By the end of 1902, Johnson had raided the National League so badly that the financially drained National League owners demanded a truce. When the truce was finally signed in 1903, the best club in organized baseball was playing in Boston, Massachusetts.

The stars of that team were Cy Young and Jimmy Collins. Young, whose name was Denton True Young, had been nicknamed "Cy," short for Cyclone, because after he once threw a couple of fastballs that damaged a wooden backstop, an observer mused that it looked as though the backstop had been "struck by a cyclone." Not much has been written about Young, the winningest pitcher of all time, except that he came from a farm and liked a swig or two of hootch before going out to pitch.

In any discussion of Cy Young, the most impressive words about him always relate to his statistics. They are simply amazing. No pitcher has pitched more innings (7,356), won more games (511), or lost more (315). No pitcher has more complete games (750).

Young's first year was 1890; that year he played only the last seven weeks and won nine games for the Cleveland Indians. In subsequent seasons before coming to Boston, he won 27, 36, 34, 26, 35, 29, 21, 24, and 26. In 1900 Young won 20 games for St. Louis, but was enticed by a $3,000-a-year contract offer to come to Boston. With the Pilgrims, he won 33 games in 1901, 32 in 1902, and 28 in 1903, when Boston won the first world championship.

Young was a large man for his era, six foot two and about 210 pounds, and as his record indicates, he was indestructible. He continued pitching for Boston through the 1908 season, hurling a perfect game against the Athletics in 1904, and when he finally retired in 1911, he was forty-four years old. He had never suffered from a sore arm. In his final big-league game, he was defeated 1–0 by a kid named Grover Cleveland Alexander.

Boston's other star, Jimmy Collins, revolutionized play at third base. He was the first modern third baseman, in that he charged the plate when he suspected a bunt was coming, and played an alert, mobile defense at third. The usual defensive technique for third basemen was to play back at a more-or-less fixed depth from one batter to another. Physically, Collins was not large. He was five foot nine and 180 pounds, but he was agile, and he could match wits with the era's craftiest managers and players.

In 1950, Connie Mack, who managed in the major leagues for fifty-three years beginning in 1894, chose Collins as his all-time third baseman. Said Mack, "He was one of the fastest men ever to step on a baseball diamond. He could hit to all fields and threw the ball like a jet-propelled rocket. I include him among the greatest baseball players I ever saw."

Behind Young and player-manager Collins, the Pilgrims won the American League pennant in 1903, and that fall they played the Pittsburgh Pirates in a set of games that would later be called the World Series. Despite the enmity of the senior National League owners, the series was played because the owner of the Pirates, Barney Dryfuss, had won an important concession from the American League owners: in exchange for the Nationals allowing a team to move to New York, the Americans promised not to place a rival team in Pittsburgh.

The negotiations to play the series were begun in August, when Dryfuss went to Henry Killilea, a Milwaukee lawyer who had bought the team from Charles Somers. Killilea went to his silent partner, Ban Johnson, to discuss their playing a championship series.

"What do you think of the idea, Ban?" Killilea asked.

"Do you think you can beat them?"

"They've got Honus Wagner, Clarke, and some other fine hitters, but Collins thinks he can stop them with Young and Dinneen," said Killilea.

"Then play them," Johnson said. "By all means, play them."

Dryfuss and Killilea agreed to play five games out of eight, splitting the gate, and because neither trusted the other, they stipulated that neither team could add a player after September 1 (which is still the rule today).

Each owner agreed to make his own deal with his players. Dryfuss had the foresight to end his regular-season contracts on October 15. The Pilgrim contracts ended on October 1. The series was to begin October 1. At first, the Boston players demanded the entire gate, but in the end they settled for an extra two weeks' pay and a small percentage of the gate.

After the series, won by the Pilgrims five games to three, Dryfuss donated his share back to the Pirates players.

Killilea was accused of "niggardly and skinflint" methods. Dryfuss and other Pirate officials were made to pay their way into the Boston park. Out-of-town sportswriters also had to pay. Some of the Boston tickets, moreover, found their way into the hands of speculators.

When the bad press continued through the winter, Ban Johnson, the power behind the league, forced Killilea out and arranged for the sale of the team to General Charles Taylor, owner-editor of the *Boston Globe,* and his son, John I. Taylor, the man who would change the name of the team from the Boston Pilgrims to the Boston Red Sox.

THE TURBULENT REIGN OF JOHN I. TAYLOR

On April 19, 1904, the *Boston Globe* reported the sale of the Boston franchise for a price "close to $150,000." According to the article, the twenty-nine-year-old John I. Taylor would do the running of the club, and would be "following the advice of manager Jimmy Collins."

What the *Globe* article didn't say was that General Taylor had bought the team for his "wild" third son to get him out of his hair and to give the boy something to do.

General Taylor, born in 1846, had grown up in the shadow of the Bunker Hill monument in the Charlestown section of Boston. At twenty-three, Taylor was already one of the top newspapermen in Boston, and in 1871, he founded a monthly magazine called *American Homes.* It was a great success until its offices were destroyed by fire the next year. Two years later, he was hired by the *Globe* to stop the paper from going under. The *Globe,* with a circulation of 10,000, was in danger of being driven out of business by the *Herald,* whose circulation was 115,000.

Taylor found a financial backer, and though he wasn't Irish, he astutely realized that Boston's Irish population was growing rapidly and needed a paper to champion its causes. Taylor changed the *Globe*'s editorial slant from Republican to Democrat, and to make the paper more affordable to Boston's blue-collar Irish workers, he cut the price to two cents and hired an Irish editor, E. C. Bailey. The *Globe* rose to prominence with its strong support of

Irish causes and candidates, and on May 20, 1874, the Boston Democratic Committee returned this loyalty, declaring that it was "the duty of every Democrat in Massachusetts to aid personally in increasing the *Globe*'s circulation and influence."

When Bailey retired in 1880, Taylor became editor and publisher, a title he held for forty-one years. An indication of Taylor's enormous success: the day after the presidential election of 1886, the *Globe* sold 424,230 papers.

General Taylor had three children. Charles H. Taylor, Jr. was on the board of the *Globe*. William O., the workaholic of the family, eventually took over the paper. John I. Taylor, however, never made it to the board. He started as a reporter, moved into the countingroom, and was put in charge of the want ads. But John I. wasn't as interested in newspapers as he was in sports and entertainment.

According to William Taylor, the current publisher of the *Globe,* "My granddad was an absolute nut about baseball." A *bon vivant,* John I. "knew John L. Sullivan and all the rest of the local celebrities, and he was a favorite of the next generation of Taylors because he would take them to Fenway Park. He had a damn good time and gave other people a damn good time."

Nevertheless, John I. was embroiled in controversy during much of his period of ownership. His first public dispute, which arose during his first year as owner, wasn't of his making. When the Pilgrims again won the American League pennant in 1904, the expectation was that the team would play the National League winner. But in 1904 the New York Giants were the winners, and the two most powerful Giants—John T. Brush, the owner, and John McGraw, the manager—were adamantly opposed to playing against a team from the upstart league.

Brush could not forgive the American League for putting a competitor, the Highlanders, into New York. He hated the Highlanders, hated Ban Johnson. And McGraw hated Ban Johnson as much as Brush did. When Johnson had owned and managed Baltimore, he'd suspended McGraw for insubordination. McGraw had jumped to the Giants, and Johnson refused to pay McGraw money owed to him, saying his unconditional release was his payment. When McGraw jumped, Johnson accused him of "treason." McGraw's reply was to call Johnson "an arrogant, overstuffed windbag."

Since late summer, Brush had been saying no to a championship series, in part because everyone had been expecting the New York Highlanders to be the American League winners. All along, Brush kept saying, "We will not play a series with the Invaders, no matter how the league races turn out." McGraw was equally hostile. "When we clinch the National League pennant," he said arrogantly, "we'll be champions of the only real major league."

The Highlanders ended up losing the pennant on the final day when New York's 41-game winner, Jack Chesbro, threw a wild pitch that allowed the winning run to score. The championship was Boston's. On October 11, 1904, Taylor sent the following telegram to McGraw:

Dear Sir—As the Boston club today won the championship of the American League, I challenge your club to play for the championship of the world. Of course, if you refuse to play, we hold the title by default, but I should prefer to win it on the diamond, in a series of five games or more.

The Giant players held a meeting and petitioned McGraw and Brush to let them play—the players wanted the money—but Brush replied, *Regret, we cannot meet you in any such series.*

In 1905, the Pilgrims finished fourth to Connie Mack's Philadelphia A's. No one had noticed that the team was getting old until it was too late. Internal dissension also plagued the team. In late December of that year, John I. Taylor was quoted in the papers denying trouble between him and his player-manager, Jimmy Collins, or between him and Ban Johnson.

About two weeks later, on January 10, 1906, a *Globe* headline proclaimed a move being made against John I. to drive him out of baseball. The article said that Taylor would be offered $125,000 for the team. The name of the purchaser was not revealed.

"If he refuses, he will forfeit his franchise right. Taylor will find himself out," said the article. The speaker was not named, but only one man was powerful enough to carry out such a threat: Ban Johnson.

The battle, it appears, was over who was to control the running of the team, John I. or manager Jimmy Collins. John I. had promised not to meddle and to let Collins run it, but it was apparent he hadn't kept his promise. Ban Johnson was lined up on the side of Collins. As stated in the article, Collins "has suffered a great deal of annoyance in the management of the affairs of the club through the activity displayed by John I. Taylor."

It continued: "Much of the erratic work of the club has been credited to this feeling, and there are stories to the effect that Taylor has been reproached for his failure to keep hands off and let the club and players alone.

"Nothing but internal dissension could operate to make any man release control of such a business prize. The players have been dissatisfied over John I. Taylor's attitude toward them. He is understood to have issued of his own volition the contracts calling for a general cut in salaries, without consultation of Collins, who disagrees with his views. The players have been grumbling ever since."

It was such dissatisfaction, the article reminded its readers, that caused some players to jump from the National League to the American.

The article also declared that there was a "coolness between Taylor and Collins the last few months. It has reached the acute stage. One or the other must go."

The article said the situation was being investigated by both Johnson and Connie Mack. Johnson and Mack met with Collins in his home in Buffalo to express their support. According to a witness at that meeting not identified in the newspaper article, Johnson is reported to have said, "Collins, the American League is back of you in this matter. You will be supported. There would have been no American League had it not been for a few men like you, and we are with you hook, line, and sinker."

Collins told friends that if John I. remained, he would go. The players pledged loyalty to Collins, who had won their hearts two years earlier when he had stood up to owner Killilea for a proper division of the world-championship receipts.

When asked to comment, Collins said, "It is no time for me to talk. If there is anything in the matter, the situation is in the hands of men higher in the affairs of the American League than I am."

From that article, it certainly looked as if John I. Taylor would be out, as Killilea had been out before him. But the next day someone evidently twisted Ban Johnson's arm—and hard. The hand of the powerful General Taylor certainly appears to have been at work, for Johnson declared, "Mr. Taylor's baseball holdings represent a very large investment, and he will receive the consideration from the organization which his pluck and enterprise justly merit him."

Nevertheless, in another article, Johnson predicted that Boston "will have a great team on the field next season with Collins in full control."

With Taylor and Collins fighting over who would run the Pilgrims, the team was in disarray. In 1906, the Pilgrims finished dead last with a 49–105 record. No championship team had ever dropped so far so fast.

The rift between Jimmy Collins and Taylor widened. Taylor was in the habit of ripping his players when they performed poorly, and so Collins tried to stop Taylor from coming into the clubhouse. But Taylor would wait in the runway to the clubhouse, and as the players walked by, he would berate them.

In the field, Collins, the peerless third baseman, was no longer fit to play every day. An ankle injury reduced him to part-time status. In June, Collins decided to step down as a player, much to the chagrin of Taylor, who ordered him to resume playing. Collins jumped the team and took a vacation without asking Taylor, who suspended him for a few days.

With eighteen games to go in the 1906 season, Jimmy Collins quit as manager. The man John I. Taylor chose to replace him was Chick Stahl, their former center fielder.

Stahl was to be the manager in 1907, but on March 26, he resigned unexpectedly. Stahl left the Little Rock spring training camp in a state of deep depression, and two days later he committed suicide in West Baden, Indiana.

One of the last men to see Stahl alive was "Nuf Ced" McGreevey, who declared that Stahl was "full of enthusiasm for the coming season" until the team reached Little Rock. "Almost from the moment we reached Little Rock, there seemed to be something on Stahl's mind. He grew moody and morose . . . Before and after the team had worked, he seemed almost in a trance.

"On the way to the grounds he sat alone in the team's private trolley car and said hardly a word to anyone. It was the same when the boys rode back to their hotel. Evenings at the hotel Stahl seemed to want to be alone, and even his old friend, Jimmy Collins, was not with him much of the time."

At her home at 39 Leon Street in Roxbury, Mrs. Stahl was prostrate with grief when she heard the news. She said she knew her husband was worrying about things, but that recently he seemed in better spirits.

Said teammate Fred Tenney, "To think that Chick should do such a thing, of all the men in the world. There never was a more merry fellow, always laughing and making fun. I cannot imagine that he had an enemy in the world."

Glenn Stout, Acting Curator, Boston Tradition in Sports collection, Boston Public Library: "Oddly enough, all through his life, Chick Stahl would come off with these off-the-wall comments that he was going to kill himself. Or, 'I may as well do away with it.' He was making comments about suicide back into the 1890s.

"It goes completely against the grain of the popular caricature that he was supposed to be this jovial, beer-drinking, hard-swinging lout. He was not quite the choirboy he was shown up to be. One time some woman tried to shoot him on the street because she wanted to marry him. He did drink quite a bit. There were several seasons where his weight ballooned and his average went down, and by the next fall he'd made a comment he was 'swearing off beer for the winter.'

"His suicide was always explained by his concern about the team. That's not what happened. What happened was that Chick Stahl had been going out with his wife for a long time. Julia Harmon was her name. And she lived right near the ballpark on Leon Street. They had gotten married in November of that year.

"On their honeymoon they went to Buffalo to see Jimmy Collins, and then something happened, because from what I was able to determine, Chick lived the rest of the winter in Fort Wayne, and she lived the rest of the winter in Boston.

"Harold Seymour and Al Stump wrote a story that he killed himself because of a Baseball Annie. Supposedly he had had a relationship with a woman in Chicago the previous year. What happened was that she got pregnant, and that next spring during spring training at Hot Springs, she started trying to blackmail him. Chick wasn't quite sure what to do with this. Now I don't know if his wife got wind of it over the winter or, and this is hearsay—I couldn't find any evidence of it—but I think he might have gotten a dose, and given it to his wife. That split them up. This other woman was on his case, and he couldn't do anything about it, so he drank carbolic acid, which he supposedly had on him because he was treating a stone bruise. If you look up carbolic acid, it's like Lysol, and back then it was used for treatment of open sores. Which could have been syphilis.

"Oddly enough, his wife, two years and a day to the day that they were married, was found dead in Boston under mysterious circumstances in the hallway of a house. That night she had been out drinking with four young men, two of whom were minors. She passed out drunk. They dumped her in a hallway. I think by that time she was a prostitute. And I think that she had syphilis too, 'cause she died of edema of the brain, which is also a symptom of syphilis.

"They had a benefit game for her and gave her all this money. But the way she was described when she was found dead, she was wearing purple, which was not a respectable color to wear, and they talked about her underwear in the newspaper story, the finest Irish lace. It's a great gothic story."

Immediately upon Stahl's death, the papers were championing Jimmy Collins's return as manager. Taylor went out of his way to deny that Collins would be back.

"It is odd that when a change is made on the team, Collins is always made manager by the newspapers," said Taylor.

Taylor lasted as head of the team for four more mediocre seasons, fighting Ban Johnson, the press, and suffering ridicule heaped on him for trading veterans like Lou Criger and Cy Young. But before he departed, he did several things that left an indelible impression on Boston baseball.

John I. Taylor started Ladies' Day in Boston, allowing women in free of charge on certain days. He changed the name of the team, declaring in 1907 that his players were to wear red socks and that in the future the Pilgrims were to be called the Red Sox. He sculpted the outfield of Duffy Lewis, Tris Speaker, and Harry Hooper, personally discovering and signing outfield stars Lewis and Hooper. And he did one more thing: he deserted Huntington Avenue Grounds and moved his team to a new ballpark of his own design, which he called Fenway Park.

CHAPTER 3

Fenway Park and the Series of 1912

The Birth of the Green Monster

In 1911, John I. Taylor announced he was building a new ballpark for the Red Sox. It would be located in an undeveloped area called the Fenway, close to Kenmore Square and only several miles from the center of downtown Boston. At the time, fans wondered why the team was moving from the Huntington Avenue Grounds. The answer: money.

The likelihood is that the man behind the move was John I.'s father, General Taylor. Ban Johnson was upset because of the rift between John I. and Jimmy Collins—and the negative publicity that resulted—and he was putting pressure on John I. to sell. The question became: how can we sell to our best advantage?

The Taylors' biggest liability in selling the Red Sox was that they did not own the Huntington Avenue Grounds. As long as they had to rent their field, buyers for the team would be limited and so would the asking price, because a new owner would also be at the mercy of the field's landlord.

At the same time the Taylors, under the name "Fenway Realty Company," owned a huge tract of undeveloped land in the Fens. By moving their team into a new ballpark built on their own property, the Taylors were not only making the land more attractive to buyers, but the club as well.

Before the construction of the park, the area was best known as being part of the Back Bay. The site of the ballpark had been a mud flat referred to as "the Fens," and the area surrounding the Fens was called Fenway. Once the Taylors let it be known that the new stadium would be called Fenway Park, the area immediately assumed a new identity in the minds of Bostonians.

The plan to move the team to Fenway Park paid off quickly. As soon as construction began and it was clear that the Taylors intended to complete the new park, they sold half their interest in the Red Sox, reportedly for $150,000—getting their original investment back while remaining owners of the ballpark.

The sale took place on September 16, 1911. The new part-owners were James McAleer, secretary of the American League and a close friend of Ban Johnson, and Robert McRoy. In a newspaper article the next day, Ban Johnson was quoted as saying, "Both are versed in baseball and have marked ability and they ought to greatly strengthen the organization."

Johnson was at the meeting announcing the sale. He "is in full sympathy with the new conditions," the article said. Johnson expressed "great satisfaction after the deal was closed to find a man of McAleer's experience connected with the local club."

In the interests of his league, Johnson had wanted John I. Taylor out and a baseball man to run the team. Taylor didn't want to go. This appears to have been the compromise.

When Fenway Park opened on April 9, 1912, the Red Sox defeated Harvard University in an exhibition game played during a snowstorm. In its major-league opener, Boston beat the Yankees 7–6 in eleven innings, as spitball pitcher Bucky O'Brien won in relief of Charles "Sea Lion" Hall (so called because of his deep voice).

The park was only partially finished at the time. There was a small section of center-field bleachers, but the bleachers in right had yet to be built and there were no stands at all down the left-field line. The area out beyond the right-field wall was a parking lot for cars during that season. (In fact, there was more parking for fans back in 1912 than there is today.) Not until the Red Sox got into the World Series of 1912 were the rest of the bleachers added.

When the park finally took shape, it featured a single-deck grandstand of steel and concrete. There were wooden bleachers in left, a right-field pavilion, and large wooden bleacher sections in extreme right and in center field.

The park was askew, built in seventeen facets, with walls and barriers breaking off at odd angles. The left-field fence was only 320½ feet from home plate down the line, and behind it was a high wall. The left-field turf sloped steeply from the wall toward the infield. The center-field fence was 390 feet away, and the right-field fence was only 313½ feet. (In the 1920s, the right-field fence was placed 358 feet from home plate, when a new bleacher section was built.)

Legend has it that the park was built with those dimensions because of the layout of the surrounding streets, and the fear that batted balls would strike nearby structures. But back in 1912, nobody ever hit the ball even as far as a fence. It was the dead-ball era, and the only home runs hit landed between the outfielders. If General Taylor had wanted to make his park symmetrical, he well could have. But first he designed the offices, and then he laid out the fences. Exactly where the fences were didn't matter, because, some experts say, they were constructed for one purpose: to keep out nonpaying fans.

The ten-foot embankment in left field was erected not to create excitement during a ballgame, but to make it easier for spectators sitting out there to see the action. On days when ticket demand was great, the ballclub sat the overflow crowd behind the left fielder. If the area had been flat, the fans in the back rows would not have been able to see over the heads of the fans in front of them. For the 1912 World Series, for instance, seats on the slope were made available. The cost was one dollar, the same as the left-field bleachers.

In later years, when more grandstand seats had been built and balls were regularly hit this far, the on-field seats were sold only in the rare event of huge crowds.

In 1934 owner Tom Yawkey removed the slope and erected a twenty-eight-foot high fence behind the left fielder, affectionately known as the Green Monster, or the Wall. It is part of the legend of Fenway Park, one of the holy shrines in American sports.

Roy Mumpton, sportswriter, *Worcester Telegram:* "I still think at the old strange ballparks, Fenway Park, Ebbets Field, which is the reverse, and Tiger Stadium, you get a much better ballgame. It sounds crazy, but you do. The games are never over until the last man is out, because you have that chance to win because of the park."

John Updike: "I had small kids for a while, and we used to go in together as a family, and though I have kept up, I have always lived in a suburb, maybe an hour away from the park. It's a headache to park around the park and sort of a headache to go in general, although once you're there, you're rewarded by the timeless American pastoral of those men in whites spaced out in that meadow. It is a wonderful thing, like entering into an Easter egg. Suddenly after the hassles and traffic jam and getting in, you do enter this world where peace and order is reigning."

Anthony J. Lukas, author, *Common Ground:* "Everybody always writes about the Wall and the size of the field and the way it hunches in, but the thing that is almost as much a symbol of Fenway Park as anything else is the Citgo sign in Kenmore Square. Over the left-field wall is this famous sign, large, flashing, neon. It's almost become a part of Fenway Park. It's the most beloved sign. A song has been written about the sign. A three-minute movie has been made of it.

"Particularly when you go there at night, that sign . . . it's too far away for even Jim Rice to hit with a ball, but it is part of the experience of going to Fenway Park.

"Also, I love the street that runs right by Fenway Park. There's something nineteenth century about that little thoroughfare, the way you come in off this little, tiny street right into that lobby. Every other stadium in this country you approach from a large parking lot with a huge facade. Here it's almost medieval. You come in off the street right into this dark, smelly warren of a lobby. It's great."

1912

There aren't many Red Sox fans alive today who were there when the Boston Red Sox won the 1912 American League pennant. Frank Gendreau, Jr., who was born in 1903, was the son of a Boston jeweler who did a lot of business with the Red Sox players back then. The elder Gendreau had a summer home on the beach at Hough's Neck in Quincy, about ten miles south along the shore from Boston. The Red Sox players used to drive their cars there after the games on Saturday or for the entire day Sunday, when playing baseball was prohibited in Boston. Frank Gendreau remembers an age that has long disappeared.

Frank Gendreau, Jr. (age 88): "My dad, I think, tried out with the Baltimore Orioles years ago, before the turn of the century. He was very friendly with the Red Sox players as a team. They were customers of his in those days, a lot of them, and they would come into the store at the corner of Summer and High streets and buy jewelry. One time, after the Sox won the pennant in 1912, at the old Fenway Park he presented the captain, Heinie Wagner, with a large loving cup as a gift from the fans before a game.

"They were always coming down to the beach to visit with us. I can remember Forrest Cady arriving in his Hupmobile and Dutch Leonard arriving in his Stutz Bearcat, and one of the other players had a Thomas Flyer. These were high-speed cars. And the players would come down and spend the day and have steamed clams. I used to go out in front of the house and dig up the clams.

"They used to play a little ball on our front yard, hit grounders to each other, and then I'd get out in a ten-foot rowboat and row a hundred, two hundred feet off shore, and they would pitch to each other, and they'd hit the balls into the bay, and I would row out and retrieve them.

"Then they would clean out all the liquor there was by late afternoon, and they'd head down to a well-known bar in Nantasket or go to Hough's Neck, which featured Taylor's ballroom, three dance halls, two bowling alleys, and also Crystal Lake, in front of the Pandora Hotel, with a bandstand in the middle, where the musicians used to play on the bandstand with the lake all around it. Hough's Neck was *the* place to go.

"Smoky Joe Wood seemed to be very close to me. I can remember one night in 1912—I was nine—it was announced that the Red Sox were going to be at Taylor's. When the locals knew that, it would bring a crowd down. Two or three streetcars at a time would be filled with people heading down there. And this one night Joe Wood was supposed to be watching me, and he lost me. The players were throwing baseballs at the African Dodger, and I was underneath the dance hall watching the bowling.

"The African Dodger got paid to duck baseballs. It was a very popular attraction with the players. They had a black fellow, and he would stick his head out of a piece of canvas, and the canvas was loose, so he had room to maneuver. I'd say this distance was about the same as from the pitcher to home plate. They'd get three balls for a quarter and they'd take the baseballs and try to hit the African Dodger in the head, and if they hit him, they got a prize.

"The trouble was the Red Sox players put a couple of them in the hospital. Because their heads weren't hard enough to stop those balls.

"Anyway, while the guys were throwing baseballs at the African Dodger, Joe Wood lost sight of me, and there was quite a commotion until they found me looking in the window of the bowling alley.

"We had a big Boston bulldog, and he used to drink beer with the players, and every once in a while one of them would spike the beer. One night they got the dog so drunk, when the dog wanted to go up the front stairs, he would start up and fall back down. We had to carry him upstairs to put him to bed. After that we kept an eye on the players.

"The players I can remember were Forrest Cady, a catcher, Smoky Joe Wood, Speaker, Duffy Lewis, Hooper I think, Dutch Leonard. My father and Forrest Cady were very close. Cady had never seen a clam before he came to Boston. I can remember the first time he ate them, he was pushing the clams around with a knife and fork, and he said, 'How the hell do you open these G.D. things?' My father had to show him. When those players left the team, which wasn't too many years after, that was the end of my relationship with the Red Sox. It was a long time ago. It sure was."

Joe Cashman, who was born in 1900 and grew up in South Boston, was a youngster who observed the 1912 Red Sox from a longer distance—a seat in the stands. What Cashman, who was a longtime Boston sportswriter, remembers best about that team was its incomparable outfield of Duffy Lewis, Tris Speaker, and Harry Hooper. It has been said that the three formed the greatest outfield of all time. They have become the standard for outfield play, much as Tinker to Evers to Chance defined infield play for the same period.

Joe Cashman: "The ball was different in those days. It wasn't lively like it is today. You never played near the walls. Few balls were hit out there.

"I don't think there was ever the equal of Tris Speaker going back for a ball. Speaker was a fifth infielder all the time. A base runner would be on second base, and that runner would look around and see the second baseman and then the shortstop, and the next thing he knew, Speaker would sneak in from center field and take the throw from the pitcher and pick him off. That's how shallow he played. There were balls hit over his head, but not many. He was uncanny the way he went after them. He would turn his back on the ball and run. He'd run to a spot, turn around, and catch the ball.

"The three of them could field, and they could throw. You couldn't run on them, couldn't take an extra base. Your life wasn't worth a nickel. Lewis was right-handed. Hooper batted lefty, but threw righty. Speaker was left-handed. Speaker started out as a right-handed pitcher. Down in Texas he broke his arm and had to learn to throw left-handed, and he became this great ballplayer. Funny thing about him: If you were going from first to third, and if he was in center field and he had the ball, he would get you out at third base. The ball leaving his hand would come toward the infield, you'd think it was crazy, but the ball would be coming directly toward second base, and when it got to second it would curve right down the line into the third baseman's hands.

"And the other guys? If you ever got hit by one of Lewis's throws right in the air, you'd get killed. Lewis, in left, never bounced the ball. It was in the air all the way. And Hooper played in a tough field. There was no night ball then. That right field was the worst in the country, for one reason. In Boston we had single-decked stands, and the sun would come in over the top, and Hooper had to play that sun field.

"All three were good base runners, and all could hit home runs. And they were consistent. I don't know why it was, but back then the players were much more consistent. Every single year you could bet your house on the first day of April on how the batting race would end: Ty Cobb, Eddie Collins, Tris Speaker. I remember one year Speaker won it and the other two finished two and three. But it was uncanny. Usually, it was Cobb, Collins, Speaker."

(The records show that Cobb, Collins, and Speaker finished one, two, and three only in the year 1914. However, it was rare during that decade that the three Hall of Famers weren't all in the top five.)

In addition to their outstanding outfield trio, the Red Sox of 1912 had another hero of legendary proportions. His name was Joe Wood.

Wood was born in 1889. At age sixteen he was paid twenty dollars a game to dress up like a woman and pitch for the Bloomer Girls, the most famous women's team of the day. He began his professional career pitching for the Hutchinson Salt Packers of the Western Association, and at age nineteen, in 1908, he played for the Kansas City Blues. That summer John I. Taylor bought him for the then-substantial sum of $7,000.

In his first three full years with the Red Sox, Wood won 11, 12, and 23 games. No one could have expected what he did in 1912: he compiled a 34–5 regular-season record with a 1.91 earned-run average. His pitching velocity was equal to that of the legendary Walter Johnson, whose American League record of 16 wins in a row was within Wood's grasp that year.

On September 5, 1912, Wood faced Johnson in one of the legendary pitching performances in baseball history. Johnson had the record. Wood had won 13 in a row. Could Johnson stop Wood and protect his record? Thirty thousand curious fans invaded Fenway Park that day to see which pitcher was superior. Thousands more were turned away at the gate.

Manville E. Webb, Jr., sportswriter: "The crowds packed the stands and the bleachers and trooped all over the outfield inside the stand and bleacher boundaries. In the grandstand the broad promenade was packed solid ten rows deep with fans on tiptoes to see what was going on. The playing field was surrounded completely by a triple, even quadruple, rank of humanity, at least 3,000 assembling on the banking in left field, and the mass of enthusiasts around in front of the huge concrete stand.

"So thickly were the spectators massed, and so impossible was it for the squadron of police to keep them back, that the players' pits were abandoned, the contestants bringing their war clubs out almost to the baselines."

The only run of the game came in the sixth inning. Speaker doubled past third, and Lewis hit an opposite-field high fly to short right field, which fell near the foul line. Washington outfielder Dan Moeller ran a long way for the ball, dove, got his fingers on the ball, but couldn't hold it. Speaker scored. Wood was credited with the victory that day, allowing him to continue to chase Johnson's record. He would later tie the record, but he did not break it.

The 1912 pennant was an easy one for the Red Sox. Under manager Jake Stahl, the Red Sox finished 14 games ahead of the Washington Nationals. Their World Series opponents were John McGraw's New York Giants, with their star pitchers Christy Mathewson and Rube Marquard, who himself had won 19 games in a row during the 1912 season.

The Giants knew that if they could beat Smoky Joe Wood, they could beat the Red Sox. Wood received a half-dozen death threats from Giant fans prior to the opening game. Each letter had a New York postmark. One letter was written in red ink, with a knife and gun drawn at the bottom of a sheet of paper. It read: "You will never live to pitch against the Giants in the World Series! We are waiting to get you as soon as you arrive in town."

Wood was unaffected. He beat the Giants in the first game. Wrote Damon Runyon: "When all is said and done, it was the chilled steel nerve of 'Smoky Joe' that lifted the Sox to a 4 to 3 victory."

The day after Wood won the opener, reporters cornered him in the lobby of the hotel and asked him for an interview.

"No," said Wood, "I have never given out an interview in my life and won't do it now or never!"

"Why?"

"It's a jinx. If I began talking and bragging about myself when I'm having a good year, then next season I would pitch rotten. I know, I tell you, and I am not going to say a word."

After a tie in Game Two and a Marquard win to tie the series, Wood won Game Four by the score of 3–1. In a column in one of the New York papers, Christy Mathewson wrote: "In spite of the fact that Wood beat us, I have nothing but admiration for Wood. His was the work of an artist."

In Game Five, Red Sox pitcher Hugh Bedient gave the Red Sox a three-to-one lead in games. After a one-day hiatus, Wood was scheduled to pitch Game Six in New York. One more win, and the Red Sox would be world champs. A typical performance from Wood would almost surely have done the trick. But there is suspicion that Red Sox owner James McAleer, who had arranged the Wood–Walter Johnson duel, didn't want the Series to end so quickly. Owner McAleer may have had his eye on the balance sheet as much as on the scoreboard. If the Red Sox were to lose Game Six in New York, with Wood resting on the bench, McAleer knew he would have one more huge gate in Boston, with Wood on the mound and 30,000 fans buying his tickets for the game.

McAleer's maneuvering may have almost cost the Sox the Series.

Sportswriter Fred Lieb was riding the train to New York with the Red Sox after Game Five. The Red Sox players, figuring Wood would be pitching Game Six, were confident of victory.

Fred Lieb: "There was jubilation in the two Pullman cars occupied by Red Sox personnel on the leisurely Sunday daytime trip to New York. They could smell the sweet scent of victory and those fat World Series checks. In the midst of the laughter in the first Boston car, Jim McAleer, president and part-owner of the club, stepped into the stateroom occupied by player-manager Stahl.

" 'Who are you going to pitch tomorrow, Jake?' asked McAleer.

"Stahl looked at his boss in surprise and said, 'Who else but Joe Wood?'

" 'Well, let's talk that over a bit,' said McAleer. 'Remember that Bucky O'Brien pitched real well in the third game. If he holds them to two runs again, I think we can win; and should he lose, it would give Joe another day's rest and he could finish it for us in Boston.'

"Stahl demurred. 'Why, all the boys are expecting Wood to pitch. Joe had told me he's ready and wants to pitch.' They discussed it some more. When McAleer left the stateroom he said, 'Think it over, but I think O'Brien deserves another chance. And remember, we always would have Wood available if we have to return to Boston.'

"There was a lot of bitterness and recrimination on the train when word spread around that Bucky O'Brien, not Wood, would pitch the Monday game in New York.

"Perhaps the feelings of his teammates upset O'Brien. He showed none of the stuff he had in Boston and was knocked out in the first inning [actually, he completed the first].

"There was more bickering and name-calling in the Boston cars of the Owl train sleeper to Boston. I heard that Paul Wood, Joe's brother, had a fistfight with O'Brien on the train and blackened one of O'Brien's eyes. Paul, expecting his brother Joe would pitch, had bet and lost one hundred dollars on the day's game."

The Red Sox still led three games to two going into Game Seven, but then came the incident in which McAleer and McRoy stripped the Royal Rooters of their customary seats. A riot ensued, Wood's arm tightened up, and the Giants won that one 11–4, to tie the Series.

By losing in Game Six, McAleer got a bonus. In addition to getting his gate for the game Wood pitched, he got yet another payday when he won a coin toss to determine the location of the final game. Unfortunately for him, only 17,000 fans showed up at Fenway because of their anger at the team's treatment of the Royal Rooters.

The final game has long been part of baseball's legendary past. There have been bizarre endings to World Series games, including Hugh Casey striking out Tommy Henrich to lose the second-to-last game in 1941 and the Red Sox losing to the Mets in the sixth game in 1986 on a ball that went through the first baseman's legs. This was a bizarre *final*-game ending.

Boston's Hugh Bedient and Giants legend Christy Mathewson were locked in a 1–1 duel after seven, and Wood came on in relief in the eighth. Harry Hooper had robbed Larry Doyle of a home run in the sixth inning when he threw himself back into an open-field box and, with some of the spectators holding him up, caught the ball in a prostrate position and grasped it tightly.

The Giants broke the tie in the first half of the tenth when Red Murray doubled and scored on a single by Fred Merkle.

New York needed three outs to be champions. Christy Mathewson was still on the mound. He induced the first Boston batter, Clyde Engle, to lift an easy fly to center fielder Fred Snodgrass.

Fred Lieb: "Any high schooler could have caught it with ease. The only possible excuse for Fred Snodgrass's finally dropping it for a two-base error was that he'd had too much time to think while the ball was in the air."

Duffy Lewis: "He [Mathewson] had us beaten when we came to bat for our last half of the tenth. A fly ball—the kind which most outfielders could take behind their back—landed in Fred Snodgrass's hands and bounced out. That started our rally. When the inning ended, we had sent two runs across the plate and Mathewson, McGraw's ace, was humbled.

"Mathewson left the park with drooping shoulders, but too much of a sport to blame anybody."

On the very next play after his mishandled fly, Snodgrass atoned by making a spectacular running catch of Hooper's long line drive, almost doubling Engle off second base. Mathewson then walked Steve Yerkes, a weak hitter, the potential winning run.

With runners on first and second, Tris Speaker lifted a high foul ball about five feet from the first-base coach's box. It was clearly Merkle's ball, but it was a windy day, and the wind had been playing tricks with foul flies. Giants catcher Chief Meyers came down from the plate to take it.

Fred Lieb: "Mathewson moved over just into foul territory, and I thought it was he who called out, 'Take it, take it, Chief, you take it.' I later learned it was Speaker who offered this 'advice.' Anyway, confusion reigned and the ball fell in foul territory in the middle of the triangle formed by Merkle, Meyers, and Mathewson.

"In returning to the batter's box, Speaker passed Mathewson and whispered, 'Matty, that play will cost you the game and the Series.'

"Tris then hit a long single to right, easily scoring Engle with the tying run and sending Yerkes to third."

Tris Speaker: "Merkle should have caught the ball, but Matty kept yelling for Meyers to take it. The old Chief was chasing the ball, and I saw he couldn't get it, and I was going to yell for him to keep after it too, but Matty was yelling so loud I didn't have to. Merkle couldn't go for it for fear of running into Meyers, and the ball fell in the coach's box.

"I singled, driving in the tying run, and took second on the throw to the plate."

*   *   *

Giants manager John McGraw ordered Mathewson to walk Duffy Lewis to set up the double play, and with the bases loaded and one out, Red Sox third baseman Larry Gardner hit a long fly to right, and Yerkes scored after tagging up.

Snodgrass's muff was recorded into the history books, even though it was the missed pop-up hit by Speaker that really cost the Giants the victory. Nevertheless, the Red Sox were 1912 world champs.

It was miraculous that the Red Sox won that final game and the 1912 World Series. The Red Sox would win three more World Series—in 1915, 1916, and 1918. After that, any luck the Red Sox would have would be bad. More than seventy years later, loyal Red Sox fans, always hopeful, inevitably disappointed, await another big break and another world championship.

CHAPTER 4

Good-bye, Smoky Joe; Good-bye, McAleer

THE EARLY DEMISE OF SMOKY JOE WOOD

Some major-league ballplayers are lucky. Many are not. Pitchers are the least lucky. Regardless of skill, every pitcher faces the same reality: the next pitch he throws may be his last.

In 1912, Smoky Joe Wood won 34 regular-season games and three more in the World Series, and was spoken of in the same category as Walter Johnson. Early in the 1913 season, Wood slipped from his exalted perch atop the baseball world, and would never regain it. In a game against the Detroit Tigers, he went to field a ground ball on wet grass, slipped, and fell on the thumb of his pitching hand. It was broken.

Joe Wood: "It was in a cast for two or three weeks. I don't know whether I tried to pitch too soon after that, or whether maybe something happened to my shoulder at the same time. But whatever it was, I never pitched again without a terrific amount of pain in my right shoulder. Never again."

Despite the pain, Wood pitched three more seasons for the Sox, winning 33 more games. In 1915, he led the league in ERA, with a 1.49. He quit

40

baseball at the end of the 1915 season, sat out a year, and in 1917 signed as an outfielder with Cleveland, a team managed by his best friend, Tris Speaker. In 1921, Smoky Joe batted .366. He retired in 1922 and for many years was coach of the Yale University baseball team.

Imagine how dominant the Red Sox teams of that decade would have been had Smoky Joe Wood not hurt his arm in 1913. Wrote Grantland Rice: "He might easily have been the greatest pitcher of all time if his arm had held up."

MCALEER'S DEPARTURE

Jim McAleer considered himself the managing owner of the Red Sox baseball team. He had the contract of sale to prove it. But in those days, one didn't own a club as much as one leased it from the league. It was your franchise—so long as you minded your own business, kept your nose clean, and didn't get in dutch with Ban Johnson, whose power over the American League owners was absolute.

Joe Cashman: "Eddie Collins was with the Philadelphia A's and was part of its Million Dollar Infield of McInnis, Collins, Barry, and Frank Baker. At the end of the 1914 season, Mack broke up the team, peddling them around to the highest bidder. Mack called up Collins one day and said, 'Eddie, I'm sorry. I had to let you go. I had to have the money. I just sold you for $50,000 to the Boston Red Sox.' Eddie told his wife, 'Honey, we're going to Boston.' She was a Massachusetts girl, and she couldn't have been happier.

"They got another call from Mack. He said, 'Eddie, I'm sorry. You can't go to Boston. You have to go to Chicago.' Collins said, 'What do you mean, I have to go to Chicago?' Mack said, 'Johnson called me up and said, "Listen, you can keep your ballplayers as long as you want. If you have to sell them, sell them, but you cannot sell Eddie Collins, the best second baseman in baseball, to a championship-caliber ballclub. They are strong enough now as it is. If we give them Collins, there will be no race. Collins goes to Chicago.' " That was all there was to it."

McAleer made a mistake when he underestimated Ban Johnson's power. Perhaps he thought he was secure because his partner, Bob McRoy, had been so close to Johnson. Perhaps he felt immune because he had managed Cleveland under Johnson when the new league was founded. Perhaps his new position brought with it blind arrogance.

McAleer's first big mistake had been to upset the Royal Rooters by selling their seats for the sixth game of the 1912 World Series. His second bumble had been in not immediately apologizing. His fatal blunder was in firing manager Jake Stahl early in 1913. Religious politics, something that would plague the Boston Red Sox through the years, apparently was at the heart of the issue.

Stahl had been Ban Johnson's choice as manager, part of the package when McAleer and McRoy had taken over the team. But as the 1913 season got under way, a split in the club arose along religious lines.

"Boston writers hinted at friction, and fans spoke of two factions on the club, the Masons and the K.C.," wrote Fred Lieb. According to Lieb, McAleer, McRoy, and some Catholic players, including Duffy Lewis, Harry Hooper, and Bill Carrigan, were lined up as part of the Knights of Columbus faction, and on the other side were the Protestant Masons, headed by Stahl and joined by Tris Speaker and Joe Wood.

Early in the season, a rumor was floated around Boston that Jake Stahl would be succeeding McAleer as the Red Sox president. An angry Jim McAleer called Stahl into his office and challenged him. Stahl told McAleer, "Jim, I'm too much your friend to say or think a thing like that. Besides, I have troubles of my own."

Things quieted down, and then in July, McAleer fired Stahl.

Joe Cashman: "In 1913, manager Jake Stahl was also the team's first baseman. The club got off to a bad start. Jake hurt his ankle and couldn't play. As the club was going from bad to worse, the team was in Chicago, and McAleer got on Stahl. They had a meeting and Jake told him, 'I can't play. If I could play, I would be out there. But I can't stand up. You think we're bad now? You should see us if I went out there and tried to play for us.'

"They were in the dining room of the hotel, and they kept arguing, and Stahl finally said, 'All right, you want me to resign?' McAleer said, 'Yes. Resign. You're fired.'

"McAleer got up and went over to the other corner of the room, where Bill Carrigan, the Red Sox catcher, was having breakfast. McAleer said, 'You're the manager of the club.' Carrigan said, 'Wait a minute. What do you mean, I'm the manager of the club? Where's Stahl? What's happened to him?'

"McAleer said, 'I let him go.'

"So Carrigan went over to talk to Stahl. Stahl said, 'That's all right, Bill. You take the club. Good luck to you. I'm through.'

"A couple of days later, McAleer got a call from Ban Johnson. Johnson said, 'The Red Sox are world champions. World champions don't fire their manager in the middle of the next season.'

"McAleer said, 'What are you going to do about it?'

"Johnson said, 'You'll find out what I'm going to do about it.'

"The Red Sox went through the season with Carrigan as manager, and at the end of the season, the American and National Leagues had barnstorming clubs that went to the Far East, to Honolulu and Japan. McAleer went along. On the way back, on a boat coming back to the mainland, McAleer got a telegram. It read, 'You have just sold the Red Sox to Joe Lannin.' It was signed, 'Ban Johnson.' McAleer never saw the ballclub after that. Johnson gave him the money from the sale, and that was it. That's the way Johnson ran things."

James McAleer's name didn't appear in the Boston papers for another twenty years. In the spring of 1931, McAleer became ill. On April 28, he put a gun to his head and pulled the trigger. The next day, he died.

CHAPTER 5

Enter the Babe; Exit Tris

Ban Johnson's newly anointed owner, Joe Lannin, came to Boston at age fifteen from Quebec, Canada, and began a career in the hotel business as a bellhop. At the time he bought the Red Sox, he was owner of substantial real estate holdings, including the Great Northern Hotel in New York City, the Garden City Hotel on Long Island, the Massachusetts House on Shelter Island, and apartment-house complexes in Boston.

Lannin had owned a piece of the Boston Braves, and he had tried and failed to buy the Philadelphia Phillies, when Johnson made the Red Sox available to him. In 1914, Lannin purchased McAleer's interest. Two years later, he bought out the Taylors.

Lannin's timing was poor. In 1914, the renegade Federal League, which attempted to become a third major league, was formed, and Lannin found he had to compete for players. The Federal League was to last two years and then fail, but while the new league was in operation, all American and National League owners had to dig deep to keep their players from jumping to the new league. Lannin's star, Tris Speaker, made $9,000 in 1913. To keep him, Lannin had to pay him $18,000 a year for two years. "What did I get into?" Lannin asked in dismay.

Though the competition with the Federal League cost Lannin money, he and his Red Sox also benefited. The Federal League had put teams into Baltimore and Buffalo, two strongholds of the farm-team International League. Because Lannin owned the Providence franchise of the International

League, it was in his best interest to keep his International League competitors solvent. In an attempt to keep the Baltimore franchise going, Lannin agreed to buy some players from owner Jack Dunn.

Dunn first had called Connie Mack, the owner of the Philadelphia A's, but Mack, who was going broke, told Dunn, "Sell [the players] to somebody who can pay you real money for them."

So on July 8, 1914, Joe Lannin bought three of Dunn's ballplayers for $8,000: catcher Ben Egan, pitcher Ernie Shore, and another pitcher, twenty-year-old George Herman Ruth, who brought with him from Baltimore the nickname "Babe." The first day Ruth reported to Baltimore, one of the coaches, a man named Steinam, had said, "Well, here's Jack's newest babe now." He was Babe from that moment on.

According to Joe Cashman, who was told the story by his close friend, manager Bill Carrigan, the Red Sox were out of the race, so Lannin sent Ruth down to Providence to help his International League club win the pennant. Ruth won nine games and led Providence to victory.

Joe Cashman: "Ernie Shore was two years older than Ruth and much farther advanced, especially up here in the head. Shore broke right into the lineup.

"The first game of both Ruth and Shore were shutouts. The next week, Ruth was sent to Providence.

"The next two years, the Red Sox were world champions. Ruth and Shore, Shore and Ruth."

At first, the two rookies roomed together. Soon thereafter, Shore called his manager and announced he was returning home to North Carolina. Carrigan asked what was bothering him.

"I can't live with that man Ruth," Shore said.

"Why, I thought you and Babe were friends," Carrigan said.

"That's right, we are," said Shore, "but there's a place where friendship stops. I told him he was using my toothbrush, and he said, 'That's all right. I'm not particular.' But that isn't all, Mr. Carrigan. A man wants some privacy in the bathroom."

In June of 1917, the two would combine to pitch the most unusual no-hitter in baseball history.

Ruth opened the game by walking Ray Morgan, the Washington Senators' leadoff batter. When home-plate umpire Brick Owens called the fourth ball, the Babe stormed toward home in a rage.

"Get back to the mound, or you're out of the ballgame," yelled Owens.

"If you chase me, I'll punch your face," Ruth said.

"You're out now," said Owens, whereupon Ruth swung a left at his head. Teammates rushed Ruth off the field.

Shore came in to pitch, and Morgan was thrown out stealing. Shore didn't allow another runner to reach base. Ruth was fined $100 and was suspended for ten days. The game went into the books as a perfect game for Shore.

In 1915, Ruth's record was 18–6. The Red Sox won the pennant. But if you look in the *Baseball Encyclopedia,* you'll notice that the only pitchers in Boston's four-games-to-one World Series victory over the Philadelphia Phillies were Rube Foster, Ernie Shore, and Dutch Leonard.

According to Joe Cashman, manager Bill Carrigan kept Ruth out of the 1915 Series to teach him a lesson.

Joe Cashman: "Bill Carrigan was a great manager. He knew human nature. He knew what you're supposed to do. And he purposely kept Ruth out of the World Series, deliberately, to show Ruth that Boston didn't need Ruth to win ballgames.

"Ruth was a fresh kid, running wild. Nobody could control him. Carrigan said to himself, 'I'll control him. I'll show him what kind of ballplayer he is.' And Ruth never forgot the lesson. He just sat there on the bench and watched the other guys play.

"Ruth was wild, but he wasn't any wilder than Dutch Leonard. When the Red Sox went on the road, Carrigan and his coach, Heinie Wagner, would have suites in the hotel. Carrigan and Leonard had one room and Wagner and Ruth were in the other room. Carrigan had to keep track of them, make sure they got in at night.

"Carrigan told me, 'I have a ballclub to run. I can't let these guys go out and get drunk every night. If they have to live with me, they won't.'

"Ernie Shore was the easiest guy in the world. The only trouble with Shore was that he wouldn't throw at batters. Carrigan told Shore, 'You have to throw at the batter if I give the sign.' He said, 'Mr. Carrigan, I've never thrown at a batter, and I won't start now. You can fine me anything you want. I will not throw at a batter.' Carrigan told me, 'What was I going to do? I couldn't do anything with him.' "

In 1916, the two star players of the Red Sox, Tris Speaker and Smoky Joe Wood, mysteriously were no longer Red Sox. History has recorded that Speaker was traded on the eve of opening day because Lannin didn't want to pay his high salary. Wood has said he quit the Sox in 1916 because of a salary dispute. Maybe.

There is evidence that Speaker and Wood may have left the Red Sox because, as non-Catholics, they didn't get along with their Irish Catholic teammates in Irish Boston.

Speaker, a Texan, was a member of the Ku Klux Klan. His best friend, Wood, was an Orangeman. Both were Masons. According to Dick Casey, who was a close friend of Duffy Lewis, Speaker in particular didn't hide his contempt for his Catholic teammates, including Babe Ruth, Lewis, and Hooper.

Babe Ruth and Speaker never got along during the fifteen years they were in the league together. Ruth was a well-publicized Catholic, even though his parents were both Lutherans. Neither Speaker nor Wood liked Ruth.

One day a ball got away from Wood and rolled toward Ruth. Wood called out, asking Ruth to stop the ball and toss it back. Like the big kid he was, Ruth bowed his legs comically and let the ball roll through them. Wood became angry, and Carrigan had to calm him down.

John Hooper, Harry's son, says he doesn't recall his dad ever having rough words about Speaker.

John Hooper: "My dad was on the quiet side. He wouldn't. But I remember my mother complaining that Speaker was quite a show-off—he'd catch a fly out there, and after he'd catch it, he'd throw the ball to Hooper and come on in, and she resented the way he acted.

"My dad was a leadoff hitter, you know. He'd get on base, and Speaker was third in the order, and Pop would be attempting to steal, and he would say, 'Every time I attempted to steal, why, Speaker would swing.' Speaker really spoiled a lot of his stolen bases.

"Another time, I remember Pop saying that the team got into a slump, and the manager changed the batting order and put Pop in third place and batted Speaker in first. After the first game, Speaker said, 'That will be all of that stuff, or else.' He didn't like that leadoff hitting position.

"Still, I never got the impression Speaker had any ill feelings toward my dad, and I have never experienced my dad saying anything, showing such feelings against Speaker.

"I met Speaker in later years in Beaumont when he came by, and he was in his usual white suit, white hat. He was always pretty dapper. I went up and introduced myself, and at that time my dad was not in the Hall of Fame, and Speaker made a quote that 'He sure belongs there. They will put him in someday.' "

According to historian Harold Seymour, however, Speaker and Hooper didn't speak to each other in all the years they played together. Speaker also feuded with Duffy Lewis. According to Joe Cashman, Speaker would deliberately knock Lewis's cap off to exhibit his "rapidly thinning" hair.

Duffy Lewis, the forgotten member of the outfield trio and the only one of the three not in the Hall of Fame, was lionized in Boston. His fans even wrote a poem about him, called "Lay On, Duffy." One verse will suffice:

> Old Duffy's No Duffer
> Not our slashing buffer
> He's there with the jazz in his mitt.

As a major league swatter
The fans simply gotter
Admit that he's making a hit.

Dick Casey was a close friend of Duffy Lewis. Lewis would sneak Casey onto the field before games and have his friend pitch batting practice to him. According to Casey, Lewis didn't like Speaker any better than Hooper did.

Dick Casey (age 92): "Tris didn't speak to Duffy or Harry Hooper for a whole season. Why? Because they were Catholics and he wasn't. And the owner of the Red Sox got $55,000 for Speaker, and because of it, Wood stayed out the whole season, wouldn't pitch, just because Tris Speaker was sold to Cleveland.

"Duffy was glad Speaker was traded. So was Hooper. They used to hate each other. Hate each other! That's why they had to get rid of Speaker. On the field he was terrible to them fellows. In the clubhouse he wouldn't speak to them at all, ignored them, moved his locker away from them over to another aisle. That's why he was traded, because he was making dissension on the team."

In 1913, McAleer had confronted Jake Stahl in what may have been a battle over religious differences, and as a result, Stahl was fired and Bill Carrigan hired. In 1916, it was two more Masons, Speaker and Wood, who would leave. The moves may have improved relations among the players, but trading Tris Speaker, one of the greatest outfielders in baseball history, certainly didn't endear management to its fans, Irish or otherwise.

Joe Cashman: "When we found out Lannin had sold Speaker, the Boston fans went crazy. But you know how lucky the Sox were? They won the world championship, so it didn't make any difference. Carrigan wasn't consulted about the deal. The team was going east from spring training, when Carrigan got a wire saying, 'Speaker has been sold to Cleveland.' He told me later on, 'You think I'm crazy to let Speaker go? He was my ballclub.' But they won without him. It showed what kind of guy Carrigan was. He won a world championship in 1915 without Ruth, and again in 1916 without Speaker."

Tris Speaker: "It was a pity. It was a young team. Every man on that '15 outfit played at least six more years of major-league ball, some of them ten, pitchers included. No telling how many pennants it could have won if it had been kept together."

* * *

Despite the success of the Red Sox in 1916, Joe Lannin became disenchanted with owning the team. The vituperation from the sale of Tris Speaker stung Lannin deeply. A bad call by an umpire late in the season set him off, and he accused the umpires of conspiring against his team. He was forced to apologize publicly for the remark. When Bill Carrigan retired, he was upset further. Bill had been his leader. His aggravation was making a heart condition worse.

After just three years, Lannin got out.

On November 1, 1916, he announced that he had sold the club to a three-man group headed by Harry Frazee, a well-known theatrical figure. The other two were Hugh Ward and G. M. Anderson. The price was announced at $675,000. "I had intended to sell out, and these gentlemen had the cash," said Lannin. Some of the cash, at any rate, because a hefty portion of the sale price was financed with notes from Frazee to Lannin.

Harry Frazee, like Lannin, had started out as a bellhop. He had worked in a hotel in his hometown—Peoria, Illinois—and then moved on to Chicago, where in time he purchased the Cort Theater. Later he added the Longacre Theater in New York, and like most theater owners, he became involved in mounting his own productions.

At the time Harry Frazee bought the Red Sox, he was flush. Charming, convivial, and shrewd, Frazee seemed to have a magic touch, though, as a Jew, he was viewed with suspicion by the Boston Brahmins and by Ban Johnson. Frazee was also a known associate of New York gamblers. He had promoted the Jack Johnson–Jess Willard heavyweight championship fight in Havana on April 5, 1915, and to this day there is a question whether or not the fight was legitimate.

On Broadway, however, Frazee was a power. Just prior to his purchase of the Red Sox, he had mounted a hit show, *Nothing But the Truth*. And though Ban Johnson was skeptical of letting Frazee own the team because of his questionable connections to gamblers, he finally agreed to allow the sale to go through.

Red Sox fans were looking forward to continued prosperity under Frazee. In his first month as principal owner, Frazee heard a rumor that the Washington Senators were thinking of selling Walter Johnson and had been offered $50,000 for him. Frazee called Clark Griffith and offered him $60,000. Griffith said no.

Joe Cashman: "When Frazee came in, there was no question about it: he didn't come here to wreck the Red Sox. People have that idea today. He didn't. He wanted a winner. He was a dyed-in-the-wool baseball fan, and he was trying to get a winner—until his financial difficulty came up."

CHAPTER 6

The Incomparable Ruth

KID AND PITCHER

There is no more colorful figure in all of sports history than George Herman "Babe" Ruth. His is an oft-told rags-to-riches saga: poor boy from Baltimore's tough streets, sent to St. Mary's Industrial School by parents who couldn't control him, raised by priests, signed at age eighteen to play for the local minor-league club, and before he was done, the number-one sports hero of all time.

One major reason for his lionization was that Babe Ruth didn't care what others thought of him. He didn't have a PR man. He didn't work on his image. He didn't try to hide his background. He was what he was, and if you didn't like him, well, that was too bad. Some of his teammates found him crude and crass, but his legion of fans didn't seem to care. He came from the wrong side of the tracks, and they loved him for it.

Babe Ruth: "My earliest recollections center about the dirty, traffic-crowded streets of Baltimore's riverfront.

"Crowded streets they were, too, noisy with the roar of heavy trucks whose drivers cursed and swore and aimed blows with their driving whips, at the legs of the kids who made streets their playground.

"And the youngsters, running wild, struck back and echoed the curses.

Truck drivers were our enemies; so were the coppers patrolling their beats, and so too were the shopkeepers who took bruising payment from our skins for the apples and the fruit we 'snitched' from their stands and counters.

"A rough, tough neighborhood, but I liked it.

". . . There I learned to fear and to hate the coppers. Perhaps it was there, too, that I learned to control my pitches. For tossing overripe apples or aged eggs at a truck driver's head is mighty good practice—although I don't recommend it to the boys of today."

Ruth came to Boston as a pitcher, and with the Red Sox the Babe became the best left-handed pitcher in the game. When manager Ed Barrow finally was convinced to allow Ruth to become an everyday player, he became "The Sultan of Swat," a world-renowned home-run hitter and the biggest gate attraction ever in sports.

Everything Ruth did appeared bigger than life. He was a sybarite of renown. He craved wine, women, and nourishment. His appetites for all three were what set him apart from less-chronicled stars. The Babe may have been vulgar, but it was always in a grand way.

Glenn Stout: "The late Bill Gavin used to tell me stories. He used to get Ruth his bootleg liquor at Johnny Igoe's drugstore on Huntington Avenue. He didn't like Ruth. Gavin said he was kind of nasty. Of course, he was just a clubhouse boy, and Ruth didn't have to cut him much slack.

"Gavin said that in Ruth's five years in Boston, regularly he was found drunk on the street, rolled by his 'friends' who he was running around with in the whorehouses. They'd take his money every night! And reportedly Carrigan would dole it out to him daily, because if you gave Ruth money in the afternoon, it would be gone by the next morning. He'd be in the street somewhere, and they would actually cart him off. In Bob Creamer's book, he mentioned that no one knew where Ruth lived in Boston. It never appeared in any directory. Or on the tax records. And sure enough, he isn't there, but that's because he was living wherever he put his hat that night.

"He frequented the area around Hemingway Street and what's now Symphony Avenue. It was a notorious red-light district beginning in the 1880s, and it's still full of streetwalkers. It's a real side of Ruth people know about but no one ever talks about."

Fred Lieb: "Just what kind of girls did Babe select as his favorite playmates? Mostly prostitutes, who in the 1910s and 1920s spoke of themselves as sporting girls. Ruth had telephone numbers of girls in all the big cities, and he knew the red-light districts of the smallest towns. Some of his visitors were semipros, bored women who came to him out of curiosity, and some were amateurs."

Bob Steele: "I was a coach at the University of Vermont and worked for Larry Gardner, who used to room with Babe Ruth on the Red Sox. Though a small man, Larry was a gifted athlete who played for ten years at third base with the Red Sox.

"Larry was once asked, 'What's it like to room with Babe Ruth?' Larry said, 'I don't know. He never unpacked his bags. He never stays with me in the room when I'm on the road. He's always living with women.'

"Larry said, 'One of the first times I saw Ruth, the guy was lying on the floor being screwed by a prostitute. He was smoking a cigar and eating peanuts, and this woman was working on him.' "

A retired Detroit police captain once phoned Fred Lieb to tell him about an experience he had had with Ruth:

"There was a house in my precinct that was regarded with some suspicion. I decided to investigate and rang the bell of the house.

"To my great surprise, one of the outstanding judges in our city answered the bell. He wasn't a little fellow, such as a police magistrate, but one of our most distinguished jurists. The house was well-lighted, and as I talked to the judge in the vestibule, Babe Ruth, with a nude girl riding on his shoulders, came down a flight of stairs. Both were singing loudly and joyously something like, 'Oh, what a gal! Oh, what a pal!' 'You wouldn't deprive the Babe of some of his fun, would you?' the judge continued with a laugh.

"I agreed to let the fun go on as long as Ruth was in town," the ex-policeman added.

Later in his career, Ruth was offered a three-year, $50,000-a-year contract, but in return he was asked to cut down on his drinking, late-night partying, and women.

Ruth said, "I'll promise to go easier on drinking, and get to bed earlier, but not for you, fifty thousand dollars, or two hundred and fifty thousand dollars, will I give up women. They're too much fun."

Constance Thomas, who was married to Fred Thomas, a third baseman for the Red Sox in 1918, well remembers Babe and his first wife, Helen.

Mrs. Constance Thomas (age 90): "Ruth was not so very well educated. He didn't save his money. He'd go out and spend it and run out of money, and the other ballplayers would have to lend him money. My husband, Fred, said Ruth used to go to amusement parks and take his whole paycheck and blow it, buying stuff for the kids, and he'd have to borrow money from other ballplayers to get back. He always took another ballplayer with him to help him get home.

"Ruth always paid them back. He was very honest, simple. He hadn't had much chance in life. Fred said he used to eat heavy. One time on the train, Fred and Babe each ordered a big steak and ate it. Babe said, 'I guess I'll order another one.' Fred said, 'Babe, you're going to die if you overeat like that.' Babe said, 'I have to die sometime.' He got another steak.

"Babe wasn't haughty. He didn't feel his talent was anything more than anyone else, as far as Fred could see. Fred said, 'Babe had the most wonderful eyes I ever saw. He knew just where the ball was going to come.' And he said, 'He not only hit them over the fences, he hit them over the houses.'

"Babe's first wife was very extravagant. She went out to the ballpark every day with a different hat on and stockings that were hand-beaded and new dresses. Everett Scott's wife was quite a good friend of hers, and she used to give her clothes and hats.

"Fred knew from the time he started baseball he was going to start a resort, and he bought a piece of property before we were married and saved his money until he got enough money to build, and then he quit baseball and built the resort. And every year the Scotts used to come up and visit, and Mrs. Scott would come, and I would say, 'Oh, Gladys, that's a pretty hat.' And she'd say, 'Babe's wife gave it to me.' "

With the Red Sox, Ruth was a left-handed pitcher. In 1915, he won 18 games, twice defeating Walter Johnson by the score of 1–0. In 1916 and 1917, he won 23 and 24 games, and as a part-time pitcher he still managed to win 13 games in 1918 and nine the following year.

In the second game of the 1916 World Series against Brooklyn, Ruth gave up a run in the first inning and then pitched thirteen innings of scoreless baseball for the victory. In the 1918 World Series against the Chicago Cubs, he pitched a 1–0 shutout in the first game, allowing six hits, and in Game Four, he pitched seven more scoreless innings—twenty-nine consecutive shutout innings, a record that was not broken until Whitey Ford beat his mark in 1961.

The Babe may have been a mound master, but by 1918, he was beginning to demand to play the outfield and to hit regularly. That year he batted .300, with 11 home runs. In 1919, he hit .322, with 29 home runs and 114 RBIs, while leading the American League in slugging percentage, home runs, home-run percentage, runs, and runs batted in.

Joe Cashman: "As a pitcher, Ruth was the best there was. In 1916, he won 23 games (1.75 ERA). He was the best left-hander in baseball. That's why I say he has to be the greatest ballplayer, everything considered. His pitching, his hitting, his drawing power. People who didn't see a ballgame, who didn't pay any attention to it, they went to see who the whole country was talking about. I don't know of anybody today where you went to a game to see one man.

"They went to see Ruth."

BABE MOVES TO THE OUTFIELD

In the winter of 1917–18, a significant number of Red Sox players, including Duffy Lewis, Ernie Shore, Herb Pennock, and manager Jack Barry, enlisted to fight in World War I. Owner Harry Frazee, in search of a new manager, chose the former president of the International League, Ed Barrow, a man known for his toughness. (As a youth in Des Moines, it was said, Barrow was put in charge of the newspaper delivery boys because he could beat them up if need be.)

Several years earlier, the existence of Barrow's International League had been threatened by the emergence of the new, outlaw Federal League, which had invaded territories and attempted to steal players. Barrow had used his influence and personal finances to help keep some of the International League franchises afloat against the stiff competition, and he'd also refused to compromise with the heads of the new league. Barrow wanted a battle to the death. He didn't want the new Federal League teams to be incorporated into the existing baseball structure. He wanted them ruined. And indeed, after two years of existence, the Federal League folded at the end of the 1915 season.

It would have been less costly to the International League owners, especially those not threatened directly by the Federal League, to make peace with the newcomers, and when Barrow refused to back down, he made enemies among some of his league owners, including former Red Sox owner Joe Lannin, who owned the Buffalo franchise at the time, and Jack Dunn, the owner of Baltimore.

When Dunn organized a block against Barrow that voted to reduce Barrow's salary from $7,500 to $2,500, Barrow quit as president.

Ed Barrow: "J. J. Lannin, who the year before had sold the Red Sox to Harry Frazee and now held the Buffalo franchise in the International League, piped up and said, 'That's fine. Good riddance!'

"I lunged for him and grabbed him by the coat lapels. Jim Price of the Newark club and Jim McCaffery of Toronto jumped in and held me.

" 'Don't hit him, Ed,' begged McCaffery, 'he's got a bad heart.'

"I didn't speak to Lannin again until 1923.

"As I stormed out of that meeting in the Imperial Hotel in December, 1917, I was in no mood to be friends with anyone. I came down the elevator and as I walked through the lobby, I saw Harry Frazee sitting in a chair, grinning like an impish kitten.

" 'Hello, Simon,' he said, still grinning. Frazee always called me Simon. 'I understand you just got fired.'

"I wasn't feeling funny.

" 'No, I didn't get fired,' I said. 'I quit.'

" 'Well, that's not so bad,' Frazee said. 'How would you like to manage the Red Sox?'

"I stopped fuming long enough to look at Frazee seriously. He had stopped grinning.

" 'Why, just to show those ———,' I said, 'I'd manage that team for nothing.'

" 'Well, you won't have to do that,' said Frazee. 'Come around to my office tomorrow morning when you're cooled off, and we'll talk it over.' "

When Barrow took over the Red Sox team at the beginning of the 1918 season, one of his toughest problems was to figure out where to play Babe Ruth. Ruth was his best pitcher, but he was also capable of hitting baseballs a long way. It had been that way ever since Ruth began playing pro ball.

Joe Cashman: "Casey Stengel used to tell a funny story about Ruth. Casey was playing for the Brooklyn Dodgers at the time. The Dodgers came up north from spring training, and they played the Baltimore Orioles of the International League in an exhibition game. Stengel was playing right field. Ruth was pitching the game against the Dodgers, and like most major leaguers, Stengel didn't pay much attention to the minor leaguers.

"Ruth got up, and Stengel said, 'He was a pitcher, and a minor leaguer, so I was playing him shallow, but I saw the way he swung the bat, looks pretty good, and I said to myself, this guy might be a fair hitter. He stands up there like a hitter, so I better not play him shallow, I better play him regularly.' He said, 'I stood there, and the ball went ten miles over my head.

" 'I chased it, and I came back to the bench, and the Dodger manager, Wilbert Robinson, said, "Where the hell were you playing?" ' Casey said, 'What do you mean, where the hell was I playing? I should have been in fifteen feet. The guy's a minor-league pitcher I never heard of. I'm supposed to play deep?'

"The next time Ruth came up, there was a guy named Hy Myers playing center field, so Casey went back not far from the fence, and he yelled to Myers, 'Do you think I'm deep enough now?' And Ruth hit one over his head, out of sight. Casey said, 'I never saw anything like it!' "

By the summer of 1918, Barrow and Ruth were at odds over where Ruth should play. Ruth wanted to play the field and hit every day, but with pitcher

Dutch Leonard having left the team to take a job in a Quincy, Massachusetts, shipyard, Barrow wanted Ruth to continue pitching full-time.

On July 1, Barrow chewed Ruth out for swinging at a bad pitch. "That was a bum play," Barrow said. Ruth replied, "Don't call me a bum, not unless you want to get a punch in the nose."

"That'll cost you five hundred dollars," said Barrow.

"The hell it will. I quit," said Ruth.

Ruth jumped the team. He wrote to the manager of the Chester Shipyards, asking what he would pay for him to play for his team, and was immediately scheduled to appear in Chester on July 4. Meanwhile, Ruth returned to his father's home in Baltimore, which is where Red Sox coach Heinie Wagner found him. It turned out Ruth had intended to play just one game for the shipyard. Wagner brought him back to the club before he got the chance. However, when Ruth returned, Barrow refused to speak to him, prompting Ruth to quit again, until Frazee got Barrow to back down.

Babe agreed to go back to being strictly a pitcher. He pitched one more game, and was sitting on the bench the game after when Barrow sent him up to pinch-hit. Ruth tripled in two runs to tie the game. The next day Ruth was in the outfield, and he stayed there until late in the season, when Barrow again asked him to go back out to the mound. He completed eight of his nine starts, winning seven games in little more than a month.

In 1918, Ruth pitched 20 games; he played 59 in the outfield and 13 at first base. He tied Tilly Walker of Philadelphia for the American League home-run lead with 11.

In the spring of 1919, Barrow was still wrestling with what to do with the multitalented Ruth. Ruth no longer wanted to pitch—at all. He wanted to play every day.

Early in spring training, Ruth was a holdout. Barrow told reporters his plan was for Ruth to "pitch and pinch-hit." Said Ruth, "I'll win more games playing every day in the outfield than I will pitching every fourth day."

The Red Sox were training in Tampa, Florida, when sports reporter Grantland Rice interviewed him in 1919. Ruth made it clear that though he may have been uneducated in terms of schooling, he was a Phi Beta Kappa when it came to understanding the mechanics of swinging a bat.

"Babe," Rice said, "I was watching your swing. You swing like no pitcher I ever saw."

"I may be a pitcher," said Ruth, "but first off I'm a hitter. I copied my swing after Joe Jackson's. His is the perfectest. Joe aims his right shoulder square at the pitcher, with his feet about twenty inches apart. But I close my stance to about eight and a half inches or less. I find I pivot better with it closed. Once committed . . . once my swing starts, though, I can't change it or pull up. It's all or nothing at all."

Years later, Ruth told Rice of the hard time his teammates gave him when as a pitcher he sought to take batting practice.

"I saw no reason why I shouldn't take my licks," Ruth told him. "I'd get them, usually, but there were times I'd go to my locker next day and find my bats sawed in half."

For his part in the making of baseball history—switching Ruth from a pitcher to a hitter—Ed Barrow takes full credit. But it would have been out of character for Barrow to have made such a radical move himself. Barrow was by nature a conservative man. He didn't take chances, especially with a property as valuable as Ruth. According to outfielder Harry Hooper, Barrow did switch Ruth to the outfield, but he did it kicking and screaming.

Harry Hooper: "It's a mistake to believe that Ed [Barrow] in his wisdom and farsightedness took Ruth out of the pitcher's box and put him in the outfield as a regular.

"He did it reluctantly and against his convictions. At the time, Everett Scott, Heinie Wagner, and myself formed sort of a board of strategy. Barrow relied largely on our judgment.

"Ruth came to me in the spring of 1919. He said he wanted to play the outfield. He thought he'd be more valuable to the club there than as a pitcher.

"The Babe kept after Barrow during the training trip. Ed didn't give him any satisfaction. Then, after the season started, we went to Ed. He gave in and put Babe in the outfield, and you know what the Bam did.

"Barrow's argument was reasonable. He protested he'd be crazy to take the best young left-hander in the league and make an outfielder out of him. He said he'd be laughed to scorn by the fans if the experiment failed.

"And I can recall Ed's words when he agreed. 'All right, I'll put Ruth out there, but mark my words, after the first slump he gets into, he'll come back on his knees begging to pitch again.'

"Ruth was always grateful to me for helping persuade Barrow to move him to the outfield."

According to Harry Hooper's son, John, there was another argument his father used to get Barrow let Ruth play every day: the lure of drawing more customers and making more money for the team. "Selling tickets to the fans was the important thing. Pop said to Barrow, 'Shoot, people come to see Ruth play. Play him every day. You'll have more people come.' And that's what happened."

Once the spring training of 1919 began, Barrow finally gave in, and Ruth became the Red Sox right fielder. In a spring exhibition game against the New York Giants, Ruth hit one home run 579 feet. Sneered Giants manager John McGraw, whose game strategy featured the bunt and the hit-and-run, "If he plays every day, the bum will hit into a hundred double plays before the season is over."

From then on during the spring, every time Ruth got a base hit, he yelled at the Giants' bench, "How's that for a double-play ball, Mac?"

In 1919, Ruth pitched on a regular basis for the last time. In July, pitcher Carl Mays quit the Red Sox and was traded to the Yankees for Allan Russell, Bob McGraw, and $40,000. Ruth had to fill in. He won nine games and had a 2.97 earned-run average. When the Red Sox brought up nineteen-year-old Waite Hoyt to take his spot in the rotation, Ruth went back to the outfield.

On Saturday, September 20, 1919, Boston played a doubleheader against the Chicago White Sox, and it was declared "Babe Ruth Day." Babe pitched and homered off Claude Williams, his twenty-seventh home run, tying the record for most homers in a season, set by Ned Williamson for the Chicago Colts in 1884. Ruth finished the season with 29.

Babe Ruth was still a member of the Boston Red Sox—and still a part-time pitcher—when he was acclaimed by the world of baseball as the greatest home run hitter ever.

TRIUMPH AND GLOOM

Harry Frazee's Red Sox won the American League pennant in 1918, and if Frazee had made a ton of money, as he should have, baseball history would have been rewritten. He didn't, however. The economy lagged, and attendance fell sharply.

World War I was raging, and with the loss of half his players to the armed services, Frazee began the 1918 season having to spend big money for replacements. He gave Philadelphia A's owner Connie Mack $60,000 and three second-stringers for pitcher Joe Bush, catcher Wally Schang, and outfielder Amos Strunk. Mack, fearing a downturn in the economy, decided to get maximum value for whatever players he could sell. There was strident criticism around the league that Red Sox owner Harry Frazee was trying to buy a pennant.

While the other owners stood pat, fearing that baseball might be stopped for the duration of the war, Frazee continued spending his money—by nature, Frazee was a gambler—and traded for A's first-base star Stuffy McInnis from Mack.

Led by four pitchers—Carl Mays, Joe Bush, Sam Jones, and Babe Ruth—none of whom had an earned-run average higher than 2.25, the Sox were in first place from July 4 on. Later in July, Harry Frazee's luck ran out. Since 1914, when the war began, there had been criticism that ballplayers should be on the front lines, not the baselines. The pressure on the government intensified, and on July 26, 1918, Secretary of War Newton Baker ordered baseball to shut down by Labor Day, September 1, or be subject to a "work or fight" order. Baker had no way of knowing it, but the war would end in just two months, on November 11.

On September 1, the Red Sox were in first place by 3½ games. Frazee's spending had won the Red Sox the pennant, but the loss of revenue from the cancellation of the September ballgames was enormous. In those days, there was no revenue from radio or television. It all came from the box office and concessions. Baker's order was the beginning of the end for Harry Frazee.

The 1918 World Series was played against the Chicago Cubs. Frazee needed high attendance at the games played in Boston to recoup his huge losses. He didn't get it.

Babe Ruth beat Hippo Vaughn, 1–0, in the opening game, played in Chicago. It was during that first World Series game that Harry Frazee made a memorable impact upon the game of baseball. Because it was wartime, he decided that during the seventh-inning stretch the band he had hired would play "The Star Spangled Banner." This was before Francis Scott Key's tune had become our national anthem. As the band played, the players stood at attention and turned to face the flag. The servicemen in the crowd saluted, and everyone began to sing. When it was over, the crowd burst into applause. The gesture was repeated the following two contests in Chicago, and when the teams returned to Boston for Game Four, Frazee had the "Star Spangled Banner" played before the first pitch. For years in Boston it would be played for special occasions, or whenever a band was present, and once electric public-address systems came into vogue, the anthem was played before the start of every game throughout the country.

After the teams split the next two games in Chicago, Ruth beat the Cubs, 3–2, in Game Four in Boston before only 22,000 fans. He had a shutout going into the eighth, giving him 29 consecutive scoreless innings in World Series play, a record Ruth believed would never be broken.

The Boston players had noted the low attendance in Boston and realized that they weren't going to get anywhere near the $2,000 promised to the winners. Harry Hooper went to commissioners Gary Herrmann and John Heydler and suggested they make up the difference by taking from the money being set aside for the second-, third-, and fourth-place teams. He was rebuffed. Hooper told the commissioners that the players on both teams would not play the next day.

The starting time for Game Five was approaching, but the players hadn't appeared on the field. Former Boston mayor Honey Fitzgerald, fearing a riot, sent for police reinforcements. The third commissioner, Ban Johnson, appealed to Hooper's honor.

"If you don't want to play, don't," Johnson said, "but, Harry, you fellows are putting yourself in a very bad light with the fans. There are going to be wounded soldiers and sailors at the game again today. With a war going on, and fellows fighting in France, what do you think the public will think of you ballplayers striking for more money?"

The players agreed to finish the series.

Chicago won Game Five before 24,000 fans in Boston, and on September 11, Carl Mays beat Chicago, 2–1, before only 15,238 Boston fans. The 1918

Series was marked by marvelous pitching and anemic hitting. In the six games, nineteen runs were scored. The losing Cubs' ERA was 1.04. The Red Sox' was 1.70. Not a home run was hit.

Though the Red Sox were victorious, four games to two, Frazee and the players from both teams came out financial losers. The victorious Red Sox ended up getting $1,108.45 a man. The Cub players each got $671.

John Hooper: "When the players had that big meeting, they agreed to go out and play on the condition that the commissioners wouldn't take reprisals against the team or the players.

"The Red Sox won the Series, and 'long about Christmas, Pop got a letter from one of the commissioners saying, 'In view of your conduct, you won't get your series emblem.' The emblem looked like a fifty-cent piece with a diamond in the center.

"Pop was always concerned that some of his less fortunate teammates never got their emblems, and until the day he died he wrote to every commissioner trying to get their emblems. Every commissioner coming by, he approached, the last one being Bowie Kuhn. No one would ever give him satisfaction."

By the end of 1918, Red Sox owner Frazee was overextended. His Red Sox had lost money during the regular season, and the 1918 World Series had been a flop financially. Moreover, his theatrical productions were bombing. *Madame Sherry* had been a hit, but several other subsequent ventures failed to catch the fancy of the public.

Harry Frazee, flush the year before, suddenly found himself in desperate financial straits.

Frazee had won the 1918 pennant with Ernie Shore and Duffy Lewis in the service, and he figured he would be able to compete without them again the next year. So he traded Shore, Lewis, and his fifth starting pitcher, Dutch Leonard, to New York for four players and $15,000. Then he looked around for more.

In July of 1919, Carl Mays, the Red Sox' moody, irascible right-hander, was pitching against the White Sox. After completing the fifth inning, he walked through the dugout and into the dressing room. He was angry. "I'll never pitch for this ballclub again," he said. During the inning, catcher Wally Schang had thrown down to second to try to throw out a base stealer. Accidentally, he had hit Mays in the head.

Mays had never been popular with his teammates. He was perhaps the meanest pitcher the game has ever known. Whenever he was behind 3 and 0 on the count, he had the attitude, "I might as well hit him with this one, because I'll walk him anyway." Mays later became the only man in the history of the game to kill a batter with a pitched ball, when in 1920 he struck Cleveland shortstop Ray Chapman in the head.

When Mays walked off the field and out of the game, manager Ed Barrow suspended him. That night Barrow got a call from Frazee. "Don't suspend this fellow," Frazee said. "The Yankees want him, and I can get a lot of money for him." Two weeks later, Frazee sold Mays for $40,000 and two players. Ban Johnson tried to stop the trade, but in 1919 Yankee owner Jake Ruppert wielded more power than Johnson. Ruppert went to court and won the right to buy Mays.

The problem Frazee faced on the field in 1919 was that money doesn't win ballgames, players do. As the other teams were gaining strength from the return of their veterans from the war, the Red Sox were weakening themselves. They finished in sixth place that year, exacerbating Frazee's economic woes.

Adding to his mounting problems was Babe Ruth's escalating salary demands. Ruth was playing under a three-year contract, but after hitting 29 home runs and driving in 114 runs to lead the league in both categories in 1919, he felt he was getting shortchanged. Ruth told Frazee he wanted his salary raised to $20,000 or he would sit out the 1920 season.

Also squeezing Frazee was Joe Lannin, who was holding the notes from the sale of the team. Lannin was demanding payment. The pressure was on Frazee.

On December 27, 1919, Harry Frazee began making ominous noises about trading his treasure, Ruth. He told reporters, "I will deal any player except Harry Hooper."

What he didn't tell the press was that the day before he had agreed in principle to sell Babe Ruth to New York.

Manager Ed Barrow was first to get the news.

Ed Barrow: "I was living in New York, at 644 Riverside Drive, when I got a call one Sunday morning from Frazee. I was taking a shower and answered the phone with a towel wrapped around me. Frazee said he wanted to see me, and made a date for six o'clock that evening for the Hotel Knickerbocker.

". . . Frazee was sitting in the cafe with Frank McIntyre, the actor. He got to the point immediately.

" 'Simon,' he said, 'I am going to sell Ruth to the Yankees.'

" 'I thought as much,' I said. 'I could feel it in my bones. But you ought to know you're making a mistake.'

" 'Maybe I am,' said Frazee, 'but I can't help it. Lannin is after me to make good on my notes. And my shows aren't going so good. Ruppert and Huston will give me $100,000 for Ruth, and they've also agreed to loan me $300,000. I can't turn that down. But don't worry. I'll get you some ballplayers, too.'

" 'Listen,' I said, 'losing Ruth is bad enough, but don't make it tougher for me by making me show off a lot of ten-cent ballplayers that we got in exchange for him. There is nobody on that ballclub that I want. This has to be a straight cash deal, and you'll have to announce it that way.' "

Waite Hoyt: "Ruth at first objected to the transfer. He had felt secure in Boston. New York was a huge, forbidding place. Ruth always said New York cost him so much dough he couldn't afford to live there. A $20,000 season's contract changed his mind."

Frazee tried to sugarcoat the sale of Ruth by blaming his star for the Sox' sixth-place finish in 1919. "It would be impossible to start next season with Ruth and have a smooth-working machine," he said. "Ruth has become simply impossible, and the Boston club could no longer put up with his eccentricities. I think the Yankees are taking a gamble. While Ruth is undoubtedly the greatest hitter the game has ever seen, he is likewise one of the most selfish and inconsiderate men ever to put on a baseball uniform."

At the time, Frazee had a show running in Boston called *My Lady Friends,* and posters for it were pasted up at the entrance to Fenway Park. A disgusted Boston fan looked at one of these signs and said, "They're the only friends that ———— has!" The next day in the papers a cartoon showed Faneuil Hall and the Boston Public Library plastered with For Sale signs.

Glenn Stout: "When they sold Ruth, the very next day signs appeared in the Boston Common and in front of the Boston Public Library that said, 'For Sale.' Because that's how struck people were with the fact that Ruth was sold. You might as well sell the Boston Common or the Boston Public Library.

"I don't think people realize looking back just how tremendously popular Ruth was in Boston. And remained so. Any time you look at an old newspaper of that era, it was Ruth, Ruth, Ruth. And selling him soured everyone on Frazee, and by guilt by association, on the Red Sox.

"When Ruth played his last game with New York in Boston in August of 1933, at the time it was the largest crowd at Fenway Park ever. The sportswriters wrote huge columns. He was wildly popular."

Babe Ruth returned to Boston in 1935, not with the Red Sox, but with the Braves. It was the Babe's final season, after his skills had mostly left him.

Joe Cashman: "I got to know the Babe real well when he came to the Boston Braves for his final season in 1935. After the last home runs he hit, three on one day in Pittsburgh—numbers 712, 713, and 714—after the game Braves manager Bill McKechnie called Ruth into the clubhouse and said, 'Babe, listen. You're being given the runaround that they're going to make you manager of this club. They are never going to make you manager. Do as I tell you. Call in the newspapermen now and announce your retirement. You're retiring from baseball. As long as the game is played, they'll say, 'Here's a home-run hitter, and on the last day he played he hit three home runs.' They will always argue over how many home runs you might have hit if you had kept on playing."

"Later on that season, Ruth was living over at the Myles Standish Hotel on Bay State Road, and I went up to see him. He said, 'Joe, remember I told you what McKechnie wanted me to do, to retire the day I hit the three home runs? If I had done that, just as he said, as long as baseball is played people would have talked about me. But I wasn't smart enough to do it."

Babe was wrong. As long as baseball is played, the fans will talk about him anyway.

With Ruth gone, the 1920 Red Sox finished fifth. Frazee's financial slide continued. He needed more money to finance his new play, *No, No, Nanette* (which featured the song "Tea for Two").

In October of 1920, Frazee advised Barrow that the ship of state was about to sink to the bottom. He also told his manager that Yankee owner Cap Huston wanted to talk with him about working for the Yankees.

"I'd advise you to see him, and anything you do is fine with me," Frazee said. Barrow moved into the Yankee front office on October 29, 1920, and during the next three years continued what historians have called "the rape of the Red Sox."

Most of the decent Red Sox players Frazee owned were sold or traded to New York. There were fourteen in all, including Ruth. In December of 1920, Frazee traded Waite Hoyt, Wally Schang, and Mike McNally. In 1922, it was Joe Dugan and Elmer Smith. And finally, in January of 1923, future Hall of Fame pitcher Herb Pennock was traded for three stiffs and $50,000.

Harry Hooper: "All Frazee wanted was the money. He was short on cash and he sold the whole team down the river to keep his dirty nose above water. What a way to end a wonderful ballclub!

"I got sick to my stomach at the whole business. After the 1920 season I held out for $15,000, and Frazee did me a favor by selling me to the Chicago White Sox. I was glad to get away from that graveyard."

The blow that well may have forced Frazee to sell the team was a divorce settlement in which Frazee was ordered to pay his wife, Elsie Clisbie, $12,000 a year, an additional $40,000 over the next two years, plus certain property.

On July 11, 1923, Frazee finally sold the Red Sox, peddling the team to Bob Quinn and three associates for one million dollars. The deal was held up when concessionaire Harry Stevens sued Frazee to collect on unpaid bills.

Coinciding with the dismemberment of the Red Sox came Prohibition. Bars, including Nuf Ced McGreevey's Third Base, closed down all over Boston and America. When Third Base was sold, to become a branch of the Boston Public Library, the Royal Rooters disbanded. In addition to not having a watering hole at which to congregate, the Royal Rooters had nothing left to root for.

Harry Frazee died on June 14, 1929, at his home in New York at 270 Park Avenue, at age forty-eight, with New York mayor Jimmy Walker at his bedside.

Cleveland Amory, author: "I remember where I was standing the day they sold Babe Ruth. I said to my father, 'Dad, you and I will never live to see it, but we will regret it to the day anybody dies.' From that moment on, being a Red Sox fan, and I presume even before that time, being a Red Sox fan means a life of sackcloth and ashes, a life of perpetual excuses, a life of misery, of sadness, of want, of penury, all of which Bostonians, underneath, really pray for. A true Bostonian craves it.

"One of the many realities was we could not be a Yankee fan. Since the day they sold Babe Ruth for a bucket of balls and a payment of a small debt, from that moment on we could not be a Yankee fan because we would win too much. And if you win too much, you will not go to heaven. The Bostonian will go to heaven because he has suffered so much here. It is very much like the Moslem religion. You must suffer in this life, and then you go directly to heaven. I'm sure, up there, whatever teams they have, all will be made up there."

A new institution was born: the Curse of the Bambino. For selling Babe Ruth to the Yankees, it was said, the Red Sox had doomed themselves, now and for all time. For their sin, the Red Sox would never again win a World Series.

And to this day, they haven't.

CHAPTER 7

The Bob Quinn Years: "Just One of Those Things"

A YOUNG BALLCLUB

It wasn't bad enough that Harry Frazee had sold most of his good players to the Yankees and then bailed out for one and a half million dollars. In addition, *No, No, Nanette,* the play Frazee sold the Sox down the river to finance, was a huge success and made Frazee about two million dollars more, causing Red Sox fans to be even more bitter and enraged.

Still, the Red Sox might have recovered if the new owners had pumped some money into rebuilding the club. But the syndicate that bought the team from Frazee turned out to be flat broke. They had bought the homestead, but they didn't have any money to furnish it.

This part wasn't Frazee's fault. For Red Sox fans, it was just bad luck. The new president, Bob Quinn, who had been asked by American League president Ban Johnson to buy the team in order to get it away from Frazee, knew the game of baseball. Quinn had been general manager of the St. Louis Browns under owner Phil Ball. In 1922, the year before he came over to the Red Sox, Quinn had almost won a pennant with the Browns, losing to the New York Yankees by only one game.

Quinn's three backers, the men with the money, were friends of his from his days as general manager of the Columbus, Ohio, team in the American

Association. One was a Dr. Drury, a surgeon, and another was a business-man named Sheinhorn. Neither of them had all that much money, but because they were friends of both Quinn and the other partner, they came along.

The man with the deep pockets was Palmer Winslow, a wealthy Indiana glass manufacturer. Winslow had assured Quinn of substantial support, including half a million for player development. But only months after the new syndicate took over the team, Winslow developed a fatal illness, and he died without having made provisions for part of his estate to go to his partners. Quinn could have sold the team before the ailing Winslow died, but he decided to hold on. It was a mistake that virtually bankrupted him.

Quinn was left with a bad team and no money to improve it. Red Sox historian Glenn Stout believes that Quinn may have been so desperate as to commit arson on Fenway Park on May 8, 1926, to collect the insurance money.

Glenn Stout: "There was a fire in 1926, when the left-field bleachers burned down. It seems clear to me that Quinn was trying to burn down the ballpark for the insurance money, because the day before, they had a big fire and two smaller fires that the fans put out with buckets of water.

"The next day they had a fire that actually burned down the left-field bleachers, and except for the Red Sox manager, Lee Fohl, who was out there with a fire extinguisher, the people who got there first to put out the fire were from the S. S. Pierce Company across the street. They were the ones who saw the flames, hooked up the groundskeeper's hoses, and started watering down the grandstand so it didn't go."

According to Joe Cashman, however, Quinn was honorable and conscientious, not the kind of man who would commit arson.

Joe Cashman: "Ty Cobb was manager of the Tigers, and he had a ball-player who Quinn wanted to buy. I forget who it was. Cobb said, 'No, Bob, you can't buy him.' Quinn said, 'I understand you have him for sale.' Cobb said, 'Yes, I have him for sale, but you can't buy him.' Quinn said, 'Put him on waivers, and I'll take him on waivers.' Cobb said, 'You can do that, but I'll get rid of him before you do that. You can't claim him.' Quinn said, 'Why not?'

"Cobb said, 'Bob, the trouble with you is that you are too honest for baseball. I can sell this guy this afternoon for $75,000. You couldn't get him for $175,000, because he can't play baseball, and I wouldn't sell him to you. He swings one-handed. He lets go of the bat. People don't know that. I know it because I own him. I'll get rid of him. I'll stick one of the other guys with him, some guy who would stick me. You wouldn't do that to me, and I wouldn't do it to you.' "

By the end of the 1920s, the future of the Red Sox seemed hopeless. The economy was slowing down nationwide, and there was no money at all to spend on the team. On January 29, 1929, Jim Price, Quinn's close friend and club secretary, committed suicide by slashing his wrist with a razor blade.

In the barren period between 1924 and 1932, when the Quinn syndicate finally sold the team to Tom Yawkey, the Red Sox were the worst team in the American League, finishing last or second-to-last in all but one of those years. At the time Quinn sold the team, he had to pay back $400,000 borrowed from the American League to keep it afloat.

The typical Red Sox players of the Bob Quinn era were either untried kids, over-the-hill vets, problem players dumped by other teams, or players with one skill: hitting *or* fielding. Few became household names. Most were out there just doing their best, glad to have a paycheck or hoping to get traded to a better team.

Billy Rogell was a twenty-year-old kid when he was signed by the Red Sox in 1924. Rogell played infield on the last-place Sox in 1925, 1927, and 1928.

Bill Rogell: "I didn't get a bonus to sign. You never heard of anything like that in those days. I got three hundred bucks a month my first year in the big leagues in '25. That spring I hit about .390, and manager Lee Fohl kept me.

"We had such a young ballclub, Charlie Ruffing and Jack Rothrock and Red Rollings, and, oh God, that Boston ballclub was so young, we'd have been much better off if we'd have gone on to some AA club. But no, the owner of the club, Bob Quinn, who was a helluva nice guy, tried to get by, and we didn't have the experience. In 1925, we lost 105 games. At one time we could have put a whole damn infield out there that wasn't over nineteen years old.

"The Sox were in a terrible financial condition. And the trouble was, they didn't pay any damn money. What the hell's three hundred dollars a month to play in the big leagues? Even in '25 that was low. Though I was happy to sign for anything to get a chance to play in the big leagues. Who wouldn't be?

"Still, I think the owner of the ballclub did everything he could for us boys. I always liked that old guy. To me, he was swell. He used to come down to New Orleans for spring training and give us talks. 'Be good boys and hustle.' He had to pinch his pennies, and he couldn't do much more. He was trying to run a big-league ballclub, for God sake, on a Class-B salary.

"We had a lot of fun, but what do you expect from a bunch of kids? Sure we wanted to win, don't kid yourself. We were out there hustling, but those old guys just outsmarted us all the time. I think sometimes if we would have taken it a little more seriously, we'd have been a lot better ballclub. But when you were in a slump, nobody ever said, 'Come on out tomorrow morning and do a little hitting, and I'll show you what you're doing wrong.'

"Lee Fohl, our manager, never got mad. He never criticized anything you did, even if you did it wrong. It was just one of those things. What the hell, you can't do anything about it. Why kill anybody? But no, we were just a bunch of young guys. We hustled. We just weren't good enough."

Walter (Wally) Shaner, who was born in 1900, played on the 1926 and 1927 Red Sox teams as an outfielder. In 1925, Shaner hit .358 with Lincoln, Nebraska, in the Western League when the Red Sox bought him. In his first spring training with the Sox in 1926, he broke his ankle sliding. He still started 69 games with the Sox.

Walter Shaner: "We had the dead ball in those days. We would get a man on base and we'd bunt him over and then try to squeeze him in, playing for one run, and at the same time the Yankees were playing for big innings, and they had the guys to do it. We didn't have a lot of good hitters on the team. We had a couple of good pitchers, Red Ruffing and Howard Ehmke. One went to New York and the other went to Philadelphia (Athletics). In Boston, as soon as they got a good player, they got rid of him—sold him. They needed the money. In those days there was no radio or television. The only way you could make money was through the turnstiles, and tickets were cheap. You couldn't make any salaries.

"The owner, Bob Quinn, was a very devout Catholic. As a matter of fact, most of the team was Catholic, and when we went to spring training there were a couple of priests who used to go with us.

"On the Sox the coaches weren't too good. Lee Fohl, a catcher, was manager, and his coach was an old-time pitcher from way back, and they weren't too good with the young players. They just didn't know enough to teach ball. Lee was a short, chubby man in his fifties, and he tried, but he didn't have a team to work with.

"In the field we had one outstanding player, Phil Todt, our first baseman. He was a smooth fielder, but he swung up around his shoulders every time, and he only hit if they threw it there. We had a second baseman, Mike Herrera, a Cuban. It was funny. Herrera was shy taking throws when a runner was coming into second. The runner would come in, and he would get out of their way. Topper Rigney, our shortstop, ended up taking all of the throws, because he would stand in there and block them off if he could.

"I didn't pal around with the other guys much off the field. We didn't play Sunday ball in Boston at that time, and we used to get on the train right after the ballgame on Saturday and go to Detroit and play a Sunday game and then catch the train right after that and then come back to Boston for the Monday game. The first time we did that, I noticed Fred Haney, our third baseman, and two or three of the other boys taking suitcases—just to go over for the day and right back. And I couldn't figure out why until we got to Detroit and found out that they had a friend who used to get Black Label beer in sacks from Canada, and each sack of twenty-four bottles fit right into the suitcase. On the next trip, one of the players asked me, 'Aren't you taking a suitcase?' I said, 'No.' He said, 'Well, take one for me.'

"It was Prohibition, uh-oh, there was drinking! At the time you couldn't make any money. If you made $4,000 for the summer you were doing good. It wasn't a lucrative thing, and so the only way you could do any good was to have a little fun out of it. Although I wasn't a big drinker myself, a lot of the guys were.

"In 1926 I stayed at the Elks Club in Boston, and on the fifth floor they had their offices, and then they had a little set of stairs in the back where they went up to a bar. The year I lived in the Elks Club the players from Detroit like Bob Fothergill, Heinie Manush, and Harry Heilmann would come to visit me all the time because I could take them upstairs to the club. And they were big drinkers, I'll tell you. They would sit and drink half the night. Manush was fighting for the batting lead, and one of the boys kept saying, 'Heinie, you can win it, but you better stay sober.' He said, 'Oh, I've been doing this all year. If I stop now, I probably won't hit anything.'

"Fothergill, oh, he was a pip too. We didn't have many pips on our team. We had a guy who had been with New York, Freddie Hofman, a catcher and a pal of Ruth. See, Ruth had a farm in Sudbury outside of Boston and he admired a gal that was a waitress in Carl Ladd's restaurant in Boston, a little place off of Huntington and Mass., [others claimed it was Landers Coffee Shop in Copley Square] and she was no good. She would get drunk. He admired her and knocked her up, and that's why he had to marry her. He kept her down on the farm. He wouldn't take her anyplace, and later on she burned herself up. She went to sleep with a cigarette.

"And what happened was, when Ruth came to Boston with the Yankees, Freddie used to tell us that he would take out a girl that Ruth told him to take, and of course he told Freddie, 'You'd better not touch her.' And at night Ruth would go up to Freddie's room. Freddie was Ruth's beard. In '27, when Ruth hit all those home runs, if we were a lot of runs behind, no chance to win the ballgame, in the later innings, Freddie would tell Ruth what was coming. He hit a couple a mile over the fence. I know, 'cause Freddie told me afterwards.

"But we didn't mind because Ruth used to fill up all the ballparks. When he'd come to Boston we'd fill the park. We couldn't get them all in. They would put the fans in the outfield. There was a bank in left field called Duffy's

Cliff, and they had people all over the bank. If they hit a ball over my head, it was a two-base hit. The crowd would be about ten feet behind me. The same way in all the towns. So everyone made money off of Ruth.

"People used to come around the clubhouse to talk to Ruth. He knew a lot of people in Boston. But Ruth didn't know the names of all the boys on his own ballclub. If he didn't know your name, he'd call you, 'Hey, kid.' I talked to him a lot of times, but I bet he didn't even know what my name was.

"Ty Cobb was exactly the opposite. When I broke my leg in spring training in '26, I was out on the field trying to get the thing in shape, and Cobb came up to me and told me that he had had a broken bone, and he said that if I would run backwards, it would strengthen my leg a lot faster. And it really did. I started doing that, getting on my toes, and I really think it helped a lot.

"In 1927, Bill Carrigan took over the Boston team. He was a much better manager than Fohl was. He was a hard loser. He wanted to win, that was for sure, and he didn't like it at all when he lost a ballgame, especially if he lost it by somebody's error or bad judgment. Bob Quinn brought Carrigan back, because he thought it might do the team some good. But he didn't do much better. We still lost 100 games."

Milt Gaston, who was born in 1896, played for the New York Yankees, the St. Louis Browns, and the Washington Nationals before he had the misfortune of having to pitch for the Red Sox in the years from 1929 through 1931. In 1929 he lost 19 games, and the following year he lost 20. After a 2–13 record in '31, he was traded to the Chicago White Sox.

Milt Gaston: "I pitched my best ball in the sandlots. They didn't know it, but I was twenty-eight when I went into the majors. They thought I was twenty-three. I had a brother, Alex, who was with the Giants. He put me wise to all the tricks in the trade. They would have got rid of me long before if they knew how old I was.

"When I came to the Red Sox in '29, Bill Carrigan was the manager. What a man! Bob Quinn was running the ballclub. He talked Bill into coming out of retirement. At the end of the year Quinn wanted to sign up Bill again, but Bill said, 'Bob, I don't want to take your money. All you got is a pitching staff, and I can't work with that.' Bill told Quinn to give it to Heinie Wagner. Heinie wanted it, and Bill wanted Heinie to have a job. Heinie wasn't a particularly good manager, but he was a nice fellow. Everybody liked him. He didn't have the goods to manage, but he didn't have anything to manage.

"Earl Webb was the only hitter we had on the Boston ballclub. He was a home-run hitter [16 in 1930 and 14 in 1931]. In those days some watch company, Elgin or one of them, used to give a watch for every home run you hit. Webby was the only guy on our club who hit home runs. Webby got one for himself and one for his wife, and when he went to bat, we'd say, 'Don't forget me, Webby, if you hit one.' We all had watches. In 1931, Webby set a major-league record with 67 doubles. He was a good hitter. But he was the only hitter on the ballclub.

"We had some good pitchers. Danny MacFayden, Jack Russell, and Red Ruffing were there then. Ruffing was like the rest of us. At Boston, he had no support. But as soon as he got over to the Yankees, he became a great pitcher. Russell and MacFayden also did better after they got away from the Red Sox. You couldn't do anything pitching for a ballclub like that, though there was no use complaining because, they were, after all, all your friends. So you just took it with a grain of salt. When Ruffing got traded to the Yankees, we were glad for him. Any time a guy left the club, we were glad for him, because he couldn't have gone to a worse club."

In the two full seasons Bob Weiland pitched for the Red Sox, he lost 16 games (in 1932) and 14 games (in 1933). Five years later, with the St. Louis Cardinals, he won 15 and then 16 games in a season. Weiland was born in 1905.

Bob Weiland: "In 1932, the team was 43 and 111. Can't you imagine? It's no fun playing on a loser. You try like hell, but nothing seems to go right for you. It seems like you get no breaks at all. A lot of times I pitched well and didn't get the win. I was a tough, hard-luck pitcher. I lost 2 to 1, 1 to 0, 3 to 2, pitching against Lefty Gomez of the Yankees, Lefty Grove, Earnshaw, Walberg in Philadelphia, against Schoolboy Rowe of Detroit. That was my lot. It was very frustrating. I did the best I could, but ended up on the short end of the stick all the time. Once in a while, I'd win. I didn't get many runs. With the Cards, I had a good ballclub behind me. Those guys could field ground balls and catch fly balls!"

Joe Cashman: "Smead Jolley was a big, strong, dumb guy who could hit the ball as far as Ruth. Smead played Duffy's Cliff. It was called that because Duffy Lewis was one of only three players who knew how to play it. The secret was, when the ball went out there, you had to be able to judge if it was catchable if you went up the cliff. If you got to the top and didn't catch it, the ball would hit the wall and bounce past you, and now you would have to run down and chase it halfway back to the infield. If you knew you couldn't catch it, you just turned and waited for it to come off, and the batter would get a single. Jolley could never do that. Sometimes he'd go up and the ball would go over his head, and as the ball would come back at him, he'd fall and roll and roll. Smead said, 'They showed me how to run up the cliff, but they didn't show me how to come down.'

"In right field Earl Webb couldn't run either. In center, Tom Oliver was a great, great outfielder. When balls would be hit to the outfield, everyone would yell, 'Get on your horse, Tom!'

"The Red Sox in those days were a lot like Stengel's Mets, except that Stengel never had a 19-game winner like Ed Morris."

BIG ED MORRIS

Joe Cashman: "The Red Sox teams in the early thirties were terrible teams. It was still fun, though. We had a pitcher named Ed Morris. I should say he was a character. From Kenniston, Alabama. The Red Sox bought him for $10,000. The Giants had turned him down. The Braves turned him down. Everybody turned him down. He had been up a half dozen years earlier with the Cubs, and he had been rolling around the minors.

"I can remember Morris coming south to join us, a big, rawboned guy. Every time he pitched an exhibition game, you never saw so many line drives in your life. Whish. Whish. He'd give up five or six in the first inning. We were watching him, and someone said, 'Where in the world did we get this bum?' But the batters were saying, 'Boys, what a pitcher you have now.' We thought it was a come-on. They said, 'This guy is going to be one hell of a pitcher.' We said, 'We've seen enough of him.'

"Just before we were to leave to go north to start the 1928 season, Bill Carrigan got a call. Morris had gotten in a fight with a cop at the old ballpark in Bradenton, Florida. Morris hated cops, particularly when he had a few drinks in him. The first thing when he saw a cop, he'd pull all the buttons off his coat, and all the time he'd get hit over the head and be in a cell.

"So Carrigan got this call that they had Morris in the jail. They wanted him to come and bail him out. He was supposed to go before the grand jury in May. Carrigan said, 'Keep him there until May!' But he went down there and bailed him out, and Ed came up to Boston with the team.

"We were playing the Yankees, and Miller Huggins was their manager. Miller told this story to Marshall Hunt, the old *New York News* writer.

"Huggins had liked the way Ed Morris had looked and at the winter meetings wanted to buy him. Huggins told Marshall, 'I got a pal in Cincinnati. He never had any connection with baseball, just a pal. We grew up together. But he's a great judge of ballplayers. He's never given me a bad steer in his life. And he told me this winter that Morris was available and that I should buy him. I told the Yankees to send the scouts out and to go and look at this Morris, but they came back and said, 'No account, no account. The bum can't pitch. All he can do is drink.'

"Huggins said, 'Marshall, what am I going to do? I know this guy is right. But we can't send two scouts out and then disregard their opinion. But I want to tell you something. Before the season is over, I'm going to be sorry we didn't sign him. And I've never seen him pitch.'

"We were in New York playing a doubleheader. He pitched the first game, and the Yankees knocked him out in the first inning. Carrigan said, 'I'm going to have to find a starter for the second game.' Morris said, 'I'll pitch.' Carrigan said, 'You'll pitch? You got knocked out.' Morris said, 'That was a mistake.' Morris started the second game and won it.

"They had no bullpen in those days. You warmed up in front of the stands. In those days, all the managers coached the lines. Carrigan was the first-base coach, and he had Charlie Wagner coaching at third. All of a sudden Carrigan would hear the sound of the ball hitting the glove. Morris would be warming up.

" 'Who told you to warm up?' Carrigan would ask. 'Nobody, but you're going to need me. I can see that. The guy is weakening. You're going to call me in.' And Bill would. What a guy! Nineteen wins for a last-place ballclub. The Yankees would have had him if they had listened to the guy in Cincinnati.

"Morris was fun to be with. He played cards, and if things were going wrong, he'd jump up out of his seat and walk around the room to chase the jinx and then sit down. And he was one of the best ballroom dancers I've ever seen. But he wasn't a ladies' man. He was a liquor man. One time a teammate, Merle Settlemire, and Ed got to scuffling because they were both drinking, and Settlemire stabbed him.

"What happened to him? More of Quinn's bad luck. The next year we were in Detroit, and he's in an elevator, and he gets into a fight with a cop, and it took two cops to subdue him, and one pulled his arm, and his career was practically over.

"In March 1932, on the eve of spring training, his pals threw him a going-away party. They had a fish fry in his honor back home. And one of his pals stabbed him. He jumped into the river that separates Alabama and Florida, and he swam to the other side. He got the chills, and they brought him to the hospital, and he died. The water was so cold it was pneumonia, not the stabbing, that killed him."

CHAPTER 8

Young Tom Yawkey Goes After the Vets

In 1932, in the heart of the Depression, Bob Quinn's woeful Boston Red Sox drew 182,000 fans, an average of 2,275 a game. The team finished last, behind New York, 64 games back. Quinn was close to bankruptcy and ready to sell, and he let that fact be known around the league.

The great Ty Cobb, the fierce Detroit Tigers outfielder, had played for an owner named William Hoover Yawkey. William Yawkey bought the Tigers in 1903 when the team was terrible. Under his ownership, the Tigers signed Ty Cobb, Hughie Jennings as manager, Sam Crawford, Donie Bush, and others, going on to win pennants in 1907, 1908, and 1909. William Yawkey had been close to his players, including Cobb. He treated them well. He gave pitchers hundred-dollar bills for winning meaningless ballgames. He would take the team out drinking. Once they barhopped and then went to the Turkish baths, and Yawkey had them stay overnight. He had the team picked up in the morning.

Yawkey had an adopted son, Thomas, who loved baseball and the Tiger players, and who as a boy had idolized Cobb. Cobb and he had remained friendly, and in the early 1930s, Tom Yawkey went to Philadelphia to visit him. Because Cobb had spent his final two years with the Philadelphia A's, Cobb was also friendly with the A's outstanding second baseman, Eddie Collins, one of the smartest men in baseball, then a coach for A's manager Connie Mack. Yawkey had always wanted to meet Eddie Collins, because Collins had gone to the same prep school as Yawkey, the Irving School in

Tarrytown, New York. One of the most coveted awards at the school was the Edward T. Collins Medal for the best scholar-athlete. Yawkey's roommate, Alan McMartin, who later played on the Canadian Davis Cup tennis team, had won it, and Yawkey had been runner-up.

Cobb introduced them, and Yawkey and Collins discovered they shared another interest: hunting birds. Yawkey owned a fifty-thousand-acre home, South Island Plantation, near Georgetown, South Carolina, which teemed with migratory game, and he invited Collins to his home. After Collins's trip, they were as close as brothers.

Later it was Eddie Collins, who described it "purely as an idle conversational subject," who told Yawkey the Red Sox were for sale. Yawkey mentioned that his father had owned the Tigers and that he'd like to own a team one day.

What Collins didn't know was that Tom Yawkey was about to come into an inheritance of staggering proportions.

Yawkey was born Thomas Yawkey Austin on February 21, 1903. His father died when he was nine months old, and his mother passed away when he was six. His last and middle names were transposed when his uncle, William Hoover Yawkey, adopted him. William Yawkey had died on March 5, 1919, and when Tom's adoptive mother passed away on February 21, 1928, he inherited four million dollars.

Now, with his thirtieth birthday coming up on February 21, 1933, Tom Yawkey was about to inherit $3,408,650, plus interests in mines and pulp and paper mills worth an estimated $40,000,000.

Joe Cashman: "In Philadelphia one day, Eddie Collins and Yawkey were having lunch together in the hotel where the Red Sox were staying, and Bob Quinn happened to come in to have lunch, and he saw Eddie Collins and he went over to shake hands and to talk with him. Collins introduced him to Yawkey, 'How do you do, Mr. Yawkey?' and Quinn went on his way. So Collins said to Yawkey, 'Listen, you're always talking about owning a ballclub. See that man you just met? That's Bob Quinn, owner of the Red Sox. And he's desperate. He's got to have money. That's a great, great franchise. If you want a ballclub, go ahead.'

"Yawkey said to Collins, 'I will buy the club if you will run it.' Collins was supposed to be the next manager of the A's. He said, 'I couldn't do that. I couldn't leave Mr. Mack. I've been with him all these years.'

"Some way or another, Mr. Mack heard about it, and he called Collins in, and Mack said, 'Listen, Eddie. If you don't go up there and run the Red Sox, I'm going to fire you anyway. So you better go quick.'

"So Collins went to Yawkey and said, 'Go ahead and buy the club, and I'll run it.' And Collins ran it for him until he died."

* * *

Cashman was there on February 25, 1933, four days after Yawkey gained his inheritance, for the closing of the sale of the Red Sox from Bob Quinn.

Joe Cashman: "When Yawkey bought the club in February of 1933, Yawkey walked into the room with his lawyer, Dafoe, and we all thought Dafoe was Yawkey. Yawkey seemed too young to have that kind of money. This was just a kid. We thought he was a secretary. Here's Dafoe looking very dignified, gray hair, a dark suit, and Yawkey's a kid.

"Anyway, they agreed to all the terms, the deal was laid out, and Quinn said, 'All right, we have the deal closed. Let's sign the papers.' Dafoe said, 'Mr. Quinn. We don't work like that. You've got to get the papers signed by the other three owners in St. Louis.' Quinn said, 'Oh no.' Dafoe said, 'What do you mean, no?' Quinn said, 'I have all the stock.' Dafoe said, 'In your name?' Quinn said, 'Every share of stock in the club is in my name.' Dafoe said, 'You mean those three left all the stock in your name? You can sell the stock to anybody?' Quinn said, 'Anybody I want.' That's how much faith they had in him. Dafoe said, 'I've never heard of a deal like that in all my life. These are businessmen, and they give you full control of the ballclub?'

"Dafoe said to Yawkey, 'Quick, get this guy to work for us.' And Yawkey kept him there as a consultant, until he went over to run Brooklyn a few years later."

Yawkey, like Lannin and Frazee before him, had offices in New York City. Yawkey was asked why he didn't buy the Giants, who were available at the time.

Said Yawkey, "Because I'm an American Leaguer myself. Me? I wouldn't own a National League ballclub."

"But what do you expect to do with it now that you have it?"

"I expect," said Yawkey, "to get a great kick out of making something out of it."

"Doesn't the reconstruction job scare you?"

"On the contrary, it's right where I'm getting my biggest wallop. I don't see how any man can get any real satisfaction out of taking a success and merely running it along. That's like landing a fish that somebody else hooked. The big kick comes from taking something that's down and seeing if you can put it up and across. That's what my daddy did. I want to see if I'm as good a man as he was."

"THE MONEY IS ON THE TABLE"

Around the time Tom Yawkey bought the Red Sox, he told journalist Stanley Woodward that he and Eddie Collins would build the team "steadily" and would spend what is "necessary to put the team on its feet."

"I don't believe that the Red Sox, having been the doormat of the American League, can be built up overnight," Yawkey said. "It would be the height of folly to dump a lot of money into the thing all at once in the hope of quick and salutary results. Even if you wanted to do that, where would you go for players?"

The young Tom Yawkey's patience lasted three months, until May. At a meeting of all the American League owners, Yawkey dispensed with the small talk and got to the point. He said, "I don't want to waste any time quibbling here. They tell me this club of mine needs players, and I have $100,000 to spend for a couple of good ones, preferably a battery.

"I don't know much about the technique of trading and buying," he said. "They tell me it is a special study in itself. I haven't the time to go through an apprenticeship. Who has any really good players for sale? The money is on the table." St. Louis Browns owner Phil Ball answered first. He said, "If you mean business, you can have [catcher] Rick Ferrell and [pitcher] Lloyd Brown."

According to James Reston, after talking a minute or two to Eddie Collins, Yawkey closed the deal with Ball.

In another deal, Yawkey made a deal certain to hearten his fans. He bought two players, pitcher George Pipgras and infielder Billy Werber, *from* the Yankees for $100,000.

Joe Cashman: "Yawkey had all this money, and in those days nobody had any money. It was the Depression. He could buy anybody, so he went out and bought them. He bought the league. It was exciting, a story every day."

One of the teams Tom Yawkey was able to buy players from was the Philadelphia A's, owned and managed by Connie Mack.

For three years in a row—1929, 1930, and 1931—the Philadelphia A's won American League pennants. Three Hall of Famers led their hitters: Jimmie Foxx, the Beast, was the first baseman, Al ("Mule") Simmons, was the left fielder, and Mickey Cochrane caught. On the mound were Lefty Grove, Rube Walberg, George Earnshaw, Jack Quinn, Eddie Rommel, and Waite Hoyt. The team was one of the best ever put together.

When the stock market crashed on Black Friday, 1929, A's fans couldn't know it at the time, but Mr. Mack's dynasty also was coming to an end. Mack lost much of his wealth, and though he struggled to hang on as long as he could, ultimately he was forced to sell his players to stay in business. Tom Yawkey, ready to buy, began purchasing A's players after the 1933 season; he acquired Grove, Walberg, and second baseman Max Bishop for two lesser players and $125,000.

In December of 1935, Yawkey hit the jackpot when he bought A's first baseman Jimmie Foxx in exchange for $150,000 and a pitcher who was 2–10 the year before. Before the 1936 season, Yawkey also bought shortstop Eric McNair, pitcher Johnny Marcum, and outfielder Roger "Doc" Cramer, the fleet center fielder, from Connie Mack, who never won another pennant.

Doc Cramer, Red Sox, 1936–40: "Mr. Mack knew the game, knew how to play it, knew the whole business. He treated everyone well. I don't think he ever had an enemy. He was like a father to you, never bawled you out on the field or in front of anybody. He'd bring you up to his office, where he'd explain to you what you did wrong. He did that with everybody.

"Connie had a scorecard to move the fielders around. When he held it horizontally, that was for the infielders. And vertically, that was the outfield. We would always watch it. He would pick one guy out and point to him, and that's the way he would do it.

"And I never saw him wrong once. He never played a game in the outfield, but he knew where they were going to hit, and he'd put you there.

"One time we were playing the St. Louis Browns, and Eddie Rommel was our pitcher. Goose Goslin, who hit with power, was the hitter, and I was in center field, and Connie kept waving me in until I was right behind second base. There were two out and three on in the ninth. Rommel threw the ball, and Goslin hit it, and I put my hands up and caught it. I never moved.

"I asked him about it the next day, and he said, 'Just a hunch.' He was a good one, the best manager I ever played for—by far.

"He lost money in the stock market. We knew Connie was in financial trouble. Sure. He told us. He said, 'I have to break up the team,' and he did it.

"I knew I was gone. He told me a year or two before. He said he was going to trade me. I asked him, 'You're not going to trade me to a tail-end ballclub, are you?' He said, 'No, I'll trade you to the number-one club.' Which he did.

"I was happy going to Boston, but it didn't make a difference whether you were happy or not. When they traded you, you were gone. But it didn't make any difference to me. I liked going to Boston because they got more money. At Boston, Yawkey treated the players very well. He was just about the finest man you ever met in your life. Yawkey was another Connie Mack. He was from the old school."

LEFTY, WES AND DOUBLE X

From the ashes of what he inherited, Tom Yawkey began to rebuild with solid veterans.

His first major purchase, catcher Rick Ferrell, was a veteran star, as were Lefty Grove, Rube Walberg, and Max Bishop of the A's. In May of 1934, Yawkey also acquired Wes Ferrell, Rick's brother, from the Cleveland Indians. Four times, Wes won 20 games for Cleveland. Yawkey had always admired him, and when he slumped in 1934, Yawkey gave Cleveland $25,000 and two lesser players.

When Tom Yawkey purchased the Red Sox, the team had no farm system. He had no farm director, and it would be several years before he would hire one. To rebuild the team and the gate, Yawkey chose the most attractive path open to him: the purchase of name players. It was to be the first of several Grand Plans to make the Red Sox world champions.

Two of those veteran stars were Lefty Grove and Wes Ferrell. They were ornery, they were colorful, and they could still pitch.

Robert Moses ("Lefty") Grove may well have been the finest left-handed pitcher ever to take the mound. He certainly was the fastest. Some who played with him say he was the fastest they ever saw. His major-league records show 300 victories and a lifetime ERA of 3.06. But Grove didn't enter the majors until he was twenty-five years old, after winning 109 games for Baltimore of the International League. At Baltimore he earned as much as $7,500 a year, more than many of his major-league counterparts.

Lefty Grove was an extremely difficult person. He wouldn't autograph baseballs. He didn't like kids. He didn't like rookies. He didn't like fans. But he sure could pitch.

Tony Lupien, Red Sox, 1940, 1942–43: "I was a rookie standing around at the Sarasota Terrace Hotel, and all of a sudden somebody came up and gave me a kick in the ass, and I went flying across the room. That was Grove. Just for laughs. An eccentric.

"He was a rough-as-a-cop mountaineer. Don't say hillbilly. Say mountaineer. He came from Lonaconing, Maryland, up there in the hills. He was a fisherman, and he was the only guy on the club who could have a whiskey bottle in his locker. The rest of us would just have a beer. When he wanted a belt, he had one.

"He was a really rough competitor who had pitched a great part of his life in Baltimore. A lot of his best years were there. Grove was a great bunter. He was a master at sacrificing the man over. Those things are all forgotten now. And he swung the bat pretty good. He was a beauty.

"I pinch-hit for him the first base hit I got in St. Louis. After you pinch-hit, you're out of the ballgame. So I sat there a minute, and I saw him go into the clubhouse to take a shower, and I said to myself, 'I guess I can shower and sit in the stands and have a beer.'

"I went into the showerbath, and I was scared to death of him. I don't know what the hell the man is going to do. He doesn't say anything. I showered, and he showered, and he said, 'You want a ride back to the hotel, kid?' I thought, 'I'd better say yes. He's liable to kill me.' I said, 'Yes,' and we walked out of the clubhouse, and he had a *St. Louis Post-Dispatch* all rolled up. A little kid came along and asked Grove for an autograph, and he hit that kid across the puss with that paper, and the kid went flying."

Gene Desautels, Red Sox, 1937–40: "Lefty didn't have much of an education, but as far as baseball was concerned, he could have had a doctor's degree. Many times I remember, we would have a runner on first, and I would call for a fastball, and he could see before he delivered the ball to the catcher that the runner was going to steal, and he'd pitch out, just because he knew the runner was going. He helped me, because I could then throw the runner out.

"He taught me a lot about pitching. By 1937, he had lost his great fastball, and he would throw the curve in on right-handers, break it down and in, and oh, he had good control. I remember the opening game of the 1937 season in Washington. Every pitch I called, I would move my glove a little bit, wherever I wanted him to throw it, and I could have caught the ball with my eyes closed. His control was that good.

"I remember there was an old professor who used to come to the ballpark, and he would try to get a picture of Lefty Grove, and Lefty would never let him take a picture. The man used to ask me, 'Would you talk to Lefty and ask him if he would please let me get a picture of him?' I would say, 'What's the matter, Lefty, the poor old guy, let him take a picture.' He'd say, 'No, he's not going to get a picture,' and walk away. And he never did let him take a picture. I felt sorry for the poor old guy, a nice old gentleman."

Bill "Lefty" LeFebvre, Red Sox, 1938–39: "In the summer of '35 I was playing for Falmouth in the Cape Cod League, and I won 11 and lost none. Hugh Duffy had gone there because he wasn't feeling well, and he saw me pitch. He was a coach for the Red Sox. He said, 'When you graduate from Holy Cross, we'll sign you.'

"I graduated, and the next day I was at Fenway Park. I signed a major-league contract for $150 a week. My friends thought I was a millionaire.

"Anyway, I bought myself a brand-new glove and a brand-new pair of spike shoes and a couple of new sweatshirts.

"Jack Barry was my coach at Holy Cross. Jack had played on the old Philadelphia Athletics, way back. He knew Grove pretty well. Barry told me, 'When you get to Boston, don't bother with Grove. He hates rookies. Stay away from him.' I said I would.

"I was in Boston six or seven days, and I never said hello to him and he never spoke to me. Finally, one day in St. Louis I was shagging flies in the outfield, and he came walking towards me, and he says, 'Hello, kid.' And you know, they never called him Lefty. They called him Moses. He said, 'You got a new glove, kid?' I said, 'Yeah.' He said, 'Let me see it.' I threw him my glove, and he threw me his, a goddamn old puddingbag. He had had it about fifteen years. It was bent backwards. He said, 'How do you like that glove, kid?' I punched it a couple times and I said, 'Geez, this is a nice glove.' He said, 'Well, Christ, keep it.' And he walked away with mine.

"I never did ask him for it. I was so glad he spoke to me.

"I was sent to Minneapolis after that, and after the last game of the season, you know how kids want a souvenir, a ball, a hat, anything. I had Grove's glove, and I threw it up in the stands to one of the kids. He punched it out twice and threw the goddamn glove right back at me!"

Grove came to the Red Sox in '34, but couldn't pitch in spring training. He developed an infection in his teeth, which created so much pain in his left shoulder that he could scarcely throw the ball. It got so bad, he jumped the team and went home for a few days.

Billy Werber, Red Sox, 1934–36: "Because he had lost so much spring-training time, the skin on the fingers of his pitching hand was still tender when the regular season opened. In an early game in Detroit, I noticed some blood on the ball when it was thrown to me at third base. After walking to the mound to hand the ball to Lefty, I saw that the inside of his middle finger was mostly raw meat.

" 'Get out of there,' I urged. 'You can't pitch with a finger like that.'

" 'Gimme the ball, and you get the hell back to third,' was his response. Back I got, and pitch he did. It was an exhibition of sheer courage, if I ever saw one. Each throw brought him burning pain."

Grove's teammates didn't enjoy playing behind him, because if a fielder made an error behind him, he'd go over and chew him out. His competitiveness was legendary around the league.

Doc Cramer: "I remember spring training my first year with the A's. I hit a home run off him in an intrasquad game. I came up to hit the next time, and Mickey Cochrane said, 'Look out, he's going to throw at you.' He hit me in the ribs. I went into the clubhouse, and after he finished his three innings, he came in and he said, 'You didn't hit that one, did you, rookie?'

"We were playing the Yankees in Yankee Stadium, a full house. We were tied for first. We had a fellow by the name of Jack Quinn pitching. We got to the ninth inning, and we had the bases full of Yankees with nobody out, winning by a run. Mack took Quinn out and brought in Grove.

"Ten pitched balls, and we were in the clubhouse. He struck out Ruth, Gehrig, and Lazzeri on ten pitched balls. Lazzeri fouled one. And that was it. We beat them. He was a pitcher, I'll tell you.

"The year he went 31 and 4, two of those losses were one to nothing. He was all pitcher."

* * *

As pitchers went, few were as dedicated as Grove.

Joe Cashman: "Grove was strictly a loner. He didn't go anywhere. He lived over at the Kenmore, and he'd walk around the corner over to Brookline Avenue into the ballpark.

"Eddie Collins once told me that he was certain that if you told Grove that if he were to walk over to Commonwealth Avenue and then down Beacon Street, and then went to the park, a four- or five-mile walk, he would win an extra game, he'd walk it every day. Collins said, 'For one game, he'd do that.'

"He was just interested in baseball. Nothing else. Just baseball.

"Grove was pitching in St. Louis one day, and we had an outfielder who couldn't play very well—I can't remember who it was—and this guy misjudged a fly ball, and Grove lost the game 1 to 0. Grove didn't speak to anyone for eight or nine days. Even to Foxx, who was his roommate. Never spoke a word to him. He'd call up and get room service, and he'd eat.

"Finally, we were leaving St. Louis, it must have been over a hundred, the heat was terrible, and there was no air-conditioning in the sleepers, and for one reason or other in the berth opposite me was Grove. I was lower seven, and he was lower eight, still not talking to anybody. We all got on the train, and he looked over to me and said, 'Have a drink?' I said, 'Sure, why not?' I went over and he took out the cups and poured, threw it down, and that broke the ice. He spoke again.

"No one hated to lose more than he did. Nobody."

In addition to buying players from the Athletics, Yawkey also bought disgruntled or hard-to-handle stars from other clubs. One of those was Wes Ferrell, a pitcher as tough and combative as Grove. After coming from Cleveland, Ferrell pitched three full seasons with the Red Sox from 1934 through '36, compiling records of 14–5, 25–14, and 20–15. When he slumped to 3–6 in 1937, he was traded to Washington.

Billy Werber: "Wes always wanted to pitch against the Indians on holidays and Sundays when fans were numerous, in order to show that Cleveland's letting him go had been the bonehead move of the decade. On this particular occasion, however, he failed to survive the first inning. He came back to the dugout, took a strong pair of scissors from the trainer's bag, and began to cut his glove into small pieces. Each time that he cut, he would grunt. Other Sox players watched in bemused tolerance, being careful not to laugh too loud—if at all.

"A game in Philadelphia provoked him even more. In the sixth and seventh innings, after we had given Wes a 10 to 0 lead, he gave up a total of nine runs, and so Bucky Harris had to take him out. Wes thereupon sat down on the dugout bench and began to berate himself in the strongest possible language. All of a sudden, he threw a right to his jaw and knocked his head against the concrete wall. When he had half recovered from this blow, and with further self-directed imprecations, he tossed a left hook to his jaw and banged his head off the cement a second time. Bucky then pinioned Wes's arms and stopped further mayhem."

Fabian Gaffke, Red Sox, 1936–39: "Wes had a terrible temper, dern right. One time he got taken out of a ballgame. He was so gol-dern mad. He wanted to throw his glove into the dugout just before he went down the steps, but he missed the dugout and threw it into the stands. He got in the dugout, and he took another of his gloves, and he ripped it to pieces."

Doc Cramer: "Wes never took it out on anybody but himself. One time Wes lost a ballgame, and he was putting his watch on, and it dropped to the floor. He just stomped on it, like that. 'Son of a bitch, it won't drop again,' he said.

"Wes would get on his brother Rick once in a while. One time he thought Rick called the wrong pitch. Rick told him, 'The hell with it. I ain't going to give you no signs. Throw whatever you want,' and he did."

Ben Chapman, Red Sox, 1937–38: "Wes had a vicious temper. He played cards, and if he lost a pot, he'd tear up all the money in front of him. I've seen him tear up five-dollar bills and throw them away. He and Grove both had tempers. I had a temper, but I was a pipsqueak compared to those guys."

Despite his temper, Wes wasn't immune from his teammates' pranks. The following story is an indication of the roughneck nature of the Red Sox teams of the 1930s.

Billy Werber: "In the spring of 1935 in Sarasota, Wes had rented a decent-looking Chevrolet to use for fishing jaunts and hopefully for dates. [He was single.] One day the car was sitting in front of the hotel and Wesley was nowhere in sight. It seemed an opportune time for a teammate—who shall remain nameless—to hide some fish heads and crab guts from the hotel garbage inside the car. There they stayed, closed up tight under a hot Florida sun.

"Wes had a date after dinner that evening, but the eye-watering stench which greeted him when he opened the car door completely altered his plans. Indeed, the odor may well have stayed with the Chevrolet for a lifetime. Next morning in the clubhouse before pitching, Wesley mounted a stool and challenged the whole club, individually or collectively, to a fight.

"We maintained a discreet, if somewhat amused, silence. Wes never knew the identity of the fish-laden prankster, and I was not about to tell him."

In the late 1930s, the Red Sox featured a home-run hitter of renown known as "The Beast" or "Double X." His name was Jimmie Foxx, and he loved the game, but had difficulty with his life after baseball.

For eleven seasons before coming to the Red Sox in 1936, Double X provided the fireworks for Connie Mack's Philadelphia A's, leading them to pennants in 1929, '30, and '31, and capturing the public's imagination in 1932 by hitting 58 home runs. Twice that year, Foxx had homers rained out when games were called. That year he hit .364 and drove in 169 runs. Though he missed the Triple Crown by three points (Dale Alexander hit .367), he won the first of three Most Valuable Player awards.

Foxx was in his prime in December of 1935, when Mack sold him to the Red Sox for $150,000.

Bob Steele: "I saw him when he was playing for Philadelphia in '33. He had this great build. He cut his sleeves off short and played without an undershirt. He had beautiful arms. He was five foot eleven, weighed about 190. He came up as a catcher when he was only sixteen. Connie Mack had Mickey Cochrane, but he realized what a great athlete this fellow was, and he put him on first base. He could play third, too. He was a *great* athlete."

Billy Werber: "I once saw Foxx grasp a 175-pound player around the ankles and lift him straight up in the air. We called Jimmie 'The Beast' in testimony to his strength and agility, but in reality there was nothing bestial about him. One could not find a better-natured, more happy-go-lucky player than Foxx."

Doc Cramer: "I was with Jimmie my whole career. He was strong as a bull. He'd take a hold of your leg right there and put the whole prints of his fingers right in it.

"I seen Jimmie hit them right on over the top of that Shibe Park. The same way in Chicago. He could hit them hard. I remember at Fenway Park he hit one over the wall one-handed.

"In 1932, I was with him in Philly when he hit 58 home runs, and of course, Ruth had 60, and when he hit number 58 he had a month to go in the season to tie Ruth, and if any of us were on second, we gave the catcher's signs. Also he was well-liked all over the league, and some of them pitchers were laying the ball in there, hoping he would hit it. But he would pop 'em right straight up.

"I was with Jimmie when his career ended. He got hit in the head up in Canada on a barnstorming trip, fall of '41.

"At the end of the season some of us would play ten to twelve games and make five or six thousand dollars. We played anybody. On this day we were in Winnipeg, Canada. The pitcher's name was Chet Brewer, a right-hander, a good pitcher. He never pitched in the big leagues. Had a good fastball and threw a screwball.

"Jimmie was with Boston at the time. Brewer hit him right in the head, and he was never any good after that. Jimmie wouldn't stay up at the plate like he used to. He bailed out all the time. He was gun-shy after that. We could see it before we finished the trip. Teddy Lyons told me, 'They got Jimmie. I'm afraid he's done.' Which he practically was."

Tony Lupien: "When I was a player at Harvard, I used to come in and work out with the Boston club, and sometimes Foxx would say to me, 'Take the infield for me.' And I'd take it in front of twenty thousand people. This was really something.

"He was such a nice guy. For instance, we'd go on from Sarasota, where we trained, to a place like St. Petersburg to play the Yankees, and we'd dress at the hotel in those days rather than the clubhouse—they were so bad—and at the hotel they'd put six of us in one room, and you'd all have to take a shower.

"Now Foxx knows I'm a first baseman, that I must have aspirations for his job. And I'd be in the room, and there would be six of us, and as soon as we got back to the room all sweaty, he'd call the desk and say, 'Send up a dozen bottles of beer.' They'd send it up, and Jimmie would pay for it. I'd say, 'Jim, can I get in on this?' and he'd say, 'Your turn will come. I've got it. I'm paying.' He was an extremely generous man. In fact, he was so lenient in his business operations that he got cleaned out. He owned the Jungle Golf Course in St. Pete, and you'd go down there and want to pay the grounds fees, and he'd say, 'No, you're a friend of mine. Play for nothing.' He was in eighteen different business ventures at one time. Everything went under. It was very unfortunate.

"Today you hear this emphasis about the weight room and lifting weights during the winter and all this bullshit, which is what it is, pure and simple. People would say to Foxx, 'What do you attribute your strength to?' He'd say, 'Milking cows and painting the barn.' He'd say, 'What do you do when you milk cows? You develop the wrists and the forearms. When you paint the house, it's like slapping the ball.' If you want to be a weight lifter, join the circus.

"Ted Williams enjoyed lifting chairs by the bottom leg. This is quite a trick. You have to have one hell of a wrist to lift up a chair that way. This is where the strength is. But Foxx was milking cows and putting the paint on the barn.

"Foxx had, all in all, a tragic life. For a man with that ability, he never made any money. He made $18,000 or $19,000 tops, and then after he quit his business ventures went bad on him. He went through a couple of marriages, a shame for such a nice, gentle man."

Bob Steele: "His first wife said he never grew up, that he was always just a boy, and that was because he got into baseball so young and didn't have other experiences that would make a young fellow grow up faster. He had this great talent, and he happened to be playing for a man like Connie Mack who was such a nice man that he maybe never did grow up."

When Foxx died in 1967, four years after suffering a heart attack, he was broke. His last job was as a filling-station attendant. The great slugger died during dinner, choking on a piece of meat that had gotten lodged in his throat.

CHAPTER 9

Joe Cronin, the $250,000 Prize: "So Where's the Pennant?"

When Tom Yawkey purchased the ballclub in February of 1933, his predecessor had already signed Marty McManus to be the manager. As soon as the 1933 season was over, Yawkey announced that his new manager would be Bucky Harris, who at age twenty-seven had played second base and managed the Washington Senators to their one and only world championship in 1924. That year the Senators beat the Yankees for the pennant by two games and went on to defeat the New York Giants in a seven-game series. The Boy Manager, as Harris was called, became the toast of the nation's capital.

When Tom Yawkey hired Eddie Collins to run the team, Collins assumed Yawkey would consult him in the major decisions, one of which, of course, was the choice of manager. However, Yawkey had admired the job Harris had done with Washington, and impulsively, without consulting Collins, he hired him.

Unfortunately, he didn't know that Collins and Harris were enemies. Now it was up to Collins to devise a clever way to get rid of Harris without letting Yawkey know what he was up to. His solution was Joe Cronin.

Joe Cashman: "George Preston Marshall, the owner of the Boston Red-skins football team, had a laundry business and made a lot of money. Marshall was a friend of Harris, and he talked Yawkey into hiring him. Yawkey never consulted Eddie Collins, so when Collins heard about it, he went crazy, because probably the two worst enemies in the league were Collins and Harris. Oh, they hated the very sight of one another from when they were players, and now Collins was the general manager and Harris was the manager, and Yawkey didn't know what the hell to do.

"The Red Sox had Harris manage in 1934, and he did a great job. They finished fourth with a bunch of misfits and bums. Anyway, Collins's one idea was to get rid of Harris, and since Yawkey was still itchy to get whatever ballplayers he could, when Yawkey asked him, 'Who is the best ballplayer in the league?' right away Collins said, 'Joe Cronin.' "

Joe Cronin was the starting shortstop and the manager of the Washington Senators. In 1933, he had led the Senators to a pennant over the Yankees. That year Cronin had hit .309 with 118 runs batted in. Only Triple Crown winner Jimmie Foxx of the Philadelphia A's was more valuable.

In 1934, however, Cronin had slumped both at the bat and in the field. He'd hit only .284, with seven homers and 101 RBIs. Cronin had broken his wrist on a Sunday in early September and had left the team early to marry Griffith's adopted daughter, Mildred Robertson, and to go on his honeymoon. Al Schacht had finished out the season as manager.

Despite Cronin's broken wrist, Yawkey was determined to buy him.

Joe Cashman: "Yawkey said to Collins, 'Go get him.' Collins said, 'You can't buy a guy like that.' Yawkey said, 'What do you mean? Go get him.' Collins said, 'Do you think all you have to do is go down and take him out of his hands? He belongs to Washington.'

"But he got Cronin, not only because Collins wanted Cronin but because Collins knew Yawkey would have to get rid of Harris. Cronin had managed Washington when they got him, and they couldn't demote him, so Collins killed two birds with one stone. He got Cronin and he got rid of Harris! And that's how that deal was made."

The call to purchase Cronin from Tom Yawkey to Clark Griffith, the owner of the Senators, came just before the World Series of 1934.

When the notoriously tightfisted Griffith got the request, he told Schacht, who saw that Cronin was slowing down as a player. Schacht advised him, "If you get enough money for him, it might not be a bad idea."

Griffith told Schacht he had never before sold a ballplayer to another big-league club. "Even when the sheriff was practically camped on my doorstep years ago, and I could easily have straightened things out by selling one or two of the few stars I had, I never even considered doing it then."

Schacht said, "I know, Griff, but listen. The wolves are already riding Cronin in Washington after this lousy season. And what with him marrying your adopted daughter . . . If you don't sell him for big money now, there might come a time when you might have to release your own son-in-law." But Griffith was determined not to sell Cronin. Schacht went off to Mexico City for a couple of weeks to perform his vaudeville act. When he returned, he learned that Griffith had indeed sold Cronin to the Red Sox.

"Let me shake the hand of a rich man," Schacht said.

"What do you mean?" Griffith replied.

"Why, you sold Cronin for a hundred and fifty G's, didn't you?"

"I'll let you in on a secret," Griffith said, lowering his voice. "It was more than $150,000. It was $250,000."

"A quarter of a million dollars!" Schacht whistled. "And you didn't want to sell him."

"I couldn't help myself," Griffith said. "I met the Boston people at the Series, and they kept after me, raising the price every day. It would have been ridiculous to hold back any longer." Then he said to Schacht, "You're in the deal too, Al."

"Me?"

"You're going to Boston with Cronin."

"What did they do," Schacht asked, "throw in a bag of peanuts?"

"Joe wants you with him," Griffith said. "Besides, they can pay you more in Boston than I can."

As part of the deal, Yawkey sent the Senators Lyn Lary. Also, Griffith made Yawkey agree to give Cronin a five-year contract at $30,000 a year.

In a separate transaction, coming to Washington from Boston to manage was Eddie Collins's bête noir, Bucky Harris.

The complaint voiced against Bucky was that he couldn't maintain discipline, a charge that would be made against most of the subsequent Boston managers. As Bucky Harris later explained, "I would have fired the drinkers in five minutes, but you don't fire high-priced name players unless you've got adequate replacements, and you can't find those in five minutes."

Bucky Harris never did learn the real reason he was let go. And, of course, in Boston it mattered greatly that Cronin was an Irishman and he wasn't. Nor did it matter that Cronin was a bad shortstop, a lousy manager, and an even worse general manager. Yawkey loved him, and so did Irish Boston.

Frank O'Neill, journalist: "Why would Yawkey pay $250,000 for a player? There were good reasons why he would, and the greatest among them were race and creed.

"Joe Cronin is Irish.

"There are as many Irish in Boston as there are in Dublin. It is in such an environment that Joe Cronin belongs. His smile and his speech and his manner place him rightfully in the midst of the blood royal of the Fighting Race.

"If Cronin could not draw the Irish of Boston through the gates, then never a man from Antrim to Kerry, nor from Clare to Kildare, could."

FAN DISILLUSIONMENT

After Tom Yawkey announced the purchase of Joe Cronin for $250,000, Red Sox fans immediately began talking pennant for '35. The acquisition of Cronin was astounding. Cronin was one of the two or three best hitters in the league; in 1930, he hit .346. He had led Washington to a pennant. He was Washington owner Clark Griffith's son-in-law. He had a lifetime batting average of .300, and he was good for a hundred RBIs a year. He had been the starting shortstop in the All-Star Game since 1933.

Though he didn't realize it, a confident Tom Yawkey was painting himself into a corner. His image radiated an aura of success. With the announcement that this young multimillionaire had purchased the team, even before Yawkey made a single move there was the assumption on the part of the Boston fans that Yawkey's resources combined with his enthusiasm soon would translate into pennants for their team. A generation earlier, the New York Yankees had bought young stars from the Red Sox and won themselves a whole string of pennants. It was only logical to Boston's fans that Yawkey would do as the Yankees had done and gain their measure of revenge on the American League. Boston fans for so long had to root for a doormat, and they were feeling that a pennant would not be long in coming.

Tom Yawkey spent freely, both on players and on the plant. He invested $750,000 to refurbish Fenway Park, adding grandstands in left and in right and erecting a new pavilion in right field. He removed the slope from the infield up to the left-field fence, ending the era of opposing left fielders tripping, falling, and rolling along the ground toward the infield as the ball caromed past. To make it more difficult to hit home runs over the now-too-short left-field porch, he erected a twenty-eight-foot-high wall.

Yawkey brought his investment in players to over a million dollars in December of 1935 with his purchase of home-run star Jimmie Foxx for $150,000, plus the additions of over-the-hill All-Star Heinie Manush and Connie Mack's fleet center fielder, Doc Cramer.

The Red Sox team in 1936 now included a lineup of All-Star-caliber players, including Wes and Rick Ferrell, Lefty Grove, Jimmie Foxx, Doc Cramer, and Joe Cronin.

Yawkey himself fueled the pennant talk by boldly predicting that under the leadership of Joe Cronin "the Red Sox would be as good as the Yankees." Yawkey, however, failed to take into consideration an element the Red Sox would be lacking throughout most of the Yawkey years: pitching depth. The

Yankees had it, the Red Sox didn't. The Sox finished fourth in '34 and did so again in '35. In 1936, despite the slugging stars, the team finished sixth, 28½ games behind the Yankees.

The team rose to second place in June 1936, but without a strong pitching staff, plummeted in the standings. Jimmie Foxx had a superhuman year, hitting .338 with 41 home runs and 143 runs batted in, but shortstop Cronin injured himself again and slipped badly to .281 with only 295 at bats. The pitching staff, aside from Lefty Grove and Wes Ferrell, was in disarray.

When the Red Sox failed even to contend in 1936, Red Sox fans "leaped to the conclusion that the pennant was in the mail," wrote Harold Kaese, a sportswriter for the *Boston Globe*. "When it was not delivered, their disappointment was as bitter as that of a boy who has not received the promised atomic peashooter for 1,000 cereal labels."

And yet, the grumbling was not aimed toward Tom Yawkey. He had made a good-faith effort in spending his millions to improve the team. The fans laid the blame elsewhere. "It was natural," wrote Kaese, "for them to take it out on Cronin."

Part of the reason was Cronin's $250,000 price tag. Like owners and fans who make the same mistake today, everyone assumed that a player's skill increases as his salary goes up. When the Red Sox paid Cronin $250,000 in 1934 dollars—the equivalent of about $2 million today—during a period when you could buy a steak for a dollar, everyone assumed he would play better than is humanly possible and bring the team a string of pennants.

Unfortunately, fans to this day have never really understood the concept that a player's purchase price, or what he is paid, is not a barometer of the skill level at which he is going to play. Whether a player is paid $10,000 or $100,000 or a million a year, he is still the same player.

With the Washington Senators, Cronin had been a franchise player, but on the Red Sox, his skills, especially in the field, slipped noticeably. Even though no one doubted his ability as a power hitter, his lapses in the field were causing Red Sox fans to grumble that he was just another overpaid ballplayer, which only served to add to his pressure and make his fielding worse.

With Boston, Cronin developed a case of "groundball jitters." The slower the grounder, the worse he kicked it. Commented Harold Kaese, "He resorted to kneeling in front of the ball as an outfielder does—the $275,000 [sic] squat. One day the ball hit the other knee and careened out to the right fielder."

"For Christ sake, Joe, if you're going to miss 'em," said second baseman Oscar Melillo, "you might as well stand up and miss 'em like a big leaguer."

Cronin was also feeling the added pressure of being a playing manager, a role he held on to until 1945, when a broken leg finally ended his playing career. Said Kaese after watching Cronin's performance for ten years, "Cronin's nerves frayed during the crucial stages of every race. Only his indomitable will carried him through. Men who lived with him on blistering western trips—when the Sox disintegrated—became prejudiced against playing managers."

SEEDS OF DISHARMONY

There is a drawback to filling a team's roster with grizzled vets. They aren't moldable. They bring their personalities to the team already set. Veterans are convinced they know how to play the game. They have very strong ideas about who should be playing and who shouldn't. And if there are no replacements in the farm system, they know the manager is powerless to control them and they are free to let their contempt show through.

And so a team of vets requires a very special man to handle them, more so than a team of fuzzy-cheeked kids. Tom Yawkey may not have known this. Perhaps he didn't care. But the vets he bought for the Red Sox, some of the toughest, worst-tempered personalities in the league, required a strong, decisive manager who could command their respect.

Yawkey's first manager, Bucky Harris, never got that respect. His replacement, Joe Cronin, had even less success controlling the team.

Because he was a playing manager, Cronin had several distinct disadvantages. The first was his $250,000 purchase price: his players didn't think he was worth it, especially since his fielding skills were so bad, and eroding further. Another problem: part of his job required him to talk to the press, and sometimes Cronin hurt himself in the eyes of his players when he criticized one of them. And Yawkey had him negotiate some of their salaries. A tough negotiator, he'd learned penny-pinching from Clark Griffith of the Washington Senators, and he was good at keeping salaries down, which made some of them bitter toward him, especially in light of his huge paycheck.

In addition, most of his pitchers resented him because he insisted upon calling all the pitches during the game. Add that his pitching staff was poor, that he was too nice a guy to be a disciplinarian, and that the players sensed that the general manager, Eddie Collins, didn't like him, and the stage was set for a situation that was to mark the Red Sox throughout the Yawkey years: raging dissension on the team.

Gene Desautels: "It wasn't only the players who didn't like Cronin. The general manager didn't like Cronin. That's the truth, because Eddie Collins used to ask me a lot of very personal questions about Cronin on the road. I was afraid to say too much. Eddie would say, 'Did he get to the ballpark on time?' Things like that. I'd say, 'Yeah, oh yeah, he's always there.' I could tell that they didn't like each other."

*   *   *

Joe Cronin, the top-paid superstar, a contact hitter who could still swing the bat with power, quickly lost the support of many of his best players. Worst, some of them, especially the former Philadelphia A's, spoke openly in the clubhouse about his lack of managerial skills.

His worst critics—superstars Lefty Grove and Jimmie Foxx—knew that they had stature and Tom Yawkey's affection and wouldn't be traded, no matter what they said, and Cronin, who had equal stature and backing, knew the same. It was a standoff. Cronin remained as manager in Boston for thirteen seasons, outlasting the carping vets who finally grew old and dropped off the team.

One incident makes clear the problems he had running the team. One year, as the season was winding down and the team was in a slump, Cronin informed the players that he was arranging for a special morning workout session in St. Louis. The next morning, he was the only player to show up. He had the clubhouse boy round up a bunch of kids, and he worked out, alone.

Cronin did have his supporters, though.

Tony Lupien: "Joe was a nice guy, just a nice guy. He let you play. Never got on your back. Expected you to do the job. I only saw him fine two or three players. Very rarely did he even hold a meeting in the clubhouse to talk over things.

"He was the sort of manager who put eight guys out there and let them play.

"Joe's idea of baseball was hitting. That's what he thought about. And when you're a player-manager, you always think, 'I can influence the game.' "

Bob Steele: "When Cronin was playing manager, when he came to bat he was very impressive. He stood up there and hit the Wall or put it over the Wall time after time, and he had no qualms about putting himself into the toughest situations. No matter who was pitching, if the situation called for a pinch hitter, he would go up there."

Gene Desautels: "Joe had a lot of patience at the plate. He was a good hitter. When I first came up, he would say, 'I want you to have a bat in your hand every possible minute.' I knew he wanted me to be a better hitter. He'd say, 'Wait on the ball and swing quick.' He was right. He knew his business."

Tony Lupien: "As a batter he knew how to decoy pitchers. He'd go up to the plate and crouch, trying to suck them in, make them think he was vulnerable to a certain pitch, as if to say, 'You're going to throw the curveball over this part.' And just as the guy would start to pitch, he'd straighten himself up again. He was an extremely shrewd hitter. He knew the pitchers and knew what their best pitch was and what they were going to throw you in a jam."

The Red Sox became a team in Joe Cronin's image: a lineup of excellent hitters. Speed took a back seat throughout the Cronin years, as it would throughout the entire Yawkey era.

Ben Chapman: "We only had three guys on the ballclub that could run, and that was Doc Cramer, Jimmie Foxx, and myself. There was no speed at all. We had a good defense—except the shortstop. The outfield was adequate, the catching so-so. We really didn't have anyone who could go from first to third on an average base hit. I didn't think we had pennant-winning clubs."

Doc Cramer: "We won in Philadelphia but didn't win in Boston for a simple reason: pitching. We didn't have any pitching. Wes Ferrell was done, Walberg done, Grove was the only one. We had all kinds of pitchers. We just didn't have any pitching, that's all. When you get beat 10 to 8, 8 to 6, it ain't the hitting. 'Cause seven or eight runs ought to win any ballgame in the big leagues. I think Collins had in mind to build the team according to the fence in Boston. But you have to have somebody to keep them other guys from hitting that fence too.

"That's why I say they went at it ass-backwards. They should have bought pitching when they were buying all this other talent. But they didn't. They bought Grove, Walberg, and Ferrell, but Walberg and Ferrell were about finished. When Mr. Mack would see something like that, he'd have young guys coming up. But Boston didn't do that. They didn't have any young guys. It's an old story. You can never buy a pennant. You can't do it.

"Joe gambled with pitchers mostly, but he had to, because he didn't have any, but it didn't seem to work out. If he thought a pitcher could get somebody out, that was his hunch, and he'd play it. It backfired an awful lot of times. And if he had one pitcher who could win, he'd use him all the time. Like Jack Wilson. Cronin burned him up by using him every day, relieving with him. Joe Heving, he was a pretty good relief pitcher, pitched good ball for us, but Cronin wanted to use him every day, and Joe Heving couldn't stand it. He was too old for that."

The best managers historically have been those players who were defensive-minded players—former catchers or infielders renowned for their defense. Great hitters rarely have had a deft touch handling pitchers. Ty Cobb, Rogers Hornsby, and Ted Williams were famed hitters who had such difficulty. Cronin was no different. Adding to Cronin's problem was a lack of quality pitching, and though the staff lacked the talent to win a pennant, Cronin made a bad situation worse by alienating most of the staff by insisting that he call the pitches. His pitchers also complained among themselves that he would second-guess them in the press.

Gene Desautels: "Lefty Grove didn't like Cronin. He never told me exactly why. But he was the sort of guy if he didn't take a liking to a guy, he would talk about him all the time. 'Hell, Cronin isn't a good manager,' he would say. And Cronin couldn't do anything, because Yawkey was instrumental in getting Lefty, and he was the one who liked him, just like he liked Jimmie Foxx and Cramer and Eric McNair and all those guys he got from Philadelphia.

"A lot of the pitchers used to think Cronin would criticize them behind their backs instead of telling them to their faces what they were doing wrong. He would go talk to the newspapermen about the pitching staff, and I know he wasn't crazy about Fritz Ostermueller and the right-hander, Denny Galehouse. Denny was a pitcher who had to have good control.

"I was the catcher, and Cronin used to tell me, 'Call for that fastball, and the hell with so many curves.' And so naturally I would try. I'd call for a fastball, and Denny'd shake me off, so I had to do something else. I'd tell Denny, 'Joe wants you to throw more fastballs.' Which should have been okay. After all, he was the manager. But Denny didn't have that good a fastball, and he wouldn't say much, but he would be thinking, 'Look, I'm pitching my own game. I've been around long enough.' And he would shake me off.

"We had poor pitching, but Cronin didn't help the pitching staff any calling the pitches. He was the kind of manager who liked to do that. He would rub his right pant leg down if he wanted a fastball and he would rub his glove hand down for a curve. I remember we had one pitcher by the name of Jack Wilson. He was a good fastball pitcher. And no curve. He couldn't get the curve over. Whenever he pitched, Cronin would just give me fastball, fastball, fastball.

"He didn't call all the pitches all the time. I remember there was one year in particular he did it a lot. Of course, Lefty Grove was there, and he wasn't going to call Lefty's pitches."

Cronin also played favorites. He seemed to be partial to players who were Catholic or who came from the Pacific Coast League—those who weren't like the former members of the Philadelphia A's, who Cronin seemed not to like at all. Unfortunately for the Red Sox, those A's players, Grove, Foxx, Cramer, and Eric McNair, provided much of the team's talent.

Tony Lupien: "Joe was a very good Christian. He went to church all the time. Joe had a coach named Mike Ryba, and we used to say about him, 'That son of a bitch would know how much you put into the collection plate.' If you went to church, he'd know if you put a quarter in or a buck or didn't go. We thought he was one of the stooges for management. And yeah, it mattered. Management was well aware. I imagine Joe was sensitive to it. When I was there, this was a pretty well Catholic-dominated club."

Doc Cramer remembers the dislike Joe Cronin seemed to have for the former Philadelphia A's players, including Doc himself. Fifty years later, it still bothers him.

Doc Cramer: "I can't recall one of the Philly players that he took to. Once during a game I heard Grove tell him that he couldn't play shortstop on a high school team. And Joe didn't like Foxx. Nooo. I don't know why. That's like not liking Ruth. Not like Jimmie? Everybody liked Jimmie. Walberg, a big Swede, a good-natured guy? I could understand how he didn't like Grove, but he sure liked them wins he had. Max Bishop was the nicest kind of guy. Eric McNair was a nice boy. Hell, I don't know. I know Washington and Philly feuded when I played for Philly, and Cronin was with Washington.

"He didn't like me. I knew that. I don't have any idea why. I didn't care too much for him either. Joe was a good hitter, that's all I will say. Did you ever see where he won an All-Star Game? I went with him to Cincinnati. I went with him to St. Louis. He didn't play me in either game. We lost both of them. And I was a Red Sox. Didn't play in either game. I didn't say a word. I didn't care. The hell with him. What did I care?"

Ben Chapman, who hit .340 for the Red Sox in 1938, was perhaps the fastest man in baseball. Between the years 1931 and '33, while with the Yankees, Chapman led the league in stolen bases. In 1931, he stole 61. Second that year was Roy Johnson of Detroit with 33. No one else in the league even had 20.

The Red Sox tried to acquire him from the Yankees, but Ed Barrow wouldn't deal him to his former employee. According to Chapman, Yawkey and Collins arranged with Clark Griffith, the owner of the Washington Senators and by now a close friend of the two men to acquire Chapman from the Yankees. The next year, the Red Sox got him in a trade with Griffith.

Chapman, outspoken, could be a hothead, stubborn and tough. He was a fighter of renown.

Ben Chapman: "When I was with the Yankees we were playing the Washington ballclub, and Buddy Myer, the second baseman for Washington, cut

Gehrig up above the knee at first base. So McCarthy said, 'Get him, and if you don't get him, I'm going to fine you.' So I went into second base and knocked Buddy from here to that television set. He said, 'If you ever do that again, I'm going to kick you right in the ass.' I said, 'All right, I'll be back.'

"So about two days later I was on base again, and I went for him and he sidestepped me and kicked me right in the butt. So we had a little skirmish around second base.

"I had to go through the Washington dugout to get into the clubhouse, and Earl Whitehill stepped up in front of me and he said, 'Chapman, you're a fatheaded . . . ,' and when he got to 'fat,' I hit him and knocked him down in the dugout, and those Washington ballplayers jumped on me, and I bet you I had twenty knots on the top of my head when they got through.

"Everybody was in the fight except Ruth, Gehrig, and Walter 'Jumbo' Brown. Even McCarthy and Gomez got it. We had a real ball."

In Boston in 1938 Chapman played in an outfield with Doc Cramer and Joe Vosmik. All three batted over .300. But despite his considerable skills, Chapman sojourned with the Sox for only two seasons.

Gene Desautels: "Ben thought he was a better hitter than Cronin, and in 1938, Ben hit .340, which *was* better, but Cronin used to talk to the newspapermen, and it would always be in his favor. Ben thought Joe was badmouthing him. I remember Joe saying to a newspaperman, 'He's a good hitter, but he hits when it doesn't mean anything.' "

Chapman and Cronin clashed openly only twice during those two seasons, once when he was given the bunt sign and he ignored it.

Ben Chapman: "I was hitting .330 or .340, doing a pretty good job in the field, and the score was one to nothing, and I had driven in the run. We had a runner on second and no outs. I looked down at Pennock, and he gives me the bunt sign. I said to myself, 'Wait a minute. I'm the guy who drove in the run, remember?'

"I backed out of the box and got back in. Pennock gave me the bunt sign again. I said, 'The hell with that.' So I got a fastball down the middle and swung. And I hit the ball, and it didn't go any higher than the ceiling, right back to the catcher. You know how I felt. So I walked back into the dugout, and Cronin said, 'Did you see the sign?' I said, 'Yup.' He said, 'Well, what was it?' I said, 'It was a bunt.' He said, 'Why didn't you bunt?' I said, 'I'm damned tired of bunting all the time.' "

*   *   *

Another time Cronin blamed him for letting a line drive fall between him and Cramer. Each time, Cronin punished Chapman by making him sit for two-week periods.

After the second incident, Chapman was on the bench late in the game. Cronin was looking for someone to bat. He had already used low-average hitters like Moe Berg and Gene Desautels, and as he was pacing up and down in the dugout, he said, "I don't have a soul to pinch-hit."

Jimmie Foxx got up and said, "What's wrong with Chappie?"

Cronin grumbled, "Go on up and hit," and Chapman got a base hit to tie the game, and Cronin resumed starting him after that.

But the two men never got along. During the winter of 1938, Chapman was traded.

Ben Chapman: "We had two arguments, that was all. I was wrong once, and I was right once. I was just dissatisfied with the way Cronin had handled me. Like I said, it was partially my fault, partially his. I remember a remark Ted Williams made one time. He said that if the Red Sox had traded somebody else instead of me, they'd have won the pennant the next year, because I was a .340 hitter, I could run, and the guy they got for me couldn't.

"After I went to Cleveland, I was on first, and I told Cronin, 'Don't you get in my way, 'cause I'm comin'.' He knew what I meant, and he got out of the way. In those days you could slide out of the baseline. If I couldn't go outside to get a fielder, then I didn't have any fun. And there was nobody I went after more than I did Cronin."

But what seemed most to hurt Cronin in the eyes of his teammates was his inability to field. Cronin was a prideful man. He didn't seem to want to give up his role as the team's shortstop. He wouldn't even move over and play third. He was a player. He liked to hit. He liked to be in the center of things. But if the pitching staff was angered by the way they were used by him, his inferior play at shortstop made them livid.

During his three years on the Red Sox, Wes Ferrell was always commenting. "If we had a shortstop, we'd win the pennant. Cronin has lost me four games already."

In August of 1936, Ferrell, backed by several other players, was set to stage a player rebellion over Cronin's shortcomings in the field. Ferrell walked off the mound in the middle of an inning without saying good-bye to anyone, even the umpire.

After the game, Ferrell was suspended and fined $1,000. It was the harshest punishment handed out by Cronin until that time. Ferrell was later reinstated, and even got his money back, but in June of 1937 Cronin got his revenge: he traded the two Ferrell brothers to Washington for Ben Chapman and Bobo Newsom.

If Cronin thought he was getting players who would be less critical, however, he was wrong.

Ben Chapman: "Bobo Newsom was pitching a ballgame one day in Boston, and he was in a little trouble, and Cronin had kicked a couple of balls, and Cronin started in to Bobo. Bobo stopped and he said, 'You play shortstop, and I'll do the pitching.' Bobo didn't pitch for about two weeks after that. So they didn't get along too well. Not at all.

"Let's just say that Joe wasn't a good shortstop defensively. They wanted Eric McNair, who had led the American League in fielding for Connie Mack's A's, playing shortstop."

McNair, nicknamed Boob, was the Red Sox shortstop in 1936, when Cronin was injured and missed most of the season. McNair, a Punch-and-Judy hitter, batted .285 in 128 games, but more important, made only 14 errors at shortstop. In 1937, after Cronin healed, he returned to short and made 31 errors. Eric McNair, meanwhile, spent a year of torture.

Doc Cramer: "McNair was a good shortstop, but what ruined him was that his wife died in childbirth. We roomed together. He was a good boy. My wife and I went to Mississippi for her funeral. Booby thought it was his fault. He was the father of the child. He never got over it. He always thought that if he hadn't made her pregnant, she wouldn't have died.

"He was less everything after that happened. He got to drinking heavy. That's why they put him with me, trying to stop it. I couldn't stop him. I couldn't."

Another former player told me the following story about Eric McNair. He made me promise I wouldn't reveal the source.

"Do you remember Gene Desautels, the catcher? One night he and I were in the Book Cadillac Hotel, and I heard a noise outside the window. There was a ledge about the width of my sofa out there. I said, 'Gene, you hear that?' And he said, 'Yeah.' I said, 'I'm going to go see what it is.'

"So I got up and raised the window, and there was Eric McNair standing out on the ledge, stiff as a hoot owl. And he had a gun in his hand. I said, 'Booby, what are you doing?' He said, 'I'm going to kill Cronin.' I said, 'No, you're not. Not as long as I'm around here.'

"It took us forty-five minutes to get him into our room."

Gene Desautels: "We were up on the seventh or eleventh floor, high up, and that ledge wasn't very wide, and we were afraid he might fall off and kill himself, because he had been drinking. If he had slipped, he would have been dead."

Ben Chapman: "Part of why McNair didn't play shortstop was that Cronin was protecting his own job, but you can't blame a man for not wanting to give it up. No question about it. Joe could hit the long ball. Joe was the star."

Doc Cramer: "Yawkey got shortstop Dib Williams from Philadelphia [in 1935], but Cronin got rid of him too. He didn't want them around. That's running the team for your benefit."

CHAPTER 10

Billy Evans Builds a Farm System

THE SALE OF PEE WEE REESE

By 1937, it had become clear to Tom Yawkey that he would not be able to buy a pennant. He decided to try Plan 2, building his team the way Yankee general managers Ed Barrow and later George Weiss had done it, by purchasing a string of minor-league clubs and stocking them with young prospects.

At that time, the Red Sox had no farm clubs and no more than twenty-five young players in development. The man Tom Yawkey hired to run the farm system was a former major-league umpire named Billy Evans.

Evans was a brilliant judge of talent and an excellent administrator. By 1941, after only four years, he had built an eight-team chain of farm clubs, with seven of those eight teams qualifying for the playoffs. While Evans was a farm director, the Red Sox acquired Tex Hughson, Mickey Harris, Dave "Boo" Ferriss, Dom DiMaggio, Johnny Pesky, Bobby Doerr, and a young pitcher-outfielder from San Diego named Ted Williams.

Tony Lupien: "Billy Evans was a perfect gentleman and an honest man. I was very happy to have known this man.

"Billy graduated from Cornell. The day after he graduated, he umpired in Philadelphia in the major leagues. He was a twenty-two-year-old kid, and Evans said that Connie Mack was on his ass something terrible.

" 'About the fourth inning,' he said, 'I couldn't stand it any longer. I went over to the dugout where Connie Mack was sitting, and took my mask and shook it in his face and said, 'Goddamn you, another word out of you, and you're going out of here.'

"And he said, 'I walked back to the plate and I thought to myself, "What have I done?" ' But, Evans said, later on one of the ballplayers on the club told him that Mack said, 'My gracious, I think the young man means it.'

"The next day Evans felt so badly about what he had done that he walked over to the bench and said, 'Mr. Mack, I want to apologize for the language I used yesterday.' And Mr. Mack said, 'That's perfectly all right, my young man. That's perfectly fine.'

"And Billy said he never had any trouble in the American League from then on.

"He wrote a book, *Knotty Problems of Baseball,* which we used to carry on the bus when I coached at Dartmouth. It had all the damn things that could happen rulebook-wise, all the little things that come up.

"After he was an umpire he was general manager of Cleveland, and then he came to Boston and then went to Detroit. He became president of the Southern League. He was a prestigious man."

One of Evans's little-noted moves was to purchase the Louisville team of the American Association to be a Triple-A farm club. In this move, Evans bought a minor-league team with a strong tradition. Equally important, Evans had bought another asset he expected would benefit the Red Sox organization greatly: an eighteen-year-old shortstop by the name of Harold "Pee Wee" Reese. Reese, a former marbles champion of Louisville, was a graceful fielder with range, speed, and quickness, and for a little guy he had a surprising amount of pop in his bat. Evans had spotted a jewel, and to get him, he had bought the entire Louisville franchise. Joe Cronin was nearing the end of his career as a shortstop, and Evans felt that with Reese, the Red Sox had their shortstop of the future. What Evans hadn't anticipated was Joe Cronin's fierce fight to protect his job and Tom Yawkey's fierce loyalty in protecting Cronin.

Tony Lupien: "When Billy was farm director of the Boston Red Sox, he made one of the greatest deals of all time when he bought the Louisville club for Tom Yawkey. He wanted Pee Wee Reese. So they got the ballpark and the uniforms and Pee Wee Reese and the whole shebang for a ridiculously low price.

"But Cronin was still playing, so all of a sudden Cronin cut Billy's legs off by selling Pee Wee Reese to Brooklyn.

"Joe didn't want to move to third base. And then Pee Wee was gone. And

Billy was livid. I ran into him shortly after that. Jesus, he went right through the roof.

"He said, 'How the hell can you run a farm system if you made a deal for an outstanding guy, and then you give him away?'

"And that move itself may have cost the Red Sox two or three pennants."

The sale of Pee Wee Reese to the Dodgers, it turned out, presaged the firing of Billy Evans as farm director.

During Harold Kaese's career as a sportswriter he kept notes, and after his death, Kaese willed his notes to the Boston Public Library as part of its Boston Tradition in Sports collection.

The following information comes from a typed manuscript marked "Evans Confidential," dated October 7, 1945, from an off-the-record interview Kaese had with Billy Evans.

On August 10, 1941, Yawkey asked Evans to move to Louisville. He said the Sox would buy him a house and he would be the general manager of the team. According to Evans, Yawkey told him, "We'll give you a $5,000 raise and ten percent of the profits there."

Yawkey then asked him if he wanted a three-year contract. Evans said he would work without a contract. Yawkey insisted on a one-year contract, and Evans agreed.

Less than a month later, on September 6, 1941, Yawkey called Evans at his Cleveland home. Yawkey told him, "Billy, we think it will be in the best interest of the Red Sox if you were to sever your connection with the club."

Evans replied, "If you feel that way, then I'll resign. I've enjoyed my association with you very much and hate to leave."

"That was all," said Evans. "It was a rough deal. I was fired over the telephone and without reason."

According to Evans, Yawkey was drunk. During the conversation, Evans said Yawkey told him, "I guess I'll call up Eddie [Collins] and fire the son of a bitch."

Said Evans, "If I had been out that night or asked Yawkey to wait to reconsider, I honestly think I'd still be working for the Red Sox."

According to Kaese, Evans blamed Cronin for his firing. His downfall, Evans told Kaese, began with the purchase of Louisville to get Pee Wee Reese. Evans had told Yawkey to buy Reese, because Yawkey said he wanted a shortstop. Yawkey said Cronin could play two or three more years. Reese started the year badly, however, and suddenly Yawkey, after discussions with Cronin, ordered Evans to sell him.

Evans said he told Yawkey, "Reese is not well, and the other clubs would shy from him, knowing the Sox didn't want him after buying the Louisville club to get him."

After June, Reese recovered from the flu and started playing well. "Sensational," said Evans. Evans begged Cronin to go see him play or send scouts.

"I'm not interested in Reese," said Cronin.

Brooklyn bought Reese for $50,000 and five unwanted players.

According to Evans, when Cronin first saw Reese at Arcadia, he said, "So that's the guy who is going to take my place. He's too small."

"Cronin," Evans told Kaese, "is too impetuous. He has too many likes and dislikes and makes up his mind too fast. Yawkey is also impulsive, and Collins is nervous and impulsive. The Red Sox need a stabilizer. Cronin lacks patience. Yawkey wants results in a hurry. He's too impressionable. If he is struck by a kid pitcher in an exhibition game in Syracuse, he never forgets it and always thinks the kid is good. If he doesn't like something about a kid, he never wants to see him again."

Evans told Kaese that Yawkey's conscience bothered him. Evans said Yawkey told others he could have fired Evans more pleasantly.

Said Evans, "I was successful, and they fired me."

As a result of these series of events, Joe Cronin got to play shortstop for the Red Sox a few years longer.

What the Red Sox lost was Pee Wee Reese, a future Hall of Fame shortstop, and farm director Billy Evans, the one man in the organization with the skill and expertise to bring the Red Sox a pennant. The 1946 pennant won by the Sox was a final tribute to Billy Evans's skill as an evaluator of young talent.

Another great irony is that it might have been the Red Sox, not the Brooklyn Dodgers, to make history with a keystone combination of Pee Wee Reese and Jackie Robinson, but that's a story for a later chapter.

LIFE IN THE BUSHES

Back in the 1940s, there was no Instructional League. Minor-league coaches didn't instruct. Their job was to pick out the best talent and just let everyone play. A young kid would begin his climb to the majors in D ball, and each year he would move up a classification or two, until he reached his level of competence, all the while keeping his eyes open, learning from experience and picking up tips along the way from whomever and wherever.

There was little glamour about playing minor-league baseball. It was a training ground, where young kids harbored dreams and over-the-hill vets came to hang on.

Tony Lupien, who graduated from Harvard College, was the regular first baseman for the Boston Red Sox in 1942 and 1943. Lupien played for Little

Rock, Arkansas, in the Southern League in 1940. His manager was a redneck by the name of Herb Brett. Brett was an embodiment of the Old South, a southerner in his own image. Lupien, who after pro ball had a long and illustrious career as a baseball coach at Dartmouth College, has never forgotten either Little Rock or Herb Brett. It was the best of times and at the same time the worst.

Tony Lupien: "I played at Scranton in 1939, and we won the pennant there, and then the Red Sox sent me to Little Rock in 1940. It was one of the goddamnedest experiences a man ever had.

"I had gone to spring training with the Sox in '40, and one night after dinner, Billy Evans, the farm director, called a little infielder named Hal Seeling and myself up to his room, and he said, 'I'm going to do something to you that I shouldn't do to a dog.' He said, 'I'm going to send you both to Little Rock.' And he said, 'I want to impress one thing on you. No matter what happens there, I'm going to stick with you all the way.' This was a hell of a send-off.

"And, Jesus, once we got there, we realized he hadn't lied to us. Little Rock spring-trained at home, and the ballpark looked like a city dump. They hadn't scraped the infield with a rake since last fall. Windows were broken in the clubhouse. There were no heads on the showerbaths.

"Little Rock was a Red Sox club, but it was privately owned. The owner was a little fat guy by the name of Thompson, an old-time southerner, and he had a box that was at eye level with home plate, and if you broke a bat, you had to bring the bat to him to get a new one. His business manager was a guy by the name of Ray Winder, and they didn't believe in spending a cent on anything.

"These were pretty tough southern people. And the two of us were both college graduates, and I was Catholic besides. In those days, that meant a lot. In Birmingham, for instance, I once went to the front desk of the hotel and asked the lady, 'Is there a Catholic church nearby?'

"She said, 'You go six blocks to the left down there . . .' There was no Catholic church. She had misdirected me. That was part of the game. And when I finally got to the church, there were three or four Catholics inside. It was a time when the South was tough.

"Herb Brett was a tobacco auctioneer from Danville, Virginia. Brett was about six foot four. He had pitched Triple A a lot and in the Eastern League and the Carolinas. Tom Yawkey had tobacco holdings in the Carolinas and Virginia, and Brett had started managing for Yawkey in Danville and gone to Rocky Mount, and then to Little Rock. He hated northerners, hated college people, and hated Catholics. Of course, he hated us.

"We were ready to open the season, and Thompson bought some of the most garish uniforms you've ever seen. The home suits were white with red raglan sleeves. It looked like a uniform from a Cuban softball team. The hat was light blue with a red 'LR' on it. Thompson and Brett began arguing whether you wear the red socks or the blue socks at home. We were sitting in the clubhouse, trying these awful things on, getting ready for opening day, and Brett said, 'We'll have a meeting.'

"He said, 'I called Judge Brabham in Durham.' Judge Brabham ran the minor leagues. 'I asked him if I could get out of this fucking contract. I don't want no part of this.' We had a young ballclub, raring to go, and boom, we had to listen to this. Brett said, 'But if I want the money, he said I have to go through with it, so what the hell, let's talk over the hitters.'

"Brett was one of the vilest men you ever met in your life. We had a pitcher on the club by the name of Jim Prendergast, who pitched a long time for Syracuse in the International League. If you look him up in the record book, you'll see he pitched a bit for the Boston Braves. And Brett hated him because he was an Irishman. Brett had piles, and he used to come into the dugout and drop his pants and stick his piles back up his ass, and then he'd take his fingers and run them under Prendergast's nose.

"We were playing in Memphis one night, and we were sitting in the clubhouse, dirty and rotten, sweating in uniforms that hadn't been washed since Christ knows when. We were in the cellar good, and it was the middle of August, and Brett said, 'What the hell, we're all on the payroll, we might as well have a meeting and talk about how we're going to pitch the hitters.' He opened a box with a ball in it, and whap, he threw the ball at Prendergast and hit him right in the chest.

" 'All right, you left-handed son of a bitch, tell us how you're going to pitch to these hitters.'

" 'Well,' Jim said, 'the first guy is Lou Bush. He's a highball hitter, and I'm going to keep the ball down on him. MaGirth is the next hitter. I'm going to sidearm him. Babe Bonner is the third hitter. I'm going to curve him.'

"Brett said, 'Stop. I want to tell you something, Jim. If you pitch one fucking hitter the way you say you will, I'll give you two days' meal money.'

"Wee Willie Duke, who was one of the minor-league characters, was sitting there, and he said, 'For Christ sake, Herb, it's hot in here.' Herb said, 'Yeah, let's just go out and beat the shit out of them.'

"So we went out, and the game was rocking along, and we got to about the seventh inning, and Prendergast was not pitching a bad ballgame. But it looked like it was time for a change. We had Butterfly Johnson, who we had just gotten from the St. Louis Browns, up and throwing.

"All of a sudden, Brett went out to the mound, and we gathered around, and he said, 'Jim, how do you feel?' He said, 'I feel great, Herb.' He said, 'Well, you look horseshit. Get your ass in the dugout right now.'

"Herb brought in Butterfly Johnson. Babe Bonner was the first hitter, and wop, he hit one over the icehouse, and Prendergast had lost another.

"This was every day, day in, day out.

"We lost 105 ballgames that year. In August we played fifty games—

twenty doubleheaders and ten singles. This was rough going. We'd lose five, win one, lose six, win one. Every night Brett would come into the clubhouse, and he'd say to Tom, the nice clubhouse man, a black guy, a Southern gentleman, 'Tom, what time does the goddamn package store close?' Tom would say, 'Pretty soon, Mr. Brett.' 'Well, you'd better get your ass down there and get me a fifth of gin before it closes. We'll be here in the clubhouse when you come back.' Every night, night after night, he'd drink it.

"We got a rainy day one day, and we were over in Birmingham, and it was coming down. You can't imagine how it rains in the South. We were sitting around in the hotel, and nobody had any money. We couldn't buy a newspaper. So Brett got a cigar and he sat down. He said, 'Let's talk about pussy.' He said, 'Who's the best fuck you ever had?' and he started going around. He said, 'I want to tell you. I played out in L.A. in the old Coast League, and I had two c——s out there who were really something. I used to take the two of them to bed with me at once. Fuck one, turn over, fuck the other.'

"If a manager did that today, he'd be banished in five minutes. He was something else.

"It was a fight every day. It was the toughest year of my life, except when you look back at it.

"One time we had a fight in our own dugout in Nashville between Brett and one of our pitchers. The pitcher, Bob Katz, was a hell of a guy. That day he was our starting pitcher, and he was thinking he had a chance to go up to Boston as a reliever. Well, they got nine runs in the first inning before you can say Jack Robinson. Balls were flying around that park and off the walls, so Katz came to the bench after the inning was over, and as he was trying to get his jacket off a nail behind the dugout, he said, 'Jesus Christ, Herb, you were a pitcher yourself. Can't you see I didn't have it tonight? What are you letting me out there for like this, getting nailed?' Brett was wearing a diamond ring on his right hand, and Brett swung at him, whop, whop, and he really cut this guy up bad.

"In 1940 in the South in this country, the Pullman company sent all the lousiest cars and trains down there. It was the trash of the world. On all those railroads, we had Jim Crow cars, which were beat-up old cars with swinging doors in the middle of the thing. We could get one for the use of the whole ballclub.

"We had played in Atlanta on a Saturday, and we were going to Knoxville, and we had two or three beers, and when it's 115 degrees, two or three beers can hit you. You can really feel it.

"We got on the train, and all the young guys were in the back half, rookies like myself, reading funny books and minding our own business, and in the front part of the car, a poker game was going on.

"Brett was playing, and he had a pretty good load on. The other guys in the game were Lefty LeFebvre, Tony Rensa, who had caught for the White Sox and Phillies and was the old head on the club, Lew Krausse, and someone else. They had five in the game, and Brett was standing up in the aisle, and the roadbed was lousy, and the chandelier was swinging back and forth. It reminded me of the movie *Stagecoach*.

"The cards were running bad for Brett. Everyone was talking and moaning and groaning and putting a nickel up or a dime, which was a lot of money. Brett got dealt a lousy hand. The bets were on the table, and he was standing up, and when he got his last card, he took the hand and tore it up and threw the cards up toward the chandelier. He said, 'This is the end of poker on the Little Rock ballclub. We're not going to play no more.'

"Now Rensa, who had a fair load in him, was sitting there, and he said, 'Herb, I want to tell you something. This is a horseshit club, and you're a horseshit manager.'

"Brett said, 'That's enough.'

"Rensa said, 'That's enough? I'll tell you again. Not only that, if I was managing this club, there would be some changes made.'

"Brett belted Rensa with his diamond ring. They got up, and it was over and under the chairs, like rats, chasing each other, and we were rolling through the night, and the porters were looking through the windows, watching the fight go on.

"Finally Brett, who was strong, had Rensa under a seat, and he had him by the neck, and he was going to choke him to death.

"We were young, and we didn't know anything. We should have held Brett and let Tony get his licks in, but we didn't.

"They stopped the fight. Their shirts were torn and covered with blood, and they looked like a couple of ragamuffins. Brett said, 'Get everybody from the ballclub in. We're going to have a meeting.'

"The ballclub huddled around. Brett said, 'Tony, shake hands.' They shook hands. Brett said, 'There will never be a word of this fight that will leave this car.'

"We got into Knoxville the next morning, a Sunday morning, and I went to church and came back, and in the lobby Brett was writing a letter. He sealed it, folded it up, and he said, 'I fixed that Rensa's wagon. I just wrote a letter to Eddie Collins and told him all about the fight.'

"When I joined the Boston club at the end of the '40 season in Detroit, Cronin and I were having a drink, and he said to me, 'That must have been a hell of a fight coming over from Atlanta.' I said, 'I don't know what you're talking about, Joe.' He said, 'Don't give me that. We knew all about it in Boston.'

"After our last home game, we were scheduled to meet in the Southern Pacific station in Little Rock after the game. We got down to the station, and we were waiting for the train, and us poor little guys, cringing rookies who don't have a nickel, we were having an orangeade at one of the concession stands, and in came Brett into the station, and he was loaded. He said to a Red Cap, 'Get me the stationmaster.' We were thinking, 'What the hell is happening?' Pretty soon, out came an official of the Missouri Pacific. 'Yes sir, Mr. Brett, what can I do for you?'

"Brett said, 'Nothing. I just want to tell you that you are the trainmaster in the worst fucking town in the United States. That's all. Good-bye.'

"When I became manager in Jamestown, New York, in the PONY League, we came up through Rocky Mount coming north from Florida, and who was running the Rocky Mount club in the Carolina League but Herb Brett. We played the game, and afterward we went up to his room and started to reminisce. I said, 'Herb, I'm just starting out to manage. Give me some signs I can use. My signs are lousy.'

" 'Well,' he said, 'I managed Fayetteville in this league last year and we won the pennant, and I'll tell you the signs we used. We used nothing but word signs. All this other stuff meant nothing.'

"I said, 'What did you use?'

" 'Well,' he said, 'the hit was always on, so we didn't have a hit sign. The take sign, when you think of taking, what do you think of—a broad. "Room 303 at the hotel." That's the take sign. "Marie?" That's a take sign.'

"I said, 'What did you use for the bunt?'

"He said, 'Any city west of the Mississippi. San Francisco? That's a bunt. Omaha? A bunt.' He said, 'People thought I was a nut. I was motioning and also telling them a name.'

"I said, 'Did it work?'

"Brett said, 'I won the goddamn pennant with it.'

" 'But,' he said, 'I got to tell you about the last day. We're playing at Fayetteville, and we have men on first and second with nobody out in the ninth inning, and Red Howell is the hitter.'

"He said, 'The bunt was in order, and I was beginning to think they were getting my signs, so I said, "Wyanachee!" And on the next pitch Howell hit one nineteen miles over the left-field fence. As he was coming around third, I said, "Didn't you hear me say Wyanachee?" Howell said, "Yes, I did, Herb, and they'll find that son of a bitch in Wyanachee." '

"The one thing we did have was laughs. We didn't get any money, but we did have laughs."

CHAPTER 11

The Kids From
San Diego

BOBBY DOERR

In 1936, Red Sox general manager Eddie Collins made his one and only scouting trip to the West Coast. While he was in San Diego he scouted an eighteen-year-old second baseman named Bobby Doerr, who later starred for the Red Sox and was voted into the Hall of Fame. During the same trip he noticed a tall, skinny teenager who could hit a baseball with impressive ability. That player was Ted Williams, the regent of the Red Sox.

Bobby Doerr remembers his own San Diego roots and his initial impressions of the eighteen-year-old Ted Williams.

Bobby Doerr, Red Sox, 1937–51: "I began playing professionally in the Pacific Coast League with the Hollywood Sheiks in 1934. I was sixteen years old, in the eleventh grade. I grew up in Los Angeles, and I played a lot of baseball out there. During the Depression days you were playing ball every day of the year.

"My brother had played with the Sheiks at one time, and then he got released and went to Portland, and whenever Portland went to play the Sheiks, I would work out a little bit and then go sit in the stands. They saw my actions enough, I guess, that they thought they'd take a chance.

"The Sheiks played in the old Wrigley Field ballpark, where the Los Angeles Angels later played. I remember that one day Portland was in town, and my dad and my brother came over after school was out to pick me up. Dad said, 'The Hollywood club wants to sign you. Do you want to sign?' I said, 'Well, sure I'd like to sign.' My dad said there was only one way he would consider letting me sign.

"He said, 'I want to make sure that you promise that you'll go back and finish up and get your high-school diploma during the winter months.' I said, 'I will.'

"So we went down to Wrigley Field and I signed a two-year ironclad contract for $200 a month, which was a lot of money then.

"In those days you played a lot of baseball and you had a lot of old players around you, so you could get by as a young fellow. Your mistakes weren't magnified like they are with young players today. The old players would pick you up if you did something wrong.

"The Sheiks moved their franchise to San Diego in 1937. That year the San Francisco Missions moved to Los Angeles and became the Hollywood Stars.

"Eddie Collins, the Red Sox general manager, came out to San Diego in July of 1936. They had an option to exercise a binder contract, and so they bought my contract, and while Collins was out here, he saw Ted Williams.

"Ted had come in June for a tryout, and San Diego liked him and signed him. At the time Collins came down, Ted wasn't playing, but Collins watched him hit, liked his swing, so he went to Bill Lane, the owner of the San Diego club, and said he would like to buy Ted's contract. Lane said he wasn't ready to sell his contract at that time and that he would wait.

"Collins said, 'Will you give the Red Sox first chance to sign Ted or to buy Ted's contract?' They shook hands on it, and that's how that came about. On a handshake. There was nothing written.

"Ted played the last month of the season. We had an outfielder named Chick Shirer. He had been a football player and had a chance to go take a coaching job. But to get the job he had to leave the last month of the season, which he decided to do, and that gave Ted a chance to go in and play. Ted had just turned eighteen on August 30.

"I remember the day Ted came in for his tryout. This big, skinny kid was standing by the batting cage. Frank Shellenback, the manager, was pitching batting practice, and we were all standing around the cage waiting for a time at bat. Shellenback said, 'Let the kid get in and hit a few.' Well, nobody knew who this kid was. And I think out of the seven, eight balls he hit, at least three went out of the ballpark, which is a pretty good poke. I don't think we had a guy on the team who could hit the fence, let alone hit it out.

"Somebody by the batting cage said, 'Boy, this kid will be signed before the week is out.' That was on a Wednesday or a Thursday. On Monday we were scheduled to make a road trip to San Francisco, and there was Ted, waiting for the train along with the rest of us.

"You know, Ted came up as a pitcher-outfielder. I remember we were playing at home, and we were getting beat pretty good. Shellenback was trying to figure out who he was going to put in to pitch. Somebody said, 'Ted claims he's a pitcher.' So he put Ted in. And he didn't do so good. I remember a fella by the name of Wes Schulmerich, who was a former major-league player, hit a home run. They hit Ted pretty good. So Shellenback said, 'Well, that's the end of your pitching career, Ted. You're going to be an outfielder from now on.'

"What I remember about Ted was that everything was done in an aggressive way. He was always in a hurry to do something. Like he'd come into a restaurant. We'd be sitting down at the table eating. It would be three-thirty or four P.M. before a night game. Ted would come in, sit at the counter, and he'd pound on the table and say, 'Waitress, I got to catch a train.' He'd rush the order, she'd get it to him, he'd eat it, and my gosh, there he'd go. I'd wonder, 'Where is he going?'

"We did hang around quite a bit. In San Diego we played all day games. A lot of times Ted would say, 'C'mon, let's go get a milk shake,' 'cause Ted was anxious to put on weight. He was six foot three, but only weighed about 145. A big, skinny kid. So we'd go and get milk shakes and go to the movies quite a bit. We both liked westerns. We hung around quite a bit, even after we were in the major leagues.

"I was nineteen in 1937 when I first played second base for the Red Sox. Joe Cronin was my shortstop. He had slowed down a little bit, but he had a good arm and could make the plays. And he did help me a lot. Gosh, he told me so many things about pitchers I was going to have to hit against and about positioning in the field. There were so many things that after all the years he played, he was able to put into me there alongside him.

"Like I remember one time he told me about Bob Feller. He said, 'Bobby, here's a guy who's a little wild. And overpoweringly fast.' He said, 'Now, don't go up there and try to protect the whole part of the plate because you're not going to do anything with the outside part anyway. Cut the plate in half, and don't confine yourself to the strike zone. If you do, the ball's going to be on you before you can decide if it's a strike or not. Even if it's a little bad, if you think you can hit it, go after it.'

"And it helped me a lot. Because if he had said, 'Look, you gotta hit strikes, and you gotta protect the plate,' I never would have hit him. The ball would have been on me. I didn't hit Feller that great, but I had better success hitting him that way.

"The majors were significantly better than the Pacific Coast League. In the Coast League some of the balls you hit would be base hits and in the major leagues they were outs. You saw better players making better plays. You saw good pitchers every day in the majors.

"Monte Pearson and Bump Hadley of the Yankees were the first two pitchers I saw, and they had good curveballs and sneaky fastballs. And then it was Lefty Gomez. Yankee Stadium was a hard place to play in, a great big monster of a stadium—I'd never seen anything before like it. In front of big crowds. And you always had a shadow between home and the pitcher's mound, and you had a white background in center field that made it hard to pick up a pitched ball. And then when you hit a ball good, it went out there in no-man's-land in left field. You just felt like you were kind of whipped when you left there.

"After I finished there I started to think, 'Well, you know that old saying, "Dear Mom, get the hotcakes on, 'cause I might be home soon," ' but as time went on, I got to where I adjusted.

"But it wasn't too much longer after that that I got hit in the head with a ball, and I started to struggle a little bit. I got to trying a little too hard. My rookie year. Nineteen thirty-seven."

Fabian Gaffke, Red Sox, 1936–39: "Bobby Doerr was my roommate when he came up to the Red Sox. Bobby was ready to quit, ready to go home. Bobby was disgusted. He had a rough time hitting, and it was affecting his fielding. They started booing him in Boston. But Cronin stuck with him. Cronin took him out and put him back in and let him regain his confidence, and there you are: Bobby got in the Hall of Fame."

His first year Doerr played in only 55 games and hit .224, but in 1938 he became the regular second baseman, hitting .289, the beginning of an outstanding career. In fourteen seasons with the Red Sox, Doerr batted .288. He hit 223 home runs over his career and drove in 1,247 runs. Six times he drove in a hundred runs or more.

Roy Mumpton: "The last time I spoke to Joe Cronin, he was very bad. He said, 'Mump, if you can do anything, get Bobby Doerr in the Hall of Fame.' Those were almost the last words he uttered."

Doerr was elected to the Hall of Fame in 1986.

TED MAKES A FIRST IMPRESSION

Theodore Samuel Williams became a Boston Red Sox thanks to his mother, May, a fervent Salvation Army worker known around San Diego as the "Sweetheart of San Diego" and the "Angel of Tijuana."

May Williams played the cornet in the Salvation Army band and entertained prisoners in the county jail for a living. She once boasted of selling more copies of the Salvation Army newspaper, *War Cry,* than anyone else. As a result, May Williams rarely was home to take care of Ted.

Wrote Ted, "My mother was strictly Salvation Army. As a result, strictly nonfamily." She was "always gone."

Sometimes May Williams dragged Ted along to march in the Salvation Army band. Gawky and introverted, he was at an age when peer acceptance was all-important, and as he marched, he felt a deep, lingering shame and would try to hide himself behind the bass drum.

Ted's father was an unsmiling, quiet man who wasn't interested in sports. A little man, he had joined the Army at sixteen and had fought in the Philippines with the Fourteenth Cavalry during the Spanish-American War. He ran a photography shop, taking snapshots of sailors with their girlfriends. According to Williams, he didn't get home until nine or ten at night.

Williams got very little direction from his father. Ted wrote, "In the real crises of my life he never once gave me any advice."

In his book, *My Turn at Bat,* Williams wrote that writers seemed to delight in calling his father a wanderer or a deserter. But, said Williams, his father stuck with his mother for twenty years before divorcing her. For the divorce, Ted blamed his mother. Decrying the fact that she was never at home, he wrote, "I wouldn't have wanted to be married to a woman like that."

Ted had a brother, Danny, who wasn't as fortunate as he. Because of sports, Ted Williams had authority figures, his coaches, but Danny was not an athlete. Surly and mean, Danny had no respect for authority and always got into scrapes with the law. "His life was just an existence," wrote Williams.

Ted's home life shamed him. He hated that his mother was in the street marching, that she was never home, and that his house was dirty all the time. He was embarrassed that his clothes weren't as good as some of the other kids'.

He also admitted to a lack of self-confidence that made him painfully shy around girls and strangers. Later, after he made the big leagues, he would keep his head bowed when he signed autographs, and the public adulation would make him uncomfortable.

It was the period of the Great Depression, and times were hard. Williams grew up living in poverty, but, outside of school, he spent much of his time in San Diego's streets and the North Park Playground, amusing himself by playing sports. It isn't hard to picture Ted Williams as a boy suffering from the want and emotional deprivations at home, but taking his satisfactions from his exploits on the playgrounds, deriving a sense of self-worth playing all the games—football, baseball, and even basketball, a game he didn't enjoy very much. However, he was especially talented in baseball, and spent hours every day swinging the bat and pitching a ball into a hole in a board.

It was an activity his mother didn't understand or appreciate. When Ted was offered two dollars a game to pitch for the Texas Liquor House team, a local semipro outfit, Mrs. Williams objected strenuously.

"Before you earn money that way, I will sweep the streets of San Diego for a living," she told her son.

One Sunday, Ted came home to tell his mother he had good news and bad. The good news was that he had been at bat with the bases loaded and had hit a ball out of the park into a second-story store window. The bad news was that he had played on Sunday, breaking the commandment to keep the Sabbath holy, and also that he had to pay for the window.

"That's what you get for breaking the Sabbath Day," she scolded.

However, Bill Essick, a scout for the New York Yankees, had seen Ted hit the ball, and the next day he arrived at the Williams home wanting to sign the seventeen-year-old. When Essick rang the bell, May Williams thought Essick was the owner of the store with the broken window. After disabusing her of the notion, Essick, the discoverer of Joe DiMaggio, offered $250 a month if Ted started in Class B and $400 a month if he began in Class A. Since Ted was only seventeen, however, May didn't want her boy leaving town. She refused the Yankees' offer. If it hadn't been for her desire to keep her son close to home, Ted would have been playing left field in New York City beside Joe DiMaggio.

And so it was in July of 1936 that Ted signed with the local San Diego team, the Padres, where Boston general manager Eddie Collins discovered the tall, lanky kid at the same time he went to see second baseman Bobby Doerr, shortstop George Myatt, and catcher Gene Desautels on the only scouting trip he ever made.

Gene Desautels: "I was out in San Diego with Ted that year. Ted lived in San Diego, so I didn't see him much after the ballgame—he was a loner—and he was also in high school, so he didn't play a hell of a lot.

"When Eddie Collins came out there, though, he asked me a lot of questions about Ted. 'What do you think of him?' I said, 'That kid is going to be a hell of a hitter.' I could tell. He could hit anything. I told him, 'He talks and thinks hitting every minute.' That's all Ted talked about. And he had the physical qualifications. He had the good forearms. Later, with Boston, he used to compare his muscles with Jimmie Foxx in the clubhouse. Ted would say, 'Hey, look at my skinny arms, and you with your muscular arms.' Jimmie would laugh and say, 'Why don't you put on some beef? Maybe you'll grow some muscles.' But Ted didn't need muscles. He could swing that bat and hit the fastball and pull it. He could pull anybody. In San Diego he told me, 'I can pull anybody. I don't care how fast they are.' He'd say, 'Nobody is going to throw the ball by me.' "

As part of the signing of Williams to the San Diego team, Padres president Bill Lane promised May Williams he wouldn't sell Ted until the young star was twenty-one. He also said he'd give her a piece when he did sell him.

Lane didn't keep his word. Ted was only nineteen when the sale to Boston for a reported $25,000 was consummated. The outraged Mrs. Williams confronted Lane, who made excuses. Lane told her that the team meal allowance was two dollars and that because Ted kept exceeding the limit, he no longer could afford to keep her son's stomach filled. Mrs. Williams contacted Eddie Collins, and later she told reporters Collins gave her $2,500.

During spring training of 1938, the Red Sox players got their first look at the nineteen-year-old phenom. Ted was unlike any rookie they had ever seen before. Where most rookies are quiet, take their turn, take abuse and never speak up, Williams was brash and overbearing.

Bobby Doerr: "I remember Ted coming in the first day into the clubhouse in Sarasota. I can't remember who introduced him to Joe Cronin, whether it was me or Johnny Orlando, the clubhouse man, but Ted greeted him by saying, 'Hi, Sport.' And that didn't go over too big with Joe."

Ted was intent on letting everyone know that he was going to be a star. He acted like he was a star. Pop psychologists might say his behavior was understandable and common, that by acting big, he was overcompensating for not feeling good about himself. Some veteran players put Williams down for being pushy and brash.

Tony Lupien: "Ted had an unfortunate childhood. He came from a very difficult family background. He had an inferiority complex about things. If you had seen him run in those days, he never looked like he ran hard into first base. I think he thought he looked awkward running, which was foolish. But he had some inferiority-complex things that he never seemed to get over too much."

There were times when Ted acted strangely, the way Jimmy Piersall did years later. That first spring training he was having trouble hitting, and to cover up his feelings of anxiety, he spoke a lot. When a fly ball came his way, he would slap his ass with his glove, and holler, 'Hi ho, Silver, awaaaayyy,' and he'd go galloping after the ball.

Doc Cramer sought to teach the inexperienced Williams the art of playing the outfield, but after a few days Cramer gave up, dismayed that the kid wasn't taking to his instruction.

Doc Cramer: "They wanted me to teach Williams how to field up there. Ted said, 'They ain't paying me to field. I'm going to get paid for hitting. The hell with this.' You couldn't do much with him. I did help him a little bit. He couldn't catch a ground ball. Used to go right between his legs. He wasn't getting ready to catch it, that was the main thing. But he got a lot better. He got to be a good outfielder."

*   *   *

But when he first came up, Ted took a high-handed attitude toward fielding his position. Manager Joe Cronin would take a look over his shoulder to check his outfield during a crucial moment in a game, and there would be Ted taking practice swings at imaginary baseballs.

Once Joe stopped the game and mimicked Ted's swings, shouting, "Hey, Bush, never mind practicing this." Then, going through the pantomime of scooping up ground balls, he shouted, "Practice this."

During camp Ted did other things that made his teammates wonder about him. Loudly he would call over to manager Cronin, "Hey, Scout," and he would constantly try to show he was smarter than the team brain, Moe Berg, by attempting to stump him with such questions as, "Can a man marry his widow's daughter?"

Ted went through the normal hazing from veterans.

Bobby Doerr: "They would rip him and everything. Ted had a lot of pride, and sometimes those guys would get a little bit rough with him. I'm sure deep down he accepted it as a fun thing. I remember in the Coast League when we broke in, we used to have one railroad car that you traveled in, and the rookies had the upstairs, up-above berths, and the starters had the lowers. And one night some of the players came in, after having a few drinks. We were getting ready to go on a road trip, and I remember they were digging him, kidding him, and fooling around with him. Finally he took a blanket, wrapped it around himself, and went into the women's room in our car. He sat there for a period of time until he could cool down, and then he went to bed."

Rookie hazing, especially for a kid with talent, was tough enough if you had a thick skin and a quiet personality. Ted had neither. Also, some of the vets couldn't have helped but resent his talent.

Bob Steele: "Nobody did anything for a rookie. 'The hell with you.' There was a certain amount of resentment. The minute you see some guy coming along who has more talent than you do, you recognize it immediately, so you do what you can to stop him, especially when it's your living and you haven't done anything else but play baseball. They are not unintelligent. They see a guy coming along who is going to take their job, they're not going to be too kind. I think that was very natural."

Ted was sensitive to the kidding by the vets, and to compensate for any perceived slight, he would always take an aggressive position. He had his antenna up, waiting to hear criticism, and when it came, he would respond with a vengeance.

When one of the veterans told him, "Wait until you see Foxx hit," Williams snapped, "Wait until Foxx sees me hit."

Doc Cramer: "He really did say that. Sure. The vets would kid him, but he asked for it. He was a good boy at heart, but Ted spoke his piece. A lot of things he said got him in trouble. He wouldn't have gone back to the minor leagues if he hadn't popped off like that.

"He was very nervous, fidgety. He put a lot of pressure on himself. And they never liked the rookie. Even when I came up. They didn't like me. I knew that. But when you showed them you could play, that was it, they were on your side. But you had to show them. You couldn't tell them."

Manager Cronin could see that the boy could hit, but Williams was so immature and irritating that Cronin sent him to Minneapolis for the 1938 season.

Tony Lupien: "Billy Evans and Eddie Collins said, 'Let's put him in that small bandbox in Minneapolis and get him some confidence.' They put him there so he could hit nine million balls out of that park. It was well-planned what they were doing."

But to Ted, going to Minneapolis was a terrible slap. Embarrassed, Williams had to have the last word.

Ben Chapman: "When Ted was leaving from the Red Sox to go to Minneapolis after they farmed him out, I remember one remark he made to Doc Cramer, Joe Vosmik, and me. He said, 'I'll be back, and I'll be making more money than the three of you put together.'

"I just laughed. It didn't bother me. I took it with a grain of salt. He was a young kid. Let him have his fun. And then he came back the next year, and from then on, he had his fun. What he said came true, you can't condemn him. That guy was one of the greatest hitters you ever looked at. Oh boy, could he swing that bat.

"When he said what he did about the three of us, I thought, 'He may be right.' "

Tony Lupien: "If we went to a ballpark on Christmas Eve and put the lights on, and it was twenty degrees below zero with snow up to your belly button, and said, 'Ted, go ahead and hit,' he'd hit. This is an animal reflex, and I say that kindly. He was a freak of nature in the sense that he had tools that the rest of us didn't have. This is not a question of a Charlie Lau theory of hitting. It's a stimulus-response thing. I put a finger up to your eye, and you blink. You throw a ball at him, and he's going to swing and hit it.

"With respect to the book he wrote on hitting, which has become something of a bible, an old-timer friend of mine, George Moriarty, said to him one time, 'You have just written this great book on hitting. You are obviously the outstanding hitting man now. Who taught you the most about hitting? You must have learned from somebody.' And Ted said, 'I guess when I was a kid in San Diego, Pat Crawford was working behind the plate one day. He said, "Kid, you have a hell of a swing. If the ball is anywhere near the plate, take a crack at it."' Well, if you can write 240 pages on that sentence, this is a hell of a trick. And this is what it amounts to. He just had that great animal eye-hand coordination that the Good Lord gives to you.

"Who has helped anybody as a hitting coach? I want to know what the name of this guy is. I talked to Paul Waner, Johnny Mize, and Hank Greenberg. Tell me a single hitter these guys made. You can tell a batter how to be shrewd, how to look for a certain pitch a certain pitcher throws, but as far as getting the bat on the ball, nobody can help you hit the ball.

"Greenberg played with Birdie Tebbetts, one of the great minds of the game. Greenberg was an astute hitting man. Why the hell didn't Birdie learn something from Greenberg? Birdie ended up hitting .270 all his life. Here is a smart man, but the Good Lord said, 'You're going to be a .270 hitter and Hank is going to be a whole lot different.'

"For Ted, it was, 'I'm going to give you .344 worth.'"

TED RETURNS FOR GOOD

Fabian Gaffke: "Ted was my roommate at Minneapolis. He was nineteen years old and quite a hitter. The kid would shake hands with you, and you'd think he'd break your hand, that's how strong he was. He'd swing that bat like a toothpick. You had to be strong to hit that ball the way he hit it.

"One time in Louisville he hit one—it was 365 in right field and they had a light pole seventy to eighty feet high up there—and Ted hit one way out of sight, over the lights and all. You couldn't see it. That's how high and far he hit that."

Dick Durrell, former publisher, *People* magazine: "I was thirteen and living in Minneapolis when the Red Sox sent Ted Williams to play for the Millers. He played right field, and you can check the statistics, but in '38 I believe he hit .366, hit 43 home runs, led the league in RBIs [with 142], won the Triple Crown, and was named the Most Valuable Player of the American Association. He replaced in right field a famous minor-league ballplayer from the Coast by the name of Buzz Arlett.

"I remember, as he did with the Red Sox, he was always asking the manager, a guy by the name of Donie Bush, to pitch. I recall he had a convertible, a Buick, because one day I was hitchhiking, and he went by. Of course, he didn't pick me up. And I remember he used to like to follow fire engines to fires.

"I used to go down to the home games with other youngsters my age, and when he was taking batting practice, most of us would stand beyond the right-field fence on Nicollet Avenue. That fence was only 257 feet but rather high, nothing like the Monster at Fenway but reasonably high, and when he was up we would go from behind home plate, where we were catching foul balls coming up and over, to around the fence, because we knew he'd be hitting a number over. We all had gloves, and we'd scramble for the balls. When we caught one, we'd take it and bring it back and get into the ballgame. That's how we got in.

"The Millers would have problems with the merchants on the street across from the ballpark, Minken's department store, the President Café. The balls Ted hit would frequently go into their windows, and the team had to pay for them.

"Everyone knew that this was an individual we'd be hearing more about. And what I remember more than any single characteristic of his playing ability was his arm. The right-field fence was short, and Williams was playing right, and he owned a rifle out there.

"But I guess what I remember most is that beautiful swing. As do many Minneapolitans my age."

Fabian Gaffke: "Ted had his ways—he was a screwy kid—but he was a good Joe. He was a little hotheaded, but he would never bother nobody. He was a ballplayer's ballplayer. He never got mad at the other ballplayers, just himself. One time in Minneapolis he popped up with the bases loaded. They had these water coolers, bottle coolers upside down where you press the button for a cup of water—he hit that SOB with the side of his fist when he came into the dugout, and the glass splattered all over the dugout. Donie Bush was the manager, and he almost threw a fit. If he had ripped a tendon, he could have been done with baseball. Oh, Jesus."

Though Williams was a great hitter, he drove Donie Bush to distraction with his sometimes strange and always arrogant behavior.

He had the habit of stalking around in the outfield and taking imaginary swings with an imaginary bat even as fly balls were coming toward him. He refused to run into walls and fences after foul balls. "They don't pay off on fielding," he would say. He threw temper tantrums. One time Williams came into the dugout after what he thought was a bad decision by an umpire and knocked the water cooler to pieces with his bat. Another time he sulked in the outfield because the trainer wouldn't give him a new baseball. Williams's lackadaisical play cost the Millers a game and infuriated one teammate who was ready to kill him.

Lefty LeFebvre: "Williams came in the clubhouse one day. We had a trainer's room that was six by ten. Doc Bowman was the trainer, and in those days there were no diathermy machines or whirlpool baths. All the trainer had was a bottle of alcohol and a couple of Band-Aids.

"Williams came flying in, lifted the team trunk open, and grabbed hold of a brand-new baseball. Baseballs cost a lot of money then, a buck and a quarter. Bowman told him he couldn't take it. And he wouldn't give it to him.

"So Williams went out and sulked all afternoon in the outfield. A couple of times balls came close to him, and he didn't even go after them. Center fielder Stan Spence had to come over and catch the ball.

"We lost the ballgame. Our third baseman was Jim Tabor, who they called Rawhide, a tough, chiseled-chin guy who always walked around with a cigar in his mouth. Tabor often would get a little booze in him, and he loved the girls.

"After this particular game, Tabor came over and grabbed ahold of Williams, and he would have kicked the shit out of him, but Donie Bush, who was managing the ballclub, told him, 'Leave him alone. He's only a kid.' He was nineteen years old. That year he hit 43 home runs."

Ted could also be contemptuous of the coaches. One day he hit a double, and when the third-base coach began to tell him what to do, Ted yelled at him, "Listen, you, I got out here by myself, and I'll get in by myself."

Donie Bush finally became fed up with this man-child. He called Eddie Collins in Boston and said, "This kid is leading the league in everything, Eddie, but I just can't take any more of him. I'm going to suspend him."

Collins told Bush, "The day Williams doesn't put on his uniform, don't you bother to put on your uniform either."

When Ted Williams left Minneapolis and returned to Boston, he returned for good, taking his position in the Boston Red Sox outfield for nineteen glorious seasons.

By the end of the 1939 spring training, Boston fans believed that Ted Williams was going to be the real thing. After years of aging veterans and failing to win a pennant, the fans were hoping that this kid from the farm system would be the catalyst to a first-place finish.

As the Red Sox were making their way north to open their regular season, the team stopped for an exhibition game at Yale University. Twelve-year-old Tiny Markle skipped school and went to the game to get his first glimpse of the man who soon would be called The Splendid Splinter.

Tiny Markle, radio broadcaster: "In those days Joe Wood was the coach of Yale baseball. Smoky Joe, the Red Sox legend. And he had scheduled a game between Yale and the Red Sox as they came north from spring training. The Sox stopped in New Haven and played the game at Yale Field.

"Every kid in New Haven's grandmother died the day before that game. The funerals were all immediately scheduled. There was no way anybody was going to school the day of that game. Not only did you have to be at the game, which started about two o'clock in the afternoon, but you had to be there early when the Red Sox got off the bus.

"I remember we all went out there, but it was important to me because I really was a Red Sox fan. The rest of them were all Yankee fans. I forget what it cost to get in. No matter. We probably snuck in. It was one of the few times in my life I saw the Yale Field filled to capacity. They had bleacher seats on the left- and right-field lines. Maybe fifteen thousand people. A lot of people for an exhibition game.

"It was time for batting practice, and here came Ted Williams to bat. That right-field line was long, 380, and it was over 400 feet in center. And Williams was awesome. He pumped about a half dozen over the right-field fence. We just stood there. I never saw anything like that. And neither did anybody else. We were all hollering, 'Hit one over the center-field scoreboard,' so he bounced a few off the scoreboard, which was a helluva feat.

"It was our first look at Ted Williams. And boy, I'll tell ya, it's the kind of thing you never forgot. He was nice to the kids. He signed all the autographs. Signed all the scorecards. I wonder if they do it today?"

CHAPTER 12

The Press and Ted: Let the Feuding Begin

During Boston's spring training of 1939, rookie Ted Williams got coverage reserved for young phenoms who come upon the scene and bring with them the sort of excitement that only home-run hitters can bring. The following was a commonplace conversation recorded between a reporter, in this case the *Boston Globe*'s Harold Kaese, and the young hitting star who glibly talked about himself and his talent. What came through was Ted's confidence and an interesting discourse on his intellectual approach to hitting.

Ted told Kaese, "No matter where I've played, I've always been one of the best hitters on the team, even back in grammar school. In high school I batted .430 in three years, although I pitched more than I played the outfield."

Kaese quoted Ted in a letter he wrote home from spring training that said, "I haven't seen any pitching yet from these big leaguers that scares me. I can see the ball all right, and I've been hitting it."

According to Kaese, Williams was constantly questioning the veteran hitters about the pitchers the Red Sox were facing. Wrote Kaese, "He comes to the park at ten-thirty to work out with Yawkey and other non-athletes and hogs their batting practice."

From the start, the baseball writers were taken with his ability. Commented reporter Tom Daly, "I've never seen anyone who was quite so loose and relaxed at the plate."

His teammates were also impressed with his ability, though they did take notice of Ted's high opinion of that ability. They got a secret kick out of Ted first bragging about what he was going to do and then doing it.

Doc Cramer: "We were playing in Detroit, and I was on first base, and Ted hit one that hit the facing of that ballpark, a pretty good drive. I waited for him at home plate, and I said, 'Ted, you hit that one pretty good.' He said, 'Yeah, next time up I'm going to hit one over the top of it.' And the next time up, by God, he did! He hit the next one right over the top, right out of the park, the only one that has ever been hit out, I think.

"And after he did that, he said, 'Didn't I tell you?' "

Ted wanted to perform feats no one else could. His confidence impressed the opposition. Early in 1939 the Red Sox were in New York, and Ted was talking to Yankees outfielder Tommy Henrich about hitting home runs.

Ted asked Henrich, "Did anybody ever hit the ball out of Yankee Stadium?"

Henrich said, "No, and don't get any dumb ideas, either."

"Why?" asked Williams.

"It's farther than you think."

Ted looked out toward right. Henrich could see Williams thinking about it.

The next time the Red Sox came into New York, during batting practice Ted hit a ball into the third deck of Yankee Stadium. Few batters could have hit one longer.

Henrich yelled over to him, "Hey, Ted, you give up?"

Williams grinned and yelled back, "Hey, don't tell anybody I said that, huh?"

The Boston fans were in love with their new phenom, as he was with them.

Bobby Doerr: "When Ted first came up in 1939, he played right field. After he'd hit a home run, he'd go out there and he'd take his cap off and hold it up, and the fans would clap, and they just loved it."

That first year was a honeymoon between Ted and the triumvirate of teammates, reporters, and fans. During a rookie year in which Ted would bat .327, hit 31 home runs, and lead the league with 145 RBIs, the press was sympathetic and often kind, even though there were signals from Ted Williams of his abrasive personality and wicked temper.

During spring training of 1939 the Red Sox were playing an exhibition game in Atlanta, and Ted missed a foul fly. He grabbed the ball after it hit the ground, and he threw it over the grandstand.

Ted, this time, was contrite. He said, "I really was so ashamed after I threw the ball that if the ground had opened up and swallowed me, it would have been perfect with me."

There was another incident in June. In one game a ball went through his legs, and it didn't appear that he hustled after it. The fans booed him. He threw the ball in, and he shouted obscenities into the crowd.

The next storm blew up in August. Ted was in a slump. Baseball is a long season—in 1939, it was 154 games—and mature players know that every year they will run up against one or two fallow periods when the hits don't fall and the batting average declines. Rookie players don't have the experience or temperament to put such slumps into perspective. Perfectionists can't stand the fact. Ted was both a rookie and a perfectionist.

On August 8, Williams popped the ball up along the third-base line. Angry and thinking the ball would be caught, he loafed down the baseline. When the ball fell fair, he was standing on first. Had he hustled, he would have had a double. Manager Joe Cronin yanked him from the game and sent Lou Finney in to replace him. The crowd booed.

The press still was not unkind. They reported that Ted was sulking because of his slump. The honeymoon held.

With the aid of hindsight, it seems inevitable that it would not last for long. Williams, who lacked self-esteem, was overly sensitive and had an antenna that was highly attuned to criticism. It is the nature of reporters to be critical. Everyone makes mistakes, and when they happen they are reported. Making it difficult for reporters to continue to be kind to Ted was his basic aloof nature and his demand for privacy. Ted was not a friendly, outgoing person. He kept to himself, seeking to be left alone.

The players were aware of Ted's penchant for privacy, but because he was a superior talent and a valued teammate, they respected him for it, much as Joe DiMaggio's teammates did their star on the Yankees. Players don't really care about a teammate's personality so long as that player performs and isn't publicly critical of them. They notice, but it doesn't affect their relationship as teammates. To the athlete, the talent is far more important than the man who has the talent.

Tony Lupien: "He was a guy you'd be in awe of, in the sense that he was aloof, and if you were in the New Yorker Hotel or the Commodore and if there were fifteen players in the lobby and you wanted to go to the movies at night, you'd ask fourteen of them, and if he was the fifteenth, you wouldn't ask him. If he wanted to go to the movies with you, he'd ask you."

* * *

Ted, an honest, outspoken person all his life, didn't hide the fact that he was a loner. He was who he was, and he wasn't ashamed of it. He was quite blunt about not wanting to spend his off-hours with his teammates.

Williams once told columnist Austin Lake, "When I look at a guy all day and am working with him, hell, I don't want to look at his mug, do I? When I'm on the field I'm one of the team, and I don't care what sort of a guy he is, or him or him," pointing at some of his teammates and not holding his voice down at all. "But when I'm through, I don't want anything to do with them. No, I'm not antisocial. I just want a change of scenery."

Reporters, when they heard that, were not sympathetic. Lake, for instance, rather than respecting the way Williams felt, employed that quote to prove that Williams was a bad teammate and a detriment to the Red Sox, a patently ridiculous charge.

Lake, of course, had his own agenda and concerns. To do their job properly, reporters rely on a player to respond to pointed questions. Reporters feel that a player has a responsibility to be cooperative with the press. Since the newspaper gives the club so much free publicity by writing about it, the thinking goes, the player's quid pro quo is to be available, open, and honest with the newspaper's reporters. And since Ted Williams was the star of the team, the reporters were relying on him twice as much as the other players. Ted didn't care. He didn't buy that he had a responsibility to be accessible all the time. He also didn't feel he had a duty to talk about his private life, and from the start he resented reporters' attempts to pry.

So long as the reporters kept to the topic of the baseball game itself, Ted would sit in his locker and answer their baseball questions. When he was tired of talking and would want to shower, he would say, "Okay, you guys, let's get the hell out of here," and he would head for the shower room. And that was it.

Ted's relationship with the press and fans, a honeymoon in his rookie year, turned sour in his sophomore year. Part of it was that people expected a spectacular performance that second year. Since he had had 31 homers his rookie year, everyone could only imagine how many he would hit the next year. In 1940, Ted hit only 23. Everyone was disappointed.

Ted Williams: "The second year they brought in the right-field fence 20 feet and right away I was supposed to hit 75 home runs. It was only 380 feet away then, and I had one of those second years. I thought I hit pretty good, .344, but I didn't hit the home runs I did the year before. I got a lot of catcalls and criticism. That just irked me enough so I got a little sour on everything and everybody."

In Boston at that time, there were a dozen papers, and every paper had a reporter who wanted to write something no other reporter was writing. As there were Republican papers and Democratic papers, soon there developed pro-Williams papers and anti-Williams papers. The anti-Williams writers could always generate the biggest headlines, and so they kept at it, with the result that Ted developed a deep hatred for many of the reporters.

Joe Cashman: "Dave Egan worked for my paper, the *Record.* How Egan could write! He was something! He could put those words together! He got those ballplayers so mad at him, and not only baseball players, but football coaches, hockey coaches, hockey players. It didn't matter who it was with Egan.

"Egan went through Harvard Law School in three years. See, Egan knew what was libel and what wasn't. He was the publicity man for Rockingham Park, and we had a guy in Boston named Parkman who was Federal Fuel Conservator. During the war Parkman ruled that you couldn't take your car to the racetrack.

"So Egan dubbed Parkman the 'Himmler of the Highways.' Can you imagine? One of the most respected men in the city. 'Himmler of the Highways.' And Egan got away with it because he knew he could get away with it.

"When Casey Stengel was managing the Boston Braves, he was hit by a taxicab, and Egan wrote that the cabdriver should be voted 'Boston's outstanding citizen.'

"And Egan got on Williams. He got on Williams all the time."

Dave Egan accused Ted of selfishness, jealousy, and a hunger for money, and when Ted refused to honor the club policy and wear a tie on road trips, he even accused Ted of contributing to juvenile delinquency! Perhaps his cruelest charge, though, was that Ted choked in the clutch—an absurd accusation against an athlete whose career record included a .344 lifetime average, 521 home runs, and 1,839 RBIs.

Egan reached his conclusion by taking what he called "the ten most important games in Ted Williams's career" and toting up his batting average. They included the seven games of the 1946 World Series, the Cleveland playoff game of 1948, and the final two games of the 1949 season. In those games, Ted hit .205. What Egan failed to take into account, deliberately or otherwise, was that Williams's wrist was sprained throughout the entire 1946 World Series. And to take ten games out of a total of 2,292—no wonder Ted was steamed!

As early as 1946, Egan was writing that Ted was a negative influence on the ballclub. "He does not associate with his [teammates]. He would not even attend the victory party [after the 1946 World Series] with them. He is utterly lacking in anything that bears even a remote resemblance to team spirit or team pride. First and at all time in between, he is for Ted Williams and Ted Williams alone."

One event that precipitated Ted's hatred for Egan and the *Record* happened early on in his career. Like his idol, Babe Ruth, Ted loved to visit the sick, young and old alike, as his mother had done, but he always insisted on anonymity. He never wanted anyone to question his motives.

Roy Mumpton: "Ted often went to visit sick kids in hospitals. We flew into Washington one day to open the season before the President of the United States. Somebody from Richmond called Ted and said he had a son who was very, very ill in a hospital there, and Ted said, 'Can I see him this afternoon?' Ted chartered a little plane at his own expense and went down to Richmond to see him.

"Then there was the incident in Boston. When Ted first came up, some father called him and said he had a boy who was dying in a hospital in Boston, and he said, 'Would you autograph a baseball for my son?' Ted said, 'Sure, sure, where is your son?' 'Children's Hospital.'

"Ted said, 'I'm tied up in the afternoon. Can I see him tomorrow morning?' The father said sure. Ted said, 'I'll be there around nine o'clock.' So Ted brings this kid a mitt, a ball, and bat. The father was so happy, he asked Ted to have his picture taken with the kid.

"And the father called the *Boston Record,* and they ran the picture in the paper the next day. Nobody knows who wrote the cutline, there was no proof, but they think it was Dave Egan. It said, 'How low will a ballplayer stoop to get his picture in the paper?'

"Ted had no idea the picture was going to appear in the paper. He thought the only reason the photographer was there was because the father was so proud, like anybody, that Ted had come.

"So naturally, Williams had trouble with the press—and the *Record."*

No one as sensitive to criticism as young Ted Williams should subject himself to the public eye, not if he expects peace of mind. Public figures who demand privacy end up living in private hells. Ted Williams lived in his own Hades until the day he retired in 1960. The Boston press helped put him there.

From the beginning, Ted was brash and spoke his mind. He was a kid, and sometimes he said kidlike things without thinking. His words, it seemed, often ended up in the papers.

In 1940 in an article about his salary, Ted told a reporter that his $12,500 salary was "chicken feed pay." He was quoted. Then, in another interview during a series in New York against the Yankees in which he wasn't hitting very well, he made the observation that he would "rather be a fireman than a baseball player." Ted had visited an uncle at a Mount Vernon, New York, firehouse, and he noticed that his uncle was sitting happily in the sun and that it looked like an idyllic life. Hence the remark.

When the Red Sox traveled to Chicago to play the White Sox, a team of bench jockeys, Chicago manager Jimmy Dykes dressed his players in firemen's helmets and cranked a fire siren in the dugout that could be heard throughout the ballpark. Ted laughed, but the reporters had a field day with it. They made Ted out to be a cad. They gave the public the impression that Ted was greedy about money and ungrateful that he was a ballplayer.

By the end of 1940, the accumulation of negative articles was having its effect on the Boston fans. In September, the Red Sox were in third place, many games behind the Yankees and Indians, and in one ballgame at Fenway, Ted was sulking and failed to run out a hit. This time the booing cascaded throughout the entire ballpark.

Wrote Austin Lake of the *American,* another anti-Williams columnist, "When Ted's name is announced, the sound is like the autumn wind moaning through an apple orchard."

With the hostile fans within earshot, Ted would stand in left field, calling back insults to his nearest detractors by curving the palm of his glove around the corner of his mouth. When Ted began doing that, a lot of fans became convinced that the columnists were right, that Ted Williams was a surly, unlikable kid. And the more the fans booed, the more defensive Williams became, until the feuding became public knowledge, which only served to incite other fans to go to the park for the specific purpose of vocally harassing Williams. In retaliation, Ted chose to ignore their existence, and the presence of every other fan as well.

Bobby Doerr: "In 1940, Ted moved from right field to left field, and when he moved, those fans were right on top of him, and all they had to do was get a little bit critical and then he decided, 'I'll never tip my cap again.' "

The fans, of course, never realized how sensitive Ted was to their slights. Ted wouldn't give them the satisfaction of letting them know. For a player, booing is a part of going to the ballpark. Every player gets booed. But to Ted, he was the best hitter in the game, and he couldn't understand why any fan would boo the best hitter in the game. Moreover, every fan who made himself heard by booing caused him to feel bad about himself.

"There will be 30,000 people cheering me," Ted told a reporter, "but up in the back row there'll be one guy booing, and I'll hear him."

Later he would swear, "Never, never will I tip my cap to those damned New England buzzards."

And he kept his promise. He became famous for it. Forever after, as a player, Ted Williams never tipped his cap, not even after the final home run of his illustrious career in 1960. In later years, he would tip it exactly twice: on his first day as manager of the Washington Senators, and on Ted Williams Day in Fenway Park in the spring of 1991.

Cronin would indeed trade Williams to the White Sox for Johnny Rigney, Taft Wright, and cash. It was yet another way for the press to minimize Williams's importance to the team.

During the winter, the skewering continued unabated. Unflattering stories appeared about Ted's mother and her work with the Salvation Army, about his father and his drifting ways. When one reporter learned that Ted was not returning to his hometown of San Diego for the off-season, he wrote, "What can you expect of a youth so abnormal that he didn't go home in the off season to see his own mother?"

The Associated Press then wrote a story out of San Diego saying that Ted had sold the furniture out from under his own mother. The Boston papers picked up the story and gave it big play. The only problem: it wasn't true. And the public's perception worsened.

Fabian Gaffke: "The way I understand it, one time Ted got some raw meat, and he threw it to the wolves out in the bleachers. That's right. They as much as called his mother a whore. I would throw something else up there to the bums like that. Don't get me wrong. It's not the Boston fans. It's the minority, the cuckoos. Good fans don't do that."

But the minority is what Ted heard. Perhaps the situation could have been saved if the Red Sox brass had stepped in quickly and firmly and come to Williams's defense. But Tom Yawkey disliked certain members of the press as much as Ted did. Austin Lake once wrote, "Yawkey gets a secret kick out of the way Ted behaves towards the press and fans." Lake may have been correct about that. This was an era before public-relations firms and information management for ballplayers. Ted was impotent to fight back.

Said his teammate, Bobby Doerr, "It was like Ted said later, 'I was immature at the time. I didn't know how to handle it.' "

IMAGES OF THE THUMPER

Two well-known writers who have attempted to deal with the subject of Ted Williams are Cleveland Amory, who interviewed him early in his career, and Roger Kahn, who sought him out toward the end. Both thought Ted different from most men, odd perhaps. Their reactions to him reflected Ted's respective treatment of them, and how they reacted to that treatment.

Cleveland Amory: "My first article ever published was on Groton School for the *Saturday Evening Post*. The only reason I was at the *Post* was that when I applied, I told the editor I had been the editor of the *Harvard Crimson*. The editor thought to himself, 'Here's a man who edited the Harvard humor magazine.' The man didn't know the difference between the *Harvard Crimson* and the *Harvard Lampoon*. So naturally he needed me.

"The second article was on Ted Williams. It was called, 'I Want to Be an Immortal.' Williams was at that time nineteen at the most. When I went to interview him at the Hotel Shoreham in Washington, he was looking out his window, and there were a lot of people by the pool. Ted said, 'How would you like to be really rich?' He was so ambitious. In those days he was already a terribly highly-paid ballplayer.

"I was fascinated with him, because all the time we were talking, he was taking a towel, wetting it, and swinging it as he was walking around the room. I never forgot it. He was studying everything about hitting, all day and all night in his mind, and as a result, he was by far the best hitter that baseball has ever seen. And remember, he did two war stints, during World War II and the Korean War, and they were not easy war stints.

"I remember when I went to Bob Feller, I said, 'How good is Williams?' He said, 'I'll tell you how good he is. When I get in a tight spot and it's 3 and 2 and the bases are full and I'm one run ahead, you just do one thing: you just rear back and try to throw that ball by them, because it's the best chance you've got. But there's just one batter you can never do that to, and that's Ted Williams, because the pitcher never lived who could throw it by him.'

"I always liked that piece. He never liked it. I knew he wouldn't be happy with it. When you're young, you do pieces that are not as fair in view of his age as I would have done now. If I were interviewing a nineteen-year-old now, I'd make allowances for things he said. But in those days you just pounced on a rather ridiculous quote. 'I would rather be a fireman.'

"I liked Ted because I saw him as a rebel. I was a very rebellious, liberal young man, and that appealed to me. Also I saw that mediocrity did not appeal to him. He would have rather quit than be a mediocre ballplayer, and he never went for anything but being the best. If it were not for missing the war years he would be probably the all-time greatest hitter who ever lived. People say, 'Mantle this,' or 'If Mantle's knees had only been right,' but I don't remember anyone else in the war flying planes against the enemy in two war stints. What other ballplayers did it?

"I feel that taking that into account, yes, I did admire him. I always knew how good he was going to be."

Roger Kahn, author, *The Boys of Summer*: "The Red Sox were making a strong run in 1955. The articles editor of *Life* magazine was Ralph Graves, who would go on to eminence in that company called Time Inc., and he asked me to do a piece about shortstop Billy Klaus. Klaus had batted in the .270s in Triple A, and now he was hitting over .300 for the Red Sox in a very tough pennant race.

"I went out with the Red Sox, and I really hadn't done that much in the American League. Klaus for those months was a hero of Boston, and writer

John Gilhooley wrote in the Boston papers a story about the Klaus family called 'The Klauses and their Houses,' where they had lived. Billy was a fiery player.

"I went to talk to Ted Williams, who I didn't know. I walked up to Williams in the batting cage, introduced myself, and I said, 'I'd like to talk to you about Billy Klaus.' And Williams said, 'One-fifteen at the batting cage tomorrow.' I found that startling, because you don't usually have to make an appointment around a batting cage. On the other hand, he was Theodore Samuel Williams. So I said fine, and I showed up the next day, and he was there.

"He was ready with a perfectly nice statement saying nothing terribly profound, that the team needed someone who could pick up ground balls and stabilize the infield, and that's what Klaus had done. I said, 'I would like to get a little beyond that, that I had heard Klaus was a sparkplug.'

"He said, 'That just sounds like writer talk. There is no such thing as a sparkplug.'

"I said, 'Who was the sparkplug on the '46 team?'

"He said, 'There was none. That's just the writers.'

"I was at a dead end. I said, 'Maybe we can look at it this way: here is somebody who was hitting in the .270s in the minors and in the .300s in the majors. You might even say he had a bad year in the minors.'

"Williams growled. 'Who are you asking, fella?'

"I said, 'I'm asking you.'

"He said, 'You're asking me about a bad year?' He said, 'Mister, I can see that you don't know very much about baseball if you're asking me about a bad year, because old T.S.W., he don't have bad years.' He looked out. He said, 'You see those guys?' There were the Boston writers standing in a picket line. He said, 'They would give their left nut to see me have a bad year. But it doesn't happen, because old T.S.W. doesn't have bad years.'

"To emphasize his point, he hurled his bat to the grass, caught it, and walked away.

"I went up to watch the game, and Hy Hurwitz, a small fellow, came over to me and he knew me a little bit from covering the Braves. And he said, 'We all heard what Williams said. And you know Williams was putting on a show for *Life* magazine. And I just want you to know that if you ever write what Williams said about us, no Boston writer will ever speak to you again.'

"It was absolutely crazy.

"The end of it was that the Red Sox dropped out of the race, and *Life* never ran the piece."

CHAPTER 13

Ted Hits .406

In his first two years, Ted Williams hit .327 and .344. He was twenty-three years old in 1941. He had eyes like a hawk, extraordinary hand-eye coordination, and amazing reflexes. Most batters were grateful for three strikes. Ted didn't feel he needed them all. Early in his career, if a fan was heckling him from the stands, Ted would waste his first two strikes attempting to hit him with a foul ball.

There was never a hitter with the confidence of Ted Williams. His rookie season, after he had the opportunity to face each American League club, his batting average hovered around .260. But Ted told himself, "I don't see no blinding fastballs or exploding curves." Williams commented, "I knew that after that one round that I could hit in the big leagues, and from July 4 on that season, I hit .380."

During spring training in 1941, newspaperman Harold Kaese interviewed Williams. Kaese asked if Ted was looking forward to the upcoming season.

Ted Williams: "Sure, I look forward to this season. How can they stop me? All right, I ask you. How can they stop me from hitting? They can't. That's all. They couldn't stop me my first year, and they couldn't stop me my second. They won't stop me my third.

"I was the best hitter on the Red Sox last year, wasn't I? Look up the records, and I missed some games in the easy parks for me, too. What's more, I bet I got the biggest raise in baseball except for maybe [Hank] Greenberg. I guess that shows what the Red Sox thought of me."

* * *

During spring training 1941, Williams chipped a bone in his ankle sliding into second base. For the first two weeks of the season he did little but pinch-hit as he recuperated. During those two weeks he didn't have to hit in the New England chill, and arranged with Boston pitcher Joe Dobson to throw him extra batting practice every day. They would pretend it was a real game, and Dobson would throw his best. By the time he returned to the Boston lineup as an everyday performer, Williams's batting skills were honed and sharp. Every ball that came off his bat was a line drive, it seemed.

By July there was talk that Williams would break Hugh Duffy's all-time one-season batting-average mark of .438. Duffy, who had been a Red Sox coach when Williams first came up, saw that Williams had a rare combination of form and power and had advised the youngster, "Don't monkey with your form."

In July, Williams demonstrated that impressive power when he hit one of the most dramatic home runs in the history of the All-Star Game. The game was played in Briggs Stadium in Detroit. The National League led 4–2 with two on and two out in the bottom of the ninth. Ted came up to bat, facing the Cubs' Claude Passeau.

Claude Passeau, Chicago Cubs pitcher: "We had an out and a man on first base, and the ball was hit by DiMaggio to the shortstop; he threw over to Billy Herman playing second base, and Herman has been quoted that he kind of showboated and threw to first base and missed it by a foot. DiMaggio was safe at first base on that play, and he should have been out, and I'd have been out of the inning.

"So Williams got a chance to hit with two on, and that was the second time I ever pitched to him—nobody ever talks about that I struck him out the first time—and I got the ball where I wanted to, inside—that's where I had to pitch all left-handed hitters. He hit the ball inside the trademark, a fly ball, but it hit the facade in right. Enos Slaughter was playing right field, and Slaughter told me, he measured on his fingers between the thumb and the index finger, about three inches. He said, 'If the ball had been just three inches shorter, it would have been a big out.' "

But it wasn't a big out. The ball hit the overhanging right-field facade, and Williams's three-run homer won the game for the American League. Joe DiMaggio, Bob Feller, and a few other American Leaguers carried Williams off the field. Del Baker, the Detroit manager, kissed Williams on the forehead in front of the surprised cameramen.

"It was a wonderful, wonderful day for me," Williams said later.

* * *

Throughout the entire season, Williams's batting average hovered above the magical .400 mark. According to Williams, the biggest thing he had going for him playing in Fenway Park was that it had a "good, green background." There were no shadows. And he had the Wall, which was a safety valve for him in the event he got a pitch that forced him to swing late. He knew that sliced hits could still go out of the park there. This knowledge enabled him to wait on the ball. As a result, he was rarely fooled. His patience at the plate became legendary. So did his selectivity. Williams was actually criticized for his habit of taking a pitch on 3 and 2 that was an inch off the plate rather than swinging at it. His critics argued that with men on base, he was the batter most likely to drive them in, and by choosing to walk, he was hurting the team. But Williams felt that if he violated his cardinal rule of swinging only at strikes, he would fall into bad habits and lose his great advantage over all pitchers.

It was Sunday, September 28, 1941, only nine weeks before Pearl Harbor and war. The Red Sox were in Philadelphia to play a doubleheader against the Athletics. These were the final two games of the season. Ted was batting .39955. For the first time since July, Ted was hitting under .400 and yet, rounded out, he was still at .400. If he sat out the two games, he would stand with the game's twentieth-century legends who had hit .400: Napoleon Lajoie, Rogers Hornsby, George Sisler, Ty Cobb, "Shoeless" Joe Jackson, Harry Heilmann, and Bill Terry. Manager Joe Cronin gave Williams the opportunity to sit out and protect his average.

Ted chose to play. He remembered that Jimmie Foxx had sat out the final day in his race with Buddy Myer and lost the batting championship when Myer had gotten two hits. Williams didn't want to hit .400 as a coward.

Bobby Doerr: "Cronin had told him that if he wanted to sit it out, he'd still hit .400. But knowing Ted, you knew he wouldn't sit out, and I'm sure he was proud of himself at what he did. This way it proved he was a great hitter and competitor. Everything Ted did was earned. I'm sure that he never gave sitting it out one single thought."

The elements that Sunday afternoon were against him. It was cold and threatening in Philadelphia. The game the day before had been rained out, setting up this doubleheader. Only ten thousand fans came to Shibe Park to see whether Williams could reach his goal.

Philadelphia A's manager Connie Mack, a ferocious, proud competitor, did what he could to stop Williams. He started a young left-hander named

Porter Vaughn, only a year removed from the campus of the University of Richmond, knowing that Williams hated to hit against an unfamiliar pitcher. Mack also instructed his first baseman, "Indian" Bob Johnson, not to bother holding on the runners at first base when Williams came to bat. Johnson played back to fill the hole between first and second.

As Ted stood in for his first at bat of the day, A's catcher Frankie Hayes told him, "I wish you all the luck in the world, Ted, but Mr. Mack told us he'd run us all out of baseball if we let up on you. You're going to have to earn it."

That was fine with Williams. His concern had been that the A's pitchers would refuse to give him good pitches to hit and prefer to walk him. He didn't mind that the pitchers would pitch him tough. For Ted, there were no pitchers he couldn't handle.

In his first at bat, Ted singled. Wrote a writer in the *Boston Evening American,* "The average ballplayer would have called it quits right then and there. With his goal reached, it was time to retire—not for Williams, though. He was going to be reproached by nobody. If he couldn't do it right, he'd rather not hit .400."

In his second at bat, Williams smote his thirty-seventh home run, then hit two more singles and reached on an error. Said the writer, "Yet, he still refused to pack up."

Roy Mumpton: "A newspaperman, Jack Malaney, who was then on the *Boston Globe,* was a friend of Cronin's. In fact, he was such a friend of Cronin's that when he got out of the paper, he became the Red Sox public-relations director. Jack was keeping track of the batting averages, and after the first game Ted was hitting .403, and Malaney went down to the clubhouse between the games and told Cronin. Cronin said to Ted, 'You're hitting .403. Do you want to sit out the second game?'

"Williams said, 'Like hell. I don't want to hit .400 that way.' "

In the second game, Williams singled, then hit a ball that struck the loudspeaker horn on top of the center-field fence in Shibe Park for a double. (During the winter, Connie Mack had to have the horn replaced.) An out on his final at bat left him six for eight on the day, giving him a final memorable average of .406.

In the locker room after the game, Williams exulted, "Ain't I the best hitter you ever saw!"

Wrote Jack Conroy of the *Evening American,* "Williams during 1941 turned in the greatest batting feat of recent years."

Even cynical Dave Egan recognized Williams's achievement. In his column, the usually acerbic Egan gushed: ". . . On both performance and precedent, Williams is entitled to the [MVP] award, and you may be sure that we'll write a stiff letter to the Baseball Writers Association if he doesn't get it . . . why the very idea."

In 1941, Ted Williams's third full season, the twenty-three-year-old phenom led the American League in home runs with 37, led the league in batting with a .406 average, led the league in runs scored with 135, and finished five RBIs behind league leader Joe DiMaggio with 120. In addition to his 185 base hits, he walked 145 times. It was a nonpareil performance, a lifetime year—but Williams would still be denied the Most Valuable Player prize.

The writers handed it to DiMaggio. It was the year of Joltin' Joe's phenomenal 56-game hitting streak during which he batted .408. Ted had hit .406 in 143 games over a full season, but the Yankees had clinched the pennant in the first week in September and won the pennant over Boston by 17 games. There was another factor as well: hitting .400 at that time wasn't unique. Bill Terry had done it eleven years earlier with the Giants. Harry Heilmann had done it eighteen years prior with Detroit.

No one could anticipate that after Ted's feat in 1941, no ballplayer would do it again.

Dom DiMaggio, Red Sox, 1940–1953: "During that period of time, it didn't really sink in that here's a man who hit .400. Only some years later did it begin to show up that it was quite an achievement. While it was happening, there was a lot of talk about it, a lot of print, but I guess I just didn't realize what a feat he'd accomplished by hitting .400.

"I take my hat off to my brother Joe, who just recently said that he would even at this late stage be happy to split the point down the middle and make two Most Valuable Players that year. I'll go along with that. Now why somebody didn't vote for one man over the other, I don't know. But I will say that Joe's statement was pretty darn to the point. Where you get two guys that close together, they should have called it a tie and said, 'Okay, the two guys will split it.' "

Bobby Doerr: "At the time I didn't think much of it, but I sure have since then. I wonder whether anybody will ever hit .400 again. It's going to be hard to do because of so much pressure. People have asked me, 'Was the media hounding Ted back then?' I don't remember that going on. It wasn't like it is now, when I was with George Brett in Toronto the night he hit the .400 mark. He was on second base with a double, and they stopped the game and let everyone applaud him for it, and I talked to George a little bit, and oh, the press was hounding him.

"He finished the year at .390, and I read that in the wintertime that he said, 'I just got a little overanxious, starting to go after bad balls.'

"Well, Ted wouldn't have done that. But it's going to be hard to do again, because of so much pressure that way."

CHAPTER 14

The Changing of the Guard

RAWHIDE AND THE PROFESSOR

The team began to alter in the early 1940s. A new infield formed around two young stars, second baseman Bobby Doerr and shortstop Johnny Pesky. Jim Tabor, called "Rawhide" by his teammates, became a fixture at third. At first base, twenty-five-year-old Harvard graduate Tony Lupien was chosen to replace Jimmie Foxx, an impossible task. Dominic DiMaggio, Joe's younger brother, became the center fielder.

Doerr, Pesky, DiMaggio, and Lupien were mild-mannered men. Jim Tabor was not. He was called Rawhide because of his toughness. He was a hard drinker and a fierce competitor who gave no quarter and took no guff from anyone, including his veteran teammates.

Bob Steele: "During one game, Tabor made an error, and Lefty Grove walked over to him and started to chew him out. Tabor challenged him right on the field. Tabor said, 'You're hired to pitch. I'm hired to play third base. Get out there and pitch.' "

Tony Lupien: "Tabor did the same thing to Ted Williams when they played together in Minneapolis. The Millers were fighting for the pennant, and in those days if you won the American Association pennant, you earned maybe an extra thousand dollars.

"Williams was having a tough time at the plate, and in the outfield during the game Ted was out there practicing his swing, while Charlie Wagner was pitching. The ball went off that tin, bang, and they got beat by a run.

"They got into the clubhouse in Minneapolis, and Tabor grabbed him. Tabor was not a star. He was a journeyman. He said, 'If you ever do that again, I'll shove you in that goddamn locker and kill you.' "

Doc Cramer: "Jim Tabor, he was a twister, I'll tell you. Tabor would drink, get drunk, and be half-drunk when he came to the park. They thought they could catch him, so they put these two detectives on him. He was in this nightclub, and he knew they were after him, and when the two detectives followed him into the men's room, Jimmy locked them in there and left."

Tony Lupien: "I played with Tabor, roomed with him, drank with him. He drank a little bit, like everybody else. I didn't think he was any worse than anybody else. But he had the unfortunate habit of drinking in public. See, you can drink in your room, and who the hell knows about it? But Jim would go to a bar or a nightclub and somebody'd see him, and that isn't good business."

In early April 1941, Tabor went to a wedding in South Boston, got drunk, and missed an exhibition game. Joe Cronin suspended him.

"I'm just a crazy old fool," said Tabor, who was twenty-four. "I ought to be kicked hard." He did not deny breaking training.

"It's just because whenever I do something, I get caught," he said. His hard living ended up costing him his career and ultimately his life.

Tony Lupien: "Those things happen. I'm not going to his defense and say he didn't drink. He drank. Who didn't? Better than those chocolate milk shake people to have around. He hustled. He was tough. He'd slide into second and knock you on your ass.

"After the war, the Red Sox sold him to Philadelphia, where we were all being dumped at the time. Then he went to Sacramento, and in 1953 he had a heart attack. Dead. He was still a young man."

Jim Tabor was tough and full of piss and vinegar. The Red Sox' new center fielder, Dom DiMaggio, was the opposite. Dom wore glasses, a rarity at the time, was soft-spoken, and evaded controversy. His teammates nicknamed him "The Little Professor."

Dom DiMaggio was the youngest of three brothers who made it to the major leagues. The first, Joe, was perhaps the greatest all-around ballplayer of his generation. The second, Vince, was a slugger who struck out often.

When Dom began playing pro ball in 1937 for the San Francisco Seals, Joe and Vince had already made it to the bigs.

The Yankees never scouted Dom, perhaps because they thought he was too small. Also, some scouts would not even look at players who wore glasses. Such players were called "four eyes." The Chicago Cubs also passed. They sent a scout to look at Dom, but ended up buying Artie Story instead.

The Red Sox, however, continuing to mine the rich lode of talent on the West Coast, did sign him. Billy Evans and Joe Cronin liked his speed, range, and skill in the field. After three years in the minors, Dom DiMaggio made it to Boston in 1940. But he injured his ankle twice that spring, and he didn't get to start until mid-July.

When the Red Sox traveled to New York's Yankee Stadium during that first season, his older brother, Joe, the Yankee star, fraternally told Dom he was playing too shallow against him.

"Balls carry further in Yankee Stadium," Joe said.

In the next game, Dom played farther back. Joe hit a ball that carried to the 457 sign in left center. Dom caught it.

When Joe passed Dom going out to center field, Joe said, "I should have pulled the ball more."

"Yeah," Dom said, "that was a tough break."

If it hadn't been for Joe, Dom would have been given far more recognition for his impressive accomplishments. Though not the dramatic slugger his brother was, Dom was an accomplished batsman. He hit .301 as a rookie in 1940; his lifetime average hovered just under .300; he could bunt, run, and steal; and his fielding was a thing of beauty.

Roy Mumpton: "Dom was a great ballplayer. He was in Joe's shadow. Joe used to say that Dom was a better fielder. That I don't know. But he was just about as good. Dom could do everything. He could run like hell. He could throw. He was very smart. He played the hitters. And he got on base all the time."

Matt Batts, Red Sox, 1947–1951: "When they named Dom 'The Little Professor,' they named him right. He never did look like a ballplayer. And to me he was as fine a baseball player as you ever want to have.

"As an outfielder he was just as good, or better, than his brother Joe, and they talk about Willie Mays and Hank Aaron, but I'll take Dom DiMaggio.

"He could come in on the ball with the best, had a good arm, knew how to play the outfield. You didn't have to tell him where to play. He knew already.

"And who can you think of who's a better second man to come to that plate? To me he certainly deserves to be in the Hall of Fame, and where is he? He's not in it."

Tony Lupien: "One thing I noticed about Dom. During practice Dom used to come and work out with the second infield, because, he said, 'The errors I'm going to make are going to be ground balls.' So he always made sure he took a lot of ground balls. Dom was like a shortstop in the outfield. Doc Cramer, his predecessor, played deep because he couldn't go back on the ball, but Dom would play shallow in the early part of the game, when the pitcher had his good stuff, and by the fifth or sixth inning, the batter would hit a gapper, and you'd say to yourself, 'He'll never get that,' but Dom would keep drifting farther and farther back as the game progressed, and he would always catch it. Dom was a great student of the game. Tremendous thought and insight. And he knew when to steal a base. He'd steal the one base that would beat you."

Though brothers, Joe and Dom DiMaggio were as different as could be. Both were private, quiet men, but Joe rarely remained secluded for long, living off his baseball reputation. Joe married—and quickly divorced—first a starlet and then the most famous woman in the world, Marilyn Monroe, and was constantly on the go with his suitcase in hand, attending golf tournaments and banquets.

Dom married, had children, and settled down outside Boston. After he left baseball in 1953, he began a business and became wealthy and secure.

Roy Mumpton: "Dom had a friend, kind of disreputable, we thought, and quite a few of Dom's friends told him to be careful of this guy. A mobster type, we thought. And he's the one Dom went in with and who made Dom a millionaire! He got in just before the war. They were making corrugated paper, and they couldn't make enough, and this man, who we all suspected, proved to be the greatest guy in the world."

Baseball teams are constantly in flux, some more than others. Careers have a finite time period, and even the greatest players lose their skills with age. With the arrival of Jim Tabor and Dom DiMaggio came the departure of two of the brightest stars of their day, Lefty Grove and Jimmie Foxx. Both had Hall of Fame careers. Both would go down in baseball's annals. But time marches on, even for the great ones. It was time for them to move on.

Lefty Grove won his three hundredth game in 1941; the following year he was released, and he retired. Sportswriter Harold Kaese went to visit the once-surly veteran at his home in Lonaco ming, Maryland. When Kaese arrived, Grove was planting potatoes on his farm.

"I'm sure happy being home," Grove said. "I've done more fishing already than in all the time I played baseball. You should see the trout."

Kaese asked the great left-hander if he missed baseball.

"I haven't seen a ballgame all spring," Grove said, "not even a high-school game. Bob, my boy, hasn't lost a game for Washington College, but I haven't gone to see him pitch. I haven't thrown a ball, haven't even had one in my hand."

"Why?" asked Kaese.

"It would only make me want to go back and play again," he said.

In June of 1942, Jimmie Foxx was waived by the Red Sox. He had been unable to hit after his beaning by Negro League pitching star Chet Brewer in that Canadian barnstorming game the winter before. Foxx didn't go quietly. He left with a cold blast at manager Joe Cronin. He asked reporters, "Why couldn't the stars who won pennants for Connie Mack win for Joe Cronin?" Said Foxx, "One manager knew what he was doing; the other didn't."

Cronin saw that Foxx no longer strode into the ball. After the beaning, Foxx would step into the bucket. He was afraid of the ball. But reporters, who loved the big guy, blamed Cronin anyway. One went so far as to say Cronin dropped Foxx because he feared Foxx was a threat to his job.

In midseason 1942, Tony Lupien replaced Foxx at first base for the Red Sox.

Tony Lupien: "Somebody said to me, 'You replaced Foxx.' I said, 'Never use that word. No one can replace Foxx.' And following him was a tremendous burden. I got caught in the same situation that Babe Dahlgren did in New York following Lou Gehrig. To follow a star is just impossible. Jesus, it's a disaster to follow a guy who can hit that ball over that left-field fence. So it was a tough struggle, and I had a bad year my second year in '43, and when my draft number came up, the Red Sox sold me to Philadelphia."

Johnny Pesky, the new shortstop, turned out to be a star. His rookie year he hit .331 and led the league with 205 hits. He and second-base star Bobby Doerr rivaled the Yankee duo of Joe Gordon and Phil Rizzuto for honors as the best keystone combination.

Johnny Pesky and Dom DiMaggio, like Doerr who had arrived before them, were star-quality players, quiet men who were all overshadowed by the Red Sox' walking and talking tornado, the outstanding batsman, Ted Williams.

As if to prove his .406 year wasn't a fluke, in 1942 Ted won the Triple Crown of batting, winning the batting title with a .356 average, the home-run title with 36, and the RBI title with 137. No one was even close in any of the three categories. The second-place finishers were Pesky at .331, Chet Laabs with 27 homers, and Joe DiMaggio with 114 RBIs.

Who won the MVP award? Joe Gordon of the Yankees. Gordon had hit .322, with 18 homers and 103 RBIs. But the Yankees had won the pennant, and the writers didn't despise Gordon the way they did Ted. Williams's enmity toward the sportswriters had cost him dearly. And so had something else.

THE WAR YEARS

After adding Jim Tabor and Dom DiMaggio to a cast that already included young Ted Williams and Bobby Doerr, the 1941 Red Sox had given every indication that the team would be a perennially strong contender for the American League pennant. The team had finished second to the Yankees that year, but there was more talent in the minors, including young shortstops Johnny Pesky and Eddie Pellagrini, and the future seemed bright.

But two months after the 1941 World Series, the Japanese attacked Pearl Harbor, war was declared, and for the next four years the Red Sox fortunes declined as their stars began to leave for the armed services, to be replaced by minor leaguers, untried kids, and fill-in players all rejected by the armed services for one reason or another.

Ted Williams's draft number was 474. At the time the Japanese attacked Pearl Harbor, Williams supported both his parents, who had separated and would later divorce. In addition to sending his mother money, Ted had set his father up in a photography business. Williams was hoping his draft number was high enough to keep him in baseball so he could continue supporting them.

"I'm the sole support of my mother now," he told Harold Kaese in March of 1941, "so now maybe . . ."

That December, Pearl Harbor changed everything.

In February of 1942, Williams's San Diego draft board changed his status from 3A (sole support of his mother) to 1A, making him eligible for the draft. When Williams requested a return to 3A, the case was sent to Washington, where General Lewis Hershey's presidential review board granted the deferment.

Had Ted Williams been beloved by the sportswriters, it is possible the writers may have been more sympathetic and supported him. But Ted's feud with the fourth estate gave them the impetus to skewer him for what they claimed was his lack of patriotism.

When Williams's appeal to change his status back to 3A was made public, the criticism in the press was negative and sharp. The writers even called Williams a coward. This was Ted Williams's personal war.

Said the twenty-three-year-old Williams in his own defense, "If I didn't think I was right and deserving, and if it were not so important to my mother that I play baseball, I wouldn't ever attempt to face this unfair criticism."

Ted got no support from the Red Sox. Management did what management always does. It listened to the knee-jerk outcry, and it attempted to do what was best for the image of the team. Manager Cronin suggested that Williams enlist at the Great Lakes Naval Training Center, where the slugger could play service ball under former Detroit star Mickey Cochrane. Tom Yawkey advised Williams not to come to spring training. Williams, however, was determined to play for Boston in 1942.

Williams, still naive about public relations, firmly believed that he was entitled to his deferment, no matter what any reporter or critic said. He was playing by the existing rules, and he felt he deserved to be exempted so that he could support his mother. He fully intended to earn what would be his first really big payday, a $30,000-a-year salary. For the first time in his life, he would be free of money concerns.

By May 1942, the write-ups in the press and the catcalls from the stands had worn Ted down. One envelope addressed to him contained an unsigned piece of paper. It was yellow. Williams finally gave in. Toward the end of the season—during which he led the league in most offensive categories, including batting average, home runs, runs scored, and runs batted in—he signed up to go into the Navy air force training program at nearby Amherst, Massachusetts.

Williams spent most of the war as a flight instructor in Pensacola, Florida. He was about to be shipped from San Francisco to Honolulu for Pacific service when the war finally ended. Meanwhile, Williams was lost to the Red Sox for 1943, 1944, and 1945.

With Ted, Dom DiMaggio, John Pesky, and most of the pitching staff off to fight, and few quality players to replace them, Red Sox fans' hopes would be dashed once again. It would be a long four-year wait before their hometown heroes came home again. Replacing them came a cast of strangers.

If the Red Sox had a star player during the war years, it was pitcher Cecil "Tex" Hughson. Hughson, from San Marcos, Texas, played for the Red Sox from 1941 through 1949, missing only 1945. His 96–54 record places him seventh among all-time Red Sox pitchers. A tough competitor who always wanted the ball, his lifetime earned-run average of 2.94 is a record for Red Sox pitchers.

After pitching for the University of Texas for four years, Hughson was signed by the Red Sox in June of 1937. He spent three and a half years in the minor leagues.

In 1940, Hughson was an ordinary 7–11 for Louisville in the American Association, when Louisville backed into the playoffs. On the final day of the regular season, it edged out the competition to garner the fourth and final playoff spot. From that point on, Tex Hughson emerged as a star pitcher.

In the first round of the minor-league playoffs, Louisville defeated Columbus and then played Kansas City, the Yankee farm team led by shortstop Phil

Rizzuto. During the regular season, Kansas City had defeated Louisville eighteen of twenty-two games.

Against Kansas City in the playoffs, Hughson pitched in relief in the first game, pitching the seventh through the tenth innings and getting credit for the win. He didn't give up a run. The next day he relieved again, going from the seventh through the eleventh inning and again winning the game. Then he started a game and won it 1–0.

The final round was a series against Newark, another Yankee farm team, for the championship of the Little World Series. Hughson pitched the only two games won by Louisville. In five playoff decisions, Hughson was 5–0. It got him his opportunity to pitch for the Red Sox in 1941.

Hughson was spectacular in his first full major-league season, winning a league-leading 22 games in 1942. That year the Red Sox won 93 games and finished second to the Yankees.

In 1943, however, Hughson was injured and his record fell to 12–15. Playing without Ted Williams and with a subpar Hughson, the 1943 Red Sox finished a dismal seventh.

In 1944, Hughson's arm recovered and he finished 18–5, with a 2.26 earned-run average. That year, the team bounced back, playing .500 ball and finishing fourth.

As Tex Hughson went, so went the Red Sox. He spent the 1945 season in the armed services. The Red Sox returned to seventh place.

Tex Hughson: "I began in Boston in 1941, was optioned out, and went back to Louisville for a brief time. I won seven straight at Louisville and was called to Boston on the fourth of July.

"I pitched my first game against the Washington Senators in Boston. The first three hitters up got doubles. I guess I was a little excited. I made a doughnut out of the ball when I was warming up. The catcher threw the ball back, and I stuck the end of my index finger plumb into that baseball.

"Manager Joe Cronin wasn't there that day. One of his sons was born, and he was at the hospital with his wife. Frank Shellenback, the pitching coach, came out to the mound to take me out. Two runners were in and there was a man on second. I asked Shellenback to leave me in, to let me get one man out.

"I ended up pitching the whole ballgame. We won.

"I was married at the time the Japanese attacked Pearl Harbor. I was visiting my wife's people that Sunday, and I was driving on the way back to my home in San Marcos, Texas, when I heard about it on the radio. We all had to register for the draft. I was fortunate to have a real high draft number. I could have gotten a deferment for agricultural production, but I didn't ask for it. I was offered it, but I told them my primary interest was baseball. I said, 'I'm not going to volunteer, but I'll go when my time comes.'

"In 1942, I had one of my better years. I won 22 and lost 6 that year and tied Bobo Newsom for strikeouts with 113, which was low, but I led the American League in nearly everything—innings pitched, wins, complete games and all that.

"I had had arm trouble at the end of the '41 season. I missed the last three or four weeks. I had hurt my arm in the second game of a doubleheader against St. Louis. The first game was one of those seesaw jobs. We won something like 12 to 10 in extra innings. The bases were loaded in the thirteenth and Ted Williams was up. I was criticizing Ted in the dugout.

"I said, 'I wish he'd hit the ball to left field.'

"They said, 'He's hitting .408.'

"While I was talking, Ted wound up and hit a home run deep into right center field over the bullpen.

"They asked me, 'Isn't that good enough for you?'

"I said, 'Yes,' and I kept my mouth shut about his not going to left field from then on.

"I started the second game, and it was called on account of darkness at the end of eight innings. I told Joe Cronin then that I was glad I didn't have to pitch the ninth inning, that my arm didn't feel good. I somehow ruptured a muscle in the back of my arm. They told me to go home and rest.

"I rested all winter, and it didn't get any better, and in the spring of '42 I spent all of spring training in Miami with Dr. Burbacker. He finally got the thing diagnosed and straightened out. I didn't spend any time with the Red Sox in spring training, but when the season began I started out relieving, pitching two innings, then three, and then four, and nearly a month after the season began I became a starting pitcher. I was fine all year long, won 22 games, and after the last game of the season, Tom Yawkey sent me a check for the same amount of money I had signed for. He just doubled my salary. That made me feel real good, for a country boy to get that kind of money.

"In 1942, my first full season, Ted Williams ended up winning the Triple Crown. I'll tell you what. Ted has asked me a half a dozen times very quietly, 'Don't you think I'm the greatest hitter that ever lived?' Just like if I had asked you for a cup of coffee. And I told him, 'You're damn right.' And I meant it. I think he was the best hitter that ever lived. Ted was criticized for taking too many bases on balls. Ted would not, did not, ever swing at a bad ball. That's the reason he hit left-handers as well as right-handers.

"In 1943, Ted was gone, and Dom and Pesky. That year I was 11 and 5 and was on the All-Star team. Then Jimmy Bloodworth of the Tigers hit a line drive that broke my pitching thumb, and I was out quite a while. When I came back, I couldn't grip the ball properly. I should have won some of the ballgames, but unfortunately we didn't get too many runs at the time, and at the end of the year I won one and lost nine. I ended up 12 and 15."

*   *   *

Eddie Lake was a Red Sox shortstop during the war years. He had come up with the St. Louis Cardinal organization, was sent to the Pacific Coast League and found himself stuck on the bench behind Marty Marion, and he was purchased by the Red Sox in time for the '43 season for $100,000. Migraine headaches kept him out of the war.

Eddie Lake, Red Sox, 1943–45: "There was a lot of pressure on the services to draft the ballplayers. The Gold Star Mothers were kicking that their sons had to go in, so why didn't the ballplayers? I took six physicals! I had four in California and two in Boston.

"The night before I went in for my final physical, I had dropped a pop fly in Boston. Dr. Cohen, who was examining me for my migraine headaches, asked me, 'Did you ever drop a pop fly in the infield?' I said, 'Yeah, I dropped one last night.' He said, 'Do you get migraines much?' Well, I did get migraine headaches all the time. He stamped Reject, Reject, Reject all over that, and I wasn't bothered again. After six physicals!

"Of course, I would have gone. The doctor said, 'Would you serve in the service if you're drafted?'

"I said, 'Sure. I'll go.'"

Francis "Red" Barrett pitched for the Red Sox in 1944 and 1945. He was also acquired from the Cardinal organization. A spot on his lung disqualified him from service.

Red Barrett: "I didn't care to be drafted, so I went down to enlist. I took my physical, and they found a spot on one of my lungs, and they wouldn't take me in because there was a possibility of my breaking out into something. They thought it might have been tuberculosis, and under certain circumstances it might recur, so they said no go. They put me in 4F. It was a surprise to me. From then on, they wouldn't have anything to do with me, so I went back to baseball."

When Tex Hughson returned to form in 1944, the Red Sox again challenged the Yankees for the pennant, but in early September the armed services claimed Hughson, Bobby Doerr, and catcher Hal Wagner. Pennant optimism died. The team stopped winning.

Eddie Lake: "We were contenders in 1944. Right up to September. One game out. But the armed forces took Hughson, Doerr, and Hal Wagner, and we folded. You lose a pitcher like Hughson, my God, you're losing half the ballclub. And he was married and had a child. They still drafted him! I don't know what the hell for. See, they were after us. We thought it was a rotten deal, but all Tex said was, 'Somebody has to fight.' "

Tex Hughson: "During the winter before the 1944 season I didn't know if I was going to be drafted. I didn't even go to spring training. I worked out at home out on the farm, the wife and I. I had a bedsheet, and I would throw at it. The day the season opened, they quit taking pre–Pearl Harbor fathers over twenty-five. I was just over twenty-five when Pearl Harbor came along, and I had a daughter born a month before Pearl Harbor.

"The first day of the season I pitched batting practice, and three days later in Boston I pitched the opening day and beat Philadelphia, 2 to 1, pitched a nine-inning ballgame.

"Then, after the Battle of the Bulge, they changed the thing, and I was drafted. Bobby Doerr and I were drafted about the same time. It was early in August and I was 18 and 5 when I left for the service. I had won my eighteenth game before any other pitcher in either league that year. Hal Newhouser ended up winning 29 and Dizzy Trout won 27."

Back in Boston, the Red Sox foundered.

Eddie Lake: "Skeeter Newsome, our shortstop, had asthma. Most of the guys had hernias or were color blind or wore glasses. When Tex was taken, our pennant chances were gone. We had to dip down to bring up replacements from Triple A, bring up our kids, and they couldn't handle the pressure.

"We had some characters on the team. Our catcher, Roy Partee, would pull jokes. He would tie your shoelaces and nail your spikes to the floor. There was a little platform in your locker for your spikes, and he would nail them to the platform. We had to buy our own shoes. We wore them with big holes in the bottom, which didn't matter so long as it wasn't raining. I always wanted to get back at him, but I could never prove he was the one who did it.

"Indian Bob Johnson lived upstairs from me. I rented him an apartment. Bob liked to drink. He would get feeling pretty good and want some company, and he would yell, 'Get up here, you little so-and-so.' But I wouldn't go. He'd say, 'You better get up here or I'll carry you up here.' I didn't drink.

"Whenever we traveled, Johnson would open his suitcase, and there would be one clean shirt, and the rest of the suitcase would be filled with booze. He'd go into the vestibule of the train and open his suitcase. Jim Tabor did the same thing.

"The guy who replaced Tabor at third base in '45, a fella by the name of Jackie Tobin, was the worst of all. I hate to say it, because the fellow is dead now, but Cronin offered this guy five thousand dollars if he wouldn't drink for three months.

"He lasted about six weeks. Tobin came to the ballpark one day soused to the gills. He was in no condition to play. Cronin said, 'Who in the hell am I going to play at third base now?' I was playing short and Skeeter Newsome was at second, and Catfish Metkovich was at first, and I said, 'I'll play third, and you can get somebody to play short.' He said, 'No, I want you at short.' Cronin said, 'I'll play.' So he called the commissioner's office and activated himself. Boy, he was mad.

"Another time we were playing against the Cleveland Indians, and shots were going right by Tobin, and he couldn't even see them. He was just out there like a statue. I went up to Joe and said, 'Gee, you better get him out of there. He's going to get killed.' Cronin said, 'To hell, let him get killed.' Boy, Boudreau hit one down that line, whooo, Holy God . . . I said, 'Joe, you better get him out of there.' And Joe had to go in and play third base. He was thirty-nine years old.

"That Tobin could have been one hell of a ballplayer. We all tried to help him, stayed with him, and then all of a sudden, you would look around, and he'd be gone. Disappeared, like the Invisible Man. We wouldn't see him until he got to the ballpark the next day.

"It was just too bad. He had all the potential in the world. He could run, hit, field, throw, had everything, but Jack would drink right up until game time. He dressed right next to me. I could smell it. I'd say, 'What, again, Jack?' He'd go, 'Aaarrrrrrrgh.' He couldn't talk.''

The major problem with the Red Sox during the last couple of war years was the pitching staff. Boo Ferriss from Shaw, Mississippi, replaced Hughson as the big winner, but he was the only reliable arm. Ferriss had been discharged from the armed services early because of asthma, and in 1945, his rookie season, he won 21 games.

Eddie Lake: "Early in the '45 season, Joe Cronin started him against the Philadelphia A's. This was do or die for Ferriss. He was behind 2 to 1, and if he lost the ballgame, he was gone. I hit a home run and we got another run, and we were leading 3 to 2 when he loaded the bases and was 3 and 2 on the hitter.

"Cronin very seldom got hot, but he was really steaming because Boo Ferriss had stuff. He was a sidearmer who could throw. Joe said, 'I don't know what's the matter with that guy. All the potential in the world and look at him out there.'

"Joe went out to the mound, and he said, 'You got to get him out, Bo.' He didn't call him Boo. Called him Bo. 'If you don't get him out . . .'

"Boo struck the batter out, went on to win the ballgame 3 to 2, and saved his job."

Even with Ferriss, the 1945 Red Sox finished seventh. The pitching staff was weak, and the team churned players constantly. Red Barrett, a relief pitcher in 1944 and 1945, recalls a line drive that almost killed Jim Wilson, one of the Sox' few steady pitchers. The instability on the team and the vagabond nature of baseball on the Red Sox toward the end of the war years was what he remembers most vividly.

Red Barrett: "Hank Greenberg hit a line drive back at Jim Wilson and hit him in the temple. They say it caved it in. He was taken to the hospital, and a silver plate was put in. He joined us much later on, but he didn't do anything much from there on out. He was never effective again.

"They had an awful lot of turnover of players, new ones coming in, old ones going out. A lot of the boys didn't produce as they had in the past. They just didn't do well. Cronin and the pitchers didn't have any rapport that I knew of. We weren't a close-knit team. The boys spent the time at the ballpark, and then everybody was like a bunch of quail. Just scattered out.

"A lot of times players would come in, and then they'd be gone, and somebody else would replace them, two or three at a time, two or three leaving, and a lot of them came in who you didn't know, who had played in different leagues, and you didn't know what to expect. And pretty soon, they'd leave, and somebody else would take their place, and maybe you might be in the next batch. There was no stability."

Tom Yawkey had purchased the Red Sox in 1933 with promises of pennants. Thirteen seasons later, the promise remained a hollow one. Red Sox fans were howling for manager Joe Cronin's scalp.

On March 23, on the eve of the 1946 season, the *Boston Globe*'s Harold Kaese wrote a scathing indictment of Yawkey's regime in an article in the *Saturday Evening Post* titled "What's the Matter with the Red Sox?" In it, he revealed the alliance between owner Yawkey and manager Joe Cronin, recounting what Cronin's critics were saying about him and questioning Yawkey for his misplaced loyalty.

Asked Kaese, "How has Cronin stayed in the saddle? He has stayed because Yawkey wanted him. Yawkey, like innumerable others, idolized Cronin as a player. Yawkey is stubborn, wealthy, and loyal. When he signed him to a three-year contract in 1944, Yawkey said, 'I'm perfectly satisfied with Joe. He can manage as long as he likes.' When Cronin was being abused as a shortstop, it was Yawkey who said, 'Instead of a better shortstop helping the pitchers, don't you think better pitchers would help the shortstop?' "

Six days after the article appeared, Yawkey was asked what he thought of it.

"I am not upset by it," the Red Sox owner said stoically.

Would the Red Sox ever win another pennant?

CHAPTER 15

Champs

Johnny Pesky, Red Sox, 1942–52: "We had a good ballclub when we all went into the service. Then when the war got over, we were still young enough, in our early twenties, and when we came back we were a lot more mature. The first month of the 1946 season I could see that the Sox had a chance to win the pennant. Tex Hughson was pitching well, Boo Ferriss, Mickey Harris, and Joe Dobson. Plus, we had good hitting. The first six weeks of the season everyone but Bobby was hitting .400. We were scoring runs. At one point we were 55 and 10."

The Red Sox won 104 games in 1946, breezing to the pennant by a full twelve games over the defending world champions, the Detroit Tigers. Finishing a distant third were the New York Yankees. Things had gotten so bad in New York that longtime manager Joe McCarthy quit the team in midseason. His replacement, Bill Dickey, fought with owner Larry MacPhail and also quit.

For the first time since Joe Cronin became manager in 1935, the Red Sox had four starting pitchers he could count on. Hughson, the ace, won 20, and Boo Ferris followed his 21-win rookie season with 25 more wins. Mickey Harris won 17, Joe Dobson 13, and Jim Bagby added seven wins.

Bobby Doerr: "Tex Hughson was about as good a pitcher as I've ever seen. He threw hard. If you wanted to compare Tex to somebody, you could say Orel Hershiser. He knew every hitter, the way that he wanted to pitch to him, and he did it. And I understand that's the way Hershiser works. He had a good sinking fastball with a quick curve. It seemed like every time Tex pitched, it was a 1 to nothing, 2 to 1 ballgame."

Eddie Pellagrini, Red Sox, 1946–47: "One day Tex called me to the mound with the bases loaded and 3 and 2 on the hitter. I was playing third. We had a rule on the ballclub, 'Don't talk to him,' because he talked a lot, just liked to talk, and he wouldn't let you up.

"He said, 'Pelli, come here.'

"I said, 'What is it?'

"He said, 'I've been pitching a long time. I've never walked a run in in my life.'

"I said, 'Well, you're not going to do it now.'

"He said, 'That's right.'

"I went back, and Tex walked him. He yelled over, 'Well, that's the first time.'

"It was a new experience for him. Join the mortals. But that's how good he was.

"Tex was a good storyteller. Texas stuff. He'd say, 'He couldn't look any more like you if you had pulled him out of your asshole with a chain.' And then he'd go and tell everyone the same joke."

Bobby Doerr: "When I came to spring training in '46, I remember the first time Boo Ferriss pitched batting practice and, man, he knocked the bat right out of my hand. Holy mackerel. He had that quick sinking fastball in on you and a good little quick slider and he was a competitor. A good pitcher. He came in in '45 and had that great year, but I'll tell you, he could have pitched in any era of the game."

Roy Mumpton: "Early in the season Joe Cronin had got his pitching staff pretty much fouled up, like some managers do when you get rain and doubleheaders. He went to Mickey Harris, one of his starting pitchers, and he said, 'I want you to do me a favor. I want you to pitch at least seven or eight innings. Even if they murder you. It's not punishment. Here's the point. I have no pitching. I have to get them straightened out, give them rest.'

"It was against a good-hitting ballclub, and Mickey hadn't done too well, but Harris went out, and they got six or seven runs off him, but all of a sudden, the Sox won the ballgame. And from that game on, Cronin would leave Harris in. As a result, Harris that year had an earned-run average higher than he would have, but Cronin kept playing that hunch, kept putting him out there and leaving him in."

Eddie Pellagrini: "One day Jim Bagby was pitching, and a ball was hit down the left-field line at Fenway, and you know how close the line is at

Fenway. Williams went for the ball, and when he did, it skipped by him, and Ted had to turn around and run, and I guess Bagby didn't think Ted ran as fast as he could.

"After the game, I was sitting in the clubhouse. Everybody was gone except Bagby, me, and Mike Ryba. Bagby was pissed off. And all of a sudden Bagby notices Ted, and he said, 'The next time, go after that fucking ball.'

"Williams said, *'What?'*

"Bagby said, 'For Christ's sake, go after that fucking ball. I have to make my living, too.'"

"Williams said, 'I don't know what the fuck you're talking about.'

"Bagby said, 'You hit four hundred and six. I ain't doing shit here. I want to stay here.'

"Williams said, 'I'll tell you what, Bagby. When you pitch, I won't play.' Bagby said, 'Is that a promise? If you don't play, I might win a fucking ballgame.'

"Williams and me were in the shower afterwards. He said, 'Do you think I hustled?'

"I said, 'I really don't know.' Maybe I didn't see it as good as he did."

Gene Desautels: "Jim Bagby and I roomed together, and when we left Florida we used to come back with the National League team and play them on the way back east. Jim was pitching in some place in Carolina, and it was a real hot day. We came in a cab together after the ballgame, and as Jim went by the porter's desk—he had this hairlip—he said to the guy, 'I'm in room 228, and I want two Schlitzes up there right away,' but it wasn't easy to understand him. We went up and took a shower, and we were waiting.

"All of a sudden, we hear a tap on the door. Jim says, 'Come on in.' He's waiting for his beer, and who walks in but two babes. Jim says, 'What the hell is this?' He went to the phone and called the desk and said, 'I want two Schlitzes. Two beers. And hurry up, I'm thirsty.'"

Leading the Red Sox, just as he had before he went away for the war, was Ted Williams. In his first year back from military service, Williams batted .342, hit a career-high 38 home runs, drove in 123 runs, and scored 142 times. Williams missed winning the Triple Crown for the second time by just a hair. Hank Greenberg hit 44 home runs and drove in 127 runs. Only Mickey Vernon finished higher than Ted in batting average, with a .353.

Williams might have achieved the Triple Crown, but he slumped badly at the end of the year. Sportswriter Austin Lake even blamed it on a conspiracy to give Williams "a lesson in humility."

"Rival athletes gradually grew sour at Ted for his aloof swagger and chill hauteur toward fellow craftsmen," Lake wrote, and so pitchers were throwing Vernon and Greenberg fat pitches at Ted's expense. "If there is a moral to point to," concluded Lake, "and I offer it paternally, it would be: Be nice to people on the way up. They are the same ones you encounter on the way down."

Despite such outlandish charges, the Red Sox star continued his amazing feats with the bat.

On July 8, 1946, Williams hit one of the most renowned home runs ever to be hit in an All-Star Game. The site was Detroit. The pitcher was Pittsburgh Pirate star Rip Sewell, who had perfected a high-arcing bloop pitch that came in at such a slow speed that major-league batters, used to eighty-five-mile-an-hour pitches, had tremendous difficulty adjusting. Ted Williams figured him out.

Roy Mumpton: "Honest to God, Sewell said he never believed anyone could hit one. Ted hit it right over the center-field wall.

"Sewell threw the ball way up, twenty feet, and we always wondered how an umpire could ever call that pitch a strike, 'cause he'd throw it way up, and it would drop straight down, a bloop. And he had great luck with it. Sewell was the only one I ever saw throw that pitch. But Ted, he hit it all right."

On July 14, Cleveland shortstop-manager Lou Boudreau gave the American sporting press something exciting to write about: a new wrinkle in an otherwise staid game. In a game in which Ted Williams hit three home runs and drove in eight runs, Boudreau adapted an unorthodox, controversial strategy that White Sox manager Jimmy Dykes had first tried against Williams in 1941: when Williams came to bat late in the game, Boudreau jogged from his shortstop position to the right side of the bag at second base, pushing second baseman Dutch Meyer into the hole between first and second. He swung the outfield around to right field, playing left fielder Pat Seery almost in center field.

Boudreau was leaving the entire left side of the ballfield for Williams to attack. Furthermore, by moving the third baseman over by the shortstop position, he was encouraging Williams to bunt—virtually a gift base hit if he did so.

But Boudreau was certain that Williams would neither hit to the left side nor bunt. He was counting on Williams's stubborn pride not to waver in the face of this challenge.

"I was playing to his ego," Boudreau once told me. And Boudreau was right about Williams. The Red Sox slugger adamantly refused to hit to left field, even when there were no fielders there. This provided the Boston press with a ready-made issue, even though that year Williams had nine home runs and batted .400 against Cleveland and Boudreau's shift.

*   *   *

Williams led the team's offense, but he had formidable help. Another slugger who spearheaded the Red Sox attack was first baseman Rudy York. York, who was acquired by the Red Sox on January 3, 1946 in exchange for Eddie Lake, was a rock in the infield, leading the league in putouts, assists, and double plays. At bat he hit 17 home runs and drove in 119 runs. He also led the league in another category: setting his room in the Myles Standish Hotel on fire. While with Boston, he did it three times.

York was a student of the game. His teammates loved him. But he had the bad habit of falling asleep while he smoked in bed.

Eddie Pellagrini: "I was speaking one night. I said, 'We have a lot of league leaders on the Sox. Rudy York leads the leagues in fires, and the year ain't even over yet.' He heard about it.

" 'You son of a bitch,' he said.

"Rudy would have a few drinks in him, go to bed smoking, and fall asleep. One time he told me, 'Someone threw a cigarette out their window, and the wind blew it into my room and set the room on fire.' In the paper the next day, they showed a picture of his room, with all the bottles on the floor.

"He was great. One night in Washington he kept me up all night. I said, 'Rudy, I have a doubleheader tomorrow.'

" 'Ah, Dago, don't worry about it.'

"He was having a few, and he had me and Pinky Higgins, Bob Klinger, and Wally Moses in there. It was a Friday, and he ordered ham sandwiches. I said, 'Rudy, I can't eat them. It's Friday.' He was pissed at me because he was drinking and I didn't drink. When it was time to go home, he wouldn't let any of us out of the room.

"The next morning, I was getting ready to go to the ballpark, and I'm feeling like I'm going to die. He sees me: 'Let's go, Dago.' He was fine.

"One night we were in Cleveland, and he said, 'Let's go get a milk shake.' I said, 'Rudy, you got to be shitting me.' He said he had quit drinking.

"So we went to a soda fountain right across the street from the hotel, and we ordered. Just about when he was ready to drink his milk shake, we heard the fire engines. He said, 'Oh, Jesus, I hope that ain't my room.'

"Where do you think the fire engines went? Right under where his room was. He said, 'Oh, Jeez.' He was ready to take the pipe. We looked out, and there was a fire in the barrels on the street.

"Rudy was one of the smartest baseball men who ever played this game. You might not think so to hear him talk—he had a deep, gravelly voice, like he had a cold all the time—but boy, did he know the game. He'd tell me what to look for, tell me what to do. He could steal signs. I picked his brain. One year with Detroit he led the league in homers and RBIs. One year with us he led the league in fires."

*   *   *

The Red Sox lost seven straight games before finally clinching the pennant on Friday, the thirteenth of September, when Tex Hughson beat Red Embree of Cleveland 1–0, his sixth shutout and fourth 1–0 win. Ted Williams got the winning hit, an inside-the-park home run hit to left field. If the Boudreau shift hadn't been on, it would have been an out.

Tex Hughson: "The Indians had the Boudreau shift on, and he hit it down the third-base line, over the third baseman's head, a line drive, and left fielder Pat Seery was playing over toward center field. The ball rolled down the line way into foul territory, and before Seery could get it in, Ted had a home run inside the park.

"Ted hadn't hit it there on purpose. He never tried to hit the ball that way."

After the Red Sox nailed down the pennant, Boston mayor James Michael Curley ordered the city's firemen to sound sirens, gongs, and bells for a full fifteen seconds. The Red Sox were American League champions for the first time since 1918. It should have been a joyous occasion, but the acrimony between the press and the Red Sox management loosed itself almost immediately.

The evening of the pennant-clinching, Joe Cronin was riding the elevator with Huck Finnegan of the *Boston Record American*. Cronin and Finnegan had been feuding. Finnegan was constantly writing that Cronin was a bad manager. Once on a train in the dining car, Finnegan began swearing at him. Cronin picked up a steak knife and waved it at him.

As the men stood together in the elevator, Cronin said to Finnegan, "What do you think now, you fucking bastard?"

"You'll never win another pennant," said Finnegan.

As the elevator door was opening at the lobby, Cronin, his face red with rage, said, "Fuck you, Finnegan."

Finnegan replied, "Fuck you, Cronin."

Reported Al Hirshberg with tongue in cheek, "This was the first public announcement by both the Red Sox and its press following the clinching of the pennant."

To celebrate the pennant-clinching, Tom Yawkey threw a party. He didn't want to invite the press, but he didn't want to offend either, so he made a Solomon-like decision and held two separate parties, one for the players and one for the press.

Wrote Al Hirshberg, "We all felt like scullery maids, banished to the kitchen while the lords and masters enjoyed themselves in the main dining room." Austin Lake refused to go along. He went into the players' party to complain and got into a shouting match with Yawkey.

Roy Mumpton: "Lake made a big stink. He wrote in the paper how snobbish Yawkey was, that he feted his players and didn't take the press. To some of us, four or five of us, it didn't matter. We all had to write stories. We were tied up for a long while. Sure, I would have liked to have gone to a party with the team, but it didn't bother me that much. I didn't even know whether other teams did it that way or not."

Though Roy Mumpton didn't mind, the writers with the most influence over the public did. Moreover, they now knew that Yawkey himself was no respecter of the press, and they were determined to punish him. For the rest of their careers, Dave Egan, Austin Lake, Hy Hurwitz, Huck Finnegan, Al Hirshberg, and a few others turned up the heat on the Red Sox whenever they could.

Wrote Hirshberg, "It cost Yawkey millions and perhaps two pennants."

And then Yawkey made an even bigger mistake.

The Red Sox had to wait for the St. Louis Cardinals and the Brooklyn Dodgers to play a three-game playoff for the championship of the National League. Red Sox management decided to keep their players sharp and to make some extra money by staging a three-game exhibition series against All-Stars from the rest of the American League.

However, they sorely overestimated the fans' appetite to see exhibition baseball, even against an All-Star ensemble. Only a thousand people showed up for the first game. Two thousand were in the stands for the second game—and then disaster struck.

The game was played in Boston on a cold, thirty-degree day. In the fifth inning, stubby left-hander Mickey Heffner of the Washington Senators hit Ted Williams with an inside curveball. The ball bore in on Williams and struck the tip of his right elbow square on. The elbow promptly turned blue and puffed up.

Said Heffner the next day; "I tried to throw a curve to Ted, but my hands were so cold I just couldn't break it off." That night, according to Ted's wife, Doris, "He was in agony all night."

The next day, despite the pain, Ted became restless and chose not to remain in his suite at the Hotel Sheraton. He and his wife went shopping. Reporters questioned how badly he was hurt and tried to insinuate he was goofing off rather than getting ready for the Series. One writer erroneously reported that Ted had gone fishing. But Ted was badly injured, though he stoically refused to admit it, and he would suffer the effects of the injury throughout the entire World Series of 1946.

A LOSS TO THE CARDINALS

In early October 1946, the Red Sox rode the train west to the most out-of-the-way outpost in major-league baseball—St. Louis, Missouri—to meet the Cardinals in the World Series.

Red Sox luck ran hot in the first game. Tex Hughson started and pitched well, but he trailed by a run in the eighth. In the top of the ninth, a ground ball went through the legs of St. Louis star shortstop Marty Marion to tie the game, and then slugging first baseman Rudy York pinch-hit a home run in the tenth to win it.

Dom DiMaggio: "In the first game, had it not been for Rudy York, I might have been made to look pretty ridiculous. I had lost a ball hit by catcher Joe Garagiola in the darkness of the crowd and couldn't get back quite fast enough to catch it. They gave him a base hit that should not have been. The ball should have been caught had I seen it.

"And so, the St. Louis Cardinals went out in front, but then Rudy hit a home run in the top half of the tenth inning and got me off the hook."

St. Louis star pitcher Harry Brecheen, who would win three games against Boston, pitched a shutout in Game Two to tie the series at one game each.

Bobby Doerr: "Brecheen threw a little screwball, a little sliding curve, and he mixed speeds. He wasn't overpoweringly fast. Our ballclub was a fastball-hitting club, a pull-hitting ballclub, and what we should have done with him was to hit him through the middle. But we didn't. And that hurt us."

Meanwhile, columnist Dave Egan, displaying a most exquisite timing, had run a story that the Red Sox were considering a trade of Ted Williams to the New York Yankees for Joe DiMaggio. The scuttlebutt was that new Yankee owner Larry MacPhail wanted to trade the laconic, stoic DiMaggio and remake the team over in his own image. The fiery Ted was certainly more in the image of the rambunctious redhead than Joe DiMaggio. Though few of the Red Sox players paid much attention to the rumors, Williams was genuinely concerned, because he didn't like Yankee Stadium. He didn't like to field there, and, worse, he felt the gargantuan ballpark provided a poor background for hitters, with its usual mob of white-shirt bleacherites and the smoky haze wafting up from center field.

"Do you think they'll trade me?" Williams asked one of the reporters. "I'd like to know. I'd like to get this straightened out."

Williams told Harold Kaese of the *Boston Globe,* "I'd hate to be traded to the Yankees. I don't like New York. I just don't want to play there."

Kaese reported that manager Joe Cronin was the man behind the trade rumors. According to Kaese, Cronin was frustrated that Williams would not hit to left field and had talked to him "until I am blue in the face." Wrote Kaese, "Cronin has decided that Williams is temperamentally unchangeable."

After the trade rumor was reported in the press, general manager Eddie Collins and manager Cronin both denied any involvement, contending that it was "a National League scheme." Collins said the stories were creations of "people working for the Cardinals."

Owner Tom Yawkey, who refused to comment on the rumors, blamed the Red Sox reporters. Yawkey resented Egan, Lake, and Hurwitz as much as Williams did, and he took it personally when three Red Sox reporters picked the Cardinals to win the World Series. The Boston owner declared he would "buy a couple of Boston papers and fire some sportswriters."

"But," Kaese reminded his readers, "no one would say that Williams would not be traded."

Ted was not traded. But the trade rumors once again put Ted Williams in the middle of controversy. To this day, fans of both the Red Sox and the Yankees ponder what might have been, envisioning the right-hand-hitting Joe DiMaggio aiming for the Wall and the left-hand-hitting Ted Williams going for the short porch in Yankee Stadium.

The Red Sox did not win the World Series. Because of his injured elbow, Ted Williams had trouble swinging the bat. Accentuating his futility was the use by Cardinal manager Eddie Dyer of his own variation of the Boudreau shift. Dyer would keep his shortstop, Marty Marion, in place and move third baseman Whitey Kurowski behind second. Other times, Dyer positioned Marion to the right of second base and moved Kurowski to short.

Williams batted twenty-five times in the 1946 Series, managing but five singles and one run batted in. If you read the papers, you would have thought Ted Williams lost the Series, which lasted seven games, all by himself.

Because Williams wasn't hitting, the reporters blasted him for his seeming unwillingness to hit to left field or to bunt. When one reporter asked Williams why he didn't bunt, Ted replied, "Because they don't pay off on bunts." Other writers suggested Ted didn't know how to bunt.

In Game Three, Rudy York, as he did in Game One, hit a home run to give the Sox a win. To prove to detractors he could do it, and to combat Dyer's defensive shift, Williams bunted once during the game and got an easy base hit. In one of the Boston papers the next day, the banner headline did not tout the Red Sox victory. Rather, it blared: "Williams Bunts." That headline by itself indicated the depths of emotion Williams created in the men who covered him in the papers.

In Game Four, the Cardinals retaliated against Tex Hughson, Jim Bagby, and four other relievers to tie the Series. The twenty-hit Cardinal outburst was led by catcher Joe Garagiola, who was a better player than he ever let on.

Tex Hughson: "That was one of those days. It seemed whatever pitcher we had, they just hit everything we threw up there. Or else everything went into a hole. We had a bad game."

Eddie Pellagrini: "Cronin brought in Bagby in Game Four, and he got the shit kicked out of him in Fenway Park. I'll never forget, he was coming toward the dugout—you could see he was pissed—and as he neared the dugout, he said, 'All my fucking life I wanted to pitch in the World Series, and the only fucking time he uses me is when he has to waste another pitcher.' And he threw his glove against the dugout wall."

The Red Sox went up three games to two in Game Five behind pitcher Joe Dobson and right fielder Leon Culberson, who homered.

The Sox needed to win only one of two games to win their first Series since 1918.

Harry Brecheen stopped them in Game Six out in St. Louis. The Cards scored three runs in the third and coasted to a 4–1 victory. Sox manager Joe Cronin wasted 4⅔ innings of shutout relief by Tex Hughson. Why he chose to pitch Hughson, rather than save him for Game Seven, was unclear.

In Game Seven, Joe Cronin proved his reputation for being a hunch manager. That hunch cost the Red Sox the Series.

With the score tied 3–3 in the eighth inning, Cronin went to the mound, took out Joe Dobson, and replaced him with Bob Klinger, a National League refugee who hadn't pitched in twenty-seven days because an illness in his family had forced him to return home.

Everyone wanted Cronin to bring in his ace, Tex Hughson, but the pitcher's position in the lineup was due up in the bottom of the eighth, and Cronin wanted to pitch Klinger in the eighth, pinch-hit for him, and have Hughson available in the ninth. Cronin's miscalculation was in forgetting that, above all, baseball is a game of pitching and defense. By the time the ninth inning rolled around, it was too late to go to Hughson. The Red Sox were already dead.

Klinger came in and immediately gave up the winning run, a hit-and-run single to Harry Walker that drove in Enos Slaughter all the way from first base. Slaughter's dash home from first has become one of the most famous plays in baseball history. Critics have said that when the throw came in from outfielder Leon Culberson to shortstop Johnny Pesky, Pesky hesitated while Slaughter continued around third, ignoring third-base coach Mike Gonzalez's signal to stop, and scored.

As a result, Johnny Pesky was tagged as the "goat" of the Series. In the great controversy engendered by Slaughter's mad dash home, Cronin, Klinger, Pesky, and Slaughter have been intertwined ever since. Slaughter's run proved to be the Cardinals' margin of victory. The Red Sox would not get into another World Series until twenty-one agony-filled years later.

Doc Cramer: "During the '46 Series, I was in Canada, barnstorming with Allie Reynolds and three or four others, and we were listening to the game against the Cardinals when Slaughter ran all the way around and scored.

"Cronin brought in a guy by the name of Klinger. A National Leaguer. Couldn't pitch any. The seventh game of the World Series, and he brings him in! And he had guys like Hughson, all those young boys, good arms, and he didn't bring them in. He lost the Series.

"When we heard Klinger was coming in, we didn't even listen. We got up and left the radio. We said, 'That's it.'

"And it was."

Slaughter's dash home from first on Harry Walker's single is indelibly etched in the minds of those who remember the 1946 Series. The frames of the memory skip from one to another quickly, but always the play ends the same way, with outfielder Leon Culberson, playing in the place of Dom DiMaggio, who had pulled a muscle running the bases the inning before, throwing to Johnny Pesky, who looks to third for Slaughter before realizing the Cardinal star is racing home, and Pesky then throwing home as Slaughter slides violently across home plate ahead of the throw.

The Slaughter dash has bedeviled the Red Sox players and their fans. The chorus of "if only" has become a litany. "If only" Tex Hughson had been pitching. "If only" Dom DiMaggio had not gotten hurt and had been in center field. "If only" Johnny Pesky hadn't held the ball.

Roy Mumpton: "Dom DiMaggio had been hurt. Leon Culberson was playing center field. The ball was hit out to him, and he hesitated throwing the ball. He took too long. He threw it to Pesky. Pesky was a very smart ballplayer. Doerr hollered at him, and he couldn't understand Doerr. He held the ball. He would have had a play on Slaughter at third base if he had thrown it. That's how much he would have been out. Doerr was hollering 'third' and Pesky couldn't understand him because the crowd was going crazy. And Slaughter scored."

Dom DiMaggio: "I was sitting in the dugout and was halfway out of the dugout when Walker hit the ball to left center. Even though he hit lefty, Harry Walker was a notorious left-field hitter—he hit to left and left center. We got Leon to move over some, but we tried to get him to move over even more. When the pitch was made, the guy hit the ball over the shortstop's head, and Slaughter circled the bases.

"Once Walker hit the ball, there was nothing Culberson could do. He threw the ball back cleanly. Had he perhaps been playing over a little further, it might not have gotten to that point. He did nothing wrong. He went over and fielded the ball cleanly and made a good relay.

"I've often wished I had been out there, and I wonder, 'Had I been there, would we have won?' "

Johnny Pesky: "I don't even want to talk about that. I got blamed for something I didn't think was my fault. It always comes up. About three weeks ago I was in the market, and a guy climbed all over me. 'You're a bum.' He was an older guy. I said, 'You weren't even there.' He said he was. I said, 'Where did this play occur?' He said, 'In Boston.' And it had occurred in St. Louis.

"I said, 'You want to blame me, go ahead.'

"It's one of those things I've had to live with. There is no such thing as a robot on the field. The ball does some crazy things out there sometimes. Joe Cronin used to say, 'It's a game of inches.' And it really is. Just a half an inch here, a half an inch there, and it's a whole different ball of wax.

"Being involved in it, I can remember it like it was yesterday. Slaughter was stealing second base, and he had a real good jump. I'm covering second base. And the ball was hit, and Slaughter, with two outs, he just kept running. I was almost at second base when the ball was hit, and now I have to retrace my steps, and I go out to left center field. I wasn't all that deep. Slaughter just kept on going. By the time I got the ball, looked around, and threw home, Slaughter scored.

"The announcer, Arch McDonald, said that I took too long to get rid of the ball, that I hesitated and all that.

"And the funny part was that in the ninth inning, with less than two outs, we had a man on first and third and didn't score.

"But those things happen, and that's what baseball is all about. And in that Series the two greatest players who ever played the game, Ted Williams and Stan Musial, had bad Series. They didn't hit a lick.

"It was a sad, sad experience. Believe me. That was the all-time low for all of us. I remember looking over at Williams and, boy, he was really down. He was almost in tears. He might have even shed a tear or two.

"To this day, I feel we had a better ballclub than the Cardinals. They had one guy who was outstanding in the Series, Harry Brecheen, and we didn't win. It's a sad thing when you think you should have won, and you don't."

CHAPTER 16
A Plague of Injuries

In August of 1946, during the hysteria of a fifteen-game Red Sox lead, the talk was of a Red Sox dynasty. After twenty-eight years of futility, very quickly everyone connected with the Sox began talking about the string of pennants the team was sure to win. Wrote *Boston Globe* writer Harold Kaese, "Declining are the Yankee and Cardinal empires. Replacing them is the empire of the Red Sox."

Tom Yawkey felt equally buoyed. In October of 1946, not long after the Cardinals' victory over his team, Yawkey boldly predicted that next season the Red Sox would win the World Series. It was a prediction that would remain unfulfilled throughout Yawkey's lifetime.

In 1947, injuries plagued the American League champs all season long. The season began badly, with a freak injury to center fielder Dom DiMaggio.

Dom DiMaggio: "I got hurt swinging on a cold day. We had a double-header, and on my first at bat, I went to swing at the ball and something popped. At first it didn't appear to be very serious. But the shoulder got very painful, and I couldn't move it. That was one year I did not make the All-Star team. It took another year or so to get over that injury. That's what I remember about the '47 season. After the pitching staff went to pot, we were no longer contenders."

In 1947, right-hander Joe Dobson had an outstanding season, winning 18 games and fashioning a 2.95 earned-run average. But the other three top Red

Sox starters—Tex Hughson, Boo Ferriss, and Mickey Harris—all came down with arm miseries. Without the services of these men, the Red Sox finished third, 14 games behind the Yankees. It is rare for three-fourths of a pitching staff to go down with injuries. In 1947, it happened to the Red Sox.

The strong beacon of light for the Red Sox was Ted Williams, who had another magnificent season in 1947. He won the Triple Crown for the second time in five years, hitting .343, with 32 home runs and 114 runs batted in. For the pennant-winning Yankees, Joe DiMaggio hit .315 with 20 home runs and 97 runs batted in. Williams should have been the Most Valuable Player in a landslide. But that's not what happened.

In fact, there was considerable controversy over just what did happen that year. In MVP balloting, the beat writers from around the league each selected ten players. A first-place vote garnered the player ten points, second place nine points, and so on. Williams was always fervently convinced that one Boston writer, Mel Webb of the *Globe,* left him off the ballot entirely—even though the *Globe*'s Harold Kaese reported that Webb didn't even have a vote that year. According to Kaese, Jack Malaney of the *Post,* Joe Cashman of the *Record,* and Burt Whitman of the *Herald* were the three Boston writers to cast ballots in 1947, and all three placed Williams first. It was a midwestern writer that left Williams off the ballot entirely, said Kaese, and Joe DiMaggio was left off three ballots.

An interesting sidelight: Two years later, in 1949, it was discovered that some of the nation's baseball writers were making small bets on the eventual MVP winner, and that as a result they were monkeying around with the voting.

In any case, in 1947 Williams got 201 points. DiMaggio got 202. DiMaggio was the Most Valuable Player. For Williams, it was just one more black mark against the sporting press.

When manager Joe Cronin took off the uniform on September 30, 1947, an era ended. He had played since 1926, performing regularly through the 1944 season. He had been a manager since 1933, the year he led the Washington Senators to a pennant.

Joe Cronin ended his career with a lifetime .301 batting average, 170 home runs, and 1,424 runs batted in. His was an enviable, productive career, and in 1956 he was voted into baseball's Hall of Fame.

Those who knew Cronin thought he would never shed the uniform. But Red Sox president Eddie Collins was slowing down, and Tom Yawkey wanted his most loyal employee to take over for Columbia Eddie as his top man. Reluctantly, Cronin agreed to the promotion from the field to the front office.

To replace Cronin, Tom Yawkey hired as manager the former Yankee skipper, Joe McCarthy. He was Cronin's choice as well. Both Yawkey and

Cronin had envied McCarthy's success, and they figured that if they hired him, some of that success would rub off on the Sox.

When McCarthy was hired to manage in Boston, Yawkey and Cronin thought they were hiring the man who had led Babe Ruth, Lou Gehrig, and Joe DiMaggio to eight pennants and immortality. What they, the players, and the fans ended up with was bitterness, disappointment, and heartache.

Joe McCarthy Takes Over

Marse Joe McCarthy, no-nonsense and taciturn, had won the National League pennant in 1929 as manager of the Chicago Cubs with players such as Rogers Hornsby, Hack Wilson, and Kiki Cuyler. With the New York Yankees, some of his players were Ruth, Gehrig, DiMaggio, and Bill Dickey, and his teams dominated the American League by winning eight pennants and seven world championships. McCarthy had quit the Yankees in the middle of 1946 after a run-in on the team plane with relief pitcher Joe Page following a tough loss to Cleveland. Tom Yawkey had offered him the chance to run the '47 Red Sox club, but McCarthy had turned him down. One season later, he accepted a two-year pact at an incredible $100,000 a year.

With the naming of McCarthy as manager, Yankee outfielder Tommy Henrich, a staunch devotee of Marse Joe, commented, "It looks to me as though the Red Sox will be the team to beat next year."

Boston was getting a tough man in McCarthy, an authoritarian figure who reportedly had a standing offer of $100 to any player who punched an opposing player in an on-field fight.

Milton Gross wrote an article in *Collier's* in which he described McCarthy's personality:

"Despite an enviable record McCarthy is neither a graceful winner nor a good loser. On the occasion of more than one victory celebration, Joe has told off certain newspapermen who didn't treat him with adjectives becoming his record.

"The fact is, Joe can't abide criticism or even conversation on a losing day, as innumerable players, waiters, bartenders, Pullman porters, hotel maids, and writers have discovered to their humiliation.

"A inconsolable, lonely man with small grace for conversation, the whimsies or vagaries of life, McCarthy regards every bad break as a personal affront. When his club isn't going right, he takes refuge in insolence and insulting remarks."

With reporters, McCarthy would chat pleasantly enough about old vaudeville stars or minor-league experiences, but when questioned about his current team's problems, he likely would turn and snap, "Let me worry about that."

He had treated the press in New York that way, but the New York writers feared and respected him and didn't dare rock the boat. What McCarthy wasn't prepared for was the Boston press. In Boston, he became a target like anyone else.

One of McCarthy's first acts after arriving in Boston was to release pitcher Bill Zuber. McCarthy's altercation with Page and subsequent resignation from the Yankees had been prompted by a loss to Cleveland. Zuber had given up the home run that had brought that loss. A few weeks later, Zuber had been sold to the Red Sox.

Now, with McCarthy running the Red Sox, he again sent Zuber packing. The Boston reporters noticed it and commented.

McCarthy was clearly a different sort of guy from the easygoing Joe Cronin. As is the case whenever a new manager comes into a clubhouse, some of the players loved the change and others didn't.

Mel Parnell, Red Sox, 1947–56: "A lot of guys feared McCarthy. I don't know why, because I thought the man was great to play for, but a lot of guys were uptight.

"There were little things he didn't like. One was a pipe smoker. Cigarette smoking was all right, but he said, 'Anyone who smokes a pipe is a contented man, and you can't be contented and play baseball.' Maybe he had a point there.

"The Red Sox made a deal with the St. Louis Browns, and Billy Hitchcock came over with us. We were standing in the lobby of the Chase Hotel in St. Louis one morning. McCarthy walked out of the elevator and started in our direction.

"We told Billy, 'Hide the pipe, because the old man doesn't like pipe smokers.' So Billy covered the pipe with his hand and stuck it in his pocket. You could see the smoke coming through the threads of his trousers. I think McCarthy did see him, but he didn't say anything. I'm sure McCarthy figured we'd get the message to him.

"McCarthy also looked down on Polish ballplayers. He said they were too dumb, said they made too many mistakes.

"He had a dress code, too. You had to have a jacket on at all times. You could wear a sports shirt, but you had to have a jacket. He always did say, 'Fellas, you're at the top of your profession. Dress like it, and act like it.'

"The one thing I appreciated about McCarthy, if you committed a wrong, he'd call you into his office and just chew your rear end out. But it was just you and McCarthy. He wasn't showing you up in front of everyone else.

"It was easier to pitch for Joe Cronin than it was McCarthy because you knew when you were pitching under Cronin. 'Today is Saturday. I'll be pitching again Thursday.' McCarthy wouldn't do that. McCarthy would put the ball under your cap. When you came to the clubhouse in the morning and you saw the ball under your cap, you knew you were the pitcher.

"His reason for that, and it was a good reason, was that he didn't want you to go home and worry about that ballgame all night and not get a good night's sleep, which some guys would do. Some guys would get a little nerved up, and they'd have that game on their mind all night and wouldn't sleep too good about it. That never did bother me. I went to bed and got up in the morning and went out onto the ballfield and gave it my best shot, just hoping my best shot was good enough. Denny Galehouse would get tight about it. Ray Scarborough would get nerved up, but he'd relax after he got out to the ballpark.

"McCarthy related to the players. If your ego got a little inflated, he knew how to knock the wind out of your sails. And if you needed a little pickup, he could pat you on the rear.

"Joe's wife used to tell me he'd come home at night and lock himself in the room and try to figure out ways to beat the opposition. She often felt he was taking it too seriously, that it was affecting his health, because he could never get baseball off his mind. Winning meant so much to McCarthy, coming from those great Yankee teams, and of course, when we played the Yankees, there was nothing he wanted more than for us to beat them. He used to say that. And if we lost, he'd go into his room, and it would get to him inwardly, but he'd never get on us about it. Maybe the next day he'd talk about some wrong we committed, which was good. He'd talk to the guys so you wouldn't continue to do the same thing over and over again. He was very much a teacher, and he had a good coaching staff, good fellas, Earle Combs, John Schulte, and Paul Schreiber."

Matt Batts: "Coming back in '48, it was more organized than the year before, even though most of them were the same ones. The difference, in my opinion, was Joe McCarthy. He was super. Oh, yeah. He didn't say much, but you just felt great with the man there. You had the feeling that you had to play your best at all times. Not that he was forcing you. It was just that you had that good feeling. It's like I try to tell my employees, 'I want you happy every day. I want you to wake up in the morning and feel like you want to go to work, not that you hate to get up and go to work at that old place, grumpy.' It was the same way with the Red Sox. When you woke up in the morning, you wanted to get to the ballpark to play ball, because you enjoyed it, and you loved the people you were with, loved the manager, loved the coaches, and of course, we had great ballplayers."

Johnny Pesky: "Joe McCarthy was the best man I ever played for. Joe was a very quiet man. He wore that long uniform, never wore a number, and he'd just stand there and look, and if something happened, he would call you over, like a teacher you fall in love with in school. That was his kind of approach to the players. He wouldn't say, 'I want you to do this,' he'd say, 'Can I suggest this to you?'

"He always moved around the field. He'd be here one time and a couple minutes later he'd be out in right field. In the dugout. He'd be talking to the

press. McCarthy knew more baseball than any other man I ever saw. But
there were some guys who didn't respond to Joe."

Bobby Doerr: "I think he felt our ballclub had been too easily handled,
and he wanted to get more firm with it. And we were the type of guys that
didn't know how to accept that type of thing.

"I didn't dislike McCarthy, but I thought he was a little harder to play for.
Joe Cronin was always kidding me, patting me on the back, and I'd break my
neck for him, and then McCarthy, I just felt kind of strained most of the time
playing for him. It wasn't that much fun.

"But McCarthy was a great manager. I'm not downgrading him. I'm just
saying that his personality was different from Cronin's, and it was hard for
me to adjust."

If Joe McCarthy had a stubborn prejudice, it was his lack of regard for
injured pitchers. Once a pitcher hurt himself, McCarthy treated him as
though he were through.

The most striking example of that had occurred back in 1926 when
McCarthy managed the Chicago Cubs. During spring training Grover Cleveland Alexander, one of the greatest pitchers in the history of the game, broke
his ankle. While "Old Pete" was in the hospital, McCarthy never once came
to see him. Once Alexander got out, he had to hobble on crutches. McCarthy
made him come to the ballpark every day, even though it pained him to
do so.

Alexander's ankle healed by June, and when the superstar pitcher finally
made it to the mound, McCarthy demanded that he, McCarthy, call all the
pitches. Nobody had ever before told Alexander, who won 373 games in his
career, how to pitch. Before the end of the season, McCarthy released him.
He was picked up by the St. Louis Cardinals, and the following Sunday he
was on the mound to face McCarthy's Cubs. Alexander beat the Cubs, 3–2.
At the end of the game, McCarthy was sitting on the bench. Alexander
passed him, looked him right in the eye, smiled, tipped his cap, and walked
on. Alexander went on to help the Cardinals defeat the Yankees in the 1926
World Series, striking out Tony Lazzeri with the winning runners on base to
end the final game.

One Red Sox player who found himself despising the new manager was
Boston's star right-hander, Tex Hughson. Hughson had undergone an elbow
operation after the 1947 season at Johns Hopkins University in Baltimore.
The doctors had told Hughson he would not be able to pitch until June, so
Hughson arranged with Red Sox president Joe Cronin for him to work out
with the Austin Pioneers, a Double-A team playing just thirty miles from his
home in San Marcos, Texas. He pitched in the Texas League for six weeks,
getting his arm back in shape.

About the time of the 1948 All-Star Game, Hughson pitched a nine-inning ballgame for Austin. He called Cronin, who said, "Tex, I want to ask you, can you help this ballclub?" Hughson said, "Joe, I'll help this ballclub if I'm used right, particularly in relief." Cronin replied, "Make your own arrangements. Come on back."

When Hughson rejoined the Red Sox, he discovered that Joe McCarthy had little interest in his services. Hughson, a likable, easygoing guy, ended up quitting the game at the end of the 1949 season because of McCarthy.

Despite his pleading to be allowed to pitch more, in 1948 Hughson appeared in just fifteen games. He had a 3–1 record. In 1949, he pitched in 29 games and was 4–2. Hughson says McCarthy never gave him the opportunity to resume his role as the ace of the staff. McCarthy supporters say Hughson wasn't the same pitcher after he returned.

To date; Hughson has the lowest lifetime earned-run average of any post-deadball era Red Sox pitcher, at 2.94. Roger Clemens is the only pitcher close to him.

Tex Hughson: "When I got back to Boston from pitching in Austin, in 1948, McCarthy didn't hardly know me. I had never done anything with McCarthy but beat his ballclub when he was with the Yankees. I held the record one time for beating the Yankees the most consecutive times of any pitcher in the American League, seven. I lost my first game to them in extra innings in 1941, and the rest of that year and '42, I beat them seven straight times.

"The first several games after returning to Boston, I pitched in relief an inning or so. I gave up one hit in seven innings. Dale Mitchell of Cleveland got a base hit off me. Then they started using me too much. My elbow would swell up and get sore from the operation. I told coach Larry Woodall in the bullpen. I said, 'I can't warm up all during a whole ballgame. I've got to throw and then I need a little time off. One of these days I'll be called on, and I won't be able to do justice to myself or to the ballclub.'

"Larry told McCarthy, and McCarthy told him, 'Aw, fuck him. He's not going to help us anyway.' That was his attitude. And what I didn't know about McCarthy was that he was an alcoholic. I didn't know it, but it was one reason the Yankees let him go. Whenever he was supposed to have slipped in the bathtub, he was riding the White Horse, and when he got on, it was for three or four days.

"Tom Dowd, our traveling secretary, who was an official in the National Football League in the off-season, was a reformed alcoholic. He traveled with McCarthy and stayed right next to him all the time, but once in a while McCarthy would get away. In St. Louis one day, Tom Dowd and I had him locked up in his room. I was pitching that day.

"In St. Louis there was no tunnel. The players had to mingle with the crowd before going to the dugout. As I was leaving the clubhouse to go warm up, just before game time, here came McCarthy. He walked up to a man in the crowd, and he thought it was Joe Cronin. He took the man by the lapel and said, 'Joe, don't get on me. I knew you in San Francisco when you were still sucking that hind tit.' He thought it was Cronin, because Cronin used to have to come down and take over the ballclub. McCarthy was so drunk that he was mistaken there.

"He brought Eddie Froelich, the trainer, from New York, and Froelich would carry his bottle with him, and McCarthy would drink during the ballgame, in the clubhouse, or down in the tunnel. Froelich had it wrapped in a white towel. Some of the players thought that was the reason McCarthy brought Eddie over there, so Froelich could carry it for him when he was drinking.

"I'm telling you, mister, I'm telling you the truth. This day that McCarthy was in St. Louis, he came back to the park, got in uniform, and came to the dugout. Vern Stephens was having a bad time hitting at the time. He had gone 0-for-20, and he hit some balls good that were caught. And with the bases loaded, he popped up.

"After Stephens came back to the dugout, McCarthy was sitting there, and he said, 'Aw, a pop-up. I never saw—'

"Vern Stephens turned around and said, 'Go to hell, you no-good, drunk son of a bitch, and get off my ass.' I'm not exaggerating. The story was written by numerous sportswriters at the time, but at that time the editors wouldn't print it.

"I could tell you stories about how he mistreated players on the ballclub. I saw Bobby Doerr, a hell of a ballplayer. McCarthy was sitting in the dugout when he was drunk and all, and he was trying to move Bobby over, telling him how to play the hitters. He finally got up and waved the white towel. He said, 'Move over, you dumb son of a bitch.' That's what he said. And I didn't appreciate that. Bobby Doerr was a hell of a good man, and a good friend of mine.

"I remember one time Sam Mele dropped a fly ball in the sun in right field. McCarthy had complete control of the ballclub. You had to go into his office to order bats. Sam had broken his last bat, and he went in there. McCarthy said, 'I thought you came in here to order a glove. Henrich would have stuck that ball up his ass.' That type of thing. I didn't like that.

"I'll be frank with you. Joe McCarthy is the only man who I've ever known in my life, and I'll be seventy-five my next birthday, who I couldn't get along with. It was a complete clash of personalities."

CHAPTER 17

1948 and 1949: McCarthy Plays His Hunches

ONE GAME

The Red Sox strengthened themselves when on November 17 and 18, 1947, Tom Yawkey opened up his checkbook and separated the economically troubled St. Louis Browns from a few of its star players. On the seventeenth, he sent six so-so players plus $310,000 to the Browns for veteran pitcher Jack Kramer and outstanding shortstop Vern Stephens, and the next day he traded three players and $65,000 to acquire pitcher Ellis Kinder and infielder Billy Hitchcock.

With McCarthy and the new players, the time was ripe for winning pennants. Moreover, the New York Yankees were ready to be taken. Dan Topping and Del Webb had just bought the Yankees from Larry MacPhail and hired George Weiss as general manager. In 1948, the Yankees seemed old and vulnerable, and the Red Sox appeared to have the manpower to overtake them.

The star of the 1948 Red Sox pitching staff was former St. Louis Browns stalwart Jack Kramer, who that year won eighteen games for the Red Sox.

Kramer had two different fastballs: he threw one about five miles an hour faster than the other, and saved it for tight situations. He also had an effective curve. His strength was excellent control. He could kiss the black on the inside or outside corner. He wasn't overpowering, but he didn't need to be.

"Batters would get out, but they would want to bat again," said catcher Matt Batts. "And he'd get them out again."

On the mound Kramer was a perfectionist, as he was in everything he did. His persnickety nature, however, used to drive his teammates crazy.

Mel Parnell: "If everything wasn't just a hundred percent perfect with Jack, he'd find fault with it. In restaurants, he would often send meals back. If it wasn't perfect, he was an unhappy person."

Matt Batts: "All of us loved to tease Jack. He was always such a goddamn pantywaist. We used to call him 'Alice.' Hell, he'd complain about everything, send food back, embarrass you. If it wasn't perfect the way he thought it should be, he'd send it back. I wouldn't eat with him. Hell, no. Not me.

"One thing he could do, he could put on a sports coat or a suit, and it could be a $5 one, and he'd make it look like a $105 one. He could make clothes look beautiful.

"Tell you a story about Kramer. In the corner of the clubhouse was his locker, mine, and then Kinder's. And Jack always had cashmere coats and fancy clothes.

"One day when I came back from practicing, my coat was laying down on the floor. I said, 'Kinder, who put my coat there?'

"He said, 'That goddamn Jack put it there. He didn't like for your sleeve to be hanging down into his locker.'

"I said, 'That was the problem?'

" 'Yeah.'

"I said, 'He didn't have to throw my coat on the damn floor.'

"So when he came in, I said, 'Jack, did you put my coat there on the floor?'

" 'Yeah, I didn't like your sleeve hanging over into my locker, so I took it down and put it there so you wouldn't be in my way.'

"I said, 'I'm going to tell you something. You know that goddamn white cashmere sport coat you got? You better not ever wear that son of a bitch to this ballpark ever again, because if you do, I'm going to pull it out of your locker and I'm going to throw it right straight across that dirty floor.'

"He said, 'Oh, no. You wouldn't do that.'

"I said, 'Test me.'

"A month later, he came in one Sunday wearing that white cashmere sports coat. He hung it in his locker, and when he went out on the field, I took that son of a bitch, and zzzzzzz, I threw it across the floor, and when he came in and saw that coat on the floor, oh Lord . . . I thought we were going to have a war. Oh Lord, he hit the ceiling.

" 'You do that?'

" 'You're goddamn right I did,' I said. 'You want to do anything about it, let's get to it. We'll go.'

"He didn't challenge me. He knew I meant business.

"One night game we played, Jack wasn't pitching, but he wanted to show off in front of Yawkey and the executives and the crowd. There was a packed house for batting practice. I was a rookie. He said to me, 'I want to warm up a little bit.' And I had to squat there right in front of the stands while he warmed up during batting practice. I had to miss my batting practice while I caught him.

"Parnell was pitching this one night. Mel and I had come up together through the minors, and he was standing there talking to me. Jack had been throwing for about twenty minutes and hadn't thrown one hard enough to hurt me.

"I said, 'Mel, you want to see me piss this son of a bitch off?'

"He said, 'Yeah.'

"I said, 'Okay, just hold tight.'

"I squatted down and I said, 'Jack, give me a good one.'

"He wound up with all that prissy shit, and he fired one in there. Yawkey and all of them were sitting right there. I dropped my goddamned catcher's mitt, caught him barehanded, didn't flinch a bit, and threw it back to him.

"He just let the ball go right by him, turned around, and walked off. And he never asked me to catch him again!

"Mel like to fell out. He couldn't believe it."

With eight games to play in the 1948 season, the Red Sox led the Cleveland Indians by a single game. During the final eight games, the Sox won five and lost three, and Ted Williams went 11-for-27, dispelling any doubt about his ability to hit in the clutch.

Meanwhile, the Indians were winning six and losing one, to take a one-game lead with one game left. On the final day the Red Sox won, and the players held their breath. Detroit beat Cleveland. The Red Sox had backed into a tie for the pennant.

The National League rules called for a playoff of two games out of three to determine the pennant, but in the American League, a single game was played. The Red Sox won the toss for home field. The playoff game against the Indians was scheduled for October 4 at Fenway Park. Almost 34,000 people jammed the park to see if the Red Sox could win their second pennant in three years. The Red Sox players were confident.

Matt Batts: "When we won and they lost to finish the season in a tie, we thought we had it in the bag. When we won the right to play at home, we knew we were going to win."

*   *   *

In the 1946 World Series, Joe Cronin had created controversy on the team by pitching Bob Klinger in the final crucial moments against the St. Louis Cardinals. In 1948, Red Sox manager Joe McCarthy created hysteria in the clubhouse when he chose thirty-seven-year-old Denny Galehouse to pitch the playoff game for the Sox.

None of the pitchers on the staff could believe it. Jack Kramer had won 18 games, Joe Dobson 16, Mel Parnell 15, and Ellis Kinder 10. Tex Hughson was healthy, but McCarthy's dislike for the big Texan kept him from consideration.

Galehouse, a mop-up man and fill-in pitcher, was 8–8 with a 4.00 ERA that season. Before the game, Galehouse had been shagging flies in the outfield. When McCarthy told him he was starting, he went to the locker room to lie down for a few minutes.

Matt Batts: "I thought of Denny Galehouse as nothing but a relief pitcher. When McCarthy picked him to start that game, the whole ballclub was upset about it. The whole twenty-five ballplayers. I don't think there was one of them that wasn't upset about it. There was mumbling and grumbling going on. You could hear the players, 'Why in the hell is he pitching him?'

"In fact, the players didn't want to make Galehouse feel bad about it, because it wasn't his fault. And hell, he went out there and did the very best he could. But it was one of those damn things."

Mel Parnell: "During the final week of the season, Denny Galehouse came on in relief and pitched very well. For that reason, when we wound up in a tie with Cleveland, McCarthy went with Galehouse. Also, the wind was blowing out to left field, and he figured the elements were against the left-hander. I think McCarthy made a mistake. I think he realized he made a mistake. It was something he just had to live with.

"I had assumed I was pitching the ballgame. The night before, I, my wife, my mother, and father were in Boston, and they were on my back to get to bed early, because tomorrow was to be the biggest game of my life. So I went to bed at nine o'clock to keep from hearing all that stuff. I was well-rested for the game.

"I went to the ballpark the next day. I looked under my cap, and sure enough, there was the ball. I figured I was the pitcher, so I took my good old time getting dressed, 'cause the pitcher doesn't have to be out on the field shagging flies during batting practice. You just have to get out there in time to take your cuts.

"While I was getting dressed, McCarthy came up from behind. He tapped me on the shoulder and said, 'Kid, I've changed my mind. I'm going with the right-hander. The elements are against the left-hander. The wind is blowing out strong to left field.'

"With that, I had nothing to do but get dressed and go out onto the field.

"In the meantime, McCarthy called Don Fitzpatrick, our clubhouse boy, and told Don to go outside and call in Denny Galehouse. He told Galehouse he was pitching, and I think it was a shock to Galehouse. He was just stunned. He didn't know what to say.

"I got dressed, ran out onto the field, and when I got outside, all the guys asked me, 'What are you doing out here?' I said, 'I'm not pitching.'

"I think we were somewhat demoralized, because everyone figured I was pitching. I had the proper rest. I had pitched fairly well against Cleveland and had everything going in my favor.

"After the game started, Lou Boudreau and Allie Clark checked underneath the stands to see if I was warming up, thinking McCarthy was trying to play a trick on them, thinking he was trying to get a left-handed lineup against Galehouse and then have me come in. But it wasn't that way.

"Lou Boudreau and Ken Keltner had big days, and it was a day in which everything worked fine for the Indians' Gene Bearden. He was a left-handed pitcher.

"Some of the press in Boston said that nobody wanted to pitch the game. That was an untruth. Anyone on the staff would have relished the chance to pitch. It was the biggest game of the year, and if you pitch and win, the next year at contract time means at least $5,000, which at that time would have been big money. It might have been more than that, because Mr. Yawkey was a very generous man. You win for him, and he's going to reward you royally.

"McCarthy made his choice, and it didn't work. After the ballgame, he said to me, 'I made a mistake. I'll just have to live with it.' Of course, he didn't tell it to the press, because they would have blown it way out of proportion. But that's what he said to me: 'I made my choice, and it was the wrong one.'

"What can you do? You can't replay it."

The Red Sox lost that final game, 8–3. Galehouse could not get through the fourth inning, when the Indians batted to a 5–1 lead. Cleveland player-manager Lou Boudreau went four-for-four and third baseman Ken Keltner drove in three runs to give the Tribe the American League pennant.

Matt Batts: "We lost some respect for McCarthy. Everybody got kind of down on him because of it."

PARNELL AND KINDER

The Red Sox were led in 1949 by Mel Parnell and Ellis Kinder, two superb pitchers but two very different kinds of men. Parnell was a conservative, solid family man, a straight-shooter all the way. He rarely drank, except for perhaps an occasional beer after pitching a ballgame. He kept himself in fine shape.

Parnell, a left-hander, had a fastball that broke in on a right-handed batter. He would throw the ball on the fist, and there was little the batter could do with it except ground out. Mel was a superb pitcher, a good competitor, and also an excellent hitter for a pitcher. Once, against Detroit, he went four-for-four.

In 1949, Parnell won a league-leading 25 ballgames, even though he pitched the entire season with a sore elbow.

Mel Parnell: "I had trouble with my arm all season. My elbow was real sore. A muscle was torn from the bone. I'd sit in the whirlpool and loosen it up and get the blood circulating. I'd get a massage, and I'd use capsiline, which is a red-hot salve, just burn the heck out of you, but it would put heat in the arm and loosen it up a bit. Other pitchers couldn't use it. Kinder tried it one day, and it burned the daylights out of him. He said, 'Never again.' "

Kinder, a right-hander, was a night owl. He loved his booze, and he loved his women. He believed he pitched better tanked up. Who was going to dissuade him? In baseball, a player can do as he wishes off the field so long as he continues to win. In 1949, Kinder fashioned a 23–6 record with a 3.36 earned-run average. His teammates were amazed by him, on and off the field.

Mel Parnell: "Kinder liked the nightlife. He'd stay out a good part of the night and get very little rest and still pitch a real good ballgame. I used to call him 'Superhuman.' I told him, 'When you die, they're going to bronze you and send you to the Hall of Fame. You do things no one else can do.'

"He had a great arm and never complained about a sore arm. He lived a real fast life, and to be able to do things he could do while living that fast life made him something separate, something different than the rest of us.

"I remember one time he came out to the ballpark just after having an accident. He failed to make one of the rotaries in Boston, cut it off, lost control of the car, and hit a pole, damaging the whole right side of his car. If he had hit the left side, he'd have been pinned in. But he accepted it like it was one of those things. He came out to the ballpark and pitched a hell of a ballgame.

"Nothing seemed to faze old Ellis."

Matt Batts: "I remember one time Kinder came out drunker than hell to pitch. He threw the first three or four warm-up pitches up in the screen. If he had turned around after I threw the ball back to him, he never would have found his way back to the mound. Hell, no.

"McCarthy sent Earle Combs out there to take him in. McCarthy didn't say the first word to him. He never ate him out about it as far as we knew.

Kinder understood. He knew what McCarthy thought, and he never did it again.

"I remember, Ellis just liked to be with women. He got where he shacked with a gal one night, and he came out the next day and won the game, and he thought from then on he had to shack up with a gal all night and the next day in order to get loosened up to go out and pitch. That's what he thought.

"He had his locker right next to mine, and that's what he told me. Any gal. He didn't give a damn.

"He came out to the park one night to pitch in Boston, and in the club-house he said to me, 'I've been after it *all* night.'

"I said, 'You son of a bitch, you'll never be able to pitch this game.'

"He said, 'Aw, hell yes. Don't worry about it.' He said, 'Look here.' His pecker looked like it had been through a goddamn meat grinder. It looked like it was bleeding.

"I laughed at the damn fool until I thought I would fall out. He went out and beat them. Hell, yes. Better believe that."

Roy Mumpton: "When we went to Chicago, the team would stay way up on the South Side, and if we went to a show, we would take the elevated train in. Well, one night Bob Holbrook of the *Globe* and I went to a show and came home, and it was summer, very hot. They had built the streets after the railroad, and to cross the street you had to go down steps to a tunnel to go across.

"We came out of the train, and it was only about two blocks from the train station to the hotel, and there was a drunk lying on the steps. I didn't pay any attention. Bob said to me, 'I think that's our new pitcher.' Kinder had joined the club two days before.

"We walked back to him, and I tried to get him up but I couldn't, so we finally got a cab, got him in, and took him to the hotel. It was the third of July, 1948. God, it was hot. It was ninety-five. We got in the hotel, got him up to bed, got his tie off and his shoes off, and left him.

"The next day they announced, 'Pitching for the Red Sox, Ellis Kinder.' Bob and I looked at each other. I had never seen a guy so out of it. But he won the ballgame. He pitched the whole nine innings in that awful heat.

"A month later, we were in Boston. He had pitched. After the game I said, 'Ellis, will you tell me something?' I wanted to ask him a question about that game. Ellis said, 'You're damn right. I will tell you and Holbrook anything you want. You two bastards not only put me to bed and took care of me, but you never told anybody.'

"I would have bet you a million dollars he wouldn't have known anybody that night. I never saw anybody so drunk. But he could pitch like hell.

" 'Give me the ball,' he would say. 'Give me the ball.' Oh, he could pitch.

"He pitched one night as drunk as could be. He threw two strikes, and the third pitch he threw nine miles over Birdie Tebbetts's head. Tebbetts went out to see what the matter was with him, and said, 'My God, he can't stand up!' Birdie said, 'I don't know what the hell to do, but I can't leave him out there.'

"Later that year, Kinder went on the wagon. He couldn't get anybody out. Joe McCarthy gave him a twenty-dollar bill and said, 'Go out and get drunk.' "

In 1949, Parnell's record was 25–7 and Kinder finished 23–6. Unfortunately, the rest of the staff was unproductive. As the season came down to the final few weeks, with the Red Sox battling the Yankees for the pennant, Red Sox manager Joe McCarthy pitched either Parnell or Kinder one day after the next.

Matt Batts: "Parnell and Kinder were all we had. They were the only two you could figure would win a ballgame for you. Tex Hughson couldn't pitch. Tex had a bad arm. Maury McDermott and Chuck Stobbs weren't ready yet. You couldn't rely on Joe Dobson. You couldn't rely on Mickey Harris. If McCarthy was going to win, he was going to win with those two."

Mel Parnell: "We were in the ballgame or in the bullpen the last nineteen games of the season. I would say we were a little overworked, but that was what we were getting paid for. He said, 'Pitch,' and you pitched. You can't say, 'No,' or 'This hurts,' or 'That hurts.' As long as you were able, you went out there and did it.

"If the rest of the pitching staff had matched our 48 wins, we would have won the pennant. But it didn't.

"People ask, 'What was the difference between the Red Sox and the Yankees?' We didn't have the team speed the Yankees had, but the biggest difference was, our bullpen was weaker. We had a chance to pick a relief pitcher by the name of Max Surkont, but for some reason, the Red Sox didn't go for him. But he could have helped us tremendously. We could have been stronger pitchers when we got down to the final two games against the Yankees. We were just both really worn out. I know I was, and I have to assume Ellis was as well."

HEARTBREAK AGAIN

With two games left in the 1949 season, the Red Sox held a one-game lead over the Yankees. The Sox had only to beat the Yankees once and the pennant would be theirs.

In the second-to-last game, the Red Sox raced out to an early 4–0 lead against Yankee ace Allie Reynolds. With Mel Parnell on the mound, victory appeared to be a cakewalk. Feeling confident, Red Sox catcher Birdie Tebbetts, always a teaser, told one of the Yankee batters that once the Red Sox won the game and clinched the pennant, the next day they were going to start a wet-behind-the-ears rookie, former Yale University star Frank Quinn.

Tebbetts was premature in his banter. Yankee relief star Joe Page, McCarthy's nemesis, had come into the game in the third inning with the score 2–0 in favor of Boston, and the bases loaded. Page walked two batters in a row to make the score 4–0, but then he struck out the next two batters on rising fastballs. After that he allowed one harmless single. After the third inning, not a single Red Sox reached second base against him. Of the three base runners Page allowed, two were erased on double plays. In all, he pitched six and two-thirds innings, shutting the door on the Red Sox.

The Yankees tied the score against Parnell, and after Joe McCarthy brought in Joe Dobson in relief, Yankee outfielder Johnny Lindell homered to win the ballgame, 5–4.

The final game of the 1949 season would decide the pennant. It was Sunday, October 2. Ellis Kinder started against hard-throwing right-hander Vic Raschi.

In the first inning, the Yankees took a 1–0 lead after a triple by Phil Rizzuto to left field that Ted Williams lost in a blinding sun.

Matt Batts: "Rizzuto hit the first pitch of the game over third base, and it got into that dang little gutter at Yankee Stadium and rolled all the way to the damned left-field fence. It went for a triple."

It was early in the game, so Red Sox manager McCarthy ordered his infield to play back on the grass and concede the run. Tommy Henrich purposefully chopped a slow-bounding ground ball toward second base, enabling Rizzuto to score.

For eight torturous, breathtaking innings, it was the only run of the ballgame.

With one out in the eighth and the Sox down by a run, manager Joe McCarthy generated heated controversy among his players for the second year in a row when he chose to send Tom Wright, a minor leaguer who had batted only three times that year for the Red Sox, up to pinch-hit for Ellis Kinder.

Matt Batts: "He took Kinder out. And damn, it was one man out, nobody on. Dom DiMaggio was coming up next. There was no sense to taking him out. Why he took him out, God knows. That was the game. Nobody knows to this day why. Kinder was pitching a hell of a game."

Roy Mumpton: "Mac figured that the Yankees had no book on the lefty hitter, Tom Wright. That was his excuse. So Wright walked, and Dom

DiMaggio hit into a double play, which was very unusual, because Dom hit into very few double plays."

Mel Parnell: "It was late in the ballgame. He had to try to do something to get runs. There was criticism of McCarthy, but it was unjust. You have to try to do something to get runs on the board. If Tom Wright could have started off an inning, it could have been explosive for us, and McCarthy would have been a genius. The way it worked out, he wasn't."

With Kinder out of the game, McCarthy sent in an arm-weary Mel Parnell to relieve. The Yankees' Tommy Henrich hit a home run. Then McCarthy brought in former ace Tex Hughson, who McCarthy rarely pitched. With the bases loaded and two out, Yankee rookie second baseman Jerry Coleman blooped a ball between Red Sox second baseman Bobby Doerr and right fielder Al Zarilla. All three base runners scored.

Tex Hughson: "Thirty days before this game, I pitched in both games of a doubleheader against Philadelphia. Then I sat. I don't know why he wouldn't pitch me. I could never understand it. But the records will show that I hadn't been in a ballgame in a month.

"I went in to pitch. Joe DiMaggio was at bat with the bases loaded and nobody out. DiMaggio hit into a double play, and one run scored. I pitched around the next man, Dick Kryhoski, a left-hander, and I walked him to get to Jerry Coleman.

"I pitched the ball just where I wanted to, on his hands, and he hit a broken pop fly between Doerr and Al Zarilla, the right fielder. Doerr went back and Zarilla came in, and they ran together, and all the runners that were on base scored, and that made it 5 to 1. We came back and scored and had men on base, but we never caught up."

The Sox scored three in the top of the ninth. With a runner on first and two outs, Raschi pitching, Birdie Tebbetts was the batter. Tebbetts lifted a high pop to the foul side of first base. When Yankee first baseman Tommy Henrich squeezed it for the final out, the Red Sox had lost the pennant on the final day of the season for a second year in a row.

Mel Parnell: "After that final game, we had to take the train back to Boston. It was the longest train ride we've ever had. I was down in the dumps. We were all pretty much drowning our sorrows. I remember going through the various Connecticut towns. The fans were out waving to us, trying to pick up our spirits.

"We had a decent reception at Back Bay Station. The fans appreciated what happened that year."

Near the end of the train ride, Ellis Kinder accosted manager McCarthy and berated him for taking him out of the game. Later, Kinder would tell writer Al Hirshberg, "Goddammit, if the old man had let me bat for myself that day we'd have won the pennant."

Matt Batts: "Yawkey had called all the wives back home in Boston to get them ready to catch the train and come to New York to have the victory party. When we lost, of course all the champagne had to go back. There was absolute gloom on the train going back to Boston. Nobody said hardly anything. It wasn't good. Of course, the discussion was mostly, 'Why did he pull Kinder?' We were some kind of hot about him pulling him out. We couldn't understand it. Two outs. Why?

"If Kinder was angry, who could blame him? If somebody pulled me out like that, I'd raise hell, too, because as great a game as he was pitching, he should have been left in to win or lose it.

"Going back on the train, one of the players said, 'Goddamn, did he want the Yankees to win or what?' I wondered about that. We thought we could win that game. Really and truly, I don't think anybody would change pitchers at that time."

Cleveland Amory: "My hatred for the Yankees is so deep, it goes back to the days of Ellis Kinder. Oh God, can you remember that game? Oh, son, you probably weren't alive when that happened.

"We went into Yankee Stadium, and we had to win one of two games. We were pitching Parnell in the first game. Parnell was the last real Yankee killer we had who you could count on. He had beaten the Yankees forty-nine straight times, and he's now 4–0 ahead of them, and somehow we lose the game. And we lose the second game, which Kinder was losing 1–0 going into the seventh. Oh, you can't imagine it!

"We were at Yankee Stadium in the high seats, way up. I don't know if you can understand what it is like to see those Yankee fans, all of whom are hunters, trappers, poisoners of animals. I try to understand them. What is it about the team he likes? Is it that he is like an Arab rooting for OPEC? What is it about them? I see them in the stands screaming and screaming. I can't understand them. I think they are dangerous. Underneath, they feel they have to win. We take vows of poverty. We have St. Francis. The Yankee fan has Attila the Hun.

"I was one little Red Sox voice in that godawful stadium, the house that

Ruth built. Well, Ruth didn't build that stadium, the Boston Red Sox built that stadium. Who built Ruth?

"As I reach the sunset of my years, I now no longer believe I will ever live to see them win the World Series. But I know that wherever I am in the hereafter, it will be in a higher position than any Yankee fan."

CHAPTER 18

The Revolving Door

MᴄCᴀʀᴛʜʏ Dᴇᴘᴀʀᴛs Sᴜᴅᴅᴇɴʟʏ

On June 23, 1950, Red Sox manager Joe McCarthy surprised the baseball world when he announced his retirement. With the exception of one season he sat out, from 1926 to the day he left the Red Sox, Joe McCarthy managed in the big leagues, a total of twenty-five seasons. During that time, he won nine pennants and his teams finished second eight times. The lowest he ever finished was fourth. He was a great manager, and his spot in the Hall of Fame attests to it.

The 1950 Red Sox had a 31–28 won-lost record at the time he announced his retirement, but they had started hitting of late. The players saw that the pressures of the game were getting to McCarthy, as they had just before he quit the Yankees. The players knew he had been drinking heavily, but no one expected or foresaw McCarthy's sudden departure from the game.

Walt Dropo, Red Sox, 1949–52: "Reflecting back, I really believe that he had reached a point in his career where he had had it. He had achieved everything with the Yankees. In Boston he had a couple of near-misses, and I don't think he wanted to subject himself to all the criticism, of them saying he was a push-button manager.

"No one knows what his true reaction was to losing in '48 and '49. He never let on. He showed no visible reaction to the way we were playing, that he was upset, though we should have been playing better than our record. But it was the middle of the season. We still had a chance. . . .

"I remember the day Joe quit. We were at the Del Prado Hotel in Chicago. We were getting on the bus to go to Comiskey Park to play the White Sox. Tom Dowd, the traveling secretary, announced that Steve O'Neill was the new manager and that Joe McCarthy had resigned. That's how we found out about it. We didn't have a reaction. It was just a matter-of-fact statement. What could we say? I'm sure within ourselves we had a lot of thoughts about why it happened. But when it happened, we didn't know. He didn't confide in us. He was a manager in a pure sense of the word.

"Some of us discussed it among ourselves. It was a shock to us. Sudden. There was no hint in the papers, nothing written in the Boston papers or in Chicago.

"Prior to coming to Chicago, we had had a bad series in Cleveland. We weren't going well. But Cleveland had a pretty good pitching staff: Feller, Lemon, Wynn, Garcia. We lost a couple games. Maybe that was the culmination.

"There was nothing you could say to each other. He didn't say anything to us individually about anything. It was just something that came out of the clear blue. 'Steve O'Neill is your new manager.' Period."

Matt Batts: "McCarthy was having trouble on the road, getting real drunk. For several days they looked for him in Detroit. They found him in the gutter, skid row. He was in real bad shape.

"I remember that one time in St. Louis he had to walk in front of the stands, and everybody could tell he was drunker'n hell. It was embarrassing to the whole ballclub. We had the greatest group of fellas you'd ever want to meet, no cliques or nothing on the ballclub. It was the greatest organization I ever played for. All the fellows had respect for each other, and they didn't want people saying, 'Goddamn, they have a drunk for a manager.' And so they just locked his butt up in the hotel room.

"He threatened to burn the room down if they didn't let him out. He finally got to the ballpark. He'd been drunk for days, and they didn't want him out there on the field drunker'n hell.

"Even so, when McCarthy quit, I didn't like it. He was the reason I got to the big leagues. He gave me the chance. I would fight for him, and he knew that. I was upset."

Mel Parnell: "His health was getting to him. The game was getting to him, wearing, tearing him up. Just like his wife told me, 'He just takes it too serious, and it's destroying him.' Finally, he walked away."

Bobby Doerr: "I think he had managed long enough. It might have been affecting his health to get down, and it got to be kind of confusing with him, nerve-wracking. Our ballclub got down to an age where they were going to have to start making some changes.

"See, what happens is, after you lose your two great pitchers like that, we weren't playing well. So many games that I can remember we'd go into the last inning or two with a run or two lead, and we couldn't seem to hold it. It finally got to him."

Tex Hughson: "McCarthy fired himself. Joe Cronin put it up to him that if he got drunk again on the job, he would fire himself. Well, he did, and they did.

"McCarthy had been the main reason I retired from baseball after the 1949 season. I was thirty-three years old. I told Joe Cronin, 'If McCarthy's coming back, get rid of me. I'm going to retire or quit. Trade me.' Joe said, 'We're going to keep you till you die.' I told him, 'No, if McCarthy's coming back, I won't be here. I won't be available.'

"They sold me to the New York Giants. I didn't report, and so I had to go on the voluntary retired list or be blacklisted from baseball. They sent Jack Kramer over there as a replacement for me.

"The day they fired McCarthy, Bobby Doerr called me. I was at the auction barn buying livestock for a meat company, and they wanted me back right then. But it was the middle of June, and I'd have to take sixty days to get off the voluntary retired list, which would have run me into September. I had retired, and I had family and business in San Marcos, so I never did play again. But I could have gone back the day he left. I was thirty-three years old. My arm was all right. Lots of times I do regret it."

Big Walt

Walt Dropo, called "Moose" because he was large and came from Moosup, Connecticut, was twenty-seven years old when he took over at first base for the Red Sox in April 1950. Dropo had played two years at the University of Connecticut, then spent two more in the service. As a member of Special Services, Dropo had played baseball against some of the best, including Ewell Blackwell and Mickey Vernon. When he returned from overseas, he went back to college and got his degree.

In 1947, Dropo, who stood six foot five and weighed 220 pounds, was drafted with Chuck Connors to play for the Boston Celtics of the National Basketball Association, and was also drafted by the National Football League's Chicago Bears. But Tom Yawkey was the man with the money— there was little money in either pro football or pro basketball then—and so Dropo took his five-figure bonus from Yawkey and joined the Red Sox organization.

Dropo climbed from Scranton to Birmingham, spent a year in a Pacific Coast League and a week at Louisville, and when he came up to the Sox in '50, he was not the usual raw rookie. He was a ready-made major leaguer who knew he belonged.

As a teenager, his idol had been Ted Williams. In 1950, Dropo played on Williams's team, hitting right behind him, and hitting as well as his hero. That year Dropo batted .322 with 34 home runs and a league-leading 144 RBIs. By the end of the year, Dropo was asking himself, "Am I another Williams? Am I another Greenberg? How good am I?" The press was asking the same questions.

The next year Walt Dropo hit .239 with 11 home runs and 57 RBIs. The Boston press treated him contemptuously. A "one-season wonder," they called him, a typical Red Sox shooting star.

Roy Mumpton: "Walt Dropo his first year hit 34 home runs. Dropo could have been one of the great, great ballplayers, but he wouldn't bother to learn how to hit the curveball. Oh, Williams gave him hell, nicely, trying to help him. He sat there one day during batting practice in Boston, and they would get kids who wanted the chance to pitch batting practice, and this one kid threw Dropo one hell of a curveball, and Dropo missed it by a foot, and Dropo growled at the kid, 'Son of a bitch.' Williams said to Dropo, 'You ought to hire that kid every day.' To learn how to hit that curveball. Finally it chased him out."

That was the press's version, but according to Dropo, that's not the way it was. Dropo believes he could have been a great slugger had he had just a little bit better luck. It had nothing to do with his inability to hit a curveball. He got hurt, plain and simple, as so many players do.

Walt Dropo: "I began the 1950 season at Louisville, and while we were in Indianapolis during the first week of the season, I got a call from our manager, Mike Ryba, who said, 'I want to see you for breakfast.' We had only started the season. I didn't know what was going on. He said, 'Pack your bags.' I said, 'Jesus, what's happening now?' He said, 'You're going to play tomorrow in Boston because Billy Goodman has broken his leg. You have to be there tomorrow morning. You're in the lineup.'

"It took me all day to get to Fenway Park. I went to the ballpark, got my gear, came back to the hotel in Indianapolis, checked out, and got on a plane to New York—that was about four hours on a piston—got to Boston about eleven o'clock at night. And the media was there, and they jumped all over me. I just wanted to go to bed.

"One of the reporters said, 'You'll be back in Louisville in a couple of weeks.' I blew my stack. I said, 'I didn't come all the way from there to listen to this garbage.' So I put myself on the spot. I said, 'I am not going back to Louisville.'

"I went to bed. I wanted to get some sleep. I didn't know who was pitching the next day. Here they are, telling me I was only here to fill in. . . ."

"The next morning I picked up the paper at breakfast. I see my name splattered: 'Dropo: I Won't Return to Louisville.'

"At the ballpark, Joe McCarthy said to me, 'You're the first baseman. You're playing. You're hitting behind Vern Stephens.' I was hitting fifth. He didn't say another word. He didn't have to. I had to play.

"And my name was written in every day that year. I knew that. And it was a relief to me. I was really happy, not because Goodman was hurt but because I knew I had the opportunity to prove myself over a period of time, not just a couple of days.

"Against Cleveland in Fenway Park, I went something like 8-for-12. I was in a groove. At that point, they didn't have a book on me. They were trying to throw the ball by me hard. The harder they threw it, the harder I hit it.

"When the writers came to me after the series, they said, 'What happened to you?' All of a sudden, I had become a miracle hitter. Nothing had happened. It was just that I had the opportunity. And so the writers started to make a big deal about how well I was hitting. Birdie Tebbetts came by, and he said, 'Listen, three days doesn't make a season, bush leaguer.'

"So I got off to a great start. The pitchers continued trying to challenge me, even guys like Reynolds and Raschi. They were testing me to see if I could hit the fastball. I just kept hitting the ball, blasting away."

After Joe McCarthy quit the team in June, Steve O'Neill, the team's first-base coach, took over. Dropo and the Red Sox hitters got hot, and the Red Sox finished the season 63–32.

Walt Dropo: "We just gelled. We could have made our move with McCarthy there. The ballplayers were the same. Under O'Neill, the same guys played the rest of the season. Hitters like myself and Stephens and Doerr, come June, July, and August, that's when we shine, because that's when the opposing pitchers get tired, when the weather gets warmer. It's tougher to hit in the spring and the fall, especially for the power hitters. The heat helps us. Your body gets warmed up and you swing better.

"Four of us made the All-Star team—myself, Ted Williams, Vern Stephens, and Dominic DiMaggio. We were tied, 1 to 1, in the ninth inning. Ralph Kiner got up and hit a long, high arching fly. Ted ran back after it, and after he caught it, he put his gloved left hand up to brace himself as he ran into the wall, and broke his elbow.

"I remember it vividly. Casey Stengel was the manager. Ted ran into the dugout, and Casey yelled out, 'Ted, you all right? You all right?' Ted said, 'Yeah, fuckit . . . Give me the bat. I'm all right. Give me the . . . I'll be all right.' And he went up and got a base hit. And Casey put a pinch runner in for him.

"Now the ballgame is over. Schoendienst finally beat us in the thirteenth.

It was around five or six at night. We were in Chicago, getting ready to go home. They had looked at Ted's elbow. It was mobile. The chips were in there, but they weren't apparent because they hadn't X-rayed it.

"We got on a plane to go back to Boston, and we were sitting there. Ted was holding his hand in his shirt, and he said, 'This goddamn thing, I think it's broken.' It was a four-hour flight from Chicago to New York, and all that time Ted was sitting there the heat of his body was going out. We got into LaGuardia—we had about an hour layover—and we went upstairs to the rotunda to have a drink. Ted said, 'Give me a double anything, Jack Daniel's, Scotch. . . .' We weren't heavy drinkers. So Vern, Dom, and I had drinks with him. He said, 'Give me a fucking drink.' Because it was really worrying him. There was no anesthesia. He didn't know it was broken even. None of us had any idea. He just knew he had injured himself. He kept saying, 'This son of a bitch is broken. It's killing me.'

"We had another two hours from New York. We landed in Boston, and I went to the hotel where I was living.

"I got up in the morning, and I read the paper: 'Williams's Elbow Is Broken. He'll be out two months.' Imagine.

"They took the chips out that night. He didn't even go home. It took him six weeks. He didn't come back until Labor Day.

"We had been right in the middle of the pennant race. With Ted, we could have won the thing. The Yankees beat us out. Let's not dwell on it, but if we had had Ted, we'd have won."

With Williams out after the seventy-five-minute operation to remove bone fragments from his elbow, Billy Goodman replaced him in left and led the league in hitting. When Ted returned, Goodman went to third and Johnny Pesky was benched. Goodman had hit well, but he couldn't supply what Williams could—the long ball and the RBIs. Losing Williams probably cost the Sox the 1950 pennant—though if you listened to Dave Egan, it was his return that doomed them.

Walt Dropo: "Those writers had personal vendettas. It had nothing to do with sports. We hated them. They hated us. We knew it, and they knew it. That's the way we lived.

"The final blow with Ted was when he gave the press box the finger. He started with the fans. Ted began, 'You, you in left field, fuck you,' and he saluted. And then he went to center field and then to right field, and then, 'You, the Black Knights of the Keyboard, take this,' and he gave them the finger. It was after the third out was made, and he was the last one in.

"That day Ted just had had enough. It had been building over a period of time. He just vented his emotions right then and there in front of everybody. He used the word 'fuck' all the time anyway, so it wasn't unusual for him.

We didn't pay much attention to it because we had our own jobs to do. It was in a hot pennant race. We just blocked out his personal antics, because we had to. When you're playing, you don't worry about someone else. Anyway, he got over it.

"For the Boston press to say we would have won without Williams was nonsense. What a statement to make! How would you like to read that in the morning in the papers—that you're a detriment to the ballclub? The greatest hitter who ever lived.

"But Egan knew Ted was sensitive. He knew he would read it. He knew it would affect him. That's what they wanted. They wanted to affect him so that he would overreact and make some foolish, idiotic statement so they could sell a paper. . . .

"At the end of the season, I barnstormed through November, playing the All-Stars with Vic Raschi and those fellas, and I did a lot of personal appearances that winter. I was getting paid. And I got out of shape. I never got a chance to calm down after the season. I was on the go all the time. Looking back, I should have taken the winter off and just gotten ready.

"Then in '51 I got hurt. We were in spring training. We were ready to break camp. I don't even recall who we were playing. The pitcher was pitching inside. I tried to get away from the ball. I threw my hands up to protect myself, and it fractured a bone in my right hand.

"Why did I get hit? Why did I get hurt? I should have gotten out of the way of the ball. I had a hairline fracture, but I was so insistent on playing that I kept strapping it up and kept saying I was all right, but it wasn't. It got worse and worse, and you know hitting a baseball is the most difficult thing to do in any sport. And to hit a baseball, your reflex acuity has to be almost perfect. And it dulled that acuity. You have to believe me.

"They all say it was the sophomore jinx, but I was hurt. There were no ands, ifs, or buts, that's what caused my downfall. I was in a cast three weeks, and atrophy set in.

"Those things happen. They can talk about how the pitchers caught up with me. They can talk about the sophomore jinx. They can talk about anything else. In '51, I never recovered. The press started getting on me. The fans got on me. 'Cause I wasn't doing what I did in '50. I was struggling. But I couldn't tell them I was hurt. You don't go around saying, 'Yeah, my goddamn wrist is killing me.' You try to weather the blow and overcome it.

"The doctor told the press, 'It isn't as bad as all that,' said it wasn't cracked. It affects the tendons that hold your wrist together.

"But the writers kept writing that the pitchers had finally caught up with me, that I wasn't the hitter I was the year before, said I should be more intelligent . . . all of that.

"I tried to block it all out, but obviously it affected me. Cronin finally sent me down to San Diego to get away from the booing. He said, 'You'll be back. Don't worry. Just get away from here.' Because he realized that part of it was psychological and some of it emotional. I said, 'Fuckit, Joe, I'm struggling. I'm trying.' Joe said, 'I know it. I can see it.' Joe had been a player. He knew what I was going through. I was fighting the fans. I was fighting the press. I was fighting everybody. I had a tough time. I hit .239. To me, that was nothing. Guys hit .239 now, and they get two hundred thousand. I hit 11 homers, but they wanted me to hit 40.

"It took me a whole season to get over it."

In 1952, Walt Dropo played 37 games with the Red Sox before he was traded to the Detroit Tigers with four other players, primarily for third baseman George Kell. That year, Dropo hit 29 home runs and had 97 RBIs. In '55 with the White Sox he hit 19 home runs. So, in fact, Dropo did have other good years. As unfair as it may be, however, his 34 home runs in his first season made the Boston fans anticipate that he was going to be a superstar. When it didn't happen, they tagged him as a one-year wonder, a characterization that always will be applied in memory to the once-mighty Moose from Moosup.

BOUDREAU'S FOLLY

Despite the managerial change of Steve O'Neill for Joe McCarthy, the Red Sox gave every indication that the team would continue its winning ways for years to come. The 1950 team had compiled a 94–60 record, finishing third behind the Yankees, who'd won 98 games, and the Tigers, who'd won 95.

In 1950, the nine everyday ballplayers (including Billy Goodman) and reserve Clyde Vollmer led the league in team batting average (.302), runs (1,027), slugging, and fielding. In the home runs department, Bobby Doerr had 27, Ted Williams 28, Vern Stephens 30, and rookie Walt Dropo 34. As for RBIs, Dropo and Stephens each had 144, Doerr 120, and Williams, who missed the heart of the season after breaking his elbow in the All-Star Game, 97. He had 80 at the time of his injury.

Here's the lineup opposing pitchers faced that year: Pesky (.312), Doerr (.294), Stephens (.295), Williams (.317), Dropo (.322), DiMaggio (.328), Zarilla (.325), and Tebbetts (.310).

Goodman hit .354, Vollmer .284 and Taft Wright .318 in 107 games.

In 1951, Steve O'Neill began his first full year as manager. That year the team won 87 games, finishing third again, eleven games behind the Yankees. It was the beginning of a slide that would take the Red Sox to the bottom. Cronin had tried his luck with a dictatorial, despotic manager, and though the Red Sox had come close under McCarthy, he would never again pick such a strongman to manage. Steve O'Neill, an easygoing company man, would be the first of Tom Yawkey's and Joe Cronin's unimaginative choices over the next ten years.

Dom DiMaggio: "Steve O'Neill was an affable sort of guy. I don't recall him ever getting angry. But as a strategist, I would have selected a guy like Cronin or McCarthy."

Mel Parnell: "When Steve O'Neill replaced Joe McCarthy, Steve was having physical problems. The man was under medication, and on occasion, Steve would go to sleep on the bench. This disturbed some of the players, because I heard a few remarks about it."

In October of 1951, the season at its end, rumors swirled around Red Sox headquarters that O'Neill was going to be fired and replaced by former Cleveland player-manager Lou Boudreau. Boudreau had been acquired as a backup shortstop earlier that year.

Boudreau came to the Red Sox in the path first taken by player-manager Bucky Harris and then by player-manager Joe Cronin. Boudreau had beaten the Red Sox in 1948 with his leadership and his bat. Yawkey admired and wanted him as part of his management team. As soon as he was acquired, the press bandied about the possibility of his taking over as manager.

Columnist Dave Egan, meanwhile, was leading the criticism of O'Neill. Egan ascribed the Red Sox failure to win in 1951 to O'Neill's "monumental stupidity." According to Egan, informed sources said O'Neill "didn't have control of the club," the phrase that's often whispered right before a ballclub wants to fire a manager.

The day before Steve O'Neill was fired and Lou Boudreau hired, the rumors began building in the press. Joe Cronin, the general manager, was pushing for former Red Sox third baseman Pinky Higgins to replace O'Neill. Cronin went out of his way to deny the rumors of O'Neill's dismissal. But Tom Yawkey wanted Boudreau to be the manager and overruled his right-hand man. The next day, Boudreau got the job.

Upon his hiring, Boudreau gave an interview to Al Hirshberg, who then wrote an article in the *Saturday Evening Post* titled "I'll Make the Rules for the Red Sox." In it, Boudreau provided a blueprint of how he was going to lead the Red Sox to the pennant that year. It sounded very Knute Rockne-ish. In a baseball context, it also sounded high-handed and not a little ridiculous.

"My primary job," he said, "is to inject speed, spirit, and the will to win into a ballclub which has seriously suffered from a lack of all three ingredients." He discussed "slugging individuals who haven't been fused into a winning machine."

He said, "Our lack of spirit, speed, and that will to win has kept us from going all the way. Speed is an integral part of spirit, and spirit leads to pennants.

"The Red Sox have plenty of talent. If they could have combined it with an absolute conviction that no one could beat them, they might have won some pennants during the past five years.

"They just haven't wanted to win badly enough."

If Boudreau's intention was to gain rapport with the veterans and to build morale, this was an unproductive way to do it.

Boudreau accused some of the Red Sox players of being prima donnas. He called them spoiled. He called Tom Yawkey "unusually generous," intimating that Yawkey was paying them more than they deserved. The net result, Boudreau concluded, was that the Red Sox players were lazy or didn't play to their abilities because of these large salaries.

"The combination is a little too much to resist for the kind of men who are easily impressed by outside influences," he said. "We will try to change the men involved. If we don't change them, we'll get rid of them."

When he took over at the start of the 1952 season, Boudreau made it clear he wanted to lift the Red Sox as high and as fast as he could. The fact was that there was little wrong with the team as it was constituted. It had won 87 games the year before. Add another pitcher, and the team would have been a contender. Moreover, the Red Sox had traditionally been a team that started slowly and then played excellently the second half of the season. A little patience would have taken the team a long way.

Boudreau, who saw himself as a messiah, wanted immediate results. He constantly shuffled the lineup, looking for the right combination, and when little seemed to work to his satisfaction, he impatiently began making wholesale changes. He backed up the moving van and by midseason had cleaned house.

In 1951, under O'Neill, the starting lineup had included Walt Dropo, Bobby Doerr, Johnny Pesky, Vern Stephens, Clyde Vollmer, Dom Di-Maggio, Ted Williams, and Les Moss.

After '51, Doerr retired and Williams returned to the service to fight in the Korean conflict. Ted opened in April, got into six games, hit a home run, and departed. Everyone else Boudreau shipped out.

The Sox began the 1952 season in first place. But on June 3, the ax fell, as Boudreau traded Walt Dropo, Bill Wight, Fred Hatfield, Johnny Pesky, and Don Lenhardt to the Detroit Tigers for Dizzy Trout, George Kell, Johnny Lipon, and Hoot Evers. It was just the beginning, as Boudreau began summoning the Red Sox minor leaguers to replace his regulars. The kiddie corps included Dick Gernert, Ted Lepcio, Faye Throneberry, Gene Stephens, and catcher Sammy White. Only White proved he could cut it.

In 1952, the Red Sox finished sixth, 19 games out of first place. In 1953, Boudreau installed twenty-three-year-old Tommy Umphlett in center field. That year the Red Sox finished fourth, 15 games out.

In 1954, the Red Sox no longer had their two aces, Mel Parnell and Mickey McDermott, who had had an 18-win season in 1953, but whose carefree, in-the-bottle lifestyle had affronted general manager Joe Cronin. An arm injury ruined Parnell's effectiveness, and in the winter of '53 the Red Sox traded McDermott and Umphlett to the Washington Senators for outfielder Jackie Jensen.

In 1954, the Red Sox finished 42 games behind the pennant-winning Cleveland Indians. Attendance dropped under a million, six hundred thousand less than its peak in '49.

By any measure, Boudreau and his movement toward youth was a failed experiment that left the Red Sox with overmatched youngsters on its parent club and few replacements in the minors. The Red Sox would not seriously contend again until 1967, a fifteen-year period of barrenness.

Years later, the vets whom Boudreau dumped looked back in derision and scoffed.

Dom DiMaggio: "I don't know why they picked Boudreau. It was the beginning of the deterioration. How could all those guys be substitutes? It was frustrating for all those guys to sit around and not play.

"I think the Red Sox had a tendency to bring up the kids a little too soon, guys like Ted Lepcio and Mickey McDermott. They rushed them up, and they should have given them more time in the minors. That was a weakness they had. Why did they do it? I think they are still doing it. They have never given them enough time to get the kinks out and mature in the minors.

"If you're going to make changes, you don't do it on a wholesale basis. You do it gradually over a period of a few years. Give them a chance to work their way up through the minor-league system. And you don't disrupt either the parent club or the minor-league system.

"I suppose Boudreau had a five-year rebuilding program going when he brought up all the young fellas and got rid of all the old-timers. But he hurt the parent club and destroyed the minor-league system. He set the Red Sox back thirteen years."

In 1953, Boudreau decided that rookie Tommy Umphlett was going to be the Red Sox center fielder of the future. He benched Dom DiMaggio. The year before, DiMaggio had watched teammates languishing on the bench, and he decided that if Boudreau wasn't going to play him regularly, he would quit.

Dom DiMaggio: "I retired on the twelfth of May, 1953, about thirty days after the season started. About five years before, I had vowed to Joe Cronin that when the day came I could not take my regular position in center field when I felt I was capable of playing, that I would immediately retire, and that's exactly what I did.

"When Boudreau didn't play me, I went to the front office and asked Cronin to trade me or release me. Cronin said he would do neither, and I said to him, 'I'll retire.' He said 'Well, don't do that.' And he talked me out of it for about two weeks. After that, I decided I had had it.

"Just before spring training I had had a little trouble with my eye, and I had been late getting to spring training. I was ready when the season started, but Boudreau decided to play Umphlett out there, and I wasn't about to be relegated to a secondary position. When I was ready to play and didn't, I just left. If they had decided to trade or release me, I would have continued."

Mel Parnell: "I didn't like some of the things Lou did. Lou used to like to call the pitches from the dugout. That I didn't go for, because he didn't have the feel of the baseball in his hand, which I did. I got into a little beef with him about that. I wanted to pitch my ballgame, not somebody else's who didn't know what was happening.

"The young guys were afraid to approach him on it. And I didn't go along with the catchers. I shook them off. If they wouldn't go along, I would keep shaking them off until I finally got what I wanted. I had a reason for wanting to throw that pitch, and I wanted to throw it. If it got hit, then it was my fault.

"We resented the fact that Dominic had left and the reason for which he left. The guys he brought in were good people, kids with talent, but in a couple of cases, they weren't ready for the big leagues."

Walt Dropo: "If Steve O'Neill hadn't been fired, it's very likely I would have stayed in Boston. Boudreau had a weird idea about what he wanted to do. I mean, he took the heart right out of the ballclub. Instead of molding them and bringing them along, he went with a total youth movement. Put a guy like Umphlett in over Dom DiMaggio? That was ludicrous.

"Jeez. He could have taken his time and taken an objective look at the ballclub and said, 'Okay, maybe some are getting older, but let's not go crazy with this whole thing.' The whole ballclub went, except Williams. And Williams was in the service. So in left he had to play Gene Stephens, who was not a major-league ballplayer.

"I remember Pesky and I and Stephens and Goodman were having dinner with him one night. We were at Anthony's Pier 4 restaurant. We had a private room, and he said, 'Lookit, I'm going with you older guys.' He lied to us. He said, 'Don't worry, your jobs are safe.' Me and Pesky were traded away a week to ten days later.

"I wasn't as old as some of the others, but he figured I was a lumbering first baseman who couldn't steal bases. I was sort of relieved when I got a call from Red Rolfe, the Detroit manager, and he said, 'We need you.' The first time the Tigers came into Boston, we beat them 3 to 2. I hit a home run. Don

Lenhardt hit a home run. I suppose I was psyched up to prove that they made a mistake.

"Two years later, it wasn't even a challenge to beat the Red Sox. Boudreau can say whatever he wants about it. He was a failure."

CHAPTER 19
Two Kinds of War

TED GOES OFF TO KOREA

Despite his damaged elbow, his previous service in World War II, and his thirty-three years, Ted Williams was called up from the inactive reserves into the Marines in 1952. He did not return to the Red Sox until late in 1953. He had lost three full seasons during World War II, and together the two wars took four and a half years out of his illustrious career.

Williams knew he was eligible to be called up. He also believed he shouldn't have to go. Senator Robert Taft was asked to intervene, but refused. Later, Ted would call President Harry S Truman and Taft "gutless." John F. Kennedy, a congressman from Massachusetts, tried to assist Ted, but at the time lacked the influence. Had it been a declared war, Ted would have been prepared to go. But the Korean conflict was undeclared, and he bristled at the unfairness of his having to interrupt his career once again.

Though Ted had broken his elbow, the army doctor who gave him the physical pronounced him healthy. He went to spring training in 1952 knowing he would not last the season. Six games into the regular season, Ted was reinducted into the service and made a captain in the Marines. The day he left was Ted Williams Day. Wrote Egan, "Why are we having a day for this guy? The Red Sox will be a better team without him."

Williams was presented with a Cadillac and a book signed by 400,000 fans. Williams homered against Dizzy Trout and left for Korea. His teammates were crushed. Dave Egan may have wanted Ted Williams gone, but it can be said with certainty that none of his teammates felt that way.

Mel Parnell: "When Ted went off to war, you didn't know what could happen, because he was a pilot. We felt he was a victim of circumstances. A lot of people were raising a fuss because he was an athlete, saying that Ted and Jerry Coleman were being sheltered, and the complaints grew to the point where the government had no alternative. That's the way it seemed to us.

"A lot of people had sons who had to go back in. When their sons were recalled, they felt, 'Hell, these guys should go too.' Of course, we felt he had served his duty.

"We missed Ted in more ways than one. Ted was a leader. He was a very underrated outfielder. He wasn't a fancy Dan, because of his tall stature. He played the left-field wall better than anyone. He was a little unorthodox in doing some things, but he got the job done.

"Did you know it was Ted Williams who introduced the glove the players wear on their hands? After he came back from the service, he was taking so much batting practice, he was getting blisters on his hands. At that time his agent was Freddie Corcoran, the golf pro. Freddie suggested using a golf glove. So Ted put one on. The other players saw the Great One using it and figured, 'What the heck, I'll use it too.'"

Matt Batts: "Ted studied the game. He knew the game. He was one of the damnedest hitters I ever saw in my life. All this hullabaloo with the sportswriters and the crowd, that guy was an angel compared to some of these damn idiots they have playing today. All he wanted was to be left alone and to play the game he loved to play."

CRAZY JIMMY

Ted was gone. One of the young players who had stepped in was a twenty-two-year-old bundle of nerves by the name of Jimmy Piersall. Piersall had played at Leavenworth High School in Waterbury, Connecticut, and had intended to go to Duke University and play for coach Jack Coombs when his father suffered a heart attack during the final game of the Connecticut schoolboy championships in New Haven. His father had to stop working. The boy had to start.

The Red Sox offered him a three-year bonus contract for $4,000 a year and agreed to pay for his father's trip to the Lahey Clinic in Boston for a complete physical. The son became the sole support of his family.

Piersall, a hyperactive kid, told himself, "I have to make money, as much and as rapidly as possible."

During the summer, he played semipro ball in Waterbury, earning $150 a week. The next spring he reported to the Red Sox' Louisville farm team. He spent two seasons there.

During the winter of 1949–50, Piersall's young wife had a miscarriage and almost died. She recovered by the spring, but had a relapse in Louisville. Until she recovered completely, Piersall suffered with stomach ailments.

In 1951, Piersall sat on the Red Sox bench under manager Steve O'Neill. Piersall begged to be sent back to Louisville so he could play, but outfielder Karl Olson had won his spot at Louisville, so the Red Sox had to send Piersall to Class-AA Birmingham, one step farther down the organizational ladder. Piersall hit .346, but his psyche was scarred.

The following winter, Lou Boudreau took over as Red Sox manager. Boudreau told a reporter for the *Sporting News* that he planned to bring Piersall to the Red Sox, moving him from the outfield and converting him into the team's starting shortstop. Piersall saw the article. The thought of switching positions made Piersall so nervous he could barely keep from throwing up.

Piersall thought to himself, "They can't shift me now. It could ruin me."

Boudreau's statement in the paper made an insecure, mentally unstable youngster go off the deep end. He drifted toward paranoia. Piersall thought to himself, "Ruin me? Maybe that's what they intend to do."

According to his wife Mary, over and over Piersall told her, "They're trying to get rid of me. This is a brush-off. Well, I'll fool them. I won't show up for their lousy spring-training camp."

As training camp neared, his inner turmoil increased in intensity. At the same time he withdrew further and further from reality. Piersall displayed paranoid-schizophrenic tendencies. He said later, "I couldn't face people. I was a pariah, a failure, neither sought after nor wanted, and everyone knew I wasn't wanted." To avoid people he knew, Piersall would duck into alleys, walk across streets, step into doorways, or even detour around city blocks.

Piersall would tell his wife he was going to the gym to work out, but instead he spent his days in movie houses, leaving just before the movie's end, sneaking out while the lights were off.

Two days before spring training, his wife had to call Piersall's father to get him to beg Jimmy to go. On the flight to Florida, Piersall began to fixate on his financial problems. As he approached the Sarasota Terrace Hotel, the self-imposed pressure became unbearable. "My heart was beating a frantic tattoo on my ribs and my head was bursting and my eyes were smarting," he said later.

Piersall paid the driver, picked up his gear, and turned toward the hotel. He crossed the patio and stepped over the threshold. From that point until seven months later, when he woke up in a room for violent patients in the Westborough State Hospital in Massachusetts, his memory was a blank.

Boudreau was true to his word. He started Piersall at shortstop. Piersall had the physical equipment to play the position. He was quick and fleet and had a strong arm. But a shortstop must also be temperamentally suited to the position. It requires quick thinking, poise, and an even temper. Piersall was rash and hyperactive.

The month of April was uneventful, but in early May there were outbursts and incidents. In one game, Piersall was thrown out for protesting too vehemently. Two weeks later, he got in a fight with New York Yankees second baseman Billy Martin.

Roy Mumpton: "Jimmy, when he first came up, was a very excitable kid. Remember that fight he had with Billy Martin? They got in an argument during batting practice. One of them was riding the other one from the bench, and then batting practice ended. They went in to change uniforms, and there was only one entrance to the dressing rooms, and they got one behind the other and got into a fight. The story as I got it was that Martin hit Piersall in the back, and two guys grabbed both of them. That was the whole fight. The rest of it was all yelling and hollering."

A few days later, Piersall had another fight, this time with a teammate, pitcher Mickey McDermott.

Boudreau became concerned by Piersall's behavior. Seeing he was under strain, Boudreau benched him. On the bench, Piersall, rather than settling down, tormented everyone. He plagued the manager to let him play, storming and screaming and one time sitting on the bench crying like a baby.

During the game, Piersall drove everyone crazy with a constant barrage of instructions to the players, coaches, and manager. He was totally out of control, but also desperate to regain that control.

In June 1952, the Red Sox swung their big deal with the Tigers, bringing in Johnny Lipon to play shortstop. When Piersall found out the Sox had traded for another shortstop, he overreacted. He felt humiliated. He broke down and cried.

Boudreau moved Piersall back to his natural position, center field. Alone amid the expanse of grass, Piersall acted bizarrely, clowning with the fans. One time against the Yankees, he mimicked teammate Dom DiMaggio's way of running, making him look silly.

On June 12, in a game against the St. Louis Browns, Boston was losing 9–5 in the ninth. Satchel Paige was pitching for the Browns. Piersall, the first batter, told Paige he was going to bunt. He did and beat it out. From the baseline, he imitated Paige's every move, jumping up and down and making noises like a pig. Paige lost his composure and the Red Sox scored six runs.

Joe Cashman: "During that game Piersall was up, and the runner kept trying to steal second, and every time Piersall would foul the ball off on purpose. Paige said, 'The runner could have stolen second base any time he wanted to, and Piersall was keeping him from stealing.' Paige said, 'That boy is sick.'

"Satchel Paige was one of the first ones to know it."

His on-field behavior became more bizarre. A few days later, in Chicago, Piersall did a hula in the outfield and had the bleacher fans make ukelele sounds. Later, when the bullpen car passed by, he put his thumb out to hitch a ride. Then, after getting a single, he flexed his muscles like a bodybuilder.

On June 27 while batting against the Washington Nationals, Piersall mocked every gesture of pitcher Connie Marrero. He took three straight strikes without taking the bat off his shoulder.

In the clubhouse after the game, Piersall became upset with Vern Stephens's young son. In the papers the next day, Piersall was accused of kicking him. Piersall denied the charge.

Mel Parnell: "It never happened. He was supposed to have kicked him in the behind. I was in the clubhouse at the time. He was chasing the kid around the clubhouse, and he wasn't within three yards of the kid when he made a kicking motion. He didn't kick the kid, didn't get close to him. I read in the newspaper the next day that he kicked the kid in the behind. I couldn't believe it. The kid admitted, too, that he didn't get kicked. He wasn't even close. The writers made it up."

The controversy, nevertheless, was too much for Boudreau, who reportedly was quivering when he went to general manager Joe Cronin.

"Joe, we've got to let Piersall go," the manager said.

The next day Piersall was sent down to Birmingham. Piersall told writer Furman Bisher, "It doesn't make no sense—me, the best thing they got, next to George Kell. How can they get along with their best outfielder in the minor leagues? That's okay, if they don't want me, there's plenty of others who do."

The Red Sox protected Piersall. Even in the early 1950s, mental illness was viewed by many with fear and loathing. The team did not reveal that the real reason for farming out their colorful young star was that he was disturbing the entire ballclub with his strange, unsettling behavior.

The Boston fans were furious when he was sent down.

At Birmingham, Piersall's behavior became even more crazed. The worst incident occurred in New Orleans. He began rushing around to teammates, whispering instructions. Before the start of one inning, he fired a baseball at close range at pitcher John McCall. McCall angrily fired it back, and when Piersall ducked, the ball rolled onto the field. The umpire ordered Piersall to go after it.

Piersall got down on all fours and crept after it like a pointer. When he got to the ball, he got up and kicked it and kept kicking it until it had rolled all the way to the fence. He then started playing catch with the scoreboard boy. The ump finally threw him out of the game.

Piersall then climbed into the stands and led cheers for himself. After returning to the locker room and changing into street clothes, he sat in the box reserved for league president Charles Hurst and heckled the umpire.

A few days later, there was an incident in which Piersall objected wildly to a third-strike call. The Red Sox counseled Piersall to return to Boston to enter a private sanitarium for observation and treatment. There he was given a series of shock treatments and released.

When Piersall returned home a few days later, all memory of the past seven months had been erased, but he was able to function from then on. Whenever he played, there was always the possibility he would do something quirky, like the time he hit his hundredth home run and ran the bases facing backwards or the time he crossed home plate, got on his knees, and kissed it. Still, Piersall went on to play a total of seventeen seasons in the major leagues.

After he returned from the sanitarium, Joe Cronin invited him and his family to spend the winter in Sarasota at the team's expense. The Red Sox picked up all his medical and hospital bills as well.

The year following his treatment, Piersall was back with the Sox, playing right field. He had a strong arm and got a spectacular jump on the ball, running at full speed with his first step. He was a daring, exciting performer who was often compared to former Brooklyn Dodger phenom Pete Reiser.

Piersall said, "The only way I can tell how tough a catch is, is by the bruises I get from hitting the wall and the amount of skin I peel off."

Roy Mumpton: "The first year Piersall played right field, he was the greatest outfielder I ever saw. Twice in one day in a doubleheader he went into the stands in the corner and took a home run away from Vic Wertz. You'd think he would get killed. He was a bit nuts and would dive right into the stands. You could see him catch the ball and then disappear from sight."

During one night game in Boston, Yankee pitcher Johnny Sain was the batter. Piersall was playing shallow. Sain hit the ball way over his head. Racing at top speed with his back to the plate, Piersall made a glove-handed catch almost at the bullpen fence. No one could believe it. The next day he robbed Mickey Mantle in equally breathtaking fashion.

Reporter Tom Meany was so taken with Piersall's play that he said of the young outfielder, "Jimmy Piersall of the Red Sox stands out like a white poodle on a coal barge."

His play in the field was so spectacular that first year that when reporter Roger Birtwell was asked to name his all-time Red Sox team, he said he was tempted to name Piersall in right field over the traditional choice, Harry Hooper.

Birtwell said, "Here I was about to select over Hooper a boy who had played perhaps fifteen full games in right field, who had been sick and mightn't have played again. Yet I was almost convinced that the Sox had never had a greater right fielder—and I had been a boyhood worshiper of Hooper."

Yankees manager Casey Stengel called Piersall the "best defensive right fielder I have ever seen. Better even than Ross Youngs." Youngs had been considered one of the best National League right fielders of all times.

Piersall's recovery was miraculous. It was a credit to medical science he could play so well after being so sick.

In 1953, Piersall wasn't chased by an umpire once. He kept his cool even though the opposition rode him unmercifully, calling him "cuckoo" and "crazyman" and other names relating to his mental illness.

In July of that year, Tom Yawkey asked Allie Reynolds, the American League player representative, to see "if the other clubs' more savage bench jockeys would discard their whips." It was the first favor Yawkey ever asked of a ballplayer. According to Piersall, the riding died down afterward.

Piersall missed only two games in 1953. He was voted Sophomore Player of the Year. He was still only twenty-four years old.

Jimmy Piersall starred in the Red Sox outfield for eight years. Though he never again was hospitalized, throughout his career the Red Sox fans nevertheless called him "Crazy Jim" Piersall.

Said Piersall thirty years later about his experience, "To this day, the first thing people ask my wife Jan, or other people who know me, is, 'Is he really goofy?' or 'What's he really like?'—meaning, 'Is he really crazy?' They've been doing that for more than thirty years now. It doesn't bother me."

In 1954 the Red Sox had an outfield of Piersall, Jackie Jensen, and Ted Williams. It was one of the best, and certainly one of the most unusual.

Commented writer Al Hirshberg, "Piersall was crazy, Jensen had a fear of flying, and well, Williams was Williams."

And in 1954, the Red Sox had another potential star performer, Harry Agganis.

CHAPTER 20

The Death of the Golden Greek

He was known affectionately as "The Golden Greek." Perhaps the greatest schoolboy athlete ever to come from the state of Massachusetts, he was a football All-American at Boston University and could have been a pro football star. Cleveland Browns football coach Paul Brown drafted him number one and offered him a signing bonus of $25,000. Instead, he chose to play baseball with the hometown Red Sox.

Before he was twenty, Harry Agganis was a legend throughout New England. At age 25, he was dead.

Aristotle George Agganis, as he was christened, first starred in football at Classical High School in Lynn, Massachusetts, a seaside town along Route 1A a few miles north of Boston up the rocky coast. At Lynn, the left-handed quarterback gained fame in football, calling signals—both offensive and defensive—and became known as a master diagnostician on the field. While in high school, he even had his own fan club.

In one game, Lynn coach Bill Joyce was frustrated because Agganis preferred to share the offensive load rather than pass on every play. Joyce ordered him to "go in there and pass all afternoon. When you stop passing, you stop playing."

"How about letting some of the other guys run?" Agganis asked.

"Never mind the other guys," said Joyce. "You pass. Remember, Harry, you come out of there if you don't."

Agganis was 23-for-32 with four touchdowns, when between the third and fourth quarters, he asked Joyce softly, "Now can I let the other guys run?"

Seventy-six colleges wanted him to play football, but he went to Boston University, in part because his father had died in 1946 and he didn't want to leave his mother alone. When he was a freshman, BU fans flocked to see the freshman team, not the varsity. Said the varsity coach, Buff Donelli, "You'll see the only eighteen-year-old in America who is ready to play football with the pros."

On the varsity, Agganis didn't disappoint, though Donelli had the same problem with him that Harry's high-school coach had had: he wasn't selfish enough. Donelli ordered Agganis to pass at least twenty-five times a game. In the middle of one game against NYU, Donelli screamed at his star, "Pass it, dang it, pass it."

BU was leading, 38–0. Agganis screamed back, "What's the matter, Coach? Aren't we scoring enough points?"

During his college career, Agganis threw for 2,930 yards and 34 touchdowns, averaged 46 yards a punt, and in 1949 made fifteen interceptions. As the starting quarterback in the North-South Senior Bowl football game, he threw two touchdown passes and almost a third, ran the ends, kicked extra points, intercepted a pass, blocked a pass, and was voted Most Valuable Player in the game.

Afterward, Cleveland Browns coach Paul Brown told him, "Any time you want, you can be my first-string quarterback."

But despite his football credentials, Agganis didn't go to Cleveland or any other pro football team. He stayed home to play baseball with the Red Sox. At the time there was little prestige in playing pro football; no other sport came close to the popularity of baseball—and Tom Yawkey had much more money than Paul Brown. In addition, though the Phils, Tigers, and Yankees were also after Agganis, with the Red Sox he could live near his mother. It didn't hurt, either, that shortly after Agganis signed, his high-school coach, Bill Joyce, was hired as a Red Sox scout.

His baseball credentials? Agganis had played baseball since he was a fourteen-year-old first baseman for the semipro Lynn Frasers, and in the Marines (he had interrupted his college career to go into the service, even though he could have claimed hardship) his Camp Lejeune base team had gone to the National Baseball Congress in Wichita, where he had been voted the outstanding player in the forty-eight-team tournament.

In 1954, Agganis was rushed up to the Red Sox. In 132 games, he hit 11 home runs, batting .251 for manager Lou Boudreau. The next year, under new manager Pinky Higgins, Norm Zauchin beat him out and Agganis began the season on the bench. Talk arose that because Agganis was left-handed, he wasn't as suited to Fenway Park as a right-hander might be, and trade rumors surrounded him. But Higgins finally switched back to Agganis on May 4, and Agganis proceeded to go on a .355 tear, raising his average to .313. He appeared on his way to stardom.

On May 16, an off-day, Agganis caught what was diagnosed to be a cold, and he was hospitalized for pleurisy as the team left for a short road trip. He rejoined the team, but did not play again until the Red Sox were in Chicago June 1 and 2. He went three-for-eight, lining out to White Sox center fielder Jim Rivera on his last at bat.

In the sleeper car on the train to Kansas City, *Globe* writer Bob Holbrook heard Agganis coughing all night in the next compartment. Holbrook suggested he see the trainer, Jack Fadden. On June 5, after Agganis complained of pains in his chest, Fadden ordered Agganis back to Boston.

Roy Mumpton: "I can remember around noon one day in Kansas City, Harry was standing in the lobby. He looked all right. He had a bad cold was all. Hell, everybody gets colds. He was waiting for a cab to take him to the airport."

Mystery surrounds the illness of Harry Agganis. When he left the team that day, he had a fever, cold sweats, and a searing pain in his cheek. Those close to him suspected he had tuberculosis.

Mel Parnell: "Agganis was with us in Kansas City, when he started spitting up blood. Jack Fadden, our trainer, called the doctor, and they contacted Yawkey, who said, 'Get him on a plane right away and get him home, and if you can't get him on one, charter one, but get him back to Boston as fast as you can.'

"Our road trip ended in Kansas City. When I got back to Boston, I talked to the team doctor, and he told me, 'Agganis will never get out of the hospital.' And he didn't. Tuberculosis. He had it bad."

But all accounts of his illness make no mention of tuberculosis.

On June 17, 1955, it was reported that Agganis was resting comfortably, confined to Sancta Maria Hospital in Cambridge with pneumonia and a lung infection. He was expected to be out for two months. Doctors said he was facing three or four weeks in the hospital and another month of convalescence at home.

On the night of June 23, Harry called his old football coach, Buff Donelli, on the phone. Donelli had been watching television, and he got up from his chair and picked up the phone. At the other end, a voice began barking BU football signals.

"Harry, you must be feeling better," Donelli said. But Harry complained of a terrible pain in his leg.

On June 26, Agganis watched the first game of a Red Sox doubleheader on TV—Red Sox pitcher Willard Nixon beat Cleveland—and that night, a Sunday, Lynn assistant coach Harold Zinman and his wife visited Agganis in his hospital room. They watched Ed Sullivan's *Toast of the Town* and *The Jack Benny Show,* and Agganis told his former coach that he was planning to refurbish his mother's home on Waterhill Street. She was in her seventies, and he said he wanted to fix up the first floor for her so she wouldn't have to climb so many stairs. He told Zinman he had offered to buy her a new home in Marblehead or Hamilton, but she had refused to leave the home in which she had lived her whole life. Harry had been born in that house. Also, she was near her daughter and her five grandchildren, and she wanted to remain near them.

The Zinmans remained with Agganis for about half an hour. Zinman was concerned because he noticed that Harry was perspiring a great deal. He didn't think his former star looked well.

Agganis told Zinman, "Being sick is an education. It gives you a better sense of values."

At 11:45 the next morning, Harry Agganis lapsed into unconsciousness and died, without warning. The end was sudden, shocking. There had been no hint that his life had been in imminent danger. According to three attending physicians, Agganis had phlebitis. The cause of death was listed as "probably a massive pulmonary embolism": in other words, a blood clot.

Roy Mumpton: "Harry was a decent, nice guy, and I don't say this because he died: I think he would have been a hell of a ballplayer. He was just coming to be a hitter. He was a fancy guy around first base.

"He was an athlete who wanted to work. He improved himself so. He was always listening for advice. If a pitcher got him out on a certain pitch, he would talk to Ted Williams. 'What am I doing wrong? What can I work on?'

"He died as we were riding the train on our way home from the West. We just couldn't believe it. It was a hell of a blow, because everybody liked him.

"When manager Pinky Higgins learned of Agganis's death, he said, 'He had it made. We thought he'd be our first baseman for ten years to come.' "

Over those ten years, the Red Sox had nineteen undistinguished first basemen, including Norm Zauchin (who had one good year), Dick Gernert, Mickey Vernon, Vic Wertz, Dick Stuart, and Lee Thomas.

Agganis's funeral was held on June 30, 1955. Manager Pinky Higgins and pitcher Frank Sullivan attended the services.

Mel Parnell: "The ballclub sent Frank Sullivan back for his funeral, and Sullivan said it was one of the saddest things he had ever seen. People were in the streets with tears coming down their eyes."

Agganis was buried at St. George Church in Lynn. Red Sox broadcaster Curt Gowdy officiated. His athletic feats were discussed, as was his wonderful character. The story was told that when the Greek community in Lynn wanted to give Harry a testimonial, he said, "I would like to give this money to the little town in Greece where my father was born, for recreational purposes."

Another time, it was related, when the BU Varsity Club and other friends wanted to give him a new car, Agganis requested that the money for the car be put up for a scholarship for kids of Greek descent.

At the gravesite his mother whispered, "Good-bye, Harry, dear Harry."

"He had a short life," said Harold Zinman, "but the things he did in it were amazing. Every youngster in America can learn something good from the life of Harry Agganis."

CHAPTER 21

Lean Years

Following the 1954 season, the Red Sox having finished forty-two games behind first-place Cleveland, Tom Yawkey fired Lou Boudreau, even though he had another year left on his contract.

The year before Boudreau had enjoyed the benefit of having Hall of Fame manager Bill McKechnie to assist him. At the end of the year Boudreau fired him. Wrote Austin Lake, "When Lou fired Bill McKechnie, this was equivalent to Lou shooting out his own brains."

Beginning in 1955 with manager Pinky Higgins and continuing twelve seasons through the reigns of Billy Jurges, Higgins again, Johnny Pesky, and Billy Herman, the Red Sox would be a mediocre and sometimes truly terrible baseball team.

Since 1933, Yawkey's attempts at building pennant winners had passed through three stages. The first was to buy name stars like Joe Cronin, Jimmie Foxx, and Lefty Grove. The second was to build a farm system, which won him a sole pennant in 1946, only to sabotage it when he fired the one man who would have sustained it and made it pay off—Billy Evans.

The third stage, which began in the late 1940s, was Yawkey's attempt to build his team by signing high-priced bonus babies. The Red Sox shelled out big money for such youngsters as Harry Agganis, Frank Baumann, Frank Sullivan, Ike Delock, Tom Brewer, Wilbur Wood, Jerry Casale, Ted Lepcio, Billy Consolo, Don Buddin, Jerry Stephenson, Ken Brett, Stu McDonald, Dave Morehead, and Carl Yastrzemski.

This attempt failed too. Tom Yawkey spent as freely as anyone, and between 1952 and 1953, the Red Sox came up with one of the most promising rookie crops in baseball. But for one reason or another, the Red Sox didn't get as much out of these investments as was hoped. Their two best talents from the farm system, Jimmy Piersall and Sammy White, were traded. So were top prospects Wilbur Wood and Frank Baumann. Harry Agganis died. Pitchers Frank Sullivan, Ike Delock, and Tom Brewer never blossomed into real standouts.

In Al Hirshberg's *Saturday Evening Post* article, "The Sad Case of the Red Sox," one American League executive gave his opinion that the Red Sox rushed some too soon and made others wait too long. He cited Ted Lepcio as an example of the former and Gene Stephens as an example of the latter.

"Lepcio was years away from the big leagues when the Red Sox brought him up in 1952. Instead of sending him back for seasoning, they kept him around, fighting for a job he wasn't ready for. He's been fighting for jobs on various clubs ever since.

"It was just the opposite with Stephens. He first came around in 1952, then went to the minors, where he belonged at the time. When he came up to stay in 1955, he was ready, but the Red Sox had no room for him. They would neither play him nor trade him. He was used five years as Ted Williams' personal substitute and got discouraged.

"Three or four years ago, we would have given plenty for him, and so would a lot of other clubs. But now he's a .250 hitter who doesn't look as good at 27 as he did at 19. The Red Sox handed him the center field job on a silver platter last year after they traded Piersall, and Stephens couldn't handle it. He had gone stale on the bench."

Other experts felt the Red Sox may have been just plain unlucky. John McHale, the former Detroit general manager who moved to Milwaukee in 1959 and later to Montreal, told Hirshberg, "When I was at Detroit, we went after most of the boys they got, and they outbid us on all of them. Five years ago I'd have said the Red Sox were the team of the future. I don't know why they're not in better shape today."

Hirshberg also contended in his article that the Red Sox put too much pressure on their young kids, labeling them "Can't miss." That's certainly what happened to perhaps the most highly rated prospect the Red Sox signed in the early 1950s, a young shortstop by the name of Don Buddin. In February 1954, Roger Birtwell of the *Boston Globe* wrote an article about this phenom. Wrote Birtwell, "Don Buddin—if nothing ill befalls him—could become one of the top ballplayers of his time."

Buddin, a shortstop, attended high school in Olanta, South Carolina, a town of four hundred. Fifteen scouts went to each game, all to see Buddin, including Mace Brown of Boston, who met with Buddin in the only room in the town that had air-conditioning, a room in the undertaker's parlor.

In 1953, after Olanta won the state championship, the scouts filed in to

meet with Buddin and his father, one at a time. The interviews began at nine
A.M., and each scout had thirty minutes to state his case. The talks were over
by noon. Mace Brown had carried the day.

Buddin chose the Red Sox because he liked the idea of hitting with the
Wall as a target. He also knew that Vern Stephens was about finished—and
Tom Yawkey gave him a bonus, somewhere around $50,000.

Two years later, Tom Yawkey revealed in an article in a Boston newspaper
that "he had a new boy on whom to pin his interest—Don Buddin. I think
the kid has a chance of being a great ballplayer."

Alas, it was not to be. When Don Buddin started at shortstop for the Red
Sox in 1956 just before turning twenty-two, he proved to be a mediocre hitter
and a less-than-satisfactory fielder. He went into the army in 1957, and when
he came out, he continued to be ordinary, though he started for the Red Sox
at shortstop from 1958 through 1961. In 1958 and 1959 he led the league in
double plays and in errors, in the latter year making 35 miscues and cement-
ing his right to the nickname "Bootin' Buddin." Nevertheless, manager
Pinky Higgins loved him and played him every day, a living symbol of Red
Sox futility.

Buddin was traded to Houston for Eddie Bressoud after the 1961 season.
He played forty games for the Colt .45s, then was sold to the Tigers, who
released him after thirty-one games. Buddin had been good enough to start
every day for the Red Sox, but he could play for no one else.

Despite his shortcomings, Don Buddin *was* the Red Sox regular shortstop
for five seasons, and during that period every New England kid who dreamed
of playing shortstop in the majors had to be satisfied with him as a role
model.

Rich Hershenson grew up in Marblehead, Massachusetts, a Buddin devotee.

Rich Hershenson, lawyer: "My favorite player was Don Buddin, and I'm
not totally sure why. I liked him, held out for him, when most of the other
Red Sox fans around me didn't. He was called Bootin' Buddin, and my
father thought he was a bum. His record wasn't good, but I remember
getting real excited one year when he started walking and his on-base percentage reached four hundred. I got a big charge when he would hit a
home run or when he'd make a really good play in the field. I'm not sure
why I liked him. Maybe because I felt he was the underdog in a way, and
I was an underdog.

"When I was growing up, I took it for granted that the Red Sox didn't have
much chance to win. It's not that we didn't want to win. It was like, 'What
can you do?' If it had been an amateur against Muhammad Ali, you can root
for the guy, but you're rooting for an upset. I had hope, but I never thought
it was even within the realm of expectation to think they were going to win.

"They were a local team, and they were our heroes. Whenever they lost, the sentiment was, 'Woe is me. They lost again.' Or if their pitcher would give up a home run, it was, 'Oh yeah, it was inevitable.' For any given year, it was hope against hope.

"The big joke was, 'Wait till next year.' My father would always say, 'If they make it to the World Series, I promise you we'll go.' He knew it was a safe bet. It was an ongoing joke. We knew, every year, the World Series meant the Yankees, which was one of the reasons I and everybody else in my family hated the Yankees.

"As a boy it seemed that the Red Sox were always fighting to stop the other team from scoring, and as a result I concentrated my imaginary play more on the defense than the offense. In my bedroom when I was imagining myself being a hero, I would always be trying to rob the other team of a home run, making a spectacular catch over the wall, saving runs, and I wonder whether that wasn't because the Red Sox stunk.

"You couldn't root for the Red Sox to win, so when I was a boy I rooted for other individual players. I liked a lot of players, players who weren't necessarily Red Sox, because of their names, guys like Lou Klimchock and Steve Boros. The Red Sox always had players with great names who came for a season or two, like Russ Kemmerer and Truman "Tex" Clevenger. I liked Tommy Umphlett, just because of his name. Since there weren't any stars on the Red Sox, you might as well like a guy because of his name, 'cause nobody was playing well enough to like him for that."

David Margolick, journalist: "It's hard to explain, but I have always identified with the team, and because the team was always losing, I thought of myself as a loser. Okay? In 1958 or '59, when I was seven, up until 1967, I came of age when the Red Sox were perpetual losers. I am convinced one's character is shaped in the first ten years. One is almost fully formed by then. It doesn't matter what they have done since. I will always feel the same way about them. When the team is in the second division, it seems perfectly natural.

"I can remember, as a boy, one series in which the Red Sox were ahead of the Yankees every game, and they lost every one. There was one series when Johnny Blanchard hit three or four home runs in a row in July 1961. It was in the summer. I remember sitting at the end of the dock, and one of the games went into extra innings, and we lost. It was meant to be.

"My father called the Red Sox the 'Red Flops.' My father wasn't a base-ball fan, but he enjoyed ridiculing me over the idea that they were losers. I took it very personally. I felt reduced. I felt humiliated.

"One story that really says it all: A friend of mine from Boston named Jonathan was going out with a woman whose father didn't approve of the relationship. Her father was doing everything he could to undermine the relationship, though he said he really didn't have to because you could see that it wasn't going to work. And whenever Jonathan would leave the house, this man would say to him, 'Good luck to you and to the Red Sox.' And that said it all. It meant that the relationship was doomed."

MALZIE'S LONG JOURNEY

The Red Sox finished fourth in 1954 and fourth in 1955 and fourth in 1956. They had played light-hitting infield prospects Don Buddin, Billy Klaus, Billy Consolo, and Ted Lepcio without great success, all the while keeping another young prospect, Frank Malzone, in the minors.

When writer Al Hirshberg was interviewing various scouts and officials to find out why the Red Sox scouting system had been such a failure, another reason, given by a veteran scout who requested anonymity, was:

"The Red Sox are always looking for the big star. They won't settle for anything less. You can't run a farm system that way. Most youngsters will never make it to the big leagues, but you need a lot of them to fill out your minor-league rosters. Besides, you never know when one might surprise you and unexpectedly develop into a star."

The Red Sox shunned doing it the way Branch Rickey and George Weiss preferred. When Rickey ran the Cardinals, then the Dodgers, and Weiss ruled over the Yankees, they both liked to sign as many prospects as they could, figuring that a certain percentage of their signees would make it, whether they received big bonuses or not. To them, quantity was the key. At one point, the Yankees had as many as fourteen different farm clubs. The Red Sox scouts sought quality in lieu of quantity—those star players to whom Yawkey could pay big bonuses.

However, baseball teams often make the same mistake fans do. They equate the amount of bonus money and salary with the quality of play. If you pay a kid a large bonus, you assume he's a better player than the kid who signs for no bonus. It doesn't usually work that way. Talent is unto itself, and it is damn hard to predict with any accuracy which kids will make it to the big leagues and which won't. Even today, if you give a kid a large signing bonus, there is no guarantee he will make it to the majors.

The money paid, especially to young prospects, results from an early evaluation that is only as accurate as the person doing the evaluating. Red Sox scouts picked the players, and Tom Yawkey paid the bonuses, but of those bonus babies only outfielder Carl Yastrzemski turned out to be the star he was predicted to be.

When Frank Malzone signed, he received a train ticket and nothing else. As a result, teammates say he was held back in the minors several years more than he should have, while less talented, better-compensated players got more of a chance than they deserved. The Red Sox tried every one of the others—Buddin, Consolo, and Lepcio—before Malzone, who wasted away in the minors in 1955 and 1956, when he should have been starting for the Red Sox.

When he finally got to the bigs, Frank Malzone was a perennial All-Star at third base. For nine years, he shone at the hot corner. Why didn't the Red Sox bring him up earlier? It's a question even the self-effacing Frank Malzone asks himself.

Frank Malzone, Red Sox, 1955–65: "I was born and raised in the Bronx area of New York City and started playing ball at Samuel Gompers High School. A bird dog whose name was Cy Phillips saw me play, and he kept following me for some unknown reason, along with a few Giant scouts, but I would say he pursued it harder than the rest of them. This fellow worked for a sporting-goods store over on Concord Avenue, and one day I went in to talk to him about buying a new pair of shoes for the summer. When I went to get those shoes, he asked me, 'Would you be interested in professional baseball?' which at the time I knew very little about. I told him, 'I think I would be.'

"He then brought a scout over to my house and they presented me with a contract. They didn't give me a nickel to sign. All it was was a contract and a ticket to go down to Florida to train at spring training.

"I got on the train riding down to Florida, and there was another player on the train who said he had gotten money to sign. I said, 'What do you mean about money?' He said, 'Well, I got X amount of money for signing the contract.' I said, 'You're kidding?' He said, 'No.' Then as I got further into spring training, I realized I had made a mistake, because I could see I was as good a player as most of these guys who got bonuses—in those days a thousand dollars, $1,200, which is what most of them got for signing their contracts, was a lot of money.

"That was 1948, the beginning of my professional baseball career. The Giants also scouted me, but they wanted me to wait a year, figuring I'd get a little bigger or stronger. I figured if I was going to go professional, I'd want to start immediately.

"In 1948, I went to Milford, Delaware, in the Eastern Shore League, which was Class D, and got off to a pretty good start, hit .315, did everything there was to be done in the game, even stole some bases. I could run pretty good when I was younger. At the end of the year, the so-called general manager of the ballclub said, 'Well, we're going to promote you to Class C next year.' I was happy about it. Got a $50-a-month raise or so. I went to Oneonta, New York, which was in the Can-Am League, hit around .310, drove in a lot of runs, and set a new record for triples in the league at 27. I probably also set a new record for errors at third base.

"As far as my career was going, I felt I was successful. I was happy with it, but the jumps were short. I would get a little disillusioned with the fact, and I'd think, 'How long is it going to take?'

"After Class C, I skipped B and went to A with Scranton, Pennsylvania. The second day of the season, I got the steal sign on a hit-and-run play, went into second, and my spike grabbed before I got to the bag. I twisted every ligament in my ankle. The trainer asked me, 'How do you feel?' I said, 'I'm all right,' but when I got up, I almost fell down again. He said, 'Get out of here.' It happened on the second day of the season, 1950. I missed the whole year. It slowed me down to where I couldn't steal like I used to, but I was thankful that I could continue playing baseball, because the doctors at the time told me they weren't sure I could play again. Ligament damage, they say, is worse than a break.

"In 1951, they sent me to Double A for spring training, but I went back to Scranton for the season, and we had a good year, we won everything. Then, at the end of the season, I got another case of good news. I got the call from the army. Another two years gone.

"I got out of the army in 1953, all ready for the '54 season, and they sent me to Louisville—Triple A! They gave me the opportunity because I was getting up in age, and they probably felt, 'If he's going to do anything, let's find out.' Mike Higgins, the manager, had a third baseman named Kenny Chapman, and he had heard I had played shortstop in the service, so he tried me out at shortstop. Kenny had a good glove, but he couldn't hit much. When Kenny got hurt, he moved me to third and Don Buddin moved over to shortstop, and we played the entire year in '54 on that side of the infield. That was the year we beat Syracuse, the Philly farm team, for the Junior World Series championship.

"You'd think that would do it, wouldn't you? But no. In '55, in spring training, I played one game with the Red Sox. It was ridiculous. I knew all along I was going back to the minor leagues. I just wasn't getting the chance. I went back to Louisville again, hit .315, and all winter I thought: ''Fifty-six is the year they are counting on me being their third baseman.' Why it took the Red Sox so long to decide, 'Hey, this guy has the ability to play third base,' I don't know.

"It's funny, years later the scouts would tell me stories, how they fought for me. Like one day Eddie Popowski and Charlie Wagner were sitting in at the meeting with Cronin and Higgins, and everyone was talking about who was going to play third. Wagner and Popowski swore that they said, 'We don't have to find anybody. We got a kid, and right now he's at Louisville. Frank Malzone.' And they told me they didn't get too good a reaction from the rest of the people at the meeting. Wagner and Popowski thought they both were going to get fired the next day. Who knows why? Maybe politics. I was a player no money was invested in. I wasn't a bonus baby like Billy Consolo, who got big money, Ted Lepcio, who got money. They were trying to make the investment in those fellows pan out. It's like that today in college. One kid gets a scholarship and the other one doesn't, and the coach says, 'He's got to get a chance to satisfy the athletic director.' When I finally made it, one of the newspapers ran a cartoon that had Joe Cronin saying, 'I found a million-dollar baby in the 5-and-10-cent store.'

"But it was after the '55 season that I got a little bit discouraged. They gave me a chance in '56, but I just wasn't myself. My daughter had passed away in December. She was a little over a year and two months. Me and my wife were not really ourselves. Heck, I was dropping pop-ups, I was doing everything wrong. But I did stay with the club until the cut-down day in June. Pinky was playing Billy Klaus against right-handers and me against left-handers. But, of course, you only face one left-hander in two weeks. In those days, there weren't too many left-handers. So I played very little, and at the trading deadline they sent me out to California to play for the San Francisco Seals, our Triple-A club. I went out there, and it did us a world of good, because we had counseling from a priest, a real good friend who sat us down and talked to us, really straightened both of us out. I can't tell you what he said, but I just know it turned our lives around, got me thinking properly again, and I went out and had a good year there. I hit .296 the second half of the season and hit about ten home runs.

"On that Seals team, we had Billy Consolo, Ken Aspromonte, Sal Teremino, Bob DiPietro, about eight or nine Italians. That's why we were a good ballclub. We came close to winning the playoffs.

"In '57, spring training was funny. I was invited to the Red Sox camp and went through the normal spring-training workout. The schedule began, we played fourteen games, one a day, and I hadn't even played yet. Higgins played Billy Klaus, Ted Lepcio, and Billy Consolo. You talk about being discouraged. I got home one night, and I said to my wife, 'It doesn't look too good. Looks like I'll be back to minor-league baseball. I have to make a decision on what I want to do with my life. I'm disgusted.'

"My wife was good. She said, 'If you want to stay in the minor leagues and play and stay in baseball, that's fine with me.' That was the extent of the conversation. So I went back to work.

"After finishing our schedule in Florida, we had four exhibition games in San Francisco. The first day in town we went out to eat, and the buildings started shaking. It was an earthquake. We were sitting at a table, the glasses were rattling, and we were all scared. The townspeople were used to it. I guess they waited for the bricks to start falling before they got scared, but it was quite an experience for me.

"That night we played the Seals. I didn't even look at the lineup card, because I hadn't played yet all spring. I was standing out at third base taking some ground balls, figuring I was going to be the last guy who was gonna hit. Pete Daley, the catcher and a good friend of mine, came over and said, 'Hey, you're playing tonight.' I said, 'What?' So I looked at the lineup card, and my name was on it. I played third base, hit sixth in the lineup, and I got a couple hits that night. I played well. And oddly enough, I played the rest of spring training and every game the rest of the season. I didn't miss a game.

I don't know what happened. I always say it took an earthquake to wake them up.

"I remember after my first full season, Joe Cronin came to me and said, 'Hey, Slug, how are you?'

"I said to myself, 'Why didn't you call me "Slug" the year before so I could play?' "

CIAO, CIAO, JERRY CASALE

Jerry Casale has a different perspective on why Malzone didn't make it earlier. Casale received a then-sizable $42,000 bonus to sign with the Red Sox in 1951, but unlike other highly prized bonus babies, Casale never received a fair shot with the Red Sox. He was sent back to the minors even while general manager Joe Cronin was choosing pitchers who were clearly not as talented. But unlike Malzone, who today holds no grudges after a relatively short but brilliant career, Jerry Casale is a bitter man.

Mike Higgins and Joe Cronin didn't treat him fairly, Casale says, for the same overriding reason it took the Red Sox so long to bring Frank Malzone to the majors; he was Italian and they were bigoted Irishmen.

Jerry Casale, Red Sox, 1958–60: "I'm sure prejudice came into the thing. When I went out to San Francisco in 1956, the first cuts were Malzone, Aspromonte, Larry DePitbo, Bob DiPietro, Sal Teremino, and Bill Renna. Seems funny, all those nice Italian boys on one team. Isn't that nice? They talk about prejudice today. There was prejudice in those days too. Why'd they do it? Who knows? Who knows? Who knows? It seemed funny. We had a team out there, an all-Italy team. And we threw a Polack in there, Sadowski.

"In 1955, Malzone and I played in the top minor league in the country. Malzone was the third-leading hitter and I was the leading pitcher, and in '57 Aspromonte was out in San Francisco and led the Coast League, and the Red Sox couldn't wait to get rid of him. They never gave that guy the chance he deserved. Kenny should have been a great ballplayer with the Red Sox. A good hitter, a good second baseman. Never got a good shot. So Malzone and Aspromonte and I were sent to San Francisco right away in '56. That's an insult. We were really good, good ballplayers. And we were all playing Triple A.

"The Sox had a guy named Billy Klaus—not to take anything away from Klaus, but he was a Punch-and-Judy hitter, a left-hander, and they needed a right-handed hitter like Malzone at third base.

"Larry DePitbo never even got a chance. He was a good first baseman. And Aspromonte should have been their second baseman for a lot of years, but with Kenny, you can only get sent here, sent there, before you start to lose your drive. And the first shot, they traded him off to Washington, got rid of him. But he was made for Fenway Park. Here's a guy who led the Coast League in hitting, and two years later they get rid of him? Why? What's the reason? If they let him play every day, he'd have been a .300 hitter. They didn't let him play.

"They didn't let Billy Consolo play. Higgins hated Consolo, but he had to keep him because he signed a bonus. If you heard the verbal abuse they used to give each other . . . It was terrible. Billy hated Higgins, and Higgins hated Consolo. Billy was a very good-looking player. He spent eight years rusting away on the bench.

"Malzie finally got a break, but what was he when he came up, twenty-seven? Frankie should have been there five years prior to that. There were others: Vince Fafaro, out of New Jersey, a good-looking third baseman. He didn't like the way he was being treated in the organization, and he just quit.

"They said it was a country club, but who was in it: Johnny Murphy, Charlie Wagner, Mace Brown, Pinky Higgins, Joe Cronin. Irish. Southern. Boo Ferriss, our pitching coach, was from the South. So they pitch old guys like Johnny Schmitz, he was 112, and Bob Porterfield, he was ninety, and they send a whole bunch of us out to San Francisco. Pitch Bob Porterfield? When you have good young arms? What's going on?

"Let me tell you one story about Mike Higgins. I don't like to say things like this, but the son of a bitch was always drunk. And he'd never talk to you. He seemed like a nice guy, but I don't think he wanted to talk to anybody, because half the time he was bombed.

"One time I saw him on the train bombed bad. He didn't even know who I was. In those days we had sleepers, and he banged into me, and he said, 'Who are you?' I said, 'Jerry Casale. I'm a pitcher.' He said, 'Oh, okay.'

"I'll tell you: if I'd have known what I learned later, I never would have signed with the Red Sox. I'd have signed with anyone but."

CHAPTER 22

Lily White

Beginning in 1947, when Jackie Robinson broke the color line and starred for the Brooklyn Dodgers, the talent of black ballplayers was demonstrated to America. Robinson, Roy Campanella, and Don Newcombe led the Brooklyn Dodgers to pennants in 1947, 1949, 1952, 1953, 1955, and 1956. Willie Mays, Monte Irvin, and Hank Thompson led the New York Giants to pennants in 1951 and 1954. You didn't have to be a genius to see how disadvantaged were teams that continued to exclude blacks.

The Red Sox had the first opportunity to sign both Jackie Robinson and Willie Mays.

At the time the issue first arose in Boston in 1945, baseball's color line still held securely. Though the city of Boston had been the home of the famed abolitionist William Lloyd Garrison, it was still largely segregated. Mixed communities existed in the South End and Dorchester, but for the most part, blacks lived in Roxbury and were discouraged from living elsewhere in the city.

However, in 1945, City Councilman Isadore Mushnick, a white representative from Roxbury, pressured both of Boston's teams, the Red Sox and the Braves, into agreeing to allow Wendell Smith of the *Pittsburgh Courier* to bring a group of black players to Boston for a tryout. Unless the teams gave the players an audition, Mushnick threatened to lead a movement to deny the teams' annual permit for Sunday baseball.

No black man had played major-league baseball since brothers Moses Fleetwood Walker and Welday Wilberforce Walker had played for Toledo in the American Association, and George Stovey had pitched for Newark in the 1880s.

In 1884, Adrian "Cap" Anson had come to Toledo with his Chicago White Stockings and ordered Fleet Walker off the field. Toledo had refused, but five years later Anson ordered Stovey off, and Newark capitulated. Anson then successfully lobbied to keep blacks from "organized baseball." As an appeasement to southern teams in the minor leagues, the northern owners joined in a gentleman's agreement not to hire black players, on the grounds that they were keeping their southern brethren from being embarrassed, lest they had to suffer the humiliation of having to play with inferior black men.

Thus, as late as 1945, blacks had to play in their own leagues, called the Negro Leagues. But despite the irrefutable fact that no blacks competed in the major leagues, Eddie Collins, who was the Red Sox general manager at the time, denied that the Red Sox practiced discrimination.

In his reply to Councilman Mushnick's threat, he said, "I have been connected with the Red Sox for twelve years, and during that time we have never had a single request for a tryout by a colored applicant."

He continued with a straight face, "It is beyond my understanding how anyone can insinuate or believe that all ballplayers, regardless of race, color, or creed, have not been treated in the American way as far as having an equal opportunity to play for the Red Sox."

No blacks would be signed by any major-league team until the following year, when Branch Rickey of the Brooklyn Dodgers would sign Jackie Robinson.

On April 14, 1945, Wendell Smith brought three star Negro League ballplayers—Robinson, Marv Williams, and Sam Jethroe—to Fenway Park to try out. Robinson was, well, Robinson, the most electrifying player of his generation, the Brooklyn Dodger star who played for ten years and finished his career with a lifetime batting average of .311. He was elected into baseball's Hall of Fame in 1962.

Marv Williams had been an outstanding second baseman for the Philadelphia Stars and a .338 batter, and Sam Jethroe was a spectacular outfielder with the Cleveland Buckeyes. Jethroe had led the Negro Leagues in batting in 1944.

Despite whatever arrangement Mushnick made, when the players arrived at Fenway Park for their tryout, they were turned away. The next day, April 15, they came again to Fenway Park, and they were turned away. The excuse: no Red Sox scout had seen them play prior to the tryout.

On the morning of the sixteenth, columnist Dave Egan wrote a scathing condemnation of the Red Sox in the *Daily Record.* He gave the qualifications of the players and chided Collins about his claim that no blacks had ever applied to play for the Red Sox.

"If [they] cannot make the grade with that classy aggregation of Red Sox we espied the other day [in 1945 the Red Sox finished seventh], room might be found for [them] in the shabbiest and lowest league in organized baseball in order that [they] might be given the opportunity to work their way up the ladder."

Collins allowed the tryout on April 16. Coaches Hugh Duffy and Larry Woodall conducted it. It isn't clear who else attended that day. Some reports had Eddie Collins there, and others said Joe Cronin observed. Ed Linn wrote in *Sport* magazine in 1956 that both sat together and watched them try out.

According to Linn, Cronin was asked about the players as he sat beside Collins. He was reported to have said, "The decision is not up to us."

The three players shagged flies in the outfield. Marv Williams batted first, and hit the ball hard. Robinson hit second, and also did excellently. Jethroe went last.

Duffy told them, "You boys look like pretty good players. I hope you enjoyed the workout." He said the Red Sox would be in touch.

The tryout got little publicity in the newspapers. President Franklin D. Roosevelt's death overshadowed all other stories.

Ten days later, not having heard from the Red Sox management, Wendell Smith wrote to Eddie Collins, who wrote back that a broken leg suffered by manager Cronin "threw everything out of gear." Later, Cronin reiterated that as manager he had no input into the signing of players. The buck had no place to stop.

Collins also fudged by saying he feared that if the Red Sox were to sign any of the players, it would constitute tampering with existing contracts signed by Negro League teams. Cronin later added a third rationalization. He said he told Smith and the players that the only openings were in Louisville, and that he didn't think it advisable to send black players there at the time.

Neither Smith nor the players heard from the Red Sox again. The players were so discouraged that they didn't even bother to try out for the Boston Braves, though Sam Jethroe did sign with the Braves and played in Boston for three years in the National League, beginning in 1950.

Joe Cashman: "I heard it from Hughie Duffy, who was a Red Sox Hall of Famer who scouted Jackie Robinson, that he told the Red Sox to keep him. Hughie liked Robinson very much, and he told the Sox to keep him. But Yawkey wanted no part of it. He didn't want to be the one who broke the color line."

Glenn Stout: "When Jackie Robinson was trying out with the Red Sox, someone yelled, 'Get those niggers off the field.' Bill Gavin said he heard it was Joe Cronin.

"Gavin remembered one time in the early sixties, after Robinson was out of the game, talking to him at spring training. He was with a group of people, and they were talking with Robinson, and he had always wanted to ask him about this incident. They were all laying down on the grass, and Gavin said, " 'What did you think about your tryout in Boston?' "

"Gavin said Robinson's face hardened, and he said that Robinson hissed and said, 'I played in the National League,' and he got up and walked away. Gavin said it was an actual hiss, seething anger.

"The odd thing is that Robinson played in Boston later that year with the Kansas City Monarchs at Braves Field. He had two hits, three stolen bases, and stole home. Satchel Paige couldn't play that day because he had gotten beat up by a black cop in Washington, D.C., and missed the game."

The animosity between Joe Cronin and Jackie Robinson lasted while both men grew old. Robinson never forgave Cronin, and Cronin continued his boycott of Robinson right to the end.

Monte Irvin: "It happened in 1972 at the World Series in Cincinnati. Jackie was dying and everybody knew it except him, and they honored him. He gave a great speech. He said, 'Things are wonderful, but one of these days I'll be so happy if I could see a black coach over at third base or a black manager in the major leagues.'

"The powers that be were going to assemble to go onto the mound as he threw out the first ball. Rachel Robinson and Chub Feeney and the commissioner were there, and they looked around, and they didn't see Joe Cronin, who was the American League president. At that time I was in the commissioner's office as special assistant. Bowie Kuhn said, 'Monte, would you search out Joe and tell him to join us on the field?'

"I looked around the stadium and finally found him under the stands having a hot dog. I went over to him and said, 'Joe, the commissioner is looking for you. He wants you to join him on the field.'

"He looked up and said, 'Tell them to go ahead. I won't be there.' I said, 'Any particular reason?' He said, 'No. I just won't be there.'

"I went back and told the commissioner, 'He won't be here.' He said, 'He won't be here?' I said, 'No. He said he can't make it.' The commissioner looked surprised, as I did when he told me. The commissioner just shrugged his shoulders and proceeded without him.

"What I figured, if you remember Jackie had had a tryout in Boston, and Jackie had said some things about him, and this was a holdover from that. Joe didn't want to have any part of that ceremony."

The Red Sox also could have signed the legendary Willie Mays before the New York Giants did. In his twenty-two-year career, Mays played in 2,992 games, batted .302, hit 660 home runs—third behind Hank Aaron and Babe Ruth—and played center field like he had wings on his feet. Mays was elected to the Hall of Fame in 1979.

Mays played for the Birmingham Black Barons, a Negro League team that had an agreement to use the ballpark of the Birmingham Barons when they were out of town. Birmingham was a Boston Red Sox farm team. In return, the Barons had first refusal on any of the Black Baron players.

According to Al Hirshberg, "The Red Sox sent Larry Woodall, a Texan, to Birmingham, to scout Mays. It rained the whole time Woodall was there. He returned without seeing Mays play."

Woodall instead signed the Black Barons' star infielder, Piper Davis, but Davis's opportunity to be a Red Sox was short-lived.

In May of 1958, Dave Egan, the *Daily Record* columnist who had campaigned for a black player in Boston for over two decades, died without ever seeing a black man in a Boston uniform. It wasn't until 1959 that black infielder Pumpsie Green made it to Fenway Park.

THE FIRST, AND SECOND

Jules Tygiel, author, *Baseball's Great Experiment: Jackie Robinson and His Legacy:* "The first black player the Red Sox signed was Piper Davis, who was the player-manager of the Birmingham Black Barons.

"Piper had been considered by the Dodgers in '45. He was a good all-around player. He could play every position. He hit line drives. But in 1947, the Dodgers didn't sign him. That year the St. Louis Browns took out an option on him, but when they dropped Willard Brown and Hank Thompson, they dropped the option on Davis too. So though Piper always was right on the edge of being one of the first blacks in baseball, he never quite made it.

"In 1950 the Red Sox signed him to a minor-league contract. By this time he was thirty-one years old. They announced they had signed this great twenty-six-year-old prospect.

"Davis could have played in the major leagues right away, but the Red Sox sent him to Class A in Scranton, Pennsylvania. The two top farm teams, Birmingham and Louisville, were in the South, and he couldn't go there.

"The Red Sox had a deal where they paid the Barons $7,500 for his contract, and if they kept him beyond May 15, they had to pay the Barons another $7,500. Davis started the season in Scranton leading the team in batting average, home runs, runs scored, stolen bases. He just tore the league apart. After all, here was a major-league player in A ball.

"And on May 13, they called him into the office. He said he thought he might be getting promoted up to Louisville. But they told him, 'We're sorry, we have to let you go for economic reasons.' Obviously they didn't want to pay the rest of the money.

"Scranton manager Jack Burns was so incensed, he took Piper down to the locker room and said to him, 'Take anything, take the bats, take the gloves, take anything you want.' Davis said he took only his hat and his hairbrush. He said all the other players used to share brushes and combs, but he had to have his own separate brush and comb in a separate part of the locker room.

"And so they cut him. On the way back home to Birmingham, he had to take the train to Washington, D.C. At Washington, D.C., in those days, you changed trains. If you were black, you could ride anywhere you wanted in the train until you got to Washington. In Washington you had to change to the all-black section.

"As he was changing cars, who did he run into but Red Sox general manager Joe Cronin. Davis asked him, 'What happened?' And Cronin told him the same thing as at Scranton. Piper said, 'You didn't even give me a ticket home.' When Cronin returned to Boston, he sent Davis money to cover a first-class ticket.

"And that was it. Piper Davis was the last black player the Red Sox signed until they signed Earl Wilson and Pumpsie Green."

Piper Davis: "They told me, 'We got to let you go because of economic conditions.' Tom Yawkey had as much money as anyone on the East Coast. I don't talk about it that much. It wouldn't help. Sometimes I just sit there and a tear drops from my eye. I wonder why it all had to happen, why we had to have so much hate."

In 1953, the Red Sox signed a young black pitcher, Earl Wilson, to a minor-league contract. Red Sox scout Tom Downey sent the following report on Wilson: ". . . he is a well-mannered colored boy, not too black, pleasant to talk to, very good appearance, conducts himself as a gentleman . . ."

The Red Sox made a couple of other unsuccessful attempts to purchase black players. In 1955, they sought to buy Charlie Neal, a young black minor-league second baseman, from the Brooklyn Dodgers for $100,000. A year later, they tried and failed to buy outfielder Al Smith from Cleveland.

Earl Wilson should have been the first black to play on the Red Sox. He had been converted into a pitcher, and in 1957 made the Red Sox Triple-A team in Louisville. That spring he beat the Red Sox in a preseason game. But Wilson was drafted into the Marines, and wasn't available for another two years.

In 1955, the Red Sox purchased infielder Elijah "Pumpsie" Green from the Oakland Oaks of the Pacific Coast League. Green had starred at El Cerrito High School by San Francisco Bay before playing for the Oaks, and looked ready—but there was still a real question as to whether the Red Sox would ever field a black player. Mike "Pinky" Higgins, a hard-boiled Texan and the Red Sox manager at the time, had been quoted by Hirshberg as saying,

"There'll be no niggers on this ballclub as long as I have anything to say about it."

In 1958, Green batted .253 for Minneapolis in Triple A, and Higgins was manager when Pumpsie Green went to spring training in Scottsdale in February of 1959. Upon his arrival at the Red Sox camp, Green was barred from staying at the hotel with the rest of his teammates. He had to stay at a hotel miles away in Phoenix. Nevertheless, he performed. That spring, the Boston sportswriters voted Green the Red Sox' top-rated rookie. He had hit three home runs and batted .444.

It seemed certain that the Red Sox would bring Green north to Boston, but then Higgins took him on a Texas barnstorming tour against the Chicago Cubs, and Green slumped badly. Before reaching Boston, Higgins returned Green to Minneapolis (over Bucky Harris's objections). The howl from the press was loud. The Boston chapter of the National Association for the Advancement of Colored People called for an investigation of Tom Yawkey and his racial practices.

Fortunately for Yawkey, Green hit well back in Minneapolis, and Earl Wilson, back from the service, led the staff with a 10–1 record. The only question then became: Who would arrive in Boston first?

On July 21, 1959, the last-place Red Sox called Pumpsie Green up from Minneapolis. He met the team at Chicago's Comiskey Park, pinch-ran in the eighth inning, and appeared in the ninth at shortstop.

The color line—finally—was broken in Boston, not by a Jackie Robinson, Willie Mays, Monte Irvin, Roy Campanella, or Larry Doby, but by an obscure journeyman with a quiet, unobtrusive demeanor.

Because the Red Sox were the last of the major-league teams to put a black player on the field, Pumpsie Green arrived in Boston to great fanfare. It was one of the few days he would make headlines.

Pumpsie Green is probably best-known to Red Sox fans for being Gene Conley's companion the day the big pitcher jumped the team and sought to fly to Jerusalem. More about that later. On the field, Green played a utility role behind the combination of second baseman Pete Runnels and shortstop Don Buddin, and after four seasons of mostly benchwarming, was traded to the New York Mets.

After the one year with the Mets, Green quit baseball and returned to Berkeley High School to coach the baseball team. Today he is a supervisor and dean's assistant at the high school. He remains quiet and unassuming. In Red Sox history, Pumpsie Green will always be known for being "the Red Sox' first black." To Pumpsie Green, it was no big deal.

Pumpsie Green, Red Sox, 1959–62: "As a kid growing up in the Bay Area, I wanted to play in the Pacific Coast League. I wanted to be an Oakland Oak. That was my dream. The Pacific Coast League was integrated. When San Diego came to town, I would go out to see the Oaks, because San Diego had

Luke Easter and Minnie Minoso and Suitcase Simpson and other guys I've forgotten, and the Oakland Oaks had Artie Wilson and a catcher by the name of Ray Noble.

"When the Red Sox bought me in the middle of 1953, I didn't give it much thought. At the time, Boston was just a name to me. I had seen a poster of Ted Williams. That's all I knew about Boston. And I found out it was in Massachusetts.

"The first year the Red Sox sent me to Albany, New York. It was the Eastern League, a tough league, but I survived it. The Red Sox wanted me to go to Birmingham, Alabama, and I said, 'No, thank you.'

"From A ball, I went to Double A at Oklahoma City in the Texas League. Oklahoma City was in the South far enough. There were teams in Oklahoma and Texas, plus one in Shreveport, Louisiana. When the team went to Shreveport, I didn't go, because they didn't allow blacks to play in Louisiana. So when the team went to Shreveport, I had a three- or four-day vacation. It didn't make me angry. In truth, I never thought about it. No black ballplayers went to Shreveport. And when you went south that time of year, it was nine hundred degrees, and if they wanted to give me three days off, well, okay, fine.

"The next year I went to Minneapolis, Triple A, and then on July 21, 1959, I was called up. They called me in Minneapolis to meet the team in Chicago, and I was there that afternoon to face Early Wynn that night.

"I'm always asked whether it meant anything to be the first black to play for Boston, and no, it never really meant a lot. I was not really aware of what it meant, because in the back of my mind I said to myself, 'Hey, they've had black ballplayers in Boston before, playing for the Boston Braves.' So it was no big deal to me—until I hit town.

"After Chicago, we went to Cleveland and then after a night game we got on a plane and flew to Boston. The plane got in around one at night. We were stepping off the plane, and I saw bright lights and cameras. I thought that was the way it is in the majors. But I found out different, because I never saw it again. I didn't know they were there to see me. It was one or two in the morning, I had been sleeping, and I just walked off the plane, getting off with the rest of the ballplayers, ready to grab my bag and go to the hotel and sleep. The reporters did what they usually do, asked a lot of questions. I was so surprised. Being the center of attention isn't really my style. Everybody would like to be a star for a day, to be on center stage, but I can take it or leave it. The next day, twenty thousand people showed up who hadn't been there all year. They roped off center field, and I was the primary reason. The ones who stood out behind the ropes were predominantly black.

"All of that made me nervous. As far as I'm concerned, baseball is a tough enough game to play without extra added pressure. These people were there to see what I was going to do. It could be positive or negative, so you get butterflies. It was the major leagues. I hadn't been there. I'm facing legends—

legends in my mind. Like when I first faced Early Wynn. I thought to myself, 'Hey, I don't feel so good. That's Early Wynn out there. I've read about him. I've seen him in the World Series. I've read about him.' And here I was, walking up to home plate with a bat to face Early Wynn.

"I was lucky my first game in Boston to be facing a guy I had faced in the minor leagues, John Tsitouris. We were playing Kansas City, and that's who was pitching for them, and that day I hit the ball all over the ballpark. First time up, I tripled high off the Monster.

"We were behind by two runs, and they brought in a left-handed reliever, and I hit another shot up against the left-center-field wall, and Bill Tuttle ran and leaned up against the wall and caught it. I was feeling great that night.

"No one on the Red Sox ever gave me any trouble, at least not outwardly. How they felt inside, I couldn't say. I felt I was friends with all of them, as friendly as you can be on a baseball diamond. Off the diamond we didn't socialize, but on the field we were like anybody else.

"I was a regular until I got hurt. I fielded a ground ball and tagged Mickey Mantle on his hip and threw for a double play, and his hip was so hard it fractured my hand. Fractured it! At night it started hurting, and I went to the doctor, and they put it in a half-cast. I had played maybe twenty games. The hand never got the way it was supposed to be. I was in and out, pinch-hit, pinch-ran. I became a utility infielder.

"I would have loved to have gone someplace where I could play every day, because one thing I found out very quick, I wasn't very good at sitting on the bench or playing once a week. My strong point was as a defensive ballplayer, and when I sat around for a week or two, I found myself not as good defensively as I normally would be. To that extent, I wished I could play every day so I could get to feel good. Baseball, to me, is how you feel. If you feel like you belong, if you feel comfortable, then you can do a good job. Every time I was out there, I was more or less an exhibit. For most ballplayers, things just don't fall into place. The pressure—you want to do so good— and you don't do it. That's the pressure I felt. I'd think, 'If I can get five, six hits, I'll be back in there tomorrow. But if I don't . . .' If I had a great day, five hits and fielded a thousand, I'd be in again, because managers are superstitious.

"I never asked to be traded. The ballplayers very seldom went to the head person for any reason. I never said anything.

"I was comfortable living in Boston. I lived in Dorchester, in the black neighborhood, and I was as comfortable as I could be. I wasn't a stranger in Boston, because I had known two of Boston's best-known citizens, Bill Russell and K.C. Jones, at the University of San Francisco. I knew them before I even heard of Boston. The first thing I did when I got to Boston was get into Russell's car, and he drove me out to Reading, where he lived. I had so many meals over his house he started to charge me. For the most part, I had a nice time in Boston.

"But it was frustrating sitting on the bench for four years. Any time there's something you want to do and don't get a chance to do it, it becomes a little frustrating. But I didn't become resentful. You have to keep yourself in playing shape, not just physically, but your mind too, in case the manager calls on you, and hopefully you'll be ready. I kept myself in the best possible shape.

"I never felt they were keeping me on the bench on purpose. I felt each manager ran the team. If Pinky Higgins or Billy Jurges had me on the bench, it was because he wanted me on the bench. I don't think Yawkey or the general manager had anything to do with it.

"When I was traded to the Mets, I was disappointed, because the Mets were a transition ballclub, and nobody knew what from who. I didn't find it difficult playing for Casey Stengel, because I didn't play much. I never got to know him or even talk to him. Back then, you never talked to the manager. He had five or six coaches. How he felt, I never knew."

Pitcher Earl Wilson was called up briefly in late 1959, right after Green. He toiled in the minors for the better part of two more years and then became a regular in the Red Sox rotation in 1962, and for four seasons was a solid performer.

Then, during spring training of 1966 in Winter Haven, Florida, Earl Wilson was refused service at a bar in nearby Lakeland called the Cloud 9. It was the beginning of the end for Wilson with the Red Sox.

Dennis Bennett, Red Sox, 1965–67: "One evening Dave Morehead, Earl Wilson, and I went to the Cloud 9 bar in Lakeland for a drink. The bartender asked Dave what he wanted and asked me what I wanted and looked at Earl and said, 'We ain't serving you. We don't serve niggers in here.' That was the first time I had ever run into any of that.

"So we got up and left the place. The sportswriters picked it up from there.

"Earl was upset at first, because he had never been refused service before. I don't think the bartenders knew we were ballplayers. To them, we were just two white guys and a nigger."

Team owners trembled when players upset the prevalent traditions in the southern towns during spring training. Going up against Jim Crow brings negative publicity to the team, since the local white supremacists tend to blame the club, not the traditions of inequality, for the bad publicity.

Wilson knew bad publicity would get him in trouble with the club. He told writer Larry Claflin what happened, but made Claflin promise not to write about it. Claflin kept his word. Another reporter learned of the incident, however, and astonishingly not only ignored the prejudice story, and the resulting ignominy faced by Wilson, but instead concentrated on the fact that Dennis Bennett, Dave Morehead, and Wilson had gone to the Cloud 9 bar to drink.

Red Sox manager Billy Herman told the press, "There have been some pretty good ballplayers who have been drinkers."

Nevertheless, Wilson was cooked with the Red Sox. On June 13, 1966, the Red Sox acquired two black players, John Wyatt and Jose Tartabull. That night, Wilson and his roommate, Lenny Green, who was also black, were joking that there were too many blacks on the team and that someone had to go.

"There was no doubt in my mind about that," said Wilson.

The next morning, the phone rang. Lenny Green was scared to answer it. He figured he was the one. Wilson picked up the receiver. Manager Billy Herman was on the other end of the line to tell him he had been traded to Detroit.

The trade involved Wilson and another black prospect, Joe Christopher, to the Detroit Tigers for Don Demeter, who had but a year left in a productive career, and Julio Navarro, who never pitched an inning for the Red Sox.

Earl Wilson had won five games for the Red Sox at the time he was traded, and that year won 13 more for the Tigers. The next season, Wilson won 22 games for Detroit and was the winningest pitcher in the major leagues.

David Margolick: "When they traded Earl Wilson away, I was embittered. Because you could see him coming into his own. I didn't know the background at the time of the racial incidents in Florida where they trained. I remember this feeling of betrayal. The Red Sox were like the Kansas City Athletics. They were trading away their best people. Kansas City had the temerity to trade their best people to New York year after year. But the Red Sox traded Earl Wilson for Don Demeter. And Earl Wilson hit more home runs as a pitcher for Detroit than Demeter hit as an outfielder for the Red Sox.

"When I spoke to Earl Wilson many years later, I was talking on the other phone and I said, 'Mr. Wilson, I'll call you back in a second, but before I hang up I just want to tell you one thing. I still haven't forgiven the Red Sox for trading you.'

"You discover early on that the Red Sox organization, if not outwardly racist, was incredibly conservative and stand-pat. The one thing you discover, the most benign explanation for all of this, is that the Red Sox are so popular they never had to please anyone. They could say 'fuck you' to the community. Even when they were lousy, it didn't make any difference, because the fans still came out and they didn't have to kowtow to anyone, and they didn't even try.

"There are still people who have never forgiven the Red Sox for being the last team to have a black. I know a friend's father who still won't go to Red Sox games because of that. He's from Quincy, and I suspect he was a Henry Wallace Democrat, an old lefty. He was well aware that the Red Sox kept blacks from joining the team, and he never forgave them for it."

CHAPTER 23

The Nadir

With Ted Williams, Jackie Jensen, and Jimmy Piersall leading the Red Sox offense, Red Sox fans spent the latter part of the 1950s with high hopes of winning an American League pennant, but in 1956 the team finished fourth, in '57 third, and in '58 third as the Joe Cronin era came to an end. Cronin was promoted to the presidency of the American League in January of 1959.

To replace Cronin as general manager, Tom Yawkey selected Bucky Harris, the man he had hired to be his manager in 1934 and then let go because of general manager Eddie Collins's enmity toward the former Washington Senators star. Yawkey had hired Harris in 1956 as a special front-office assistant and superscout after the Detroit Tigers had fired him as manager.

Harris, like all general managers, wanted his own manager. In the middle of the 1959 season, he fired Pinky Higgins and hired Billy Jurges over thirty-three-year-old wunderkind Gene Mauch, who was managing the Red Sox' top minor-league club in Minneapolis. Harris feared that Mauch would not be able to control the Red Sox' temperamental star, Ted Williams.

Jurges, unfortunately, was the one who was temperamentally unsuited for the job. Jurges had been a fine ballplayer, but was high-strung, nervous, and a perfectionist who took every loss personally. By the end of the 1959 season, Jurges was on the verge of a nervous breakdown.

The Red Sox players didn't feel that Jurges was on top of the game, that he made the right moves at the right times, and it all spilled out on July 25, 1959, in an article by Ed Rumill of the *Christian Science Monitor*. An unnamed Red Sox player pointedly criticized the infield play around second base (the aging Pete Runnels was at second and Don Buddin was at short) and the fact that the Red Sox needed a first baseman who could hit the left-field fence at Fenway. The unnamed player (who by process of elimination was probably Jackie Jensen) also claimed that some of the pitchers weren't bearing down.

"The Red Sox need a manager who can rule with an iron fist," the player said.

The next day, Jurges called a meeting and asked the unnamed player to come forward. No player stood up. Jurges, who had asked Rumill to the meeting, demanded that the reporter reveal his source. Rumill refused. Jurges asked Rumill, "Why can't we live together and be happy? You guys eat with us, travel with us, and we hang around together. Why can't we be happy?"

In the story, Rumill described his source as "a veteran and intelligent." Commented one Red Sox player, "That eliminates nineteen of us right away."

Frank Malzone: "Billy Jurges was basically a good coach. But Jurges couldn't handle men. He got nervous. He was very high-strung. He wanted to do new things, try innovations. One night I was in the hotel in Detroit, and he called me in his room. Don Buddin was the shortstop at the time, and he had been making a lot of errors and hadn't played well. Jurges called me in his room, and he said, 'You're going to be playing shortstop tonight.' I said, 'Okay. I've played short before. I can handle it. No problem.' He said, 'I just wanted you to be prepared for it.' I said, 'Fine,' and I left the room.

"When I got to the ballpark, Jurges called me into his office. I said, 'What's the matter?' He said, 'You're playing third.' 'Why the change?' He said, 'We had another meeting and you'd be better off playing third base.'

"What had taken place, I found out later, was that Mr. Yawkey said, 'Leave Frank Malzone alone.' Jurges had gotten a call from Bucky Harris, who told him, 'You're not playing Malzone at shortstop. He's playing third.' These are the sort of things managers have to put up with.

"What I realized about Billy was he was not manager material, that's all. Jurges was a good coach; he could teach people. But managing? He was no leader. Every player worked on his individual stats, what he ends the year with. You have a goal, and you want to hit those figures.

"Team concept loses out. And we're talking about a time when the Yankees won it pretty much every year. They'd get off to a big lead, and before you know it, you're floundering in third or fourth place, and you say to yourself, 'You better start thinking about your own personal goals.'

"Billy felt he was doing the job, but everyone knew he was nervous doing it. He was a nice man. During spring training, he would drop by my room and say hello to me and the wife. But it was better he was not managing the Red Sox anymore."

*   *   *

The criticism continued. On April 26, 1960, yet another anonymous source critiqued a recent game against the Senators. For instance, said the player, look at what had happened in the eighth inning. With right-hander Al Worthington pitching for the Red Sox, the left-handed hitting Julio Becquer appeared on the field for Washington. Becquer was swinging a couple of bats. Immediately upon seeing Becquer, Jurges waved for left-hander Ted Bowsfield to come in from the bullpen and pitch. Bowsfield was announced and began warming up. But because Becquer's name had not been announced, the Washington manager, Cookie Lavagetto, did not have to use him, and so Becquer went back to the bench and Lavagetto sent up a righty batter. The players snickered.

And so it went. In May of 1960, the Red Sox were foundering. Jurges, seeing he was going to be the scapegoat for the ineptness of the team, tried to walk the fine line between being a good soldier and defending himself. Jurges knew that management was woeful, that the farm system was weak, and that general manager Bucky Harris seemed to have little interest in extricating him from the bind he was in by acquiring a couple of new players.

On May 26, 1960, he told Clif Keane, "I know what's wrong with this club, but I can't do anything about it. My hands are tied." That very day, Tom Yawkey and Bucky Harris demanded Jurges issue an apology. His days were numbered.

On June 8, 1960, Billy Jurges left the team. Two days later, his departure became public when the Red Sox announced he was leaving as manager because of illness.

With no one else under consideration, Tom Yawkey returned to the tried and true, rehiring an old buddy, Pinky Higgins.

The Red Sox had not helped themselves, either, by some of their recent trades. On December 3, 1959, Red Sox catcher Pete Daley was traded to the Kansas City A's for washed-up pitcher Tommy Sturdivant. Many observers felt that Daley had gotten his walking papers not because the Red Sox didn't need him, but because of an incident during a game with the Yankees during the summer.

Daley had been the Red Sox batter when Yankee reliever Ryne Duren came into the game. Jurges, coaching at third base, beckoned Daley for a conference. When the two met halfway up the line, the Red Sox manager told him, "Be ready. He's real quick."

Since Duren was known for his tremendous fastball, this redundant bit of advice so tickled Daley that he couldn't wait to relay it to his teammates. "Be ready" became a team catchphrase to indicate their contempt for Jurges, and for the rest of the season the Red Sox ballplayers uttered it often in ill-concealed stage whispers. It never failed to draw a laugh.

If the trade of Daley was an act of vindictiveness, the trade of the other catcher, Sammy White, was one of stupidity. White, who was adored by the young pitchers, was dealt to the Cleveland Indians for a lesser catcher, Russ Nixon. Incensed, White refused to go. He retired from baseball and opened a bowling alley in Brighton, a town north of Boston.

Mel Parnell: "Sammy was the best catcher I ever had. Usually in a ball-game I would check with my catcher after the first inning and ask, 'What seems to be moving the best?' He would tell me, and that would be my out pitch. Or if I had two strikes, I'd go to that pitch. Sammy always could give me a quick answer."

Jerry Casale: "In 1959, my first year with the Red Sox, we had the nucleus of a good, good pitching staff: myself, Bill Monbouquette, Ike Delock, Tom Brewer, big Frank Sullivan, good young arms. So what do they do? They trade Sammy White away to get a guy like Russ Nixon. Nothing against Russ, but Sammy White was a great catcher, great with young pitchers. He was a monstrous help to me, calmed me down, would come out and talk to me, 'Jerry, you got to pitch Mantle this way.'

"When they traded Sammy White, he didn't even report to Cleveland. He quit. How do you get rid of a first-string terrific catcher? And we ended up with Jim Pagliaroni, not taking anything away from him either, but you can't have a young pitching staff with a nineteen-year-old catcher. Let the kids stay under a guy like Sammy for a couple of years, then move him. To me, they just threw the guy out.

"If you check, you'll see that Sammy hit .284 in 1959. Come spring training, and they get rid of him to Cleveland for a left-handed hitting catcher. What the hell sense did that make? Now you have a left-handed hitting catcher, a kid coming out of high school, who doesn't know the pitchers. Is this what you're going to put in the big leagues? In Fenway Park? How the hell?

"I couldn't say anything. How do you get rid of a catcher that's so good? It couldn't have been because of his hitting. We had Jensen, Malzone, Runnels, Ted Williams. God, we had some good hitting. What we needed was defense."

Just before the start of the 1960 season, Cleveland Indians general manager Frank Lane predicted about the Red Sox: "They'll finish sixth just by showing up. Bad as they are, the Athletics and Senators are worse. But they won't beat anyone else."

They finished seventh, 32 games behind New York. Only the Kansas City Athletics trailed them.

By the end of the season, the Red Sox were again led by Pinky Higgins. What the Sox desperately needed was a teacher and a leader. Little teaching was going on in the minor leagues, but it was Higgins's belief that once a player got to the major leagues, he was supposed to know all he needed to know. As a result, Red Sox players were not accustomed to carrying out the more exotic executions of the game such as the bunt, the hit-and-run, and the steal.

Not that it mattered. Higgins didn't manage that way anyhow.

Gene Conley, Red Sox, 1961–63, who also played for the Boston Celtics: "Pinky Higgins believed that when a guy reached the majors, it was a bat, a ball, and a glove, and if you didn't know it by the time you got there, well then, work your way out, because I haven't got time to teach it to you now. So he probably wasn't a great manager.

"Baseball is a detail game. Red Auerbach did that in basketball. Red was the type of guy that when you went into a ballgame, he didn't just say, 'Go in there and take so-and-so's place.' He would say, 'Go in there and make sure you screen so-and-so off and make sure you release the ball out to the side when you get it.' You had a couple things on your mind. You didn't just go in and give somebody a breather. I had to block off Chamberlain, and if I grabbed the ball, I had to hit Cousy on the side quickly, or my ass would be out of there. You always had to do something.

"It wasn't that way on the Red Sox."

Ed Bressoud, Red Sox, 1962–65: "The Giants organization, where I came from, as well as the Dodgers, were known as very good teaching organizations. I cannot say what the Red Sox organization was like, because I was never involved in it, but it appeared that the players in the Giants organization were more fundamentally sound when they got to the big leagues than the players with the Red Sox.

"I've been in baseball seventeen years, and I managed two seasons in the minor leagues, and I learned more about baseball managing than I ever did as a player. I know what it takes to win. The simple commodity is that a good team makes productive outs, and a bad team does not. On the bad team with a runner on first base and less than two outs, the batter strikes out or hits a line drive to the third baseman or pops out to the infield. The good team makes an out, and the base runner moves up.

"On the Red Sox, we made unproductive outs. The rationale of managers at that point in time was such that we were not concerned with making a productive out. When he was manager of the Giants, Bill Rigney used to say, 'I want to manufacture a run.' That means getting a base on balls, advancing him to second on a bunt, advance him to third on a ground ball to the right side of the diamond, and he scores on a wild pitch or a balk. Or with a runner on second and no outs, you advance him home on two infield ground balls.

"I can recall when I was in the Giants organization playing for Eddie Stanky. We had a runner on third and less than two outs, and I hit a bullet of a line drive at the third baseman. Stanky screamed bloody murder. Had I hit a weak grounder to shortstop, the runner would have scored, and we would have had a run. That's what I'm talking about.

"We didn't do that when I was with the Red Sox those years. Rigney always used to say, 'The winning team is going to score more runs in one inning than the losing team is going to score in the course of the ballgame,' and it constantly happens. If you can generate two manufactured runs early in the ballgame, the other team has to score three, and they don't do that very often.

"The other problem was our pitching staff wasn't real deep. Fenway wasn't kind to pitchers. My God, they didn't have a left-handed pitcher who was successful from the time of Mel Parnell to maybe Bruce Hurst. And they kept trying to find somebody. They brought in all kinds of left-handers. Wilbur Wood was there and was not successful, and then went over to the White Sox and won twenty games for a number of years.

"Most left-handers, because of the way the ball tails, start the ball over the middle of the plate and hope you hit a ground ball to the shortstop. You didn't do that in Fenway, because most of the batters stood on top of the plate a little more, and that ball that tailed away was no longer on the outer two or three inches of the bat, it was more on the meat of the bat, and the batter would hit it off the left-field wall.

"So very few left-handers would come in and run you off the plate in Fenway. 'Cause they were afraid if they made a mistake, it was downtown.

"As a result, the load went to the right-handers, and we had Bill Monbouquette and Earl Wilson. Earl was a little bit wild. He'd walk a couple, and it would create more pressure on him, and now he'd make a mistake, and give up a homer.

"Don Schwall was Rookie of the Year in '61, but he did not pitch well after that when I was there. He didn't get the ball over very well. He threw a very heavy sinker, but in '62 those pitches were balls, and it was ball one, ball two, and now he had to get the ball up a little higher, and when the ball comes up, it doesn't move as much, so instead of getting the sinker around the knees, it was up around the belt, which most players can hit. Somebody would jerk one off the Wall.

"If you're a sinkerball pitcher, and the umpire is calling that pitch a ball, you're in big trouble, especially if that's the only thing you've got. And Don didn't have a pitch going in the opposite direction to keep the hitters honest.

"When I arrived in Boston, and before and after, the Red Sox were referred to as the 'country club of baseball.' Mr. Yawkey paid very good salaries. The club was not a contender. They fell out after Ted Williams left in '60, and without Williams's influence the club suffered a setback for a number of years."

CHAPTER 24

Ted's Last Hurrah

As long as Theodore Samuel Williams wore the flannel Boston uniform with the red number nine on the back, the fans could be certain something exciting would occur at or away from Fenway Park.

On September 25, 1960, the Red Sox announced the unthinkable: Ted Williams would retire at the end of the year. He was playing in his final season.

Roy Mumpton: "I was climbing the steps to the press box—they had no elevator then—and I felt a tug on my coat. I turned around, and it was Yawkey. He said, 'Mump, I'll tell you something.' This was when the Yankees announced that Joe DiMaggio was getting $100,000 and was the highest-paid player in baseball. He said, 'The Yankees don't have the highest-paid player in baseball, I do.' And he added, 'I'm not going to tell you how much I'm paying him, whether a nickel more or a hundred dollars more or five thousand, but I have the highest.'

"Williams and I always got along good. We fished together. We were buddy buddies. We were at a dinner at Manchester, New Hampshire, a few years ago, and we were alone. I asked him, 'Did you do all your negotiating with the Red Sox?' He said, 'Yes.' 'Did you ever have trouble?' 'Never. They were very good to me.'

"And he said, 'I'll tell you this. After we got through with the contract and I had signed it, Tom Yawkey would always say, "Are you sure you got enough? Are you sure you're happy?" And I would say, "Fine," until the last one I signed.'

"We were sitting around having a drink—Ted never drank anything but beer until about his last year playing baseball—he was having a cocktail, and Ted said, 'Tom Yawkey asked me the same question. "Are you sure you're happy?" and I took the contract and tore it up and threw it on the table.'

"Ted said, 'You should have seen them. They asked, "What's the matter? What do you want?"'

"Ted said, 'Make me out a contract, thirty thousand less. You've been very good to me. This is my last year. I'm forty-one years old. I could get hurt easily. I might not be much help. Make me one out for $100,000, and I'll sign it.'

"I said to Ted, 'So you were getting paid $130,000?'

"He said, 'I didn't mean to tell you that, but I was.' So he signed that last one for $100,000, and of course, he had another great, great year, and at the end of the year Yawkey gave him a fifty-thousand-dollar going-away present.

"Later I went to Dick O'Connell to check it out, and he told me, 'Absolutely true. Exactly the way it happened.' "

Mel Parnell: "Ted was the greatest hitter of all. They talk about Ty Cobb. If he was better than Ted, I'd have to see it to believe it. Ted had the best bat control of anybody I've ever seen, and he had great eyes.

"I remember one time he was called out on strikes in Fenway Park. After he was called out, he came back to the dugout and he was as mad as can be. He said to general manager Joe Cronin, 'By gosh, if you would get off your duff and get this ballpark in line, I wouldn't have been called out on strikes.'

"All of us pitchers who heard this were laughing like mad. But Ted kept up his argument with Cronin. Finally, Cronin agreed the next morning to check home plate and see whether it was out of line.

"At nine in the morning, the ground crew was out there, and they checked, and it *was* out of line. It was an inch or two off. We didn't notice anything. But Ted did."

Frank Malzone: "Nineteen fifty-seven was my first full year, and I made the All-Star team behind George Kell, who was voted in by the fans. Casey Stengel picked me as the alternate. The only other Red Sox player was Ted Williams. My first year, and Ted's played forever.

"We were sitting on the plane going to St. Louis, Sportsman's Park. I didn't know what to expect. Ted said, 'This is important to the American League. You're going to be playing against the best in the other league.'

"Ted was always willing to give advice, to help. He's always been that type of individual. When he talked about hitting, I used to listen, just to grasp things I thought could help me.

"One day during a game, I was waiting to hit. The pitcher was warming up. Ted said, 'Don't stand so far away. Get as close as you possibly can and look at what he's throwing so you know what kind of fastball he's got.' I said to myself, 'That makes sense.' And by doing so I spotted a few things I wouldn't have known about. Ralph Terry, the Yankee pitcher, had a habit. His last pitch warming up would be his first pitch of the game. If his last warm-up was a slider low and away, I'd look for it the first pitch. If I hadn't been watching, I wouldn't have noticed. And I did hit Ralph pretty good, and a lot of times it was on the first pitch.

"Ted would preach, 'Take a pitch. Gauge the fastball.' I told him, 'I need three strikes, not two, Teddy.' He understood that.

"Even today he will laugh and say, 'Yeah, I know, everybody would say you were a high fastball hitter, but I watched you, and you used to make them think you hit the fastball and you'd sit on the curve.'

"I said, 'You noticed that, huh, Teddy?' He said, 'Yeah. You sat on the curve. You hit it as good as the fastball.'

"Today he tells me, 'You saved me a lot of running by catching those balls down the third-base line.' He didn't tell me then.

"During the four years I spent with him, Ted was outstanding. Two of his home runs stand out. His 500th. It was in Cleveland. He hit it to the opposite field, left center; his other home runs were long and deep to right field.

"And then there was the last one off Jack Fisher at Fenway."

On September 28, 1960, Ted Williams ended his illustrious career in storybook fashion. He hit a home run in his final appearance in a major-league uniform. It was home run number 521, and it has become a cherished memory in baseball history.

Frank Malzone: "It was a cold day, the wind was blowing northeast, in from right field, the kind of day you say, 'No one's going to hit one out.' He had hit two balls good previously; the first one got into the wind in the right-field corner and was pulled back and caught by the right fielder. The next one he hit to right center and the center fielder caught it. The next time up he hit one a little lower and a little bit better, and the wind didn't hurt it, and it made the bullpen.

"Ted trotted around the bases and came in, and Ted's handshake was kind of a limp arm. He never gave you that good handshake. He'd give you a little oomph and that little smile of his. Ted was figuring Pinky was going to take him out, but he let Ted run out to left field, and then he sent Gene Stephens out. Ted got a standing ovation.

"It was a shame it had to take place during a time when the club wasn't involved in a pennant. There were maybe twelve thousand people there. Realizing this could have been Ted's last ballgame at Fenway, there should have been more.

"After the game, Ted wasn't around. He knew what was going to take place as far as the press, and he wanted to avoid that. Why? That was his makeup. He liked to aggravate them. I think he got a big kick out of it.

"After Ted retired, they had some lean years at Fenway. It took the '67 season to bring them back."

Roy Mumpton: "The last week of the season, he told me, 'If I could just hit one good home run, I'm going to quit.' The Sox were out of the race, going nowhere. He said, 'I have it fixed with Yawkey. If I can hit one home run, that's it.'

"He came up in the late innings, and he hit it nine miles over the bullpen to win the game, and afterwards he told me, 'I was on the verge of tipping my cap. I wanted to, and yet I didn't. I always felt sorry that I didn't. Running around the bases, I really wanted to, but I didn't.' "

Jerry Casale: "Teddy was just wonderful to me. I was a young guy coming out of the army, and he knew I didn't have any money. I had made ninety dollars a month for two years. I was always broke. Ted was making a film on hitting, and he said to me, 'Come to the ballpark the next few days.' One day I threw ten pitches, the next day twenty. It was nothing. He handed me two hundred dollars. And two hundred dollars in those days, wow, it was like two thousand dollars today. It was nice for him to do that.

"Teddy couldn't have been more a help to me than my brother or father would have been. I remember one time in Chicago I was facing Early Wynn. I was a young guy facing a future Hall of Famer, and I wanted to beat him, because he was a mean guy, very mean. First two times I get up to the plate, I can't get the bat off my shoulder. The umpire is calling all these high sliders strikes. They're outside by a foot, and the catcher, Sherm Lollar, is saying, 'Nice pitch, Early, nice pitch.' They're a foot outside! I can't even reach them. Strike one, strike two, strike three. Being a rookie, I dropped the bat and didn't say anything. The second time, I couldn't have hit those pitches with a flagpole. And Lollar is saying, 'Nice pitch.' Strike one, strike two, strike three. I threw the bat in the bat rack and sat down. I said, 'Teddy, those fucking pitches are not strikes.' He said, 'Bush, move up in the box and start swinging, because that's Early Wynn.' I said, 'I'll bet you ten to one he wouldn't call those strikes against you.' He said, 'That's right, but on you he's going to call them.'

"So the next time I went up, it was still a 0–0 game, and without Wynn noticing me, I moved my left foot facing him, and I went with the slider and hit it into the right-center-field seats in Comiskey Park. Wynn cursed me all around. He cursed my mother, my friends, my uncle, my grandfather, everybody. And Teddy was right there to congratulate me when I came in. 'Attaboy, Bush.' And he came up the same inning and hit one into the right-field seats.

"I had them beat, 2 to 0, bottom of the eighth, and I got tired, and Mike Fornieles, a knuckleballer, came in. He got out of the eighth, we went to the bottom of the ninth, a walk, a dribble up the third-base line, a sacrifice bunt, and Nellie Fox blooped one to right, and we lost the game, 3 to 2. I never did get to beat him.

"But as for Teddy, he was always there. 'Bush, you're not bending your arm. You're not doing this. You're not doing that. Watch how this pitcher throws the ball. He'll throw this in this situation.' He was always good to anybody who wanted to get better. He didn't like the know-it-all guys like Gene Stephens or Marty Keough or someone who wouldn't go over and ask him things. If I was a hitter, I would have lived with Teddy. I would have asked to room with him, just to get inside his brain and find out how he thinks and how to get a pitcher set up.

"I remember opening day we were facing Camilo Pascual, who to me had the greatest curveball I've ever seen. Teddy took that curveball right over the center-field fence. He hit Herb Score like he owned him. Teddy was just so good. And I caught him at the end.

"I felt sorry for him in 1960 because his legs weren't there anymore. He tried like hell, but he couldn't get to the ball, and guys would take extra bases on him. The man was so perfect, but he just wasn't able to do it anymore. I actually felt sorry for him, and that year I couldn't get Molly Putz out.

"I remember one day Ted couldn't get to a ball, and it fell in, and the runner slid in for a double. Ike Delock was the pitcher, another tough son of a bitch. Ike was out of Detroit, and he didn't take any nonsense if a guy was dogging. But Ted wasn't dogging it. He was up in age. He just couldn't get to the ball.

"When they got in the dugout, Ike said, 'Catch the goddamn ball.' And Ted yelled, 'Pitch the goddamn ball right.' I was sitting in the corner thinking, 'This is the big leagues?' Ike grabbed a bat and said, 'Come on, you big bastard, I'll show you. I'll knock your head in for you.'

"The day he hit his final home run, I was in the bullpen. We all knew it was his last game. We were pulling for that ball to be hit out of there. I know I was, along with the rest of the boys in the bullpen, Leo Kiely, Fornieles, a guy named Ted Wills, Ted Bowsfield. We were all pulling, 'Come on, Teddy, hit it.' And then he did, and I had chills. I had a beautiful feeling. It was a real thrill.

"After the game, he was gone. He had left before we were in the clubhouse. And I never saw him again. It was the last time I laid eyes on Teddy as a ballplayer."

John Updike, author: "Ted Williams did a lot to antagonize a certain kind of fan. He was somewhat combative himself in his statements, and he was vulnerable in being very sensitive and being a perfectionist. He wanted to be the best, and any mistake he made, any strikeout, was very painful to him, and so people will tend to heckle somebody who is heckleable, and Ted was supposed to have rabbit ears. In fact, he never tipped his hat to the fans.

"Of late Williams seems to be coming out of his shell. He was asked about the hostile attitude of the sportswriters all those years, and he said that he hadn't liked it, but he wondered if it didn't make him play better, that he just went up there mad, and it seemed that whenever there was an assault on him in the press, he would go out and go four-for-four. So it might have been that that atmosphere of antagonism gave him an edge as a ballplayer. I certainly wouldn't have wanted to have stood out there and heard abuse, but I'm not Ted Williams.

"He wasn't allowed any private life. But you don't get anything for nothing, and for the average fan like me who wasn't in on locker-room scenes, never met the man, never hoped to, the fact that he had these detractors in the stands and in the press just made Williams all the more appealing. It made you like him more and root for him harder. It gave him a heroic ethos.

"I don't think it hurt him much with New England at large. I think part of his hold over the New England fan was this atmosphere of tragedy and opposition and anger that circled around him. He seemed to really need it, because whenever there was a long, quiet lull, he would do something to get it going again. I think he enjoyed being the center of attention, to be honest.

"It seemed to me he was almost mythical, certainly heroic. It was very different the way Boston treated Williams and New York treated DiMaggio.

"DiMaggio was always the other superplayer who was held up against Williams as being a great all-around player. It was part of New York. The New York temperament rallied around Joe. He was kind of classy and they liked that, and they liked his going to the nightclubs. They liked what they knew about him. A lot of it might have been blown up to be unattractive, he too was a kind of loner after all, but that was played down, and the smile, and the fans seemed to be entirely behind DiMaggio. You cannot say that of the Boston fans and Ted. But the run of us certainly were for Williams and admired him all the more because he seemed to be carrying all these handicaps, broken bones, angry *Herald* columnists, all these loud fans, double war service, divorce problems. One time he took a fall off of a clog in a shower, just an inch fall, and injured his heel so he was out for a month or more. He never had a smooth season where he just played ball and everything just fell into place. There was always something going wrong. And that also kept you interested."

It would be stretching the truth some to say that Ted Williams made John Updike famous, but for many baseball fans who have never read any of his novels or enjoyed his poetry, Updike's tribute to Ted Williams in the October 22, 1960, issue of *The New Yorker* magazine, entitled "Hub Fans Bid Kid Adieu," might be one of his most notable works.

The piece was written by Updike by happenstance. Updike had witnessed Ted's farewell, not because he was on assignment, but because he was a fan. The moment so thrilled him that he just wrote the article and sent it to his editor at *The New Yorker*, William Shawn, who of course found room for it. Without ever meeting Ted Williams, Updike penned one of the great pieces of literature and journalism ever written about sport. Just about every anthology of sports literature has reprinted it.

One paragraph reads: "Like a feather caught in a vortex, Williams ran around the square of bases at the center of our beseeching screaming. He ran as he always ran out home runs—hurriedly, unsmiling, head down, as if our praise were a storm of rain to get out of. He didn't tip his cap. Though we thumped, wept, and chanted, 'We want Ted' for minutes after he hid in the dugout, he did not come back. Our noise for some seconds passed beyond excitement into a kind of immense open anguish, a wailing, a cry to be saved. But immortality is nontransferable. The papers said that the other players, and even the umpires on the field, begged him to come out and acknowledge us in some way, but he never had and did not now. Gods do not answer letters."

If Williams's final home run made some Red Sox weep, so did John Updike's rare ability to combine words to describe it. Updike is immensely proud of "Hub Fans Bid Kid Adieu" and he smiled often as he reminisced about the background of the piece.

John Updike: "There was no assignment the day of his final home run. One of Harold Ross's many prejudices at *The New Yorker* was that he didn't like baseball, although *The New Yorker* had columns about polo and the race track and tennis. This was all pre–Roger Angell. It was my idea to go to the ballpark. It was a late-minute impulse. I happened to be in town. I knew that this was Williams's last game.

"The game was not especially well-attended. It being a kind of nothing team and the end of the year, a chilly, gray September day, the stadium was only half filled. I got a pretty good seat, and it was only as the game developed, ending with the home run, that it seemed worth writing about. It was so exciting, the whole day, the way it mounted, the fans applauded at the end, and I found that very moving. The left-field stands were quiet at last, saying good-bye for all these years of entertainment and class, the applause, and his ignoring all of this was somehow nice too, not tipping the hat, still trying to operate in this vacuum of the nine men on the field. I was by no means sure *The New Yorker* would want it, but I had time, nothing pressing on my desk, and I sat down and wrote it in five days.

"I didn't have much by way of reference material, not an awful lot about his early career, just what I remembered, and maybe that makes it a more interesting piece, because it's not all that résumé. So I wrote about him in my own longhand, plus a record book or two that I was able to find, and I sent it down, and [editor William] Shawn called me up and very sweetly, in this shy, small voice of his, he said, 'In addition to your other accomplishments now, you have written the best baseball story *The New Yorker* has ever run.'

"I had thought it was the *only* baseball story *The New Yorker* had ever run! It was gratifying to me that my one sports story ever has given me the reputation of something of a sportswriter, and I'm still being approached by *Sports Illustrated* and newspapers to write a story about this and that as if I really know a lot about sports. I basically don't.

"Ted read the piece and liked it enough to invite me to write his biography, but that I thought was too broad a detour from my chosen path. I've never met Ted, though people have offered to get us together. I'd just as soon think of Williams as he was to me, a man of statistics and an apparition on the baseball field, seen at a distance, a name in the daily box scores.

"I never met him, but I have watched with interest that he has mellowed. He usually has nice, wise things to say to the press. It's one of his traits that were not allowed to surface in the years he was an active player. He does have a great theoretical love of the game and he's willing to talk about it with ballplayers on his side or the other side. He has a strong sense of those who can play major-league baseball belonging to a really charmed club. He's for all of them. He liked them all. So the love of baseball is what you get our of the older Williams that is very nice. He has not turned his back on it. He managed for a few years. He shows up at the Red Sox spring training camp. He has become a nice old-timer, which you might not have thought when he was such a cranky, erratic and surly, even antisocial player."

When Ted Williams retired, his lifetime batting average stood at .344407. He hit 521 homers off 224 pitchers. His homers won 99 of the 2,292 games he played. He hit 17 grand slams. He homered every 14.8 at bats.

Month by month, his final career batting statistics were:

MONTH	HITS	HOMERS	*RBIS*	AVG.
April	156	31	108	.333
May	436	95	341	.335
June	502	97	378	.336
July	545	108	345	.354
August	544	101	367	.341
September	461	88	293	.358
October	10	1	7	.500

He batted .361 at Fenway, .327 on the road.

He was the Kid, the Thumper, the Splendid Splinter, Teddy Ballgame. He used to say, 'I'm Ted Fucking Williams, and I'm the greatest hitter in the world.' And he was. His teammates loved him, and the press hated him. The fans didn't quite know what to think except that they will never again behold another quite like him.

CHAPTER 25
After Ted

With the corpus of Ted Williams having retired to Florida after the 1960 season, Red Sox fans for the next half-dozen years had to be content with his memory. There would be a dry period, a time of deprivation, but the average Boston fan would seek the great performance or perhaps the one outstanding at bat in a ballgame and focus on that one play or one player and be satisfied. With the first post-Ted year of 1961, however, they would be witness to the birth of another glorious career.

YOUNG YAZ

Carl Yastrzemski came from a family of potato farmers who lived about thirty miles from the eastern tip of Long Island. Yaz's father and uncle Tom inherited the farm from their uncle Vincent Zaluski. Carl never picked potatoes. He was too busy practicing to become a major-league ballplayer.

Carl's father had tried out with the Cardinals and Dodgers, but when the Dodgers offered him a Class-D contract, he decided his responsibilities at home were too great, and he declined and fanatically transferred his major-league ambitions to his son. Since Carl was about six years old, his father pitched tennis balls to him after supper every evening. When Carl got old enough, they practiced for an hour each evening after dinner on a big lot with a real baseball. As a boy, Carl Yastrzemski got more batting practice than most professionals get during a career. To supplement his hitting of the hardball, he played stickball. He would pretend he was Ted Williams or New York Yankee first baseman Joe Collins. He pretended to be Williams because

Williams was Williams and Collins because he was Polish. For hours he also
hit a ball attached to a pipe, as in T-ball.

Carl performed farm duties, but his father let him perform only the tasks
that would strengthen his wrists and arms for baseball. Carl moved irrigation
pipes, tied cauliflower, cut cabbage, picked cucumbers, and helped to load
trucks as the potatoes were picked by hand and bagged.

His father coached the Babe Ruth League team, for which Carl pitched
and played shortstop. The team won the state title. His father also founded,
managed, and ran a local semipro team made up mostly of family members,
and Carl played for that from the age of fourteen. On the team were Yastrzemskis and Skoniecznys and Jasinskis and Bortkowskis. The one non-
Polish player was Bill Stravopoulos, a high-school teammate of Carl's. The
double-play combination was Yastrzemski to Yastrzemski to Stravopoulos.

Yaz was a small boy when he entered high school, and, as a freshman,
bunted a lot to get on base. To gain strength in his arms and shoulders, he
practiced during the winter swinging a lead bat. The next year he hit .650.

As a senior, he was a metropolitan New York All-Star. His father told him
he could sign a professional contract if a team offered six figures, plus paid
for college tuition. Carl's father had quit school in the eighth grade, and he
demanded Carl go to a Catholic college even if he were to sign.

The New York Yankees called first. Carl had always wanted to play for the
Yankees. He imagined the lineage—Ruth, Gehrig, DiMaggio, Mantle, Yastrzemski. He was invited to Yankee Stadium and was brought into the
Yankee clubhouse, but he ended up dressing by himself and wasn't introduced to any of the players. The batboys who dressed near him ignored him.
He listened to the players talking to each other, and suddenly he felt very
lonely.

He went into the batting cage to hit, took ten swings, hit four out, and went
to see general manager Lee MacPhail.

The Yankees offered $40,000.

"It isn't enough," said Carl's father. Carl couldn't believe his father, who
had never made $10,000 a year his entire life, had turned it down.

"It's more than the Yankees have ever offered a high-school boy before,"
said MacPhail.

"It still isn't enough."

"Take it, Dad. It's the Yankees."

"I'll have to think about it."

Back home, Carl's father consulted Father Joe Ratkowski, their spiritual
adviser. Ratkowski had known Gil Hodges and some other ballplayers and
fancied himself an expert on baseball. All along, he had insisted that Carl was
worth six figures.

A couple of days later, Yankee scout Ray Garland returned with an offer
of $45,000. Carl begged to be allowed to sign the contract.

His father wrote on a sheet of paper in large letters "$100,000" and then pushed it over to the scout.

"That's what it will cost you to sign him," he said.

Garland grabbed a pile of paper, some pencils, contracts, and scratch pads and threw them all up in the air.

"The Yankees never offered that kind of money to anybody, and they won't give it to your boy," he said.

"Then they won't get him," said Carl's father.

And they didn't. For years, Yankee fans cried over that one. The Milwaukee Braves offered $60,000 to make the boy a pitcher. They were rebuffed. The Giants wanted him to be a catcher. His father vetoed the West Coast and the position of catcher.

Bots Nekola was the Red Sox scout. He was the only one who ever took the Yastrzemski family out to dinner, and he had other points in his favor as well. Nekola had graduated from Holy Cross, and had once pitched for the semipro Bushwicks against Carl's father. The elder Yastrzemski felt comfortable with Nekola, and that helped him to reject the rest of the offers.

The Los Angeles Dodgers said they'd top all offers.

"If only you were still in Brooklyn," said Mr. Yastrzemski.

Father Joe recommended that Carl sign with the Red Sox or the Philadelphia Phillies. Both Tom Yawkey and Bob Carpenter are known for their generosity to players, he advised.

The Philadelphia Phillies offered $95,000 plus a big-league contract, a total of $102,000. Carl's father demanded an extra $10,000 if Carl didn't graduate from college in six years. Phils owner Bob Carpenter balked. Carpenter had no control over Carl's study habits. Why should he be penalized if Carl should fail to get his degree?

The Reds offered $100,000 plus tuition. By now, his father's asking price had jumped to $150,000. The Reds' offer rose to $125,000. It was rejected. The father turned down $80,000 from Detroit.

Carl began to see that his father's loyalty was to Bots.

Two days after receiving the $125,000 offer from the Reds, the Yastrzemskis flew to Boston to negotiate with the Red Sox. Nekola recalled bringing his young star to see Fenway Park for the first time. Twenty years later he even remembered the date—November 28, 1958.

"They drove up to Boston in the middle of this damn blizzard," said Nekola. "It was dismal, snowing like hell, and Fenway Park was the last place in the world you'd try to entice anybody with." Yastrzemski walked the park while the scout waited nervously. He studied the fences, then finally walked back to Nekola.

"I can hit in this park," he said.

Red Sox farm director Johnny Murphy offered the boy $100,000 plus college tuition. Yaz's father dropped his price from $125,000 to $115,000.

Said Murphy, "We'll give you $108,000 plus a two-year Triple-A farm contract at $5,000 a year, plus the rest of your college expenses."

The deal was done. And that's how Carl Yastrzemski became a Boston Red Sox.

After the contract was signed, they went to meet general manager Joe Cronin, who was surprised to see that the youngster was only five foot eleven and 170 pounds.

When they were introduced, Cronin said, "He doesn't seem very big."

Wrote Yastrzemski of the meeting: "Then he walked out, shaking his head like a man who had met a midget when he expected a giant."

Joe Cronin didn't realize it at the time, but Carl Yastrzemski would be the one megastar culled from his unproductive farm system. This time Tom Yawkey's big bucks would pay dividends. Beginning in 1961, the player called Yaz would be the successor to Ted Williams in left field and the heart of the Red Sox team for twenty-three seasons.

Frank Malzone: "Yaz was replacing a great player and was expected to do more than he could do when he first came up. During his first spring training, he asked me what to expect. I said, 'It's no different. You're going to find the same players as in the minor leagues. Just do the things you're capable of doing.' "

Gene Conley: "When he first came up I would throw against him in batting practice, and his ball came off the bat quicker than all of them. Jumped. Like Hank Aaron. Certain guys, when they hit back at you in practice, the ball gets smaller. He hit the ball up the middle a lot, but he popped it.

"I called him 'Stosh.' He reminded me of Stan Musial, 'cause I had pitched seven years against Stan, and I knew how he hit, and Carl was the same type hitter, though Stan was a little better. Musial hit through the middle, lacing them here, lacing them there. Hit a home run. Yaz was the same type ballplayer.

"Yaz was kind of a loner. He hung around with a guy named Chuck Schilling who he knew from Long Island. He had his few beers. Yaz liked beer. He never mingled much with the veterans, because he was a kid. Yaz was a personable guy. He had a smile and a laugh that you really enjoyed. You could just see he was going to blossom."

THE GOLDEN BOY RETIRES

When they traded Mickey McDermott and Tommy Umphlett to Washington for outfielder Jackie Jensen at the end of the 1953 season, the Red Sox acquired an athlete of uncommon ability. Jensen was one of only two professional athletes—Earle "Greasy" Neale was the other—ever to perform in the Rose Bowl, the World Series, and a professional All-Star game. He was blond and handsome, married to a former Olympic diving champion—truly a golden boy.

There was only one problem: at the time of the trade, Jensen didn't want to play baseball anymore. He had a wife and two babies, he didn't think he was making enough money to compensate for his having to be away from his family so much, and he was considering retirement to some kind of well-paying, be-near-home job in Oakland.

Originally, Jensen had signed a $75,000 bonus with the New York Yankees, and for a number of games in 1951, the Yankee outfield was rookie Mickey Mantle in left, Joe DiMaggio in center, and Jensen in right. He played intermittently, however, and after two years of mostly bench-sitting, he was traded to Washington in 1952 for outfielders Irv Noren and Tom Upton. After two ten-home-run seasons with Washington, years in which he drove in 82 and 84 runs for a bad team, he seemed on the verge of stardom. Instead, he was ready to quit. A complex man, Jensen was a perfectionist who always felt he should be better than he was. The pressure of the game made him unhappy, he had a terrible fear of flying, and he was a homebody who hated to be away from his family. In baseball, family usually comes second.

After the trade, Red Sox general manager Joe Cronin sought to talk him out of quitting. He pointed out that Fenway Park would be tailor-made for his swing, and even offered Jensen an extra thousand dollars to join the team. Finally, Jensen talked it over with his wife, who told him, "If you quit, I don't think you'll be proud of it later."

Jensen continued with the Red Sox for seven seasons, twice quitting the game he was never certain he wanted to play in the first place. Despite his problems, Jensen managed a lifetime batting average of .279, hit with power, and in 1958 with Boston was voted the American League's Most Valuable Player after hitting .286 with 35 home runs and 122 RBIs. He was a team leader, a matinee idol who was more serious about life than was the average ballplayer.

Frank Malzone: "Jackie was quiet and reserved, an intelligent man who kept within himself pretty much. He didn't mix with too many of the other players. I roomed with him for half a season, and he wasn't much of a gambler, he wasn't a run-around guy, and he didn't drink much. Jackie seemed like an easy individual to live with. Who knows what takes place?

"I do remember that Jackie came out and said a few things about Ted Williams getting privileges that other players didn't get, which did happen in those days, 'cause Ted was the big honcho. Matter of fact, when we wanted something, we would go to Ted so we could get them. Little things, like maybe you're going on a flight, and you want a beer on the plane. Club rules said you didn't do that. There was a rule we couldn't play cards in the clubhouse. Ted would say to us, 'Don't you think we ought to do this?' We'd tell him, 'Tell the people in charge.' And naturally, they would agree with him. He would make the effort for us, which we always appreciated. But Jackie would get upset because Ted got preferential treatment."

In February 1959, Jensen indicated that his interest in the game of baseball was cooling again. He told a gathering at a sports banquet in Palo Alto, California, "I have only one life to live, and I'll be happier when I can spend it with my family. Being away from home with a baseball team for seven months a year doesn't represent the kind of life I want or the kind of life my wife and children want." He had been a major leaguer for nine seasons. In May of 1959, he told Harold Kaese, "It takes a certain breed of guy to be happy with a ballplayer's day-to-day existence. I'm not the type."

Contributing to his unhappiness was his uncontrollable fear of flying.

Frank Malzone: "When Jackie got on a plane, he would grab the two armrests, and his hands would be sweating. Jackie was absolutely scared. He'd just sit there and hold on to his seat. After a while, he'd relax a little, but the plane would hit a little turbulence, and he would be in trouble again."

According to Harold Kaese, his fear began as a result of a near air collision on a trip to the Orient with Ed Lopat's All-Stars in 1954. In an attempt to conquer his phobia, he hired not only a personal psychiatrist, but a hypnotist as well.

One time, according to Al Hirshberg, Frank Malzone was nursing a bad leg that stubbornly refused to get any better. It was suggested that Malzone go to Jensen's hypnotist.

Al Hirshberg: "Before the game, in the trainer's room, the great experiment took place. The whole team gathered 'round.

" 'You must cooperate,' the man said. 'That is essential. Cooperate. Trust me. Put yourself in my hands. Relax. Cooperate. I will help you, but only if you cooperate.'

" 'Okay,' said Malzone, 'I'm cooperating.'

"The hypnotist pulled out a shiny coin and moved it gently back and forth in front of Malzone's face.

" 'You are getting drowsy . . . your eyes are closing . . . you are thoroughly relaxed . . . you are going to sleep . . . sleep . . . sleep . . .'

"The soft voice droned endlessly, repeating the words while the observers watched, half fascinated, half skeptical. Pretty soon, Malzone's eyelids grew heavy, and at last his eyes closed. The hypnotist continued to croon softly, his voice sugary, the words never changing. This went on for perhaps twenty minutes.

"Then, in the same soothing voice: 'When you wake up, you will get off the table and lean all your weight on your foot and it won't hurt . . . remember . . . it won't hurt . . . it won't hurt . . .'

"Now the only sounds in the room were the hypnotist's voice and Malzone's regular breathing. The words were repeated over and over until at last the man said, 'Now you will wake up when I count to three . . . three . . . three . . . and when you put your foot on the floor it won't hurt . . .' Over and over, the hypnotist repeated the words. Then, his voice rising, he counted.

" 'One . . . two . . . *three.*'

"Malzone stirred, his eyes fluttered, and he woke up. While everyone watched, completely captivated, he sat up, letting his legs swing over the table. After a short pause, he leaned on his hands and jumped off, landing hard on both feet.

" '*Chee-zus Kee-rist,*' Malzone howled.

"As he scrambled back onto the table, holding his leg in anguish, the hypnotist turned away and muttered, 'Wouldn't cooperate.' "

The incident was humorous for Malzone and the Red Sox players in attendance, but not for Jensen, who was never cured. On January 27, 1960, after a year in which he had driven in 112 runs, he announced his retirement, shocking the baseball world.

Jensen sat out the entire 1960 season. He was coaxed back in 1961 for a little while, but his fear of flying was too great. After a month, he walked out again. He felt he could no longer produce to his high standards.

When Jensen deserted on the final day of April, 1961, he didn't tell anyone on the Red Sox. He was certain they would attempt to talk him out of it. Instead, he confided in Lin Raymond, a reporter for the *Quincy Patriot Ledger.*

In his room at Cleveland's Hotel Statler, he told Raymond, "I believe I have given Mr. Yawkey value for value since I have been with the Red Sox. Now, I feel I can no longer do that, so I don't want to take his money under false pretenses. I can't run anymore, I can't throw, and I can't hit. There were times I felt so ashamed of myself I dreaded going back to the dugout . . . I just felt that young fellows like Carroll Hardy can help the team more than I can, so I'm dropping from the scene. I don't want my friends to go on defending me."

He had a bellboy take his bags down on the freight elevator and out to a cab in the back of the hotel.

The bellboy told him, "There was another man in your room."

"That's my roommate, Carroll Hardy. What did you tell him?"

"I told him I was just moving your baggage to another room."

"That's great," said Jackie. He asked the bellboy to accompany him to the train station.

Jensen had asked Raymond to inform manager Mike Higgins he was leaving by train from Cleveland to his home in Crystal Bay, Nevada.

"Tell Mike why I'm leaving. I would do it myself, but I know Mike will argue with me and that would only make things worse for all of us," Jensen said.

Eight days after he departed, a sheepish Jensen returned to the team and completed the 1961 season. After two spectacular seasons in which he led the league in runs batted in with 122 and 112, that year he hit only .263, with 13 home runs and 66 runs batted in. His flying phobia had hurt his confidence and taken away his enjoyment of the game. At the end of the year, Jackie Jensen quit baseball for good. He was thirty-four years old.

CHAPTER 26

On to Jerusalem

After losing first Ted Williams and the next year Jackie Jensen, the Red Sox of the early 1960s were rudderless. Carl Yastrzemski was talented but just a baby. Hard times were at hand. Bill Monbouquette, Gene Conley, and Dick Radatz led the pitching staff, but the offensive talent was so thin that by June the team was headed for deep in the second division. The players felt free to occupy themselves with non-baseball activities.

Manager Pinky Higgins loved his liquor. Many of the players followed his lead. When the Red Sox came to town, there was no telling what might happen. In July of 1962, Gene Conley, the six foot eight pitcher, made headlines when he disappeared for five days after walking off the team bus on its way from Yankee Stadium to Newark Airport. The bus had stopped in traffic near the Lincoln Tunnel, and Conley walked off, ostensibly to go to the bathroom.

No one could find him anywhere. He had vanished. Upon his return, he told an astounded press that during his hiatus he had attempted to catch a flight to the Holy City of Jerusalem. Conley was a great athlete, a pro baseball and pro basketball player. But he will always be remembered best as the man who left his team in the middle of the season to fly to Israel.

Few American athletes have been talented enough to play two professional sports successfully. In recent times, sports fans remember Dave DeBusschere, a great basketball player but a mediocre pitcher. Pitcher Ron Reed of the Braves and Phillies played two seasons with the Detroit Pistons. Danny

Ainge played three years with the Blue Jays before turning to basketball with the Celtics, and most recently with the Portland Trailblazers. Deion Sanders tried both football and baseball, but hasn't hit well enough yet to star in baseball. Hip injury or not, Bo Jackson has been an incredibly successful two-sport athlete.

The most famous two-sport pro star was Jim Thorpe. Thorpe played pro football and also the outfield for John McGraw's New York Giants. After Thorpe, the next to play two sports successfully was Gene Conley.

In basketball, Conley was a productive member of the world-champion Boston Celtics and the New York Knicks, a veteran of both the NBA and the ABA. He played with Bob Cousy and Bill Russell and against George Mikan and Wilt Chamberlain. In baseball, he pitched in both the American and National Leagues as a star with the Milwaukee Braves, Philadelphia Phillies, and Boston Red Sox. He roomed with Robin Roberts and pitched on teams with Warren Spahn and Hank Aaron.

After signing with the Boston Braves at age twenty, he was voted the Minor League Player of the Year in 1952 and again in 1953. Called up to the big leagues in 1954, Conley was runner-up for National League Rookie of the Year behind Wally Moon. Hank Aaron was third.

His sophomore year, he was selected to the first of three All-Star squads. Days before the All-Star Game, he threw an overhand curve to the Phils' Granny Hamner, and his shoulder popped so loudly, catcher Del Crandall could hear it. His fingers went numb. He relieved in the All-Star Game, was tagged with the loss, and then had to sit out the rest of the season. For the rest of his career, he got by on guts and cortisone.

Conley got the win in the 1955 All-Star Game and pitched two innings for the National League All-Stars in 1959. Meanwhile, during the winter, he toiled for the championship Boston Celtics. He went from baseball to basketball and back with hardly a break. Ultimately, all that work took its toll.

In 1962, Conley compiled a 15–14 record, with a 3.95 ERA, on a Red Sox team that finished twenty games behind the Yankees. He was the ace of a staff that included Bill Monbouquette, Ike Delock, Earl Wilson, and Don Schwall. But all of that is largely forgotten because of what he did on the hot summer afternoon of July 27.

Roy Mumpton: "Gene Conley and Pumpsie Green were sitting right behind me on the bus. We had come out of Yankee Stadium, and we were going to Newark Airport. It was a fast ballgame, and because it was around six, we got into this awful traffic jam. We sat there for an hour, and the bus never moved.

"I could hear Gene. He said, 'Pumpsie, come on. We'll get a beer.' Pumpsie said, 'All right.' Two or three other guys went out and bought sandwiches. But we weren't moving. So nobody paid attention.

"We got to the airport, and there was no Gene or Pumpsie. A day later,

Pumpsie came back. He and Conley weren't close. He just happened to be sitting next to him when Gene said, 'Let's go.' "

Pumpsie Green: "People ask me about the time I got off the bus and went with Gene Conley. If you're wondering what was said, 'Hey, since this bus is sitting here and we're not moving anywhere, see that place down there, let's find a restaurant and go to it and then we'll get back on the bus.' 'Cause the bus was sitting in New York traffic on a one-hundred-degree day, and during those days after a ballgame you always have a couple of beers, so it was time to find a rest room. That was the only intention.

"We went into the restaurant, hung around for a while in New York, had a few beers. For the record, it was really no big deal. The next day I showed up in Washington. Afterwards, I heard things that were amazing to me. The guys asked me, 'Were you and Conley going to Israel?' I don't know how that story got out. I don't know what he was doing. They ask me and I say, 'I don't know,' and I didn't know. I still don't know."

Gene Conley: "I had played thirteen straight seasons in the big leagues in both sports, baseball and basketball, and hadn't stopped. The Milwaukee Braves were a championship team and then the Celtics were always world champions, and the competition was so strong, so tough, that I just ran out of gas physically, and it affected me mentally as well. I don't mean I went crazy, but I needed a rest, whether or not they wanted me to, regardless of the fact that it was in the middle of the season. To me, it didn't make any difference.

"We were playing the Yankees. Ralph Houk was the manager, and the manager of the American League All-Star team, too. I had played in three All-Star Games in the National League, with the Braves twice and the Phillies once. It was '54, '55, and '59, and at the time I thought, 'Wouldn't it be great coming over to the American League and being able to make an All-Star team in the American as well?'

"And at the time my record was good enough that Houk could have picked me. I had nine or ten wins at the time, and I was pitching a lot of innings. I hadn't beaten his club, but one time Ralph Terry beat me, 1 to 0. We even had the bases loaded in the ninth inning with nobody out, and we still got beat, 1 to 0. Another time I got beat by Bob Turley in Fenway Park, 2 to 1, so Houk knew I could pitch.

"I was tired, you gotta realize. I had already put in eight or ten seasons of sports without stopping. In four or five days Houk was going to choose his pitchers, and I thought, 'If I could turn in a good performance, the son of a gun just might pick me.'

"Well, that day everything went wrong. We had two or three errors. Yastrzemski missed a ball in left field that I could have caught, and at least four or five runs were let in, not knocked in, *let* in. I went out of the game about the fourth or fifth inning, and I thought, 'Well, that's the end of that, 'cause Ralph certainly isn't going to pick me.'

"I was disgusted from the game. I was tired from sports. Because of the All-Star Game, we had four, five days off. In the clubhouse, I started drinking beer. By the time the game ended, I was pretty well smashed. And I could care less.

"So we got on the bus in New York. There we were. We got in this traffic jam, on our way to going through the Lincoln Tunnel, and with all that beer in me, I said, 'You know, I've got to go to the bathroom.' We were on a bus with no toilet. I started up the aisle, and Pumpsie looked like he needed to take a leak. Everybody had a few beers after the game in those days, and I guess I just wanted someone to go along with me to make sure they held the bus. I should have known better. I could have taken six guys in there, and they wouldn't have held the bus. I hit Pumpsie on the shoulder. I said, 'Pumpsie, you gotta take a leak?' He said, 'Yeah.' I said, 'Come on, this bus is gonna set here for fifteen minutes. Let's run into this little place.'

"Well, we went in there, and would you believe the traffic jam opened up, and the bus kept going! And we were inside this little restaurant.

"We didn't stay and have a beer or nothing. We just went in to go to the bathroom. We must have killed five minutes, but some truck probably opened up and let the bus through. When we came out, the bus was gone. The driver couldn't care less. He was probably hot and tired and concerned, and he couldn't sit there and wait for us and hold up New York's traffic. So he left.

"There we were, in New York City. And because I was the starting pitcher, I had four days off before the All-Star Game. The only thing I could do was chew tobacco and watch the Washington Senators play the Red Sox for three days, and then I'd have had a break at the All-Star Game. So I really had five or six days off.

"When I saw the bus had left, I said, 'Pumpsie, here we are. What do we do? We're in New York City. The bus is gone. We'd certainly be foolish to go to LaGuardia and fly into Washington. The game isn't until, when, tomorrow night?' I said, 'Let's go downtown and have some fun. Let's do something different. And then perhaps we'll go to Washington later.'

"We went in to see Toots Shor, who was always nice. Every time I pitched in a World Series or an All-Star Game, he always sent me a telegram and wished me good luck personally. That was the type of guy he was. I said to Pumpsie, 'Let's go in to Toots Shor's and meet Toots Shor. Say hello.' He said, 'Really?' I said, 'Sure, why not?' So we went in to Toots Shor's and stayed there four or five hours. Willie Hartack was there, and a couple of writers, and they were asking, 'What the heck are you guys doing in town?' We said, 'We just played the Yankees, and we got a day off.' We just blew them off a little bit. It was hot outside. And who cares, you know?

"So the next thing I knew, we were both pretty well smashed. We got a bottle of booze and checked into the Commodore Hotel. We even got our baseball rate. I'm sure they were wondering, 'These guys just left here. What are they doing checking in again?' We got us a room, had a few drinks, and we talked about a lot of things. Baseball, sports, his brother. He has a brother named Cornell Green, who played football, made all-pro for several years.

"Then, I think, I was too far gone. I said, 'Let's take a few days off and go to Jerusalem.' He said, 'You're crazy.' I said, 'No. Let's go to Jerusalem. Let's get out of this country. Let's relax. The heck with baseball. The heck with sports, period. Let's just let 'em know that we're taking a vacation.'

" 'Oh, no,' he said. 'Oh, no. You're crazy.'

"So I said, 'Pumpsie, quit it. I'm trying to have some fun. Come on, Pumpsie, what's the matter?'

"He said, 'No, no. We're both smashed.'

"I said, 'I don't know about you, but I'm going, Pumpsie.'

"We slept it off, but the next morning we were at it again. We had a couple of Bloody Marys. Pumpsie said, 'I'd better be thinking about getting back.' I said, 'Pumpsie, the heck with it. Don't worry about it.' I was about half smashed again.

"Pumpsie said, 'I think I'd better get back. You go ahead. Have a good time, but I'm gonna go back.'

"I said, 'Are you sure, Pumpsie?'

"He said, 'Yeah.' And he left.

"I didn't have any money, but I had a few bucks in the bank, not much, but a couple thousand. I went to the manager of the Commodore Hotel, who I knew over the years, and I said, 'Would it be possible if I cashed a check for a thousand dollars?' I was guessing what it would cost to go to Jerusalem. He said, 'I don't know. I'll have to check with your bank.' And would you believe my bank okayed a check for a thousand dollars? All this time my wife was off at a church camp with my kids. She wasn't even around. She had no idea what was happening. She just knows I got beat by the Yanks. I got the thousand, and I went down to the Israeli tourist place to get an airline ticket. They sold me the ticket. I'd never been overseas, or anywhere, for that matter. So there I was with my ticket in my pocket. Pumpsie was gone. I'd made a commitment to go, and so it had built to where, 'Hey, I've gone this far, by golly, I think I really will go. I ain't hurting anybody. I'm by myself. I'm gonna relax a few days. I've got a few bucks. How can I get in trouble?'

"I went back to Toots Shor's, and I told everyone, 'Hey, I'm gonna go to Jerusalem. I'm going to Bethlehem. I'm going to the Promised Land. I'm gonna get everything straightened out between me and my Savior.' And they looked at me like I had three eyes. I started flashing my ticket around. 'See, I am going.' A few guys said, 'Conley, forget it. Get a good night's sleep. Go back to Washington.' I said, 'No, I'm going to go.' I left there, and I went to a place called Al Schacht's, stayed there, talked ball a lot. I let the word out where I was going, and I had 'em call me a cab.

"I got a cab, and I went to LaGuardia Airport. When I got there, there were newspapermen and photographers. They figured they really got a story. But when I got there, the guy at the counter said, 'Sorry, fella, but we can't let you go without a passport.'

"I was so disappointed, you just wouldn't believe it. I thought, 'Oh, what the heck.' Otherwise, I would have been gone.

"Why Jerusalem? Oh, I don't know. Maybe it was because I was kind of at the end of my career. Maybe I was worried about what was going to happen to Gene Conley and his family. I'd had chronic arm trouble for five or six years, so I didn't know how long I had left. And the next year, I *was* out of ball. I hadn't saved much money. Even if I hadn't had a beer occasionally, there wasn't all that kind of money in those days. So I was concerned about my family and the whole ball of wax. 'Cause I was very much of a family man, but I did like to have a little tea once in a while.

"I got in a cab and I said, 'Well, if I can't go to Jerusalem, I'll go first class. I'll check into the Waldorf Astoria. I didn't want to show myself back at the Commodore. I spent two nights at the Waldorf. First class. Must have cost two or three hundred dollars. Lots of room service. I just hid out in my room for two days.

"I was starting to straighten out, and I began to become ashamed of myself. Not afraid. Ashamed. 'What have I done? I gotta have more pride than that.'

"I got on the phone and called my folks. I couldn't call my wife 'cause she was away at this camp. I called my mother and dad. They said, 'Son, where are you?' I said, 'In New York.' 'Well, are you all right?' I said, 'Yeah.'

" 'You realize you've been on TV? You've been on radio? We're worried to death. We thought something happened to you.' I said, 'I'm real ashamed of myself, but I had a few beers and was gonna leave the country for a few days.' My mother was crying. She said, 'Mr. Yawkey, the owner of the Red Sox, has called several times. He's quite concerned about you, son.'

"I said to myself, 'Isn't that something? Here you are, you big jackass. You're having a great year. Mr. Yawkey's a peach of a guy. Here he is concerned like you're his son, calling all over.' I thought, 'What am I gonna do now? How am I gonna face this? The guys in Washington are either gonna laugh or think I'm nuts. My goodness, what am I going to do?'

"Somehow I got ahold of my wife. I told her I was coming home, that I was considering quitting baseball. That's how bad I felt. Can you imagine? Three or four days earlier, I thought I'd be in the All-Star Game.

"I took a train to Providence and met her there instead of Boston, 'cause I knew there'd be a lot of writers. She said, 'I think you should relax for a couple of days and get back on the ball and get your bearings.' She was very sympathetic. Always has been. We headed back to her camp, and we stopped in a little diner, and I could hear people saying, 'There he is. He's in town up here.' Like, 'Holy mackerel, what have I done?' I was marked. They thought I was kidnapped or killed or lost.

"I stayed at the camp for a day, and I said, 'Katy, we gotta go home. We gotta get back.' At the time I was living in a trailer in Foxboro. I said, 'I've got to figure something out.'

"When we arrived at the trailer, it was surrounded by newspapermen. Cameras. Everything. I couldn't hardly get inside. There I was, barefooted. I looked like an old Okie. We pulled down the blinds. They were trying to look in the windows. I couldn't believe what was going on. I thought, 'Boy, all this publicity for a guy throwing a four-day toot.'

"I did let in a couple of reporters to try to explain the story, but they couldn't get it straight. They just thought I was a drunk, but I couldn't have been a drunk if I was going to be an All-Star pitcher. I was leading the team in innings. I was a workhorse. They didn't get the idea that I had been concerned about my arm. They didn't see I was thirty-two years old and that the grind of pro sports had tired me out and that I was ready to dump it all. No one understood that for all I had done, I had nothing to show for it. I had no future. I didn't have a college education. I wasn't going to be a coach. After acting like this, they certainly wouldn't let me be a coach. So I was depressed and wanted to get away. And maybe I was getting a little religion, starting to see the light or something.

"I called Mr. Yawkey. He had left messages for me to call him. He wanted to see me in his office. Just a sweetheart of a guy. And I called Mike Higgins, whom I really admired. I explained that I really felt ashamed of myself and that I had considered quitting. Mike said, 'Things like that can happen to anybody. No one will even care. You haven't missed anything anyway. You're starting in a couple more days.' After I hung up, I thought, 'He must have died laughing.' I felt everyone was laughing at me. But they didn't know how serious it was.

"I went up to see Mr. Yawkey. I said, 'Most people have at least an off-season with their families, but I don't have one, and I haven't seen them winter or summer for four or five years, so I don't even know them hardly, and I think I'll just get a job and rough it out for the rest of my life.'

"Mr. Yawkey said, 'Sit down.' I sat down on the couch. He said, 'You know, fella, you've had it tough, haven't you?' I said, 'What do you mean, Mr. Yawkey?' He said, 'You're just kind of worn out, I got a feeling. I know the feeling you have. You're over there trying to play basketball and you're playing baseball. I know the feeling you have. You've probably been drinking a little too much. You know,' and he smiled—he was shaving in the mirror—and he said, 'Do you really want to know the truth? There are times I'd like to do the same thing. But I can't do it because of who I am. When you're in the limelight, you can't do things like this because the publicity's bad, and it's just not done. And you probably don't understand what kind of influence you really have on the public and the kids.'

"I said, 'You're absolutely right in what you're saying, Mr. Yawkey.' He said, 'Now, I'm gonna have to fine you, 'cause the papers are gonna be asking questions—"Sir, did you give this guy a fine?"—so I'm gonna have to more or less act like I'm gonna discipline you. I'm going to fine you as much as I fined Ted Williams the time he spit at the crowd.' I said, 'What is that, Mr. Yawkey?' He said, 'One thousand, five hundred dollars.' I said, "Mr. Yawkey, I don't have that much money.' He laughed. He said, 'We're just going to have to take it out of your paycheck as you go.' He said, 'I'll tell you this: if you behave yourself and not pull any more antics like you did and straighten yourself out and show me that you really are concerned about your pitching and your welfare and your family, I'll give it back to you at the end of the season.'

"I said, 'Mr. Yawkey, you got a deal. And I really appreciate it, because you won't have any more trouble with me.'

"I won about six more games, and I pitched real good ball, and with luck I could have won 17 or 18 games. As a matter of fact, on the last day of the season, I lost 2 to 1. I worked hard right to the very last day. Mr. Yawkey called me up and said, 'You got your money back, Gene.' He said, 'Congratulations, you really straightened yourself out.'

"The next year I got a sore arm, and I was out of baseball after that, but I saw him several times after I was working for a living in Boston. I'd go to Fenway Park, and I'd run into him walking around the bleachers. He'd always stop and talk to me, and he'd never bring that up. He'd always say, 'It's sure good to see you,' and 'How's your family?' A peach of a guy.

"After I returned, I had the support of the players. They were sympathetic. I got teased a little. We'd go on the road, and if somebody got a couple of base hits when I was pitching, somebody'd holler, 'Now don't get mad and go to Jerusalem.' Then they'd laugh.

"And when I got out of baseball, I went to work for a company out of New York called Tuck Tape. I played center alongside Roger Kaiser and Tony Jackson in the ABA. I called on accounts all over the New England area trying to sell tape, and all the purchasing agents wanted to talk to me about was that incident, and they'd say, 'This is the greatest story we've ever heard in our lives. Give this guy an order.'

"It's been thirty years, and twenty-year-old kids ask me about it. And people who don't even know me as a ballplayer, I mention my name, and they say, 'You're the guy who got off the bus in New York and wanted to go to Jerusalem. Did you want to go to Bethlehem?'

"And I say, 'Yeah, that's right.' "

CHAPTER 27

A Tale of
Two Players

THE MONSTER

When a team is consistently out of the pennant race in August and finishes far back in the standings, its fans look to the individual performers for their gratification. The Red Sox teams in the early sixties didn't play .500 ball, but the fans still went to Fenway to watch the batting style of Carl Yastrzemski, their young outfield star, or to watch their most popular starter, Medford's Bill Monbouquette, who on August 1, 1962, pitched a 1–0 no-hitter against the Chicago White Sox. Monbo threw a hard slider, was smart and savvy. In 1963, he became the first Red Sox pitcher since Mel Parnell in 1953 to win 20 games.

The fans also went to Fenway in the hopes that the Red Sox would have a lead late in the game so that they could have the experience of watching their overpowering relief pitcher, "The Monster," Dick Radatz, mow down the opposition.

Ed Bressoud: "The three years I was there, Dick Radatz was the most overpowering pitcher that I ever saw. He just threw the ball by everybody. If Dick had been on a competitive ballclub, he would have been the premier pitcher in baseball. When I was with the Red Sox, he threw strikes all the time. He was amazing."

* * *

Radatz, at six foot six, 240 pounds, had been a multisport athlete at Michigan State University. He played one season of basketball at MSU alongside Jumping Johnny Green, who would later be a Knick regular for fourteen years, but when his grades slipped precipitously, Radatz decided to stick to one sport—baseball. As a starting pitcher for MSU, Radatz compiled a 10–1 record, averaging a strikeout an inning in 1959. He had the lowest earned-run average in the NCAA—1.10—and was named second-team All-American.

At the end of the school year, Radatz signed with the Red Sox. He got bonuses of $5,000 to sign, $5,000 if he made it to Class A, $5,000 for Double A, and another $5,000 if he made it to the majors. A year and a half later, he jumped to Triple A and picked up $10,000 in bonuses. The following year, he went to the majors and got the rest.

Dick Radatz became a star because the Red Sox had an outstanding coach and teacher in their minor-league system. His name was Johnny Pesky, the former Red Sox shortstop and third baseman. Johnny Pesky knew what was best for Dick Radatz. Johnny Pesky made him a star.

Dick Radatz, Red Sox, 1962–66: "I can remember after coming out of Michigan State, All-American, I went down to Raleigh and won my first game. I was a starter at the time. Three weeks later, I was 1 and 6 with a 2.10 ERA. I lost three games 1 to 0. The crowning blow was my sixth loss. I had broken the Carolina League record for strikeouts in one game with nineteen, had a perfect no-hitter with two outs in the ninth inning. A fellow hit a home run off me. I lost the no-hitter, the shutout, and the game.

"I decided I was going to quit. I was going to go back home and teach. A couple of the players on the club, Russ Gibson being one of them, talked me out of it. I said, 'I can't take this.' Gibby said, 'There will be better days.' And he was right. I stayed on and won my last three games. We won the pennant by 17 games. I was the only guy on the staff who had a losing record.

"I went back to Raleigh the following year. I was 12 and 3, led the league in strikeouts, ERA, and wins, and in the middle of the season they called me up to Minneapolis, our Triple-A farm club.

"The following season, in my first appearance in spring training in 1961, I started and struck out 11 or 12 in four innings. The next day, Johnny Pesky brought me into his office and said, 'Dick, I'm going to take you to Seattle.' I said, 'Gee, that's great, John.' He said, 'We're going to take you as a relief pitcher.'

"I said, 'Don't do me any favors. Send me back to Allentown,' our A farm club. 'I want to start.' Back then, if you weren't good enough to be a starter, you were shipped to the bullpen. Relief pitchers were not nurtured or trained in the minor leagues.

"He said, 'No. I'm going to take you with me and teach you to pitch every day.'

"I said, 'I can't do that.'

"He said, 'I'm going to teach you to do it.'

"As it turned out, it was the best thing that ever happened to me. If you're going to be a starter, you should have the command of three good pitches. I had a great fastball and a decent enough slider to keep them honest, but I didn't have enough to become a starting pitcher.

"My anger subsided when I discovered Pesky was going to pitch me a lot. And I did pick it up rather quickly, though I didn't feel part of the ballclub. I felt like I was an extra who was being dragged along. The year before, I had been in B ball, and the fact I was in Triple A was inspiring to me. I was on the brink of being a major-league ballplayer, so that also took the anger away.

"And I loved Johnny Pesky. He understood the plight of ballplayers, understood their problems. He was your boss, but also a confidant. He'd say, 'If you're having a problem on the road and want a beer, we'll talk about it.' He was almost like a father away from home. I got very close to Johnny very quickly.

"I came up to the Red Sox in '62. Mike Fornieles had led the Red Sox in saves the year before, and he was my biggest booster. He told me how to pitch to the batters. In fact, Mike helped me take his job. He knew he was coming to the end. He also saw I had a chance to be pretty good, and he did the best he could to help me.

"Playing in the majors was a rush. But because of my demotion from starting to relieving, even my first year, after I won the Relief Pitcher of the Year Award, I didn't feel I was part of the ballclub. I still felt I was an extra, an add-on. I didn't realize I wasn't. It took me a couple years to get into it. And all through my career I got a bigger kick out of saving games for the starter than winning them myself. Because when I did that, I felt I was helping someone else on the ballclub instead of helping Dick Radatz. Until my last day in the big leagues, I always had the feeling, 'If I could save this one . . .'

"The worst feeling in the world was coming in after a fellow left me a 2–1 lead, and I'd blow it for him. I didn't want to look the poor fellow in the face. He's trying to make a living, and I screwed it up for him. But I overcame that, too. If I blew a game, I'd say to one of my starting pitchers, 'Gee, I'm really sorry.' They'd say, 'The next five you're going to save for me. Don't even worry about it.' But I did.

"And I did have a big year in '62 [9–6, 2.24 ERA, 24 saves]. I got a lot of ink. I was twenty-five. I had only been in pro ball two and a half years, and here I was with guys like Frank Malzone and Pete Runnels, established stars. I don't know if I can even put that first year into words.

"One day I came into the locker room in Fenway, and there was a rotund gentleman in my locker sitting with his back to me. I thought to myself, 'Who the hell is that sitting in my locker?' I said, 'Excuse me. You're in my locker.' He turned around. It was Mr. Yawkey.

"I said, 'Gee, I'm sorry, Mr. Yawkey.' He said, 'No, Dick, let me get the hell out of here. This is your locker.'

"I said, 'No, Mr. Yawkey, please. I'll get another stool.'

"He said, 'Dick, can I get you a beer?'

"I said, 'No, I'll get you one,' and we had a beer together.

" 'Dick, it's wonderful having you here,' he said. 'You've done a great job for my ballclub. If there is anything you need, feel free to give me a call, and I'll do my utmost to get it done. We appreciate all your efforts.'

"After he left, I thought to myself, 'Isn't this something?' It was like the president of General Motors coming down to some guy on the line and asking, 'What can I do for you?'

"Before the 1963 season, Pinky Higgins, who was the general manager, took me into his office and doubled my salary, which was absolutely unheard of. I went from $7,500 a year to $15,000, which is what they make every inning now, and they gave me a $5,000 bonus for having such a good year, and I was on top of the world. It was beyond my wildest dreams. I felt I was filthy rich, not only monetarily, but mentally too.

"I remember one particular game that year. I relieved Earl Wilson against the Yankees in Fenway Park. I was on a roll, cocky, Radatz in the paper every day. Earl left me with the bases loaded and nobody out against the Yankees in Fenway with a 2–1 lead. It was the ninth inning.

"Earl was aware I was warming up. Johnny Pesky came out of the dugout and asked Earl how he felt. The stock answer for any starting pitcher is 'Fine.' Earl said, 'Fine.' Johnny said, 'Well, if you feel good, stay out there.' He started walking away, and Earl stopped him. Earl said, 'Wait a minute. Are you sure the big guy is ready?' Johnny said, 'He's ready.' He said, 'Maybe you better bring him in, then.' So he did.

"I'll never forget that moment. I got to the mound, and I told Earl, 'Why don't you just go and crack me a beer? I'll be in in a minute.'

"I struck out Mickey Mantle, Roger Maris, and Elston Howard on ten pitches. And that day I threw my hands over my head, I was so exhilarated. I didn't know I had done that. Everybody came out onto the field. It was like the World Series. It was probably the greatest single rush I had in one ballgame. And there was Earl at the clubhouse door waiting for me with a beer.

"Our announcer, Curt Gowdy, came up to me the next morning and said, 'Do you realize what you did last night?' I said, 'Yeah, I struck out Mantle, Maris, and Elston Howard with the bases loaded and nobody out.' He said, 'Over and above that. Did you know you threw your hands above your head?'

"I said, 'No, I didn't.'

"He said, 'The fans loved it. Why don't you continue doing it if you're so moved?'

"And that became my trademark. I did it all the years I was with the Red Sox. When I went to the Cleveland Indians, Birdie Tebbetts said, 'The heck with that Fenway-over-the-head-arms thing.' So I left it back in Fenway. But I missed it. I really did.

"It was special playing in Fenway Park. Fenway Park is so intimate it's like playing a slow-pitch game in your neighborhood. And when you're on a roll, the fans are with you. And because I knew the fans were with me, it put a couple of extra inches on the fastball. They would roar with every pitch. In '63 and '64, it got to the point where they would chant in the seventh inning, 'We want Radatz.' Thank God my starting pitchers understood and never came down on me for it. It was a little embarrassing. But it was a love affair.

"As a team, runs were not our problem. Giving up runs was our problem. We had people who could move the ball, but it was the 12–10 losses, as opposed to the 2–1 losses, that killed us. I pitched a lot of games: 62 games in '62, 66 in '63, 79 in '64, and I shudder to think how many games I would have pitched had we been in them in the end.

"Was there satisfaction winning 16, saving 29, and finishing eighth? There was. I'd be lying to say otherwise. But as the years went on, they became less and less important when I saw friends of mine walking around wearing World Series rings. I'd think to myself, 'Why the hell don't I have one of those?' I pitched in two All-Star Games. I took a lot of pride in that. But I missed the big ring. It's upsetting, but what could I do about it? I did the best I could. I busted my can for every ballclub I played for, and I'm not sure every ballplayer can say that. I can take that to my grave and feel good about it.

"Playing on losing teams was terrible. We'd be going into September fifteen games out of first place, standing no chance whatsoever. You'd start talking about what you're going to do in the off-season. You start talking about fishing trips. 'I'll meet you in January. Where are you going to be on Christmas?' Everything but baseball. A terrible attitude.

"Most of the fellows felt, 'We're going to finish seventh or eighth. Let's bust and see how much money we can make. Because a lot of ballplayers won't admit it, but I will: come August the writing was on the wall where we were going to end up, and it wasn't first place. So it was salary-drive time. It's 'the hell with the ballclub, let's see how good I can do so I can make some money' time. You start thinking individually. It was the overall attitude of the ballclub.

"But it's a natural thing. Losing is very, very boring. You've already played 130 games, and the last 25 are absolutely meaningless, except for the fellows hitting .295 who have a chance to hit .300. You'd rather be anywhere except at the ballpark where the people boo you and call you everything but a baseball player. It wasn't a pleasant situation."

BIG STU, OR THE SABOTAGING OF JOHNNY PESKY

The Red Sox hit bottom when manager Pinky Higgins led his ragtag bunch to an eighth-place finish in 1962. With the team in last place, there was great pressure from the press and the fans for Tom Yawkey to change managers. Yawkey did not want to get rid of Pinky, his longtime friend, so he fired general manager Bucky Harris and promoted Pinky in his place, and then to replace Pinky, appointed Johnny Pesky, who had created a sensation with his dynamic managing in the minor leagues.

Though Higgins and Pesky had been teammates years earlier, clearly they did not get along. During the two years Pesky was manager, Higgins rarely spoke to Pesky.

In Johnny Pesky, Tom Yawkey had hired a man with enthusiasm and determination. A Red Sox star for eight years, Pesky taught the game and sought to instill the best values into his players. Johnny Pesky could have been a great manager. But no manager can be successful without the support of his general manager. Without that support, the players are quick to view him as a figurehead, and take advantage.

It seemed that Pinky Higgins did what he could to make sure Pesky would fail. Whenever Pesky requested that Higgins acquire just one or two spare parts that could make the team a contender, Higgins refused.

When he had been manager, Higgins had engendered an undisciplined, loose atmosphere in the clubhouse. The same eight players went onto the field every day and played nine innings. Then most everyone would hit the bars. They didn't play winning baseball, but under Higgins the players sure had a good time.

Those who had played for Pesky in the minors figured he would bring with him his hard-driving personality and change the offense to more of a hit-and-run, bunt-and-steal type of offense. That had been his game in the minors at Seattle, and he had been wildly successful.

But Pesky knew he needed support from Pinky Higgins to effect change. Without it, Pesky saw he had no clout to reach players who had no intention of veering from the status quo. Whether it was a conscious decision or not, with the Red Sox Pesky dropped his rah-rah approach and toned himself down in an attempt to get along better with the veterans on the team. As a result, Johnny Pesky was never the manager with the Red Sox that he had been in the minors.

Dave Morehead, Red Sox, 1963–68: "Playing for Johnny Pesky in Seattle was a great experience. He was almost like a father to all of us. He was always supportive, consistent, fair, but he was very tough. The game had to be played his way. He had a couple of pet peeves: giving up base hits on 0–2 counts and failing to get a runner in from third with less than two outs.

"I can remember him flaring up at postgame meetings. He was very fiery. After a game, he'd take his uniform off and come out in his sweatshirt and maybe his jock, and he'd start walking around, holding a bat, and he'd talk situations. He'd say, 'You gotta get a ball you can drive.' He'd even swing at trash cans. All he was doing was trying to make the players concentrate. That was his way of teaching.

"One good thing about Johnny: he'd get on your ass, and you usually had it coming, you deserved it, but the greatest thing about him, something that struck with me my whole life, was that after it was over with, he never brought it up again. It was forgotten, like it never happened. It was something I respected him for.

"But when he went to Boston, he wasn't the same kind of manager. Guys would talk. 'Well, he won't be able to manage that way here.' Or 'Yaz won't put up with that BS.' And Johnny *didn't* manage that way. He stopped teaching. I don't know whether he thought when you got to the big leagues you should already know that, but there was no doubt he was not the fiery catalyst he had been in Seattle. I have to assume he didn't think it was needed or that people told him he couldn't act that way at the big-league level."

During spring training his first year, Pesky tried an experiment. Knowing the good teams are strongest up the middle, he wanted to see if left fielder Carl Yastrzemski could play in center. By the end of the exhibition season, Pesky decided Yaz was better off in left, where he had begun. When the experiment was abandoned, the twenty-three-year-old Yastrzemski's ego was bruised. Yastrzemski, who had enjoyed playing under Higgins, quickly became disenchanted with Pesky.

Yastrzemski told writer Larry Claflin, "Yes, I was disappointed. I thought I was doing okay. To begin with, you can't judge everyone as a center fielder in Arizona because of the bright sun and the high sky. A long time after that, Pesky told me he was afraid I would crash into a fence if I remained in center field. I don't crash into fences."

The players could sense Pesky was on a limb, and some of them, like newly acquired first baseman Dick Stuart, took full advantage. In 1963, Pesky had the Red Sox in contention as late as the end of June, but when the team headed into a tailspin, Higgins's lack of support anticipated his firing Pesky a year later. A man who might have been a great manager was disempowered right from the start.

If the actions of one ballplayer illustrated perfectly Johnny Pesky's dilemma in running the team, Dick Stuart's did. Stuart had a fluid, powerful swing that was capable of driving baseballs over Fenway's left-field wall. But Stuart was a one-dimensional player who was not interested in improving himself. His fielding was atrocious, and he seemed to care little for anything except his own statistics and what they would do for his pocketbook. As Al Hirshberg wrote, "Dick Stuart insults waitresses and stewardesses, heads for the nearest bar, shows up hung over, and ignores training."

But because Johnny Pesky had no backup from his general manager, he was powerless to harness Stuart in any way. Stuart knew this, and he made a point of getting into arguments with Pesky and making his manager look silly in front of the other players. When Johnny Pesky requested that Stuart be traded because he was a bad influence on the club, Higgins refused.

Dick Radatz: "Johnny Pesky made one glaring mistake. Dick Stuart would try to take advantage of people. Dick was a big, good-looking guy, dressed to the nines, and he was very proud of himself. That's all right. No problem with that. But I can remember in New York, opening day, 1963. We had been rained out the first two days, and they were going to play on the third day, come hell or high water, just to get in one game of the series.

"Stuart lived in Connecticut at the time, and he came to the team meeting. It was still raining. The field was covered, and Stuart walked in—I'll never forget it—with a beautiful burgundy blazer on, black pants, alligator shoes, looking like something right out of *GQ*. We were in the middle of a team meeting, and we were trying to figure out how to get Mickey Mantle out. Stuart stood in front of the clubhouse door and said, 'Here I am, boys, eat your heart out.'

"Pesky told him to 'get to your locker, get your uniform on, and get with it.' Near the end of the team meeting, Pesky said, 'For you fellows who haven't played for me before, it's going to cost you $500 if you're caught out after curfew the first time, $1,000 the second time, and so on.'

"Dick raised his hand, and Pesky called on him. Dick said, 'Is that tax deductible?' And with that, everybody fell off their stools in the clubhouse.

"Poor Johnny. I always felt that he should have stopped it right there. But Johnny would argue instead of saying, 'I'll see you in my office in five minutes.' He would go back and forth with Dick, and Dick was quick. Not that Johnny wasn't, but Stuart would usually get the best of him.

"Another example. We got on the team bus. As you know, the manager always sits in the front. And Stuart would sit up there also, because of Johnny, to get on him. Stuart liked an audience, and he had a captive audience on the bus. Stuart would sit down next to Johnny and say, 'Johnny, those aren't really your clothes you're wearing, are they?' Things like that. Stuart would say them just to get a rise out of Johnny.

"And instead of Johnny saying, 'Listen, smart guy, I'll see you in my room,' Johnny would start to banter with him, and nine out of ten times Stuart would get the best of him, at least in the ballplayers' eyes. I thought it was demeaning to Johnny.

"I do remember this: We were at Fenway, and I was pitching the game, so I was in the dugout at the time. Stuart came up to bat, and we had the winning run on base, and Stuart had not been hitting particularly well, striking out, and Pesky ordered Stuart to bunt. Three times in a row, Stuart disregarded the sign, on purpose, and struck out. He got back to the dugout, and Pesky told him, 'You big son of a bitch. I put the bunt on three times and you disregarded it. It's going to cost you.'

"Stuart said, 'Let me tell you something, Needle. I get paid to do one thing on this ballclub, and I do it very well, and that's hit the ball out of the ballpark. Don't you ever give me the bunt sign again as long as you live.'

"I don't know what happened after that. Stuart was way out of bounds, but the way he said it . . . that was Dick Stuart.

"Here's a funny story. We were playing the Twins the last series of the year, 1963, and Dick and Harmon Killebrew were tied for the American League lead in home runs with 40. And Killebrew was coming into Fenway for a four-game series. Neither club was going anywhere, so it was a personal rivalry inside a series to see who would lead the league.

"Stuart hit two. Killebrew hit five. The last day of the season, Stuart said in the paper, 'Hell, Killebrew had a distinct advantage. If I could have hit against our pitching staff, I'd have hit ten.'

"That set real well with the pitching staff. But that's how Stuart was."

Gene Conley: "I was pitching against the Yankees one time. This was 1963. My arm bothered me quite a bit that year. I'd say to my wife, 'How can I ever win a ballgame?' but the score would be 8–6, and I would be the winning pitcher. I thought, 'Am I lucking out?'

"But anyway, we were playing the Yankees, it was a Sunday-afternoon game at Fenway, and when I got to the park, the flag was starched, blowing straight out. And New York came in with Maris and Mantle and Yogi and Howard and Blanchard, the whole ball of wax. They were all there, loaded. Kubek, Richardson, Boyer. Ugh.

"Well, my arm was not feeling very good, but I wasn't the type to say, 'I can't pitch today.'

"So we started the game. Packed house. Everybody wanted to see the Yankees. That day Dick Stuart didn't even take infield. Jack Fadden was giving him a back rub instead. Half the time Dick didn't take infield. And that ticked me off, even though I didn't get into arguments with players.

"So I started to the mound to start the game. Dick caught me before we got across the foul line. He said, 'It looks like a lot of white shirts over there behind Malzie today. If you throw over, be very careful, because I can't see the ball too good.'

"Here I was, my arm was bothering me, they're bringing in this crew, with the wind blowing out, and this guy was telling me that if somebody gets on first, don't throw too hard over there! He's telling me he might miss the ball if I throw it!

"I thought, 'Holy shit, get over there and just hide behind the bag.'

"I lost the ballgame. They hit three or four home runs off me. They took me out of the game. I understood that. But I'll never understand the statement he made."

Ed Bressoud: "Dick Stuart was not a predictable person. I can recall we played a ballgame against the Yankees in Fenway. Chuck Schilling was the second baseman, and I was the shortstop. The Yankees had the bases loaded, and Johnny Blanchard hit a pop fly right to first base. It was almost going to hit the bag.

"It went up, and Dick didn't move much. Chuck Schilling sauntered over. I moved over a little bit and got a little closer. Schilling was watching Dick, but nothing was happening, and we recognized that Dick was not going to try for it.

"Both Schilling and I dove for the ball, we collided, and the ball fell. It was a two-run double.

"Stuart's comment was, 'God, did you guys look funny.'

"I don't know if Stuart intentionally tried to undermine John. John was not as strong a leader as maybe he had to be, and that's why I say that maybe the problem was not the ability of the manager to lead as it was with the ability of the team to follow. If you take a look, Dick Williams was a player on that team. And when he took over as manager, he became a tyrant. He thought to himself, 'If I become manager, you will not do that to me.' "

Carl Yastrzemski: "I could never understand why Pesky took it. He was the manager, and for a while he had been a good one. I thought he could have shut Stuart up by taking away some of that $40,000 salary in fines.

"Then he would have regained the respect of us all and maybe salvaged something from the season's mess. In fairness to Pesky, I heard later that he actually did fine Stuart a few times, but the front office wouldn't back him up, which may or may not have been true. Whatever the story, it was a pretty sad situation."

In 1964, the Red Sox finished eighth. With two games left to go in the season, Pinky Higgins chopped off the head of Johnny Pesky.

When it came time to analyze the whys behind the firing, the writers looked first toward Carl Yastrzemski. Yaz had won the American League batting title in 1963 playing under Pesky, but the supersensitive Yaz was the sort of man who liked his manager best when he was left alone and was never criticized, even when he made mistakes and deserved it. Pinky Higgins had been that way. Pinky was like a parent who never scolds or reprimands his child, no matter how outrageous his behavior. If the child turns out to be a monster, the parent shrugs his shoulders and says, "I'm not to blame." And he means it.

Yaz, moreover, had been unofficially adopted by Tom Yawkey. His teammates knew that Yaz had Yawkey's ear. True or not, beginning with Pesky, Yaz would be blamed for the firing of several Red Sox managers.

The rift between Yaz and Pesky came in 1964 when Yaz's best friend on the team, second baseman Chuck Schilling, broke his hand. When his hand healed, Pesky kept him on the bench. By July, Yastrzemski wasn't talking to Pesky. The summer was also soured for Yastrzemski by Boston writers who constantly compared the batting records of Pesky and Yastrzemski. Their conclusion: Pesky, a lifetime .307 hitter, was better. It was a ridiculous comparison; Yaz was just a kid starting out. But the kid's ego took a beating, and it made him bitter.

But if Yaz had a role in Pesky's firing, he was no more responsible than anyone else. This was a team molded by Tom Yawkey and Pinky Higgins. Dick Stuart fit the Tom Yawkey player prototype: he hit home runs, packed the stadium, was overpaid, and lost more ballgames than he won. And worst of all, he infected everyone around him with his negative attitude.

The Red Sox players had become used to being left alone, to being allowed their slovenly work habits. Johnny Pesky didn't stand a chance.

CHAPTER 28

The Kids

TONY C.

Tony Conigliaro was born on January 7, 1945. As a young boy he was restless, impulsive, fearless, and bad-tempered. He hated school. Once he skipped kindergarten classes a whole week, and when he got caught, received his first beating from his mother's wooden spoon. When he was in the second grade, his teacher locked him in the closet as punishment, and at the end of the day forgot about him. Then there was the time at St. Mary's High School when he kept getting picked on by one of the nuns because he was a star athlete. Tired of the merciless taunting, Conigliaro enlisted two friends to help him beat her up.

During class, the three boys crawled toward her desk. When he got to her chair, Conigliaro discovered that his two friends had chickened out. When the nun caught him, he didn't know what to say.

Of his boyhood Conigliaro says, "It's a good thing I was so interested in sports—or else I don't know how I would have wound up. When I wasn't playing ball, I was getting in trouble."

What he could always do well was hit a baseball a long way. He practiced for hours hitting the pitches of his uncle Vinnie Martelli. At age nine, in his very first organized game, he batted fourth, even though he was the youngest kid on the team, and in his first at bat hit a home run.

At St. Mary's, Tony C. attracted serious attention from professional scouts. He hit over .600 his junior and senior years, won sixteen games as a pitcher, and hit long home runs. Small wonder that fourteen major-league teams sent representatives to see him.

He signed with the Red Sox. The team discovered, however, that he brought them not only talent but also a bad-boy reputation. The day before he was to leave for his first minor-league assignment, he was talking to a girl who at the time was dating the captain of the high school football team. The other boy saw them together and began swearing at him. Tony C., incapable of walking away, drove to the boy's house, went inside, punched him in the face as hard as he could, and took a rain of blows from a rolling pin wielded by the boy's mother. When Tony finally got outside, his white pants were covered with the blood of the other boy, and the bone of his right thumb was sticking up through the skin.

Tony's father concocted a story that Tony had broken the thumb during batting practice, and Uncle Vinnie took the rap for the bad pitch. For about a month, however, Tony's father refused to talk to him.

Tony ended up missing two months of his first minor-league season. Nevertheless, at the end of a year in which he played only 83 games for Wellsville, he had hit .363, with 24 homers and 84 runs batted in, and was Rookie of the Year and Most Valuable Player in the New York–Penn League. Conigliaro was still only eighteen years old. Figuring he could beat out any of the Red Sox outfielders except Yastrzemski, Conigliaro fully intended to make the Red Sox at nineteen.

He was invited to the parent club's spring training in Scottsdale, Arizona. However, his ability and temper continued to march hand-in-hand. For one thing, he was hurt that the veterans treated the rookies coolly. Early in camp during practice, a ball whizzed by his head. Dick Williams shouted at him, "Watch where you're going, Bush." Conigliaro took the incident as a hostile attack. The next day as Williams came out of the dugout, Conigliaro fired a ball at the veteran's head. "Watch where you're going, Bush," Tony C. yelled. Williams charged him, but Dick Stuart intercepted Williams. "Watch where you're going, Bush," Stuart yelled at him, shoving him away and keeping the two apart. Conigliaro had made a friend.

He was also making some fans. During the exhibition games, Conigliaro's hitting was the talk of camp. In one game against the Indians, he hit a 572-foot home run off Cleveland pitcher Gary Bell. He impressed everyone with his hustle on the bases and in the field.

Before the end of spring camp, Red Sox manager Johnny Pesky announced his outfield: Yaz in left, Lu Clinton in right, and Tony Conigliaro in center.

Said Pesky, "He can be another Joe DiMaggio."

But unlike DiMaggio, Tony C. was going to get his apprenticeship in the big leagues.

Ed Bressoud: "One of the differences between the San Francisco Giants and the Boston Red Sox was that because the Giants were usually pretty good, the players got to develop in the minor leagues. The Giants did not have great turnover with young players.

"It seemed to me that Tony Conigliaro came up to the Red Sox with very little experience. He had tremendous physical skills, a strong arm, and the ability to pop the bat like nobody in the league at that time, but he needed experience. He needed to know how to throw to the cutoff man, when to pull the ball, when not to pull the ball, and Tony didn't have that. But he came along quickly. The major leagues are likely to do that to you."

Frank Malzone: "I remember the first year Tony came to spring training. You could see he had all kinds of talent, but even though you didn't know whether he was ready for the big leagues, you knew Johnny was going to keep him.

"It was late in spring training during a game. I was sitting on the end of the bench with Tony and a couple other guys. Something happened on the field, and some of the guys started laughing, and it really didn't call for laughing, but it was the atmosphere that was there.

"I can remember Tony got up, a fresh rookie, and he said, 'No wonder you guys lose all the time.' The older guys shut up.

"I sat there and smiled a little bit, because this kid was going to be a player. I could see it. He was so enthused with winning.

"When he said it, I chuckled to myself. I thought, 'He's right.' "

One reason Tony C. succeeded was his supreme confidence. He was consumed by his belief in his ability. In one game against the California Angels, pitcher Bob Lee came to the mound in relief. As Lee approached the mound, someone said, 'This guy is tough.'

Conigliaro turned and said, "I got 11-for-14 off him in the New York–Penn League last year."

A few minutes later, Tony popped up, and as he returned to the bench, a teammate said, "That's 11-for-15." Conigliaro said nothing. In the ninth, he came to bat with the bases full, two out, and the Red Sox a run behind, and hit the first pitch to left center to win the ballgame.

When he came back to the dugout, all Conigliaro said was, "That's 12-for-16."

Gerry Moses, Red Sox, 1965, 1967–70: "Tony had great self-confidence. He believed in himself more than any other player I ever knew. Conig would stand at the plate and challenge you to throw a fastball by him. He would get right up to the plate. And pitchers don't want you up on the plate. They'll knock you off.

"Well, they couldn't knock him off. If you knocked him down, he got right back up.

"One day he told Tiger pitcher Fred Lasher, 'If you throw at me again, I'm coming to the mound.' The next time, Lasher hit him, and Conig went after him with karate chops and spikes. He said, 'You're taking my living away from me.'

"Two years in a row, he got his arm broken from being hit with fastballs inside. Because they had to get him off the plate. They weren't trying to hit him. They were just trying to get him off the plate.

"I've heard other people say it, and I believe it: 'If I had to have one person go to bat for me to save my life, I'd rather have Conig than anybody I ever saw.' Maybe Tony Oliva would be second. If he had been 0-for-20 and you needed a home run in the bottom of the ninth to win it, he'd get it.

"In Seattle in '69 he hit a home run, and when he hit it, everyone was watching the ball go out. They looked back, and Tony was bent over at home plate. He had pulled his back.

"Dick Williams, the manager, ran over and said, 'No problem, we'll pinch-run for you, and whoever runs gets credit for the home run.' Tony said, 'I think I can make it,' and he walked all around the bases, and he took himself out. He missed a week.

"He had a flair for the dramatic."

David Margolick: "I used to go downtown after school, and I remember going to the Montgomery Ward store, where there were a whole bunch of televisions on. It was opening day, 1964. I had never seen Tony Conigliaro before, and I remember him holding that bat and swinging, and it was the most beautiful swing I had ever seen. He held the bat extending his muscles. He wasn't holding it in a comfortable way. It looked unnatural, but there was a mightiness to that swing that I had never seen before. And that day, his first game, he hit a home run. It was the most beautiful, natural swing, epitomizing mightiness and youth and promise, which was fulfilled."

RICO

Tony Conigliaro was not the only kid on the Red Sox. During spring training in 1965, it was manifest that the team would be starting another talented Italian youngster up from the minors, a sensitive, skittish rookie by the name of Americo (Rico) Petrocelli. The haunted Petrocelli, who one year would hit 40 home runs as a shortstop for the Red Sox, was insecure and needed continual assurance that he had the talent to stay on the team. Both Conigliaro and Petrocelli needed a manager like Johnny Pesky or Gene Mauch, one who understood kids and could nourish their appetite to learn and feed their fragile egos.

General manager Pinky Higgins instead hired William Jennings Bryan "Billy" Herman, the former Chicago Cubs and Brooklyn Dodgers infield star who had been a Red Sox coach under both Higgins and Pesky. Herman had managed the Pittsburgh Pirates to a seventh-place finish in 1947. Higgins and Herman were friends.

Unfortunately for Conig and Rico, and other youngsters like pitchers Jim Lonborg and Dave Morehead, Billy Herman chafed at having to play kids, preferring the vets because they made fewer mistakes. But on this Red Sox team, he had to play Conigliaro and Petrocelli. They had too much natural talent not to play.

From the start, Herman made it clear he didn't like Petrocelli. He would pointedly ignore the boy, except for outbursts of criticism. According to writer Al Hirshberg, Herman had "an almost pathological dislike" of Petrocelli. Commented Carl Yastrzemski, "Of all the Red Sox ballplayers, the one Herman disliked most was Rico Petrocelli."

Petrocelli was traumatized by Herman's treatment of him, and often during his rookie season talked of getting out of baseball. Yaz, whose locker was near Petrocelli's, had to keep bolstering the youngster's ego, telling him how great a shortstop he was, stopping him a dozen times from quitting.

One time, after Herman benched him, Petrocelli told Yaz, "I can't make it. I'm going to quit." Yaz told Rico he thought he would be the best shortstop in the league in a couple of years.

"Herman doesn't think so," he said.

Yaz told him he didn't care what Herman thought.

Once, Rico had a premonition something was wrong at home, and left in the middle of a game without getting permission from Herman. His wife had been sick, and Petrocelli kept concocting scenarios in his mind that her condition was turning more serious.

Leaving in the middle of a game is scandalous, and after the game, Herman, Yawkey, and Mrs. Yawkey met to discuss the situation. Herman demanded Rico be traded immediately. Tom Yawkey invited Yastrzemski to the meeting to explain why Petrocelli would do such a thing. Yaz told him about the boy's penchant for worrying. Yawkey was still somewhat mystified that Rico would walk out on the team in the middle of a game.

"Trade him," Herman barked. "Get rid of him. He doesn't want to play ball."

Petrocelli and his wife were found at Union Hospital in Peabody. His wife was indeed suffering from a stomach ailment. Even so, Herman fined Petrocelli $1,000, a huge sum that amounted to one-ninth of his salary.

To this day, Petrocelli refuses to talk about his relationship with Billy Herman.

Herman's relationship with Tony Conigliaro was no better. Part of the problem was that the generation gap was so great, there was no way the conservative, traditional Herman could possibly understand or relate to this new generation of young, wild, hip, free-spirited ballplayers.

Conigliaro, who had cut a hit record in Boston called "Playing the

Field"—and two others: "Little Red Scooter" (it goes *putt putt*), and "Limited Man"—enjoyed bringing his portable record player with him on the road. Conigliaro, Petrocelli, Tony Horton, and young pitcher Jerry Stephenson all liked to listen to rock-and-roll music on the plane rides. Herman and a few of the veterans hated the sound of it.

On one trip, Herman came to the back of the plane and said to Conigliaro, "I wonder how that thing would sound on a bus between Toronto and Toledo." Then he benched him. Conigliaro told a reporter, "Baseball is everything in my life, and it looks like somebody's trying to get rid of me."

The somebody, of course, was Herman. At the end of the season, Tony had to go into the army reserves for six months, and Herman told reporters, "If any of you writers have any pull with the army, see if you can get them to take Tony for two years instead of six months." He added, "We're trying to develop minor leaguers into major leaguers while they're wearing major-league uniforms. It's no good."

The remarkable thing was that this was the year Tony Conigliaro won the American League home-run championship. He hit 32 homers that year, despite missing twenty-four games after getting hit on the right wrist by a pitch thrown by Wes Stock of the Kansas City Athletics, Conigliaro's fourth broken bone in three years as a pro. At twenty years of age, Conigliaro was the youngest player in the history of the league to win the home-run title. But still Herman was after his scalp.

It should come as no surprise that Herman and Carl Yastrzemski didn't get along either. Herman rarely talked with his players, except about golf: club selection, driving, chipping, putting, golf courses. Yaz resented his golf chatter. Said Yaz, "It just seemed to me that if you're trying to turn a team around, the team should be thinking about baseball. So should the manager." And if Yaz had resented Johnny Pesky for not playing his friend, Chuck Schilling, he never forgave Billy Herman for trading Schilling to Minnesota. The ill feeling was mutual.

With Conigliaro, Petrocelli, and Yastrzemski, the heart of the team, unhappy, morale sank. The team finished the 1965 season with a 62–100 record, good for ninth place. Through it all, Billy Herman refused to take any responsibility.

Wrote Red Hoffman of the *Lynn Item*, "I'm reminded that when the Third Reich began its plummet, Adolf Hitler blamed it on everyone but himself. So did Nero when Rome was being converted into ashes. Herman is making Pesky look better and better every day."

Billy Herman had taken over as manager at the end of the '64 season. One of his first moves when the season ended had been to unload first baseman Dick Stuart. The following January, the sadistic Boston baseball writers invited the colorful and quick-witted Stuart to speak at their annual banquet.

Looking down the head table at Herman, Stuart said, "Well, Billy, I hope you're having a good winter. You sure had a horseshit summer."

CHAPTER 29

September 16, 1965

One day during that miserable year lives in memory, however, as a monumental day in Boston Red Sox history, though the importance of it wasn't apparent at the time. The story of September 16, 1965 began when a young right-handed pitcher by the name of Dave Morehead threw a no-hitter for the Red Sox.

Morehead, from San Diego, had been 16–0 his senior year in high school in 1961, averaging about fifteen strikeouts a game. The seventeen-year-old signed with the Red Sox for an $85,000 bonus. Said Morehead, "I saw the Red Sox weren't playing very well, and I saw it as an opportunity to advance fast."

He started in Class A, went to Triple A under Johnny Pesky, and in 1963 went with Pesky to the Red Sox. Morehead was just a thrower, but he was a hard thrower. In his first game, which was against the Washington Senators, he pitched a five-hit shutout and struck out ten. Then he began learning how to pitch. That first year, he finished 10–13 with a 3.81 earned-run average. He was twenty.

In 1964, Morehead dropped to 8–15 and his earned-run average soared to 4.97, but at age twenty-one he was still a baby with a great deal of potential.

At the start of 1965, Morehead pitched well, but in part because of the lack of support from Billy Herman and in part because of the defensive weakness of the team playing behind him, he began to press and lost his rhythm. Pitching coach Mace Brown continued to work with him, and by early September he had regained his confidence and his rhythm.

On September 5, his twenty-second birthday, Morehead beat the Yankees,

1–0, in New York. He came back to Fenway and threw another good game, and on the sixteenth he was in a groove. He threw a no-hitter in front of about fifteen hundred fans at Fenway Park.

Dave Morehead: "It was a day game. Dick Howser led off for Cleveland. Ed Runge was the umpire behind the plate. I was taking my warm-up pitches, and Runge was standing to one side, getting ready to dust off the plate. Howser was taking his warm-up cuts. The Indians weren't going anywhere, and we weren't going anywhere.

"Runge said out loud to Howser, 'That kid out there on the mound is from San Diego. I'm from San Diego, so get in there and start swinging.' He was joking. That started the day.

"I don't think I had better stuff the whole month. I was hitting good spots. There weren't many tough chances. In about the sixth inning, Rocky Colavito hit a high bouncer over my head. Shortstop Eddie Bressoud ran behind second base and made the defensive play of the game. If it had been anyone but Colavito, it would have been a base hit. That's where the luck comes in. Other than that, there weren't many sharp-hit balls. A close friend of mine, Lu Clinton, came up in the ninth inning and flied out to center field for the second out. He ran by the mound and said, 'I hope you get the son of a bitch.'

"The last batter was Vic Davalillo. He pinch-hit. Birdie Tebbetts, the Cleveland manager, was trying to disrupt me. I threw two fastballs for strikes. Davalillo went and ran to the dugout. I don't know if Birdie called him back. I just stood there. I wouldn't look at Bob Tillman, my catcher.

"While Davalillo was doing that, Tillman came out and Eddie Bressoud came in.

"I said, 'It's 0 and 2, what should I throw him?'

"They said, 'You're calling the pitch, not us.'

"I said, 'Okay, I'm going to throw him a curveball down. I'll try to keep on top of it.'

"It was a good pitch, and he hit it back to me. I went to catch it, and I was going to run over to first the way Mel Parnell did in his no-hitter, either step on the bag myself or hand it to the first baseman so I wouldn't take the chance of throwing it away.

"In my haste, the ball hit the heel of my glove and I started to run without the ball. The ball lay on the mound. I went back to pick it up and threw it to first base real quick. The throw was low in the dirt, and Mad Dog Lee Thomas scooped it out. I had my no-no.

"The next day, Tom Yawkey called me up and gave me a $1,000 check, even paid the taxes on it."

* * *

Riding the wave, the Red Sox called a press conference right after the game—but it didn't have anything to do with Morehead's no-hitter. It was to announce the firing of Pinky Higgins as general manager.

Higgins's replacement was club vice president Dick O'Connell. O'Connell, unlike Higgins and Joe Cronin before him, was both baseball-knowledgeable and confident in his own ability to make a trade. Neither Cronin nor Higgins had liked to trade. Trades can backfire. But if you don't deal, it's much more difficult to improve. Cronin and Higgins chose not to do anything rather than risk being wrong, but O'Connell had no such fear and proved himself to be a shrewd trader—with the result that since his appointment on that fateful day, the Red Sox have been a powerful contender.

But Dick O'Connell was not even his own first choice. After Higgins was fired as general manager, O'Connell offered longtime Pittsburgh Pirate manager and guru Danny Murtaugh the general manager's job. Murtaugh, who lived in Chester, Pennsylvania, turned it down. He didn't want to move. So O'Connell, who had graduated from Boston College in 1937 and begun his baseball career in 1946 with the Lynn Red Sox, succeeded Pinky Higgins. Along with Higgins's departure, most of the deadwood scouts hired by Joe Cronin were also fired, as Dick O'Connell began the rebuilding of the farm system. One of his appointments was former catcher Haywood Sullivan, who on November 28 was named vice president and director of player personnel.

When it was announced after the game that Higgins had been fired, Red Sox management was criticized for overshadowing Dave Morehead's feat with their headline-making news. What wasn't explained was that the Red Sox had a pressing reason for making their announcement. Throughout his reign, Higgins had fed stories to his friend Bob Holbrook of the *Boston Globe*. It had incensed the competition, but there was nothing they could do about it. By announcing the firing the day the decision was made, O'Connell prevented Higgins from scooping everyone else.

The next year Dave Morehead had a great spring. In his second start, which was against the Detroit Tigers on Patriot's Day, he was throwing as well as he ever had. It was cold, thirty-eight degrees. There was a little drizzle, and the footing on the field was poor.

In the fifth inning, Morehead was ahead, 2–0. He had struck out nine. There was one out, and Tiger slugger Willie Horton was up. Morehead made a pitch, and Horton hit it. Morehead's left foot gave out as he came down. He felt something in his arm, sort of a pop, as he described it. He called time and asked if he could throw a couple of pitches. Satisfied that he was all right, Morehead decided to stay in and struck Al Kaline out on three pitches to retire the side.

The Red Sox scored four more runs in their half of the inning, which required about twenty minutes. When Morehead went to take his jacket off to start the sixth, he couldn't lift his arm.

Every five or six days Morehead attempted to throw, but he could barely propel the ball thirty feet. He couldn't even comb his hair. Six weeks after he hurt the arm, his shoulder had turned black and blue in the socket and blood had started to ooze. It had been hemorrhaging deep inside and taken that long to work its way to the surface.

He was only twenty-four. He never threw the same after the injury. Morehead hung on with the Red Sox through 1968, winning only six more games for Boston. He was traded to the Kansas City Royals and played a final two years, winning only five more.

As for Pinky Higgins, life took a wrong turn on February 27, 1968. He was driving his automobile near Ruston, Louisiana, when he swerved and ran over a chain gang of workers along the side of the highway, killing one and injuring three others.

He pleaded guilty to charges of negligent homicide and driving while drunk and was sentenced to four years in the Louisiana Penitentiary.

Higgins entered prison in January 1969 and was paroled on March 19. He returned to his Dallas home, and, two days later, suffered a fatal heart attack in the emergency ward of St. Paul's Hospital.

CHAPTER 30

The Evolution of the Red Sox

DENNIS THE MENACE

The Red Sox began to change. But it was a gradual process. For instance, if they thought trading away Dick Stuart in the beginning of 1965 would help tone down the team's wild ways, they were very mistaken. The player they acquired for him was a pitcher named Dennis Bennett.

Dick Radatz: "Dennis Bennett used to carry a gun with him in an attaché case. I could never understand why. One night in New York we were in the Commodore Hotel. I was rooming with Galen Cisco. Galen and I had come in around two in the morning. We came back with Lee Thomas, Mad Dog, if you will. Lee was rooming with Dennis.

"Shortly after Bennett came in, we could hear Bennett and Thomas talking. The walls were paper-thin. 'Where have you been?' I heard Lee say, 'Turn off the light.' Bennett: 'You turn out the damn light.' 'No, you turn out the goddamn light.' 'No, you.'

"All of a sudden, I heard a 'pow.' A gun went off. Galen and I jumped out of bed. I said to Galen, 'For Christ sake, Bennett shot Thomas.'

"We ran out, and there was Thomas running down the hall in his underwear. He yelled, 'The man is crazy. He shot the light out.'

"All I could think of was, 'What about the people on the floor above?' What did they think when they saw a .38 slug coming through the ceiling?"

Jerry Stephenson, Red Sox, 1963, 1965–68: "Dennis and I lived in an apartment above the Playboy Club in Boston in 1966. This was before either of us got married, needless to say. I better not say too much about that.

"Dennis was a great friend of mine. I got married in January of 1967. I said, 'Dennis, I'd like you to be at my wedding.' He was living in Boston during the off-season. He said, 'Fine.'

"I said, 'How are you getting out? I can't afford to fly you out.' He said, 'No problem.' I asked, 'How are you going to get from Boston to Anaheim?' He said, 'Don't worry about it. It's a secret. Just pick me up at the airport. I'll be there.' He gave me a flight number.

"He arrived, and I asked him, 'What's the big secret?' He said, 'I know a stewardess.'

"Turns out he got on a plane and sat in the men's room the whole five hours. He was a stowaway! The stewardess had hustled him on an hour before and stowed him away in the men's room. They put an 'Out of Use' sign on the door. That's how he got to my wedding! Ballplayers just don't do that kind of stuff anymore."

Dennis Bennett began his career with the Philadelphia Phillies. In 1963, his second season, he led the National League in earned-run average with 2.64, but because he hadn't pitched enough innings he didn't qualify for the title. He began the 1964 season with a 9–3 record, helping the Phils, who experts said would finish last, to a first-place lead at the All-Star break. Then, in a game against Cincinnati, his arm began to pain him. Doctors could find nothing wrong, but he lost his next eight games in a row.

He went to the mound every fourth day, and in the two games he pitched without pain, he managed a 1–0 victory over San Francisco and a 2–0 shutout of L.A. During his other outings, the discomfort returned, and so did his lack of success, which contributed greatly to the Phutile Phils' famed collapse of 1964.

During that winter, Bennett was skiing in the Poconos. He walked into the lounge of the ski lodge to have a beer, when a girl he knew informed him he had been traded to the Red Sox. Bennett couldn't believe the Phils would trade him. He waited for the six o'clock news for confirmation.

"Sure enough," Bennett said, "I got traded for Dick Stuart even up. I don't think Dick Stuart could ever live that down."

Only after Bennett came over from Philadelphia, however, did the Red Sox learn Bennett's arm was dead. Philadelphia owner Bob Carpenter, who was an honorable man, offered to nullify the deal, but Higgins was satisfied just to dump Stuart and didn't want him back. The deal of a leading slugger for the sore-armed Dennis Bennett stood. Only in Boston.

Dennis Bennett: "The Red Sox didn't know at all that I had a bad arm. It was funny how they found out. I was invited up to the Boston sportswriters' dinner. During dinner I was talking to Dick Radatz, and I was telling him about my arm problems. He said, 'Nobody around here knows that. You're supposed to be healthy.' I said, 'I'm not.' And so it came my turn to give a speech, and Curt Gowdy, the emcee, was comparing me to Mel Parnell, my being a left-hander. I got up and I said, 'I don't know how you can compare me to Mel Parnell. He's already accomplished so much, and I hope to if my arm comes around and I can throw . . .'

"You should have seen those sportswriters staring at me. There was mumbling going throughout the audience. After I got through talking, I was surrounded by reporters asking, 'What do you mean?' And the next thing I heard, they were going to try to send me back to Philly.

"There had to be truth to the story that Higgins didn't want Dick back, because I know Dick and Pinky didn't get along, and in 1965 I pitched the whole year for the Red Sox. I started 34 games, and I ended up 5 and 7, and basically I couldn't have won in Double-A ball the way I was throwing. I'd have a man on second or third with one out, and I'd pitch around two right-handers, intentionally walk them, to get to a left-handed hitter, because I knew I could get the left-handed hitters out.

"When I first came up to the big leagues, I was throwing ninety-four miles an hour. I was a power pitcher. In '65, I'll bet I wasn't throwing eighty miles an hour all year. The only reason they kept me was to save face over the trade."

In 1965 and 1966, Bennett began to see some changes in the Red Sox.

Dennis Bennet: "When I came over, they were not a good ballclub. There were three big stars—Radatz, Yaz, and Conig. The pitching staff was Monbo, Earl Wilson, and myself. After the trade, everyone said, 'You're getting traded to the country club, huh?' And that's exactly what it was, in the respect that a lot of the players cared more what happened after the game than during the game.

"In 1965, we trained in Scottsdale, Arizona, a fantastic town. Me and Earl Wilson and Felix Mantilla were in Tucson playing the Cleveland Indians, and we decided to go to Nogales, Mexico. We were going from nightclub to nightclub, and all of a sudden Felix disappeared. Well, Felix had the keys to the car. About four in the morning, we didn't know what to do. We had to be at the ballpark at ten for a game. Nogales was three hours away. We couldn't find Felix. He had met a senorita and took off with her and forgot about us. We jumped into a cab. It cost us $112!

"One time in spring training, I ran into this girl, and she gave me a ride back to the Ramada Inn in Scottsdale. I was driving. In front of the hotel I started to turn in, and bang, a car broadsided me. Will McDonough of the *Boston Globe* had the room next to mine. He was peeking out the window when the cops came. It wasn't my fault.

"McDonough wrote about it, and it ticked me off. Three nights later, I was throwing rocks at his door. He opened it. I said, 'Will, come here. I want to talk to you.' He walked over and said, 'What do you want?' I said, 'Get your head over here. I want to show you something.' He put his head around the corner, and I laid a .38 right over his head and touched off six rounds.

"So me and Will didn't see eye to eye for the rest of my time there.

"I always carried guns in my suitcase. Another time we were in Detroit. I had about five guns, a 9-millimeter, a couple other pistols. It was an off day, so Dick Radatz, Butch Heffner, Dave Morehead, and I decided to go to a bar, and we started playing pool. We were beating all the locals, playing five dollars a game. Radatz was cleaning up, and pretty soon the bartender came over and said, 'Hey, you guys better get out of here. They're sending some boys down.' I said, 'What do you mean?' He said, 'The bad guys are coming down here, and they want to shoot a little pool.' The mob.

"We thought we were big and strong. So I called my roommate, Lee Thomas, and I said, 'Hey, Mad Dog, get my suitcase and bring me my guns.' Twenty minutes later, Mad Dog came into the door, and he had five pistols stuck all over him.

"Pretty soon, the bartender said, 'You boys may think you're tough, but you're fooling with the wrong people. You better get your asses out of here.'

"We looked at each other, and Radatz said, 'Let's go.' We were in over our heads. Out the door we went.

"In '66, the Red Sox went to Winter Haven, Florida. There was nothing there. One field to practice on. An old, beat-up clubhouse. I remember the disappointment when we got there. There was one bar outside of town called the Bikini-A-Go-Go, and that was the only place in town to fool around. Maybe that's why they brought us there.

"Nothing against Billy Herman. I thought he was a fine manager, but he was just a nice guy in the wrong situation, and most of the players took advantage of that fact. You'd party every night. You'd do just about what you wanted to do. There was no set curfew. There was no bed check.

"You'd have four or five players and some girls, and you'd have a party. And it might go until six, seven in the morning, and maybe you had a day game that day. And the thing was, you'd get on the bus, and Billy Herman would be sitting in the front seat, and everybody would talk about the party the night before or the girl the night before—'I got laid five times'; 'I got home in time to change my clothes and get on the bus'—and Billy would sit there hearing it all, but there wasn't too much he could do about it because some of your stars were the ones doing the talking, and he didn't have any control over the ballclub whatsoever, because the stars do about what they want to do. They run the club. The organization is not going to get rid of them. They are going to get rid of the manager, and so the manager doesn't have any room to come up to a star and say, 'I want you in on time, and that's it.' Because they know they aren't going anyplace, and he would get fired. Which eventually happened anyway. So Billy let them do whatever they wanted.

"And everybody else did what they wanted to, because they saw the stars getting away with it, so they figured, 'If they can do it, I can too.'

"Besides, we weren't going anyplace in the pennant race. Everyone could see we were going to finish sixth or seventh. But then, in the second half of '66, some of the young prospects came around—Joe Foy, Jim Lonborg, Jerry Stephenson, Dave Morehead—and about halfway through the season, most of us started to realize, 'Hey, we've got something here. We're going to surprise some people.'

"And halfway through the '66 season, the attitude began to change. The partying slowed down. I won't say it stopped, but it definitely slowed down. You start taking a little pride in yourself. You start putting the club ahead of personal stats.

"I can remember when we were going bad, I was never a selfish player, but it seemed you didn't care whether you won or lost unless you were pitching the game, and guys didn't care if we won or lost so long as they got their two hits or drove in two runs. After the game, it was, 'Let's get dressed and go out on the town.' Until the second half of '66.

"I, for one, started realizing, 'Hey, this club has some potential.' Radatz got traded. We had Petrocelli, Foy, Lonborg, Conigliaro, and Yaz was always a great player. We saw the potential, and anticipated the 1967 season.

"I felt, 'Maybe we have a shot at it next year.' "

THE END OF THE COUNTRY CLUB

There was another reason for the change in the Red Sox.

The day before the start of the 1966 season, Billy Herman called a meeting of the players to elect a team captain. Carl Yastrzemski, who preferred to lead by doing rather than talking, objected. He suspected that if a vote were taken, he would win the election, since the best player usually will win an election of any sort, and he didn't want the job. He voiced the opinion that the manager ought to select his captain. Yaz was outvoted, and, as he had expected, in a secret ballot, won the captaincy. Yaz still didn't want the job, but now he was in a bind. His teammates had elected him. He couldn't well refuse.

Usually the manager handles most of the players' petty gripes and hassles, but Billy Herman, who shunned personal interactions with his players, had called this election specifically to delegate that responsibility. For the rest of the year Yaz had to listen to the complaints, the pleas for money, the sour grapes over a benching. As Yaz put it, "If a guy got out of bed on the wrong side in the morning, he came to me."

The election made Yaz's life difficult, because his position gave him special access to the manager and added reason to confer with owner Tom Yawkey. Some players considered him to be a management tool. But at the same time they would ask him to put in a good word with Yawkey concerning an advance, a loan, or a personal problem.

For about a week Yastrzemski discussed players' problems with Herman, but after about ten days, Herman instructed Yaz to stop bothering him. Yaz, in a situation he'd wanted nothing to do with in the first place, resented Herman for making his job harder than it should have been and for abdicating what should have been his responsibility.

Their dislike for each other intensified during the season. A blowup between them in the first days of September turned ugly when Herman accused Yaz of loafing. Yaz denied it.

Yaz replied, "If you're here next year, I don't want to be." At the end of the day, Yastrzemski was convinced he would be gone, and the subsequent trade rumors in the papers fractured his concentration to such an extent that he was no longer playing very well.

Forced to choose between his manager and his star player, Tom Yawkey chose Yaz. The Red Sox owner fired Billy Herman on September 8, 1966, and veteran Pete Runnels, two-time American League batting champion, took over on an interim basis. Runnels was asked to take the job in 1967, too, but declined. A couple of years later, he told Red Sox pitcher Darrell Brandon, "I had the chance to take the ballclub, but I had ulcers and I didn't want to do it because of my health."

The Red Sox played .500 ball for the last sixteen games of the 1966 season under Runnels. It enabled the Red Sox to finish ahead of the New York Yankees for the first time since 1948. Unfortunately, in 1966 the Yankees finished tenth. The Red Sox were ninth.

On September 28, 1966, Dick Williams, who had played on the country-club teams of 1963 and 1964, and who had led the Red Sox Triple-A club in Toronto to the Governor's Cup championship two years in a row, was named manager of the Red Sox.

The country club was about to turn into a chain gang.

CHAPTER 31

Dick Williams Takes Charge

Dick Williams: "I signed with the Brooklyn Dodgers in 1947 after graduating from Pasadena High School, and I learned how to play the game of baseball from Branch Rickey. I learned how to play it as a team, the rules, how to be thoroughly versed in fundamentals. Half the people playing the game today don't know the rules.

"We had to go to lectures at Dodgertown at Vero Beach. We'd be quizzed on them from time to time. Three times a week, we went to the auditorium for an hour's lecture. Instructors lectured us on base running, hitting, pitching, stealing. We had to keep notes. Then we'd go out to the diamond. That was how I was brought up, and that was the way I always instructed.

"My last two years as a player in Boston in 1963 and '64 helped me know what had to be done. There was no discipline. If you're getting paid good money, a player should give an honest day's work.

"At Toronto, we had gone through the fundamentals thoroughly. We had gone from base to base, talking about all the possibilities, offensively and defensively, the things that could happen there. And that's what I did with the Red Sox my first year in Boston. We went back to the basics. We worked from square one.

"I laid down the law the first day of spring training. I knew about the lackadaisical play, but I'd have to say that was management's fault. Most of the players are going to do the least amount of work they can do unless you stay on them.

"When I took over the ballclub, I felt it was very important that I establish who was boss. When I was a player, we had too many people running the ballclub. I decided we wouldn't have a captain anymore. Yaz had no problem not being captain. Captain's a mythical thing anyway. He had enough work to do just playing left field and leading by example. He went out and had a year that I have never seen a player have before or since. It was phenomenal what he did.

"And the other thing I did: I like Ted Williams very much. He's one of the best hitters I've ever seen. But every year Ted would come and work with the outfielders, hit fungoes, talk to the hitters.

"When I came, we had a strict program, something we never had before. Everybody had to be at a certain place at a certain time. I even had my pitchers playing volleyball so they wouldn't be standing around, clogging up the outfield, bullshitting. Which Ted laughed at.

"Anyway, Ted was talking to all our pitchers about the slider, but the pitchers were supposed to be someplace else, doing something else, and I said, 'Ted, we've got things we've got to do.'

"And it must have upset him, because after that day he packed and left. So we had somebody else hit fly balls to the outfielders."

Darrell Brandon, Red Sox, 1966–68: "Going from Billy Herman to Dick Williams was like going from night to day. Dick Williams had control of that ballclub. I saw a manager who wasn't going to take any crap. If you showed up five minutes late, you knew you were going to be fined or called on the carpet for it.

"The players understood they weren't going to get away with some of the things they had gotten away with, the lackadaisical play, not running out ground balls, giving excuses for not playing in certain ballgames.

"I remember one game where Yaz said, 'I can't play.' And after the game Yaz said to Dick, 'I want to take extra hitting.'

"Dick said, 'If you're not able to play, you're not going to get extra hitting.' End of conversation.

"More fundamentals were taught. The organization was a lot better. And a lot more emphasis was put on winning."

Ken Brett, Red Sox, 1969–71: "I always thought Dick was fair. He got on my case a few times. One time in '69, when I was playing with Louisville in Triple A, I was in the army reserves. The meetings were held in Boston once a month, and so after this reserve meeting I was expected to go to Fenway Park and work out, so when I got back to Louisville, I would still be in shape.

"I was in the Red Sox offices talking to Neil Mahoney, the minor-league director, and I ended up walking out onto the field at five minutes past five. The players are supposed to be on the field at five.

"I moseyed out at five after to shag and run. Dick Williams called me over and said, 'If you're ever late again, there will not be a uniform for you, son.'

"I almost melted in my pants. I said, 'I was up talking to Neil.'

"He said, 'I don't give a fuck where you were. If you're late again, there won't be a uniform waiting for you.'

"And he just walked away. I was never late again my entire career.

"I liked Dick. Dick didn't get on you if you did your job, were on time, and gave a hundred percent. If you have only eighty percent to give because you're hurt or hung over, that's okay. So long as you give a hundred percent of what you've got. Do that, and you've got a friend. He'll stick up for you.

"He'd say, 'If I ask you to bunt, try to get the runner over.' Now, if that's being too tough, then he's too tough.

"He didn't care if the players liked him. He just wanted them to play for him. 'Cause he got the credit, and he got the blame."

Jerry Stephenson: "Dick was more than fair to me. He gave me a chance to pitch, and I didn't do the job for him. He just wanted you to do the job, and if you didn't do it, he'd let you know. It would be nothing for him to come to you and say, 'You stink.' Which in my case was true.

"I never hated the guy. I have no complaints. He and Yastrzemski used to have words. Yaz was the star, and they didn't get along. They let each other know how they felt about the other. Dick didn't go out of his way to be nice to anyone. He wanted to win and wanted you to do the job.

"In 1967, he played a bunch of young kids who were with him from the minors—Reggie Smith, Mike Andrews, George Scott, Jim Lonborg. And Rico, Tony Conigliaro, and Yaz were still young. It was a young team. Joey Foy, Mike Andrews, and Petrocelli were all twenty-three. Sparky Lyle. Dave Morehead. Myself. And he gave the young guys a chance. That's why we won. Look at that team. We were all the same age. It was like when Tommy Lasorda came to the Dodgers. He played all those guys he had in the minors.

"You have to go with the young guys. He wasn't afraid to play them, whereas the Red Sox for a long time went with the older crowd.

"The guy can manage. He's a no-nonsense guy. Go out and play and do the job, and if you didn't do the job, he'd let you know about it."

THE QUEST

Dick Williams set down the rules in 1967 spring training much as Lou Boudreau, Johnny Pesky, and Billy Herman had laid down their rules at the start of their reigns. The difference this time was that Williams forced his players to obey them.

"I'm not here to make friends," he said. "I'm not in a popularity contest. I want to win, and I want a ballclub full of other guys who want to win."

The age-old Red Sox double standard for stars and lesser players vanished. One of Williams's rules was that single players and players whose spouses had returned home before the end of camp had to stay in the team hotel. Only players whose wives were in town could get their own apartments.

When Carl Yastrzemski's wife left to go home before the end of spring training, everyone looked to see whether Yaz would comply. Obediently, Yaz moved into the team hotel, sacrificing the rest of the rent paid on his apartment. Yaz's attitude was excellent. Yaz had put himself through an exhaustive off-season exercise program, and when he came to camp, he was in top shape. On the field, he performed and hustled as he never had before. Whatever Dick Williams asked him to do, he did willingly. On some level Yaz sensed that Dick Williams could make this group of young, talented players into a contending team, even though it was predicted that the 1967 Red Sox would finish in the second division.

Though Dick Williams could be harsh, he was smart and sensitive enough to do something to help shortstop Rico Petrocelli through his bouts of insecurity. Petrocelli had adored Eddie Popowski when he'd managed him in the minor leagues, and Williams hired Popowski as a coach and placed his locker right next to Petrocelli's.

As Yaz said about Williams during this honeymoon year, "To Williams, each player was an individual, and he handled each in just the proper manner."

Williams set up a weight chart and insisted that every player adhere to it. Williams particularly rode hard two of his young players, Joe Foy and George Scott. He felt he had no choice. It was Williams's hardest task, because he knew the other players judged him to be too tough on the young players. Williams cared only about the end result.

Dick Williams: "The roughest hump I had to get over in '67 was dealing with George Scott. We constantly talked to George about his weight problem. If he didn't watch it, he would really balloon up. He loved to eat and loved to play ball, and could play ball. But if he got a little heavy, he couldn't move as well and didn't do things as well. So I told him if he reached a certain weight, he wasn't going to play.

"We went in to play Anaheim a three-game series. We had had an off-day prior to that, and he packed on some pounds and didn't get the weight down, and he didn't play. I pinch-hit him, and that was it. We lost all three games, and one of the players with the Angels was Jim Fregosi, now managing the White Sox. Bill Rigney was the manager there, and Fregosi said, 'The Red Sox have nine managers and one dietitian.' After we won the pennant, I made sure that they told Mr. Fregosi that the dietitian won it."

Dick Williams had another rule: show up on time. Pitchers Dennis Bennett and Bob Sadowski showed up thirty minutes late for one of Williams's early spring-training workouts. They said the hotel had failed to wake them up. To

Williams, lateness was a sign of disrespect. He chastised them in front of the rest of the team, and then he ordered the hotel to call each player at seven A.M. every day. Sadowski didn't make the team, and Bennett was traded to the Mets by the end of June.

By the end of spring training, Dick Williams was finding the job demanding and not much fun. Said Williams, "After six weeks in Winter Haven, when spring training finally came to an end, I thought, 'When is this supposed to get fun?' I had pissed off an entire team, alienated its greatest star ever [Ted Williams], and—oh, people in Las Vegas were saying we were 100-to-1 shots to win the pennant."

Ever the realist, Williams predicted to reporters only that the Red Sox would win more games than they would lose. In other words, he was predicting a first-division finish. He would end up doing a lot better than that. The players could see the difference in attitude under Williams.

Dennis Bennett: "I always felt that the change on the ballclub came when we played Detroit, not more than a month into the season. Jim Lonborg was pitching, and Joe Foy, who usually started, for some reason didn't start this game. And you know when a regular gets sat down, he's not real happy. Joey was down and angry and mad.

"But Lonborg was pitching and it was the sixth inning, and we were ahead. The Tigers had the bases loaded and no outs. Everyone was sitting on the bench nonchalant, saying, 'Here we go again,' and all of a sudden Joey got up and hit the edge of the bench with his fist and started yelling. He turned around and said, 'Hey, come on. Get up here. Let's get Lonnie through this. Let's root for him. Let's get him out of this situation.'

"For a regular who was benched to say that, it really brought the club together. And Lonnie got out of it.

"Maybe no one else even considered this. Maybe they don't remember it, but I do distinctly. From that game on, we took off. From then on, everyone was pulling for each other instead of everyone sitting back on the bench and thinking their own thoughts. And every game on, everyone was standing up, yelling and pulling for each other. You didn't see that before. Before that, a lot of times Yaz would hit a home run and run past Conig and Conig would barely even acknowledge it. Conig would hit one, and Yaz would think, 'Ah, Christ, there he goes hitting another one.' Yaz would hit one, and Conig would think, 'There, he's gonna get all the glory.'

"But now when Conig would hit one, everybody would pound him on the back. Yaz would hit one and it was 'let bygones be bygones.' Let's forget everything and go.

"And everybody started pulling for everybody else in '67. Joey Foy leading the cheers to me was the turnaround. In my eyes, that was the turnaround of the whole year.

"Before I was traded [for having one too many run-ins with Williams], I just knew the ballclub was going someplace. At that time we were only a couple games out of first, and you could feel it. It was two weeks before the All-Star break. There was a sense that instead of being the last one at the park, everyone was showing up two hours before you were supposed to be there."

The country club disappeared. With the backing of general manager Dick O'Connell, Dick Williams could set the rules and the tone without having to worry that the front office wouldn't back him up. He was a bastard every day, giving no ground, accepting nothing less than perfection, and railing at the players and in the press when he didn't get it. He fought with umpires as though he hated them. His goal was to inspire his players. He wanted everyone—including the umpires—to know the Red Sox were serious about winning. When he was thrown out of a game at Fenway Park, the fans leapt to their feet to cheer him.

Meanwhile, for the first time in his career, Yastrzemski was showing signs of being a Hall of Fame player. In June, Chicago White Sox manager Eddie Stanky commented that Yaz was an All-Star "from the neck down." The next day in a doubleheader, Yaz went six-for-nine and homered his final at bat. As he headed for home, Yaz tipped his cap to Stanky.

In Washington one night, Yaz was supposed to take the night off. Williams wanted him to rest. But Yastrzemski insisted on playing and homered in his first at bat and in his last. In Detroit, he tied a game with a homer in the ninth. Dalton Jones won it in the tenth. In 1967, Yaz arrived.

Three months into the season, the Red Sox were playing about as well as Williams had predicted. On July 13, the team was at 42–40, and they were no longer patsies. They were just six games out of first place.

Beginning on July 14, the Red Sox won ten games in a row. Following the tenth win, the team was one-half game behind the Chicago White Sox. When the plane arrived from Cleveland at Boston's Logan Airport, ten thousand cheering fans were waiting.

Joked Yastrzemski, who had never seen such a reception before, "Does anyone know if they're hostile?"

CHAPTER 32

Tony C. Is Beaned

Just when the momentum of the Red Sox seemed unstoppable, tragedy struck. It is a day remembered by every Red Sox fan: the beaning of Tony Conigliaro.

Dave Morehead: "I was sitting on the top step of the dugout, charting pitches, right there by the corner closest to the on-deck circle. I was talking to Fitzie, the clubhouse man. Tony was up. I was watching him. [The Angels'] Jack Hamilton threw the pitch, and Tony never moved a muscle. He had to have lost sight of the ball. There was a lot of talk it was a spitter.

"The ball hit him right in the cheek. It was frightening. His left eye was closed before our trainer, Buddy Leroux, got to him. They carried him off on a stretcher."

Darrell Brandon: "Tony C. once said to me, 'I'm the best fastball hitter in the American League.' He believed it, and he had the perfect swing for Fenway Park. In my mind, he would have hit 600 home runs if he hadn't gotten injured. No doubt in my mind.

"I was in the bullpen that night. Jack Hamilton was the pitcher who hit him, and later I played with Jack in Triple A in Tucson. We were sitting in a bar talking about the fact that it happened and that Tony had so many problems after that. He had had a few drinks, and that night he admitted to throwing a spitball. Jack said he hated that it had happened. Believe me, it bothers him to this day that he did that. He didn't mean to hit him, believe me. It was a pitch that got away.

"A spitball is a dangerous pitch. That's the reason they outlawed it. Because if you throw it, it moves about a foot, in any direction, straight down, straight up, depending on where you release it from, and of course, Tony C. never gave an inch to anybody. He protected the inside part of the plate and dared you to throw inside. And when you did, he'd turn and take you into the net.

"But that night, the ball ran in on him and got him. He didn't have a chance to move. It hit him in the area just under the left eye, shattering it."

Dick Williams: "My heart nearly stopped. I raced to the plate and saw a man lying motionless, with blood rushing from his nose and a left eye already beginning to blacken and swell as we watched. In a few minutes he started flipping his legs around in agony, and we could no longer watch. While all of us stood around looking at something else, anything else, a stretcher was finally brought out and Conigliaro was carried off. Tony and I had our disagreements, but at this moment I actually prayed."

Tony Conigliaro: "Funny, you never go up there thinking you're going to be hit, and then in a fraction of a second you know it's going to happen. When the ball was about four feet from my head, I knew it was going to get me. And I knew it was going to hurt, because Hamilton was such a hard thrower. I was frightened. I threw up hands up in front of my face and saw the ball follow me back and hit me square in the left side of the head. As soon as it crunched into me, it felt as if the ball would go in my head and come out the other side; my legs gave way and I went down like a sack of potatoes. Just before everything went dark, I saw the ball bounce straight down on home plate. It was the last thing I saw for several days."

Gerry Moses: "I remember Buddy Leroux telling me, 'He was very lucky. He could have died that night.' Before they got him to the hospital, some people were concerned he might. The ball hit him about a half-inch from where it would have killed him."

Frank Malzone: "He would have broken a lot of home-run records if he hadn't gotten hurt. He had a great swing for Fenway, and he hit balls a long way on the road. But he got beaned and lost his eyesight and went into a coma and had a heart attack."

Rich Hershenson: "The Don McLean sentiment, 'The day the music died,' comes to mind.

"The consequences couldn't be felt when it happened. It was, 'Oh, he's beaned, and it's terrible,' but I was hoping he'd be back in a week. And then it became more and more sickening when he couldn't come back, though the Sox did manage to pick up Ken Harrelson, who picked up the slack in a totally different way. He just wasn't exciting the way Conigliaro was.

"Then, in later years, it was sickening when he came back. It was incredible he could still hit thirty homers one year after that, but what I was noticing, he was actually moving both feet before the ball came in. He was never the same again."

THE HAWK

Nevertheless, the Red Sox persevered. One reason the Red Sox contended all year round was that general manager Dick O'Connell communicated with manager Dick Williams constantly, listened to what he had to say, and acted. O'Connell was one general manager unafraid to make a decision or a trade. A baseball club needs spare parts all season long as injuries and fatigue and slumps take their toll. Whenever Williams needed a man, O'Connell was there to supply him.

Dick Williams: "Dick O'Connell was the best man I've ever worked for. He was a business person, but he would go with the baseball people's ideas. I'd say what we needed, and he'd say, 'Can you use so-and-so?' I'd say, 'If you can get him.' "

O'Connell's first stroke in 1967 was to trade pitcher Don McMahon to the Chicago White Sox for infielder Jerry Adair. At the time, the White Sox were five games in front. The year before, Baltimore had traded Adair to the White Sox. That year, Baltimore won the pennant. Adair took a ribbing. He pondered missing out on two pennant winners two years in a row.

The Red Sox also needed another starting pitcher, so the next day, O'Connell risked the displeasure of Tom Yawkey by trading Tony Horton, one of his young potential stars, for veteran righthander Gary Bell. Yawkey had paid $125,000 to sign Horton, but after the trade, Gary Bell won twelve big games the rest of the way. Along with Jim Lonborg, Bell became a mainstay that year.

Gary Bell, Red Sox, 1967–68: "I got off to a 1–5 start for Cleveland in 1967, and the Indians felt it was my time to start going downhill. I had no idea the Red Sox were going to do anything. They hadn't done much in many years. One of the main reasons they got me was that I had always pitched pretty well against them in Fenway, and when you pitch well against a team, your value may be greater to them. It turned out the trade was good for Mr.

Yawkey, even though he didn't really want to give Tony Horton up. But they took a shot at winning the pennant one year and losing a player who could play five or six years. And it turned out that way. I won twelve games after coming over on June 15, and we won it by one, so obviously it helped.

"In the first five games I pitched, we won four, and then I got shut out 1–0. Coming to a new club and doing well right out of the chute, that breaks the ice, makes you feel comfortable and part of the team.

"We had a young club—Conigliaro, Yaz, Reggie Smith, Mike Andrews, and Rico—and hell, they were good ballplayers, young and full of vinegar."

Then, on August 3, O'Connell acquired veteran Yankee catcher Elston Howard. In April, with the Yankees, Howard had broken up a no-hit try by Red Sox rookie pitcher Billy Rohr by singling with two outs in the ninth inning. Howard had plenty of experience in postseason play and would be a settling influence on the young Boston pitching staff.

And finally, faced with having to replace a terribly injured Tony Conigliaro, O'Connell acted quickly and decisively. He signed Ken "Hawk" Harrelson, the star first baseman for Charlie Finley's Kansas City A's, to fill Conigliaro's spot in right field. It was a dramatic, important move that boosted the morale of the Red Sox team and kept it in contention for the pennant.

The Red Sox got Hawk Harrelson because of the turbulent nature of Kansas City owner Charlie Finley. Harrelson had begun his career with the A's in 1963. In 1965, he had a salary of $8,000. When he ended up hitting 23 home runs, he asked for a $16,000 contract for '66, but settled for $12,000. The problem was, Harrelson needed more money than that to feed the lifestyle to which he aspired. To buy a house, he borrowed about five thousand dollars from Finley, and agreed to let Finley take some money out of his paycheck each pay period. Finley did just that—and left him so little in his checks that Harrelson's list of angry creditors grew.

The two men clashed on other issues as well. Finley, a rare owner who knew talent and who put together one of the most powerful teams in the game's history, could be neurotically cheap and petty. He steamed because Harrelson was in the habit of throwing practice baseballs to fans in the stands. He steamed because he wanted the players to wear their socks down low, and Harrelson refused. After one game, Finley fined him a hundred dollars because of the way he wore his socks. Now it was Harrelson's turn to fume. Finley, of course, got the last laugh. In June of 1966, he traded him to the Washington Senators, where Harrelson clashed with manager Gil Hodges.

Then, in June 1967, the mercurial Finley bought Harrelson back. Harrelson hit over .300 for the two and a half months he was in Kansas City, but

Finley made Harrelson's life miserable by once again deducting large sums of money from his salary. Sometimes his paycheck contained as little as $150. A's manager Alvin Dark went to Finley and begged him to stop. His star hitter was suffering from depression, he said. Finley refused.

On August 3, on a flight from Boston to Kansas City, Harrelson and pitcher Jack Aker sat in the back of the plane and drank. Aker was upset. He wasn't happy with the way he was pitching, so Harrelson, doing most of the talking, tried to get Aker to relax and offered tips to make him a better pitcher. Apparently someone complained about the drinking, because on a flight from Kansas City to Washington on August 18, Finley ordered that no drinks be served to the players. When the plane landed, the players were astonished to learn Finley had suspended and fined pitcher Lew Krausse for being drunk and disorderly on the August 3 flight—no mention was made of Harrelson and Aker—and that night at the ballpark, a letter written by Finley was read to the team. The letter, which accused unnamed players of "deplorable" behavior, made the papers.

The next day, the players responded, calling Finley's charges unjust and asking him not to undermine the manager and the coaching staff. Every A's player signed the response, and, of course, that hit the papers too. Finley demanded a retraction, the players refused, and the stage was set.

Finley promptly fired manager Alvin Dark, as Dark knew he would . . . then, a couple of hours later, Finley assured Dark he would get a new, two-year contract . . . then, an hour later, after Dark had gone to bed, Finley changed his mind and fired him again.

Ken Harrelson was very close to Dark, and when the reporters came around for comments, Harrelson lowered the boom. Finley's actions were "detrimental" to the game, he said, and Finley himself was a "menace" to baseball. That ought to take care of him.

When Harrelson read the story the next day, however, he began to worry that maybe he had gone too far. He decided to retract the word "menace," hoping that would end the situation. He was wrong. Finley wanted Harrelson to retract *everything* he had said. Harrelson refused. Finley threatened to send him to the minors. Harrelson told him he couldn't. Finley told him he would suspend him. Harrelson told him to go ahead. Finley asked if he wanted his release. Harrelson said no. He was too scared he would be blackballed.

But Finley released him anyway, unconditionally. It was unprecedented. Finley had rashly fired his hottest hitter. Now Harrelson was scared. He blinked back tears. Was he through? Harrelson wondered.

Minutes after he learned he had been fired Harrelson's phone rang. It was Chicago White Sox general manager Eddie Short informing him that Finley had put him on the irrevocable waiver list, which meant that after four days, Harrelson was free to sign with anyone he wished. Short asked how much

Harrelson wanted, and Harrelson suggested $100,000. Short said he would get back to him.

Now Harrelson's spirits were buoyed: There would be no blacklist! He was officially out of Finley's clutches—though he had to admit that he wanted to stay in Kansas City. It was his home, after all. Maybe Finley would call back and say it was all a mistake. The call never came.

Several other teams called that day, but none made an offer. Haywood Sullivan, the player personnel director of the Red Sox, asked to meet with Harrelson that night at the Baltimore airport. Harrelson and Sullivan had played together and were old friends. The Detroit Tigers called too, asking him not to sign with anyone until he spoke with them.

In the afternoon, Harrelson returned to the A's locker room in Baltimore to pick up his gear. Luke Appling, the A's interim manager, tried to convince Harrelson that Finley hadn't meant to fire him.

Said Appling, "You know how he is—he lost his head this morning. He wants you back. I want you back. We all want you back." Harrelson, offended that Finley hadn't called him personally to apologize, turned Appling down.

At their meeting that night, Sullivan offered Harrelson a package totaling around $88,000. Thank you, Harrelson said, but he had to talk to the other clubs first. That was when Paul Richards, a golfing buddy, called him from Atlanta. Harrelson, a Georgia boy, liked the idea of playing for Richards and the Braves, and decided that if the Braves would give him $100,000, he'd take it. They offered him a package worth $112,000.

That was more like it! Harrelson called Sullivan and told him he had an offer from another club worth over a hundred thousand and was taking it. Once Sullivan learned that the club was in the National League, he wished Harrelson luck. Both Detroit and Baltimore said they would give him more than the Braves, but Harrelson decided he'd have more fun with Richards. Money was important, but not *that* important.

And that was when Dick O'Connell called. Harrelson told O'Connell he had made a commitment to another club, that he had already turned down Sullivan's offer, but O'Connell refused to let Harrelson get away. He said, "You don't understand, Kenny. We've got to have you here. How much money would it take for you to play in Boston?"

"A hundred and fifty," Harrelson said, exhaling.

"You've got it," said O'Connell. Plus a three-year pact.

Harrelson wondered what O'Connell would have said if he had said two hundred and fifty. He called Paul Richards, who told him the Braves could not match the Red Sox's offer. The next day, the player they called the Hawk flew to Boston to play baseball rather than to Atlanta to play golf with Paul Richards, thanks to Dick O'Connell's perseverance and Tom Yawkey's money.

That O'Connell was able to replace a star like Conigliaro with a player of Harrelson's stature and skill was incredible to both Red Sox fans and players. For the first time in memory, the Red Sox front office was acting as a team. Dick Williams and Dick O'Connell were consulting frequently, aggressively keeping the team in contention, fighting to win a pennant. The days of a Johnny Pesky having to beg Pinky Higgins for a player, only to be told to do the best he could with what he had, were over.

The day Ken Harrelson reported to the Red Sox, two games separated the four top teams in the American League. Minnesota, Chicago, Detroit, and Boston would battle through the final week of the 1967 season. The Hawk would fly high in Boston, where he would be the center of attention, a media darling, and a hero, and he would love every precious minute of it. In 1967, he played in twenty-three of Boston's games and drove in 13 runs, many in important situations. Harrelson was unique, and the players, the young players especially, remembered him with awe.

Ken Brett, Red Sox, 1967, 1969–71: "Ken Harrelson was a great guy. He was worldly. He was mannered, cultured. He made putting on his uniform an art. The tongues of his cleats were always folded down several inches, and he'd have a big 'Hawk' written on them in parentheses. His shoelaces were just so. He was perfectly dressed.

"When Nehru suits became popular, the next day he had a closet full of them. Hawk was the first guy I ever saw wear slacks and a sports coat and a tie that were outlandish. Beautiful. And no socks. He was years ahead of his time."

Joe Lahoud, Red Sox, 1968–71: "Ken Harrelson and myself became the best of friends. He used to call me The Kid. Matter of fact, when I first came up, Harrelson and I were both living in the old Somerset Hotel. He had two rooms, one for himself and one for his clothes! It was astounding. There was no bed in that other room. I remember one of those huge foot-lockers was just full of socks. There was a closet just full of shoes, stacked up on each other. Then he had clothes racks on which all his shirts would be lined up. They brought in extra dressers for his shirts and ties. The man was unbelievable.

"He took me under his wing, as Yastrzemski did. But Hawk was never in one clique. He was in all the cliques.

"We would go to a place called the Sugar Shack. At eleven o'clock, he would call a cab and send me back to the Somerset. He didn't want me out past eleven-thirty so the press could write about me. He didn't care about himself, because he had that reputation. And it was a reputation he enjoyed.

He liked playing that role. He liked that charisma. It made him perform better."

Harrelson played in Boston for only one year and a month. In 1968, he was a genuine star. When Tony Conigliaro returned in '69, the Hawk was traded to Cleveland, causing his fans to march in protest around Fenway Park.

CHAPTER 33

The Impossible Dream

YAZ IS UNREAL

As the season entered its final weeks, a feeling of euphoria permeated the Red Sox, largely owing to the player who had made it possible for the Red Sox to remain in contention throughout that magic season: outfielder Carl Yastrzemski. During his first few years, Carl had been a line-drive hitter who hit mostly to left field. Before 1967, the year he led the league with 44 home runs, the most round-trippers he had ever generated in a season was twenty. In 1967, for the first time, Yaz held his bat high—batting coach Bobby Doerr suggested it in mid-May—and with his new stance he was consistently able to turn on the ball and pull it high and deep to right.

In the third game of the year, Yastrzemski had demonstrated that this was indeed a different season. Rookie pitcher Billy Rohr had a no-hitter going into the ninth against the Yankees at the Stadium. The first batter, Tom Tresh, hit a drive over Yaz's head. Yaz broke back, ran as hard and far as he could, and dove in full stride, extending his glove hand as he grabbed the ball just before it hit the ground. He landed, tumbled, and held the ball up in triumph. That Rohr lost the no-hitter didn't diminish in the least Yastrzemski's effort in his behalf. The kid still won the game, 3–0.

In the 1967 All-Star Game, Yaz, Conigliaro, Petrocelli, and Jim Lonborg represented the Red Sox. Yaz, who all year long played best when the most was on the line, that day got three hits and walked twice.

Even when Yaz wasn't hitting, he was contributing with his glove and his arm. There was the game in which Don Mincher of the Angels tried to score the winning run late in the game on a hit to left field. Yaz snared the hit one-handed, like an infielder, and threw it on a line home to Russ Gibson, who blocked the plate and kept Mincher from scoring. The Red Sox won in extra innings.

Two days later, against the Twins, Yaz threw out two more runners, including Ted Uhlaender at home, in a game won by the Red Sox in the eighth. There was the game against the Angels when the Red Sox trailed, 8–0, only to rally and win the game. A Yastrzemski three-run home run was a key blow. A home run by Jerry Adair won it. In the team's second-to-last August game, Yaz homered off Yankee pitcher Al Downing in the eleventh inning with the score tied 1–1. It was his thirty-fifth home run of the year.

Carl Yastrzemski and Frank Robinson of Baltimore were having tremendous seasons. Each was capable of winning the Triple Crown. Frank Robinson had been a dominating player for a long time. Yaz had become one. What had brought the change in Yastrzemski? His off-season weight program certainly had a role. But teammates suspected that that bastard, Dick Williams, also played an important role.

Gerry Moses: "Dick Williams challenged the players to be as good as they could be. For this, he was disliked terribly. He pulled players to the greatest heights they ever had. He challenged Yaz. He put Yaz in a position where he could excel, or he could fail. Yaz had never put it together. He had had spots of greatness. But Dick didn't baby him. He treated him like the rest of the guys, and from that point on, Yaz grew up.

"Maybe it was Yaz's time to grow up, and Dick Williams gets credit for it. Sooner or later, it was bound to happen. But Williams played a part in it."

Under Billy Herman, Yastrzemski had been elected captain. But under Dick Williams, Yastrzemski actually *became* the captain. As a youngster, Yastrzemski the perfectionist would play with a quiet desperation punctuated by bursts of powerful emotion—busting up clubhouses, shattering bats, protesting called strikes.

In 1967, Yaz proved himself steady and cool.

"Yaz reminds me of John Wesley Harding, the outlaw," said Ken Harrelson. "Wes Harding was a quiet man, the most feared gunman because of his great cool—he'd never draw wild, but he was known as the quickest. See, Yaz is the dead opposite of most people. He's uptight *until* the moment of crisis, until something extreme must be done, then he lowers his metabolism."

Yastrzemski admitted as much. "I always feel tense right before a game— that's the time to feel tense," he said. "When the game starts, I relax."

In the past, the Fenway fans had booed him. He was distant, unemotional, and sometimes seemed not to care, though nothing could be further from the truth. If anything, he cared too much, as many perfectionists do. As a result, he sometimes loafed on the field and sulked. As fans are wont to do, they would boo. One day, as the booing mounted, Yaz suddenly dropped his glove and reached into his ears, where he pulled out two wads of cotton and held them up for everyone to see.

In 1967, Yaz changed. Teammate Ken Harrelson could see the change.

Ken Harrelson: "Up until 1967, you'd see him dog it out there sometimes, not running out ground balls, going out of control emotionally. He'd sit in the clubhouse perfectly still, then get up and walk around in a crazy little circle, then sit back down again.

"But in '67, he got over the hump. He proved to *himself* that he could maintain control under pressure—the hell with the fans. It's like a chain-smoker giving up cigarettes: Who else gives a shit? Nobody. But *he* does, and other people respond to the change in him."

On Saturday, August 26, 1967, the Red Sox were in first place. No one thought it was a fluke. No one was talking about the Red Sox choking. The players, loose as champions, knew they were good enough to win the pennant. They demonstrated the confidence of old pros, even though few of them had ever experienced such success, and they played selflessly, with the élan of the young kids that they were. Every day at the ballpark seemed like a carnival.

Darrell Brandon: "During the course of the season, I don't think we ever got uptight. We simply didn't know what was happening. No one ever said, 'We're going to win the pennant.' If someone had said that, maybe we would have gotten nervous."

Russ Gibson, Red Sox, 1967–69: "I wasn't personally disappointed when Elston Howard came. It wasn't like that. Elston helped the club. He had been there before. He handled the pitchers real well. He was a nice guy. He fit right in. We could have used him.

"We were all for one thing, winning the pennant, and whoever could help us, that's the way it went. As far as the catchers, we all got along great, we did everything we could to help each other out. Everybody pulled for everybody else. There was no animosity among the ballplayers."

Gerry Moses: "I never before had experienced the closeness among everybody on the team. We had been picked to come in last, and now we were fighting for the pennant. Baseball is a team sport played by individuals. If you hit, you hit alone. If you pitch, you pitch alone, and you hope everyone does his part. The '67 team was the greatest relationship I have ever seen. Guys who were playing behind other guys were pulling for them. They weren't saying, 'Miss it, so I can get in.' Or 'Strike out, so I can get a chance.' Everybody was pulling for one another. There was the greatest closeness I have ever seen on any team I had ever been on.''

Dave Morehead: "There was no pressure in '67. It was fun. You had the camaraderie and no bitching and moaning, 'cause you're pulling for one thing, to win, and that's what was really exciting. I tell you, it was fun to be wrapped up in a pennant race, probably the most exciting pennant race that has ever been.

"I remember we were out in Los Angeles with about two weeks to go, and they put up the standings, and there was a half game separating the first five teams. It was phenomenal and exciting."

As the season wound down to its nail-biting conclusion, Carl Yastrzemski was asked whether the pressure was getting to him. The question was first met by thoughtful silence. Then he said, "There shouldn't be any pressure in a pennant race. You should enjoy it. My first six years here, I played on teams that finished thirty to forty games out of first place—*that's* pressure. In a pennant race, you can play at a higher level, you can go beyond yourself. When you're forty games out and make a great catch, who cares? It won't have the same meaning. Nothing you can do will have much meaning. Knowing that is the worst pressure of all.''

In the final twenty-seven games, the Red Sox won sixteen. In those twenty-seven games, Carl Yastrzemski was 40-for-96—.417. In those twenty-seven games, he drove in 26 runs and scored 24.

In the final two games of the season, Carl Yastrzemski would make himself forever immortal in Boston.

THE FINAL STRETCH

Dick Williams: "At the start of the final week of the season, there were four clubs involved in the race—the White Sox, the Tigers, the Twins, and our club. We played on Tuesday and Wednesday against Cleveland, managed by Joe Adcock, and we lost both ballgames. It looked like we were going to be knocked out of the race.

"Well, the White Sox, who were in first place, went in to play Kansas City a doubleheader on Thursday, and they faced two young, unknown kids, Chuck Dobson and Catfish Hunter. The White Sox lost both games, and that put us back in the race. And they went to Washington and they lost the next day. Which eliminated them, even though two days before they were in first place. That's how close the race was.

"Detroit, which was playing the Angels in Detroit, got rained out on Thursday, so they had a doubleheader scheduled for Friday, and I'll be doggone, we were off Thursday and Friday, and they got rained out on Friday, so they had a doubleheader Saturday and a doubleheader Sunday.

"Minnesota was in first place, and we had two games against them. If Minnesota wins one of them, they win it, unless Detroit can win three out of four."

Williams started Jose Santiago against the Twins' Jim Kaat on Saturday. Yastrzemski and Twins slugger Harmon Killebrew were engaged in a duel for the home-run title. Before the game, Santiago promised Yastrzemski that Killebrew wouldn't hit a home run. The two were tied for the home-run lead at 43. Yaz promised Santiago he would hit one. They shook hands.

The Twins scored a run in the first inning on a walk and three singles. Kaat struck out four in the first two and two-thirds innings and looked unbeatable. Then, unexpectedly, Kaat called time. The trainer came out to the mound. He had pulled a tendon in his pitching arm. It had never happened to him before.

Darrell Brandon: "If Jim Kaat hadn't hurt his elbow, we might not have won the pennant. He blew out his elbow. He was pitching unbelievably that Saturday. Jim Kaat just shut down Yaz, who was on a roll.

"They brought in a reliever, and it was all over."

Luck would continue to play a part in the race. In the fifth inning, Reggie Smith led off with a double to left center. Williams sent Dalton Jones to pinch-hit for Russ Gibson. Jones hit a soft bouncer to rookie second baseman Rod Carew, but the ball took a bad hop and hit Carew in the left shoulder. Everyone was safe.

With two out, Jerry Adair singled in one run. Yaz then hit a bouncer toward Killebrew at first. Killebrew couldn't reach it. But Carew could. He looked to throw to first for the out. But pitcher Jim Perry forgot to cover. Yaz got a base hit and an RBI, and the Twins never recovered.

In the sixth, George Scott hit a 450-foot homer for a 3–2 lead, and in the seventh the Twins again shot themselves in the foot. Mike Andrews got an infield hit on a short roller. Then Adair hit a ball right back to pitcher Ron Kline, who threw to second, where shortstop Zoilo Versalles dropped it.

Yaz stepped in. Lefty Jim Merritt relieved Kline. On the 3–1 pitch, Merritt threw a high fastball. Yaz was guessing high fastball. He swung, and the ball soared into the Fenway bleachers. In the box seats, Massachusetts senator Ted Kennedy was jubilant. Minnesota senator Hubert H. Humphrey, who was there that day too, was glum.

The Red Sox led, 6–2. Yaz and Santiago both had kept their promises to each other.

In the ninth inning, Gary Bell was pitching for the Red Sox against Killebrew. With the Red Sox lead at four, there was a runner on second base and two outs. Williams went to the mound and ordered Bell to let Killebrew hit the ball. An intentional walk would have allowed the Twins an added base runner. Williams wanted to make sure the Twins earned their runs.

"Whatever you do," said Williams, "let him hit it."

Killebrew hit a long home run, allowing him to tie Yaz for the home-run lead at 44. After the game, Williams celebrated the victory and at the same time apologized to Yaz and later to Yaz's wife for calling the fastball that Killebrew hit out.

Commented Williams, "It was one of the first, and last, times I have ever done that [apologized to a player for strategy that forsakes an individual title]. Just the sound of it [his apology] makes me sick."

The Tigers beat the California Angels in the opening game of their double-header and led by four runs in the second game. And then they blew the game for a split.

At the end of the day the standings read:

	W-L	PCT.	GAMES BACK	GAMES LEFT
Boston	91-70	.565	—	1
Minnesota	91-70	.565	—	1
Detroit	90-70	.563	1/2	2

The final Sunday would decide it all. The Red Sox would have to defeat Dean Chance (20–13), a sinkerball pitcher who seemed to dominate the Red Sox. Dick Williams would start Jim Lonborg, who went into the game with a 21–9 record, but who was 0–6 lifetime against the Twins. The Tigers would have to win *both* their games to force a tie.

Yaz couldn't sleep. He was worried. He fretted about Dean Chance and which way the wind would be blowing at Fenway. Yaz was feeling the Red Sox didn't deserve what they were on the verge of accomplishing. When you are a loser your whole career, the thought of winning can be scary.

At three in the morning, he got in his car and drove to the deserted seacoast of Gloucester on Route 128. Then he drove back. He got no sleep on this the most important day of his career.

Jim Lonborg didn't sleep in his apartment either. He wanted to change his luck against the Twins and spent the night in Ken Harrelson's vacated room at the Sheraton Boston Hotel. He hoped it would make him feel he was pitching a road game. Lonborg fell asleep reading *The Fall of Japan* by William Craig. He felt confident when he got to the ballpark.

Before the game, Dick Williams gathered his players around him. He said, "I want to congratulate you men right now on a great season. I want to thank you for all you have given me. I know that you feel you can beat Minnesota today. So do I. Let's go get 'em."

The Red Sox allowed two unearned runs early. A George Scott throw home was high and wide to allow a run in the first, and Yaz made an error charging a hard-hit ground-ball single to allow another run in the third. Dean Chance, meanwhile, seemed invincible.

In the bottom of the sixth, with the score 2–0 in favor of the Twins, Jim Lonborg led off. Dick Williams was faced with a dilemma. It was the same choice manager Joe McCarthy had faced in 1949 when he had taken out pitcher Ellis Kinder for a pinch hitter. Kinder had been invincible, but the Red Sox trailed by a run. Kinder came out. The Red Sox didn't score. That day the relief pitcher cost the Red Sox the pennant.

On this day, with Dick Williams calling the shots, he chose to rely on Jim Lonborg's heart and desire. Said Williams, "If anyone could figure out how to pull our ass out of the sling . . . well, he could."

On the first pitch from Dean Chance, Lonborg surprised everyone by bunting. Cesar Tovar raced in, but bobbled the ball. Lonborg was safe. Fenway Park went into an uproar. Adair and Dalton Jones singled to load the bases. Yaz was the batter.

It was almost impossible to homer off Chance's hard, tailing-away sinker. Yaz had to choose between doing the selfish thing and going for the ultimate, the grand-slam home run, or being satisfied with just trying to hit the ball hard somewhere, even if it meant *only* tying the game. He was greeted with a wall of noise.

Yaz opted for good sense, and he singled sharply up the middle to tie the score. It was then that Dick Williams knew the Red Sox were going to win that day.

Darrell Brandon: "Chance was done. It looked like he was shaking on the mound. Then Zoilo Versalles fielded a Hawk Harrelson ground ball and completely lost it, threw it home too late, and a run scored. And then Al Worthington came in and threw two wild pitches and runs scored. They completely blew. Like they couldn't handle the pressure. We handled it. But we had Fenway fans screaming at them, and that made a big difference."

Dave Morehead: "The excitement is what stands out. I came to the ball-park that final day of the season, and the fans were going crazy. It was a very festive, exciting atmosphere. We didn't know what was going to happen. All we knew we had to win or it would be all over for us. All game long, we were watching the scoreboard. Detroit was playing the Angels a doubleheader. If we won and the Tigers split, we won. If the Tigers won two, we tied.

"In the final game, we thought that if we could stay close, we'd have a shot. Lonnie threw a hell of a game. After it was over, I remember running in from the bullpen. We were going one way toward the dugout, and Lonnie was in a sea of people, and he was going the other way towards the right-field line as the fans carried him away.

"The people poured out onto the field. All at once there was a huge mob, and Lonnie was up on the shoulders of a couple of fans. A couple of guys picked him up, and this wall of people started moving. We were coming in, and he was going out. He was on his own.

"For the players, it was 'See ya later, Lonnie.' We just hightailed it to the clubhouse."

Ken Brett: "We won our last game against Minnesota, and we were listening to Detroit play California on the radio. Everybody in the locker room was there, still in their uniforms, half dressed, listening. If Detroit won, there would be a playoff. We were thinking, 'We did our job. We hope somebody else does their job.' But in the back of our minds we were thinking playoff. There was almost a gloomy atmosphere. 'Oh, no, we don't want a playoff.' Any time something went wrong, it was, 'Oh, shit, the roof's gonna fall in now and pack your bags. We've got a game tomorrow.'

"And then Detroit lost, and it was over."

Dick Williams began shouting, "It's over. It's over. It's over." Tom Yaw-key, who hadn't had a drink in several years, raised a glass of champagne and said to Williams, "I will drink to you." Then he started to cry.

"Mr. Yawkey," replied Williams, as tender as he would be all season long, "I'd love to have that tear."

The final score was 5–3. Yastrzemski had thwarted a Twins rally in the eighth inning. With two outs and two men on, Bob Allison had come to the plate, the tying run. Allison hit a hard drive into the left-field corner. Yaz grabbed it backhanded, and as the third Twins run scored, he got the message in his head: Stop Allison from getting to second. He set his back foot against the Wall and fired. The throw went swiftly towards second baseman Mike Andrews. Allison tried a hook slide. Andrews placed the tag. The umpire swept up his right arm as the Fenway following erupted in a frenzy. Of all of his great outfield plays that season, it is the one I will always remember.

In his final 13 at bats of 1967, Yaz made ten hits. It was a once-in-a-lifetime season for Carl Yaz. He won the Triple Crown that year, even though he had to settle for a tie with Killebrew for the homer title. At the end of the season, he was named the American League Most Valuable Player.

After the pennant-clinching game, Dick Williams told Yastrzemski, "I've never seen a perfect player, but you were one for us. I never saw a player have a season like that."

CHAPTER 34

On to the Series

It was the first time since 1946, a span of more than two decades, that the Boston Red Sox would be appearing in a World Series, and only the second time since 1918. Their opponents, as they had been in 1946, were the St. Louis Cardinals, a team that presaged the modern post–reserve clause era. The Cardinals featured Orlando Cepeda, who'd come from the San Francisco Giants; Lou Brock, who was from the Chicago Cubs; Curt Flood, from Cincinnati; and Roger Maris, whom the panicked Yankees had traded even-up for an obscure third baseman named Charley Smith.

With Maris playing on one Series competitor and Elston Howard on the other, and neither wearing a Yankee uniform, the dynasty that had reigned in New York since Boston traded Babe Ruth was over.

The Cardinal star was a pitcher, Bob Gibson, who had missed two months of the season with a broken leg. Roberto Clemente had hit a line drive off Gibson's right shin, breaking a bone. Gibson nevertheless completed a 13–7 season with a 2.98 ERA. In the four prior years, Gibson had won 18, 19, 20, and 21 games, and in the three seasons following, he would win 22, 20, and 23. In 1981, he would be elected to baseball's Hall of Fame.

Because Red Sox ace Jim Lonborg had pitched in the final game of the American League season, he would not be ready for the Series opener. It was a handicap the Red Sox couldn't quite overcome.

Dick Williams selected pitcher Jose Santiago, who started the first game and homered, and gave up only two runs on ground outs. But Santiago's home run was the only run the Red Sox were able to manufacture against Gibson, who threw hard and inside.

Russ Gibson: "Bob Gibson was more overpowering than I thought he'd be. The first game he struck me out twice, but I didn't feel bad. He got Yastrzemski twice, Rico twice. Punched out ten of us. Heat. And he had a good curveball, too.

"He was the best pitcher we faced all year, that's for sure."

Lonborg, who finished the regular season with a league-leading 22 victories, also led the league with 39 starts and 246 strikeouts in 273 innings. He had had 15 complete games. The future for this 25-year-old bulldog seemed limitless.

Lonborg overpowered the Cardinals in Game Two. He didn't allow a hit until two out in the eighth, when Julian Javier doubled cleanly into the left-field corner. It was the only hit he allowed. Yaz hit two home runs and drove in four of the five Red Sox runs.

The extravaganza traveled to St. Louis for the next three games. In Game Three, the Cardinals retook the Series lead. Nelson Briles angered the Red Sox when he hit Yaz in the leg with a fastball in retaliation for the two home runs the day before. He allowed just two runs and beat Gary Bell, who lasted only two innings.

Gary Bell: "I got beat up a little bit in the first inning of Game Three. Lou Brock got a triple, and he scored on Curt Flood's single. In the second, I hung a curveball, and Mike Shannon hit it out for two more runs. Hell, that was it. When I came to bat, Dick pinch-hit for me. I was gone."

After the game, Dick Williams was still furious that Briles had nailed Yaz. "The St. Louis Cardinals are as bush as the name of the beer company that owns them," he said.

Bob Gibson returned for Game Four. The Red Sox got five hits and didn't score a run. Jose Santiago suffered an elbow injury and didn't last through the first inning. The Red Sox were one game away from elimination.

Dick Williams wasn't worried about Game Five. He knew he had Lonborg. But after Lonnie?

Lonborg threw a three-hitter, beating Steve Carlton. In two complete games, he had allowed four hits, a World Series record.

The Series moved back to Boston. Williams made a bold move when he started rookie pitcher Gary Waslewski in Game Six. Rico Petrocelli homered in the second inning, the Cards came back with two in the second, and then, in the fourth inning, three consecutive Red Sox batters—first Carl Yastrzemski, then Reggie Smith and Rico—homered. The Red Sox led by two.

The Cards tied the game 4–4 in the top of the seventh, on Lou Brock's two-run home run against John Wyatt. After a four-run Red Sox rally, it was up to Gary Bell to keep the team alive.

Gary Bell: "I was in the bullpen. John Wyatt was on the mound, and he threw up a home-run ball to Brock that would have passed the spaceship *Discovery*. My God, it went over our bullpen and fifty rows back up into the center-field bleachers. Geez.

"I came in, and they were hitting me again. I had Yaz plastered against the left-field wall. He was stuck against it with these shots, but we got them out.

"The last pitch of the game, I had a runner on base and Orlando Cepeda was the hitter. I threw him a sinker, and he hit right on top of the ball. It was down the third-base line right on the chalk, and I had to run over, grab it, and throw him out. I grabbed it, and I didn't have a good feel on the ball, but luckily he wasn't a fast runner. I threw him out.

"I breathed a sigh of relief there."

So did all of New England. Dick Williams's gamble had paid off. For Game Seven, a rested Bob Gibson was the scheduled Cardinal pitcher. Williams chose to go with his ace, Jim Lonborg, on two days' rest.

Gary Bell: "Of course Dick had to start Jim Lonborg. He had two days' rest, which normally isn't enough. If Dick hadn't started him, they'd have hung him. It was one of those things that had to be done. There were other pitchers more ready than Lonnie, but because of the year he had and the success he had in the World Series already, Dick had to go with him. I do think he went a little too far with him. I really do. And that's not second-guessing. He had five or six guys in the bullpen who were ready to pitch. Lonnie didn't have his good stuff."

In view of the drama of the World Series up to then, it was an anticlimax. Lonborg gave up ten hits and seven runs in six innings. Gibson only allowed three hits and two runs all day. The Red Sox were well and thoroughly beaten, and the St. Louis Cardinals were the World Champions.

Dave Morehead: "It was unfortunate Lonnie couldn't start the first game with Gibson, and then they could have pitched three games against each other.

"Gibson's performance was one of the most amazing things. We saw that firsthand. He was overpowering. I don't think we could have beaten him if we had played ten times. We were beaten soundly. We did the best we could. Everybody took it like a man and was proud of what we accomplished."

Gary Bell: "It was disappointing. We got so close. We took the Cardinals to seven games, and we weren't even supposed to be there. To be honest, being in the World Series was anticlimactic. Getting there was the biggest thrill of all. No one expected us to be there. You'd like to win, but going seven games with them was icing on the cake.

"The fans were proud of us. That was a great year in Boston. My God, I can still remember clinching the pennant that last day, coming out of the parking lot, and there must have been ten thousand people just raising hell, hollering and going down Commonwealth Avenue, and I was raising hell with them."

Darrell Brandon: "I was not a star on that '67 ballclub, but the Boston fans still remember me, remember games I pitched. They remember situations I don't remember as a player. Boston fans are the most knowledgeable I know of. They really love their baseball. And it's amazing to me what they remember. You don't realize what that year did for the New England area. That year put baseball back into the forefront in New England."

The joy for Dick Williams, a driven man, did not last very long. He had won a pennant, and had lost a closely fought World Series, but it was not long after the final out of the '67 Series that he began the mental preparation for the following year in the expectation that he would lead the Red Sox to a world championship. Williams always believed in himself and believed in running a ballclub "the right way." Williams was convinced that for his success to continue he needed a three-year contract, proof of a firm commitment from the Red Sox management to him.

Several days after the Series, Dick Williams drove to the Red Sox offices to talk to Tom Yawkey about a new contract. Williams's animosity toward Yawkey and his wife Jean had simmered during the season. Williams was the first manager in many years who hadn't been his buddy. Williams wasn't a hail-fellow-well-met type, and as a result felt he wasn't Yawkey's kind of manager. It bothered him that for the first three months of the season, Yawkey never as much as called him once.

Then, after not seeing Yawkey much at all the first half of the season, Williams chafed when, during the second half of the season, the owner showed up in the clubhouse every day, coming around the batting cage, chatting and joking with the players. Said Williams, "His presence in our domain late in 1967 wasn't just a distraction, it was an insult."

Williams was also sensitive to the fact that Jean Yawkey kept track of how often his wife Norma came to the ballpark. According to Williams, when Norma would show up, Jean Yawkey would say, "Where have you been? I haven't seen you for a while." Williams said he was lucky Norma kept her counsel and didn't speak her mind.

Now, with the season over, Williams and Yawkey had to talk contract, and it wasn't easy for either of them. Williams and general manager Dick O'Connell both said they wanted it to be for three years. Yawkey insisted it only be for two.

Williams thought sarcastically, "Maybe, more likely, he'd decided on another steambath buddy for the job."

Finally, Yawkey gave in. After Williams left the meeting, he went down onto the field, where he discovered that a large section of sod was being dug up and was to be transplanted in Carl Yastrzemski's backyard as a token of appreciation from Yawkey.

Thought Williams, "How about that. Yawkey didn't want to give me a piece of his lousy bank account, but he was giving Yaz a big piece of his heart." Williams never gave Yawkey an inch, but *he* still wanted to be first in the owner's heart. Williams was so upset, he left the ballpark without his son. Only after he crossed the Mystic River Bridge did he remember he had left him behind.

Williams had gotten the contract he demanded, but he had such a strong belief in himself that he felt he was *owed* Yawkey's allegiance. As always, it was Williams's way or no way.

The Red Sox held a press conference to announce that they were giving Dick Williams a three-year contract at an estimated $50,000 a year. Williams, talking about the season, said among other things, "We made some mistakes."

A reporter asked him, "What mistakes did *you* make, Dick?"

"I didn't say the manager made any mistakes," he said. "I was talking about the team."

"Did the manager make any mistakes?"

"No," Williams said without a hint of a smile.

CHAPTER 35

The Final Days of Dick Williams

Jim Lonborg, who had just won the Cy Young Award, went to the Red Sox offices to sign his new contract that winter after the '67 season. During the meeting, Lonborg told general manager Dick O'Connell he intended to go skiing. O'Connell advised him that he risked the loss of his salary if he were to become injured on the ski slopes. Lonborg assured him he would not get hurt.

On Christmas weekend, Lonnie was skiing down a slope in Vail, Colorado, when he toppled awkwardly, wrenching his knee and tearing ligaments.

Joe Lahoud: "Lonnie was the doll of the media. He was six foot five, a very attractive man, blond hair, blue eyes, and very well-spoken. He was called 'Gentleman Jim.' Jim was always a favorite. Whatever Jim did, even if it was a mistake, was never criticized.

"No one ever read a lot of information about Lonborg's accident. There wasn't anything printed other than he had a skiing accident and hurt his knee.

"When he came back for rehabilitation, nothing was said about it, not even among the players. Other than feeling sorry for him, 'cause he had had such a super year. But there was no doubt, his injury had a big impact on the Red Sox in 1968, since we basically had the same ballclub."

Gerry Moses: "Lonnie was my first roommate in Boston. Those who faced him before he hurt his knee say his stuff was as nasty as anyone who ever played the game. It was a shame that he got hurt, that he lost his velocity, because his ball was hard. You hurt your hand when you caught him. He threw a heavy ball that came burrowing in on you, down and in. And he threw very hard, harder than most people gave him credit for.

"Lonnie's greatest asset, beside his arm, was his mind. He was a real competitor. Jim's reputation as a gentleman is earned, but it fits him off the field, not when he's pitching. He and Ray Culp were the most serious pitchers I ever caught. He was tough. He knew what he wanted to do. He didn't need a catcher to call the game.

"Sometimes, when a pitcher shook me off, I wouldn't let him. If Lonnie shook me off, I did what he wanted. We had the highest respect for him as a pitcher and a person. He was right up there with the best of them.

"Off the field, Lonnie is a lot of fun in a wonderful, quiet, gentlemanly way. Witty as hell, but he's not an entertainer. He's my dentist, and he's as good a dentist as he was a player. Everything he's done in my mouth is still there.

"I'll tell you what I heard about the skiing accident. Lonnie was the type of guy who didn't want people telling him what to do. He didn't want anyone telling him he couldn't go skiing. He was, and is, his own person. He's going to live to his own mind-set.

"Jim was young and single, and the rumor was he was chasing a young gal down the slope to see what she looked like. Some people said it was Jill St. John. I wasn't there, but if it had been Jill St. John, I would have been chasing her down the mountain too. I don't blame him.

"But if you injure your knee, you begin to favor it, and then you hurt your arm. You learn to live with the pain. Most players have pain. And you can handle that. But he didn't have the same velocity. The ball still moved. He was still a good pitcher. But he was not the Great Jim Lonborg he was in '67."

Jim Lonborg would return, too soon, in 1968, and he would compile a 6–10 record with a 4.29 ERA. It was a year, remarked manager Dick Williams, that indicated he never really returned at all.

Nineteen sixty-eight was the beginning of what was to be a two-year nightmare for the crusty manager. When Williams showed up in Winter Haven, he knew it would be without his ace. And after his arrival, he saw that first baseman George Scott, who had hit .303 with 19 home runs, was obese and slovenly. Scott always talked about the "taters" he hit. All Williams could think of was the "taters" he had eaten.

Thought Williams, "He looks as though he ate Christmas dinner every night of the week." Williams would not forgive Scott for what he considered his unprofessional behavior. Beginning in spring training, Williams gave

Scott the cold shoulder. His teammates felt that Williams's treatment of the Boomer hurt him badly. In 1968, George Scott hit .171 in 124 games.

Joe Lahoud: "George Scott and I were really good friends. George was never in any clique. He would fit in with anybody. Everybody liked the Boomer. I remember when I first came up to the Instructional League, he'd wake me at 7:15 in the morning, drag me out of bed, and we'd be at the batting cage at 7:35. Me and him would just throw to each other in the cage.

"He'd be running with a wet suit because he had an overweight problem, which he was always aware of, and I remember Dick Williams used to just hound him about it. 'Don't eat potatoes. Don't eat meat.' And if he didn't perform well, Dick would say, 'Did you eat a pound of potatoes last night?'

"And that bothered George, so he worked harder and harder. The guy lots of times couldn't perform because he was dead tired. Totally exhausted. The man would run two, three miles in a rubber suit before a ballgame, and then after the ballgame run another two, three miles. People didn't understand that.

"Even the players got on him about his weight. And he was very sensitive about that.

"George Scott was a likable, nice guy. If you humiliated or took away some of the confidence from George Scott, he became one-third the ball-player he would be if you just patted him on the back and told him how great a job he was doing. Nobody worked harder than George Scott. He was outspoken, but supersensitive.

"George needed all the moral support he could get, because he was never that sure of himself. He knew he could hit the taters, and he knew he could play first base, but he didn't know if he could do everything that was expected of him."

Gerry Moses: "George Scott went from .301 in '67 to .171 in '68. At the end of the year, I asked Scotty about it. Scotty was from Greenville, Mississippi, and I was from Yazoo City, so we used to call each other 'Home Boy.' I sat with him and said, 'George, what's wrong? What's happening?'

"He said, 'He won't play me. The guy just won't play me.' I didn't know what he was talking about. I said, 'Boomer, you've been up 400 times.' He said, 'Yeah, but he doesn't have any confidence in me. He won't put me out there and leave me alone.'

"George was a great defensive player. He was a good offensive player. He could get some big hits. He was also an entertainer. People loved to watch him play.

"But in his own mind, he was the kind of guy who had to be built up. You can't knock him down. And Dick would beat him down. Dick destroyed his confidence.

"Once you get to the big leagues, there is only one thing to work out, and that's between your ears, your psyche. And you can't afford to let anyone destroy that. Most great athletes have the inner strength that makes them excel. Boomer lost that in '68. Dick really hurt him. Great managers handle individuals to get them to play to the best of their ability. Dick handled everyone the same way.

"Dick complained Boomer was overweight. He was. Boomer was always struggling with his weight, and that hurt him during the season. He'd come to spring training in a sweatsuit, and between the whirlpool and the sweatsuit, he'd be worn out.

"I don't think you can blame Dick Williams for doing that to George Scott. You have to blame George Scott for allowing someone to do that to him. You can't do that. You just say to him, 'Whatever you think, I don't agree with you. If you don't play me, fine. You are not going to run me down.'

"And you have to keep saying it in your mind over and over again. For every negative thought, if you put two positives there, you'll overcome it. You have to say to yourself, 'I can do it. Dick Williams can't stop me.' You may have to ride the bench for a year and get traded, but eventually you'll overcome. You can't allow anyone to do that to you."

Williams also had problems with Reggie Smith. Smith was a hard-nosed, no-nonsense man who took little guff, even from his manager.

Joe Lahoud: "Reggie was the type of player who wouldn't take anything from anybody. If he had to fight to survive, he would fight.

"I remember a fight we had with the Yankees. The pitcher was Thad Tillotson. Yastrzemski was on first, I was on second, and Reggie was on deck. Scotty was hitting.

"We were doing a pretty good job on the Yankees, and somebody hit a batter, and a fight occurred. Yaz and Pepitone were on first, and Yaz had Pepi in a headlock, and I came running right over to help Yaz, because I didn't know if it was real or not, and Pepi was saying, 'Polack, listen, you can fuck with me, but don't fuck with my hair.'

"I was laughing like hell. And I turned around, and here comes the Yankee bullpen running in. And I looked over toward the mound, and Reggie Smith was holding Thad Tillotson over his head, and Tillotson was a big man! And Reggie threw him, and he landed on his feet. I thought, 'Holy Christ.'

"In 1971, Billy Martin was managing the Tigers. I hit a home run, and Yaz hit a home run, and Reggie came up. And the Detroit pitcher got the word from Martin. Martin was screaming, 'Nail him, nail him.' You know how couth he is. And Reggie stepped out and he said to Martin, 'If he nails me, I'm going to get you.'

"The pitcher nailed Reggie right between the shoulder blades. Well, as soon as he did, Bill Freehan grabbed Reggie. Reggie was dragging Freehan toward the mound, knowing that Billy Martin would come out. Billy was notorious for getting the first shot in. We all knew that. And there was a little guy on our ballclub who couldn't stand Billy Martin: Rico Petrocelli. Rico, being from the Bronx, would fight at the drop of a hat and knew all too well how to do it.

"Anyway, Reggie was dragging Freehan out, and the Detroit pitcher saw that his hands were down, and he dropped his mitt and pulled back, and just as he did that, Reggie, who is trained in karate, made a quick move, sent Freehan on his ass, and he just nailed the pitcher, boom. Meanwhile, Martin came running out, and just as he crossed the line, who did he run into but Rico. Rico went bam-ba-bam-ba-bam-bam, and Martin was down on his ass.

"Everything settled down, and now Martin began screaming and yelling, and I yelled back at him 'cause he was on everybody. He said to me, 'I hope you can fight as good as you can talk.' Reggie stood up in the dugout, and he said, 'You want me, you come and get me right after the game. I'll be waiting for you underneath the stands.'

"If you've been to Fenway Park, you know the visiting clubhouse is on the left-field side, and the Red Sox on the first-base side. But they used to park the buses behind right field, and they were leaving to go out of town that day. So they had to walk from their clubhouse around behind home plate and up the right-field line to the bus, going right by the Red Sox clubhouse. Reggie waited.

"I said, 'Reggie, come on. Let's go. Don't get yourself in trouble. It's not worth it. Let's get the hell out of here.'

"He said, 'No. I'm going to get that son of a bitch. If that man had hit me in the head, he could have ended my career. And he was the one shouting out to nail me.'

"An hour and a half after the ballgame, we were under the stands, Reggie and myself, and here comes Billy Martin, and the whole Detroit press. Five or six guys. Martin was laughing, joking, with a beer in his hand.

"Reggie said, 'Here I am.'

"Billy said, 'You want me?'

"Reggie said, 'Yeah, I want you bad.'

"They started to approach each other, and a middle-aged gentleman from the Detroit press jumped in between them and said to Reggie, 'The guy has a bad leg. He's a lot older than you. What the hell is the matter with you?'

"And now Martin began saying, 'I'll kick your ass.'

"Reggie looked at him and looked at the reporter and said, 'Billy, you did the right thing. You brought all the reporters with you. Now you can't lose, and I can't win.' Reggie added, 'But there will be a day when they're not going to be around, and I'm going to kick your ass.' And Reggie walked away.

"Reggie was very moody, very temperamental, very hard to deal with. If

Dick Williams got on his case, Reggie would say, 'Fuck you, I'm doing my best,' or else he'd go into his shell. And then, because of Williams not saying something in a more understanding way, Reggie would do squat for three or four games. Just loaf, dog it.

"There were times when I hated Reggie. And Reggie and I were good friends. Reggie was a nice human being. But Dick Williams would say in the papers, 'If Reggie didn't dog it in center field today, we might have won,' and you'd read the headlines, 'Reggie Dogs It in Center,' and Reggie read the papers. Reg said to himself, 'Okay,' and the next three games he would do nothing. *Nothing.*

"It would be, 'Fuck you, I'll show you. I won't do a fucking thing. I won't do a thing. What are you going to do about it? You want to bench me, bench me. Who are you going to have playing center field better than me?'

"So Dick didn't bench him. Who was he going to put out there, Joe Lahoud?

"Reggie didn't talk about it, but Reggie would let you know his feelings in his own way. Batting practice would be a perfect example. He would go up there and take four or five swings and go sit in the dugout or go back into the clubhouse. And you knew, right then and there, it was his way of letting you know, 'I don't give a fuck today.' Or he wouldn't take infield practice.

"But when Reggie was feeling up, goddamn, he could do anything he wanted to do on the ballfield."

It wasn't just George Scott and Reggie Smith. Dick Williams thought that all the players were too relaxed and self-satisfied. He wondered whether they cared as much as they had the year before. He didn't think so, so to combat their smugness, he ran roughshod over them harder even than the year before.

This was a year in which Dick Williams would fight with the writers, the players, the owner, and even his loving wife. Dick Williams became a monster. He screamed at mistakes the moment they were made, chewed out players in full view of teammates, and shuttled players in and out of the lineup as his doghouse became filled with bodies.

Once, early in the season, Williams climbed aboard the team bus after losing a game. There was a burst of laughter from a player in the rear. Williams thought it was Lee Stange. Stange told Williams it wasn't he. Williams still held it against him.

"There is no way you can like that man," said Hawk Harrelson about Williams. "He doesn't give you a chance to like him."

The players were hurt most by Williams's sarcasm. Said pitcher Don McMahon before he was traded to the White Sox, "If you had a bad game, here came the wisecracks. He'd never let up. I dropped a double-play ball in the eighth inning of one game, they tied it up, and we lost in the eighteenth. He got an expression on his face like I smelled bad or something and he had it all the time I was there."

Over the winter, Williams had disparaged the ability of pitcher John Wyatt. Wyatt wrote a letter to the *Boston Record American* to refute what Williams had said. Wyatt was sold on May 18 to the Yankees.

Said Wyatt, "I been sold not because of my ability, but because of a personal thing. If that man is your enemy, forget it."

Dave Morehead: "When Dick Williams was manager, he was hard to play for. He was insulting. That was his style, his personality.

"I remember one time in Washington, we were playing a game. Whenever I threw to the plate, my follow-through would take me off to the left side of the mound toward third base, like Bob Gibson and Jim Bunning. I made a pitch, and there was a ground ball hit right back over the mound under my hand. I didn't have my glove there, and I didn't make the play. It ended up costing a run.

"I knew I could have gotten it if I hadn't fallen off. I surely didn't do it on purpose, but when I came back to the dugout Dick's first words were sharp and critical. 'That ball has to be caught.' It was in the tone, the way it was said. He was very, very tough."

In 1968, the injury parade didn't stop. Jose Santiago, the team's best pitcher, won nine games in his first eighteen starts and then was lost for the season. Backup infielder George Thomas missed all but twelve games of the season. Mike Andrews was lost for two weeks. Tony Conigliaro had tried to play in spring training, but because he had lost the vision in his left eye, it was too dangerous for him to continue playing.

Despite all this, the Dick Williams–driven Red Sox won 86 games, only six fewer than they won in '67. Hawk Harrelson played full-time in right field when Tony Conigliaro was forced to sit out the season, and hit 35 home runs and led the league with 109 runs batted in. Carl Yastrzemski led the league in hitting at .301. But with Denny McLain winning 31 games, the Detroit Tigers finished seventeen games in front of the Red Sox.

The next year, 1969, it was the same story. Tony Conigliaro miraculously returned and hit 20 homers and drove in 82 runs, and the team actually won one more game than it had in '68. It was only the second time the team had won that many games since 1951.

Despite the winning seasons, however, the enmity continued to grow between Williams and Yawkey, and also between Williams and Yastrzemski. Fueling this was Williams's resentment of the close relationship forged between the owner and his star player.

Joe Lahoud: "Mr. Yawkey loved the town of Boston, loved his players. He was a person who loved the game of baseball and loved the people who played for him. The players were not employees. You're not dealing with a commodity. You're dealing with a family. If you ever needed to talk to Mr. Yawkey, his door was always open. And he always went out of his way to come by and say hello to everybody. He was a very unpretentious, likeable guy, and he just lived and died for the Boston Red Sox.

"Dick Williams most definitely resented the relationship between Yawkey and Carl. Dick made it so perfectly obvious. Many times Yawkey would call Yastrzemski up after a game to talk over the ballgame, not Williams. He would come down before a game or after and go down and talk to Yastrzemski before he went to talk to Williams about it. Yawkey loved his players. He loved Yastrzemski more than any of them. And he loved his players more than he loved his managers. Always. He would side with the players before he would side with Williams. Which is why the Red Sox are one club with a lot of managers through the years."

By mid-1969, Dick Williams had lost rapport with the front office. In July, *Boston Globe* reporter Clif Keane asked Yawkey to rate his manager on a scale of 1 (excellent) through 4 (poor). Yawkey rated Williams a 2 (good).

Convinced he was the perfect manager and that he deserved a top rating, especially after winning for Yawkey his first pennant since 1946, Williams was deeply offended. Coach Eddie Popowski had advised Williams not to say anything. Williams, stubborn and stung, wouldn't listen. He felt he had to speak his mind.

He said, "Mr. Yawkey, I don't care about myself, but this doesn't help the ballclub one bit. I didn't think your coming into the locker room as often as you do helps either. Too many times I've eaten someone out for a mistake and then seen you put your arms around his shoulders as if to comfort him."

According to the *Globe*'s Keane, Yawkey said about the incident: "Williams was in my office at 9:40 the next morning. We discussed it. 'Hell, what did you want me to say? That you're a combination Stengel, McGraw, and Connie Mack after just two and a half years?' I didn't mean it to be a slap in the face to anyone, but I can't tell him he's the greatest manager that ever lived in a short time like that."

Williams lost Yastrzemski's support when, against Oakland in a game on August 1, he benched and fined Yaz $500 for loafing. Yaz had had a bad ankle all season long. According to Yastrzemski, Williams knew his ankle was bad. The day of the incident, Williams had asked Yaz to play despite the injury, says Yaz.

In the first inning, Yaz was on third base with two outs. A ball was hit back to the pitcher, Blue Moon Odom. Yaz limped home from third on the hit, and when Odom threw home, Yaz was tagged out easily.

Williams started screaming at him as he came back to the bench. He threatened to take him out of the lineup. Yaz thought Williams was kidding, but learned otherwise when Joe Lahoud went out to take his place. Asked Yastrzemski, "What are you talking about? You knew before the game I wasn't even planning to play."

Williams threatened a $100 fine. Yaz screamed, "Hell, make it $200." Soon it was up to $500.

Yastrzemski headed for the locker room, furious at having been shown up in front of the whole team. After the game, Yaz stormed into Williams's office and offered to fight him. Williams said, "We're not doing anything like that." Yaz had a beer can in his hand. He fired it against the wall and walked out.

It wasn't the end of the incident. Dick Williams always got even.

Joe Lahoud: "At the time of the confrontation, I was rooming with a young pitcher by the name of Mike Nagy. You have to realize that at this point Yaz and I had many times roomed together on the road, went out to dinner all the time. We became that close. And Williams despised that. Dick felt I should have been more loyal to him and less loyal to Yastrzemski, because Yastrzemski was totally loyal to Yawkey. All of a sudden, I'm friends with Yastrzemski, and Dick Williams really resented that. And he didn't think a rookie should be hanging around with a veteran ballplayer of Yastrzemski's stature. A couple of times prior to this, he came to me and said, 'I don't like the relationship.'

"I said, 'Dick, I'm a young kid. He's a friend of mine. We don't do anything. We go out to dinner. I don't understand.'

"He said, 'You'll see.'

"About two in the morning of the night of the incident on the field, Dick came to my room, banging on the door. 'Room check, room check.' I mean, he was drunk out of his tree. He knocked on the door. 'Dick Williams. Open the door.' I opened the door.

"He said, 'What are you guys doing?' I said, 'We were sleeping.' He said, 'You got any women in there?' I said, 'No, we don't have any women in here. We've been sleeping.'

"He went and looked under the beds, looked behind the curtains, all the time yelling and screaming, 'You'll learn. You'll learn. You keep hanging around with the Big Guy, and you're going to be sorry.' He went and looked in the bathroom. Finally, he said to me, 'You keep hanging around with the Big Guy, your ass will be in Louisville so fast. You better start doing things my way, or you're not going to be doing them at all.'

"He wasn't able to get Yastrzemski, so he came to me, because he didn't like our relationship to begin with. I'll never forget that. Mike Nagy was sitting in bed. The kid had just come up. He was in complete awe.

"Williams haunted me throughout my whole career. In 1974, I happened to be in California, had a super year, and he came in in '74 after they fired

Bobby Winkles. I was hitting .319 in August, and he came in and sat me the first twenty-one days he was there.

"After that night, I was up and down the rest of the year. I felt like a yo-yo between Boston and Louisville, and to this day I believe that given a chance to play day in, day out, I could have been a full-time ballplayer. Dick Williams was the main reason I wasn't one. And I resent him for that, even though he was the one who brought me to the big leagues.

"I think at this point Williams was beginning to outwear his stay. A majority of the ballplayers did not enjoy playing for Williams.

"Later on, guys I talked to who played for him in Montreal said he changed, that he was a totally different person. But he had to change a hell of a lot, like the Devil becoming a newborn Christian."

Gerry Moses: "I see nothing wrong with the fact that Yaz had a rapport with Tom Yawkey. I see nothing wrong that Yaz offered him suggestions and ideas. Other players may disagree, but they should look into their own lives and compare it to what he did. I think Yaz had every right to do that. As a playing leader, he knew what we needed more than most of the people in our organization. And I do not agree that by doing that, he was undermining the manager. And if it happened, it was Tom Yawkey's fault, and not Yaz's.

"Dick wanted Yawkey out of his clubhouse. There is a right and a privilege of someone who owns something. Yawkey paid a lot of money. It was an investment. He has the right to do what he wants to do. The person you hire must listen to you.

"The only successful people in any walk of life are the winners. Nobody pays a loser. We won in '67. We didn't win in '68 or '69. Whose fault was that? You can blame it on Lonnie getting hurt, or Santiago or Conig getting hurt, or 'I didn't motivate the players.' Or maybe it's a trade they didn't make. Most likely, it was a combination of all three.

"I do not believe Dick Williams allowed anyone to undermine him. Dick, because of his personal attitude, undermined himself."

Three weeks after he benched and fined Yaz, Dick Williams was fired. There were nine games left in the season. The date was September 22, 1969.

Dick Williams: "Usually after each roadtrip before the first game of our homestand, I would go in and talk with Dick O'Connell, and this day was no different. We were in the process of trying to get another coach. Al Lakeman had left, and we needed a bullpen coach. We were looking at Charlie Lau. He was unhappy with Baltimore, and he would have loved to come with us and I was trying to solidify that.

"I said to Dick, 'What about Charlie? Did anything further happen on it? I'd sure like to have him. And my coaches are coming back, aren't they?'

"He looked at me. I said, 'I'm not coming back.' He nodded his head. He hated to tell me. But Yawkey had left town and had left instructions to terminate me.

"It wasn't just a firing, it was more like a shooting. More than twenty years later, talking about it still makes me snarl, thinking about it still makes me hurt."

When Williams was fired, not all the players were pleased to see him go.

Russ Gibson: "When Dick got fired, the Red Sox realized I was upset, and they traded me. Mike Andrews was sad when Dick left. It was tough, after what Dick had done, taking a last-place club to first place, turning it around, and then getting fired. It was a pleasure playing for him. He was a great manager. It's too bad. Baseball is funny. You have to win every year. One year is not good enough.

"I lived across the street from Dick in Peabody. He called me in the morning and told me he got fired. I said, 'Go back to sleep. You're having a bad dream.' He said, 'No. I've been fired.'

"I said, 'I'll be right over.' He said, 'No. Don't. You'll get in trouble.'

"I said, 'The heck with it. I'll be right over.' I owed everything I had to him.

"I was mad, and maybe the Red Sox felt it would be bad for the club for me to stick around. But the Red Sox treated me well, and I was happy to have the chance to play with them."

Bill Lee, Red Sox, 1969–78: "Dick was frustrated, upset with the way things were going. We were having trouble with pitching. We had a lot of guys who had army duty. He had to do a juggling act. The war in Vietnam was picking up. A lot of his players—Dalton Jones, Jim Lonborg, Ken Brett, myself, Bill Landis—were all on military duty. He had a hard time jockeying things around.

"One thing Dick did, he made fun of you, and you had to be able to take it, and the guys weren't able to take it anymore. And they got down on themselves. Ballplayers have tremendous egos, and the manager's job is to get the most out of them. Williams could hand-ride certain guys, whip other guys and get along, but after a while certain guys couldn't handle it and they rebelled. They went to Yawkey, and Williams was expendable after that. And that was too bad, because he was a great manager. He was the best in the big leagues. He had the ability to handle pitching real well. He never let a guy get beat out there. He always brought in someone fresh. He was consistent. He put the right people in the right places at the right time. He uses his players well, and his record proves that.

"I liked him. He was surly and mean, but he was honest."

CHAPTER 36

Young Guns

One reason the success of 1967 wasn't repeated by the Red Sox was the continued run of bad luck to outstanding pitching prospects. Two of those pitchers were Jerry Stephenson and Ken Brett.

Stephenson was the son of one of the best Red Sox scouts, Big Joe Stephenson. Jerry, who came from Fullerton, California, pitched four straight no-hitters in American Legion competition between his junior and senior years in high school. In two games, he struck out all twenty-one batters.

In 1961, both the Chicago White Sox and New York Yankees offered Jerry six figures to sign. When Tom Yawkey learned that the son of one of his own scouts was going to sign with another team, he ordered the rest of the scouting staff to give the boy a tryout. If he's as good as the other clubs think, Yawkey said, sign him.

Jerry Stephenson: "You always heard about the great talent signed by the Los Angeles Dodger organization, but the Red Sox had more good young kids than anybody.

"They signed great young players, and then a couple years later, you ask, 'What happened to them?' I don't have an answer. The Red Sox have a horrible history of great pitching prospects. I was one of them.

"My first year in pro ball I pitched for Winston-Salem, Class B, and pitched very well. I was eighteen, made the All-Star team, and struck out more batters than I had innings pitched.

"In '63, I went to spring training and made the Red Sox club. I could throw hard. I was nineteen."

330

* * *

Stephenson traveled with the Red Sox for a month and was sent down to Seattle of the Pacific Coast League. He was wild, on and off the field. His nickname was "Teens" because he loved *Teen* magazine. He loved the Beatles and wore turtleneck shirts. Once he peroxided his hair. It ended up with a green tint.

In some games, he would strike out twelve and walk twelve. When Stephenson went to manager Mel Parnell for advice to cure his wildness, Parnell told him that the Red Sox brass had ordered him to "just let you throw." It was all the instruction he was to get.

Said Stephenson, "Thinking about that, maybe that's one reason the young pitchers never did come around. I suppose there is something to helping yourself, but I needed a lot of help, and I never did get it."

After half a season, Stephenson was sent farther down, to the Eastern League, where he would face younger players. In 1964, he returned to Seattle. For the first two months of the season, he led the Pacific Coast League in virtually every pitching category. Then he hurt his elbow.

Jerry Stephenson: "I was pitching in San Diego, and they had had an ice show at the ballpark the night before. They had leveled the mound, and then rebuilt it, and I was pitching the first night back, and it was like pitching at the beach. It was sandy, and about the fourth inning, while making a pitch, I slipped and hurt my elbow."

Stephenson was told he needed an operation. His father told him it would be preferable for him to pitch in pain. If he couldn't do that, then he'd have the operation. Stephenson went to the Red Sox spring training in '65 and pitched by taking Darvon and aspirin to kill the pain.

"I spent the year with the Red Sox," he said, "but half the time I couldn't throw the ball ten feet." Stephenson changed his motion to alleviate the pain. Though he did manage to remain in the major leagues for seven seasons, he never became the great pitcher everyone thought he'd be.

Gerry Moses: "Jerry Stephenson had more God-given talent than any other pitcher I ever caught. He had dainty little fingers and hands, and yet he had a tremendous arm. He threw the ball harder than anyone, and it was more lively.

"The Red Sox had some great young arms: Dave Morehead, Jim Lonborg, Dave Gray, and Pete Charton. Stevie had the best arm of all."

Jerry Stephenson: "Strange things happened to our young pitchers. There was a guy named Stu McDonald who never got to pitch for the Red Sox.

They signed him out of Seattle in 1961 for $100,000. He went right from high school to the Seattle Rainiers of the Pacific Coast League, and this was back when the Coast League was a good Triple-A league, not like it is now.

"Stu won ten games in a half a year, right out of high school, and he hurt his arm and never pitched again. The next year when he went to spring training, he could barely throw the ball sixty feet.

"We signed a guy named Dave Busby out of Oklahoma. He went to Waterloo, Iowa, won 21 games right out of high school, hurt his arm, and never pitched again.

"Dave Morehead signed out of high school, got a lot of money, pitched a no-hitter for the Red Sox, and hurt his arm. If you had seen him, you'd have said, 'This guy is going to be a twenty-game winner ten straight years in the big leagues.'

"And my dad signed Ken Brett."

Ken Brett was another high-school phenom, a left-handed pitcher who could throw a baseball ninety-three miles an hour. As a hitter, Ken had rated even better than his younger brother, George. The scouts rated the youngster from El Segundo, California, as one of the best pitching prospects in the nation.

In June 1966, Brett was the fourth player chosen in the free-agent draft, behind catcher Steve Chilcott (Mets), Reggie Jackson (A's), and Wayne Twitchell (Astros). The Red Sox gave Brett $72,000 to sign. In his first full season in the minors, Brett indicated his greatness by winning ten games and striking out 142 batters in 125 innings. His ERA was 1.80.

Near the end of the 1967 season, Red Sox manager Dick Williams brought him up for a look-see. He made two appearances in the World Series against the St. Louis Cardinals. Ken Brett could have been a superstar like his brother. But at age twenty his luck ran out.

Ken Brett: "As soon as the 1967 season was over, I got my draft notice. I was a healthy white male, so I was classified 1A. I called the farm director, Neil Mahoney, who proceeded to get me into the reserves.

"By the time the World Series was over, I had about ten days to go home and revel in my glory before going to basic training in western Massachusetts. I didn't get out of the service until about April 1.

"I had thrown some in the Army, but I made the fatal mistake of trying to catch up a month of spring training in about a week. They sent me to Triple A in Louisville, where Eddie Kasko was the manager. I hadn't pitched in any games. The first game I pitched in Syracuse, New York, in the cold. I went eight innings, which in retrospect was total stupidity on their part as well as mine.

"The second time out, I went out and pitched eight again. It was in cold weather in Columbus, Ohio, in April. And afterwards, I couldn't lift my arm. I had serious elbow problems. I was out the rest of the year.

"I blame it more on them than I do on myself. I wanted to get back. They should have worked me into it. They should have known better. They had a real investment in me."

Gerry Moses: "When I caught Ken in '67 in Double A, I never saw anyone throw the ball harder with more accuracy. He was in the nineties, knee-high. He had great control, could move it in and out. He didn't have much of a breaking ball, but he was working on it. In Double A, no one could touch him.

"We played the first four games in Syracuse, New York, and it was twenty-eight degrees. He pitched opening day, and his arm was never right after that. A potential Hall of Fame career was ended."

Ken Brett remembers what it was like for a left-hander with a sore arm to pitch at Fenway Park. His most vivid memory is turning around and seeing the Monster rising up close behind him.

Ken Brett: "I only pitched two or three good games at Fenway Park my whole career. I pitched a nine-inning shutout against the Yankees late in the season. They were not real strong. Horace Clarke was the leadoff hitter. To take the bat out of his hands, all you had to do was throw a strike.

"But I can remember standing on the mound and getting the ball back from the umpire and turning around facing the left-field wall and thinking, 'Goddamn, that wall is so close I can touch it.' You rub the ball and think, 'I don't want to throw it. I just don't want to.' Especially when you look up and see Frank Robinson or Frank Howard, Willie Horton, Bill Freehan, any of those guys. Frank Howard was so big it looked like he could reach out and touch the Wall with his bat. He'd stand at the very far end of the batter's box, the very deep end, and he'd take the bat and bend over and touch the other side of the plate, just to let me know he could get there. And you'd say to yourself, 'I can't pitch him outside because the bat goes six inches over the plate. That's where the meat is. Now what am I going to do?' I had to blow the ball by him.

"The Wall just totally intimidated. And I didn't know how to pitch to it. I tried to pitch away. And right-handers normally would crowd the plate and pull the outside pitch. They'd hit a line drive or a little fly ball which would go off the Wall or over it.

"To be successful, left-handers would have to pitch in. And nobody ever told me that. So sometimes I just didn't want to throw the ball, because I knew they were going to hit it. It's a bad feeling. You don't have a whole lot of confidence when you got that ball in your hand and it feels like glass and you're rubbing it up, and it still feels that way. You think, 'I'd like to throw a curveball, but the ball's gonna slip out of my hand. I gotta throw a fastball.' "

CHAPTER 37
The Yaz–Conig Feud

PART I

With the dismissal of Dick Williams, the dynamics of the Red Sox team changed dramatically—back to the way it had been before his arrival. Under Williams, there had been no cliques and the players didn't feud. Rather, they had concentrated their efforts on hating the manager. Once Williams left and the easygoing Eddie Kasko replaced him, the players were once again free to concern themselves with the petty rivalries that occur on most baseball teams.

The most obvious rivalry on the Red Sox was between the two marquee names on the team, Carl Yastrzemski and Tony Conigliaro. Both were outstanding baseball players, and each resented the other's success. Yaz became a Hall of Famer, and Tony C. would have been one had he not been beaned. No one expected him to return after the injury, but he did. He became the youngest player ever to hit one hundred home runs. By the end of the 1970 season, when he was only twenty-five, Conig had hit 160 home runs, despite missing all of 1968. In his first five years with the Red Sox, he had home-run totals of 24, 32, 28, 20, and 20. In 1970, even after suffering that terrible injury, he managed 36 round-trippers.

Nevertheless, despite Tony C.'s success, Carl Yastrzemski ruled the Red Sox clubhouse. Yaz was tight with Tom Yawkey. Yaz was the Big Guy. And Tony C. wanted to be the Big Guy.

These were the only two on the team who could be king of the clubhouse. Each tipped big. Each expected deferential treatment and got it. Other players went for a beer. Yaz and Tony C. were brought a beer. Other players packed their own bags. Yaz and Tony C. had their bags packed for them. And each had a clique that revolved around him.

Joe Lahoud: "The Red Sox, for some reason, have never been able to participate as a team. There have always been cliques. One group included Mike Andrews, the Conigliaros, Russ Gibson, Rico Petrocelli, and Mike Ryan. That whole crowd lockered together, slept together, ate together, partied together. The other crowd included Reggie Smith, Carl Yastrzemski, Gary Peters, Ken Harrelson, and Doug Griffin, the second baseman. Then you had your pitchers, who always had their own clique. The pitchers stuck together.

"As a rookie coming in, the love-hate relationship between the Conigliaros and the Yastrzemskis was very noticeable to me. And as a rookie coming in, you fall someplace, or you don't fall at all. Yaz took a strong liking to me, mainly because people were comparing my stance and my batting style to his.

"You have to remember that the whole life and blood of that ballclub was Carl Yastrzemski. Whether it was true or not, if the team did well, Yastrzemski got credit, and if the team did poorly, he got blamed for it. The manager was secondary. A lot of that was brought on by Tom Yawkey. Yawkey loved Carl Yastrzemski. He was like his son. He would come down, and they would sit, and Mr. Yawkey would have his arm around him, and Carl would always go up to Yawkey's office. Some of the players resented that."

In temperament, Yaz and Tony C. were two men who were very different. Yaz was internal, rugged but not handsome, and he could be shy. Baseball was something Yaz *worked* at. He was constantly taking batting practice, striving to make himself better. He feared losing his skills, in case someone was gaining on him. When he signed autographs, sometimes he would sign, "Work Hard, Carl Yastrzemski."

On the other hand, Tony Conigliaro was flashy, outgoing, handsome as a movie star, a man who could light up a room. He was also a practical joker.

Ken Brett: "Back in 1970 we had to wear coats and ties to the ballparks on the roads. I went out and invested some money in a green sports coat with a beautiful green tie with a pocket square to match. I didn't know how to tie ties in those days, so I had to have my roommate, Gerry Moses, tie it for me. I'd take off my tie by loosening it, putting it over my head, and hanging it on a hook in my locker.

"Well, after batting practice one day I came in and somebody had cut my beautiful green tie in half.

"Tony walked up to me and said, 'What's the matter, Kenny?' I said, 'Somebody cut my . . .'" and I showed him.

"He said, 'That's unbelievable. I'm gonna find out who did this to you, and I'm going to bring this person to justice.'

"A couple of days later he said, 'I found out the guy who did it.' But he never did tell me the name.

"Tony was the one who did it."

To the players, their rivalry was open and obvious.

Dennis Bennett: "There was a lot of dissension between Tony C. and Yaz. You could see it in the clubhouse and in some ways on the field. They didn't talk to each other much. They didn't run around at all together. Tony had his group of friends, and Yaz had his. Yaz was a bit of a loner. If there were four guys and Yaz was with you, and you say, 'Let's all go down to Pier 4,' and Yaz says, 'No, let's go someplace else,' well, if you vetoed Yaz, he'd go his way anyway. He'd say, 'You guys go there. I'll go to the other place.' It was his place or no place. If you ran around with Yaz, you did what Yaz wanted to do."

The player Yaz ran around with most for a couple of years was Joe Lahoud.

Joe Lahoud: "Yaz's influence on the team was huge, even if he didn't say anything. Yaz was one of the type of people, like Frank Robinson and George Brett, just having him around made you try much harder. 'Cause you knew everything he did, he did with complete dedication. And that rubs off on a ballclub.

"A lot of players respected him and didn't understand him. Not that I was a psychology major. Yaz liked to have fun, but his idea of having fun was *doing it* on the field. When he went out and busted his ass going from first to third, bled up his knees and his ass from sliding, got strawberries, that was fun for him. The more strawberries he had, the better he liked it. Whether the team was winning or losing.

"Yaz was very likable. I always found that in life people respect certain things. One of them is strength, the other is ability, and Yaz had both. He wasn't a Punch-and-Judy hitter, a Pete Rose who hustled, hustled, hustled, and hit singles. Yaz hustled *and* hit the ball out of the park. Plus played the outfield. He could do it all. So right away, the players respected him for that.

"Yaz was always refining his tools. I remember one year I was living in Boston, and Yaz said to me, 'I want you to come with me in the off-season and work out with this trainer I use every day. He gets me in shape for spring training.' Well, let me tell you, I went through ten minutes of his workout, and I thought I was having a heart attack. It consisted of push-ups, aerobics, weights, no stopping for thirty-two straight minutes. I'm nine years younger than he is. I did ten minutes, was on the floor. That's what I'm saying about dedication.

"I heard Mantle took hours and hours of batting practice until his knees couldn't take it anymore. And Yaz did it all the time. We'd be on the road, and he'd call, 'C'mon, we're going out to the ballpark.' I'd say, 'Christ, it's only one o'clock. The game's at seven.'

" 'C'mon.' He lived, breathed, ate, slept baseball. If he went oh-for-four, he couldn't live with it. He could live with himself if he went one-for-three. He was happy as shit if he went two-for-four. That's the way the man survived.

"If he took an oh-for-four that day, oh my God, it was unbearable. We'd go out to dinner afterwards, and he'd order a lobster, steak, pork chops, two different types of fruits, a bottle of wine. We'd drink the wine, and he'd pick at the lobster. We wouldn't say fifteen words in an hour and a half. I'd say, 'Are you through?' He'd say, 'Yeah,' and I'd have a meal like you couldn't believe.

"After the good nights, he was a totally different person. We'd go out and have dinner, drinks, fun, a totally different person, and at twelve-thirty, boom, back to his room. I don't give a shit where we were. I'd go to the bathroom, and he'd be gone.

"That man cost me more money than my wife. He never had any money on him. We'd go out and have a $150 dinner, and he'd say, 'I don't have any meal money.' 'You just got your meal money.' 'I left it in the room.' 'Don't you have any credit cards?' 'I don't carry credit cards. Pay for it. I'll take care of you later.' So I paid for it. If we had to take a cab, it was, 'Give him the ten dollars.' After two days of a ten-day road trip, I'd be broke. I'd have to get out my checkbook and write a check. And he was making $150,000 and I was making $22,000.

"But I got even. One day in Boston I took his American Express card. I went all over Boston, bought clothes, went out to dinner. I had it for one week. When he wanted to know where his card was, I said, 'I got it, you fuck. You owe it to me.' He laughed. He didn't care. Finally, he said, 'Give me back that goddamn card.' I gave it to him. 'How much did you spend?' 'About $2,500.' He shrugged. But the next road trip he got me again.

"For twenty-four years of his life, Yaz was in baseball, and now he's without it, and he's having a tough, tough time. He has all the money he needs in the world, but it's difficult for him to accept he's no longer in baseball. The best thing in the world for him to do would be to get back into it, as a batting instructor, or possibly a manager. But pride won't let him do that."

Part II

On October 11, 1970, Tony Conigliaro was traded to the California Angels. Tony C.'s eye problems had returned, and the Red Sox had determined he could no longer play right field, despite his home-run production. That should have been the end of the rivalry, but, ironically, it only got worse. The two men vying for Tony's starting job were two youngsters with great potential: Joe Lahoud and Tony's younger brother, Billy Conigliaro.

Billy C. had been born in August of 1947, Lahoud in April of that year. Both were young, handsome, and talented. The Red Sox had high hopes for both. Neither panned out. In four years of playing part-time for the Sox, Lahoud hit 26 home runs, including 14 in 1971, but he batted only .205. Billy C. played three years, hit 33 home runs, including 18 in 1970, and batted .269. They would be traded together to Milwaukee after the 1971 season. They were significant figures only inasmuch as they were pawns in the war between the cliques.

Ken Brett: "I played with Billy C. in the minors. He was a friend of mine. Billy was always Tony's brother. Billy always had a little chip on his shoulder, thought the Red Sox were out to get him. I don't know why, and it wasn't true, but he always thought he wasn't being treated fairly, and that Tony hadn't been treated fairly. Billy had a tendency to look at things in the negative more than the positive. He was a good player, but he blew all the opportunities he ever had to play in Boston. He was stubborn, very stubborn.

"Billy didn't like Lahoud. It was personal, something about a girl. Guys should never fight over girls. There are plenty of girls to go around.

"Billy was always out chasing it. He liked the women. He didn't have time for the guys. And one thing that was really hilarious: If Billy went out with a girl, and she wouldn't give it up, he wouldn't waste time on her. If she did give it up, he'd say, 'This girl is too easy.' You couldn't please him.

"And he had a way with women. He wasn't afraid to walk up to a girl and be forward with her. We'd be in a bar, and he'd say, 'I'm going to get that one,' and he'd walk over. 'Hey, can I buy you a drink? Let's get out of here. Let's . . .'

"I was always shy. I couldn't do that. I thought, 'My God, I can't do that. I have to get home and go to bed.'

"You couldn't please Billy. We were playing a game, and he laid down a sacrifice bunt. The fielder got the ball, looked at second, and walked toward Billy with the ball. Billy backed up, so the fielder took a swipe at him. And Billy took a swing at him. 'You can't do that to me. Who does the guy think he is?'

"He's Italian."

Joe Lahoud: "When Hawk was traded to Cleveland, there was a new rivalry. It was then that everything started cooking. A real nonhuman being by the name of Billy Conigliaro came around. When we first met, Billy and I were the best of friends. What set it off was that Billy had an ego as big as Boston—no, as big as the state of Massachusetts. Mine was as big as Boston. And I was getting a lot of press coverage as the one who was going to fill Tony Conigliaro's shoes. Billy resented that.

"Billy and I liked to party. We liked to have a good time. We were together for the first time in '69 spring training, vying for a spot on the team. He was going to a place called the Marina in Sarasota, and taking out the singer there, and I didn't know it. Well, one time I was there and I met her, and I ended up going out with her. Billy and I got into a big fight about that.

" 'Did you take so-and-so out?'

" 'Yeah.'

" 'Did you know I was taking her out?'

" 'No. She didn't even mention your name. She just said she knew a couple guys on the ballclub. But she never said she was going out with anybody.'

"He said, 'Yes, you did. You did this on purpose, just like you think you're going to be the right fielder for Boston, taking my brother's place.' He had all this inside of him. It was really eating him, but I guess I never realized it. Then it built from there. He was obnoxious to me. And I was to him in return.

"We had a few fights, drag-outs where they had to pull us apart. I remember one time getting coldcocked in the back of the head.

"The Lahoud-Conigliaro rivalry began that spring, 'cause Dick Williams said at the time it was 'fortunate he had competition between two good, young ballplayers.' To me, the competition was on the field. To Billy, the competition was on the field, off the field, in the press.

"I remember one time I had my batting helmet on and was on deck, and then the next thing I knew, somebody hit me over the head with a bat. It was Billy. Don't ask me! Right across the batting helmet! He would go crazy sometimes.

"A couple times in the elevator I'd be coming down or up, and he'd get in, and he'd want to start fighting. He'd look at me and say something. Rico pulled us apart a couple times. And I got to the point where I used to laugh at him. I really did feel sorry for him, because he added pressure to himself. He had such a strong rivalry with me, and he had to live up to the reputation his brother had.

"The ironic part was that Tony Conigliaro and I were the best of friends. Tony and I used to go out to dinner together. Tony once said to me, 'What the hell is it between you and my brother?'

"I said, 'Tony, don't ask me. I really don't know.'

"And the media pushed young players like us into that type of rivalry.

They wrote about the competition. Dick Williams loved it. It was blown up to the point where it was unbelievable.

"It got so crazy I wouldn't look at him. He wouldn't look at me. We'd walk in separate directions. I wouldn't even fly in the same plane with him sometimes. I remember one time I took a train back from Cleveland to Boston. It was so stupid. But to this day he totally resents me. As we got toward the end of our careers, as we got older, we tolerated each other. I played a little longer than he did. He should still be playing today with the body that he had.

"Billy had a lot of extra pressure on him because of Tony. He wanted to be better than Tony. In fact, he had more ability than Tony had. What he didn't have was Tony's Fenway Park home-run swing. You could throw a pitch at Tony's elbow, and he was going to hit it into the net. Otherwise, he wasn't the outfielder Billy was, didn't have the speed, didn't have the arm, didn't have the same baseball savvy. Billy also had extra pressure on him because he was from the Boston area, and from his family, and because of the competition with me and the other clique.

"Whenever the Red Sox would send him down and keep me, it was like someone took a barbed knife and twisted it in his heart, because in his mind he felt he was a superior ballplayer. He felt the only reason he had been sent down and not me was my relationship with Yastrzemski. He even said it in the paper. 'If I was friends with Yastrzemski and not Lahoud, Lahoud would be the one being sent down.' But if you look at the stats, that's not true.

"And then the *Boston Globe* did a two-page Sunday centerfold on me. Big picture of me, one of Boston's most eligible bachelors. Remember, he wasn't just competitive with me as a player. Everything he did in life, he felt he was competing with me.

"And what made it harder for him was the Red Sox trading his brother in 1970. Now his sounding post, his pillar, was no longer there. Now he had nobody to turn to. Nobody at all.

"And it got to the point where he just cracked. He went crazy. There was one day when he threw the helmets and bats out of the dugout. He want batshit, because I *pinch-hit* for him.

"It was the late innings. We were behind by one or two runs with men in scoring position. I was sent in to pinch-hit for him, and that's what set him off. He threw the helmets and bats, kicked out the water cooler, went into the locker room and broke a couple of lockers.

"Rico went after him to calm him down. Rico was close to the Conigliaros. Rico was close to everybody. He was just a super guy.

"But even though Rico tried to calm Billy down, there was a fight that took place in the locker room between Billy and Reggie and Yaz. I was up at bat, so I didn't see it. But I do know that Billy was saying stuff like, 'You get rid of my brother, and now Lahoud's pinch-hitting for me and he can't carry my jockstrap.'

"And Yaz said, 'What the fuck are you talking about?' And Reggie, who couldn't stand Billy and who was friends with Yaz, went after Billy. Yaz was not involved in the fisticuffs. Yaz went to get Reggie away from Billy. Because Reggie would have killed him.

"Reggie was the only guy in baseball, other than Willie Horton, that when a fight broke out, his eyes were as big as golf balls, and the whites of his eyes would turn red. And if you look at any top prizefighter with a killer instinct, it's the same way. Reggie had that killer instinct. With his tools, I'm glad he liked me."

It all came to a head in the summer of 1971. In June, the Red Sox were playing a day game against the California Angels at Fenway Park. Billy was playing center field deep. A fly ball dropped in front of him and a run scored.

After the game, the writers asked Yastrzemski whether Billy was playing *too* deep. Yaz declined to answer. The writers left him, except for Clif Keane of the *Boston Globe*. Yaz told Keane that the few times he had played center, he had played shallow, figuring the balls hit over his head would hit the bleacher wall and bounce back to him. But Yaz said that Ken Berry, the Angels' center fielder, played deep, and Berry was a better center fielder than he was. Yaz suggested Keane talk to Berry. Yaz had said nothing about Billy Conigliaro, but somehow other writers re-created Yaz's discussion with Keane, misquoting Yaz and writing about the "dissension" on the team.

That same evening, a writer asked Reggie Smith whether the Red Sox might benefit by shaking up the lineup. Smith replied, "You always shake up the lineup a little when things don't go well. Do something. Maybe play Lahoud a few games." Again, Smith had intended no disrespect toward Billy Conigliaro, but the writers made it sound as if Smith was suggesting Billy be benched and Lahoud inserted into the lineup. The writers added gasoline to the fire by going back to Billy for his comments on what they had "said." That night Billy passed both Yastrzemski and Smith, growling.

Sensitive to his feelings, Yaz and Smith went to manager Eddie Kasko, and all four met in Kasko's hotel room to discuss the misunderstanding. Yaz and Smith each explained to Billy what had been said, saying that neither had criticized him. Bill responded by saying how much he missed his brother Tony and had depended on him. Kasko told the three he hoped this would be the end of the problem. He advised all three to talk out any differences. The first skirmish was over.

And then on July 10, 1971, the Red Sox lost a game in Yankee Stadium with two outs in the ninth because Billy was again playing too deep. In the locker room after the game, Billy shocked reporters by openly accusing Yaz and Smith of being responsible for the trade of Tony by the Red Sox.

The next day, Reggie Smith responded by saying that Billy should be suspended. Smith said he didn't want to play with him anymore. Tony C., who had never expressed any negative feeling for Yaz in public, apologized to Yaz in writing for Billy's remarks. Billy also apologized publicly in writing. But Yawkey had had it.

On October 11, 1971, Billy C. was traded to Milwaukee along with George Scott, Jim Lonborg, Ken Brett, Don Pavletich, and—in yet another irony— Joe Lahoud, for Tommy Harper, Pat Skrable, Lew Krausse, and Marty Pattin.

In June of 1972, Billy C. retired temporarily. He quit for good the next year. Joe Lahoud continued to play part-time for seven more seasons with Milwaukee, California, Texas, and Kansas City, before himself calling it quits.

CHAPTER 38

Sparky and the Spaceman

In 1970, Eddie Kasko was brought in to manage the Red Sox. Most of his players say Kasko was a terrific guy, a fine person and a competent manager—easygoing, witty, with a dry sense of humor. If Kasko had a fault, it was his inability to relate to the new brand of rebellious youth that had sprung up from the protest era of the Vietnam War. The Red Sox had brought up a couple of young, talented left-handed pitchers who were outspoken, rebellious, and outrageous people. They were tough competitors on the field, but were carefree and had little respect for authority. Their names: Sparky Lyle and Bill Lee.

Sparky Lyle came up to the Red Sox in 1967. He was a cocky left-hander with a hard-biting slider, and in his five years with the Red Sox he recorded earned-run averages of 2.28, 2.74, 2.54, 3.90, and 2.77. During those five seasons, he recorded 69 saves, including consecutive seasons of 17, 20, and 16 saves, and the crowds loved his flair on the mound. But Lyle was also a crass and unruly character who rode around on a motorcycle, stayed out late at night, and enjoyed torturing his teammates in the clubhouse by sitting naked on birthday cakes sent them by their fans. Though most of his teammates loved being around him, Eddie Kasko was not amused by his deviltry.

Gerry Moses: "In A ball, I roomed with three other players—Dave Gray, Bob Montgomery, and a kid named Dick Kratz—in a $500-a-month apartment. On the other side of the hall was Sparky Lyle and three other guys. And we were always playing pranks on each other.

"Sparky gagged and tied up one of his roommates, Ed Vetters, in a closet and wouldn't let him out for twelve hours. We thought that was really funny. The poor kid could have killed himself if he had claustrophobia."

Gary Bell: "Sparky was famous for sitting on cakes. The first time he did that, it blew me away. Rico Petrocelli had received a birthday cake from his fan club. And he tried to hide it from the rest of the guys. He put it in his locker and covered it up.

"One of the eagle eyes caught him and didn't say anything, and when Rico went out onto the field to take batting practice, the culprit snuck back into the locker room, took the cake out, and sat it on a bench out in the open. The culprit, of course, was Sparky.

"When Rico hit the door, Sparky was standing next to that cake, naked. Rico was about thirty feet away when he saw him. Rico yelled, 'Not my cake.' But before he could get to it, Sparky squatted on top of it.

"Sparky said, 'Would you like a piece?'

" 'No, thank you.' "

Joe Lahoud: "I was rooming with Sparky Lyle, and it was great. It was like rooming alone. I never saw him. I could bring my girls back and I had no problems. Sparky would be gone for the night.

"This one night I was out partying, and I came back to the Holiday House in Cleveland, and there was Dick Williams and Eddie Popowski and one of the other coaches sitting in the lobby. Ordinarily, everyone was on their own, and Dick handled it like we were adults. 'Take care of yourself, 'cause if you don't, you'll just be shortening your career.' But there were times when Dick was pissed off at us or drunk, and there would be a curfew. This was one of those nights.

"I went up to my room and got right on the phone. Sparky was out, and I knew it was getting close to curfew, and he had gotten nailed a couple times already.

"I called the Caravelle, and I couldn't get through, so I went down the fire escape, got in a cab, drove over and got a hold of him to tell him Dick was waiting in the lobby. It was only a ten-minute trip to downtown Cleveland. The only nuts out in that town were the ballplayers.

"I said to Sparky, 'Come up to the side of the hotel and come up the fire escape, and I'll leave something to keep the fire-escape door open.' So I did, and he did.

"I don't know what time it was, but Dick didn't catch him. Sparky said, 'Thanks. You really saved my ass.'

"Some guys, like Sparky, were flamboyant. He was a reliever. He could be in seven games in a week. But Sparky didn't give a shit about anything. He wanted to go out and pitch and be on that mound, and he would do a damn good job. And Sparky was such a likable guy, such a funny guy, that reporters liked him. Even the reporters who hated baseball players liked Sparky. He was well-liked by everybody."

Not quite everyone.

Sparky Lyle, Red Sox, 1967–71: "Eddie Kasko was hired to manage the team in 1970. Kasko was the only big-league manager I ever played for who I didn't like. Kasko lost total confidence in me, which is a terrible thing to happen between a manager and a ballplayer. He didn't think I could get left-handers out after Boog Powell, who is left-handed, beat me up in Boston on two consecutive nights. The second night Boog hit a little pop-up that landed right on the left-field foul line. It was in the newspapers the next day: 'Kasko: Lyle Can't Get Lefties Out.' Kasko didn't like me much anyway because of my lifestyle. He wanted Sunday school–type ballplayers, and he wanted me to curtail my staying up late, which I had been doing since I'm old enough to remember. I just can't fall asleep at one in the morning. It's too early for me.

"If you were in a bar after a game, you could talk with him, but he acted like he was noticing how many drinks you were having. Plus, he didn't want you talking about pussy. He wanted you talking baseball, and I'm just not that way. To me, when the game is over, it's over. Talking about it isn't going to change it.

"But what really burned my ass was a meeting Kasko held. He said, 'If you have anything to say to me, come to my office and say it to my face. Don't talk behind my back.' A couple of days later, Kasko fined me for being overweight and gave the clubhouse boy a message to give to me. The clubhouse boy forgot to give it to me, so when I went into the clubhouse the next day, he said, 'I forgot to give you this.' It was the message from Kasko that he had fined me. I went bananas. I stormed into Kasko's office yelling and carrying on, and I reminded him of his speech about saying things to guy's faces. I said, 'You don't have enough respect to me to tell me about this fine to my face? I have to find out from the clubhouse boy?'

"That night I went to the racetrack with Red Sox pitcher Ray Culp, and while we were there, we ran into Kasko, Eddie Popowski, and trainer Buddy Leroux, and they didn't talk to me. Culp said, 'Uh-oh, something's up. There's a trade brewing.' I said, 'Yeah, they sure are acting funny.'

"The next day the Red Sox traded me to the Yankees for first baseman Danny Cater."

With the Red Sox, Danny Cater played three seasons, 1972 to 1974. In those three years, he hit 14 home runs and drove in 83 runs. He played a final year with St. Louis in '75. The Boston fans never forgave him for being the man the Red Sox had traded for Sparky Lyle.

Ken Tatum, Red Sox, 1971–73: "Danny was very quiet. He took a lot of things personally. He couldn't understand why the fans disliked him, because with the Yankees he had been a pretty good hitter. Even though he was trying his best, he couldn't understand why the fans were still on his case, and he took things badly. Eventually the booing affected his play. I've heard players say, 'I don't pay attention to the crowd,' but anyone who says that isn't telling the truth. How can you not hear 37,000 people?"

Tack Burbank, attorney: "Danny Cater was booed right from the beginning. I know that because he was the next-door neighbor of my friend, Bill MacCrellish. It was very hard on Danny and his wife and family. They moved up here and got booed right out of the box. He never performed. He was only with the Sox a couple of years. He never hit for them, never did anything. Bill MacCrellish never derived any status from living next door to Danny Cater. If he had lived next door to Sparky Lyle, that would have been worth something. But not Danny Cater."

Eddie Kasko managed the Red Sox to third-place finishes in 1970 and 1971. Nineteen sixty-seven was becoming a fond but distant memory. Red Sox fans, now thinking the Impossible Dream might well have been a fluke, wondered whether the team would ever finish first again, never mind win a World Series. The Lyle trade added to their feelings of frustration.

Tack Burbank: "I was getting impatient. I was beginning to feel the way I felt all the rest of my life before '67, like it would never happen again.

"I had grown up as a Red Sox fan. I went to my first game in '54—Bob Feller shut out the Red Sox. They lost, 7–0. Kids hope for everything. They are always optimistic, by definition dreamers, but as a kid growing up in the fifties and sixties, I never had any expectation that the Red Sox would ever win the pennant, and around 1971 those same old feelings returned. I just figured '67 was it; that I would suffer the fate of my mother, who waited in vain her entire life to see the Red Sox win a World Series.

"In '71, the Red Sox traded away George Scott, and during spring training the next year, in order to fill the vacancy at first, they traded Sparky Lyle to the Yankees for Danny Cater. I thought it was a terrible trade. Cater basically was a singles hitter playing at a power position, and Lyle became one of the best relief pitchers of all time."

BILL LEE

Bill Lee, who pitched for the Red Sox from 1969 through 1978, was a rabid perfectionist. He demanded it from himself, but what continually got him in trouble was that he also demanded it from his manager and his teammates. He was bright, outspoken, and spoke up without ever considering the ramifications. If you screwed up during the game, chances are you'd hear about it from Lee. Not even the manager was spared his sharp tongue.

Ken Tatum: "You're talking about a fierce competitor, good Lord. Bill had an opinion on everything, and he would voice it even to Kasko. He'd say, 'This is a stupid move.' Bill was not the easiest athlete to have to manage, not at all. Bill cared, and he would voice his opinion, and sometimes he was right.

"But on the mound you could always depend on him."

Lee had the nickname of "The Spaceman," a sobriquet that he has always firmly rejected. In fact, when asked for an autograph, Lee will sign his name and then write in bold letters, "EARTH." A graduate of the University of Southern California, Lee had a dual nature. He was as tough a competitor and as willing a street fighter as anyone in baseball, and at the same time he was morally a pacifist, an antiwar activist, and a critic of the nation's dog-eat-dog mentality.

Lee enjoyed tweaking the stuffy suits who ran baseball, especially commissioner Bowie Kuhn, a joyless, self-important man. Lee once told Kuhn he didn't smoke marijuana, but he sprinkled it on his Wheaties. Kuhn fined him for his words. No wonder that to many, particularly Boston collegiates, Bill Lee became a cult hero.

Turmoil always seemed to be swirling around the Red Sox, however, and often it seemed to be swirling about Lee. Here is a typical Bill Lee situation:

Bill Lee: "In the winter of 1972, I went to Puerto Rico. My manager was Luis Aparicio. I was playing for Mayaguez, and I was pitching against Caguas at home. I gave up a three-run home run to Willie Montanez in the late innings to lose the ballgame. The next guy up was catcher Ellie Rodriguez. He was taking a big swing, and I had had enough of this. On a 2–2 pitch, I drilled him right in the hip intentionally. I hit him right on the bone, and he was hurt bad. He was stunned for a second, and then he charged the mound with the bat. I stood, held my ground in a stretch position, and he came running at me. The minute he put the bat down, he leaped at me like he was going to kill me. I stepped inside him and hit him with a left hand on the button. I dropped him cold right on the mound. Cal Ermer said it was the greatest left hand he had ever seen. The fans stood up in jubilation.

"Next thing I knew, Rodriguez was getting to his feet. I was standing at the back of the mound. The trainer was holding my hand, because I had split a knuckle. Rodriguez got up, stunned, looking for me. He ran right behind me, didn't even see me, and then he turned around, and all hell broke loose.

"Four days later, we were going to play Caguas in Caguas. We had played in San Juan the night before. I came out late and brought my bags onto the bus. The players told me, 'Don't go to Caguas. This guy is crazy. He's going to kill you.' I said, 'No, people don't do that kind of stuff.' They said, 'No, Bill, don't go.'

"We got to Caguas. We were coming toward the ballpark, and the bus was having trouble with the soft dirt. We were stuck there for five minutes. A big crowd gathered around the bus. Finally, the driver got it going. He had about a quarter of a mile to the park. My feeling was that if someone in the crowd was going to jump me, I would get off the bus quickly and get into the ballpark.

"I jumped down the flight of stairs and started walking into the ballpark. Three guys were standing beside the bus, a little, short guy and two big guys, but I didn't recognize them. One of them was Rodriguez, who wasn't dressed. The next thing I know, I've lost four teeth. He had jumped behind me and hit me in the head, and boom, threw me into a steel pole. One guy had a knife, and Ron Woods and Pete Koegel saw it and grabbed him. Woods grabbed the other guy, who was about ready to knife me. Ron picked me up and got me to the ballpark.

"I got a letter from the Mayaguez owner. 'If you come back, I'll give you $3,000 if you fight a three-round preliminary before our game with Caguas against Eddie Rodriguez. We'll pack the place.'

"In May of '73, the Red Sox were playing Milwaukee. Reggie Smith was on the bench. He had a dislocated finger on his nonthrowing hand. He was taking the day off. Early in the ballgame we were ahead of Milwaukee, and our second baseman, Doug Griffin, had his wrist broken by the pitcher from Milwaukee. Smith started yelling at me about retaliation. I told him, 'Lookit, you're not even playing in this game, Reggie. You're sitting out with a hangnail.' I said, 'I'll pick the spot. I'll wait.'

"We had a five-run lead, and Ellie Rodriguez came up to the plate. I said to myself, 'Wow, this is a good time.' I threw him a hard slider and drilled him in the hip again.

"He charged the mound. Our catcher, Bob Montgomery, got him real fast. He went to first base, and two pitches later, I picked him off first base with a real tricky move. He was pissed. He ran by the mound, yelling and scream-ing at me. I looked at him and said, 'That's once. I'm going to hit you again.'

"He went and sat in the dugout. They had a little shortstop up at the plate. I got ahead of him and threw him a good straight change, and while Ro-driguez was in the dugout putting on the catching equipment, the batter fouled it off and smoked him. And I was laughing. I thought, 'Geez, if that ain't poetic justice.'

"I came into the dugout the next inning, around the fifth or sixth, and Reggie Smith was mad as hell at me again. He wanted to fight me right there in the dugout. I had hit a nonwhite player. He was all over me. But I hadn't hit Rodriguez because he was a Puerto Rican. I had a grudge against Ro-driguez. He had knocked four of my teeth out. If he had been from Mars, I'd have hit him.

"And Kasko broke it up.

"In the eighth inning, I went up into the clubhouse because I had a bad cold and I wanted a hit of Cheracol. Someone must have known something might be happening, because Pete Cerrone followed me. I got to the club-house, and Smith came at me and threw a right. I turned to the side, and he hit Cerrone right behind me and broke his bridge and his teeth. And, boom, Smith picked me up, dumped me upside down into the bat rack, and kicked me in the side of the head.

"I was woozy. I took another hit of Cheracol, finished the ninth, one, two, three, thinking it was all over. I came into the clubhouse. I was mad. I saw Smith sitting down. His locker was next to Yastrzemski, and his head was down. So I went into the clubhouse and made a left into the trainer's room, and that was the last thing I remember.

"He jumped up, hit me in the back of the head and the side of the ear and knocked me into the bulletin board and knocked me out. If I could ever get hit straight-on, I can take a punch. I always seemed to get hit behind the head. I don't have a lot of protection there. Plus I wear glasses.

"Smith and I had a tempestuous relationship. He intimidated other people, but he didn't intimidate me. He was brash and demonstrative. Smith was always on me. I knew he wasn't playing with a full deck.

"After that we got along real well, because he got traded to St. Louis. He calmed down in St. Louis, but then he went to San Francisco, where he got into fights with people in the stands. He went to Japan and had a rough time there.

"The further I am away from him, the better."

CHAPTER 39

In Contention

Step by step, the Red Sox began to put together a team again.

In 1972, an old, over-the-hill pitcher with little promise captured the hearts of New England. In 1968, he had won 21 games with the Cleveland Indians, with an earned-run average of 1.60. The next year, he was 9–20, and after a trade to Minnesota (7–3, 3.39), he was released in April 1971. Signed to the Atlanta Braves' Richmond farm club, then acquired by the pitching-needy Red Sox, who sent him to Louisville, he was promoted to the parent club, where he won exactly one game and lost seven.

Who could have anticipated that Luis Tiant would star for the Red Sox the next seven years? During that span he compiled records of 15–6, 1.91; 20–13, 3.34; 22–13, 2.92; 18–14, 4.02; 21–12, 3.06; 12–8, 4.53; and 13–8, 3.31. The flamboyant El Tiante became a Boston icon.

Mark Starr, journalist: "Unequivocally, the most popular ballplayer at the time was Tiant. Boston has not been an ethnic paradise for ballplayers, but his was such a great baseball story. He was virtually out of baseball when the Red Sox signed him, and he pitched his way back to the Red Sox. Luis had so much charm, he was a man who loved the game in such a demonstrative way, and as far as pitchers go, he was as much fun as anyone to watch."

Another surprise performer who blossomed in 1972 was twenty-four-year-old catcher Carlton Fisk, New England's own. Carlton Ernest Fisk was born in Bellows Falls, Vermont, and lived in Merrimack, New Hampshire. In 1972, his first full season with the Red Sox, he hit .293, with 22 home runs.

Tack Burbank: "I identified with him immediately. I never saw a catcher who looked like him. He *looked* like he was from New Hampshire. He always had a chaw then, but Carlton's uniform was always clean and white and his face clean. Thurman Munson also chewed tobacco, but he always had tobacco juice all over him.

"Fisk was so tall. He looked like a power forward, just a wonderful-looking athlete. He was striking from the beginning.

"Fisk had had a mediocre minor-league career, and it surprised everyone when he came up as a rookie catcher and was Rookie of the Year. He had a great year at bat, and defensively, what a great defensive catcher! His whole career, Fisk was a guy who hated players who dogged it. He would chew out a player on the team if he was dogging it. He had this real Yankee work ethic that all us New Englanders could relate to."

Mark Starr: "The most important aspect of Carlton Fisk was that he was homegrown. Remember, this isn't California. We're provincial up in New England, and we don't produce that many ballplayers. To whatever extent the Red Sox fans are fanatics, there is a sense that if you're born in New England, you're born to be a Red Sox fan, so when a homegrown player comes up, which is rare—Harry Agganis, Tony Conigliaro, Jerry Remy, Jeff Reardon—it means something to them and it means something to us.

"And Fisk was not only a local boy, but a terrific player as well.

"Carlton was always a wonderful Fenway Park hitter, which isn't always the case with righties. It's one of the big myths that Fenway benefits right-handed hitters. Fenway is actually a much better park for non-pull lefties, those who know how to spray the ball. All the batting-crown guys, Pete Runnels, Boggs, Williams, Freddie Lynn—Yaz learned—they were all lefties, except for Carney Lansford, who won it one year.

"Fisk was more of the Rico Petrocelli type. He hit fly balls over the Wall. The Wall never helped Jim Rice, who hit line drives that would have gone out in any other park, but it was a wonderful place for Fisk.

"Fisk had charisma. He looked like a young Ted Kennedy, but he was reliable, unlike Ted Kennedy. He was stoic, but there was a sense he was in command. It was hard to believe he left this town."

In 1972, the top Red Sox relievers, Bill Lee and Bobby Bolin, managed just five saves each, and Don Newhauser four, while Sparky Lyle was leading the league in New York with 35. That year there was a strike at the start of the season. The Detroit Tigers canceled six regular-season games as a result. The Red Sox canceled seven. That one game would make all the difference.

Tack Burbank: "I remember 1972 for the strike, the emergence of Carlton Fisk, and Luis Aparicio rounding third, falling down, and getting tagged out.

"The strike cost the Red Sox a week of games. It was depressing, but quickly forgotten, because the team was bolstered by the addition of Fisk.

"The Red Sox didn't win in '72 because Luis Aparicio fell down. The Tigers had come in for a three-game series at the end of the season. The Tigers won the first game, and the Red Sox needed to win the last two. It was late in the second game, the Tigers were ahead by a run, and Aparicio was on second. Yaz singled, and with Luis's speed, it was clear he was going to score, so you already had the run in your column if you were keeping score at home, and I was watching it on TV. But Luis hit the outside of the bag rounding it, and he fell. The throw came in behind him, and as he was returning to third, Yaz was also running for the base. One of the two had to be out, and it was Yaz, and that killed the rally. That was the kind of thing we Red Sox fans had to endure. It was the kind of thing that ruined my week. There would be other things that happened later that destroyed major parts of my life."

Fans remember Aparicio's slip at the end of the season. For pitcher Bill Lee, it was something even more: it was déjà vu (all over again).

Bill Lee: "I can remember we went into Detroit for opening day in 1972. We didn't know if we were going to play the ballgame. It was a real misty day. Tommy Harper was our leadoff hitter. He got on base and stole second. Aparicio singled him in. Yastrzemski hit the ball in the gap up against the fence. Aparicio rounded third, and he was going to score easily, but he hit the wet bag and slipped and fell into the wet grass surrounding third base. He scrambled to his feet and dove back to third, only to have Yastrzemski round second base with his head down chugging into third with a sure triple. Both of them were standing on third base.

"They got the out. We only scored one run in the inning, and we got beat by a run.

"And now it's the *end* of the season and we're going into Detroit. We had to win two out of three games to win the pennant. It was a tense situation.

"In the first game of the series, Mickey Lolich started for the Tigers, a must-win game for us. Tommy Harper got on and Aparicio got a base hit. Here came Yastrzemski up to the plate. It was a misty day, boom, Yastrzemski hit the ball in the gap up against the fence, Aparicio rounded second, went into third, he was going to score, hit the bag, slipped, fell down, got on his feet, dove back into third, and Yastrzemski was running with his head down into third base—again. And I was going, 'I don't believe this.'

"The next day, we went out, and Tiant got beat by Woodie Fryman. So we were not destined to win that year. The gods were definitely against us."

The next year, 1973, the Red Sox finished eight games behind the Baltimore Orioles, with a record of 89–73. During one streak late in the season, the Red Sox won eight games in a row, but couldn't gain any ground on Earl Weaver's club.

Red Sox management lost patience. Eddie Kasko was fired and Darrell Johnson replaced him.

In October 1973, the Red Sox made a trade they hoped would lead to a pennant. They traded the difficult Reggie Smith and pitcher Ken Tatum to St. Louis and acquired All-Star pitcher Rick Wise and a twenty-six-year-old outfielder named Bernie Carbo.

Wise was the key. A nine-year veteran, in 1973 he had been 16–12 with a 3.37 ERA, and had been the starting and winning pitcher in the 1973 All-Star Game. A trio of Tiant, Bill Lee, and Wise gave Red Sox fans hope that their team had enough pitching to catch the Baltimore Orioles. For Rick Wise, though, it was not to be. He places the blame on the shoulders of the gods and manager Darrell Johnson.

Rick Wise, Red Sox, 1974–77: "We opened up in Milwaukee in '74. We had a Friday, Saturday, Sunday series, and Tiant and Lee pitched the Friday and Saturday games, all fine and dandy. I was ready to pitch the Sunday game, and we woke up Sunday morning to a snowstorm. The game was postponed, we moved on to Boston, and the storm followed us. And we were snowed out for quite a bit of time.

"I figured that as soon as the weather broke it would be my turn to pitch, but Darrell Johnson started making September pennant moves in April. He bypassed me and put Lee and Tiant back ahead of me. Obviously, I was not happy with that decision.

"I told Darrell rather bluntly of my dissatisfaction. I was wondering what was going on. I said, 'You traded for an All-Star pitcher, and this is April, the third game of the season. What's going on?' Well, I didn't get any satisfaction and the decision stood. I didn't get to pitch until twelve days after breaking spring training.

"It was a backup Game of the Week against Detroit. The regularly scheduled game was postponed, and so this game was going to be played at all costs, and so I pitched in thirty-eight-degree, cold, drizzly rain. I did win, pitched a complete game, did very well considering the conditions. Then the next start I was pitching against the Yankees in the Stadium. I pitched five shutout innings, and all of a sudden I felt discomfort, felt myself weakening, and I knew something was wrong.

"I had never been hurt before. I had a torn tricep muscle and as a result of trying to alter my throwing motion, developed tendinitis. I could not throw without pain and was not anything near what I was the previous years, wasn't even close. I had averaged 250 innings a year. I was in my prime. I pitched 49 innings that year."

Despite Wise's injury, however, the Red Sox seemed to have caught fire. Luis Tiant pitched brilliantly. Newcomers Reggie Cleveland and Diego Segui buoyed the staff. Rick Burleson at short, Cecil Cooper at first, and Dwight Evans in the outfield provided a youthful nucleus to go with the other outstanding performers—Carlton Fisk, Yaz, Tommy Harper, Juan Beniquez, and Bernie Carbo. Late in August, the Red Sox were leading the American League East.

And then a funny thing happened. The hitters stopped hitting. It was a burden too great for the pitching staff. The lead started to dwindle.

Tack Burbank: "By 1974, I was thinking that we could win the whole thing. I was thinking we had a good team, with guys like Fisk and Rico, Yaz, Juan Beniquez, who had tremendous talent, but even with Bill Lee, Luis Tiant, and Reggie Cleveland, we were still a little thin in the pitching staff.

"Late in August, the Sox were six and a half games in front. I went on a camping trip and disappeared for about two weeks up to Nova Scotia. I was in places where you couldn't get radio reception, and the newspapers were local, small, and didn't have the box scores.

"I remember we drove back to Maine, and the first thing I did was look for a newspaper and check the standings—they had been way in front when I left, and now they were seven games *behind!* I thought, this is unbelievable."

Rick Wise: "The same thing happened to me in Philadelphia in 1964. We played well, but the other teams in contention played great. Funny things happen. It can't be explained altogether. We weren't hitting, and we'd make critical errors, wouldn't do the fundamentally correct things, moving runners over or getting runners in with less than two outs. Those things snowball and the skids start getting greased, and all of a sudden you're going backwards or treading water instead of moving forward."

Bill Lee sometimes speaks in parables. His explanation of what happened to the Sox in '74 is as informative as any.

Bill Lee: "In 1974, we lost the pennant because all the hitters got the flu on the same day. It was a rare disease. It happened in Minnesota in late

August. We had a six-game lead over the Yankees, and led the Orioles by even more. We finished third.

"That day we had a four-run lead against the Twins in the fifth inning, and then something really weird happened. The wind came out of the north and the temperature dropped thirty degrees. And every hitter caught a cold. It affected all of them, except the two rookies, Jim Rice and Fred Lynn, who weren't playing at the time and were well-protected from it.

"Our manager, Darrell Johnson, couldn't recognize the symptoms, and he kept playing the guys who had colds. And he had these two young healthy guys, and he wouldn't play them. If he had played them, we would have won in '74. There's no doubt in my mind that would have happened. But he didn't.

"Our next stop was Baltimore. We lost four in a row. Then we played them in Boston and lost four more. We just couldn't beat them. And that was it. That year I made every start, went nine, went eight, went nine, and I'd lose by a run. I got shut out three times and got one or two runs scored for me the other two times.

"I remember the day the season was over I couldn't get out of bed. Neither of my arms worked. The phone rang, but I couldn't answer it. I couldn't brush my teeth. I had a water bed, and when I awoke, I thought I was paralyzed. I had to roll off the bed, and I landed on the floor. I couldn't move.

"It was from the fact that my kidneys had shut down taking so much butazolidine and therazolidine, so I had no natural capacity for producing things that keep you going. During the year I had also taken Indicin, Clineral, and Orazime. I'd get hit with a line drive, and I'd take something to thin my blood down. Constantly. I could pitch in the American League, but I couldn't have run in the Kentucky Derby. I'd never have passed the urine test.

"I had to have a shot of Benadryl to get my body back in shape. It scared me.

"Some guys don't like to play hurt. Others do. Everybody has heard the Wally Pipp story. Pipp missed a game with a cold, and Lou Gehrig took his job away. No one wants to be Wally Pipp. So you want to play. But by the end of the season a pitcher is worn down. So they gave me those drugs.

"When I first came up, Buddy Leroux used to give me Librium before I'd go out to the mound. He thought I was hyperactive and it would quiet me down. I'd fall asleep in the third inning.

"I liked Darrell Johnson fine, though a lot of people didn't. He was my first pitching coach, and he gave me some basic knowledge that I used a lot. A lot of times he didn't show up at the ballpark because he was drinking back then, but we all drank because the pressure in Boston is unbelievable. You have so many knowledgeable writers and you are totally surrounded with this tradition, and it's very hard. Dick Williams handled it better than most. Ralph

Houk handled it because he was a major, and he didn't take any shit from nobody."

In 1975, Darrell Johnson would prove he didn't have to take any shit either.

CHAPTER 40

On to Glory: 1975

THE PENNANT

By 1975, the press was beginning to give up a bit on the Red Sox. Mindful of their August swoon the year before, and their missed opportunity in the split-season year of 1972, they concluded that the team just couldn't hack it.

But they had a surprise coming.

Under manager Darrell Johnson, the Red Sox won 95 games in the year 1975. Bolstered by the return to form of Rick Wise, who won 19 games, and two wonderful rookie outfielders, Fred Lynn and Jim Rice, the Red Sox took the lead on June 29 and never lost it. Lynn that year hit .331, drove in 105 runs, and hit 21 home runs. Rice hit .309 with 102 RBIs and 22 home runs. Coming off the bench, Bernie Carbo hit 15 home runs, and on the mound, Wise, Bill Lee, Luis Tiant, Reggie Cleveland, and Rogelio Moret pitched the team to victory.

It was a classic Red Sox team: powerful offense, good starting pitching, no speed on the bases, and an inconsistent bullpen. Dick Drago was the ace of the pen with 15 saves.

Rick Wise could sense it coming even before they took the lead.

Rick Wise: "I led the team in total wins and in starts and tied Bill Lee for the ERA lead. The fact that I came back from a debilitating injury was a really big boost for me mentally. I spent a lot of long hours in rehab with the question mark in the back of my mind, 'Will I be able to pitch again?'

"I remember in '75, we weren't picked to do very well that year. In the early games I was pitching without pain, doing well, and I ran off the longest consecutive wins in my career with nine, culminated by a near no-hitter in Milwaukee.

"I should have had a no-hitter. I had Billy Sharp struck out with two outs in the ninth and didn't get the call. It was a knee-high pitch across the plate and I didn't get the call, and to this day I don't know why. George Scott was the next batter, and you never want to give a hitter like Scott a chance to bat. And I was tiring. It was 98 degrees and muggy in June.

"Anyway, Scott caught a fastball and drove it good and broke it up. I ended up with a two-hitter and we won, which was the most important thing, because we were riding high. It was my ninth straight win, and I was on a roll and pitching very well. We were playing good baseball.

"We had a veteran staff. Tiant was a consummate performer. Bill Lee was a pro. We knew what we were doing. Our catcher, Carlton Fisk, was very intense, very knowledgeable, and always in the game. If your mechanics weren't quite right or you were making bad pitches or getting the ball up in the strike zone, Pudge would come out and tell you. Just remind you. 'Finish it off. Get the ball down.'

"For the younger kids, he had to be more forceful. 'You're not concentrating. You're getting lazy. Let's go. Bear down.' But we knew what had to be done. We had experience.

"We knew Boston had a history of losing leads. The year before was a pretty graphic reminder. We all thought, 'This is ours to win or lose. If we play the way we're capable of playing, we'll win it. No one is going to beat us if we play right. We'd have to lose it ourselves.'

"We didn't."

One of Dick O'Connell's quiet moves in April of 1975 was his dealing of shortstop Mario Guerrero to the St. Louis Cardinals for a player to be named later. In mid-summer 1975, that anonymous player, whose name was Jim Willoughby, joined the Red Sox as the tenth arm on the staff. He got to pitch because relief aces Diego Segui and Dick Drago came up lame and pitcher Dick Pole was injured by a line drive to the face. Willoughby, a starter by trade, was immediately thrown into the closer role by manager Darrell Johnson. Few pitchers do well at first when their role is suddenly switched. Willoughby, a sinkerball control specialist, thrived. He proceeded to either save or win most of the games played in his first two weeks. His presence shored the staff when it needed him most.

Jim Willoughby, Red Sox, 1975–77: "I came up to the Red Sox in early July. They were percentage points in first place when I was told to report. I knew I was going up to the big leagues, but when Ken Boyer called me into his office, I was expecting the call to St. Louis. When he said, 'You're going to Boston,' my response was, 'Where's that?' I knew Boston from my American history classes. I knew it was in the East somewhere.

"The Red Sox had the reputation for being real aloof. I went into the clubhouse that first day, and the first guy who came over to welcome me to the club was Yaz. We were never great friends on the team. Players of his stature tend not to hang out that much with other players because of privacy problems, but in the clubhouse Yaz was a great guy.

"I found out an interesting thing about Yaz that year. He was being used as a DH, and it can get cold sometimes in the summer in Boston. If he was DHing, he'd spring into the clubhouse before he had to bat, and our clubbie, Vince Orlando, would wad up tape balls, and one of the batboys would throw them to him, and he'd take full swings to get some extra practice before he went up there, to make sure he was loose.

"Yaz and Doug Griffin were always setting each other on fire. I remember one time Griffin was sitting at his locker reading the newspaper. Around the clubhouse were spittoons filled with cat litter, and Yaz pushed one over underneath his chair, wadded up a whole bunch of newspapers, and soaked it in alcohol. By now everyone in the clubhouse was watching. He set it on fire and it burst into flames, which were actually above Griffin's feet. He still didn't see it, and those Fiberglas plastic chairs got red hot, and even though Doug got blisters on his ass, he thought it was funny.

"Yaz had a raincoat that he wore that looked exactly like the one Peter Falk wears all the time. It was just as beat up and old. One time we were coming out of the ballpark going to the airport, and the whole back half of it was cut off. Griffin had done that. Of course, at the same time Griffin was wearing slacks cut off above the knees. They were always doing that kind of stuff to each other.

"I had pitched a nine-inning complete game for Tulsa the day before I joined the Sox. They told me they wouldn't use me for three or four days, but I ended up pitching the next day in the second game of a doubleheader, when the Sox went through every pitcher in the bullpen. I had an auspicious beginning, gave up three or four runs. The next day we went back to Boston and had my introduction to the local press. I picked up the newspaper and it said, 'Red Sox Looking for Pitcher, Find Willoughby, Still Looking.' I thought, 'Jesus Christ. So this is what everybody was talking about.'

"I had a day off, and the nature of the health of the pitching staff was such that they had to throw me back into a game the next day. I pitched a couple innings, got a save, and I ended up my first two weeks getting five saves and two wins on our way to the division championship.

"I wasn't aware of pressure affecting anyone in an obvious manner in '75. A guy like Rick Burleson was a super-intense person on the field all the time during the stretch drive every year. He would lose fifteen pounds from midseason to the end, but you try to put him on the bench for a day to give him some rest, and he'd go bananas. He had to be out there.

"There were times he needed to lighten up a little, and on the Red Sox we were fortunate to have Luis Tiant, who had the ability to get people to relax, to step back from the intensity of the moment, look around, and see what the real values are, thereby freeing them to perform.

"You play best when you can relax your mind and let your body and mind do what they can do. And Luis and Rick Wise were two great guys to have around the clubhouse because of their sense of humor.

"I remember in September against Cleveland, we had a couple of games when we weren't playing that well. We always had trouble with Cleveland late in the season. Rick Burleson struck out, and then he went out to his position in the infield and made an error, and he was storming around totally out of control. The whole dugout was quiet, everybody concentrating, the manager pacing, a typical high-pressure situation, and Tiant was at one end of the dugout and Wise at the other end.

"They were talking to each other in one-liners. Luis said something like, 'Nice hands,' and then Wise said, 'That's an All-Star play.' Little putdowns, but laughing at it, and Tiant came back with another cutting comment, and pretty soon the entire dugout was laughing and rolling around, and even Darrell was laughing.

"And everyone loosened up, because Luis and Wise knew everyone was too tight. And they would do that constantly.

"Carlton Fisk was a real steady kind of guy. He was a family man, in control all the time. He very seldom became angry or frustrated. That picture you see of him in the sixth game waving at the ball, to people who know him well that's out of character. He would be excited about something, but never demonstrative. He was one of the solid members of the team that held it together. Him and Rico Petrocelli. If Rico hadn't been at third base, I wouldn't have been a successful pitcher that year. I was a control pitcher, a sinkerball pitcher, not a strikeout pitcher, so I needed a defense behind me, people who can turn two, come up with a good play, and at third base Rico made play after play to get me out of jams. Rico really was a significant factor in my success that year.

"Jim Rice and Freddie Lynn in '75 were the two best players I ever played with. Though Rice never quite developed as an all-around player, he made himself into a very good outfielder because he worked on it every day, and Freddie, I don't know what it was with him, he kind of backed off a little bit. He didn't want to kill himself running into walls like he did in spring training, and that was a significant turning point in his career. He could have been a Ted Williams kind of player. And it was never realized. He just became an excellent baseball player.

"With a month left in the season, my elbow started getting a little tight. I asked Darrell for a three-days rest. The Yankees were coming to town, and though I would blood-and-guts it with the best of them, I didn't think I would be effective the way my elbow was, and I didn't want to be in the position to go out there when someone else could do the job and I couldn't, and we'd lose. I told Stan Williams, the pitching coach, 'Sorry it's the Yankees, but I need a couple days here.'

"It took me a week or so to get back in form, and I was ready to go the last three weeks of the season. And by the time the Series came around, I had it all together and pitched well."

Jim Willoughby finished the year with five victories and eight saves. Until Segui and Drago were able to return, it was Willoughby who held the staff together for the stretch run to the Eastern Division championship.

Bill Lee: "Nineteen seventy-five was the most boring year we ever had. Being successful every day is pretty boring. But no one was better than Freddie Lynn that year, with the exception of maybe Jim Rice. Freddie did everything well. Jim was raw power.

"Freddie Lynn went to USC as a freshman in '69. It was the first year freshmen were allowed to play on the varsity. USC won the College World Series. In '70 he won the College World Series, and again in '71 and '72. In '74 he was in the Red Sox organization, and in '75 he won the pennant and won the Most Valuable Player award. Freddie was the greatest ballplayer to come along since Babe Ruth and Ted Williams. He had five of the greatest years, and the next year he slid back into second base and jammed his ankle, and he was really never the perfect ballplayer again.

"Jim Rice was one of the best left fielders I ever had out there. He could go and get the ball. In one ballgame, he leaped up and robbed Glenn Borgmann of two home runs and in the same ballgame Freddie Lynn robbed someone else of a home run, and I ended up throwing a four-hitter and won the game, 3–1.

"Jim Rice was an incredible talent. He was a powerful home-run hitter, but the fans never liked Jim Rice. No one could like Jim Rice. Jim Rice had one of the biggest egos I've ever seen. He treated people so abruptly, just had no need for anybody, gave no time back to the fans, just was not a nice person. And the fans all knew that. If you have all your bridges sealed off so that you have yourself completely shut off from people, why should he think he should be treated nicely? And then he generated more and more hostility.

"He complained about Fred Lynn, because Lynn could string three words together. Rice was always defensive, stand-offish. Lynn's no real popular guy. But it had nothing to do with any black-white thing. It was all coming from Jim Rice.

"Freddie ran into Jerry Kapstein at Providence University. Jerry became his agent, and I think when ballplayers have agents, they fall from the graces of God, and they cannot develop into the ballplayers they would have. It's a strange belief I have. A lot of people think I'm crazy. But when ballplayers hire agents, they cease to speak for themselves. They isolate themselves from the fans and alienate themselves from the general manager, and baseball has never been the same.

"Everything we did in '75 on the field, off the field, was unbelievable. The presence of young talent forced the older players to play well to save their jobs. It just kept people going. The greatest thing that happened to Carl Yastrzemski was Fred Lynn and Jim Rice coming to the team to push him for his last few years.

"Show me a club with veterans with a bunch of young kids coming up pushing them and I'll show you a club that's going to go somewhere. Especially if the veterans suck it up and go out and do the job. And manager Darrell Johnson did a great job by blending the old with the new.

"He had the ability to do that after '74, because the old guys hadn't done the job. That allowed Darrell to experiment and use the younger guys in '75, and that's what did it. There was no club in major-league baseball that had more talent than the '75 Red Sox. We had six outfielders who could start with any ballclub: Rice, Lynn, Yaz, Juan Beniquez, Bernie Carbo, Dwight Evans, and Rick Miller. All of them could go and run and get it, all could throw, and they could all play every position.

"I called Darrell Johnson 'the cat' because he kept falling out of trees and landing on his feet. When you have a ballclub like he had, it didn't matter who he put in. He wasn't going to make a bad move. Great ballclubs make great managers. Let's put it this way: he was a nice guy and he drank, so I liked him.

"We didn't have much of a bullpen in those days, but we didn't need one. I could start and finish, and so could Luis Tiant, who was one of the hardest-working men I ever knew in baseball, who had one of the most tenacious, killer instincts in the game. That's what made him a great pitcher. He never gave in to the hitters. He knew when to trick hitters. He knew when he had a guy on the ropes, to bury him. Come the seventh, eighth, and ninth innings, you'd yawn and go back to sleep. Tiant closed them down.

"We also had Rick Wise. He threw good. But he would also have a seven-run lead going into the third inning. When you know you're going to get runs, it makes you a relaxed pitcher. When you have a good offensive ballclub, if you make a mistake, you don't let it worry you, you don't get tight, you don't let it bother you. He gave up a lot of solo home runs, but they never beat us.

"We ran right through the damn league."

*   *   *

The Red Sox coasted to the division championship by 4½ games. Could they keep it going?

THE WORLD SERIES

In the American League Championship Series, the hero was the veteran Carl Yastrzemski. Yaz had hurt his shoulder badly during the season, and he would never hit with the same power again. He was also saddled emotionally. His mother had cancer and was dying. She was supposed to die in six months. But she was tough. She lasted three more years. And her son was equally tough. He bit his lip and went back to work.

Tiant had suffered a back injury during the summer, coming back on September 11 after three weeks of inactivity to beat the Tigers and then shut out Jim Palmer and the Orioles. Then he shut out Cleveland to all but clinch the pennant.

Against the powerful Oakland A's, Luis Tiant pitched a three-hitter to win the opener, 7–1. Yaz singled to start the winning rally.

In the second game, the A's led 2–0 when Bert Campaneris walked with two outs in the third. Sal Bando drilled a hit off the wall, and Yastrzemski turned, faced the Wall, and waited for the carom. He fielded it cleanly, whirled, and threw to third. Campy was erased on the play.

At bat, Yaz had had to find a new stance. His shoulder injury didn't allow him to hold his hands high anymore. In the fourth inning of the second game, Denny Doyle singled against Vida Blue, and then Yaz went the other way and hit a home run over the fence in left center. Then, in the bottom of the sixth, with the score tied, Yaz doubled and scored the winning run on a hit by catcher Carlton Fisk.

Yaz's magic continued in Game Three. Rick Wise pitched the Red Sox to a 1–0 lead in the fourth, when Reggie Jackson lined a ball down the left-field line. Yaz sprinted toward the corner to intercept the ball, and as he gloved it, he saw Jackson heading for second. Yastrzemski spun and fired perfectly. Jackson was called out.

He wasn't done yet. In the eighth, with a 4–1 lead but Wise faltering, two A's runners on and no one out, Reggie Jackson stroked a line drive to left center. When it was hit, Yastrzemski didn't think he could even cut it off, but at the last moment he made a lunging dive for the ball, which bounced once. His body flew sideways, his right arm fully extended, and the ball stuck in the webbing of his glove.

Only one run scored. Jackson was held to a single, which enabled reliever Dick Drago to get the next batter to ground into a double play. The Sox won, 5–3. The dispatching of the mighty Oakland A's had come with surprising ease.

Jim Willoughby: "It happened so fast and seemed so easy. We were in control in all three games."

Rick Wise: "We weren't given a chance to beat the three-time defending world champions. It was a wonderful feeling. And they said we didn't belong on the same field with the Reds. As far as we were concerned, there was never any doubt we were going to win the World Series. No team goes into postseason play thinking they're not the best. It's unthinkable, even though again we weren't picked to win."

The 1975 World Series opponent was the Big Red Machine of Cincinnati. The indomitable Reds had finished 20 games in front of the second-place Los Angeles Dodgers. The team featured a lineup of potential Hall of Famers: Tony Perez, Joe Morgan, Dave Concepcion, Pete Rose, Johnny Bench, George Foster. Six of its starting pitchers had won ten games or more. In the bullpen, Rawly Eastwick and Will McEnaney had 37 saves between them.

It was a daunting task, but the Red Sox felt like destiny's children.

In the first game, Luis Tiant pitched a five-hit shutout. He was masterful, entertaining, and at the top of his game of control and deception.

Tack Burbank: "In Game One, Tiant was unhittable. It was a great experience to see the Big Red Machine shut down. We had heard so much about them in the press. They were so good and so brash, all of them, including their manager, Sparky Anderson, so you had the sense they thought the Red Sox couldn't beat them.

"Tiant was a Cuban in Boston, and normally the Latin players don't have much of a following in Boston. Luis was different. He had a wonderful personality, was eminently quotable, and he was the most entertaining pitcher the Red Sox ever had. After the game, he would be in his locker with a cigar in his mouth, drinking a beer and talking. He was very open, and the fans loved him.

"I remember Joe Garagiola and his call of the '75 World Series saying, 'How can you hit a guy who doesn't even look at you when he goes into his windup?' He had a whole assortment of deliveries and pitches, and every pitch was an adventure."

Jim Willoughby: "Luis Tiant was the quintessential professional in that he knew what he could do, was the master of his whole repertoire, threw a dozen different kinds of pitches from three different positions, and he threw them all for strikes without even looking at home plate.

"Tiant was fascinating. He threw sidearm, overhand, three quarters; sliders, knuckleballs—he threw knuckleballs! What starting pitcher throws an occasional knuckleball? Forkballs, screwballs, just amazing!"

In the second game, Bill Lee had the Red Sox ahead 2–1 going into the ninth inning. Fate then intervened.

Tack Burbank: "We ultimately lost the World Series because of a rain delay during Game Two. Bill Lee, who was probably my favorite player on the team, had absolutely handcuffed Cincinnati, and after eight innings there was a long rain delay. When Lee came out to pitch the ninth, he gave up a hit, and bing, bing, bing, the Reds scored twice, and to me that was the turning point of the Series."

After the delay, Reds catcher Johnny Bench doubled, and manager Darrell Johnson brought in Dick Drago, the Red Sox stopper. Drago got the first two batters. The Red Sox were one out away from a two-game advantage, but Dave Concepcion singled in the tying run, stole second—shortstop Rick Burleson got the tag down, but the umpire called Concepcion safe—and a double by Ken Griffey put the Reds up for good and tied the Series.

In the next game, the Red Sox got jobbed even worse. At first it looked hopeful, when outfielder Dwight Evans tied the game with a surprise two-run home run in the top of the ninth.

Rick Wise: "When Evans hit the home run, I jumped for joy. I said, 'All right, we have a chance to win this thing now.' We didn't, but nevertheless it gave recognition to our club as one that would not fold, one that had a lot of heart and character, a club that had the talent and ability and the where-withal to be on the same field as the mighty Cincinnati Reds."

However, Evans's dramatic home run only set the stage for a controversial play, one that shall be rued by Red Sox fans for all time. In the bottom of the tenth inning, with a runner on first, pinch hitter Ed Armbrister bounced a sacrifice bunt high in the air just in front of the plate, and then somehow entangled himself with Carlton Fisk as the catcher stepped forward to make the play. Fisk's problem was that Armbrister was standing there—he hadn't run, so he was blocking Fisk's path to throwing the ball to second.

Fisk caught the ball, pushed Armbrister out of the way—without trying to tag him—and then threw to second, seeking a double play, but the collision affected his throw, and the ball sailed off Rick Burleson's glove and into center field. The runner on first, Cesar Geronimo, went to third and then eventually scored.

Clearly, it was interference on the part of Armbrister, but umpire Larry Barnett ruled, "It was a simple collision," saying that an interference call was proper only if the collision was intentional.

The rulebook, however, clearly indicates that intention has nothing to do with it. Section 7:09: "It is interference by a batter or a runner when (1) He fails to avoid a fielder who is attempting to field a batted ball . . ." Which is what Armbrister did. Armbrister should have been called out, and Geronimo should have been made to go back to first.

Rick Wise: "I've looked at the play a hundred times. I don't know why interference wasn't called, and I never will. I thought Fisk got the ball in time to get the force at second, but he made a high throw to second base. His thoughts might have been scrambled, thinking he was going to get a call. He wasn't in good position to make the throw, as a result kind of hurried it as he waited for a call that never came.

"The throw sailed into center field, and that gave them some impetus to go on and win the ballgame."

Jim Willoughby: "I was on the mound. There was a runner on first, and Armbrister pinch-hit. He was bunting. The bunt was in order. My responsibility was to cover the first-base side of the mound. Being left-handed, he was going to bunt that way.

"When he squared to bunt, it was no surprise. I was ready. But he bunted a ball that bounced on the plate and went straight up. The problem was that as he squared around, he was over the plate, and he didn't move. Fisk had to push him out of the way to get the guy at second, and he threw it away.

"It was my opinion we should have gotten a double play. At least they should have called the interference and made the runner go back to first. One out and a runner on first is a hell of a lot different from a runner on third and first and nobody out.

"I couldn't believe it. I was really dumbfounded. By the time I got to the clubhouse, I was yelling and screaming.

"Larry Barnett made a bad call. He got death threats from Boston fans the next day and for weeks. The way baseball umpires are, when they make a decision and put their heads together and decide, it's never reversed. Everybody has to save face, and it wasn't going to be changed, especially in the spotlight they were in, bad call or not.

"That was a bad call, but you try to go beyond that. At that point Darrell took me out and brought in a left-hander, Roger Moret, to pitch to Joe Morgan, and we got an out, and then there was a sacrifice fly that scored the winning run."

Roger Angell: "There were curses and hot looks in the Red Sox clubhouse that night, along with an undercurrent of feeling that manager Johnson had not complained with much vigor.

" 'If it had been me out there,' " Bill Lee said, " 'I'd have bitten Barnett's ear off, I'd have van Gogh'ed him.' "

Luis Tiant struggled to win Game Four. He made 163 pitches, left men on base at every turn, and proved his gutsiness. He won 5–4, evening the series at two games each.

The Reds' Don Gullett won Game Five, as Cincinnati retook the lead. The two teams returned to Boston, where it rained for three days. When the downpour finally ceased, the nation would witness one of the greatest baseball games ever played.

The Sixth Game

In Red Sox lore, there are no world championships to celebrate after the year 1918, when Armistice Day ended World War I. That year, the Eighteenth Amendment to the Constitution proclaiming Prohibition was passed.

No, in the intervening years there are no world championships to relive, but there have been legendary games. There were the no-hitters pitched by Howard Ehmke in 1923, Mel Parnell in 1956, Earl Wilson in 1962, and Bill Monbouquette less than two months later that same year. Dave Morehead also pitched one in 1965.

Then there were magical games, such as the pennant clinchers in '46 and '67 and the final doubleheader of the '41 season, when the Splendid Splinter made six hits in eight at bats to finish the season at .406, and of course Williams's final game at the end of '60.

Then there is the drama and the excitement of the sixth game of the 1975 World Series. It was like a heavyweight fight, two great teams duking it out. For Red Sox fans—and many others—it was the greatest single ballgame ever played.

Three days of heavy rain had preceded Game Six. The Red Sox players were on edge.

Rick Wise: "Everyone was on pins and needles from the anxiety of waiting, waiting, waiting. That famed New England weather was holding up the greatest sports event in all of sport."

*   *   *

The delay allowed manager Darrell Johnson to start his ace, Luis Tiant. In the first inning, Fred Lynn, the Sox's wondrous rookie, who New York Yankee manager Bill Virdon had said would be "the next DiMaggio," hit a three-run homer. Tiant pitched a shutout into the fifth inning, when he walked Ed Armbrister to open the way for the Reds to tie the game. George Foster drove in two runs in the seventh, and a Cesar Geronimo homer made the score 6–3 Reds. Tiant left the game, trailing by three seemingly insurmountable runs.

In the bottom of the eighth inning, all seemed lost. Fred Lynn, who had almost knocked himself out running into the center-field fence chasing Ken Griffey's triple, started things with a single. Rico Petrocelli walked. Reds manager Sparky Anderson brought in right-handed relief ace Rawly Eastwick, who got two quick outs.

Boston manager Darrell Johnson sent left-handed batter Bernie Carbo to pinch-hit. Carbo had lost his outfield job to young Dwight Evans early in the season and had been used mostly as a pinch hitter. Though Carbo hated that Evans was playing instead of him, he had been successful in his limited role, three times during the season hitting pinch-hit home runs. The Reds were within an inning of winning their first World Championship since 1940. Bernie Carbo stood in their way.

Eastwick threw him a high fastball, out over the plate, and Carbo swung . . .

Bill Lee: "Carbo was the greatest clutch hitter I ever saw. He could come off the bench and deliver in a clutch situation. He had nerves of steel. Nothing bothered him. I've seen him come out of a dead sleep and hit.

"I remember in the Hall of Fame game at Cooperstown, Bernie was out behind the fence sleeping at the scoreboard during the game because it didn't mean anything and he was getting some rest. Don Zimmer got really mad at him and tried to show him up. He woke him up and had him bat, figuring he'd do bad. Bernie walked up, hit a home run, ran around the bases, and went back to sleep.

"Managers hated that."

Rick Wise: "I loved Bernie. Bernie was way before his time. He was a free spirit, and we didn't have a lot of free spirits back then. Bernie was an off-the-wall kind of guy. He didn't seem like he was serious. He never took the game that seriously, but when he played, he was very good. He had a hell of an arm, was a good outfielder, and had tremendous power. He hit like a right-hander. His power was to left center and center field. For such a small guy, he generated tremendous bat speed and power. But he was never serious. He didn't take the game home with him when it was over.

"I was out in the bullpen at the time of Bernie's home run. All the pitchers were in the pen. It could have been the last game of the Series. I watched that ball soar majestically into center field. When it landed in the stands, it was absolute bedlam. It was really one of the most dramatic home runs ever. We were down three runs and there were two outs in the eighth, not looking good, because Cincinnati had very good closers, and they usually finished off a team when they got in that position in the late innings. They didn't lose many games.

"How often do you see pinch-hit home runs? It's very difficult even to get a base hit in a pinch-hitting role. Bernie was able to go deep in the World Series and tie it up."

Jim Willoughby: "Bernie had been in one of those slumps where he was pulling his head out when he was swinging, and he kept coming up to me during the Series: 'If I get in, maybe I should swing this way, maybe I should step out, maybe I should use this stance.' He was one of those hitters who would always change his stance around when he was struggling.

"Before the game we were talking, and he said, 'What should I do, Willow?' I said, 'Bernie, see the ball. Hit the ball. Wherever it is, just see it good.' That's a very basic statement, but Bernie took it seriously. He said, 'Yeah, that's what I'll do. I'll just see the ball.'

"After he hit the home run, he told me, 'I saw that one real well.'

"Diego Segui was sitting next to me in the bullpen when he hit it. He was so excited, he turned and grabbed my arm and squeezed it, and if you know Diego at all, he's one of the strongest men around, and he left bruises on my arm.

"But Bernie was capable of doing that kind of thing, stepping out from out of nowhere and hitting it out."

Tack Burbank: "When Carbo got up to hit, I felt as though the Series was over. There were two strikes on him, and he got totally fooled by a pitch that was inside, and somehow he just about dug the ball out of the catcher's mitt to foul it off. He got just a little piece and looked pathetic doing it.

"Well, on the next pitch he hit the sucker into the triangle up in center field to tie the game and save the Series. It was unbelievable.

"I was seated in front of my TV at home with my wife Christine. Our first summer of marriage, 1971, we had lived two blocks from Fenway in the fifth story of a five-story walk-up, and we went to thirty-seven Red Sox games. We sat in the bleachers. It was a great place to go on a hot night. She was a fan.

"So when Carbo hit it out, Christine and I were just jumping up and down screaming, and already we knew it was the greatest game that had ever been played, and we hadn't even played the ninth."

Bernie Carbo: "I wasn't looking to hit a home run. I wasn't thinking home run. There were two runners on. I worked the count to 3 and 2.

"What happened was, he threw me a slider, and I thought it was going to be a fastball. I went out to get it, and I saw it was going to be a slider, and I fouled it off. At the same time, the umpire called it a ball. Johnny (Bench) turned around at the umpire and said, 'That was a strike. That pitch was a strike. The ball had two inches of the plate.'

"I stepped out of the box. I figured, 'He's going to be thinking I'm going to be looking slider, so instead I'm going to be looking fastball.'

"Eastwick got the fastball up and away, where I was looking. I knew I would be swinging. I wasn't going to be taking. I knew I would commit myself to where it would be difficult to stop my swing. I got the pitch, and I hit it.

"When I started running to first base, I didn't know if the ball was going to go out of the park, because I knew that center field was a long ways. I figured it might be off the wall, and I ran to first and started for second, and I could see Geronimo turn his back, and that's when I knew the ball was gone. The game was tied."

The Red Sox should have won the game the next inning. They loaded the bases in the ninth with nobody out, but there was a short fly ball on which Denny Doyle tagged and was thrown out on a perfect throw by left fielder George Foster. Don Zimmer, the third-base coach, was shouting, "No, no," but Doyle thought Zim was telling him to "Go, go." Doyle wasn't even close.

In the tenth, Red Sox reliever Dick Drago hit Pete Rose's uniform. Griffey bunted, and catcher Carlton Fisk bravely threw Rose out at second. Morgan then connected solidly. Everyone thought the ball was going out of the park and into the right-field seats, but Dwight Evans sprinted backwards after it, and at the last second pulled the ball in over his head at the fence. Then he bounced off the wall, spun, and threw the ball quickly in to the infield. First baseman Carl Yastrzemski took the relay and threw to Burleson, who had raced from shortstop to cover first. Griffey was easily doubled off first. Evans's catch, old-timers said, was as great as any made by Tris Speaker or Duffy Lewis, or, heaven protect us, even the great Harry Hooper. Not bad for a player the writers and fans had been trying to trade for three years.

There was no scoring in the eleventh inning. Then came the twelfth.

Carlton Fisk was facing the Reds' Pat Darcy. Darcy was a low-ball pitcher. Fisk was a low-ball hitter. Fisk was looking low. He got it low and hit the second pitch into the darkness above the lights down the left-field foul line of Fenway Park.

Adding to the drama was the question of whether the fly ball pulled by Fisk would curl foul or stay fair as it approached the pole. After striking the ball, Fisk took a step toward first. When he realized he had hit the ball far enough for it to go out of the ballpark, he stopped and watched. Everyone stopped and watched. Like thirty-five thousand insecure grooms who had just asked the loves of their lives, Will you marry me? everyone in the ballpark held very still, expectant, waiting for an answer. Fisk started to wave his arms: Go fair! Go fair!

Yes or no? Fair or foul?

When the ball finally dropped down and struck the innermost edge of the netting on the pole at 12:34 A.M., the Red Sox catcher threw his fists above his head and performed a balletic leap of grace and style. Serenaded by the loudspeaker's blare of Handel's "Hallelujah" Chorus performed on the Hammond organ, Fisk completed his circuit of the bases accompanied by hundreds of fans who felt compelled to run along with him. When he arrived at home plate, he jumped on it with both feet.

Fisk, his teammates, and millions of Red Sox fans across America celebrated one of the Red Sox's most climactic and exhilarating victories. The fans reacted as though the Sox had won the Series, not merely tied it up.

Jim Willoughby: "My approach to the whole game of baseball as a job was to remove myself emotionally from it. I performed best as a mechanic. But about the tenth inning of this game, I started hoping. Where before I was saying to myself, 'We've got to win this game,' I started thinking, 'I hope we win it. We *should* win it.'

"From the bullpen when the ball went up, you can't tell whether it's fair or foul. And Fisk was standing at home plate, so we knew it was close. And then when everyone went crazy, we went over the wall. Nobody waited to go through the gate. We jumped the bullpen wall and headed straight for the field.

"We were on our way before he crossed the plate, because he didn't do a fast trot. He was savoring the moment.

"What a high! Wild jubilation. Everyone was so excited, especially after we got screwed in the third game. We had been in a position where it would have been easy to set yourself up for a lot of negative thinking.

"We were underdogs to start with. Nobody gave us a chance against the Big Red Machine and all that crap. We knew that was a media hype more than anything else. We knew we could play with anybody if we were on our game, and we did."

Tack Burbank: "When the ball stayed fair, Christine and I jumped up and down and were shouting and shouting, jumping up and down screaming, and then we just started hugging each other. It was very emotional. It was a great moment in our marriage."

Red Sox fans have treated this game as the Big One of modern-day baseball. It is celebrated in Boston the same way the Civil War was celebrated in the South, as though there had not been a Gettysburg. By that point, the southerners knew they weren't going to win the war. But they sure were thrilled when the Rebs kicked the crap out of the North at Chickamauga.

So it was with the Game Six victory over Cincinnati's Big Red Machine. It had been such an epic struggle that baseball's Homer, Roger Angell, waxed thusly:

Roger Angell: "I suddenly remembered all my old absent and distant Soxafflicted friends (and all the other Red Sox fans, all over New England), and I thought of them, . . . and I saw all of them dancing and shouting and kissing and leaping about like the fans at Fenway jumping up and down in their bedrooms and kitchens and living rooms, and in bars and trailers, and even in some boats here and there, I suppose, and on back-country roads (a lone driver getting the news over the radio and blowing his horn over and over, and finally, pulling up and getting out and leaping up and down on the cold macadam, yelling into the night), and all of them, for once at least, utterly joyful and believing in that joy, alight with it."

Game Seven pitted two left-handers against one another, Bill Lee against Don Gullett. Before the game Lee was asked by reporters to compare himself to the Reds' ace.

"After the game, Don Gullett is going to the Hall of Fame," Lee said, "and I'm going to the Eliot Lounge."

The Red Sox gave their faithful a playful tease. They were leading 3–0 in the third inning, but against Don Gullett they had already stranded nine runners. One added crucial hit would have put the Reds away. It never came.

Bill Lee held that 3–0 lead until the sixth inning, when the indomitable Pete Rose hit a leadoff single. With one out, Bench bounced a double-play grounder to Burleson, who threw to Denny Doyle just as Rose slid high and hard. Doyle's throw to first went into the Boston dugout. With Bench standing on second, the next Reds batter was first baseman Tony Perez.

Tack Burbank: "Tony Perez had had a horrendous first half of the World Series. He had gone 0-for-15 in the first four games, terrible, looked awful, and my wife Christine was feeling very sorry for him, and she started talking about it, because she said Tony Perez seemed like such a nice guy. I was getting mad at her. I said, 'Wait a minute. Let's feel sorry for him after it's over.' "

Lee threw an off-speed blooper pitch, but placed it badly, and Perez emerged from his early-Series slump by propelling the ball over the Wall to close the gap to 3–2.

Jim Willoughby: "In the three years I pitched against the Reds for the San Francisco Giants before coming to the Sox, Tony Perez never gave me any trouble, because I never gave him any strikes to hit, nothing where he could get the ball on the bat.

"Bill had never pitched against Perez, but he was the one guy in Cincinnati, and maybe the whole National League, that you would never throw the eephus pitch to. You throw him sliders in the dirt to strike him out. You don't want to throw him that pitch. He was a free swinger with bat control. He could wait and stride and take a half-swing and still have the power to hit it out."

Bill Lee: "I was throwing pretty good in Game Seven, but I gave up a two-run homer to Tony Perez after we failed to turn the double play, which most fans don't realize. I had a runner on first base and one out, and I got Bench to hit a nice two-hopper to short, and Doyle threw the relay over the first baseman's head.

"They had moved Doyle out of double-play position because Bench had hit me to right field. The scouting report had changed. I didn't know at the time I threw the pitch that Doyle was that far into the hole. Burleson had the chance to get it to him, but Doyle had to come from so far away that he didn't have the chance to make the good pivot and throw, even though he had plenty of time.

"And now I have Perez up and two out. I let it bother me, and out of the stretch I threw a curveball too hard and hung it, and he hit it about forty miles. And now we have a one-run lead."

An inning later, Lee developed a blister. Ken Griffey walked when Lee couldn't get the ball over the plate, and Lee had to come out. It signaled the end for the Red Sox.

Bill Lee: "I tore the skin off my thumb, and the rest was history. But we could have had six or seven runs in the first three innings of that game. We were just pounding the ball, but we couldn't score any runs. We kept stranding people at second and third with one out. We just couldn't break the game open, didn't put them away, and when you don't put a team like Cincinnati away, they're going to come and get you.

"I just wish I could have thrown strikes after my thumb went. But I couldn't. I hated to bleed on the ball like that."

Darrell Johnson brought in Roger Moret. Griffey quickly stole second, and then the great Pete Rose, who finished the Series getting on base eleven out of fifteen at bats, singled in the tying run. Johnson went back to the pen and brought in Jim Willoughby to get the final out in the seventh.

Willow, who in the Series pitched six and a third innings of no-run baseball, retired the Reds easily in the eighth. In the Red Sox eighth, with the score still tied, Dwight Evans led off with a walk. Shortstop Rick Burleson tried to bunt him to second, but failed. He grounded into a double play. The next batter scheduled was Willoughby.

Darrell Johnson had a hard decision. Should he leave Willow in to hit for himself, or should he pinch-hit for him and use another, less effective pitcher in the ninth? It was Tom Wright batting for Ellis Kinder in 1949 all over again.

Johnson decided to do just what Joe McCarthy had done. He batted for his pitcher. He took out Jim Willoughby, who had handcuffed the Reds, and sent to the plate Cecil Cooper, mired in a 1-for-18 slump. Cooper fouled out.

Rick Wise: "There were two outs, and Darrell went ahead and made a change. Willoughby had pitched real, real well and was throwing a nasty sinkerball they were pounding into the dirt. He took a calculated chance. It didn't work. Obviously, Darrell was trying to win just as badly as we were. I don't ever want to say that he wasn't. We had the hammer. We were home. If you get something going, next thing you know someone hits one over the Wall, and it's over. I would never want to second-guess a manager. It's something he has to live with."

Jim Willoughby: "I was the scheduled batter, and I was swinging the bat. In the National League and all through my career all the way back to Little League, I was a good hitter. And I had this dream—the night before the seventh game I was rehashing the whole season. In March I was wondering whether my career was over, and here I was going into the seventh game of the World Series.

"I fell asleep, and I dreamed that in the seventh game I came in and saved the game and hit a home run in the bottom of the ninth to win it. It was one of those fantasy dreams that you have. The Fenway wall is only 315 feet, and I'm capable of hitting them out of there.

"So when Darrell pinch-hit for me, the disappointment was more that I didn't have the chance to live the fantasy than the reality of the situation. I didn't have a problem intellectually with Darrell taking me out. Even though Cecil Cooper was 1-for-18 at the time, and he popped up. Under those circumstances, I would bet on him as opposed to betting on me."

Tack Burbank: "I never would have pinch-hit for him. How could he have done that? Willoughby had pitched beautifully, and he was their premier reliever down the stretch. He pinch-hit for him with two outs and nobody on. It didn't make any sense.

"There were a couple of turning points in the Series. One was the rain delay in Game Two, and then lifting Willoughby for a pinch hitter was a big mistake. I said it then. I said it as it was being made. And I continue to say it. Hell, I've only been saying it for sixteen years."

The 1975 World Series was settled in the very last inning, and the Red Sox did not win it. The true Red Sox fans did not expect to win it. As Roger Angell described it, "Fenway Park was like a waiting accident ward early on a Saturday night."

Having removed Willoughby, Darrell Johnson needed a new pitcher to toil in the ninth. His choice: rookie Jim Burton.

Jim Willoughby: "There were plenty of comments about the move, especially from writers after the game. We had to bring in a rookie pitcher, although people forget he led the team in ERA and was a strong member of the bullpen all year long. With hindsight came the second-guessing from the players. That's the thing about hindsight. Who can tell? My feeling was that most of it was sour grapes."

Rich Hershenson: "In the end, it all came down to Jim Burton. Burton had barely played. He had been called up late in the year. They must have had somebody better. When I saw him coming in to pitch, I thought it was a joke. And then I was hoping, the same kind of hope I had growing up, that even though this pitcher was bad, somehow he would hold up the team. But I wasn't very optimistic."

Burton began the inning doing just what a relief pitcher isn't supposed to do. He walked Reds outfielder Ken Griffey, who went to second on a sacrifice bunt and then on to third on a groundout by pinch hitter Dan Driessen. Pete Rose walked. Now there were runners on first and third. Burton was an out away from extricating himself from the jam. The rookie ran the count on Joe Morgan, who would be named the National League's Most Valuable Player that year, to 1 and 2, and then threw the Reds' second baseman a tough outside slider. Morgan protected with the bat, and the ball blooped out into the very short center field well in front of Fred Lynn as the go-ahead run scored.

Rick Wise: "It wasn't a mistake pitch. It was a good pitch, and it was a good bit of hitting on Morgan's part. It's just the way it goes."

*   *   *

In the Red Sox ninth, Will McEnaney retired the Sox one, two, three. With two outs, Carl Yastrzemski, who had also made the last out in the 1967 World Series against the Cardinals, flied out weakly to Reds center fielder Cesar Geronimo.

The players of the Big Red Machine were champions of the world, but though the Sox lost, it would be a Series to be cherished in the minds of Red Sox fans forever.

Rick Wise: "They won it. We didn't lose it. We didn't give it away. Look at the box scores of all seven games, and you can see what a well-played Series it was. It was a tremendously played Series, and credit should go to all the players involved. Someone's got to lose, someone's got to win. After what had to be a psychologically crushing loss for the Reds in Game Six, they had the character to come back and beat us in the ninth inning of the seventh game. You have to give credit where it's due. You can't plead, 'What if? What if?' Everyone gave his best and was a great credit to the game."

Roger Angell: "The games have ended, the heroes are dispersed, and another summer has died late in Boston, but still one yearns for them and wishes them back, so great was their pleasure.

"A[ny] recapitulation and re-examination of the 1975 Series suggests that at the very least we may conclude that there has never been a better one.

"In six of the seven games, the winning team came from behind twice.

"In five games, the winning margin was one run.

"There were two extra-inning games, and two games were settled in the ninth inning.

"Overall, the games were retied or saw the lead reversed thirteen times.

"No other series, not even the celebrated Giants–Red Sox thriller of 1912, can match these figures.

". . . This year the splendid autumn affair rose to our utmost expectations and then surpassed them, attaining at last such a .level of excellence and emotional reward that it seems likely that the participants will in time remember this Series not for its outcome but for the honor of having played in it, for having made it happen."

Rich Hershenson: "That was another year that bum Yastrzemski made the last out of the World Series."

Mark Starr: "After the seventh game ended, I went into my living room with a bottle of Jack Daniel's, put on the Allman Brothers' 'Whipping Post,' and blasted it, turned the lights out, and drank myself into oblivion.

"My ex-wife came over and told me I was a 'Herculean asshole.'

"I said, 'No, I'm just from Boston.'

"We lasted another five years. We made it through Bucky Dent, and then we split up."

CHAPTER 41

End of an Era

TURMOIL

One month after the end of the '75 Series, pitchers Andy Messersmith of Los Angeles and Dave McNally of Baltimore were declared free agents by arbitrator Peter Seitz. Indentured servitude in baseball was dead. By the next summer, Red Sox owner Tom Yawkey also would be dead. Over the next few years, Carlton Fisk, the Red Sox hero of the Series, shortstop Rick Burleson, outfielders Freddie Lynn and Bernie Carbo, and pitchers Jim Willoughby, Bill Lee, Luis Tiant, and Rick Wise all would be gone.

The day of a player holding out for an extra ten thousand dollars was over. Starting ballplayers would soon average half a million dollars a year in salary. If they held out, it would be for millions.

And team loyalty to and from the Red Sox players would largely become a thing of the past.

The year 1976 began with so much promise. General manager Dick O'Connell added pitcher Ferguson Jenkins, a future Hall of Famer, to a starting rotation that already included Bill Lee, Luis Tiant, and Rick Wise.

But all teams, including the Red Sox, were affected by labor turmoil once Peter Seitz ruled that the reserve clause no longer bound a player to a team forever. Under the ruling, when a contract was up, the player would be free to sign with another team. Owners could no longer treat their players like dirt if they so desired. Now they would have to kiss the players' behinds or risk losing them. The Revolution had begun.

At the start of spring training, the owners announced they would lock out the players until a new basic agreement was reached. Training was delayed until March 19, when Commissioner Bowie Kuhn forced the owners to allow the players to practice. The new agreement was signed in July.

On the Red Sox, starters Freddie Lynn, Rick Burleson, and Carlton Fisk were threatening that if the Red Sox did not give them lucrative contracts they would play out the year, become free agents, and go play for other teams. All three had hired tough-talking agent Jerry Kapstein to represent them. Management had never been faced with such a challenge before, and the negotiations turned ugly.

Around the league, the baseball owners, including Tom Yawkey, didn't fully appreciate that a new era in player relations had been forged. Yawkey had always been generous with his players, had treated them as family, and here were star players, his beloved boys, refusing to negotiate in the spirit of we're-all-in-this-together.

For a long time, the Red Sox refused to negotiate with the three. Rumors abounded that Lynn and Fisk would be traded to the Oakland A's for Charlie Finley's potential free agents, including Vida Blue, Joe Rudi, Gene Tenace, and Sal Bando. A trade never materialized, and once a new basic agreement with the players was signed, all three Red Sox players did eventually sign staggering five-year deals with the Red Sox. But all through the spring, the contract issue contributed to a lack of team unity, and, worse, the unhappiness of the three cast a pall over the clubhouse. "Business" was the new operative word, as players talked more about money—and less about baseball.

Jim Willoughby: "At the time when I was asked whether the holdouts of Fisk, Burleson, and Lynn affected the team, my answer was, 'No, it didn't,' because I didn't see it specifically. But as you get older, you get wiser—maybe—and I believe it really did affect the whole atmosphere of the ballclub, because we didn't have the same feeling that we had in '75.

"Those guys were under a lot of pressure. I know at times it was affecting Fisk, just because we'd be out after games, and I could tell in our conversations it was a more troubled Carlton Fisk. He had weight on his mind that he didn't need. He wanted it to be settled.

"Freddie was a real mellow Southern California guy, and he handled it best of all. It wasn't in his hands, so he could divorce himself from the day-to-day part of it.

"But it affected the rest of the team. Our run production was down a hundred runs from the year before. The team didn't hit, which affected my stats. I led the team in ERA and saves with ten. But I also tied with Tiant for losses with 12. I was 3–12. I had an eight-game stretch where I came in and pitched in relief, and the team did not score a run. If you're the last pitcher in the game, and your team doesn't score, you don't win. I lost eight in a row without a run being scored. It was a real strange year."

Nevertheless, by May, the raw talent of the Red Sox players made itself felt. Everyone appeared optimistic they could repeat as American League champions, as the Red Sox traveled to New York to play in the newly renovated Yankee Stadium for the first time. The new-look Yankees, featuring Mickey Rivers, Willie Randolph, Thurman Munson, and Graig Nettles, led the Red Sox by six games.

On May 20, Bill Lee started the opener of the series, facing the Yankees' Ed Figueroa. Lee had not won a game since the previous August 24, but against the Yankees he looked as sharp as ever. He was trailing 1–0 in the sixth inning. Outfielder Lou Piniella was on second base. Otto Velez singled to right. Piniella sought to score.

Red Sox right fielder Dwight Evans made a perfect throw home to catcher Carlton Fisk. Piniella arrived at full speed and banged into Fisk's chest with his upraised knees in an effort to jar the ball loose. Fisk held on, but the violent crash sent both players sprawling. Fisk set off a prolonged and extremely ugly fight when he began punching Piniella. From the mound, Bill Lee charged into the melee, throwing fists. Yankee outfielder Mickey Rivers began pummeling Lee with punches to the back of his head. When Lee finally got up from that first beating, Yankee third baseman Graig Nettles began exchanging punches with Lee. In the ensuing wrestling match, Nettles dumped Lee to the ground, and Lee badly injured his shoulder.

Once order was restored, Lee stirred it up again by saying something to Nettles, who slugged him. A massive pile of bodies followed. Lee was lost for most of the year. It was the beginning of the end for the '76 Red Sox.

Jim Willoughby: "The fight was in two parts. They had the original confrontation, and then the two sides backed off and were milling about. Lee's shoulder was separated. He couldn't defend himself. He was walking around, and he walked over and called Nettles a neofascist pig or something like that. He wasn't threatening Nettles, but he was ranting, and Nettles just coldcocked him right there.

"I grabbed Nettles from behind and went down, and there were thirty guys on the pile at that point with Mickey Rivers running around the outside taking cheap shots at everybody.

"Bill never was effective. He came back at the end of the year, but we were out of it by then."

Bill Lee: "There's a picture in the paper when the fight was just breaking out. Don Zimmer, the third-base coach, is seen looking at the umpires for help, instead of sprinting into that action and grabbing his starting pitcher and pulling him away and protecting him. And that's the contempt I hold for Zimmer. He didn't do the most logical thing a general is supposed to do, and that's to save his starting pitcher. His pitcher shouldn't be in that shit. We don't swing the bat for a living. We're defensive specialists. Brawls are for offensive specialists.

"The Red Sox players and the Yankee players really didn't like each other. Fisk and Munson were competitive. They came up the same time and they both thought they were the best catcher in baseball, and they were both out to prove it. They had both played in the Cape Cod League, and they were mortal enemies from the beginning.

"Rico hated every Yankee. I don't know why. Maybe his in-laws were from New York. He just liked to kick ass in New York. Rico liked to fight anyway. He'd fight over a bar of soap in the whirlpool if he had a chance. Rico was one of the better handlers of himself.

"I always hated the Yankees. I still do. If we had a ballgame, I'd drill the first two guys just to set the tempo. I do hate them. Billy Martin was a terrible person, nasty, bitter, just a real nasty guy, a man who was born with no liver. Got to be a nasty guy, because none of the poison gets recycled. He sucker-punches everybody. I tell people, 'If you meet Billy Martin, don't have your hands in your pockets, because you'll never get them out quick enough. He'll drop you in a heartbeat when you least expect it.' "

Losing Bill Lee to injury was one blow. In early June, the front office further affected morale when it traded the ebullient 1975 Series hero, Bernie Carbo, to Milwaukee for relief pitcher Tom Murphy and outfielder Bobby Darwin.

The outspoken Lee questioned the motives of the Red Sox front office. Lee was aware that owner Tom Yawkey was dying of cancer. He wondered who was minding the store in his absence.

Bill Lee: "In the year 1976, the Red Sox sent Bernie Carbo to Milwaukee. That year they got rid of a lot of talent, Juan Beniquez, Cecil Cooper. I think what was happening, Tom Yawkey was ill, and they were cutting bait. Maybe it was profit-taking. I don't know. It didn't seem logical. I don't know why they did it. They were by far some of the worst decisions I've ever seen a ballclub make. I'd like to have been a fly on the wall to find out who was doing it."

It wasn't logical to accuse the Red Sox of penny-pinching in light of the next unexpected development. Charlie Finley, who had no intention of paying any of his players multimillion-dollar salaries under the new era of free agency, offered to sell the Red Sox both star relief pitcher Rollie Fingers and outfielder Joe Rudi if Yawkey would pay him one million dollars in cash for each player. Tom Yawkey agreed. When the Red Sox learned Finley wanted to sell superstar pitcher Vida Blue (whom the Red Sox needed desperately) to the Yankees for $1.5 million, general manager Dick O'Connell told Finley they'd buy him too. The date was June 15, 1976.

According to O'Connell, Yawkey was thrilled. Yawkey had begun his reign as owner of the Red Sox by purchasing the best of Connie Mack's Philadelphia A's, and who could forget that he had paid an incredible $250,000 for Washington Senator shortstop Joe Cronin back in 1934. Then, in 1947, he had paid $65,000 for Ellis Kinder and $310,000 for Vern Stephens and Jack Kramer. Buying the A's star players was in character for the Red Sox owner. In fact, when Yawkey was told he had purchased Rudi and Fingers, O'Connell and team treasurer John Harrington claim the deathly-ill owner replied, "How come you didn't get Bando too?"

Jean Yawkey and general manager Haywood Sullivan, who had been demoted to scouting director at the time, dispute Dick O'Connell's version of these events, however. When Tom Yawkey died a short while later, Dick O'Connell, the most competent executive to run the Red Sox since Billy Evans, was fired, and they say it was this episode that led to O'Connell's dismissal. According to Jean Yawkey and Sullivan, Tom Yawkey had wanted both Lynn and Burleson traded before the June 15 deadline, choosing to retain Fisk because he was from New England. According to them, not only was O'Connell derelict in not dealing the two stars, but, against Yaw-key's wishes, went ahead and offered all that money for Rudi and Fingers. According to them, Tom Yawkey was outraged and ordered O'Connell, the man who had rebuilt the Red Sox, to be fired.

Somebody's not telling the truth. History supports Dick O'Connell. Tom Yawkey had never shied from paying top dollar for talent before, nor had he been antagonized by contract demands from his players. It wasn't in his character. The story provided a good excuse, however, to fire Sullivan's nemesis after he and Mrs. Yawkey took over the team.

In the end, the Red Sox didn't get either Rudi or Fingers. Nor did the Yankees acquire Vida Blue. Unfortunately for the Red Sox and their fans, A's owner Charlie Finley had a big mouth. Rather than just take the millions quietly, before the deal went through Finley began boasting around the league that he had struck gold. He even called Fingers and Rudi and boasted how much he was getting for them. Their first call was to their agent, Jerry Kapstein, who told them not to sign anything.

Perhaps if it had been another owner, the sales would have been allowed to go through. But it was Finley, who held himself to be smarter than the other owners, and let them know it. The next day, another Finley enemy, baseball commissioner Bowie Kuhn, vetoed the deals, saying he was doing so in the best interests of baseball.

Rick Wise: "I remember we were out in Oakland, and Fingers and Rudi were sitting in our dugout in Red Sox uniforms. I thought, 'This is amazing. This is great. We got Joe Rudi? Rollie Fingers?'

"They didn't play, but they stayed with us a couple days. And then it was nullified by Bowie Kuhn.

"The players were thinking, 'What happened? Why?' It was like a mirage in the desert. They were there, and then they disappeared. And then there was no use worrying about it. It was out of your hands. So we had to concern ourselves with the team we did have and keep playing."

Despite Commissioner Kuhn's intervention, baseball was turned upside down. The not-quite sale of Joe Rudi and Rollie Fingers to the Red Sox gave a hint of what was to come. The economics in the game had changed forever.

THE DEATH OF TOM YAWKEY

On July 9, 1976, Tom Yawkey died in New England Baptist Hospital. He was cremated. There was no service. In death, as in life, the emphasis was on privacy.

Before his death, Tom Yawkey, beloved for his traits as a loyal, decent sportsman who had helped raise millions of dollars for the Jimmy Fund to help cure muscular dystrophy, talked about his legacy. The longtime Red Sox owner had been aware that some people saw him as a man who had been handed a fortune at a young age only to spend his time and his money in the pursuit of frivolity, running a baseball team. Yawkey refused to apologize.

"Perhaps some people think I have wasted my life," Yawkey told Al Hirshberg. "I can't help that. I was always taught to help others, that those of us fortunate enough to be born with material abundance should do what we can for those who are not. I do what I can. In forty years I have tried to provide jobs, to give pleasure, to treat human beings like human beings."

Yawkey admitted once that he made the mistake of treating employees like associates, rarely firing them even if they failed to demonstrate competency. He added that he did not consider the players themselves to be associates. The reason he gave seems to provide the underlying reason for his paternalistic behavior toward them.

"Players are the most helpless people in the world," he said. "If you told them to go to San Francisco by themselves, they might wind up in Mexico City. I guess we could have really used a resident s.o.b. in the organization. There hasn't been one since Eddie [Collins], and he wasn't one really."

Despite his admitted flaws as an administrator, Yawkey was philosophical about his relative lack of success. He told another reporter, "In baseball, just like in hunting, you have to be patient and take the good with the bad. There's a lot of luck involved. After all, it's only a game."

With the death of this gentle man, baseball in Boston went from a sporting endeavor to an enterprise with a strong emphasis on politics and the bottom line.

Two factions emerged for control of the team. Tom Yawkey's widow, Jean, backed one; Dick O'Connell, the team's general manager, headed the other. It wasn't difficult to figure out which one was going to gain control of the team.

On one side were Jean Yawkey, James Curran, and Joe LaCour—trustees appointed by Yawkey and backers of her unofficially adopted son, Haywood Sullivan—and former team trainer Buddy Leroux. The financing for the purchase by Sullivan and Leroux was to come from money borrowed from banks.

On the other side was O'Connell, along with former Red Sox star Dom DiMaggio and his brother Joe, insurance magnate Bernard Baldwin, and San Francisco mayor Joseph Alioto.

Another group, headed by William Gardner, Yawkey's nephew and a close friend of Carl Yastrzemski, was also mentioned. So was a challenge from Jack Satter of the Colonial Provision Company, which provided hot dogs in Fenway Park. Another bidder was the A-T-O Corporation of Ohio.

The three trustees made it appear as though the Red Sox really were up for sale, but it was clear to anyone vying to purchase the team that Mrs. Yawkey wanted to retain ownership.

Dom DiMaggio: "I found out early that there wasn't much of an opportunity for me to get the team. And eventually when I made the proposal, it was really halfhearted, because I knew the handwriting was on the wall. I just knew it was. She retained it herself, along with Haywood Sullivan and Buddy Leroux. She put the whole package together."

For over a year, the trustees left the Red Sox intact. Business was conducted as usual. On November 4, 1976, the first free-agent draft was held. General manager Dick O'Connell, knowing that Tom Yawkey had been willing to pay a million dollars each for Joe Rudi and Rollie Fingers, decided to enter the free-agent market in a major way. Aware that the Red Sox' biggest weakness was the lack of a dominant closer in the bullpen, he drafted Minnesota Twins relief pitcher Bill "Soup" Campbell.

In relief, Campbell had appeared in 78 games for the Twins in 1976, and had gone 17–5 and earned 20 saves, with an earned-run average of 3.01. For his efforts, he had asked Twins owner Calvin Griffith for $27,000. Griffith, who until he sold the team chose to act as though the reserve clause had never been overturned, would only go to $22,000. Campbell opted for free agency. O'Connell and the Red Sox signed Campbell to a five-year deal worth $1,050,000 before other teams could get his name on the dotted line.

O'Connell was jubilant. He felt the signing of Campbell would propel the Red Sox to another pennant. It did no such thing, but it did provide more leverage for Haywood Sullivan to stab him in the back, convincing Mrs. Yawkey (if indeed she needed convincing) that Dick O'Connell was a profligate who should be fired for his free-spending ways.

When O'Connell set off to sign another free agent, either second baseman Bobby Grich or pitcher Don Gullett, he learned that Jean Yawkey was not Tom Yawkey. Through Haywood Sullivan, she ordered O'Connell to stop spending *her* money.

On September 29, 1977, the "mystery" of who would own the Red Sox ended. The Yawkey executors "chose" former vice president Haywood Sullivan, and former trainer Buddy Leroux to own the Red Sox for $16 million. The problem was that $15 million of that was borrowed money. The deal created a furor from competitors who had offered more, with more cash up front. Other American League owners also howled. When they made it clear that they would not approve the deal, Jean Yawkey then included herself in the arrangement, pledging her name, Fenway Park, cash, and a loan to Sullivan. Buddy Leroux got coal baron Rogers Badgett to increase his investment to five million dollars, and in May 1978, Jean Yawkey, Haywood Sullivan, and Buddy Leroux officially took control of the Red Sox.

What makes the choice of Buddy Leroux as part owner particularly odd is that earlier Tom Yawkey had actually fired Leroux as trainer.

Roy Mumpton: "I was up in the press room. Tom Yawkey told Dick O'Connell, 'Get Leroux out of there. I don't give a damn if he does own the machines. We'll buy the machines. Throw him out.'

"I found out afterward what happened. See, Buddy was a promoter. He was going after the Red Sox players, trying to get them to take their money and put it into his investments, and Leroux was driving them nuts. When they complained, Yawkey told Buddy, 'Leave the players alone. Just take care of them.'

"And this day a couple of the players complained again, so Yawkey fired him. And Mrs. Yawkey knew this.

"When it came time to sell the team, why in the hell would she let Leroux in on a thing like that?

"Now, Dom DiMaggio, who also wanted to buy it, was one of Yawkey's real great friends. Dom and he met almost once a week. So when the club was up for sale, Dom told some of us he was going to try to buy it. His partner was the mayor of San Francisco, Alioto. I said to Dom, 'Has Alioto got deep pockets?' He said, 'All he has is money. He has so much money he doesn't know what to do with it.'

"Later on, in one of the Boston papers, Mrs. Yawkey was asked about Dom's buying the team, and she said, 'Over my dead body.'"

"She took Leroux in, whom her husband had fired, and she wouldn't have anything to do with Dom, who is the greatest guy.

"Dom used to go to spring training every year, and he'd be the first one in that ballpark, and he'd work with the youngsters for nothing. Since then, he hasn't been back."

A month later, on October 24, 1977, just ten days before the scheduled meeting for league approval of the new ownership group, the executors fired not only Dick O'Connell, but his two lieutenants, assistant general manager John Claiborne and vice president Gene Kirby.

When O'Connell moved up to general manager in 1965, the Red Sox had not played .500 ball for seven years, or drawn a million fans since Ted Williams had retired in 1960. In the eleven seasons under O'Connell, the Red Sox had averaged 88 victories and 1,720,000 customers a season. But Dick O'Connell had made a fatal mistake. He had sided with a dead man.

Jim Willoughby: "Dick was honest and a first-rate front-office guy. If he said something, you took him at his word. I had grown up where my word meant something. It's a hard lesson to learn, that to a lot of people the only thing that's good is what's written. So when you come across a guy like Dick O'Connell, you can appreciate it, because it's the exception.

"And when Mr. Yawkey died, I couldn't believe they got rid of him. I knew Haywood Sullivan was Mrs. Yawkey's guy. When you looked into the press box, he was with her. When there were business dealings I would hear about, it would be Sullivan and Mrs. Yawkey. At that time I didn't have anything to do with Haywood Sullivan. It wasn't until after he took over and took control that I found out I didn't like him very much.

"In '75, I saw what we had with Rice and Lynn as rookies, and Yaz still had some good years left, and Rico was the greatest third baseman I ever played with, and I had the feeling that we were going to be pennant winners for three or four years, that we were going to be the Oakland A's or the Yankees for years, and then in '76, when everything fell apart so fast, we never recovered as a team after that. The opportunity was there, but it slipped out of the front office's hands. They had the makings of a perennial winner, and it just didn't happen. And you can trace those failings right upstairs.

"From the time Tom Yawkey died, the power struggle went on a long time, a lot longer than it ever should have, and the fact the players would talk about it, comment on it in the usual conversation, meant it was affecting play one way or another."

*   *   *

The battle for control would not end there, however. There was one more twist to come, and a bizarre one it was.

On June 5, 1983, a reunion of the 1967 Red Sox was held. It was Tony C. Night—an effort to raise money for the comatose Tony Conigliaro: Conigliaro had suffered a heart attack in January 1982. He would die in 1989. In the press room in Fenway Park, the players from 1967 were reminiscing. When the talk turned to Tony C., eyes misted over. It was inconceivable that this young, vibrant Boston hero had been cut down in the prime of his life, much like Harry Agganis had, nearly thirty years earlier.

Amid the laughter and the sadness, the Red Sox called a press conference for four-thirty that afternoon. A few minutes past the scheduled starting time, Buddy Leroux walked in. At his side were Dick O'Connell, of all people, and one of the limited partners, James Curran. Curran was also Leroux's attorney. Leroux announced that he, Curran, and Kentucky coal baron Rogers Badgett had merged their limited partner shares to form a majority, and that they were *firing* Haywood Sullivan and naming *Leroux* as "managing general partner," and reappointing Dick O'Connell general manager.

The meeting took about half an hour. Dick Bresciani, the publicity director, then announced there would be another press conference shortly, at which time Haywood Sullivan informed the gathering that Leroux's actions were *invalid* and that they would go to court to get an injunction in the morning.

All amid what should have been a sacrosanct celebration of the team's hallowed Impossible Dream and of its star slugger.

The two sides spent the summer of 1983 in the Suffolk County Superior Court. During the trial, Mrs. Yawkey was painted as a vindictive old woman, and was even accused by Badgett of embezzling funds. Sullivan was accused of being a complete and utter incompetent.

Superior Judge James P. Lynch ultimately ruled that the takeover by Leroux was invalid. Haywood Sullivan, with the backing of Jean Yawkey, emerged the victor. Initially, he intended to be his own general manager as well as chief executive officer, but he discovered that two hats were one too many. Only the hiring of Lou Gorman as general manager in 1984 saved the Red Sox from certain disintegration.

THE GERBIL

With the death of Tom Yawkey, it was out with the old, in with the new. After a tough loss to Kansas City on July 18, 1976, Red Sox manager Darrell Johnson, who was cracking under the strain of his job, asked Carl Yastrzemski and Rico Petrocelli whether it would help the team if he resigned. Both said no.

On July 19, general manager Dick O'Connell, still in power at the time, called him to say he was fired. On the road only two days before, some Red Sox players had reportedly been involved in a wild all-night party, with naked men and women seen running through the halls of the hotel. Somebody blew the whistle. The word was out: Darrell had lost control. The pink slip followed.

Jim Willoughby: "In 1976, Darrell's drinking got in the way of his managing. And yet when Darrell drank in '75, no one seemed to mind. What happened was that the team didn't do as well in '76, and so the drinking was more obvious. In baseball, when you're on top, you make your own rules. I saw it with players all the time. It's a classic, traditional double standard that's part of baseball. If you're doing well, you can do what you want. As soon as you fall from favor, you might be living the same way, but you're under the gun now, and how soon they forget. You read about the trouble Earl Weaver got into in Baltimore, but he was a winner. It was only later when the team had problems that he talked about retirement. And the same thing happened to Darrell."

The third-base coach, Don Zimmer, a Jean Yawkey favorite, took Johnson's place. Zimmer immediately acted to restore order. One of Zimmer's first acts was to crack down on curfew breakers on the road. He got rid of twenty-one-year-old Rick ("Too Tall") Jones for being "irresponsible," and sat Rico Petrocelli for what he said was insubordination, instead playing at third base Butch Hobson, a youngster from Pawtucket whom he favored. The Red Sox responded to the new manager's toughness by winning fifteen of their last eighteen games in 1976.

It wasn't enough. The Red Sox finished the '76 season 15½ games behind New York. Without Bill Lee, lost after the pummeling by Graig Nettles, Boston didn't have enough pitching.

In 1977, the Red Sox unleashed an awesome display of power, as a team hitting 213 home runs, seventh all-time. Jim Rice hit 39, George Scott 33, Butch Hobson 30, Fred Lynn 18, Yaz 28, and Carlton Fisk 26. With those kinds of bats, all Don Zimmer had to do was keep the pitching staff happy, and the Red Sox would have been champions. But he couldn't, in large part because the pitchers disliked their manager intensely. Zimmer took it personally.

To a man, the starting pitchers hated the way Zimmer was using them. Luis Tiant bitched that because Zimmer went with a five-man staff early in the season, he "ruined all our control." Bill Lee, Fergie Jenkins, and Rick Wise complained that Zimmer didn't leave them out long enough. Wise said that Zimmer's handling of the staff was "a joke." Zimmer resented Bill Lee so much that he wanted to release him outright in late July, only to be thwarted by the front office.

On September 18, Jenkins and Zimmer had a big row in Baltimore. Zimmer ordered Jenkins to warm up, but Jenkins was nowhere to be found: he was watching a football game in the TV truck out by the bullpen. Zimmer blew up, though Jenkins swore coach Walt Hriniak had known exactly where he was. Wise, who had won 19 games for the Red Sox in '75, also dropped into the manager's doghouse. Zimmer vowed neither Jenkins nor Rick Wise would ever pitch for him again. And they didn't. Both were traded before the '78 season.

And so the Red Sox went down the stretch in '77 with their pitchers in rebellion. The cancer eating at the team was a clash of cultures between manager Zimmer, a meat-and-potatoes, old-fashioned conservative, and a group of players who were called the Buffalo Heads—pitchers Bill Lee, Fergie Jenkins, Jim Willoughby, Rick Wise, and the carefree Bernie Carbo, who had been reacquired by Dick O'Connell in December of 1976. Jenkins had founded and named the group the Buffalo Head Gang, because according to the big right-hander, Zimmer looked like a buffalo and "buffaloes are the ugliest animals alive." Also dumb. The press had shortened it to the Buffalo Heads, which in the midst of a prevalent drug culture gave it a different connotation entirely.

These players were hip, liberal iconoclasts. Lee, especially, made his contempt for Zimmer public. Even though these players were crucial to the success of the Red Sox, Zimmer could not curb his feelings about them and he retaliated by trading away the Buffalo Heads one by one.

Tack Burbank: "The Buffalo Heads were modern players for the time, and Zimmer was a guy who got hit by too many pitches, was completely inflexible and from another era. What I saw in those players was a part of me that found expression in the sixties and early seventies in the Vietnam War protest. They were late-adolescent rebels, as so many of us were, and they would say and do things that were not out of the old-time mold, and it drove Zimmer crazy to the point he didn't use them the second half of the season nearly as much as he should have. And that ultimately cost them dearly."

Rick Wise: "It's erroneous to say the Buffalo Head Gang was synonymous with not liking Don Zimmer. We were in his doghouse at one time or another, but the club wasn't formed to take up arms against Zimmer per se. At least I didn't feel that way. A couple of us were growing beards that Zimmer didn't like—myself, Spaceman, Pudge. But that didn't have anything to do with how we tried to perform when we were called upon.

"I remember in Baltimore, before one of the big series, Zimmer called in eight of the pitchers for a meeting and did not call me in. I had just led the club in total victories two years before, and I was not invited to be at this meeting. I was in his doghouse. Simple as that. I don't know what I did, and I didn't go talk to him because I would not have gotten any satisfaction.

"As far as I was concerned, I guess Zimmer got his way with me. Talk about someone being banished! I was traded to Cleveland! And I don't mean to slight the fine citizens of Cleveland, but talk about going from championship teams and perennial winning teams to the toughest, roughest existence in professional baseball. Damn!"

Jim Willoughby: "The pressure on the manager in Boston is intense, and you see over the years the way different managers have not handled it. Don Zimmer would listen to all the talk shows on the radio and, boy, that's the biggest mistake you can make because there are three or four of them, and it's a real competitive market. Any angle you get, you jump on, and there were some nasty guys on the radio. Zimmer couldn't handle it, and he'd call them up. Boston is a tough, tough area for press. You have to be able to take the bad with the good. Zimmer had real trouble doing that.

"He did not like pitchers categorically. He wears a metal plate in his head from being beaned, and all those metal-detector jokes he hears are all because of pitchers. The animosity between the pitchers and Zimmer was palpable. I can remember on a team bus in Chicago, we were leaving to go to the airport after a game. Dick Pole was in back, and he was down on Zimmer. Dick was trying to come back from an injury, and he figured he was going to be traded, because he and Zimmer already had had some words. He was playing the Eagles on his tape player, and one of the songs was 'Already Gone.' He had it going full blast in the back of the bus and was singing along with it, and every time the words 'I'm already gone' came around, he would scream it out specifically for the front of the bus. It happened to all of us in different forms.

"I was traded to Chicago the last minute of spring training in '78. It was an hour before we were supposed to leave the ballpark in Winter Haven to go to the airport to fly to Boston. Peter Gammons of the *Boston Globe* told me they had sold my contract. I haven't heard from the Red Sox to this day."

Bill Lee: "Zimmer was definitely a noncommunicative type. He was a belligerent terrier, a Gila monster, a great third-base coach. It was the Peter Principle one more time. 'Always keep dumb-ass people below your general manager.'

"Anyway, when Fergie made the statement about Zimmer being dumber than a buffalo, it became a club. Everyone wanted to join. We were going to sell franchises. Even though Fergie was the one who said it, Zimmer felt I was behind it. Fergie was six foot eight and black with a nasty right hand. Zimmer walked quietly by Fergie's locker. Fergie was not a self-conscious, insecure black from the South who had faced years of prejudice.

"I *was* the one who called him 'the gerbil,' but affectionately so. The interview started when I was asked, 'What is Billy Martin?' I said, 'Billy Martin is a no-good dirty rat.' The interviewer asked, 'What's Don Zimmer?'

I said, 'He's a gerbil. He has fat, pudgy cheeks and kids like him.' And then everyone said, 'You said Don Zimmer's a gerbil.' And he got really pissed. Because he must have thought he looked like one.

"A kid wrote me a letter and said, 'Mr. Lee, I'm afraid you're wrong. Hamsters are the ones with big, puffy cheeks. Gerbils are the skinny things that run around and multiply real fast.' So I stood corrected, but 'gerbil' stuck, and I was history."

Despite all the turmoil and hard feelings, the Buffalo Head Gang and "The Gerbil" and all the rest of it, the team did manage to win 97 games, thanks mostly to their heavy hitters. But, by 2½ games, they lost the division to the Yankees. Again. Next year, they swore, would be different. If it was the last thing they did, they would beat those goddamn Yankees.

CHAPTER 42

The Great Collapse of '78

In the spring of 1978, the Red Sox looked ready. The offense was again a powerhouse, and the pitching, though not deep—and the loss of Jenkins and Wise aside—was experienced and dependable, with a staff that included Dennis Eckersley, Mike Torrez, Bill Lee, Luis Tiant, and Jim Wright.

Left fielder Jim Rice proved to everyone he was one of the game's great players. In 1978, he hit .315 and led the American League in home runs with 46, triples with 15, runs batted in with 139, and a slugging average of .600. Playing every day, he batted 677 times that year. The man was incredible. With a lineup that included Rice, Lynn, Fisk, Yaz, Dwight Evans, George Scott, and Butch Hobson, it seemed likely that this time the Red Sox would finally make good on their oath.

At the June 15 trading deadline, however, the first shadow of a bad omen appeared: the Red Sox sold Bernie Carbo, the team's premier pinch hitter. Carbo hated authority, and he could be a pain in the ass to management. Because he was pinch-hitting and not playing, Carbo didn't bother taking fielding practice before games, which angered Don Zimmer. That Carbo was a Buffalo Head didn't help his standing either.

Nevertheless, Carbo was one of the game's great pinch hitters at the time, and to his teammates his sale seemed vengeful and senseless. The Red Sox lost an important bat. To this day, Bernie Carbo has not gotten over the fact that the Red Sox broke his heart not once, but twice.

Bernie Carbo: "In 1976, Mr. Yawkey died. He had given me a two-year contract, $75,000 for '75 and $95,000 for '76. I went and bought a house in Framingham. After Haywood Sullivan took over in '76, I went to Darrell Johnson, and I said, 'Am I going to be traded?' He said, 'No, no, you're not going to get traded.' I had two little kids. I said, 'You know, my wife is pregnant.' He said, 'Don't worry.'

"The Red Sox traded me to Milwaukee.

"I didn't show up for twenty-two days. My wife talked me into going back into baseball. I didn't talk to nobody. I didn't talk to the press. I never talked to my mother, my dad, no one. I took the phone off the wall and I hibernated in my room. My apartment was on 808 Memorial Drive, so I could see the lights of the ballpark.

"Milwaukee sent me telegrams and telegrams. Finally, Susan said, 'Call them up.' I called Milwaukee. They said, 'Come on, we'll fly you out, get an apartment, get doctors, get you set up.' Milwaukee did an outstanding job. I didn't appreciate them enough. I didn't give the owner, Bud Selig, enough credit in my life, when at that time I was ready to have a nervous breakdown.

"Anyway, I was with the Brewers, and when Don Zimmer got the manager's job in Boston, he came up to me and said, 'I don't want you to tell anyone, but I'm trading for you.' So Boston traded Cecil Cooper for George Scott and myself, and I went back to Boston. I had a real good year in '77, hit .289, hit 15 home runs, including three pinch-hit home runs.

"The next year, 1978, I felt that I was going to be traded. Every ballplayer can feel it. My contract ran out at the end of the year, and that spring I walked into Haywood Sullivan's office and said, 'Just offer me a contract, any contract.' Just to stay in Boston. But he would not do it.

"On June fifteenth, Don Zimmer called me up and he was crying. I could tell he had tears in his eyes. I said, 'You don't have to tell me. Where am I going?'

"He said, 'Cleveland.'

"I said, 'For who?'

"He said, 'Nobody.'

"I said, 'You're not getting a fucking ballplayer for me? Who in the fuck are you going to replace me with? I hit .289 and had fifteen home runs. What the fuck is going on?'

" 'We sold you to Cleveland,' he said.

"I said, 'You people must be fucking crazy.'

"And I knew right then that Haywood Sullivan was busting up the team. Look who he got rid of. He got rid of Reggie Cleveland, Diego Segui, Fergie Jenkins, and myself and didn't get a player. They sold us off."

With the sale of Bernie Carbo to Cleveland on June 15, 1978, only one Buffalo Head remained on the Red Sox—Bill Lee—and to show his disdain for their sale of Carbo, he not only criticized Zimmer and the Red Sox management to reporters, he then staged a one-day strike.

Zimmer had sought to release Lee the year before, but had been stopped by management. The pitcher had returned to prove his manager wrong about him, winning ten games going into July of 1978. But Lee underestimated how much Zimmer resented his constant criticism. Zimmer bided his time.

When the Red Sox built a fourteen-game lead in July, Zimmer benched his tormentor, with the expectation that the Red Sox would win the pennant without the Spaceman. It was what Boston manager Bill Carrigan had done to teach the young Babe Ruth a lesson many years earlier.

But this time Zimmer figured wrong.

Bill Lee: "Management didn't know how to handle Bernie because he was a free spirit, easygoing, had no real goals in life other than to have a good time and hit pinch-hit home runs in the World Series. Establishment people tend to trade away people they don't understand.

"On June 15 when Bernie was sold to Cleveland, it was a sad day. The night after the game on the fifteenth right before the trading deadline, I figured we had both made it. Nothing had happened. And then I found out the next morning in the *Globe* that Bernie got sold at two-thirty Hawaii time. I said, 'Sold? Sold for half the waiver price? That's fifteen grand.' I asked myself, 'Why would Zimmer do that?' We were so far ahead. It had to be a punitive measure. It was totally illogical, so I went nuts.

"When he was sold, I didn't show up at the ballpark. When they called me, I said I wasn't coming in. I told them I had had it. I told them to go shit in their hat and told them that their trading Bernie was the worst thing I had ever seen. I said, 'Here's a pinch hitter who does everything for you, and you sell him to Cleveland?' I said, 'You didn't even trade him.'

"Bernie and I got drunk that night. We went to the Lucky Garden and ate Chinese food. Bernie said, 'You've got to go back. Not for me, but for all the ballplayers. You're the player rep. You have to stick up for our rights. You have to speak out, and the only way you can do that is by showing up and going out.'

"I said, 'Bernie, if you want me to go back, I'll go back.'

"I went to the ballpark the next day. They called me in right away. They said, 'You have to go up and see Haywood Sullivan.' They gave me a towel, because I had just run five miles and it was really hot, and I was sweating all over their desk.

"Haywood started yelling and ranting and raving at me, 'Why did you do this? Do that?'

"I said, 'You can't do this to the ballclub. You sold Bernie Carbo for half the waiver price. You did it to punish him. That's the most unjustified thing. You got rid of him in '75 when his wife was pregnant. After that season, you promised him you wouldn't get rid of him. In spring training this year, you promised him he'd be on the ballclub. Two days before spring training, he bought a house. Now, boom, you trade him to Cleveland.'

"Haywood said, 'That's none of your business.'

"I said, 'The hell it isn't. I'm the player rep. What you did to him was uncalled for.'

"He said, 'We're going to fine you five hundred for missing that ballgame yesterday.'

"I said, 'Fine me fifteen hundred and give me the weekend off.'

"That's when he came across the table and tried to drill me. And Mrs. Yawkey was sitting in the back room, rocking back and forth, knitting.

"Leroux smoothed things over. I went down and saw Don Zimmer. He yelled at me, and I called him a horse's ass and a lying cocksucker because he got rid of Bernie Carbo. I said, 'You said Bernie was like your son. You don't sell your son to Cleveland.' Zimmer said, 'Yeah, get out of here.' He hates left-handers. He hates left-handed breaking-ball pitchers. He hates left-handed breaking-ball pitchers who throw curveballs late in the count. And that's me. Psychologically that remains in his head. You always remember things that you hate most.

"I went out and pitched, but my heart wasn't into it. We were way ahead anyway. I lost three or four ballgames in a row, and Zimmer took me out of the starting rotation.

"In '78, I was 10–6, and I lost four straight to go 10–10, and Zimmer took the ball out of my hand. He said, 'That's it. You're finished.' He said, 'We don't need you, Lee. We can win it without you.' And he didn't give me the ball again except two times in September against the Yankees in Fenway Park. I ended up 10–10. The next year I went to Montreal. I was 10–6. I lost four ballgames in a row, and what did Dick Williams do? He gave me the ball. I won my last six games in a row, and we missed the pennant by two games. I ended up 16–10. All Zimmer had to do was give me the ball three times, and the Yankees don't catch us. But Zimmer wasn't thinking of the ballclub. We had a big lead. So I sat back in a chair the rest of the season and watched the lead dwindle away."

The Red Sox shooting star reached its apex on July 19. The won-lost record was 62–28. The starting five pitchers were a combined 44–13. The Sox led the Yankees by 14 games. Two days before, the Yankees seemed to have self-destructed, when Reggie Jackson defied Billy Martin's order to bunt and was suspended for three days. The Red Sox appeared to have a lock on the pennant. There were seventy-two games to go.

Tack Burbank: "It was in the bag at that point. I couldn't wait to get up in the morning to watch that day's game. It wasn't even a question of losing. The Sox pummeled everybody. There was one game when we were behind

9–0, and we won. The team had power up and down the lineup, and so it was the way they won. It seemed unprecedented. The team was so good."

In the next few weeks, the team slipped a little, but with forty games left, the Sox still led by 8½. The Sox players then began to break down. Yaz suffered back and shoulder ailments in mid-July, then pulled ligaments in his right wrist. In two months, he hit three home runs. Carlton Fisk had a cracked rib. Butch Hobson had cartilage damage in both knees and bone chips in his right elbow. His fielding suffered. Dwight Evans was beaned on August 29 and suffered from dizzy spells. Bill Campbell, who in 1977 had won 13 games, more than any other pitcher on the Red Sox staff, and led the league with 31 saves, vindicating Dick O'Connell, had a sore shoulder all season long. In '78, he had only four saves.

In August, the Red Sox traveled to the West Coast, and losses in close games became the norm. The pitching continued to be reliable, but suddenly the big bats that had been so dominating went silent. At the same time, the Yankees won 13 of 15 and arrived at Fenway Park for a crucial four-game series beginning on September 7. The lead was down to 4½ games.

The Red Sox were in Seattle for their final game of the disastrous road swing. Pitcher Mike Torrez was talking with manager Zimmer when Lee came over. Lee asked, "Hey, Skip, is it all right if I do my running? I'm supposed to pitch the first game in Boston, right?"

Zimmer replied, "You're not pitching. We're bringing in Bobby Sprowl from Pawtucket. You're pitching in the bullpen now."

Mike Torrez, Red Sox, 1978–82: "I thought he meant they were going to pitch Sprowl for just one game. We had a big lead at the time, so it's no big deal. But I'm wondering what he's going to do that for. Bobby Sprowl never beat anybody."

Bill Lee, who had a career 12–5 record against the Yankees, didn't start any of the four games in Boston, and the Red Sox lost all of them. All were routs: 15–3, 13–2, 7–0, and 7–4. Butch Hobson's throwing error opened the gates in the first game. Evans was dizzy and dropped a fly ball in game two. In that game, Fisk threw two balls away for errors.

In the third game of the series, Lou Piniella and Bucky Dent scored a couple of runs against ace Dennis Eckersley on dinkers, and then there was a walk, an error, a wild pitch, and a passed ball, and suddenly it was 7–0, Yankees. Bobby Sprowl started the finale. He began by walking Mickey Rivers and Willie Randolph, lasted two-thirds of an inning, and was charged with three runs. The Yankees quickly led 6–0, and coasted to victory.

The Red Sox were outscored 41–9 and outhit 84–29. The four starters selected by Zimmer—Torrez, Wright, Eckersley, and Sprowl—retired a total of twenty batters.

The series became known as the Boston Massacre. Panic began to set in.

Tack Burbank: "I had tickets to all four games of the Boston Massacre. Even though the Sox had played poorly on the West Coast and the Yankees had been playing well, it seemed impossible we could do worse than a split. I was still very confident the Sox would win the pennant. In fact, I figured they would win three of four.

"What I remember, the Yankees scored early and often with lots of Red Sox errors, and the line scores were unbelievable. I never saw such a mismatch. Watching that unfold was a major source of depression, and after the third game I was so disgusted I gave my tickets away for the fourth game on Sunday.

"That day I did actually turn the TV set on, and I saw the Yankees go ahead, and that cinched it for me. And at that point I actually gave up on them. I had never given up on them before, but I was so hurt, I had been through too many seasons of this, and then to have this happen, it seemed like a mortal wound, a narcissistic injury somehow, so I stopped following them. I didn't watch or listen to another game until the last weekend of the season."

With fourteen games remaining in the 1978 season, the Red Sox actually *trailed* the Yankees by 3½ games, a swing of 17½ games. Then, suddenly, unexpectedly, and to its fans, quite remarkably, once again Boston couldn't seem to lose and won twelve of the final fourteen contests. It was an astonishing swing from utter dominance to humiliating failure to mastery once again. And the Yankees kept pace. The Red Sox had to play extraordinarily well in September to stay in contention. Fascinated, all of baseball watched.

On the final day of the season, the Yankees still had a one-game lead, with Catfish Hunter pitching against the relatively unknown Cleveland pitcher, Rick Waits. For the Red Sox, Luis Tiant faced Toronto, and won. All eyes were on New York.

Waits gave up two runs in the first inning. And then Cleveland lit up Catfish Hunter and scored nine runs, while Waits pitched shutout ball the rest of the way.

Tack Burbank: "I arrived at the finish line of the Dartmouth Marathon, the first and only marathon I ever ran, and I ran it much too fast and went into shock. It was a cold New Hampshire day, and I started turning purple, and they threw heated blankets around me, and all I was concerned about was the score of the Yankees-Indians game. I knew the Sox had won. Tiant pitched, and there was no way he was going to lose. And when I found out that Waits had beaten the Yankees, I couldn't believe it.

"Because now there was going to be a one-game playoff, and it was going to be at home, and there wasn't any way we could lose. I was confident except that we had Mike Torrez on the mound, and that worried me.

"Mike Torrez had won 14 games for the Yankees before he came to the Red Sox, but basically he was a fourth starter. Yeah, he'd pitch a lot of innings for you, but check his ERA. He always gave up runs.

"He was healthy. He always wanted the ball. He wasn't a bad pitcher. But he was the kind of pitcher who threw home runs. So I was very excited going into the playoff game, but I did have some trepidation. They were starting Ron Guidry, and we were starting fucking Mike Torrez."

THE MIKE TORREZ GAME

And so the 1978 season came down to a one-game playoff. This game, played on October 2, 1978, matched 16-game winner Mike Torrez against the New York Yankees' left-handed ace Ron Guidry, the winner of 24 ball-games.

Early in the game, the wind blowing in from left field saved the Red Sox three runs. Reggie Jackson would have hit a three-run home run in the first inning, but the air currents blew the ball back, and Carl Yastrzemski made a great catch in the left-field corner.

The Red Sox took the early lead in the bottom of the second, when Yaz turned on a Guidry fastball and pulled it just inside the foul pole in right field for the lead. Guidry had given up just one home run to a left-handed batter all season.

The Red Sox scored a second run in the sixth inning on a sharp single by Jim Rice. The Fenway fans sensed victory. Through the middle innings they gleefully, arrogantly chanted, "The Yankees suck!"

In the sixth inning, Fred Lynn came to bat, with two runners on and two out. On this day, Ron Guidry was not overpowering. A home run by Lynn would have clinched it. Guidry threw Lynn a slider on the inside. Lynn guessed inside. He was way out front and pulled it. Right fielder Lou Piniella was playing Lynn a few steps closer to the line than usual, because catcher Thurman Munson had told him that Guidry's breaking ball was hanging.

Lynn lined a ball in the air toward right. Piniella lost it in the bright afternoon sun. If Reggie Jackson, the usual right fielder, had been out there, he probably wouldn't have made the play, and the Red Sox probably would have won the game. But Yankee manager Bob Lemon opted for a stronger defense, so he had Piniella in right, with Jackson inserted into the batting order as the designated hitter.

Piniella ran to where he thought the ball was going to drop. He stuck out his gloved left hand, blindly—and the ball lodged in the webbing. The two extra, desperately needed Boston runs were prevented from scoring.

Jonathan Schwartz, writer and broadcaster: "Piniella's catch was an indignity. He had appeared bollixed and off balance, lurching about under the glaring sun in the right-field corner. That Lynn had unleashed so potent a smash and would go unrewarded, that I would go unrewarded, that the game itself would remain within the Yankees' reach, struck me as an ominous sign that things would not, after all, work out in the end."

Mike Torrez battled the Yankees and kept them from scoring through six innings. At this point, looking back, Don Zimmer should have brought in a fresh arm to finish up. Bill Lee probably would have gotten the job done. But Zimmer wouldn't pitch him. Torrez remained in the game.

Bill Lee: "It boiled down to the last game, and he sure needed me the last three innings. I was one of the better relievers they ever had. Those last three innings the wind started changing. Before that, the wind had been blowing in from left field, and nothing was going to get out of that ballpark. Reggie Jackson hit a ball that would have been a home run in the first inning, but Yaz ran it down in the corner.

"About ten-thirty in the morning before the game, I told Al Jackson, our pitching coach, 'About the fifth or sixth inning, the wind is going to start blowing out to left.' He said, 'What?' I said, 'Yep, the wind is going to stop blowing in after the fifth inning, and it's going to change dramatically and blow out in the sixth or seventh.' And that's exactly what it did."

Leading 2–0 in the seventh inning, Torrez gave up singles to Chris Chambliss and Roy White. He had two outs when Yankee shortstop Bucky Dent came to the plate. Dent was a singles hitter. He was hitting .240. He had hit all of four home runs in 1978.

Dent hit a foul ball back behind home plate and then fouled a ball off his instep. Torrez stood on the mound, rubbing up a new ball. Four minutes went by as the Yankee medicine men administered to the banged-up foot of the light-hitting Dent. He seemed in such pain that it was a wonder he was able to return to the batter's box, but Dent stepped back in.

Torrez threw a slider. Dent swung. As the ball headed toward left, Torrez began walking off the field, figuring it to be an easy fly-ball out. He could see Yaz in left patting his glove. But the wind, an ill wind as Bill Lee had predicted, had changed and was now blowing out hard.

The ball continued to carry and struck the net atop the Wall for a three-run homer.

Bill Lee: "Torrez threw that horseshit slider that is still sitting there in the middle of the plate, and Bucky Dent hit it right near the end of the bat. I couldn't believe he hit it out, but he did."

Tack Burbank: "The pitch before the home run Bucky Dent fouled off his foot, and he went down hard. He really looked like he was out of the game. It was a serious hurt. And then he got up, and he tried to walk it off, he was limping, so I wasn't worried. Here was Bucky Dent, the number-nine hitter, he was hurt, and then the next thing you knew, the ball was in the screen. And I just said, 'Fucking Mike Torrez.' Those were my words. I shouldn't have blamed Torrez. But you have to blame somebody, and he was as good a candidate as anybody."

Dent's cheap three-run home run in the top of the seventh made the score 3–2 Yankees. Torrez, his composure lost, walked Mickey Rivers, who immediately stole second. Yankee catcher Thurman Munson was the batter. Torrez had struck out Munson three times. Nevertheless, Zimmer replaced Torrez with Bob Stanley. Munson lined a ball off the Wall, making the score 4–2.

In the bottom of the seventh inning, Zimmer made a move that reminded everyone how much the Red Sox missed the presence of their nonpareil pinch hitter, Bernie Carbo. After Haywood Sullivan sold Carbo to Cleveland, the Red Sox went for a stretch of 122 games during which not one Boston pinch hitter came off the bench and hit a home run or even knocked in a run. This game was part of that streak.

With a runner on base and two outs, Zimmer pinch-hit right-hander Bob Bailey, one of his favorite players, for second baseman Jack Brohamer. With Carbo gone, Bailey was the best Zimmer had to throw at the Yankees.

In response to Zimmer's move, Yankee manager Bob Lemon took the ball from Guidry and brought right-handed reliever Goose Gossage into the game. Gossage said to himself, "Thank you," when he saw Bailey come to the plate.

Gossage threw three fastballs over the plate. Bailey took a seat.

When Reggie Jackson homered in the eighth into the center-field bleachers, the Sox' deficit rose to three.

Jonathan Schwartz: "I affected bemusement as I watched him round the bases. I thought: Let's see, just for the fun of it, how big it's going to be. What does it matter, anyway? It's only a game."

In the eighth, the Red Sox showed their fortitude, scoring two runs off Gossage, but the beefy reliever retired two right-handed batters, Butch Hobson and the slumping George Scott, to end the threat.

One more inning to go. Dwight Evans pinch-hit for Frank Duffy, who had replaced Brohamer, flying easily to left. With one out in the ninth inning, Rick Burleson walked. Red Sox second baseman Jerry Remy then lined a ball into right field. Lou Piniella, unable to see this ball in the sun, stood stock-still as he waited for it to come down, making Burleson believe he was in position to make the catch. Burleson could not take the chance of getting doubled off first to end the inning.

For a second time in the game, Piniella could see the ball of sun, but not the horsehide sphere, and had to guess where the ball hit to him was located. Again, Piniella somehow anticipated where it was going to land, and he took it on one hop, keeping it from skipping past him and getting the ball in quickly enough to keep Burleson on second. Had Burleson reached third, he would have scored on the next play.

But runners were only on first and second with one out. The two hitting stars, Jim Rice and Carl Yastrzemski, were the batters. Rice hit a long fly ball to Piniella in right. This time, the Yankee outfielder saw the ball all the way. He caught it about twenty-five feet from the fence. Burleson tagged and moved to third.

The Red Sox were ninety feet from a tied ballgame.

There were two outs in the ninth. The batter was Carl Yastrzemski. Yaz had made the final outs of both the 1967 and 1975 World Series. He had led the team to their surprise victory in '67, winning the Triple Crown that year, but he had never again been as dominating, and with the emergence of Fred Lynn, Jim Rice, Dwight Evans, and Carlton Fisk, Yaz was no longer the singular focus of so many of the Red Sox fans. Here was an opportunity for Yaz to return himself to the premier position he had attained in 1967. A hit would tie the game. A home run would win it.

Tack Burbank: "When Yaz came up to the plate against Goose Gossage, I knew he was going to make an out and it was probably going to be a pop-up, 'cause that's what he specialized in. I realize it was hard for him, because he couldn't replace Ted—Yaz was a great player based on a lot of athletic ability and tremendous hard work, but he didn't have Ted's elegance and ability. Ted was a god and Yaz was pretending to be a god. And when Yaz came up, the game was over in my mind. I didn't think Yaz would get around on the pitch."

Jonathan Schwartz, who loved the Red Sox and their star dearly, also didn't hold out much hope for a Yastrzemski base hit. Schwartz felt that because it was late in the day, he would be tired and overmatched. From his vantage point on the roof of Fenway Park, Schwartz began screaming for Yaz to bunt the ball, figuring a surprise bunt would tie up the ballgame.

Burleson danced off third. Yaz held his bat high waiting for Gossage's first pitch.

Jonathan Schwartz: "I thought: Freeze this minute. Freeze it right here. How unspeakably beautiful it is. Everyone, reach out and touch it."

Alas, time stands still for no man or fan. The first pitch was a ball. The second pitch blazed across the inner edge of the plate. Yastrzemski swung, attempting to hit the ball in the hole between the first and second baseman.

Carl Yastrzemski: "The pitch came in, on the inside, just at the knees. My pitch. I swung, but just as I got the bat out, the ball exploded on me, coming in quicker than I had thought. I tried to turn on it, but I got underneath the ball."

The ball rose in the air in the vicinity of Yankee third baseman Graig Nettles, who stood still and then squeezed the ball tight. The Red Sox had saved and then blown the pennant in what turned out to be Yaz's last chance at a pennant and a World Series.

After the game, Yaz stood in the Red Sox clubhouse, answering endless questions about the pitch, crying at times. Often he told reporters, "You don't always *make* an out. Sometimes the pitcher gets you out." This was one of those times.

Jeffrey Lyons, film critic: "On the morning of October 2, 1978, I got up pretending that I would be playing in the game. I know that ballplayers get to the park four hours before game time, so four hours before the game, I began pacing in front of my television set. I knew my friend Jonathan Schwartz was up at the game. I wanted to be in front of the TV. I wanted the perspective of television.

"I sat and I paced, and an hour before game time I started to loosen up. I sat down and made my own scorecard.

"At the beginning of the game, everything was neat and firm and with confidence, because the Red Sox were out in front. Yaz hit a home run.

"And then at the end of the game, when not only Bucky Dent hit a home run but Reggie Jackson, too, my writing was indifferent, and I felt that the walls were closing in on me, and I didn't answer the phone. After the game, I began to perspire profusely. I never had anything like that happen before. There was never a great tragedy in my life, until then.

"When Yastrzemski hit the home run early, I said, 'This is it. We've won it.' I really thought we did. And then Bucky Dent, of all people, and with a borrowed bat! I can remember when the game was over I actually had a nauseated feeling in my stomach. I took a shower and went to bed.

"It was five in the afternoon. And that night I had to work at WPIX, the Yankee flagship station. Our sportscaster, Jerry Gerard, is a fanatical Yankee fan, and over the air I gave him a bottle of champagne. I tried to put it behind me.

"And then WPIX assigned me to cover the arrival of the Yankees at Newark Airport. They arrived on the tarmac eight miles away, and I was surrounded by five thousand Yankee fans, who recognized me as a Red Sox fan. It was like being assigned to Lebanon."

Mark Starr: "It was depressing, always depressing. That may have been the worst, in truth, of all of them. Bucky Dent at Fenway. Yaz up against Goose. Nineteen seventy-five had been painful but not that bad. We weren't supposed to be there. The sixth game was so titanic. The Carbo and Fisk home runs. It was such a great Series. 'Seventy-eight was even worse than '86, worse than any of them.

"There was a feeling we had it, that this was a terrific team, a well-put-together team, that with Eckersley, Torrez, Tiant, and Lee in the starting rotation and Campbell, Drago, and Stanley in the bullpen, this was a team with pitching. This was a real team.

"Let me put it this way. When Yastrzemski got up against Gossage, being a true Red Sox fan, I didn't for a second think he was going to do anything. There wasn't a moment when I really believed Yastrzemski was going to do something heroic.

"I also remember odd little things, the worst being that the Gerbil took Torrez out right before Thurman Munson came up. Torrez had struck Munson out two or three times, made him look bad each time, but Zimmer took him out, and whoever came in gave up a double and it turned out to be the winning run that they needed, and it was just a sense that, with the exception of Dick Williams, there is never a manager who makes the right move. There are always these old company men who don't seem that bright, and they just pull the wrong trigger.

"I remember a numbness. I mean, getting beaten by the Yankees was far worse than losing to any National League team. They had all these riches, and had had such a meager start, and here they were stealing one more from us. Even to the extent that after blowing it, we had that late streak and caught them from behind. It was the perfect setup for disappointment."

Rich Hershenson: "It was horrendous those years, the way they lost. Especially having to live in New York with all those New York assholes who lorded it over you and laid into you. At the end of the playoff in '78, it was like, 'It doesn't do any fucking good to get ahead. Sooner or later, somewhere down the line, we're going to lose.' Especially against the Yankees. I'm going to lose, the Red Sox are going to lose, and the Yankees are going to win. Even though the Yankees were far from their glory years, it was inevitable."

Tack Burbank: "I watched the game at the home of my friend Dan Ford. When Yaz popped out, I left the house. It was the kind of thing where your mind kept going back to it. I couldn't be rid of it for a long period of time. I kept seeing Bucky Dent lying in the dirt next to home plate, apparently having broken his foot with a foul ball.

"And then I would see the ball on the screen.

"Understand, I was almost thirty years old. I had gone to my first game in June 1954, and from then on, with the exception of the three weeks after the Boston Massacre, I was the kind of fan who would watch, attend, or listen to 140 games a year and certainly read every box score.

"But when I walked out of Dan Ford's house, I did not listen to, attend, or watch another baseball game until 1986. I cold-turkeyed them for eight years. I just felt so jilted. It was like I had come home and my wife of twenty-something years was in bed with my best friend. It was like I was never going to love again. I felt to survive psychologically, I couldn't be a fan anymore."

CHAPTER 43

Up and Down with the Red Sox

IN A DAZE

Immediately after the '78 playoff loss, the Jean Yawkey/Haywood Sullivan regime made it clear that saving money was its primary concern. Tom Yawkey wasn't just turning over in his grave; he must have been spinning like a top down there.

Sullivan offered star pitcher Luis Tiant a one-year contract. Buddy Leroux attempted to scare him into signing it when he told El Tiante, "Before you think about becoming a free agent, think about your age. I hope you have a lot of money in the bank."

Tiant said later, "They never took me seriously in those negotiations. They treated me like some old fool, but I was wise to their bool cheat."

Tiant, challenged, shunned the Red Sox offer and on November 13, 1978, signed instead with the hated New York Yankees. Commented Carl Yastrzemski, "When they let Luis Tiant go to New York, they tore out our heart and soul."

The irreverent Bill Lee had been the hero to every college kid in New England. On December 7, 1978, a day that will live in infamy, he was traded to Montreal for light-hitting infielder Stan Papi. In 1979, Lee went 16–10 for Montreal. Back in Boston, left-handed starters won exactly one game during a dismal season in which the Sox finished 11½ games behind Baltimore.

For Bill Lee, a prickly thorn in the side of management but a sensitive, hardworking performer, getting traded from the Red Sox has brought a bitterness that he will carry with him all the rest of his days.

Bill Lee: "On December 7, 1978, I was traded to Montreal. Zimmer had the guts to tell me he thought they had made a good deal when they got Stan Papi.

"I said, 'That's how much you know, Don.'

"I came back to Boston, and every subway station had written on it, 'Who's Stan Papi?' I felt bad for poor Stan Papi. I talked to him afterward. It had hurt him psychologically.

"We could have won a lot of pennants. All we had to do was not have a manager for about five years, just let us do it on our own. But tradition says you have to have a manager. I would have taken the ashes of Casey Stengel and just sat them on top of the bat rack. That would have been good enough for me."

Without Tiant and Lee, the team became mediocre, and worse, dull.

After the 1980 season, Sox stars Rick Burleson and Fred Lynn were traded to the California Angels. In exchange for Burleson and Butch Hobson, the Red Sox acquired third baseman Carney Lansford, outfielder Rick Miller, and relief pitcher Mark Clear, a fair swap, but for Lynn, the return was a sore-armed Frank Tanana, an over-the-hill Joe Rudi, and a guy named Jim Dorsey, who never made it.

The trading of Burleson and Lynn signaled a trend, a break with the loyalty-at-all-costs tradition that Tom Yawkey had held so dear. This disturbing trend continued when the Red Sox failed to tender their beloved catcher Carlton Fisk a contract by December 20, 1980. Pudge, who despised Haywood Sullivan, was declared a free agent. Fisk signed with the Chicago White Sox, changed his number from 27 to 72, and became a legend in a second city on the way to a niche in the Hall of Fame.

Behind the scenes, Buddy Leroux and Haywood Sullivan played out their feud, with Sullivan, backed by Jean Yawkey, coming out the winner. The losers, of course, were the Red Sox fans.

The Red Sox finished fourth in 1980, 19 games out of first place. In 1981, the season split by strike, they finished fifth in the first half, four games back of the Yankees, and second in the second half, a game and a half behind Milwaukee. In 1982, the Sox were third, six back. The Yankees won the East in a playoff in '81, the Brewers in '82. The big drop came in 1983, when the Red Sox finished under .500 for the first time since 1966. At 78–84, Boston was 20 games behind Baltimore, sixth of seven teams in the American League East.

When Yaz arrived in 1961, the Sox were losers. In 1983, his retirement year, they were losers again. Despite his excellence over a long, illustrious career, some perverse fans would dwell on his magical moments of failure. To them, Carl Yaz symbolized his era. To them, Yaz and his Red Sox, despite pennants in 1967 and 1975, were sources of disappointment.

When he retired, Yaz admitted that he couldn't believe the Red Sox hadn't won two or three World Series with all the talent they had had in '75. Ironically, a number of those Red Sox players from '75 did go on to success with other teams in the postseason, including Cecil Cooper, Carlton Fisk, Fred Lynn, Rick Burleson, Juan Beniquez, Bill Lee, and Rick Miller. Unfortunately for Boston fans, none of them did their playing for the Red Sox.

Black players continued to find it difficult playing for Boston. Players like Jim Rice and Ellis Burks found themselves targets of racial name-calling from fans. Ferguson Jenkins and Reggie Smith found the atmosphere stifling and left Boston with bad feelings. Blacks complained that their families couldn't go to games because of abuse by white fans.

Tommy Harper lost his job as a minor-league instructor because he revealed that a private club in Winter Haven invited the white players for free meals but not the blacks.

At the same time, certain white players could get away with a great deal. The unequal treatment of the Red Sox players was noted by some fans.

Danny Frio, journalist: "In 1975, there were two automobile accidents involving Red Sox pitchers. They happened late at night on days before they were scheduled to pitch, under questionable circumstances. One was Roger Moret, who was a black Latin, and the other was Reggie Cleveland. Take a look at how the *Boston Globe* treated both incidents. Take a look at how the management reacted to both players, what their punishments were, and I can assure you from going to the games that the fans didn't give Cleveland any grief, and they gave Roger Moret a lot of grief. And I blame the media for the way the fans reacted. Moret was on the front page. The other was a little item on the sports page.

"Take the parallel between Orlando Cepeda or Tony Perez and Bill Buckner. There was no tolerance for Orlando Cepeda's slow wheels in the latter stages of his career. He hustled and did the best he could. Perez put in a couple of productive years with the Reds post–Red Sox. Perez hit 25 homers, drove in 105 runs his first year with the Sox, but they weren't real tolerant of his slow speed.

"And Bill Buckner, he stayed and played, and no one said very much. Until the ball went through his legs.

"The Red Sox tolerated a lot of grief, even open insubordination by Bill Lee toward the manager. And you know there is no way in hell that a black player would ever come close to doing that.

"The level of tolerance for behavior is unequal. One of the most enlightening things you can do is look at the press that Jim Rice and Fred Lynn got in 1975 when they both had full years with the Sox. It's no wonder Rice doesn't talk to the press, because the press built up Lynn's accomplishments a hell of a lot more than Rice's. Lynn got more ink than he deserved and Rice got less than he deserved.

"Mario Guerrero got traded. The Latin players get a year or two, and if they're not superstars, they're out. Guerrero, Julio Valdez, Luis Alvarado, Jackie Gutierrez, Rey Quinones, all out.

"I can't figure out how they got Luis Tiant. That's unusual for the Red Sox. Tiant's pretty bitter about the way the Red Sox treated him. When he signed with the Yankees, he had been told they had a managerial or administrative position for him, that he was going to be in the Red Sox organization forever. And after he quit playing, he asked about it, and they said, 'Forget it.'"

Mark Onigman, journalist: "There is a long history of Irish media in Boston. Not that these guys are guilty of anything. No one is saying that. But when you start adding it up and look at the Sox management, the Sox media, the writers, it's Boston. This is the home of Honey Fitz and John F. Kennedy. There is not a lot of cultural diversity."

YAZ RETIRES

Carl Yastrzemski somehow had aged before our very eyes. Suddenly, he was almost forty, and where had the years gone? Yaz went into the 1979 season with 383 homers and 2,869 hits. He needed 17 homers and 131 hits to become the first American League player to achieve 400 homers *and* 3,000 hits. Three others—Stan Musial, Willie Mays, and Hank Aaron—had done it in the National League.

The mathematicians predicted that Yaz would hit the milestones in early July, but he suffered from painful Achilles tendons. When he hit, he had little feeling in his legs.

"When I got set in the box, I had to look down at my legs to see if they were positioned properly because I couldn't feel them," he said.

After hitting home run number 399, Yastrzemski went an agonizing 16 games before hitting another. Finally, on July 24, he hit number 400 off nineteen-year-old rookie Mike Morgan of the Oakland A's. Number 400 put Yaz at number eighteen all-time, one ahead of Detroit's Al Kaline.

Getting hit number 3,000 was much more difficult. He was getting old, and with the Red Sox out of the race, all the attention was on him. Yaz stopped being selective. He went 90 at bats without a walk, and was only 17-for-79 at the time he finally got that 3,000th hit.

Part of the added pressure he put on himself was that he wanted hit 3,000 to be a home run. He wanted to be remembered as Ted Williams had been. The hit came on Tuesday, September 12. Catfish Hunter was the Yankees starting pitcher in that game. Catfish announced it would be his final game.

The great right-hander walked Yaz once and retired him the next two at bats. In relief, Jim Beattie retired Yaz to deepen his slump to 0-for-10, but in the eighth, Yaz hit a hard ground ball between first and second. Willie Randolph made a stab for it, but the ball rolled into right field.

Once Reggie Jackson fielded it, the game was stopped. A microphone was brought out. Yaz made a flat joke about enjoying all the standing ovations he had been getting from the fans while they were waiting for his 3,000th hit, then he thanked manager Don Zimmer and his teammates, especially Walt Hriniak, the batting coach.

In closing, he thanked his two biggest boosters, the late Tom Yawkey and his mother, who had died of cancer not long before. He broke into tears and could say no more.

Yaz had talked of retirement during 1983, but as the year wore on, he changed his mind and decided to retire in 1984. What initially had been his retirement day was changed to Carl Yastrzemski Appreciation Day.

Baseball had been his entire life, and even though he would have a post-baseball career as a spokesman for Kahn's beef, the game had been all he knew.

By the end of '83, however, Yaz had lost his desire for the game. The Red Sox were out of the race, and he was bored. He told manager Ralph Houk, "Baseball just doesn't mean that much to me anymore unless we're in a pennant race. I think it's left me."

Yaz asked Houk, "Do we have a shot at a pennant next year?"

Houk, honest always, replied, "I don't think so." Then the Major told him, "Yaz, I managed and played with some great ones. Get out at the right time if that's how you feel."

On October 1, 1983, Carl Yastrzemski bid Boston good-bye. Yaz knew it was time to go. He always said that his reflexes would tell him when to quit. He didn't want to go out as Willie Mays had, struggling to be adequate.

Before the game, he stood out on the field with his wife, Carol, his children, Governor Michael Dukakis, and Senator Ted Kennedy.

He began, "This is a very special day for me." He gulped and had to stop. When he resumed, he spoke of his being honored by the fans, whom he called the greatest and most loyal. He talked of the spirit of Fenway Park, calling it the best place to play baseball in the world. He spoke of his pride in the Red Sox uniform, and what a privilege it was to be a Red Sox longer than any other player.

"I will miss you," he said.

He spoke of being blessed by his family and called baseball the finest of all games. He said people had asked him how he would like to be remembered, and he said he hoped people would remember him as a winner, "because I feel just playing one game at Fenway Park makes me a winner." He spoke of his love of competition, that he always did his best.

"I might not have had the greatest ability in the world, but I got the most out of it," he said.

Yastrzemski admitted to no regrets. He said he hoped he had represented Boston and New England with class and dignity. Then he asked for a moment of silence for his mom and for Tom Yawkey.

A bell sounded in their memory. When it ended, the silence continued to waft over the old park. Few eyes were dry.

Yaz said, "New England, I love you."

It was a magical moment. And then the usually unemotional Carl Yastrzemski did something unforgettable. As the audience stood and cheered for this man who had meant so much to them, Yaz decided he would show the fans how much they meant to him. He ran toward the stands along the first-base line and started shaking hands with the men and women who had come to honor him. He then ran along the edge of the field toward the right-field stands, waving, bowing, showing his appreciation, and then he ran into center field and over toward left along the Wall, toward the fans who had sat behind him all those years. As he ran, Carl Yastrzemski began crying, and he didn't hide the fact. He wanted them to see how he felt. They cried, too. It was the end of an era at Fenway. Carl Yastrzemski was leaving them forever.

On the final day of the season before the game, his teammates gathered in the clubhouse. While Yastrzemski sat in front of his locker, Dwight Evans presented him with a retirement present, an expensive rod and reel.

"You've got no excuses now," Evans told him. "Go get 'em."

On that final day, Yastrzemski wanted to do something dramatic, as Ted Williams had when he retired. Yaz's dream in his final game was to throw a runner out at the plate. The best he could do was hold a Toby Harrah hit off the Wall to a single. The fans gave him a standing ovation.

Yastrzemski's final at bat was against the Cleveland Indians' Dan Spillner. Hitting a home run was in the back of his mind. The count went to 3–0. Spillner threw another pitch, high, that would have been ball four, but Yaz swung and lifted a harmless pop-up to the infield.

When he was removed in the eighth by manager Ralph Houk, Yaz stopped in front of the dugout to wave to the crowd and headed for the clubhouse. Perhaps Yaz remembered Ted Williams, who had never tipped his cap to the fans. But on his way out of the game, he noticed a small boy sitting with his parents in the box seats near the dugout.

Yaz took off his cap, and he handed it to the boy. The boy and Yaz exchanged smiles, as number 8 went down the steps of the dugout for the last time.

Jeffrey Lyons: "Rooting for the Red Sox, I watched how many guys failed, how many Lee Stanges there were, how many Sonny Sieberts came and disappeared. And why a guy like Yaz endured forever. Yaz only played for the Red Sox. How many players today only play for one team over such a span? There just aren't players like that. His last game, he ran around the park hitting the hands of the fans, like a bullfighter. I was crying when I watched that.

"In '67, he was the complete ballplayer, and he had one of the great stances. The only other player I can remember with a stance like that was Milt May, who was a journeyman outfielder whose father was Pinky May, a .270 hitter. I batted like that all through high school, with my hands above my ears. For me it meant too many pop flies to left field. But Yaz could do it. I copied his every movement. And whenever I played in the park, someone would shout, 'Yastrzemski, get your hands up,' and I knew a kindred spirit was watching.

"Yaz followed Williams in the hallowed tradition. I love traditions like that: Jimmy Brown, then Larry Czonka, then Floyd Little, three greats. It was once that way in center field at Yankee Stadium. But left field to me is hallowed ground, and to have someone like Yaz, a self-made man, follow Williams, who was born with the ability . . . But Yastrzemski made himself a hitter, made himself the greatest. I saw him make a catch in the Washington Senators' old stadium in an All-Star Game, leaping up over the chain-link fence and catching the ball and pulling it down.

"He was a normal guy who made himself, and I was always convinced that if I had had the time and the wherewithal, I could do the same thing.

"Yaz is not the most loquacious person in the world. This is not Abba Eban we're talking about, but you don't expect him to be. That's not his job. His job was to be the best of us. He's not a proud athlete the way Dave Winfield is. He made himself play the game.

"The thing about Yastrzemski, unlike any other aging athlete, he never put on weight. If you see ballplayers in the later part of their careers, their faces begin to sag, their bodies begin to fall. His didn't. I always marveled during the last years of his career that he was always slim and weighed the same as he did when he was a rookie.

"And he was also the last ballplayer who I can think of who got down on one knee in the on-deck circle. Ballplayers don't do that anymore. It's not cool. He was the last player to do that. You will never see that again. And so I do that when I wait on the deck in the park in games.

"To see this man toward the end of his career making himself a first baseman, making himself into a designated hitter, which is a completely different mentality than being an everyday player, and seeing a younger man play the position he owned, to me showed that there was somebody who was very special indeed.

"And in his last game he played left field, and thank God it was a season they didn't win. They could let him play left field one more time. That to me no other franchise would do for no other player. It showed there is a love from this city for that team.

"They will never move from Fenway Park. The towel guy, Buddy Leroux, the guy who cleaned the towels, owned the team. The owner's son was a catcher who hit .185. No other team would do that.

"Being a film critic, I once wrote to the Red Sox and asked them, 'Would you please ask Mr. Yastrzemski what is his favorite film of all time?' If I were a player, I would say something like *Citizen Kane* or something by Fellini, highfalutin, just to catch somebody's eye. I'd be a colorful interview if I were a player. But the guy who was doing public relations wrote back, 'Mr. Yastrzemski does not go to the movies. He concerns himself mostly with fishing.'

"Well, okay. Please, all I did was ask. Make up a movie. Tell me he likes *The Seven Little Foys* or *Take Me Out to the Ballgame.* Don't say, 'Mr. Yastrzemski only concerns himself with fishing.' What does Yaz do now? Does he go to the Sorbonne to take courses? Is he relaxing and fishing? I hope so."

CHAPTER 44

Resurgence: 1986

THIS TIME FOR REAL

The resurgence of the Red Sox came with the trade to the Chicago Cubs in May 1984 of pitcher Dennis Eckersley and minor leaguer Mike Brumley for first baseman Bill Buckner.

Said the newly appointed Red Sox general manager, Lou Gorman, "We have to do something to regain the fans' confidence." The Sox had finished twenty games out in 1983. And after the loss of Fisk, Lynn, and Burleson, and then Carney Lansford, many Red Sox fans stopped coming to the park and watching on television.

Getting Buckner was a signal to the fans that the Red Sox would once again compete on the open market for players. To acquire Buckner, who had played thirteen full seasons in the majors and seven years for the Cubs, they first had to get his permission to leave the Cubs and come to the Red Sox. He demanded a $300,000 signing bonus and got it. In acquiring Buckner, the Red Sox were agreeing to pay him what he was making under his Cubs contract—$600,000 for 1984 and $710,000 for '85—and then to add another $750,000 for 1986.

Gorman, who had worked for the New York Mets under Frank Cashen, came to Boston in the nick of time. After checking the winds, he pointed the sails of the Red Sox ship straining toward competitiveness again.

New blood came surging to Boston from the farm system. A third baseman by the name of Wade Boggs came up to the Red Sox in 1982, and in 104 games hit .349. Was it a fluke? The next year he was a regular, banging out 210 hits and batting .361 to lead the league. Then he reeled off seasons of .325, .368, .357, .363, .366, .330, and .302. He is a hitting machine, which in part explains why Boggs is admired but not loved.

Mark Starr: "I have very little emotional connection with Boggs. He's a very skilled, technical hitter. His skill commands admiration, perhaps some respect, and the conventional wisdom that he has improved his defense is certainly true, he has worked at it, but he's not an easy player to love. He's neither particularly charming nor supremely intelligent, and his off-the-field exploits certainly haven't helped. I can remember fifteen hundred of his hits, yet I can't remember any one of them.

"He seems the classic throwback to what they've always said about the Red Sox, which was, 'Twenty-five players, twenty-five cabs.' No one ever had a sense he went for power to win a game when it might be needed or that he gave himself up when it might be needed. There was a famous play a few years back, when the Red Sox were trying to rally late in the game, and he took a pitch on a hit-and-run, and later didn't say he missed the sign, implying he doesn't swing at the first pitch, no matter what. It didn't fit into his personal ethic. And the runner, of course, being a Red Sox base runner, was thrown out."

At the end of the 1980 season, the Red Sox had repeated history by hiring a former New York Yankee legend. In the late forties, Joe McCarthy had been hired. For 1981, it was Ralph Houk, the Major. Houk had led the Yankees to pennants in 1961, 1962, and 1963, and then stepped up the ladder to become Yankee general manager. When the team collapsed in 1965, he returned as manager, continuing as Yankee skipper from 1966 to 1973, when he could no longer abide the meddling of owner George Steinbrenner. Houk managed Detroit from 1974 to 1978 and retired. He came out of retirement when Boston called.

Houk, who managed Boston from 1981 through 1984, had the youngest pitching staff in the league: Bruce Hurst, Bobby Ojeda, Dennis ("Oil Can") Boyd, Al Nipper, and a youngster from the University of Texas by the name of Roger Clemens. Under Houk, the Red Sox finished fifth and second in the split 1981 season, then third, sixth, and fourth.

After the 1984 season, John McNamara took over as manager. McNamara was from the old school of Red Sox managers, Irishmen with little imagination. Under McNamara in 1985, the team played .500 ball and finished fifth. Wade Boggs that year hit .368 and drove in 78 runs, and with

Tony Armas hitting 23 home runs, Jim Rice 27, and Dwight Evans 29, there was plenty of offense, but Roger Clemens was plagued with arm woes, and Oil Can Boyd, Bruce Hurst, Bobby Ojeda and Al Nipper weren't a strong enough staff to contend.

In 1986, however, Clemens established himself as the best pitcher in all of baseball. After signing off the campus of the University of Texas, Clemens became the team stopper in 1986, winning 24 games and losing only four. He had a two-year, 14-game winning streak before it was stopped in early July. In 1986, he struck out 238 batters. In one game against Seattle in late April, the Rocket Man struck out 20 batters and walked none. His earned-run average for the season was a league-leading 2.48. At the end of the year, he was voted both the Cy Young Award and the Most Valuable Player of the American League.

Mark Starr: "I love Roger Clemens. He reminds me of Luis Tiant and the great pitchers in that he is a ferocious competitor. You get the sense that he is in synch with the team, that he comes out to the mound and says to himself, 'I'm going to pick up the team.' And he's not just a thrower. He's a pitcher. You see him some days with really mediocre stuff. The other team is getting singles and there are base runners every inning, and he still keeps them off the board and keeps the team in the game.

"I love his competitiveness. His competitiveness leads him to act like a jerk sometimes, and I don't admire that jerkiness or find it particularly appealing, but I love his intensity, love how visibly he cares. The old expression, 'He wears it on his sleeve,' applies. He *does.*

"I like the emotion in Clemens. He's going to battle you. He'll come inside. He'll get himself tossed out of the game for the team. Other star pitchers might say, 'They can't afford to lose me.' But I remember one game against Detroit he gave up back-to-back home runs to Rob Deer and Pete Incaviglia early, and he obviously didn't have good stuff, and then he plunked John Shelby and clearly could have gotten thrown out of the game, and maybe he should have, but he then settled down and they didn't score until after Boston was in command. That was really impressive."

On Good Friday, March 28, 1986, the Sox added character and one of the best designated hitters in the game when it acquired Don Baylor from the Yankees for Mike Easler. On June 29, the Sox added more character when they acquired legendary pitcher Tom Seaver. Seaver was expected to lend stability to the pitching staff. Clemens had been seven years old when Seaver led the Mets to a championship in 1969. Seaver became the first 300-game winner to take the mound for the Red Sox since Cy Young. That day, Lou Gorman also promoted a promising right arm, Calvin Schiraldi, from Pawtucket.

The Red Sox led the league by eight games in early July. Red Sox fans were jubilant. Past disappointments were forgiven (though not forgotten, never forgotten).

Tack Burbank: "I hadn't watched a Red Sox game since 1978, and then about halfway through the '86 season, I thought to myself, 'Jesus, this team has pitching. This team can win it!' So I took it hook, line, and sinker, and by midseason I was into it again, watching all the games."

Everything was going smoothly until the All-Star break, when pitcher Oil Can Boyd began acting strangely. It had not been the first time a Red Sox pitcher succumbed to life's pressures. After all, Gene Conley had jumped the team to go to Jerusalem. And in the late 1970s, Rogelio Moret, after brilliant years of 13–2 and 14–3 records, had begun having episodes of bizarre behavior, staring at walls and going into a fugue state, before being dealt away.

In 1986, the Red Sox had another pitcher who appeared to be nearly as unstable. Oil Can Boyd, who was facing financial problems, was counting on a $25,000 bonus he was to get if he made the American League All-Star team. But American League pilot Dick Howser, faced with having to choose players from each team in the league, decided not to pick Boyd, and when Oil Can learned of the snub in the middle of a game against California, he threw an unforgettable tantrum, berating his own manager John McNamara, the team physician, and his good friend, teammate Al Nipper, whom Boyd accused of being a "redneck."

Boyd stormed out of the clubhouse and left the ballpark. McNamara suspended him for three days without pay and ordered him to apologize to his teammates. Boyd checked into a Boston hospital for observation and treatment, and during the first two weeks he was away, the team went into a tailspin, dropping eight of ten, and its lead was cut to 2½ games.

In the last fourteen years, the Red Sox had been leading the division seven times at the All-Star break and had only one pennant to show for it—1975. Visions of Bucky Dent and 1978 hung over the Red Sox.

In early August, however, the Red Sox continued to hang on. The *Boston Globe* ran a story on page one. It began, "A fatalistic gloom hangs over Boston. It's August and the Red Sox are in first place."

But newcomer Don Baylor professed not to care about the past. "I don't care what happened in 1978. This club wants to win so bad. To have people telling you you're going to fail . . . You can see it; they expect us to choke . . ."

General manager Lou Gorman continued to fine-tune. On August 17, he acquired shortstop Spike Owen and outfielder Dave Henderson in a trade with Seattle for shortstop Rey Quinones. Owen had played on the same University of Texas team with Clemens and Calvin Schiraldi. Dick Williams, who was managing the Mariners, had buried Henderson in his doghouse. Henderson's acquisition would make history.

The Red Sox celebrated September by winning eleven games in a row, nine of those after trailing. Jim Rice hit 18-for-46, with five home runs, during the streak. Clemens won his twenty-second game and went to the White House to meet President Reagan, along with some teammates. Reagan regaled Clemens with tales about his playing Grover Cleveland Alexander in the movie *The Winning Team.*

The streak gave the Red Sox a nine-game cushion. The rest of the season was a cakewalk. A contrite Oil Can Boyd clinched the division title on September 28 with a complete-game victory over Toronto.

In the playoffs, the Red Sox had to face the veteran-laden California Angels without the services of forty-one-year-old Tom Seaver, who had injured his knee. But, for once, the Red Sox were favored, because they had the home advantage and Roger Clemens pitching in the first game.

The first game did not work out exactly as planned—the Angels rocked Clemens, 8–1—but Bruce Hurst, who pitched brilliantly the second half of the season, evened the series with a 9–2 victory in Game Two. The unpredictable Oil Can lost Game Three, and then suddenly the Red Sox were on the brink of extinction when, after leading 3–0 in the ninth inning of Game Four behind Roger Clemens, Jim Rice lost a fly ball in the lights, the roof fell in, and California won.

Then, on Sunday, October 12, with the Angels leading three games to one, California had a 5–2 lead in the ninth behind the superb pitching of Mike Witt. Billy Buckner led off the ninth and singled up the middle. Don Baylor homered, making the score 5–4, giving Red Sox fans just enough hope. But at the same time Red Sox fans reminded themselves that the Sox had lost the Bucky Dent game in '78 by the same score.

Catcher Rich Gedman was the batter. He had already produced a single, double, and home run against Witt.

Gene Mauch, the California manager, had been a victim of bad karma during much of his career. Mauch, known as the most brilliant manager never to win the pennant, had blown the 1964 pennant for the Phils and he'd done it again in 1982 with the Angels. Mauch was often referred to as a baseball genius, but he tended to overmanage, and as often happens, his weakness tended to pop up in moments of stress.

Mauch came to the mound and removed Witt. He brought in left-handed control specialist Gary Lucas to face Gedman, a left-handed hitter. Gedman called time and asked the umpire to remove a banner hanging over the outfield wall.

The banner read, "Another Boston Choke."

Lucas hit Gedman. It was the only pitch Lucas threw. Mauch then brought in his closer, right-hander Donnie Moore, to face reserve outfielder Dave Henderson. Since coming over from Seattle, Hendu had hit one home run and delivered three runs batted in.

Joe Sambito, Red Sox, 1986–87: "All the pitchers from our team, seven or eight of us plus the coaches, were in the bullpen. We were all standing there watching. Nobody was warming up. There were two outs. The grounds crew was standing there and all kinds of security were all crowded in there. The bullpen in Anaheim is almost pie-shaped—very narrow at the fence and then it widens as it goes back—so everyone was funneled up to the front. I was standing six or seven people deep from the fence, but I was able to see over shoulders and heads, and I was watching.

"The fans lined both sides of us, hooting at us, yelling at us, pointing. I had my jacket wrapped up and stuffed into my glove. I had my glove under my arm.

"The California Highway Patrol was there. One of the troopers came over to me and said, 'When the game is over, we'll take you guys underneath the stands and around the tunnel to your clubhouse. Don't go across the field, because there will be a lot of people out there, and we'd rather you don't go out there.' We agreed. There was a 2–2 count to Dave Henderson."

Moore was one pitch away from victory. In the dugout, outfielder Reggie Jackson was hugging Gene Mauch. Moore threw a forkball, low and away. Henderson hit it high and deep.

Joe Sambito: "Hendu swung, and here came this ball toward us, and it went over the left-field fence, and we all started cheering, but everyone else was stunned. The Angels fans were in utter silence. And then we started hooting at the fans. I mean, we got on them just as they were getting on us. I said to myself, 'How often do you see a game like this?' "

Tack Burbank: "We were down to the Angels three games to one, and in Game Five when Henderson got up to bat, there were two outs in the ninth, we were losing by a run, and I had given up hope. I was disconsolate, couldn't believe we were going to lose to the Angels, because we were a much better team, and I had figured it would just be a formality beating them.

"When Dave Henderson came to the plate against Donnie Moore, I had zero expectation. So when Henderson hit the home run, it was like when Bernie Carbo hit his pinch-hit home run in the 1975 World Series, the same feeling, like I was a little boy, jumping up and down screaming. I couldn't stop, and then the Red Sox brought in their big right-hander, Steve Crawford, an incredibly scary inning, the kind of ninth inning where California could have won it if Gene Mauch had any luck at all. Crawford gave up a run and the game went into extra innings, and we ended up winning on Henderson's long sacrifice fly.

"And after that, California totally disintegrated. Boston won the last two easily. They were laughers."

The scores of the final two games were 10–4 and 8–1. Oil Can Boyd and Roger Clemens wiped up. The Red Sox were winners of their fourth pennant since 1918. Their opponents in the World Series would be the New York Mets.

ONE STRIKE AWAY

Tack Burbank: "I went to Game Seven of the ALCS and saw the Red Sox win, which was a great thrill. After the victory I hung around Kenmore Square with my friend Dan Ford and partied, as I did in '67 when they won the pennant. That year, I walked out of Fairweather Hall at Dartmouth, and hundreds of people were walking around the green, skipping and dancing. People just wanted to be together. And it was the same way after the Sox beat the Angels.

"When the Red Sox won the first two games in New York against the Mets, I was figuring with Clemens scheduled and three games to play at Fenway, well, I don't know if I felt they had a lock on it, but I was pretty confident."

Bruce Hurst, who had once quit while pitching in the minor leagues because he didn't think he'd ever make it, defeated the Mets' Ron Darling, 1–0, in the opener. Dwight Gooden was bested in Game Two. The Red Sox were rolling. It looked like the jinx was finally beaten.

The Mets won Games Three and Four, but that was all right. Hurst came back and beat Doc Gooden, 4–2, in Game Five. The Red Sox were one game from winning their first World Series since 1918. Just one game.

Before the Sox' return to New York for Game Six, Dwight Evans told reporters, "It's at hand, but it's not over. We're not going to celebrate until the last pitch and the last out."

In Game Six, Boston led 2–0, as Clemens pitched no-hit ball through four innings. In the fifth, the Mets tied it up. Each team scored a single run as the game went into the tenth inning.

Dave Henderson homered in the top of the tenth and the Sox added an insurance run to give them a 5–3 lead, as the Mets came to bat in the bottom of the tenth. Rookie Calvin Schiraldi, who had a 1.41 earned-run average and had saved nine games since being called up from Pawtucket, went out to nail

down the Red Sox' first Series triumph since Carl Mays had beaten Lefty
Tyler and the Chicago Cubs sixty-eight years earlier. By now, even the most
cynical Red Sox fan had been won over. All the little doubts and hesitations
had been put away. The day had finally come. The Red Sox were going to
win the World Series.

Tack Burbank: "Dan Ford came over to my house to watch Game Six. He
always questioned the chemistry when the two of us were together watching
Red Sox games. You can't believe how many times they've lost in the late
innings when we were together. But we decided we had to win it together, so
Dan, whose family owns a package store, brought over a vintage bottle of
champagne. We put it on ice, and it sat in a big ice bucket the whole game
on the kitchen table.

"So we were watching the game in our little TV den, and Danny espoused
the theory of the 'deadly aftershock.' The 'deadly aftershock' is scoring a run
to go ahead and then hitting them again by scoring an insurance run. It gives
you a little bit of a working margin.

"The Red Sox had gone ahead 3 to 2 in the seventh, but the Mets scored
in the bottom of the eighth inning to make it 3–3. And then in the top of the
tenth, Henderson homered and we scored another run, and Danny said,
'That's it. The deadly aftershock. The game is won. The World Series is won.'

"I began thinking about my mother. She became a fan in grade school
around 1920, and through her adult life she was a true fanatic. She was one
of those New Englanders who sat by the radio and listened to every game,
and once they were televised she would watch them, even though she preferred the games on the radio. It was more comforting to her. But the Red
Sox never won a World Series in her entire life, and I was feeling so glad for
my mother and so glad for all the Red Sox fans just like her, and feeling so
glad for me.

"And then something strange happened. It was surreal. There were two
outs. We were one out away from winning our first World Series since 1918.
Then Gary Carter hit a single. All right, there are two outs and one guy on.
But once they got the second single—Kevin Mitchell hit it—I started to feel
it go. I started to feel like this was fate. I always wondered what fate was. This
was it."

Mets third baseman Ray Knight followed Carter and Mitchell with a third
single—on two strikes, no less—to close the gap to one run. Kevin Mitchell
stood on third base. The tying run was ninety feet away. The two outs
remained.

Bob "Steamer" Stanley came in to replace Schiraldi. Stanley had been a
target of the Red Sox fans because of his inconsistent performances, but he
vowed the fans would remember him in the World Series. They would.

Mookie Wilson was the batter. The big right-hander ran the count to 2–1, then Wilson fouled off two pitches. One strike away. He fouled off one more.

Stanley came inside with a fastball that was supposed to come back over the plate. Only, the ball didn't fade. Instead, it continued to bore in on Wilson, searching for his ribs. At the last moment, Wilson reacted, backing away, momentarily blocking catcher Rich Gedman's view of the ball. Too late, Gedman watched the ball heading for the backstop. Kevin Mitchell scored easily to tie it up. Knight went to second.

Red Sox fans watched, continuing to disbelieve what was happening before their eyes. What *was* this?

The count was still 3–2 on Wilson. He fouled off the next pitch. At first base, Bill Buckner stood thirty feet behind the bag. Wilson wondered whether he could beat Buckner to the bag if he hit it in his direction.

Billy Buck, standing guard at first, was a heroic figure. In a sixteen-season career, he had amassed 2,464 hits and had established a reputation for being a clutch player. During the season, he had expressed the hope he could play long enough to collect 3,000 hits and earn consideration for the Hall of Fame. But in the final game of the playoffs against California he had torn the Achilles tendon of his right foot. All season long, he had suffered with a left ankle that pained him terribly. He took cortisone shots to alleviate the pain. For the last eight seasons, Buckner had soaked his feet in ice before and after every game. Billy Buck was the Ultimate Warrior, and the Red Sox fans loved him for it.

Stanley threw again, and Wilson did hit the ball toward Buckner. Okay, said the Red Sox fan, this is okay. Billy's going to field it, step on the bag, and we go to the eleventh. No problem. The ball went bounce, bounce, and as it neared Buckner, no bounce. It skipped sideways under his glove and through his gimpy underpinning, out, out onto the field. Ray Knight of the Mets ran home on winged feet.

Ask a Red Sox fan to recount that fateful inning and you're asking a lot. It's like asking him to recount the death of a close relative. It's painful, very painful.

Peter Gammons of the *Globe* wrote in *Sports Illustrated* that fall: "When the ball went through Bill Buckner's legs, 41 years of Red Sox baseball flashed in front of my eyes. In that one moment Johnny Pesky held the ball, Joe McCarthy lifted Ellis Kinder in Yankee Stadium, Luis Aparicio fell down rounding third, Bill Lee delivered his eephus pitch to Tony Perez, Darrell Johnson hit for Jim Willoughby, Don Zimmer chose Bobby Sprowl over Luis Tiant and Bucky (Bleeping) Dent hit the home run."

David Margolick: "I was sitting at home with my friend, Jonathan, watching the game on TV, and when the first batter for the Mets got a single with two outs, I looked at him, and he looked at me, and we both instantly knew what one another was thinking. 'This thing is not over.' Nevertheless, we did not think it would turn out as horrifically as it did.

"And I remember when it was over, I put it off immediately. It was too traumatic for me. When the ball went through Buckner's legs, and the guy came around to score, I put it off. I didn't want to hear the postgame summary and hear the cheering. I quickly turned the TV set off.

"I had gotten a call in the top of the inning from a Mets fan. We were talking on the phone as it went along, and he said, 'Well, you did it.' He wasn't egging me on, though I was probably interpreting it that way, because he wasn't thinking the same thing I was thinking. He was behaving the way a normal baseball fan would behave. When a team is losing by a couple runs late in the game, ninety-nine times out of a hundred it's over. And I was humoring him, hedging. But for him, the game was over.

"Yet, I was responding in a cautionary way. I wasn't saying, 'Yeah, it looks like Mudville for you guys.' In fact, I thought I was tempting fate even to be thinking about winning. It's like talking about a no-hitter. You just don't do it. And when the Mets started to get the hits, Jonathan and I looked at each other and at this point I didn't even want to talk to him. I retreated, and when the game was over, I went into my room and closed the door. I wanted to be left alone.

"I did watch the seventh game, but only halfheartedly. There was absolutely no doubt in my mind that the Red Sox were going to lose. If somebody had offered me tickets to the seventh game, I wouldn't have gone. What was the point? What's the point of going to an alien stadium and being there when the barbarians won?"

Tack Burbank: "The game was over, and I was sitting with my wife, Christine, and my friend, Dan Ford, and not a word was spoken from the time of the wild pitch to the end. Not a single word was uttered by the three of us. In silence we watched the ball go through Buckner's legs. We watched the postgame celebration. We watched the postgame show.

"It's late now, about eleven-thirty, and the local affiliate came on with the news. We sat there staring at the TV screen, but we were not watching. Without saying anything, Christine got up and went to bed. So Danny and I were left there, and the news ended and a *M*A*S*H* rerun came on, and we sat there, and now it was an hour since the game ended, and we haven't said anything, and I turned to my friend Dan Ford, and the two of us have been on the verge of tears, which is why nothing had been said, and I mustered the emotional energy to say, 'Danny, just how bad is it for you?'

"Now Danny, who is a Superior Court judge and one of the finest trial judges in the state of Massachusetts, he's a very thoughtful guy, and I can see him considering the question. Danny is an only child, and both of his parents are deceased. Finally he said, 'It's somewhere between the death of my father and the death of my mother.'

"Those were the only words that were spoken. We sat there silently for another fifteen minutes, and Danny got up and left the house. I got up and turned off the TV set, and I went to bed and didn't sleep that whole night, and I didn't get a good night's sleep for several nights. I kept replaying the game, replaying the tenth inning in my mind again and again and again and again. It was six months before I got over it, and that was when I developed the Holy Grail Theory.

"Under this theory, I feel sorry for the Mets fans of '86 because I wondered what they could ever look forward to again. I decided that a world championship was the Holy Grail and that a large part of the Boston mystique was that we had been chasing it so valiantly for all these years. It's why we're different from Cubs or White Sox fans. For the most part, they have had lousy teams. But the Red Sox have had so many good teams, and they've come so close to the Holy Grail and then failed. There is something very spiritual about it, and I think that if they ever won a World Series, a lot of the religion would be gone.

"Having said all that, I still follow them, and I still go to games, but because of Game Six in '86, a part of me has been killed."

For the players, the loss was equally devastating, but they were not up to blaming Billy Buck for the loss. Some felt manager John McNamara should have replaced him defensively in the ninth or pinch-run for him in the tenth after he was hit by a pitch. But McNamara hadn't pinch-hit for Buckner all year, and the only time Dave Stapleton played for him on defense was early in the Series, when Buckner's Achilles tendon hurt him too much for him to play. Said McNamara in his own defense after the game, "He has good hands, and he was running well tonight."

His teammates saw how gutsily Billy Buck had served the Sox all season long, and in the end they could not bring themselves to blame him.

Sammy Stewart, Red Sox, 1986: "I was sitting in the bullpen during Game Six. Bob Stanley was on the mound. Our bullpen coach, Joe Morgan, was telling me the whole time in the bullpen, 'You're warming up, because you have the best arm right now, Sammy.' He saw me. He said, 'Don't get down about this. It's not the end of the world. You're going to get to pitch in this Series. Don't worry about it.' And it kept going, kept going.

"We had heard through Joe Morgan that McNamara was going to put in Dave Stapleton for Buckner, but Morgan told us that Buckner said, 'No, I want to stay in there. I want to be there and finish the game.' He kind of talked McNamara into it, and so he *was* there to finish the game.

"We thought it was a good ground ball and were ready for him to make an out. We jumped up, ready to holler, and then, 'No. No.'

"From Day One, when I went to the place where I shopped at in Boston, they would say, 'You guys are going to blow it again.' I said, 'Wait a minute. This is my first year here. I'm coming over from the winningest team in the last twenty-five years, the Baltimore Orioles. I'm a winner, and you have to feel you're going to give us a chance.' They said, 'No, forget it. You guys will blow it again.'

"And that's when I said, 'They know what they're talking about. They got more than clam chowder up there.' Oh, but it was amazing. I thought, 'Now I have to go home and listen to "We told you so." ' "

Joe Sambito: "I was in the bullpen with my brother. It was the ninth inning of the sixth game. He asked me, 'How will I get in the clubhouse?' I said, 'Here's my hat and glove and some catching equipment.' We had a small TV down there, and I said, 'Carry this TV. And here's a bag that says Red Sox, carry this stuff into the clubhouse, open the door, get in there, and I'll see you inside.'

"So he's holding all this stuff, waiting for the game to end, ready for the last pitch. There were two outs. Nobody's on. The bullpen gate is unlatched, and we're ready to run across the field. There was a base hit. My brother said, 'Uh-oh.' I said, 'Relax, it's only a hit.' Then there was another hit. And then everything's a blur.

"You know, I've never watched that Series highlight film—but the next thing I know, there's a wild pitch, the ball goes through Buckner's legs, and we lose the game.

"My brother, with all that stuff in his arms, carried it back to the club-house. When he got there, he put it down, went up against a wall, and just sank to the floor. It was as if he was the losing pitcher. He took it harder than I did. He was shattered.

"I admired Buck. I could never blame Buck for losing, and anybody who pointed a finger and said, 'Buckner lost the Series,' to me is a very shallow person. I had seen what Buck went through every day just to play the game, and I gained a whole lot of respect for him, and I really enjoyed playing with him because I always thought of him as one of the best competitors I ever played with.

"I felt bad for him because, of anybody on the team, you certainly didn't want something like that to happen to him. He was such a gamer. With Buck I felt so bad because it's not supposed to happen to a guy like him who played so long, did so well, put up with what he had to put up with just to make himself physically ready to play.

"People blamed Buckner for making the error, and people blamed McNamara for not taking Buckner out, and that was more valid than blaming Buck, but I don't blame McNamara either. That's baseball. Anybody who knows baseball and has played the game understands that errors are going to be made."

*   *   *

Oil Can Boyd had been scheduled to start Game Seven, but rain put it off a day, and McNamara broke the Can's heart by starting Bruce Hurst. McNamara promised Boyd he'd be the first pitcher to come in from the bullpen if needed.

Hurst led, 3–0, going into the sixth, when the Mets tied it. The rookie Calvin Schiraldi came in, not Boyd. Ray Knight homered to make it 4–3, Mets, in the seventh, and then the Mets scored two more against Schiraldi and Joe Sambito.

Then, in the eighth, the Red Sox rallied for two runs. A double by Dwight Evans closed it to 6–5.

Manager John McNamara needed a pitcher to keep it close. He could have chosen The Can or even Sammy Stewart. Boyd, a sixteen-game winner, hadn't pitched in six days. Stewart hadn't allowed a run in twelve innings of World Series play, but Stewart was in McNamara's doghouse after the former Baltimore bad boy had spit on traveling secretary Jack Rogers, who had left Stewart behind when he was seconds late for a bus.

McNamara picked Al Nipper, despite his 5.38 earned-run average for the season. It was shades of Denny Galehouse from 1946.

After Nipper came in to pitch, Darryl Strawberry homered. Nipper also allowed relief pitcher Jesse Orosco to drive in another run, and it was all over.

After the game, Oil Can Boyd sat on his stool, sobbing. "I wanted the call, but I didn't get the call," he said.

The Red Sox had come within a hairbreadth—one strike away three times—of winning their first world championship since 1918.

Said pitcher Bruce Hurst, who had pitched brilliantly, "As much as the fans hurt, we hurt. Maybe even more."

CHAPTER 45
Ad Infinitum

Since '86, the Red Sox continued to be powerful, entertaining. But they still hadn't won a world championship. Roger Clemens, Wade Boggs and Mike Greenwell continued to provide the leadership and skill to bring Boston fans exciting, first-rate baseball, but as in the past, events seemed to conspire to keep the Red Sox from winning a world championship.

The year 1987 proved to be a disaster. During spring training, Clemens walked out when general manager Lou Gorman wouldn't give him what he (and the rest of the modern world) felt the Rocket Man deserved. Clemens sat out spring training and had a subpar start.

Pitcher "Oil Can" Boyd raised eyebrows in Winter Haven when he was arrested for stealing some videocassettes of movies from a local store. One movie was *Nudes in Limbo*. Pundits called it "Can's Film Festival." That year, saddled with neck and shoulder ailments, Boyd won one ballgame.

Catcher Rich Gedman didn't get to perform for the team until May. The All-Star catcher declared himself a free agent, only to discover that collusion kept all other owners from signing him. When no one would sign him, he was forced under the rules to wait until May 1 to sign. The interim catcher? Marc Sullivan, Haywood's son. Tom Yawkey would have been proud. The only problem was, Marc couldn't hit. Gedman returned, but he was never the same player again.

Manager John McNamara alienated his players during spring training by telling them, "Don't even think about making it to the seventh game of the World Series."

Tensions built. Don Baylor expressed his deep dislike for what he felt to be Jim Rice's lackadaisical attitude. Bill Buckner was released in July. Baylor and Dave Henderson were discarded on September 1.

Rookies Mike Greenwell and Ellis Burks gave Sox fans hope, and then Cubs manager Don Zimmer enabled the Red Sox to return to championship form by trading away his monster reliever, Lee Smith, in December 1987. Smith, a profane man, uttered the word "motherfucker" once too often for Chicago general manager Jim Frey's sensibilities. Zim thought Smith had bad knees and wouldn't last another season.

The offer to Lou Gorman: Smith for Calvin Schiraldi and Al Nipper. Gorman lost his breath. He accepted before the offer could be rescinded, and called a press conference to announce the trade before anyone could talk the Cubs out of it.

The year 1988 was best remembered for two very distinct things. The first was a woman named Margo Adams, who helped get manager John McNamara fired and who created such controversy among the players that before the season was out there would be a fistfight on the team bus over her between Wade Boggs and Dwight Evans.

It turned out that for four years Boggs had taken Ms. Adams on road trips and had claimed she was his wife. Later, Adams charged that Boggs had promised to leave his wife and marry her. Adams went on the *Phil Donahue Show* to say that Boggs had snuck into the rooms of his teammates on the road and had taken photos of them with other women. She said he had called the operation "Delta Force." Boy, did she make everyone nervous. She sued Boggs for $6 million in palimony. She ended up famous, a curiosity in *Penthouse* magazine, but not rich, when a court ruled she could sue only for lost wages and out-of-pocket expenses incurred while traveling with Boggs. She never became Mrs. Boggs. Mrs. Boggs stayed Mrs. Boggs after he swore to her he would never do it again.

McNamara got the ax on Bastille Day, July 14, 1988. Jean Yawkey wanted him out. Joe Morgan, a little-known career minor-league manager and a bullpen coach under McNamara, took over the Red Sox on an interim basis, while top brass conducted a search for a replacement. And thus began the second memorable event.

Morgan's Red Sox won nineteen of their first twenty games under him, tied for first in early August and roared to the division flag. Boston had found a new hero. Before the streak was over, Morgan had a contract for '89.

The most impressive aspect of the Sox' 1988 division title was that the team was able to conquer despite the Boggs-Adams affair. Most impressive was Boggs himself. He was hitting .310 when Adams went public. Amid the storm of publicity concerning revelations about Boggs's active sex life, the man himself acted as though it was no big deal. For the rest of the season the five-time batting champion batted .380. He finished with a league-leading .366.

The Red Sox lost the 1988 American League Championship series to the Oakland A's in quick order, however. Former Red Sox starter Dennis Eckersley, the man Lou Gorman had traded for Billy Buckner, had been turned into a relief pitcher with Oakland. Eckersley was credited with saving all four Oakland victories.

Before the 1989 season, the Red Sox suffered the loss of starting pitcher Bruce Hurst. Hurst, a religious man, had been upset with the notoriety brought to the team by Margo Adams. He also felt the Red Sox players drank too much. He wanted out of Boston. Hurst's defection would be a tough loss for the Red Sox. That Hurst felt as he did prompted Roger Clemens to tell reporters, "If you take a family man like Bruce is, there's too many obstacles there in Boston to be able to overcome that....There are a lot of things that are a disadvantage to a family there."

Clemens was referring to the Margo Adams incident, but his inelegant prose made it seem as though Boston was a bad place to raise a family. While the press was vilifying Clemens, Hurst was taking less money than the Red Sox had offered to pitch for the San Diego Padres.

A few months later, Clemens further alienated himself from the media when he said, "I don't appreciate reporters writing about my family, and somebody's gonna get hurt one time doing that."

After Clemens was advised it was in his best interest to keep his comments to himself, the Rocket arrived in spring training declaring he would no longer talk to reporters.

In February 1989, *Penthouse* printed the first installment of its interview with Margo Adams. It was tame, but Boggs' teammates were forced to sweat it out until it was published. During spring training, Boggs was asked whether Adams' charges would affect his play. Boggs told reporters, "This stuff didn't affect me last year, and it's not going to affect me this year. When you step over those white lines, you've got a job to do. It's called being a professional."

It wasn't too long before stories of Steve Garvey's illegitimate children surfaced, and the sex life of Wade Boggs faded as fodder for the press.

The most startling true confession came from Boggs, who declared that he was "addicted to sex," endearing him further to most of the Red Sox fans. Oil Can Boyd, who had been forced to see a psychiatrist in 1986 after several scrapes with the law, said about Boggs, "Who needs a psychiatrist now?"

The Red Sox suffered a blow when, in May, it was discovered that Boyd had a blood clot in his shoulder. Then pitcher Mike Boddicker went down. Young outfield star Ellis Burks got hurt. Jim Rice got hurt. Dwight Evans was in traction.

With all the injuries, in 1989 the Red Sox finished third, six games behind the Toronto Blue Jays.

In 1990, the Red Sox again won the Eastern Division, this time behind Roger Clemens and a patchwork pitching staff of retreads and no-names. Jeff Reardon was signed as the closer, and then Lee Smith was traded to the St. Louis Cardinals for Tom Brunansky. The Sox won despite an off year by Mike Greenwell and a poor season for Dwight Evans, who was released at the end of the year.

In the playoffs, though, the Red Sox were again rolled over by the powerful Athletics, who were in turn rolled over by the Cincinnati Reds in the World Series. Roger Clemens cornered the attention by getting himself thrown out in the second inning of the final playoff game. The hardworking, nonpareil Clemens loosed a string of swear words at the vicinity of home plate umpire Terry Cooney after the veteran ump ruled a pitch to A's second baseman Willie Randolph had been ball four. Cooney, who many think should have kept his cool, tossed the Rocket before a stunned national audience. After that, the Red Sox succumbed meekly.

And so, another year passed without the Sox capturing the golden ring, increasing the time elapsed between the last Red Sox World Series victory in 1918 and the present.

The year 1991 began with players coming and others going. Mike Boddicker headed for Kansas City and Dwight Evans for Baltimore, while Lou Gorman shelled out $11.8 million for Houston pitching ace Danny Darwin, $6.35 million for pitcher Matt Young and $8.7 million for brittle slugger Jack Clark.

Darwin and Young both became lame early and pitched little, and the pitching-poor Red Sox struggled to play .500 ball when a lineup that included Boggs, Greenwell, Ellis Burks, Clark, Tom Brunansky and catcher Tony Peña, who suddenly stopped hitting for about a month in midsummer. The year was also marred when pitcher Jeff Gray suffered a mysterious stroke in July and had to leave the team. The team perked up a bit in August and made a strong run for it, but still ended up finishing in second place, seven games behind the Toronto Blue Jays.

They actually managed to close the gap from a seemingly insurmountable 11½ games to a razor-thin one-half game by September 22nd, and momentum seemed all on their side. Fans' hearts were stirred. But then they suffered three consecutive losses when: 1) they gave up a game-winning home run with two outs and two strikes in the bottom of the ninth; 2) they made a crucial run-producing error after a black cat jumped in and out of their dugout; 3) they walked in the game-winning run. Only the Red Sox. For his sins, manager Joe Morgan was fired at season's end and replaced with Pawtucket manager, former Red Sox third baseman and former manager of the Winter Haven Super Sox in the Senior Professional Baseball League, Butch Hobson.

Hobson, however, had no magic formula, as the Sox finished last in the American League East in '92. Roger Clemens finished 18–12 with a 2.41 ERA, but he didn't have much help. Mo Vaughn, the big first baseman in his second season, led the team with but 57 RBIs.

Compounding the team's woes was the death of Jean Yawkey, who passed away on February 27 at the age of 83. Her death marked the end of an era in Boston history. When Mrs. Yawkey died, it was thought that the trustee, whether it was Harrington or Sullivan, was named for the purpose of selling the team.

Red Sox fans expected the estate to be sold to a giant, wealthy corporation. Instead, its control was left to the winner of a battle between two of Mrs. Yawkey's most trusted executives, John Harrington and Haywood Sullivan. When Harrington won out, Sullivan sold his shares back to the trust and retired to Florida. After more than a decade has passed since Mrs. Yawkey's death, Harrington continued to run the team with no purchaser in sight. It was rumored that under the trust the Sox had to be sold after a finite period of time, but no one seemed to know for certain.

In 1993 the Red Sox improved to 80–82, good for fifth place, as Mo Vaughn began making an impact. Mo hit .297 with 29 homers and 101 RBIs. The team would have been better, but during the summer Roger Clemens was bitten on his pitching hand by his dog, as his record fell to 11–14 with a subpar 4.46 ERA.

In January of 1994 John Harrington hired as his general manager Dan Duquette, the former GM at Montreal. Duquette had run a bargain-basement operation in Montreal, selling off high-paid players and signing subs from the slap-heap of rejects, over-the-hillers, suspects and never-were's. Critics wondered whether Mrs. Yawkey had left enough money to let Harrington run a first-class organization and questioned whether Duquette was hired to run the Red Sox as a small-market team by selling its stars and using low-priced replacements.

Under the new three-division setup that began in 1994, no team could finish lower than fifth. The Red Sox were mired in fourth place at 54–61, seventeen games worse than the New York Yankees, when on August 12, the players were forced by the owners to go on a strike that wiped out the rest of the season. John Harrington, the victor in the struggle to run the Yawkey estate, incurred additional fan ill-will when he was named the official spokesman for the team owners during the length of the impasse, which did not end until April 1995, with the owners finally agreeing to go back to the status quo. Harrington's boldest move while Fenway stood silent and empty was to fire Butch Hobson as manager and replace him with Kevin Kennedy, who had led the Texas Rangers to a second-place finish in '93 and had the once-lowly Rangers in front of the AL West in '94 when the strike cut short the season.

Because the strike was not settled until the late winter of '95, spring training was only a couple of weeks long. One casualty was a sore arm suffered by Roger Clemens, who was unable to pitch until early June.

The pundits foresaw disaster for the Red Sox in '95, but with Kennedy in control, the team surprised everyone as they took the lead in the American League East on May 13 and never relinquished it, winning the division title by seven full games over the New York Yankees. On August 2, the Sox led the Yankees by 4½ games and then won twenty of their next twenty-two ballgames. Everyone in New England was elated by the unexpected turnaround.

In addition to the hitting of Mo Vaughn, who batted .300, hit 29 home runs and led the league with 136 RBIs, his Seton Hall teammate, John Valentin, also starred. The talented shortstop hit .298, hit 27 homers and drove in 102 runs. Jose Canseco, whom Duquette acquired from the Texas Rangers, at first had trouble hitting before the Green Monster, but as the season moved into summer, he got hot. Canseco provided power and excitement, as he batted .300, hit 24 home runs and added 81 RBIs.

Duquette had built a reputation for rescuing players from the scrap heap. Knuckleballer Tim Wakefield, drafted by Duquette after being sent to the minors by the Pittsburgh Pirate organization, at one point was 14–2 with a 2.30 ERA. His 16 wins led the staff. Erik Hanson, another reclamation project, finished 13–4. Clemens who suffered from a swollen right elbow, had but ten wins. The staff was bolstered by the addition of closer Rick Aguilera, who led the team with 20 saves.

The Red Sox faced the Cleveland Indians in the first round of the 1995 playoffs. In the opener, which the Sox lost, Aguilera slipped on a muddy mound in Cleveland and pulled a hamstring muscle. Two straight defeats followed, leaving the Red Sox fans once again dismayed and disappointed.

In February 1996, the Sox announced the signing of Mo Vaughn to a three-year, $18.6 million contract, which seemed to indicate that the Red Sox would compete in the marketplace against the richer teams. But during the '96 season, grumblings of unrest and revelations of infighting within the Red Sox organization began to surface. When marquee players Roger Clemens and Jose Canseco began complaining about Duquette's hardball negotiations, manager Kevin Kennedy took the players' side, a certain kiss of death for any manager, even a winning one.

While the Red Sox slipped to an 85–77 third place finish, Canseco made a public demand to be traded, and Mo Vaughn ripped into Duquette for what the big first baseman saw as disrespect toward Clemens, long the team mainstay. Clemens had been the most popular Red Sox since Carl Yaz, and Duquette was running him down in negotiations and in the press. Clemens, who won the Cy Young Award in 1986, 1987 and 1991, felt he deserved better treatment, and so did Vaughn.

Duquette's stock dropped even farther at the start of 1997, when he allowed Clemens and Canseco to leave as free agents, refusing to match the money offered Clemens by the Toronto Blue Jays. To add insult to injury, he also fired their popular manager, Kevin Kennedy. After being turned down by first Jim Leyland and then by Whitey Herzog, Duquette hired former Toronto manager Jimy Williams. Blared the headline in the *Boston Herald*: "Sox Fans Say Jimy Who?"

With the Red Sox plummeting into (78–84) fourth place in '97, Blue Jay Roger Clemens made Duquette look very bad as he raced to a 10–0 record (1.65) by June 1. Talking about his final season with the Sox, Clemens told reporters, "It was disheartening. The experience I had the last year, year and a half, wasn't pleasant."

Worse, Clemens' $4,850,000 replacement, Steve Avery, the NLCS MVP in '91 but sore-armed afterward, was so ineffective that in early September he was yanked from the starting rotation—the move seemed logical until it was revealed that he was one start away from automatically earning a $3.9 million salary in '98, as provided for in his contract. Duquette looked like a welsher, even when the move seemed appropriate.

Avery's '97 statistics were 6–6 with a 6.57 ERA. Duquette's bête noire, Roger Clemens, meanwhile, won his fourth Cy Young Award in Toronto as he compiled a 21–7 record, with a 2.05 ERA and 292 strikeouts, all league bests. Hal Newhouser last accomplished this pitcher's triple crown in 1945. (Clemens would win his fifth Cy Young the following year.)

Adding to the drop in esteem of the Red Sox were two midseason incidents involving players. Mo Vaughn was accused (and later acquitted) of punching a man in the face at a strip club in Cleveland, and Wil Cordero was arrested for hitting his wife in the face with a telephone, threatening her life and violating a restraining order. When Cordero refused to apologize and plead for his career, he was suspended for the rest of the season and then released to go to the White Sox.

If the '97 season had a bright spot, it was the play of rookie sensation Nomar Garciaparra, who was named American League Rookie of the Year. Garciaparra was a rare commodity, a fine-fielding shortstop who cold hit with Ernie Banks–like power. To make sure the youngster didn't pull a Clemens, Duquette signed him to a long-term contract.

Duquette showed Red Sox fans that he had the money to operate with the big boys when he went on a spending spree. He raised eyebrows when he signed free agent reliever Dennis Eckersley. Duquette had refused to sign expensive free agents. Critics accused the GM of being cheap, but Duquette insisted that he didn't sign free agents because it was against his philosophy of swapping highly prized draft picks. Eck was the first player drafted by Duquette for such a draft pick.

And in addition to signing Garciaparra to a long-term contract, Duquette also signed Troy O'Leary, Tim Wakefield and Tom Gordon, spending somewhere around $150 million on salaries. The only player not signed was Vaughn, whose drawn-out contract negotiations with Duquette seemed to be following the same path as Clemens'. Vaughn wanted $11 million per year, and when Duquette offered $9, Vaughn was offended.

"Either the club wants to pay a fair-market deal or they don't," said Vaughn. Adding to Vaughn's anger, Duquette surprised his fans when he traded Carl Pavano and two other minor leaguers to Montreal for Pedro Martinez, and then signed Martinez to a six-year, $75 million contract. It was the kind of money Vaughn was seeking and far more than what Clemens got from Toronto.

All through the summer of 1998, Vaughn's contract negotiations made headlines. Behind the scenes, it was rumored that the reason Vaughn hadn't been signed was that John Harrington was offended that Vaughn liked to go to strip clubs. He thought this the wrong image for one of his players. Prudishness and political correctness would cause the Sox to lose its star and soul.

At Harrington's request, Duquette made Vaughn a low-ball bid of four years for $37 million, knowing he'd turn it down. In July, Duquette and Vaughn agreed to put off negotiations until after the season. Duquette vowed it would not be "another Roger Clemens fiasco," meaning that this time he would get someone back in a trade rather than lose his star to free agency. But how could he possibly trade his superstar in the middle of a pennant race? He couldn't, and didn't.

Vaughn turned up the heat even more when he accused Duquette of hiring private detectives to follow him. Duquette denied the charge, but the bickering left a worse taste in everyone's mouth than any strip club activity by Vaughn.

The controversy almost obscured the fact that for a second time during Harrington and Duquette's sorry reign, the Red Sox battled for a playoff berth. Vaughn, who had an outstanding season, was a big factor. Another was the rehabilitation and return of Bret Saberhagen. This was perhaps Duquette's finest coup. Saberhagen, who had not pitched regularly in the major leagues since 1995, finished the year 15–8 and was named Comeback Player of the Year.

Another coup was the success of relief pitcher Tom "Flash" Gordon, a failure as a starter, who took over the closer role from an over-the-hill Dennis Eckersley and became one of the dominating relievers in the league. Gordon would save 43 games in a row, a new league record, en route to a season in which he saved 46 games.

The Red Sox met the Cleveland Indians in the first round of the playoffs. Expectations were high in Beantown. With Vaughn, Garciaparra and Valentin leading the offense, and Duquette's grunts: Troy O'Leary, Darren Bragg, Darren Lewis and Damon Buford, the Red Sox were among the league leaders in hitting. With a rotation of Pedro Martinez, Tim Wakefield and Bret Saberhagen, fans were looking forward to a repeat of the 1978 matchup between the wild-card Sox and the league-leading New York Yankees.

A week before the playoffs, Mo Vaughn sent a shock wave through New England when he told reporters he intended to see what other teams had to offer before he would re-sign with the Red Sox. Everyone suspected the post-season games would be the big slugger's last hurrah as a Red Sox.

"It won't matter (what the Red Sox do)," said Vaughn. "I'm going to test the waters. I owe it to myself."

The playoff opener took place at Fenway. Pedro Martinez started, and he didn't disappoint as the Sox defeated the Indians, 12–3. The win broke a streak of 13 straight playoff losses. It was the Sox first playoff win since the 1986 debacle against the New York Mets when Mookie Wilson hit the ball that went through Bill Buckner's legs.

It was the only game the Red Sox would win. The Red Sox seemed in fine shape in Game Two when Indians starter Dwight Gooden was tossed from the game for arguing balls and strikes in the second inning. But Tim Wakefield gave up five runs in the second inning, and the Indians won 9–5. Then in Game Three Bret Saberhagen pitched well, but Manny Ramirez hit two solo home runs that gave the Indians a 4–1 lead going into the bottom of the ninth. A Nomar Garciaparra two-run shot was too little, too late.

The Indians needed to win but one more game and started rookie sensation Bartolo Colon. Pedro Martinez pleaded with manager Jimy Williams to start, but Williams went instead with Pete Schourek, a journeyman lefty purchased from Houston after the Astros acquired Randy Johnson.

Boston reporters screamed that this was a repeat of 1948, when Red Sox manager Joe McCarthy started Denny Galehouse instead of Mel Parnell, but this time Schourek made his manager look brilliant as he pitched the Sox to a 1–0 lead with 5⅓ innings of shutout ball.

The Sox would have scored a second run or more had John Valentin not been thrown out a home by Cleveland outfielder David Justice in the sixth. Had Valentin stayed at third, the Sox would have had the bases loaded and one out. Indian reliever Jim Poole struck out Troy O'Leary to end the inning.

Williams made another controversial move when he brought Flash Gordon in to start the eighth. All season long Gordon had pitched only in the ninth. It was a first. But Gordon had saved 43 straight, and Williams wanted the ball in the hands of his best.

Kenny Lofton and Omar Visquel singled to start the eighth, and then David Justice hit a 400-foot double to score them both and give the Indians a 2-1 lead.

Mo Vaughn almost tied it up when he sent a soaring shot toward the Green Monster, but the ball hit high on the wall and came back toward the infield. Vaughn, who hit .412 in the series, had to settle for a double. When he didn't score, the hopes of the Red Sox and their long-suffering fans were dashed, and the Nation sullenly watched the rest of the playoffs on TV.

After the game, Vaughn went by the lockers of each of his teammates and told them the playoff defeat "can never take away from what this ballclub accomplished."

It was his way of saying good-bye. On November 25, 1998, Vaughn signed a six-year, $80 million deal with Disney's Anaheim Angels. At that moment, he was the highest-paid player in all of baseball.

With the departure of Vaughn, there was no one to replace him as the big-name stars opted to go elsewhere. Albert Belle went to Baltimore, Bernie Williams stayed in New York, Rafael Palmeiro moved to Texas and Will Clark shifted to Baltimore. It was musical chairs, but the last one standing didn't end up wearing Boston colors, except for Brad Clontz, a sore-armed pitcher formerly with Atlanta.

With Mo gone, fans wondered what Dan Duquette would do for a power-hitting first baseman. His replacements were either Mike Stanley or Jose Offerman. Said Tony Maserati of the *Boston Herald*, "They have taken a huge step backwards. A year ago at this time there was a pretty positive feeling about the team. Then at the end of this season they lost Mo. They are spinning this as, 'Everybody is coming back,' but I don't think you can underestimate the impact of that loss. It's a huge loss in every way imaginable."

To add insult to injury for Red Sox fans, on February 18, 1999, the Toronto Blue Jays traded Boston's former pride and joy, Roger Clemens, to the already-powerful New York Yankees. This was the same Clemens who once struck out twenty Seattle Mariners and ten years later repeated the feat against the Detroit Tigers. Clemens, the winner of five Cy Young awards, for years inspired Fenway fans to string signs—K-K-K-K-K-K-K-K-K-K—along the back of the bleacher walls.

Finally, the Red Sox fans had something to make them forget the loss of Mo Vaughn. And oh, yes, Clemens set another American League record when he won his 20th consecutive victory, against the Cleveland Indians on June 2, 1999.

By midsummer the Red Sox fans began to heap scorn on general manager Dan Duquette. "Red Sox fans can and do grow old waiting for a winner," wrote Ernie Perelmuter of Chelmsford, Massachusetts. "How many fans does Duquette think are still alive who remember the last Red Sox world championship in 1918?"

Toward the end of July, the Red Sox' chances of returning to the playoffs lessened when closer Tom Gordon went on the DL with what turned out to be a broken hand. Controversy arose when it was discovered that it took thirteen days for the X-rays to get from team doctor Arthur Pappas in Massachusetts to specialist Dr. James Andrews in Alabama.

"Our doctors are killing us," said Nomar Garciaparra when he learned that Gordon would miss the rest of the season.

Then on Saturday, August 14, more controversy erupted when Pedro Martinez showed up late for work. An angry Jimy Williams replaced Martinez with Bryce Florie, and then with the Sox down 5–1 with two outs in the fifth inning against Seattle, Williams brought Martinez into the game. Pedro pitched four shut-out innings, but the Sox lost.

The next time Martinez was scheduled to pitch, a hoard of Boston reporters arrived to see whether Pedro would show up on time. He did, and he was furious—at Jimy Williams.

"Is he going to come over?" asked Martinez. "Is he going to apologize? Is he going to shake my hand?"

After the game Martinez pleaded with the reporters to let the whole thing go. "Let me handle Jimy," Pedro said. "Let me handle my clubhouse."

As much as the Boston fans wanted to find fault with Duquette and Williams, the two ended up with the last laugh in 1999. By the end of August the Red Sox, helped by the hitting of two players Duquette signed off the scrap heap, Troy O'Leary and Brian Daubach, tied for the lead for the wild-card spot. The Anaheim Angels, who had signed Mo Vaughn away from the Sox, causing so much wailing in Boston, were twenty-four games out of first. And Vaughn was hurt all season. Red Sox fans began wearing "Mo Who?" T-shirts.

On August 31, Duquette bolstered his stock when he traded left handed reliever Mark Guthrie and a player to be named later to the Cubs for closer

Rod Beck. Beck had saved 51 games the year before, then developed back problems. With Derek Lowe in the closer's role, the move gave manager Jimy Williams more maneuverability.

"If Dan Duquette ever decides to switch careers, he could always find a home on Wall Street," wrote two *Boston Globe* staff writers. "Whether he knows it or not, the Red Sox general manager is a superb value investor."

The flamboyant Señor Martinez was the Duquette acquisition who, more than anyone, was making the fans forget about the beloved Mo and Clemens. The '99 season was the *ano de Pedro*. In July, pitching two innings at Fenway in the All-Star game, Martinez struck out Barry Larkin, Larry Walker, Mark McGwire, Sammy Sosa and Jeff Bagwell—four MVPs plus McGwire. Martinez was named the game's MVP in the American League victory.

Two months later, on September 10, Pedro one-hit the Yankees in Yankee Stadium and struck out 17. Yankee pitcher David Cone called it "the best-pitched game I've ever seen."

"He had three completely dominant pitches, a great fastball, a knee-buckling curve and a parachute changeup. Other than that, what else do you need?"

He would finish the year an awesome 23–4 (third-best winning percentage in Red Sox history) with a sparkling ERA of 2.07. His 291 strikeouts bested Clemens for most in a season in Red Sox history. Pedro was the unanimous winner of the Cy Young Award, only the third pitcher to win it in both leagues.

With Pedro—Dan Duquette acquired him after the 1997 season from the Dodgers for Carl Pavano and Tony Armas Jr.—and Nomar Garciaparra—Duquette's first draft pick after he was hired by Boston in 1994—leading the way, the Red Sox clinched their second-straight postseason berth with a win over the Chicago White Sox on September 29. After Nomar stepped on second and threw to first for the double play to end the game, Pedro rushed out of the dugout and did a cartwheel on the field. It was the first time they accomplished the two-playoff-years-in-a-row feat since the Babe Ruth–led Red Sox went to the World Series in 1915 and 1916.

The Red Sox won 94 games in 1999 and finished four games behind the New York Yankees. The Sox' opponent in the first round of the 1999 playoffs was the powerful Cleveland Indians, which won the first two games. Making things worse, Pedro and Nomar both were hurt and had to miss Game Three. The Sox' fans and press blasted the team for its lack of power and its bad pitching. The reporters pointed out that in the nine Division Series, only the 1998 Seattle Mariners had ever come back from a 2–0 deficit.

The 1999 Red Sox became the second team. After tying the series at two games apiece, they won Game Four by the score of 23–7 as John Valentin hit two home runs and drove in seven. In Game Five Troy O'Leary hit a grand slam home run and then, with the score tied 8–8 in the seventh, hit a three-run home run to help defeat the Indians 12–8 to complete one of the most improbable comebacks in playoff history. O'Leary had been put on waivers by the inept Milwaukee Brewers, and Dan Duquette noticed his name in

1995. Couldn't hit for power, couldn't hit lefties, was the knock on O'Leary. Duquette thought otherwise.

Pedro Martinez, suffering from a strained muscle in his back, entered the game in the fourth inning and pitched six innings of no-run, no-hit relief. He ended the game striking out Omar Visquel on three pitches. Only one Indian hit the ball out of the infield.

The win meant that Boston would meet the New York Yankees for the first time since the one-game playoff in 1978 when Duquette, a sophomore at Amherst College, sat in the Fenway grandstands and watched Bucky Dent's home run beat them.

As the champagne flowed, Latin music could be heard throughout the Red Sox clubhouse. Said a sober John Valentin, "We're excited to go to the next level. It's going to be tough, but you know, it's also going to be fun trying to beat them." Valentin added a plea to Boston's skeptical fans, "Please, please, believe in us. Don't be so negative. Mistakes happen. It's part of the game. We want you to be on our side."

Wrote Michael Holley in the *Globe*, "Based on what this improbable team has displayed, you would have to say they are on their way to the Series for the first time since 1986. Maybe they'll win the thing. Seriously."

They didn't.

Wrote Dan Shaughnessy of the *Globe*, "It is going to happen. The Boston Red Sox and their long-suffering legion of followers have been granted an opportunity to avenge eight decades of hardball indignities."

They didn't.

The Sox lost each of the first two games at Yankee Stadium by a single run. In Game Three it was Martinez versus Clemens. Pedro pitched a two-hitter. Clemens was shelled. It would turn out to be Boston's only win.

When the Red Sox lost the next two, once again the wailing could be heard throughout the land.

In the postseason Jimy Williams was named American League manager of the year. He did not, however, get a contract extension from general manager Duquette, whose stock rose even higher in December when he signed left-hander Jeff Fassero to a contract.

Then in mid-February 2000, Duquette acquired switch-hitting center fielder Carl Everett from Houston for a couple of prospects and signed him to a four-year deal. The year before Everett hit .325, hit 25 homers, drove in 108 runs and stole 27 bases for the Astros. The trade for Everett seemed like another coup for Duquette. Dan Shaughnessy of the *Globe* went so far as to call him "Wonderboy." He touted Everett as the best Boston center fielder since Fred Lynn.

After basking in the glow of optimism about the coming season, Shaughnessy revealed his true colors when he wrote, "I remain cynical. I am a veteran. And they are still the Red Sox."

In March, *Sports Illustrated* predicted the Red Sox would win the 2000 World Series. Gordon Edes of the *Globe* went into the clubhouse of the New

York Yankees to see what those players thought about that. The Yankees had finished a 5–18 spring, and Edes was being cheeky. Paul O'Neill, the Yankee outfielder, noted the Yankees had a chance to win every year because of George Steinbrenner's deep pockets.

"And no magazine cover is going to change that," wrote Edes.

But by the end of spring training, Edes was reporting what was blowing in the wind: the Yankee century was over, and that "this, at last, is the year."

By the end of May the Red Sox were in first place, one game ahead of the Yankees. The players were scrapping, hustling and everyone was optimistic. Then on May 29, Pedro Martinez defeated Roger Clemens of the Yankees 2–0 in an epic duel. With two men on, Pedro retired Paul O'Neill, Bernie Williams and Jorge Posada to end the game. The balance of power, the Boston reporters reported, was shifting toward the Red Sox.

Then Dan Duquette wrecked all the goodwill he had built up. Infielder John Valentin ruptured a tendon in his knee and had surgery by a doctor not approved by the Red Sox front office. Duquette hinted he was thinking of voiding Valentin's contract.

"Really, wouldn't it have been easier to send flowers?" asked Michael Holley of the *Globe*, who characterized Duquette's response as "diabolical."

On June 25 the Red Sox fell out of first place for good. The Yankees beat them 22–1, and then they beat Pedro 3–0 on three solo home runs. With a 6–13 downward spiral, Shaughnessy wondered if Oil Can Boyd and Bobby Sprowl might pitch for the Sox.

Then on July 16, Carl Everett took the focus off the team and placed it squarely on his back. Everett, who would hit 34 homers and drive in 108 runs for the Sox, twice head-butted umpire Ronald Kulpa, then erupted in a loud obscenity-laced tirade at his teammates, Bret Saberhagen, Tommy Harper, Wendell Kim, Jose Offerman and others, bashed water coolers, and tossed a bat. When Dan Duquette justified his behavior as that of a "very intense competitor," the press bristled.

Everett was suspended for ten games by MLB's top cop, Frank Robinson. Things were mostly quiet until a week later, when the Red Sox players raged over Duquette's unceremonious release of first baseman Mike Stanley, arguably the most popular player on the team.

Said Nomar Garciaparra, "I think it's horrible for our ballclub. He's been such a great leader. You shouldn't get rid of a guy who is such an integral part of this clubhouse." Stanley had been on the disabled list for three weeks, even though he wasn't injured at all.

"He's so valuable," said Garciaparra. "I don't know what the deal is." Duquette was playing musical chairs with his roster, and this time Stanley was left standing without a chair.

The most vocal Red Sox to complain about Stanley's treatment was infielder Jeff Frye, who called Stanley's release an "injustice."

"Is that how you get rid of your leaders?" he asked. "When I see Mike Stanley yesterday leaving the clubhouse with almost tears in his eyes and to know what he meant to this team, it kills you. I just want [Duquette] to be accountable."

On July 25, Duquette defended himself, and on July 27, Jeff Frye was traded to the Colorado Rockies. Said Dan Shaughnessy, "Duquette must have majored in Machiavelli at Amherst College."

Carl Everett returned on August 6 from his enforced vacation. While everyone waited for him to say he was sorry, Everett shocked everyone by shouting and cursing at Jimy Williams. Michael Holley opined that the Red Sox were turning into the WWF. Of course, the rest of the Boston press corps refused to leave well enough alone. They all noticed that manager Jimy Williams had been placed in an untenable position by Everett and by Dan Duquette's refusal to publicly rebuke his star outfielder. The writers all seemed to think Williams should resign. Williams, who was making more than $1 million per season, never quite saw it that way.

In mid-August the Sox awakened their fans when they won a string of late-inning games. The forgotten Brian Daubach hit a home run with two outs in the ninth to tie the score, then hit a single in the 11th to win it against the Angels. It was the third time in eight games the Sox had won in their last at bat. When September began, the Sox were five games behind the Yankees and chasing the Cleveland Indians for the wild card.

Then it was Rico Brogna's turn to cry uncle. Duquette, he said, didn't want him to play because he had been asked to go on the DL when he wasn't hurt and refused. The night Brogna refused, he hit a grand slam, but he kept a constant seat on the bench ever since. Brogna, a 30-homer hitter for Philadelphia, was mystified at his treatment. When Duquette said he was sitting on the bench because his bat was slow, Brogna felt he had to speak up. Brogna said he wanted out of Boston.

Another Carl Everett eruption came next. Given that Everett had a low boiling point, this outburst was not entirely Everett's fault. Everett, who had a sore left quadricept, didn't arrive to the park on time because he was sure Jimy Williams knew he was too hurt to play. When he arrived and saw he was in the starting lineup, his temper got the better of him. He openly cursed Williams. When teammate Darren Lewis spoke to Everett about the disrespect he showed the team by arriving late and by not taking treatment for his injury, Everett took offense and got in his face. Coaches had to break it up. Everett ranted obscenely about Lewis for another five minutes.

Duquette backed Everett, saying, "The bottom line is how you perform on the field. He is a highly productive baseball player for the Red Sox."

Jimy Williams then challenged Duquette to hire a manager whom he would back.

That prompted the *Globe*'s Gordon Edes to write, "Duquette yesterday sent a clear message that Carl Everett is now in charge of the team."

He wasn't, of course, but it gave the media a chance to write about the "feud" between Duquette and Williams, which was never as bad as the writers felt it was.

Gordon Edes pleaded with John Harrington to intercede on Jimy Williams behalf in his feud with Duquette.

"Maybe it's not too late to save your team," he wrote.

But it was. Pedro Martinez had a second-straight Cy Young season, finishing the year with a 18–6 record and an ERA of 1.74, lowest since Luis Tiant's 1.91 for the Sox in 1972. Nomar Garciaparra, who was hitting .403 on July 20, ended the year at .372, winning his second straight batting title. But the rest of the team wasn't good enough to reach the playoffs, even though the Yankees lost their last seven games and fifteen of their last eighteen. The players blamed Duquette's revolving door, including the release of Mike Stanley and the distraction caused by Carl Everett's anti-social behavior. In 2000 the Yankees would play the Mets in the first New York City subway World Series since 1956.

"It would be so great," said Trot Nixon, "to go into Yankee Stadium the next time and not have to hear that '1918' crap any more."

By mid-October Red Sox CEO John Harrington had had enough. He was sitting in church, grief-stricken during the funeral of John McCafferty, the man who got Harrington his job with the Red Sox when he recommended him to Red Sox GM Joe Cronin more than thirty years ago. He decided that life had become too short. After running the Red Sox under the Yawkey Trust after the death of Jean Yawkey in 1992, Harrington decided it was time to sell.

"Time for a change," intoned Dan Shaughnessy. "Time for new ownership." But Gordon Edes wondered who would buy a team in the middle of the Everett-Williams-Duquette imbroglio. It would take a whole year to find out.

"It's [going to be] hard to leave something with so many wonderful memories," said Harrington. "But to grow, sometimes you also have to go."

At the end of the 2000 season, Dan Duquette made a list of the potential free agents coming on the market. Among the marquee names were the Orioles Mike Mussina, the Royals' Johnny Damon, the Indians' Manny Ramirez, the Mariner's Alex Rodriguez and Atlanta pitcher Mike Hampton.

On December 1, 2000, the Yankees signed Mussina. Chided Dan Shaughnessy, "Any day now you can expect general manager Dan Duquette to announce the signing of free agent righty Jack Billingham. Are Gary Peters and Steve Ontiveros still breathing?"

Asked the *Globe* scribe, "Just how much are the citizens of the Nation supposed to take?" Red Sox fans were in a state of anguish when they learned that Mike "Moose" Mussina had signed with the hated Yankees.

Dan Duquette was under the gun. He had announced a steep rise in ticket prices. If he wanted to avoid a fan revolt, he had better bolster his lineup.

Five days later Duquette began a marathon six-day negotiation session with Jeff Moorad, agent for Cleveland slugger Manny Ramirez. The question was whether the 28-year-old Ramirez would return to Cleveland or sign with the Red Sox. For the last three years Ramirez averaged better than an RBI per game, with 432 in 415 games. But would the Red Sox step up to the plate and spend the money to sign him?

For a while, it looked like the Red Sox were going to win. They offered Ramirez $122.5 million for seven years. Then on December 11, the Texas Rangers announced they had signed shortstop Alex Rodriguez to a contract worth $252 million for ten years. All bets were off.

But John Harrington and Duquette refused to let Manny get away. By the end of that same December 11 date, the Red Sox announced they had signed Manny Ramirez to an eight-year contract worth $160 million.

Ramirez said he chose Boston over Cleveland because he felt the Red Sox were closer to getting into the World Series.

When the deal was announced, Bob Ryan of the *Globe* didn't congratulate Duquette. He congratulated the Red Sox fans.

"Duquette was just the negotiator," he wrote. "He didn't bring Ramirez here. You did."

Dan Shaughnessy was more gracious. He wrote, "Dan Duquette has gone from doofus to genius in less than 24 hours. Same for John Harrington. The Sox have made themselves the must-see team in town, and their overpriced tickets will be harder to get than PlayStation 2.

"How many days till the start of spring training?"

As an extra added attraction, Duquette also signed starting pitcher Hideo Nomo, once the darling of Los Angeles, but at 31 on the downside of a fine career. Nomo, a free agent, had pitched decently for the Detroit Tigers. He had averaged 200 strikeouts over his six-year career. But after arm surgery, his fastball was less than it once was, and if he didn't have his control, batters would sit on his fastball and hit long home runs.

"We thought he was the best starting pitcher available to us," said Duquette. With Manny, Pedro, Nomar and the combative Carl Everett, Red Sox fans were expecting a lot. So was Duquette.

"I feel a responsibility," he said, "to create a sense of hope for Red Sox fans that we're progressing toward the ultimate goal of a World Series championship."

The year 2001 brought a spring of "rabid hope" for Sox fans. The one negative thought was, "After Pedro, who was going to pitch?"

Then on March 7, as the team bus prepared to go from Fort Myers to Clearwater, Carl Everett was a no-show at the 7:45 A.M. departure deadline. The bus took off without him. A few players were upset. Most were not. The writers noted Everett's lack of responsibility. As an issue, though, it paled compared to the one swirling around Nomar Garciaparra's right wrist. All spring the All-Star shortstop was in pain. When Dr. Frank McCue was asked whether Nomar should have surgery to repair a split tendon, McCue said he should. But Sox PR director Kevin Shea told reporters otherwise, and in later interviews, McCue changed his opinion. The writers and Sox fans worried that Nomar would be lost for a long time.

"In other words," said Dan Shaughnessy, "get used to Lou Merloni, Mike Lansing and maybe Craig Grebeck."

Shaughnessy was absolutely right. Garciaparra was operated on the day before Opening Day. He would be lost until July, and perhaps beyond.

Then Manny Ramirez announced he would not play left field, and a few days later pulled a hamstring. Would he be another temperamental troublemaker like Everett? With Garciaparra out, the season was shaping up to be a tumultuous one.

Jimy Williams added to the drama when he announced that three of Dan Duquette's high-priced starters, Jose Offerman, Dante Bichette and Mike Lansing were being replaced. Observers wondered whether Williams would last the season.

Pedro lost the season opener in Baltimore, and then on April 4, 2001, the second game of the second century of Red Sox baseball, Hideo Nomo pitched a no-hitter against the Orioles at Camden Yards. It was the first no-hitter for a Sox pitcher since Dave Morehead no-noed the Indians in 1965. It was also the first shutout thrown by a Sox pitcher not named Pedro since 1997.

When the team returned for the Fenway opener, everyone was upbeat. "We expect a lot," said catcher Jason Varitek. "We're just like the fans. We expect to win, and we're gonna win."

Going into June, they were winning, a first-place team winning consistently. But then on June 5, manager Jimy Williams pulled Pedro after six innings and 90 pitches, a game the relief corps blew 7–6, and then Dan Duquette went on the WEEI pregame radio show and blasted Williams for taking him out. That allowed the Boston writers to blast Duquette with a venom not seen previously.

"Too bad he was born without a personality," Bob Ryan had written earlier. He added, "Duquette isn't just humorless; he is bloodless. It is as if John Harrington went to a store specializing in robots and came away with the general manager model."

Dan Shaughnessy accused Duquette of wanting the Sox to lose a little more so he could fire manager Jimy Williams "without too much bloodletting."

"This is the way it's always been around old Fenway," wrote Shaughnessy. "Remember Buddy versus Haywood, Buddy versus Mrs. Yawkey, John McNamara versus Everybody, the Duke versus Kevin Kennedy."

By July the team continued to win and to be dysfunctional. Everett had hurt his knee and was hors de combat on June 22. By July 7, Trot Nixon was pleading with him to work harder to rehab himself and to come out and play.

By the All-Star break the Sox had eleven players on the DL, including Nomar, Everett, Pedro and Jason Varitek. However, the Sox, led by Manny Ramirez and three second-line pitchers, Tim Wakefield, Hideo Nomo and Frank Castillo, managed to remain close to the Yankees for the division title, going an outstanding 51–36 at the break.

The credit went to manager Jimy Williams, who penciled in 71 different lineups in the first 87 games.

"There's got to be an edge," said Toronto manager Buck Martinez. "I'd suggest from afar that [Williams] is that edge. They're missing an All-Star pitcher, and All-Star center fielder, an All-Star catcher, and an All-Star shortstop. And he's got them [near] first place."

Two days after Bret Saberhagen won his first game in two years, Nomar Garciaparra returned to action on Sunday, July 29. When his name was announced in the line up, the Bosox fans gave him a standing ovation. In the game, Nomar earned greater applause when he tied the game with a home run in the sixth, and then with the bases loaded, singled in the winning runs in the seventh inning.

"That Nomie," said Trot Nixon. "He just gets out of bed and hits. It's a beautiful thing."

On August 16, 2001, with the Sox trailing the Yankees in the Eastern Division by five games and the Oakland A's in the wild-card race by just two games, Dan Duquette surprised everyone when he fired manager Jimy Williams. Duquette had waited for the opportunity, and a Sox streak of six losses in seven games gave it to him.

"Over the last ten days, I just really didn't like the look of the team," said Duquette. "It looked to me like everybody was standing around waiting for the club to make a change." The power struggle was over. No surprise, the GM won.

"I don't have anything to say," said Williams, who rarely had anything to say.

He was replaced temporarily by pitching coach Joe Kerrigan, a man with zero managing experience. A major reason Kerrigan was hired was his love for matchups, tendencies and probabilities based on statistics. He also said he preferred a set lineup every day.

When in his first day on the job Kerrigan used Urgueth Urbina to close instead of Derek Lowe, Lowe called Kerrigan an obscene name.

"It only took one day," said Kerrigan. Urbina gave Kerrigan the game ball.

The Sox were six games behind the Yankees, when on August 29, Nomar Garciaparra had to go back on the disabled list. His right wrist was hurting him again.

The next day Kerrigan took a lot of grief in the media when he took starter Frank Castillo out of the game after seven shutout innings. He brought in Derek Lowe, who got lit up and lost the game.

Kerrigan, who said he took Castillo out because he had thrown 89 pitches, managed "like an over-his-head" rookie, wrote Michael Holley in the *Globe*. "This is not a time for pitch counts." Kerrigan started rookie Israel Alcantara at first base. When Duquette brought Alcantara up, he asked Jimy Williams to play him. Williams refused. Kerrigan, the good soldier, went along. After Izzy Alcantara dropped a throw from third in the eighth, Jorge Posada homered off Lowe, dooming the Sox.

"This is not the time for Triple A kids against the Yankees," wrote Holley.

By early September, the writers had given up on the season. Adding to the turmoil, some players were grousing that Kerrigan was Duquette's puppet.

"Duquette should just put on a uniform and come down here and manage himself," said an unnamed player. The writers began petitioning for Duquette to pick a manager with major league experience for the 2002 season.

On September 2, things got crazier when Duquette demoted new pitching coach John Cumberland to bullpen coach. No reasons were stated, but the rumors were that Cumberland took one drink too many for Duquette's taste.

Responded Nomar Garciaparra, "That's why nobody wants to come play here."

Three days later it was Pedro Martinez' turn to be furious. He had gone on the DL for two months without being told he had a tear in his rotator cuff. The club had told him he had an inflammation. Martinez then went to Dr. Lewis Yocum, team doctor for the Anaheim Angels. Yocum disclosed the tear. Martinez had come off the DL and was pitching again. But Martinez' furor grew when Duquette's went on the radio and said that Pedro wasn't hurt and should remain in the rotation because "we're paying him a lot of money."

But Martinez said his arm still hurt. "I have the same symptoms as before I went on the DL," he said. "It's getting fatigued and heavy."

The next day Pedro labored for just three innings in a 3–2 loss to the Yankees. His pitches were flat. The Yankees batted around in the third.

When Dan Duquette refused all interview requests, Dan Shaughnessy in the *Globe* said he was "hiding in the cowardly John Harrington bunker." Shaughnessy then recommended Pedro be shut down for the rest of the year to let his arm heal. Two weeks later the Sox did just that.

In that same issue, reader Alan Amiralian wrote a letter to the *Globe* saying he will never buy another ticket to a Red Sox game as long as Duquette is general manager. He ended his anti-Duquette diatribe with, "Sleep well, George Steinbrenner. Dan Duquette is on the job."

On September 11, 2001, there was a terrorist attack on the World Trade Center in New York City. That day Trot Nixon was flying from Tampa to Boston, when his plane was diverted to Norfolk, Virginia, after the attacks. His wife was due to give birth to their son, Chase, and Nixon had to drive from Norfolk to Boston, too late to be there for the delivery. For Nixon, 9/11 was memorable in more ways than one.

Baseball was suspended one week, and on the first night back Carl Everett showed up late for the pregame workout.

Since taking over as manager, Joe Kerrigan had gone out of his way to befriend Everett, calling him on his cell phone to chat about his health. When Everett showed up late for a workout, Kerrigan, who was hitting fungoes, ordered him to leave the ballpark, prompting Everett to launch into one of his patented obscene rants. Among other accusations, Everett accused Kerrigan of being a racist and a drunk.

This time Dan Duquette didn't take Everett's side. He suspended Everett for four games without pay.

When the four days were up, Everett wasn't back. His right knee still hurt him. He was fined $140,000 and never again put on a Red Sox uniform.

Everett's loss contributed to the 17–26 record under manager Joe Kerrigan, who never had the players' respect. One time Manny Ramirez got on the team bus playing his radio too loud for Kerrigan's sensibilities. The manager ordered him to turn it lower. Ramirez obscenely told him what he could do to himself. The radio stayed loud.

The focus of the fans' fury was not on Everett or Kerrigan, but rather on Dan Duquette, the architect of this madhouse. Before the final game of the sad season, a year in which the Sox finished barely over .500, Dan Shaughnessy wrote, "The Red Sox Disgrace Across America Tour closes tonight in Baltimore."

Who would buy the Red Sox became the hot topic of the 2001–2002 Hot Stove League season. Among those mentioned was John Henry, the billionaire owner of the Florida Marlins. Henry, a money manager whose genius in understanding mathematical formulas enabled him to reap a fortune in commodities futures and hedge funds, announced in mid-November he was selling the Marlins (to Jeff Luria, owner of the Montreal Expos) so he could join forces with TV mogul and former San Diego Padres owner Tom Werner, skiing entrepreneur Les Otten and former Maine senator George Mitchell. Henry visited Fenway Park on November 27. A week later Peter Gammons wrote a column in the *Globe* discussing how close the three potential owners were with baseball commissioner Bud Selig. The article mentioned that Henry was going to hire Larry Lucchino, another of Selig's confidents, to run the team if he succeeded in buying it.

A second group, headed by Joe O'Donnell, a close friend of Texas governor George W. Bush, also was in the running, Gammons said.

Dan Shaughnessy of the *Globe* expressed his view that the fix was in for the Henry-Werner-Otten team.

"Of course," he wrote, "the Henry deal was part of the Bud Selig-Oliver Stone, Marlins-Expos-Red Sox bag job that was supposed to put the Sox in the hands of Messrs. Werner, Otten, Henry, Lucchino, Mitchell, Crosby, Stills, Nash and Young."

Shaughnessy also opined that Dan Duquette "should be handing out résumés" rather than trying to make deals.

"It's like General MacArthur giving orders after he was relieved of his command in Korea," he wrote.

But that was exactly what Duquette, who expressed a desire to keep his job under the new ownership, was doing. On December 14, he got rid of his problem child, Carl Everett, trading him to the inept Texas Rangers for left-handed pitcher Darren Oliver, whose ERA for the Rangers was 6.02.

A week later, on December 20, 2001, John Harrington sold the Red Sox to the Henry-Werner-Otten group for $700 million, more than twice the highest price ever paid for a Major League franchise. The Yawkey stewardship, which began in 1933, was officially over.

CHAPTER 46

The John Henry Era Begins

I first met John Henry in 1989, when he was the owner of the West Palm Beach Tropics, one of the eight Florida teams in the Senior Professional Baseball League. Dick Williams was his manager, and Dave Kingman and former Minnesota shortstop Ron Washington were two of his star players. The team was powerful, talented and drew well. His players were happy, and the organization ran smoothly and without controversy.

The league folded after only a season and a half. Henry bought one share of the New York Yankees, and then he bought the Florida Marlins from Wayne Huizenga. The Marlins he built would go on to win the World Series in 2003.

It didn't seem possible. Huizenga had won the World Series in 1997, but then dismantled the team when the voters of South Florida refused to build him a new stadium. When Henry took over ownership, the team looked almost as inept as the cross-state Devil Rays. But Henry and General Manager Dave Dombrowski rebuilt the franchise, stocking the farm system with talented arms and signing such talents as All-Star catcher Ivan Rodriguez.

But Henry, as competitive as he was smart, decided he wanted a situation where he had a better chance of winning a world championship. He tried to buy the Anaheim Angels, but Disney wanted more than Henry felt the franchise was worth. Then he began negotiations with John Harrington.

Even though Dan Shaughnessy of the *Globe* chided Harrington for selling the team to Boca Raton's Henry and not to Bostonians Joe O'Connell and Steve Karp, history now tells us that Henry and Co. was the right choice.

They were also the right choice because they were the only group of the six potential purchasers who wanted to improve Fenway Park and not tear it down. Every other group wanted a new park on the water. John Henry and Tom Werner believed in tradition and felt that Fenway Park was as important a national monument as Independence Hall or the White House.

A BREATH OF FRESH AIR

On December 21, 2001, the Henry–Werner ownership group took possession of the keys to Fenway Park. Larry Lucchino, who had run both the Baltimore Orioles and the San Diego Padres, was named to head the front office. Lucchino declared that the group would build a team worthy of fan support, renovate the park to preserve all that is good about it and be active in the community. And finally, he said, "This isn't so much a wish as it is a commitment. We will extinguish the curse of the Bambino."

Talking about the makeup of the team, Lucchino, who rebuilt the Padres into a World Series team, said, "One thing I have learned as a baseball executive is that the game is about pitching, pitching, pitching. You never have enough pitching."

Lucchino made one other pronouncement: "There will certainly be changes in the Red Sox organization." In other words, bye-bye Dan Duquette and Joe Kerrigan.

Duquette was fired on February 28, 2002, in Fort Myers. He was replaced temporarily by an assistant, Mike Port, who once was GM of the Anaheim Angels. Duquette was sure Henry would retain him, and the man known for his cold-blooded ways had tears in his eyes when he spoke just before departing.

The next day John Henry, Tom Werner and Larry Lucchino met with the players. They invited the press and even allowed photographers after the meeting. They said their doors were always open, that if a player had a complaint, no matter how trivial, he should drop by. When they finished speaking, the players applauded.

GRADY ARRIVES

On March 5, 2002, Joe Kerrigan was fired and replaced on an interim basis by Mike Cubbage. Then, on March 11, Larry Lucchino announced his new permanent manager, Grady Little, a fifty-two-year-old cotton farmer and career minor league manager who was chosen over Felipe Alou and Cubbage. Little was bench coach for the Cleveland Indians when he was picked. He and Manny Ramirez had been close there. Little also had been Jimy Williams' bench coach with the Red Sox from 1997 through 1999. Lucchino said he took Little over Alou because he knew the Red Sox system, personnel and the league. Little had managed for 16 years in the minor leagues. He won championships at every level, and Baseball America had named him the best minor league manager of the last 20 years.

"When I come to this ball club as a manager," said Little, "I'll bring a little bit of Jimy Williams with me, a little bit of Bobby Cox, a little bit of Charlie Manuel, and a little bit of Bruce Bochy, and I'm going to bring a whole lot of Grady Little."

When asked whether the Boston fans would allow him a honeymoon, he replied, "I don't want one. I'm all about winning. If they give us a chance to come in there and show them what we can do before they start voicing a bunch of opinions, they might like it if we're winning. They might not like me too much if we're losing. "I like that. I feel the same as they do because losing is not an option here."

When Little was introduced to the Red Sox players, there was a roar of approval. Little had a simple message for them.

"Buckle up," he said. "We're getting ready to have a good ride."

Wrote Bob Ryan of the *Globe*, "This was the Big One, and now the focus is off ownership and back down on the field. Shine that spotlight on the (high-priced) talent."

Before the season started, in Dan Duquette's last move as GM, he added another star to its galaxy. It signed free agent Johnny Damon, a center fielder and leadoff hitter for the Oakland A's. Damon signed with the Sox because he was aware of the Bambino Curse and the utter frustration of the Red Sox fans over not having won a World Series since 1918. Damon wanted to be part of the team that broke the curse.

SPIRITS SOAR

With the addition of Damon, and thanks to the goodwill engendered by the new owners, excitement for the Red Sox was never higher.

Opening Day at Fenway was on April 2, 2002, and as the 33,520 faithful flocked through the gates, they were greeted by the Red Sox players, including Nomar Garciaparra, Manny Ramirez and Pedro Martinez, in uniform. Unfortunately, as befitting most of Red Sox history, this era of good feeling brought by this memorable PR stunt was eclipsed by Pedro's terrible performance against the Toronto Blue Jays. In three innings, he allowed nine hits, two walks, and seven earned runs. In 2001 Pedro had had a sore arm and had only won seven games. The question whether he was healthy hovered over Fenway Park like the ghost of Babe Ruth. Fans knew that no amount of goodwill could make up for a damaged Pedro Martinez.

As starts went, this one could have been better.

As it turned out, Pedro was fine, and the Red Sox rotation turned out to be solid. Derek Lowe, who had been yo-yoed between starter and reliever, was inserted into the rotation by Little, and on April 27, in a game against the Tampa Bay Devil Rays, Lowe pitched a no-hitter, the first no-no at Fenway

Park in 37 years. Three weeks earlier Lowe had flirted with a no-hitter against the Orioles.

In April and May the Red Sox surged to a 40–17 record. The one negative occurred on May 11, when Manny Ramirez fractured his left index finger sliding headfirst into a base. He went on the DL and missed a month.

The Sox continued to win without him. June began with the Sox taking two out of three from New York in Yankee Stadium, with Derek Lowe and Frank Castillo shutting down the powerful Yanks. Lowe improved to 8–2 and boasted the best era in the league at 1.95. In Castillo's 7–1 win, Rickey Henderson made a leaping catch of Enrique Wilson's liner to the left field wall. Henderson, who homered earlier, hurt his lower back when he hit the wall and had to go to the hospital. The win gave the Sox a two-game lead over the New Yorkers.

The Sox traveled to Detroit, where Pedro gave up four runs in the first inning in an extra-inning loss. Since Pedro had been rocked in Toronto, the worry birds were flocking around him.

The road trip was completed with a Derek Lowe shutout, and the next day Cuban defector Rolando Arrojo, who replaced Darren Oliver in the rotation, won to give the Sox a 25–6 record on the road. Would this be the year? It certainly appeared that it would.

The Red Sox returned to Fenway to start a long interleague series against Arizona (the world champs), Colorado, Atlanta and Los Angeles. Manny Ramirez, still on the DL, missed the team flight back to Boston. The press publicly wondered where he was while Grady Little said, basically, it was nobody else's business.

Then the interleague games began, and the Red Sox, facing some great pitching, fell on their faces. They began with two losses to Arizona. Darren Oliver, in his last effort for the Sox, lost, and the next day Curt Schilling, who started in the Red Sox organization and was traded away, beat them 3–2.

After the game a fan shouted to Schilling, "Wish you were with the Red Sox?"

The big pitcher replied, "I was."

"Please come back," the fan pleaded.

The Sox managed to win two of three from the woeful Colorado Rockies, but against the Atlanta Braves they couldn't overcome their lack of power without Manny, losing 2–1 to Kevin Millwood and 4–2 to Greg Maddux. Both Pedro and John Burkett pitched beautifully, but not good enough.

On the Coast, they won two of three from San Diego. Pedro won the finale 5–0 and struck out 11. Leading the Sox was center fielder Johnny Damon, a favorite in the MVP balloting. Damon was leading the league in runs scored with 57, and his 16 stolen bases led the team.

After getting swept by the Dodgers, the Sox were 5–10 and fell a half game out of first behind the Yankees. Theo Epstein released Darren Oliver and sent

Casey Fossum, the pitcher he wouldn't trade for Bartolo Colon, back to Pawtucket. The one question on everyone's minds after the string of close losses: when would Manny come back? After splitting with the Indians, the Sox hosted the Atlanta Braves. Manny returned, but the Braves swept the Sox in three games anyway, as the Sox fell two games behind the Yankees in the American League East. The Sox completed their interleague play with a 5–13 record, and finished June an ugly 10–16.

The press and fans began to panic, but even after Kevin Millwood beat them 2–1, Jason Varitek remained a bastion of sanity.

"We're gonna score," he said. "This won't last forever. We're going to score."

Added Trot Nixon, "We're not panicking, and the fans shouldn't either. Sooner or later, we'll be fine."

When the Blue Jays came to town the next day, Pedro Martinez helped Sox fans forget a lost June and reminded everyone how special he was with a 14-strikeout shutout in a 4–0 win. Martinez, whom everyone continued to worry about in any game when he wasn't overpowering, ran his record to 10–2. The next day Alan Embree earned both saves in a doubleheader sweep against the Jays, and first baseman Tony Clark, silent most of the season, lined a pitch into center field in the eighth inning to score Rickey Henderson for the win. In that game Johnny Damon reached base five times, twice stealing second. Derek Lowe won big to complete a five-game sweep, as the Sox remained just one game behind the Yankees.

CHAPTER 47

Good-bye Ted, Hello Theo

A rare home run by Johnny Damon beat the Tigers on July 5, 2002, the day Ted Williams, the "Splendid Splinter," passed away at age eighty-three of heart failure in a hospital near his home in Inverness, Florida. His death marked the end of an era for Red Sox fans. During years of futility for the Sox, Ted was the shining star. In his final at bat at Fenway, he had hit a home run. He crossed home plate, ran into the dugout, and retired. Then he lived forty-two more years, and during that time the crusty curmudgeon softened and became one of the most beloved figures in all of sports.

His hope was that one day people would say, "There goes the greatest hitter who ever lived," and in New England, the affirmation of that fact was made by Sox owner John Henry.

"I know that everyone who is a Red Sox fan today is in mourning," Henry said. "He accomplished the one thing that he set out to do, and that was to become the greatest hitter in the history of the game."

"He was the greatest of all Red Sox, and the greatest hitter of all time," said Larry Lucchino, "and also a larger-than-life American hero. We deserve to celebrate that."

"My dad was a big fan of Ted Williams," said Grady Little. "He always used to talk about him being the greatest hitter."

"He was like my brother," said Johnny Pesky. "I just can't believe he's gone."

Before the game that night against the Tigers at Fenway, a bugler played "Taps." When the last note was played, there was a silence as players on both teams stood, hats off, during the National Anthem. When the ceremony ended, Nomar Garciaparra, who would get phone calls from Williams in the clubhouse from time to time encouraging him or tutoring him in hitting, embraced Johnny Pesky. Tears were shed throughout the Red Sox Nation. We would not see the likes of No. 9, "Teddy Ballgame," ever again.

A week later Ted would be back in the news. Ted's thirty-three-year-old, ne'er-do-well son, John Henry Williams, who had made a living solely from selling memorabilia signed by his dad, shipped Ted's remains to a cryonics lab in Arizona. Though Ted had told his closest friends that he wanted to be cremated in the Florida Keys, his son produced a piece of greasy paper pulled from the trunk of his car with Ted's signature on it. The document said that Ted wanted to be frozen for eternity so he could be brought back to life when advances in medical science made it possible. Ted's daughters suspected that their brother had gotten Ted to sign a blank piece of paper on which he then wrote the terms he wanted above it. They also accused him of wanting to sell Ted's DNA. Considering that Ted's DNA had produced John Henry Williams, it was hard to imagine anyone paying for the privilege. If John Henry Williams had wanted to sully Ted's memory, he couldn't have been more effective, as Red Sox fans were forced to picture his remains hanging upside down in a tube frozen in dry ice. Meanwhile, jokes abounded. He became the "Tedsickle." There were jokes about Ted one day telling Walt Disney he wasn't opening up his hips enough on his swing. When John Henry Williams died of leukemia a year later at age thirty-four, no tears were shed. Truth is stranger than fiction, that's for sure.

In the final game before the All-Star break, the Sox lost to the lowly Detroit Tigers 9–8. When asked what he would have changed in the first half, Garciaparra said, "I wish we were undefeated. That's what I'd change."

The Sox were spectacular the first half, finishing at the break with a 52–33 record. Only the Yankees, at 54–31, were better. The Sox sent six players to the All-Star Game, including Pedro, Derek Lowe, Ugie Urbina, Shea Hillenbrand, Manny, and Nomar. Bud Selig would call the game in a 7–7 tie after 11 innings when both teams ran out of pitchers.

When play resumed, Grady Little called a clubhouse meeting. Some players were nervous over the many trade rumors. Little told everyone to stay positive. After splitting series with two of the weaker teams, the Blue Jays and the Tigers, they swept two from the Devil Rays. Lowe won his 13th game, and Manny homered in a comeback win.

The Yankees were next, and Pedro, who beat Mike Mussina 4–2, improved his record to 12–2. He allowed five hits in 7⅔ innings and K'ed 9.

"I love when they dare me to do something," said Pedro.

Cy Young had had a 75–25 record with the Red Sox in his first one hundred decisions. Pedro was 78–22.

"Man," said Michael Holley, "I say they should give you the Cy Young right now."

But the Yankees won the next two games by identical 9–8 scores. Dustin Hermanson blew a lead in one game, and in the bottom of the ninth of the second game, Jason Giambi hit a ball to Trot Nixon in right field with runners on first and second. As the ball was rolling toward him, Nixon picked up his head to check the runners, and the ball sped under his glove to tie the game. With the tying run scoring, the winning run advanced to third. Little walked the next two batters to load the bases, but Ugie Urbina walked Jorge Posada to force the winning run home.

"I don't know if it's just us being snakebit," said Grady Little, "or them having some Irish luck."

A FINAL SALUTE

Because John Henry Williams had shipped his dad to a cryonics lab in Phoenix, Ted Williams never had a funeral or a wake. His friends and fans never had a chance to say good-bye. Owner John Henry and the Red Sox decided to do it for him. From 9:00 in the morning until 9:00 at night, more than 32,000 fans passed through Fenway Park to pay their respects. At night, 20,500 paid to attend a memorial service, with the money donated by the Red Sox to the Jimmy Fund.

During the ceremony, the scoreboard only listed one team, Boston, and under the words "AT BAT" was the number 9.

The Sox owner John Henry was introduced as "John W. Henry" so no one would confuse him with John Henry Williams, the reviled son.

"I am saddened by the turmoil of the current controversy," Dom DiMaggio, Ted's teammate, told the gathering, which erupted into one of the loudest cheers of the night. "May he rest in peace."

For the finale, all the lights were turned off in the park, and the façade of the nearby Prudential building was lit in the shape of a number nine. While a trumpeter played "Taps," fifteen or so Red Sox players, old and new, laid down roses in a garden in left field.

A recording of Ted's last home run blared. Jack Fisher, who threw the pitch forty-two years earlier, stood on the mound spotlighted. Curt Gowdy, who called the home run, stood at home plate and reenacted the moment.

"There's a long drive to right field," said Gowdy. "That ball is going, going, gone. It's a home run."

A spotlight then lit up a number 9 jersey in center field. The players saluted, and "Auld Lang Syne" played, as Red Sox Nation mourned. In one night John Henry was able to undo much of the harm done to Ted by John Henry Williams.

The next day, Ned Martin, who broadcast Red Sox games from 1961 through 1992, died at age seventy-eight. Martin was traveling from Boston to his home in Virginia when his heart stopped. The genteel, beloved announcer, whose catchphrase was "Mercy," had attended the Ted Williams memorial the day before. For longtime Red Sox fans, Martin's passing only brought more sadness.

Meanwhile, the Sox could not get out of their win-one-lose-one slump. When they lost two out of three to the Devil Rays, who were 30½ games out of first, doubt began to arise whether the team had too many weaknesses to make it into the postseason.

The Sox took off west for a fateful road trip. During yet another one-run loss, this time to the Angels, Jose Offerman was asked to pinch run late in the game. His reply: "I'd rather not."

When Mike Port made a trade for former Marlin outfielder Cliff Floyd a few days later, Offerman was designated for assignment. When he found out, Offerman let loose with a tirade against Port and against the reporters, whom he blamed for ruining his career in Boston.

At the time the trade for Cliff Floyd seemed like a move that would lift the team to greater height. Floyd had been an All-Star the year before, and he was hitting .287 with 18 home runs and 57 RBIs when Montreal acquired him July 11. But Floyd had been a bust in Montreal, hitting just 3 home runs in 53 at bats. Montreal had hoped Floyd would improve its playoff chances, and when he didn't, the cash-strapped team traded him to Boston for two Korean pitchers, Seung Song and Sunny Kim. Floyd had been John Henry's first acquisition after taking over the Marlins, and he had helped lead them to a pennant. Henry was hoping he could do the same thing for his Red Sox.

By August, there was talk of another strike as the owners fought over whether to have mandatory drug tests for steroids, raise the minimum salary to $300,000 and impose a luxury tax on teams spending far more money on players than the average. The scuttlebutt was that a strike date would be set for September 16.

August began with a 19–7 pasting by the young and talented Texas Rangers. Johnny Damon led off the game with a home run, but Frank Castillo, who replaced John Burkett, allowed 11 hits and 10 runs. Carl Everett, shipped to Texas by the Sox, hit two long home runs and drove in seven runs.

Derek Lowe pitched a 13–0 shutout, but then the Sox gave away the match game when Shea Hillenbrand fielded a Carl Everett bunt and threw it away, allowing the winning run to score. Pedro won, but the A's then took two out of three.

The Sox came home and continued playing .500 ball. On August 20, they lost a particularly crushing defeat when they led the Texas Rangers 2–0 going into the eighth, but blew it on a costly error by Nomar, followed by a game-tying home run that Ugie Urbina gave up to Ivan "Pudge" Rodriguez in the ninth. Red Sox reliever Willie Banks then allowed Todd Hollingsworth to hit one out to end it. After the game Grady Little held a closed-door meeting with his players to ask everyone to dedicate themselves harder to making the playoffs.

The Sox responded by winning three in a row, but then the Angels won the first two games of their series at Fenway. They would have swept it except for the heroics of Johnny Damon, who in the 10th inning hit a walkoff home run off Scott Shields.

Hope died in late August when David Wells and Mike Mussina pitched consecutive shutouts against the Sox, the first time that had happened since 1943. The Yankees' lead grew to nine games.

No Strike

On August 30, MLB and the players announced they had agreed on a new contract. The Players Association, aware of the fans' intense anger over the long strike of 1994, had not set a strike date, and an accord was reached.

"It came down to us playing baseball or having our reputations and life ripped by the fans," said Steve Kline of the St. Louis Cardinals. "Baseball would have never been the same if we had walked out."

Any team paying more than $117 million in salaries would be hit with a luxury tax. Observers feared that an increase in the luxury tax would mean that the Red Sox would have to slash payroll. Red Sox observers chortled that Yankee owner George Steinbrenner, who was paying $180 million in salaries, would be paying a huge penalty to the crappy, poorly run teams. They also noted that there was nothing to prevent those owners from pocketing the money.

By September, Sox pitching had collapsed. Pedro wasn't Pedro, and John Burkett, who had been elected to the All-Star team and had declined to go, suffered from a dead arm the second half of the season. It got so bad Grady Little even took him out of the rotation for a time.

The Sox had one final chance to climb back in the race when the Sox traveled to Yankee Stadium for three games. After winning the opener, Frank Castillo, filling in for an injured Pedro, pitched well, but not as well as Roger Clemens. An error by Rey Sanchez opened the gates to a Yankee win. Andy Pettitte then outpitched Derek Lowe in the finale.

Sox Collapse

By early September the Sox were 9½ games out of first place and 7½ games behind in the wild-card race. It would be the third consecutive season the Red Sox failed to make the playoffs after so much optimism about outdoing the Yankees.

And by September, Dan Shaughnessy of the *Boston Globe* was discussing the possibility of Larry Lucchino firing Grady Little if the team's fortunes didn't pick up.

Wrote Shaughnessy, "Ken Macha is loosening in the on-deck circle. Poor Grady. Hard to believe he may not even last as long as Angelina Jolie and Billy Bob Thornton."

Michael Holley had another take on the season that took everyone by surprise when the team went into the toilet. Wrote Holley, "It's hard to remember them fondly now. They are like the guy who died before paying off a $10,000 debt. Each time his name comes up, all you can think is, 'That [expletive] owes me something.'"

Holley ended by saying the collapse was not Grady Little's fault. (Despite the late-season crash and burn, the Red Sox finished the 2002 season with a 93–69 record. Obviously, the expectations were so high that 93 wins without making it to the playoffs had become unacceptable. Talk about pressure!) He called on Larry Lucchino to hire a talented general manager "who can remix and resuscitate the Sox."

To that end Lucchino tried to hire J. P. Ricciardi, the GM of the Toronto Blue Jays. Ricciardi recused himself and signed a long-term deal with the Jays. Lucchino then offered the job to Billy Beane, the Oakland GM. Beane would be lionized for his sabermetric approach to scouting in the brilliant book, *Moneyball*, by Michael Lewis. In that book, Lewis painted a scene where Beane called together all his scouts in a room. Also with him was an assistant who had analyzed the stats of the country's college players. Beane asked the scouts for their recommendations. Then he asked who the stat guy liked the best. Beane ended up firing all the scouts and drafting all the picks of the stat guy. Had a great draft, too. Player procurement would never be the same.

As an indication that the Red Sox were thinking along the same lines, Larry Lucchino drew the attention of Fantasy Baseball addicts everywhere when he signed Bill James, the first and most famous Roto-geek to a job as the team's statistical advisor.

"The way we try to look at players is through two lenses," said Theo Epstein, the kid assistant GM. "One lens is the traditional scouting method. The other lens is objective analysis. We find we get the truest evaluation by using both lenses."

Lucchino put the full-court press on Beane, who—for a second—accepted the job at a contract worth $2.5 million a year for five years. To seal the deal Tom Werner had his main squeeze, Katie Couric of the *Today* show, call Beane's wife and sing "Happy Birthday" on her answering machine.

But Beane was concerned that by taking the Red Sox he would be making life harder for his wife and daughter, who loved their California lifestyle. He decided to remain in Oakland.

Exactly two weeks later Henry and Lucchino chose their new general manager, someone who had been recommended highly by Ricciardi, Beane, and San Diego general manager Kevin Towers. To the shock of many, they picked their own assistant GM, twenty-eight-year-old Theo Epstein, the youngest general manager in baseball history. He was, in fact, younger than all but two of the players in Boston's 2002 starting lineup.

"It will be clear to you over time that this is a gifted person with a real opportunity to have a profound impact on this franchise," said Lucchino.

Epstein, a Yalie, is the grandson of Philip Epstein, who with his brother Julius, wrote the screenplay for the movie *Casablanca*. His father Leslie is a novelist and the head of the creative writing program at Boston University.

Theo's creative writing got him his first job in baseball. He wrote a letter to fellow Yalie and Dallas Cowboys football star Calvin Hill, who was vice president of the Orioles, and was hired as an intern in the PR department. It was Epstein who conceived the idea of the first Negro League players reunion, a highlight of the 1993 All-Star Game.

Epstein then jumped to the Padres with Lucchino, who saw his potential and suggested he go to San Diego Law school. He graduated, though he was working seventy-hour weeks for the Padres and never went to classes. He passed the bar on his first try. Padres GM Kevin Powers appointed Epstein the director of baseball operations. When Lucchino took over the running of the ballclub in Boston, Epstein again went with him, this time as assistant GM.

Epstein defended the choice, saying there is a difference between "youthfulness and inexperience."

"I'm going into my twelfth season in major league baseball," he said. "I'm qualified for the job. I'm ready for it. The Red Sox are very much in my blood. I grew up second-guessing Red Sox general managers. There's a certain familiarity. Being a Red Sox fan is different."

Epstein vowed to deliver a world title to Boston.

"It's going to happen," he said. "We're going to become a championship organization and win a World Series."

"The Red Sox are taking a bit of a gamble here," commented Dan Shaughnessy, "but it's bold and daring and makes them more interesting than they were yesterday."

CHAPTER 48

A Work in Progress

THEO IN CHARGE

With Theo Epstein calling the shots, Red Sox fans everywhere sat back and waited to see him work his magic. He announced that for 2003 he intended to upgrade the team at first base and in the bullpen, add outfield depth and make one big move. To have money to effectuate his plan, Epstein shed $33 million in salaries, getting rid of Ugueth Urbina, Jose Offerman, Tony Clark, Dustin Hermanson, and Darren Oliver.

Epstein's first move was the acquisition of second baseman Todd Walker from the Cincinnati Reds. Epstein clearly did not want to start the season playing rookie Freddie Sanchez. Epstein said he expected Walker to be the two-hitter behind Johnny Damon. With one year left on his contract, Walker came at a reasonable cost.

The next player Epstein sought was Cuban defector Jose Contreras, a strong-armed right-hander, but Contreras' agent suddenly cut off negotiations. Meanwhile, the New York Yankees had announced their intention to cut their league-high payroll, but in mid-December the Yankees announced the signing of Japanese outfield star Hideki Matsui to a three-year deal worth $21 million. Then the day before Christmas 2002, they offered Contreras $32 million for four years. When Contreras accepted the offer and ended the auction, the Yankees were looking more indomitable than ever.

"It's very difficult to bid against a team that has an unlimited budget," said John Henry. "It doesn't matter how many outfielders or how many starters they already have. With an unlimited budget, you can buy anyone you think you need."

Imagine how the rest of the league felt.

RANT AGAINST THE EVIL EMPIRE

Larry Lucchino was furious. He called the Yankees "the Evil Empire," a reference from the *Star Wars* movie saga. Red Sox fans had visions of Yankees owner George Steinbrenner as a porky Darth Vader, armored in black and holding a lightsaber.

If the enmity between the Red Sox fans and the Yankees weren't bad enough, Steinbrenner, a bully incapable of letting any slight go by, especially one that is accurate, responded with his own venom. He accused Lucchino of operating behind John Henry's back, of deserting both Baltimore and San Diego and of "not being the kind of guy you want to have in your foxhole," as though Steinbrenner, who spent the Korean War as the athletic director of the Lockbourne Air Force Base in Columbus, Ohio, knew anything about foxholes.

Said Lucchino, taking the high road, "I made it a New Year's resolution not to respond to George's petty personal attacks and gross mischaracterizations of my record. But I may underline those dates when the Empire visits Fenway Park."

The Montreal Expos, stepchild of major league baseball, couldn't sign both its star pitchers, Bartolo Colon and Javier Vasquez. For more than a month Epstein sought either, but got neither. Every time Omar Minaya, the Montreal GM asked for minor-league phenom Casey Fossum, Epstein countered with Shea Hillenbrand and Freddie Sanchez. But Minaya said he needed a pitcher in return. Ultimately the reason Colon, a top-flight starter, didn't become a Red Sox was that the Yankees did everything in their power to keep him from landing in Boston.

On January 15, 2003, a three-way deal sent Colon from Montreal to the Chicago White Sox. The Yankees sent Orlando Hernandez and $2 million to Chicago, which in turn traded Hernandez to Montreal for Colon and a minor leaguer. The Yankees received an inconsequential relief pitcher, Antonio Osuna, a minor leaguer and the satisfaction of watching Colon go somewhere other than Boston. The deal also kept Vasquez in Montreal.

Brian Cashman, the Yankee GM, denied making the trade—one which helped the White Sox and the Expos but did little to improve the Yankees—to hurt the Red Sox.

"Sure," wrote Bob Hohler in the *Globe*, "and the Cross Bronx Expressway is paved with gumdrops."

"Right," wrote Dan Shaughnessy, "and all those gorgeous women date Donald Trump because they dig his hairstyle."

"It goes back to 1919," said Johnny Damon. "Steinbrenner is willing to win at all costs. They have deeper pockets, but they fear us and that's why they are making these moves. And the year we win the World Series, it's going to get back at all 26 they've won."

With the Red Sox Nation growing more and more impatient for victory, frustration was setting in New England. Wrote Shaughnessy, "It would be fair to say that Sox rookie GM Theo Epstein is not exactly on a winning streak so far."

THEO SIGNS MILLAR, MUELLER AND ORTIZ

Epstein, however, showed he could be ruthless if he had to be. He was able to waylay infielder Kevin Millar, put on waivers by the Florida Marlins for the purposes of shipping him off to Japan for the Chinichi Dragons to sign him to the richest contract in Chinichi history. When Epstein claimed Millar, a .300 hitter with some pop, it broke the unwritten code between teams not to interfere when a team wanted to sell a player overseas. The Marlins were furious. Millar swore he would go to Japan, but the Sox paid everyone off, and Millar, whose left-handed swing proved perfect for Fenway Park, ended up a valued member of the 2003 Red Sox.

Few in Boston knew anything about Millar or the next acquisition, Chicago Cubs third baseman Bill Mueller (whose name for some reason is pronounced "Miller"), and two relief pitchers: Chad Fox, the former Brewers closer who was recovering from elbow surgery, and the hard-throwing Mike Timlin. Then very quietly, Epstein completed the rebuilding of the Red Sox infield with the acquisition of free agent David Ortiz, a six-foot four-inch, left-handed, power-hitting first baseman.

Ortiz had hit 20 homers and 75 RBIs in 2002 but had suffered a broken wrist sliding into home plate and then had to undergo knee surgery. He also suffered emotionally when his mother died in a car accident.

Epstein had coveted Ortiz when he was with the San Diego Padres. Not an hour after Ortiz was released by the Minnesota Twins, fellow Dominican and good friend Pedro Martinez, playing matchmaker, called Epstein.

"This guy can give you 30 jacks and 100 RBIs," said Martinez. "And a lot of people don't realize that David is a young kid."

Pedro also worked on Ortiz to sign with the Sox. Said Ortiz, "Pedro is like my father to me."

The always-thorough Epstein got on the phone just to make sure there were no surprises concerning Ortiz. When everything checked out, Epstein signed the big Dominican.

"From one to nine, we have some tough outs, on-base skills, and power as well," said Epstein about his revamped lineup. "I think we're going to score a lot of runs."

If there was any weakness, the expects saw, it was that the Sox didn't have an established closer. They had let Ugueth Urbina go and never replaced him. For years Bill James had preached that a team didn't really need a closer if it's relief staff was strong, and Theo Epstein was going to be the first GM to test James' hypothesis.

The first test was a disaster. The season opener on March 31, 2003, was played at Tropicana Field against the Tampa Bay Devil Rays. Pedro Martinez started and was brilliant. After Ramiro Mendoza pitched a 1-2-3 eighth for the Sox, they were leading 4–1.

Lefty Alan Embree came into the game and gave up a single, then a two-run pinch hit home run by a bench player named Terry Shumpert, the 25th player on a team with too many Rule-5ers. After giving up another single, Grady Little replaced Embree with Chad Fox, who got two outs before giving up a walk and a long game-ending home run into the right-field bleachers off the bat of kid outfielder Carl Crawford.

Closer by committee? Puleeeeze. Pedro told reporters he could not understand why Urbina was let go. Wrote Dan Shaughnessy, "It was like a cruel April Fool's joke, one day early. The Red Sox are now 0–1 lifetime in March. Sheer madness. The closer-by-committee system is a bust, and the sky is falling inside the Teflon roof of Tropicana Field."

Shaughnessy, who tended to predict the coming of the Apocalypse any time the Sox lost two games in a row, this time was right. Two weeks later, a Red Sox pitcher saved a game. He was a twenty-three-year-old rookie by the name of Brandon Lyon, a kid signed by Toronto who Epstein picked off the waiver wire in October.

On May 29, Theo Epstein, realizing the Yankees had in Mariano Rivera the one chess piece he lacked—a dependable closer—traded young third baseman Shea Hillenbrand to Arizona for Byung-Hyun Kim, a submarining right-hander with nasty stuff who won 8 and saved 36 games for the Diamondbacks in 2002. In two seasons the fireballing Kim struck out 205 batters in 182 innings. The move was important for two other reasons: it allowed Bill Mueller, who was leading the league in hitting and doing so with power, to play every day at third, and it provided more playing time for David Ortiz. Of the many moves Epstein made in 2003, this was the key one.

With Brandon Lyon saving games regularly, Pedro Martinez on the DL, and kid starter Casey Fossum struggling, the Red Sox badly needed Kim to start, and in his first appearance as a starter, against Pittsburgh, he pitched seven innings of quality ball in a win.

The pen blew two games in a row in two losses to Pittsburgh and Milwaukee. Then on June 7, Casey Fossum pitched one inning, gave up five runs and went on the DL. In that game the Sox came back and beat the Brewers 11–10 on consecutive home runs by Trot Nixon and Jason Varitek. Kevin Millar added a grand slam and in the next game hit a pair of home runs to beat the Brew Crew, and the Sox climbed back into first place.

Against the Cards on June 10, the Sox scored seven runs but lost when Brandon Lyon, who had converted all six save opportunities, allowed two runs in the ninth.

Pedro Martinez stopped the wailing and teeth-gnashing by the press and fans by returning in style, pitching three classic innings in a 13–1 win over the St. Louis Cardinals. While Pedro was out, the Sox record was 9–13. The Sox clung to first anyway.

"Being back in first place in the middle of June doesn't mean anything," said Todd Walker, "but having Pedro out there meant the world."

The Sox returned home for two games against the Houston Astros. David Ortiz, playing more since Hillenbrand was traded, hit a bases-loaded double to win the first game, and on Father's Day, the Sox won in the 14th when Todd Walker singled, Nomar bunted him over to second and Manny Ramirez drove Walker in.

All the talk was about Nomar. He had hit three doubles and a triple, and in a bunting situation, he did what was best for the team. He bunted.

"I've been around a lot of superstars that won't put the team first," said Todd Walker, "and Nomar's not one of those guys. He's a special person and a special player."

Pedro then went out on June 16 and pitched well, striking out Frank Thomas with the bases loaded to protect a 2–1 lead. Unfortunately, another of Theo Epstein's relief candidates, Ryan Rupe, gave up a three-run home run to Joe Crede. The Sox lost, and they dropped out of first.

John Burkett started the next day, pitching as though his job was on the line, which it was. Burkett had the bad habit of giving up a bunch of runs in the first inning, and Grady Little was losing patience. On this day Burkett won and saved his job. "You guys were writing my obituary, weren't you?" Burkett asked the writers after the game.

In a game against the Angels on June 17, Trot Nixon made the highlight of *SportsCenter* every day for a week when, with a runner on base, he caught a fly ball hit by David Eckstein and then tossed it to a fan in the right-field stands. Unfortunately, there was only one out when he did it. A runner scored and the gaffe allowed the Angels to win the game.

If the bullpen was submarining anyone, it was Pedro Martinez. Pedro had a 2–1 lead over Philadelphia when he left the game, then Mike Timlin allowed a home run to Jim Thome. It was the fourth time the pen let a Pedro win get away. Thome hit another home run in the 12th to retie the game, and in the 13th Todd Pratt hit a homer off Rudy Seanez to win it.

"That's the thing that's killing us this year," said Todd Walker. "We're not winning the games that [Pedro] starts."

After the Sox swept the hapless Detroit Tigers, the Florida Marlins came to town. In the first game the Sox scored 14 runs in the first inning in a 25–8 pounding. The Sox scored 10 runs before pitchers Carl Pavano, Michael Tejera and Allen Levrault of the Marlins could get an out. Bill Mueller had six RBIs. Johnny Damon tied a record with three hits in the inning. In all, the Sox finished with 28 hits, tying a Boston record.

The next day the bullpen gave it right back. The Sox led 9–6 in the ninth, when Brandon Lyon allowed a run on three hits before giving up a home run by Mike Lowell. It was Lyon's first blown save, and the Sox dropped three games behind the Yankees.

Talking about his relief staff, a frustrated Grady Little told reporters, "There's probably a few guys out there whose wives shouldn't be buying green bananas."

The Sox continued playing .500 ball. The next day the Red Sox hit six home runs to help Derek Lowe beat Florida 11–7. The day after that Brandon Lyon blew his second save, this time against the lowly Devil Rays in the 11th when he threw the ball away and allowed the winning run to score. In his struggle to find some consistency in his pen, Theo Epstein signed Todd Jones, once a star reliever for the Tigers, after he was released by the Colorado Rockies.

The Sox rebounded with a win over the Rays on a two-run home run by Kevin Millar, followed by a heartbreaking loss when Lyon gave up a two-run home run to Al Martin in the 10th. Lyon's reign as closer was coming to an end.

When the Red Sox invaded Yankee Stadium on July 4, George Steinbrenner's birthday, the Yankees had won 16 of their last 19 games. Alphonso Soriano led off the game with a long home run off Derek Lowe. The hand-wringing was excruciating. But Jason Varitek hit a three-run home run of David Wells, Manny hit a two-run dinger and David Ortiz homered to lead off the fourth. Then Bill Mueller and Varitek hit back-to-back homers, and when Wells left, he threw his glove and cap into the stands in disgust. In the ninth the stadium stands were half empty, and chants of "Lets Go, Red Sox," reverberated as the Sox won 10–3.

The next day they won 10–2. Ramiro Mendoza, a former Yankee, defeated Roger Clemens. Back in September 1996, when Clemens was a Red Sox, Mendoza beat him, the last Yankee pitcher to do while he was in a Red Sox uniform. Mendoza was sharp, pitching five shutout innings.

Prior to the game Manny Ramirez was teasing David Ortiz, calling him "Juan Pierre," after the Marlins Punch-and-Judy leadoff hitter. Coming into the Yankee series, Ortiz had five home runs in 189 at bats. Against the Yankees he would hit four home runs in nine at bats.

Sox fans were praying for a sweep, but Andy Pettitte and Mike Mussina took care of that, pitching masterfully in 7–1 and 2–1 wins. Pedro lost the 2–1 game, which was marked by controversy when Pedro hit both Alfonso Soriano and Derek Jeter in the hands on 1–2 counts.

After the game George Steinbrenner was furious at Pedro. He told reporters, "If Pedro threw at them to try to deliver a message, he delivered the wrong fucking message, in my opinion."

Pedro played coy. "That's exactly right," he said, "he can't do anything about that, whether I was trying to send a message or not. Only I know."

Later Pedro said he hadn't meant to hit anyone, that Soriano "is my kid from the Dominican." He said, "There's no way I would want to hurt him. Jeter's another nice guy. I have no reason to hurt him. He's had plenty of hits. I've never hit him, not that I remember."

Then Pedro discussed Steinbrenner. "He'll probably buy the whole league," he said, "but not my desire and my heart, unless he buys me along with the whole league. He's not going to put any fear in my heart. He doesn't have the money to buy fear and put it in my heart."

The Red Sox then ripped off five wins in a row against the Blue Jays and the Tigers. At the All-Star break the team had a 55–38 record and was two games out of first. Garciaparra was having a fine season offensively, hitting .319 with 125 hits, 13 home runs, 73 runs, 24 doubles, 12 triples, and 60 RBIs, the last statistic tying him with A-Rod.

After the break, the Jays were threatening a three-game sweep when, in the third game and trailing 4–3 in the ninth, Nomar walked, stole second and scored on a single by Manny Ramirez. The Sox won in the 10th when Trot Nixon singled to score Gabe Kapler, another player who Theo Epstein had salvaged from the scrap heap. Epstein signed Kapler, a hulking moose of a guy, after Colorado released him. Theo kept churning his roster when, on July 22, he sent Brandon Lyon and a minor leaguer to the Pirates for left-handed relief specialist Scott Sauerbeck and another minor leaguer.

The Sox swept the Tigers, and beat up on the Devil Rays 10–4, as Trot Nixon hit two home runs, including a grand slam in the seventh to help Tim Wakefield win. Grady Little started Ramiro Mendoza against the Rays in the next game, and he allowed seven runs on nine hits in a 15–9 loss.

Then it was back to Fenway for three games against the Yankees. The series started badly when the Sox were beaten by Yankee spear carrier Enrique Wilson. Why was it always the 25th guy who killed them? Wilson led off the seventh and singled, went to second on a wild pitch, stole third and scored on a Bernie Williams single. In the ninth, Wilson singled, stole second, went to third on a grounder and scored the winning run on a sacrifice fly. Pedro threw 128 pitches. The critics wondered whether his arm was going to fall off.

And again, with a tough loss to the Yankees, there was moaning, groaning, second guessing and threats of suicide. But this was a Red Sox team with a lot of heart. It had indomitable characters like Johnny Damon, Kevin Millar, Jason Varitek, Bill Mueller and of course Nomar, Manny, Pedro and its newest star, David Ortiz.

With the Sox up 4–3 in the eighth of the second game, Byung-Hyun Kim allowed a run. He pitched a scoreless ninth, and then Ortiz singled in the winning run for an important victory. The Sox won the rubber game, 6–4, on home runs by Jason Varitek and Johnny Damon and a two-run triple by Ortiz.

The game ended on a terrific backhand catch of a hard line drive hit by Jorge Posada by left fielder Manny Ramirez. After he caught it, the always-entertaining Manny laid on his back, giggling as the Fenway fans rejoiced as though they had won the pennant. The fans knew how good the Yankees were. Now they were discovering that the Red Sox were just as good. They could smell defeat for the Evil Empire. They could envision the breaking of the Curse. They were in their glory.

A day before the July 31 trading deadline, Theo Epstein acquired fireballing closer Scott Williamson from Cincinnati for a couple of minor leaguers and a ham sandwich. Grady Little, who had started with no closer in April, now could choose between Kim and Williamson. Since July 1, Kim was 1–1 with a 1.15 era. Williamson had been 5–3 with 21 saves for Cincinnati.

A few days later the Pirates complained about the health of Brandon Lyon's arm, and so Theo Epstein made another deal with Pittsburgh. He sent Lyon back and acquired starter Jeff Suppan, the former Red Sox wunderkind, further strengthening the team. Red Sox Nation had never seen anything like this. John Henry and Epstein had promised to do everything in their power to bring home a winner and, by God, they were doing just that. Fans saw the match up between Steinbrenner's money and Theo Epstein's brain.

Four straight losses in early August—three to the Rangers and one to the Orioles—dropped the Sox 4½ games behind the Yankees. After hitting six homers to beat Baltimore, the Sox returned home and swept the world champion Angels. Everyone contributed. In the first game, Nomar and Kevin Millar hit three-run homers in a 10–9 win. Pedro followed that by pitching a beauty, and Nomar homered in a 4–2 win. In the seventh inning of the third, Adam Kennedy hit a liner toward the wall. Johnny Damon chased the ball to the warning track, leaped as high as Kobe Bryant, made the catch, banged into the wall, and crashed to the ground in a sitting position with the ball in his hands. John Burkett beat the Angels 9–3 in the final game of the series, sparked by yet another Nomar home run and a Jason Varitek homer off Troy Percival. The Sox, at 38–16, had the best home winning percentage in all of baseball.

Theo, meanwhile, kept shuffling the deck. He acquired David McCarty, a flashy-fielding, hard-hitting first baseman, on waivers from Oakland, and he brought Casey Fossum back from Pawtucket and sent Ramiro Mendoza down.

Baltimore took two of three, and then Tim Hudson pitched a shutout, moving the A's into a tie for the wild-card spot. When the A's beat the Sox 5–3 the next day, the Sox were in danger of letting the postseason slip away.

It was up to Derek Lowe, the ace of the staff much of the season. In the fifth inning Lowe had bases loaded with two out and slugger Erubiel Durazo at bat. When he threw strike three, Lowe celebrated publicly, thrusting his fist into the air, then staring into the A's dugout.

They were tied again, and then it was Tim Wakefield's turn to keep Oakland at bay. He allowed two hits in six innings, but the A's led 2–1 in the ninth. Against Keith Foulke, Manny Ramirez went deep into the count, fouled off pitcher after pitch, and then homered to tie the game. Byung-Hyun Kim pitched two perfect innings, and in the bottom of the 10th Bill Mueller hit a sacrifice fly to drive in the winning run.

The Sox then traveled to Seattle to face a Mariner team that won three out of four. Only Pedro won, giving up one run in seven innings. Returning home to play a key series against wild-card foe Oakland, the Sox lost the series opener when Scott Sauerbeck walked two batters and Scott Williamson gave up a home run to Ramon Hernandez.

The next night the A's beat the Sox again in a very ugly ballgame. Byung-Hyun Kim blew the save and was booed lustily by the Fenway Faithful. After the game Kevin Millar blew up at the press and the fans, chastising them as doomsayers driven by the team's tortured past.

"It baffles me that all the media and all the fans want to bash us in August," said Millar. "There's a lot of baseball left."

Millar, from Beaumont, Texas, then made a speech that will go down in Sox history.

"I want to see somebody 'cowboy up' and stand behind this team one time and quit worrying about all the negative stuff and talking about last year's team and ten years ago and 1986," he said. "I don't know any better, man. I'm here to win and to have fun. [The past] makes zero sense to me."

"Cowboy up," which in cowboy talk means the same as "when the going gets tough, the tough get going," became a Sox rallying cry. Mike Timlin made shirts with the slogan on it for his teammates. Ryan Reynolds wrote a song titled "Cowboy Up," which the Sox began playing on the PA system.

CHAPTER 49

Cowboy Up

On August 20, 2003, the Yankees led the Red Sox by 7½ games. By early September, the Sox had closed the gap to 4½ games. But when the Yankees came to town, Manny Ramirez was sick and unable to play. The Yankees took two out of three, leaving the Red Sox 5½ games back with 26 games to go, and negativity reigned. In the wild-card race, the Sox trailed Seattle by 1½ games. Sox fans were getting ready to become emotionally involved with Tom Brady and the New England Patriots.

It's hard for a Red Sox team to go through a season without controversy, and in 2003 they made it as far as Saturday night, September 1. Manny Ramirez, who had absented himself from the ballpark during the three-game Yankee series because he said he was too sick to play with a severe sore throat, was seen in the bar of his residence, the Ritz-Carlton Hotel, sharing a table with Yankee infielder Enrique Wilson.

That the Yankees were in first place made Manny's absence seem even worse. Dan Shaughnessy, who was always quick to find a reason to fire a Red Sox manager, opined that Grady Little's lack of discipline would cost him his job.

At that point the Sox offense, including Manny, caught fire. But it was a Manny's spectacular defensive play that left his teammates talking. During the game at Yankee Stadium on September 4, Manny raced to the left-field wall and robbed Bernie Williams with a spectacular over-the-shoulder catch. He then flipped the ball into the stands and raced toward the dugout. The only problem was that his catch was the second out. Fortunately, there was no one on base. The laughter on the bench showed how loose everyone was.

The Red Sox won that game 9–3, and the next day the Sox led 8–0 after three innings against Roger Clemens on the way to an 11–0 rout. The win moved the Sox to within 1½ games of the Yankees.

Red Sox Nation came alive with expectation. The Patriots could wait. Now they were wondering, will the Yankees blow it this time? Will the Red Sox be avenged for Bucky Dent, whose home run was hit on this day twenty-five years earlier? Can anyone stop the Red Sox? Can the fall of the Evil Empire be imminent? There was one thing about Red Sox Nation: no one was middle of the road. The frustrations since 1918 had left everyone subject to extreme emotional swings. No one disliked the Yankees: they *hated* them. No Red Sox fan was immune from the dangers of fanaticism. After all, extremism in defense of Ye Olde Towne was no vice. Paul Revere, or maybe it was John Hancock, had said that a couple hundred years before.

On September 8, Yankee starter David Wells showed why the Yankees were so hard to beat when he defeated the Red Sox 3–1 with a masterful performance. The Yankee rotation in 2003 included Roger Clemens, Andy Pettitte, David Wells and Mike Mussina, one of the most formidable staffs of all time. The Red Sox took comfort in the great game pitched by Jeff Suppan, the number-five starter, a late-season Epstein acquisition from the Pittsburgh Pirates.

MOST HOMERS EVER

On September 9, David Ortiz hit a 430-foot home run off Damian Moss of the Orioles, the 214th home run hit by the Sox in 2003, a new club record, which was set by the 1977 Sox featuring Yaz, Jim Rice, Fred Lynn, George Scott and Dwight Evans. Theo Epstein in the spring had predicted that this would be a hard-hitting, exciting team, and he was right.

The Sox took two of three from Baltimore and took two from the White Sox, beating Bartolo Colon and Mark Buehrle. After they took two from Tampa Bay on the pitching of Pedro and Derek Lowe, the Sox had a 2½ game lead over Seattle for the wild-card with only a dozen to play.

"We're about to be in the playoffs," announced David Ortiz.

By the time Ortiz' pronouncement came to pass, he had become one of the prime reasons for the team's surge in hitting. David Ortiz, who had played so little in May that he considered asking to be traded, was being considered for MVP. In the first fifty games, Ortiz hit three home runs. By mid-September he had 26, including a stretch that month of 10 home runs and 28 RBIs in 15 games. Pedro had predicted Ortiz's season stats almost exactly: 31 home runs and 101 RBIs to go with a .288 batting average and a high on-base percentage.

The Sox provided drama in almost every outing. On September 23, the Sox trailed the Orioles by three runs with two men on, two outs, and two strikes on Todd Walker in the bottom of the ninth. Even though the Sox were losing, few fans had left. It was as though the fans were expecting a home run. Fenway was still packed when Walker lined the ball over the Green Monster in left to tie the game, and the Red Sox went on to win the game on an electrifying home run hit by David Ortiz. When the Angels lost, the magic number for the wild card dropped to two.

WILD-CARD WINNERS

Two days later, on September 25, the Red Sox clinched the wild-card spot before 34,526 wildly cheering Sox fans, defeating the Orioles 14–3. Nomar and Kevin Millar hit three-run homers. The Sox led 12–0 in the fourth, and the rest of the day was spent celebrating.

During the final inning, the players left the dugout to wave to the fans. After the final out, they stormed onto the field, surrounded Ramiro Mendoza, who had thrown strike three past Brian Roberts for the final out, and celebrated.

The PA played the song "Dirty Water," which goes, "Well, I love that dirty water / Oh, Boston, you're my home," and as everyone sang along, you could feel the love for the city and the team.

Kevin Millar went to the mike and sang a few bars of "Born in the U.S.A.," and then he spoke to the fans.

"It's time to cowboy up," he concluded. "We love you."

"Could this be the year?" asked Bob Ryan.

The Sox finished the 2003 season in record fashion. Theo Epstein's offense finished the year with a slugging percentage of .492, two points better than the vaunted 1927 Yankees with Babe Ruth and Lou Gehrig. Finishing with a record of 95–67, the Sox set Major League records for extra-base hits (649) and total bases (2,832). Had the bullpen not blown a dozen or so games, it's conceivable the Sox might have won 110 ballgames. As it was, despite Theo Epstein's best efforts, the relief corps finished the year with a 4.83 era, third worst in the American League.

Manager Grady Little was praised highly by everyone, though members of the media wondered why Larry Lucchino and Theo Epstein had chosen not to extend his contract, which was to run out at the end of the season. Everyone proclaimed it not to be an issue. When asked, Epstein would reply, "I just don't want to talk about it right now." After the Red Sox made the playoffs, Little's job seemed safe, but it made people wonder.

The team the Sox had to play in the first round of the playoffs was Billy Beane's Oakland A's. By the fall of 2003 Theo Epstein's star had eclipsed Beane's, the featured subject of Michael Lewis' *Moneyball*. Epstein, with the acquisition of Kevin Millar, Bill Mueller, David Ortiz and Todd Walker to go along with Nomar, Manny, Johnny Damon and Jason Varitek, built a more potent offense than the legendary Yankees' Murderer's Row. The switch-hitting Mueller would lead the league in batting with a .326 average, and Ortiz would be right behind him at .325.

But could the team overcome its defensive and pitching deficiencies?

Oakland won the series opener 5–4 on a bases-loaded bunt in the 12th inning by catcher Ramon Hernandez.

Pedro Martinez outpitched Tim Hudson as the Sox led 4–3 in the eighth, but relievers Byung-Hyun Kim and Alan Embree let the A's tie it on a walk, a hit batter and a single.

In Game 2 Barry Zito pitched seven sterling innings to help defeat the Sox 5–1. Oakland's defense was stellar, and it looked like curtains for the Sox.

The saving grace was that the Sox were going back to Fenway, where the team didn't lose often.

"We're going back to Fenway Park, where we kill the baseball," said Kevin Millar. "We're ready for our fans to be behind us. Sox Nation. We're going back to our place, and I think it's going to be a different atmosphere."

"They've got to win three straight," said Dan Shaughnessy, "or those 'Cowboy Up' T-shirts go into the closet next to your 8-track collection and those 'Dukakis for President' bumper stickers."

Game 3 began under leaden skies. It had rained all afternoon, and water was puddled in the outfield. In the clubhouse, Kevin Millar decided the Sox had to change their luck. They had lost four games in a row, the last two games of the regular season to the Devil Rays and the two playoff games to the A's. They decided that the luck changer would be to have everyone shave his head. Fifteen players submitted to Millar's clippers.

Derek Lowe pitched a gem, and the score was tied 1–1 in the 11th inning when Trot Nixon pinch hit with a runner on base. Nixon had pulled a calf muscle in mid-September and was fighting to regain his health and his stroke. The A's Rich Harden threw a 1–1 fastball, and Nixon hit it high and long toward the center field wall. Center fielder Eric Byrnes ran back, reached up, but the ball kept carrying. It cleared the fence, scoring Doug Mirabelli in front of him. Shades of Bernie Carbo. Nixon's heroics saved the Sox from elimination. It was the most memorable home run since Carlton Fisk's 1975 homer off the foul pole.

But the drama didn't end there. In the bottom of the eighth inning of Game 4, David Ortiz, in an 0-for-16 slump, faced Keith Foulke, Oakland's usually unhittable closer, trailing by a run. If any pitcher was a sure thing, it was Foulke, who in 2003 saved 43 out of 48 games. With runners on the corners, and two outs and two strikes in the ninth, Ortiz hit a pitch deep into right field for a two-run double to give the Sox a 5–4 win over the A's and a tie in the series. Scott Williamson, acquired by Theo Epstein down the stretch to bolster the bullpen, then gave the Sox a 1-2-3 ninth to save the victory. After being down 2–0, the Sox players were very much alive and well, having won two games in a row with at-bats in the final inning.

After the game, Sox owner John Henry cried unashamedly.

"How could it get any better than this?" asked Kevin Millar. "This is how guys are made heroes. And now we've got Pedro."

The Game 5 matchup, played in Oakland, pitted Pedro Martinez against Barry Zito, two of the finest pitchers in the league. Martinez had won only 14 games, but he would have had at least five more wins had the Red Sox had a reliable closer. Some felt Martinez should have been the Cy Young Award winner anyway. His 2.22 era led the league.

Martinez pitched masterfully. The score was tied 1–1 with two on in the sixth, when Manny Ramirez homered off Zito over the Verizon ad in left to put the Sox on top. Before the game Manny had predicted to David Ortiz that Zito would make a mistake, and he would hit one out. After he dropped his bat, he looked into the dugout and nodded to Ortiz.

"JUST IN TIME"

The Sox took a 4–3 lead going into the ninth. The season would come down to the skill of one of Theo Epstein's closers. In the spring it had been Brandon Lyon, then Byung-Hung Kim, and now it was in the hands of Scott Williamson, who started the ninth by walking his first two batters. A sacrifice bunt moved the runners into scoring position.

Grady Little took out Williamson and brought in Derek Lowe, who had started Game 3 and who had been told by Grady Little while jogging in the outfield to be ready to pitch with the game on the line. Lowe had been a reliever during the Dan Duquette regime, but in 2003 he won 17 games as a starter. Up by a run with one out and two runners in scoring position, the Sox needed Lowe to cowboy up, and he responded in style, striking out Adam Melhuse, a backup catcher for the A's, on a sinker. The next batter was Terrence Long. Once again Lowe reared back and threw a sinker for a called third strike, ending the game and sending the Sox to the next round of the playoffs.

When Long took strike three, Lowe demonstrated with a now-patented windmill fist pump what his joyful teammates called "the Tiger Woods pump." Angry A's players accused Lowe of modifying it into a vulgarity. Lowe went into the A's clubhouse and apologized.

"It wasn't directed toward anybody," said Lowe.

After the game, the champagne flowed. Teammates surrounded Manny Ramirez and poured the bubbly over his head. CEO Larry Lucchino walked over and hugged his big outfielder.

"Just in time," Lucchino said to Ramirez. "Just in time."

Said a gleeful Theo Epstein, "I think we put a few things behind us history-wise, winning this kind of game and this kind of series."

Blunting the excitement was a head-to-head collision in the seventh inning between center fielder Johnny Damon and second baseman Damian Jackson. Both players were knocked out after the crash, and the rest of the Red Sox players on the field ran and gathered around them.

Jackson walked off, while Damon, who was unconscious for three or four minutes, had to be placed in a neck brace, strapped to a stretcher and wheeled off in an ambulance to an Oakland hospital. Damon lifted his right hand and waved as he was being lifted into the ambulance. Doctors said he suffered a concussion. Later he would say he thought he was walking off the field wearing an Oakland A's uniform. It would be several hazy days before he returned to the land of the *compos mentis*.

After the final out, pandemonium reigned in the Fenway area, as fans poured out of the local bars and went wild. Two sisters were arrested for baring their breasts. Several fans turned over cars and set them afire. Three Emerson College students were arrested for trying to steal a Red Sox banner from atop City Hall. A riot broke out at UMass at Amherst as two thousand students celebrated. One group of fans broke into Fenway Park and ran around the field before police came and chased them out.

It was high time for the Sox to break the dreaded curse, but the next round would take pluck, and luck, coming against George Steinbrenner's New York Yankees. They had met nineteen times in 2003, and the Yankees had won ten, the Sox nine. The two teams were very close in skill. Both had front-line starters. Both had All-Star hitters. The Yankees had one player, Mariano Rivera, the nonpareil closer, who the Red Sox could not match.

Could the 2003 Sox become only the second AL wild-card team after the 2002 Angels to reach the World Series? Red Sox fans were betting on it.

CHAPTER 50
One Game Away

The opening game of the 2003 American League Championship Series pitted Mike Mussina, one of the Yankees' horses, against Tim Wakefield, the knuckleballer who didn't get any respect, except on nights like that. Wakefield shut down the Yankees on that night, making them look silly as they swatted at his 68-mile-an-hour flutterball. The score was tied at zero in the fourth when Manny Ramirez singled, and David Ortiz, Theo Epstein's best buy, worked the count to 3–2, fouled off a couple pitches and then hit a long home run to right field into the third deck of Yankee Stadium. Ortiz had been 0–20 in his career against Mussina before that. In the fifth inning Todd Walker, who hit 13 home runs during the regular season but five in nine playoff games, homered off the foul pole. Manny Ramirez also hit one out as the Sox won 5–2.

In Game Two, the Sox could not get past Andy Pettitte, who allowed only two runs in six and two-thirds innings. Jose Contreras, the big pitcher Steinbrenner signed in the off season, finished the job en route to a 6–2 Yankee win. Mariano Rivera closed it out 1-2-3 in the ninth. Sox starter Derek Lowe gave up six runs to take the loss.

ZIM GOES FLYING

The series moved to Fenway Park, and Game Three featured beefed up security and an ugly I-hate-the-Yankees mood. Thousands of frustrated Red Sox fans packed the streets around Fenway Park before the game, many wearing "Cowboy Up" T-shirts, while Boston policemen on horseback patrolled. The screams of "Yankees Suck" could be heard everywhere.

The foul mood of the fans spilled over into the game itself. In the fourth inning Pedro Martinez walked Jorge Posada, then allowed hits by Nick Johnson and Hideki Matsui. Martinez then threw a high fastball close to the head of Yankee right fielder Karim Garcia, hitting him in the shoulder. When Alfonso Soriano grounded out in a double play, Garcia retaliated, sliding hard into Sox second baseman Todd Walker. There were a lot of words, but no action.

The action didn't come until the next inning when Roger Clemens threw a high fastball in the vicinity of Manny Ramirez. Clemens had two strikes on Ramirez, and Clemens swore he was trying to strike him out. But Manny well knew Clemens' habit of pitching with intent to intimidate, and he was angry enough to cause a scene that cleared both benches. One of the players who ran out from the dugout to near home plate was Pedro Martinez, who turned in time to see Yankee bench coach Don Zimmer charging toward him. Zimmer had been manager of the Red Sox in 1978 when Graig Nettles dumped Bill Lee upside-down during a brawl, injuring the Red Sox pitcher. Zimmer now was the Yankee bench coach, and this time he decided to get involved. When the furious Zimmer, 72, reached Martinez, the pitcher casually grabbed him by the neck and shoulders and, with a push, let Zimmer's forward motion propel him headlong into the dirt.

Jorge Posada, upset at seeing his elderly coach lying on the ground, had some words with Martinez.

"The next time," said Martinez, "I'm going to hit you in the head."

It was not Pedro's finest hour.

The madness wasn't over. In the ninth inning a Red Sox groundskeeper whose job it was to manicure the pitcher's mound in the Yankees bullpen, began swinging a towel around as he exhorted the Red Sox on to victory. Yankees reliever Jeff Nelson took offense and went after him. Karim Garcia, who was in right field, ran to help Nelson pummel the outmanned groundskeeper, who ended up in the hospital.

The Sox lost 4–3. It was Martinez' first-ever postseason loss. If anyone had forgotten how bitterly hard-fought the Red Sox–Yankees series had become, this game was a vivid reminder. Martinez was fined $50,000, Manny $25,000, Garcia $10,000, and the martyred Zim $5,000, which he made up many times over in appearances, commercials, and book deals.

The next day the field was too wet to play, and the game was postponed. When the series resumed, Tim Wakefield diffused the tension by holding the vaunted Yankees attack to just five hits and one run in eight innings. A slow relay on a potential double play by Alphonso Soriano allowed the Red Sox to take a 3–1 lead in the seventh.

With one out in the ninth, Scott Williamson allowed Ruben Sierra a home run, the first run allowed by the Boston bullpen in the series. But Williamson then K'ed David Dellucci and Alfonso Soriano to end the game and even the series at two games each. Wakefield's win made him the only knuckleball pitcher in baseball history to win a postseason game. Joe Niekro won one for

Houston in 1981, but unlike his brother Phil, Joe was not strictly a knuckeball pitcher. With two wins Wakefield had positioned himself to pitch in Game Seven and perhaps reserve for himself a singular place in Red Sox history.

Red Sox fans' hopes were high before Game Four. It was the finale at Fenway, but David Wells, who allowed just four hits in seven innings, was too good for the Bald Sox. The Red Sox fans took out their frustration on Nomar Garciaparra, who had batted .170 in September and who was batting .105 in the ALCS. With runners on second and third and two outs, Garciaparra struck out swinging in the third, ending the Sox' chance to score in a 4–2 loss. He also grounded out in the fifth with runners on first and second. Gordon Edes of the *Globe* wondered whether Nomar was "hurt, tired, or preoccupied with his wedding to Mia Hamm next month—on the face of it, a preposterous notion for someone as single-minded as Garciaparra is about baseball." Callers to the radio station WEEI suggested that Nomar ought to be benched in favor of Lou Merloni.

"Nomar wasn't having a slump," wrote Bob Ryan, "he was having a midlife crisis."

Said Garciaparra after the game, "I never give up. This team hasn't given up, and I'm not going to."

Making things seem even more grim was the knowledge that Red Sox killer Andy Pettitte was starting Game Six against John Burkett in hostile Yankee Stadium.

"IT DOESN'T GET ANY BETTER THAN THIS"

The Red Sox faced elimination late into the game. They were trailing 6–4 in the seventh inning when the Sox rallied for three runs against Jose Contreras, who had struck out the side in the sixth. They scored two more in the ninth to win 9–6, stretching the series to a seventh game. Nomar Garciaparra had four hits, ending the criticism about him.

"I've never been around a club quite like this," said manager Grady Little.

"We're going to have some cocktails, get some rest, and be ready to take on the Babe and the rest of the Yankees," said Johnny Damon after Game Six.

It was time for the Miracle Comeback in the Bronx. Pedro Martinez against Roger Clemens. The Armageddon game.

"We've been on a collision course for a hundred years," said Theo Epstein. "It definitely seems appropriate, definitely meant to be, and certainly poetic. It's special for both teams and both franchises, regardless of the result."

"This is what we worked so hard for," said Kevin Millar. "It doesn't get any better than this."

CHAPTER 51

Five Outs Away

Sox Lead

It felt like a repeat of 1946, 1949, 1967, 1975, 1978, and 1986 all over again. The Red Sox were on the top step, knocking on the door. In 2003, seventeen torturous years since the ball rolled through Bill Buckner's legs, the Sox were in a position to beat the Yankees and go back to the World Series, where every Red Sox fan was sure that the first series triumph since 1918 was inevitable.

One reason Red Sox Nation was so sure of victory was that Pedro Martinez was starting. Earlier in the year, when asked about the Ruth curse, Martinez spit in the Babe's eye, saying, "Wake up the Bambino. Bring him back, and I'll drill him."

Facing Martinez was Roger Clemens, once loved in Beantown, but fiercely despised for leaving town (never mind that Dan Duquette didn't want him anymore, saying he was too old to continue to be effective). He had taken George Steinbrenner's filthy lucre and pitched better than ever. (Clemens, who had won six Cy Young Awards—two with the Yankees—would retire at the end of the season, then come out of retirement in 2004 to win his seventh Cy Young with the Houston Astros.)

On that day, the Red Sox knocked out Clemens in the fourth with nobody out and took a 3–0 lead. Mike Mussina, who hadn't relieved since high school, replaced him and gave up two runs. The Sox scored four runs on home runs by Trot Nixon, Kevin Millar and David Ortiz, and added a fifth on a throwing error by Yankee infielder Enrique Wilson.

Martinez was masterful as he took a 5–2 lead into the eighth. Two solo home runs by Jason Giambi were the only damage he suffered.

GRADY LEAVES PEDRO IN

When the eighth inning began, Pedro Martinez stood on the mound, ready to face Derek Jeter. He had thrown 115 pitches, and the TV announcers on Fox were telling the rest of the country something every Red Sox fan knew well: Martinez was far less effective after his first hundred pitches. After a hundred pitches, Tim McCarver as much said, Pedro is batting practice. Throughout New England, Red Sox fans were screaming at manager Grady Little through their television sets to take Martinez out and bring in a reliever. Alan Embree, Mike Timlin and Scott Williamson were armed and ready. But Grady Little wasn't a stats guy. He was a touchy-feely, sentimental guy. Grady Little decided to go with Pedro Martinez' heart—breaking everyone else's.

Pedro got an out. Five outs from victory, the game seemed in hand. Then Derek Jeter hit a long double, and Bernie Williams hit a laser shot for a single to make the score 5–3.

Hideki Matsui was up. Little went to the mound to talk to Martinez. The armchair managers throughout Red Sox Nation were standing on their feet, trying their best to channel Little to get him to take Martinez out. Pedro told Little he had the stuff to finish, which was what Pedro told Little every time he or pitching coach Dave Wallace went to the mound.

When Little returned to the dugout, Sox fans went looking for a rope and a tall tree.

Matsui doubled hard to right as Williams went to third. No Grady Little. No relief.

Jorge Posada, a switch-hitter, batted next. Martinez threw and Posada blooped a shallow hit into center field in front of Johnny Damon to score the two base runners and tie the game. (It was a carbon copy of Reds second baseman Joe Morgan's bloop into center field off Jim Burton to win the 1975 World Series.)

At that point, Little came in and gave Pedro the hook.

Though Red Sox Nation knew it was time to turn off the TV, like abused children, most watched until the painful end.

The Red Sox still could have won, but they couldn't score against Mariano Rivera, who dominated for three innings. David Ortiz doubled in the 10th with two outs, but Kevin Millar popped out to end the inning.

Tim Wakefield, pitching in relief, was equally effective, but there wasn't a Red Sox fan alive who felt that Wakefield could hold off the Yankees forever. One flutterball that didn't flutter, they knew, and it would be all over.

Aaron Boone

The game was in Yankee Stadium, and Aaron Boone, the Yankee third baseman, led off the 11th with the score still tied 5–5. If a casual baseball fan was asked to name the Yankees starting lineup, he could name Giambi at first, Soriano at second, Jeter at short, but the third baseman? Hmmmm. Boone had come to the Yankees from Cincinnati mid-year. He was good, but a hero? Hardly. He was kind of like Bucky Dent, only stockier, one of the last guys you'd think would win a historic ballgame.

Wakefield threw, and without warning, like a thundershot, Boone hit a long fly ball that carried into the left field stands. Somewhere, the Babe was smiling. North of Hartford, the whole world was in mourning. The Evil Empire had prevailed—again.

"It might be the closest we'll ever get to the World Series," said Johnny Damon, "without actually getting there."

Said Dan Shaughnessy, "A new generation of New Englanders has learned the risk of rooting for the Red Sox."

As for manager Grady Little, the players didn't feel he had done anything wrong. Pedro had gotten two strikes on each of the five batters he failed to retire. He was throwing 93 miles per hour. So he had lost. That's baseball. As far as the players were concerned, Grady Little had done everything right from beginning to end. To them, losing the way they did was no terrible thing.

But outside the Red Sox dugout, the rest of Red Sox Nation was as vengeful as a crowd of angry Frenchmen outside the Bastille before the French Revolution. Bob Ryan seemed to have the final word on Little.

"He has become," wrote Ryan, "the managerial Bill Buckner."

After the final game, no one in Boston talked about Aaron Boone. The sole topic of conversation was Grady Little and his decision to leave Pedro Martinez in the game.

"What was Grady thinking?" became the battle cry.

Ten days later, the manager who had done such a fine job combining personalities and leading his troops to within five outs of going to the World Series was fired.

John Henry, Tom Werner, Larry Lucchino and Theo Epstein met to decide his fate. The vote was unanimous.

Before he was fired, in one of his last interviews, Little said to Gordon Edes of the *Globe*, "If Grady Little isn't back with the Red Sox, I'll be another ghost, fully capable of haunting."

The ghost of Grady Little walks. *Whoooooooooooooo.*

CHAPTER 52

The Psyche of the Red Sox Fan

David Margolick: "I feel the same sense about baseball in general and the Red Sox in particular that I do about my religion. It was something I was born with, and it helps define my identity as an American and an individual, and these feelings of community are very precious. And the same time I feel them very privately. I can't cheer lustily when I go to the ballpark. I feel it privately. And so I never abandoned it. It's like some element in your blood. It doesn't matter how many different phases you go through. It's utterly instinctive. There is some kind of germ you are inoculated with early on, and you cannot get rid of it. I cannot understand people who ignore it. It's too much to ignore. It becomes a fundamental part of your personality so much so that there have been particular periods in my life when I wasn't around Boston and wasn't that much connected with the team, but it never went away. It receded in my consciousness, but it never went away. And now it is coming back again. And I'm sure when I have children, it will come back even more.

"As a youngster, I used to get very upset when the Red Sox lost, slamming the door, going to bed angry, turning off the game in disgust. I remember one game after I had turned it off in disgust, they came back and won. But someone else had to tell me. I wasn't around to see it.

"I had favorite performers. I think about Yastrzemski and his beautiful swing and all those home runs he hit to right. As for the rest, I think more about players blowing it. If I thought about Dick Radatz, I would think about all the games he lost rather than the ones he won. He was there during the low period. They were in the cellar. I'm much more likely, if forced to call upon my memory, to think about the games he lost.

"You've heard of players to root for? These were players to get frustrated over. I see the beauty in the game much more now. It was much more of a masochistic thing back then to watch them, because they always lost, and they were very novel about finding ways to lose. Now I can watch the Red Sox and watch Boggs get a hit and marvel at his talent, but back then I didn't do much marveling. It was mostly excruciating. It wasn't just an exercise in frustration.

"I remember a game in which Boog Powell of the Orioles hit three home runs against the Red Sox. One scene embossed in my mind is the ball hit by an opposing batter going into the net in left field or over the Wall, though I do remember Don Buddin hitting a grand slam. Just that image of balls going over the Green Monster. I don't remember games the Red Sox won. I remember another game when they were in a scoreless tie and Tom Brewer was pitching for the Red Sox against Cleveland, and Francona, the elder not the younger, hit a long foul ball in the ninth, foul by inches, and the next pitch he hit a home run.

"And every year the Sox would start out by losing their first few games to the Orioles or the Tigers. Five hundred was always a magical number to me. And they were always below five hundred through all those years. And to this day, five hundred is a measuring rod for me for almost everything. If the team is above five hundred, I consider them a success. It was a pleasant surprise whenever they won.

"As a result, I always felt that fate was very fickle, that basically if all other things were equal, that things would go badly, and that when things went well, it was a fluke. This is what happened in 1967. The Red Sox had been a second-division team every year of my childhood, and then they miraculously won the pennant.

"And then I remember watching Gary Waslewski pitching in the World Series. I had the feeling that they were playing beyond their ability, and they were just going to fall a little bit short. And it always happens. Even once they turned the corner and became a contending team, they would always fall a little bit short. I remember the '67 World Series when Lonborg started on two days' rest. They would always start running thin toward the end.

"Rooting for the Red Sox gave me a notion of hubris. I didn't know what the word meant, but a Red Sox fan knows what hubris is. Hubris is expecting to win everything, and you are destined to doom if you feel that way. You don't take anything for granted. And that is what rooting for the Red Sox did to me psychologically. I don't take anything for granted. Good fortune is a blessing, but it is also a fluke. One's natural state is difficulty and defeat. When you win, there is something freaky about it. It has made me very fatalistic.

"When the Red Sox were ahead by fourteen games in 1978, my brother, who was a fanatical Yankee fan, was utterly convinced the Red Sox were going to lose. There was no doubt in his mind that they weren't going to win. I was in Europe that year, and I would buy the *International Herald Tribune*, and the Sox were winning and winning and winning, and then they started their collapse, and it was something that everybody expected.

"It's an incredible notion that a team has character. I don't know metaphysically how that works. I don't know why the Celtics have a certain character. Or the Red Sox.

"I well remember I was in Yugoslavia, and you couldn't get the *International Herald Tribune* there, and I remember one day coming across three issues, and in each paper the Red Sox had lost. For me, on one day, the Red Sox had lost three games. It was as if they had played a tripleheader and lost all three games. Never has a collapse been more tangible to me. And again, unsurprisingly. Utterly unsurprisingly.

"I could even see coming what happened in the sixth game of the Series in 1986.

"Before that, though, I was thinking that my relationship with the Red Sox was founded on tragedy and disappointment and dashed expectations, and if the Red Sox had won, it would have been like when they changed the formula for Coca-Cola. I was very upset when they did that, because there are certain things that you can count on, certain sensations that should never be altered and that should be left alone. It's very precious, and when you open up a Coke, it should taste a certain way. For the same reason, part of me didn't want the Sox to win. I mean, I wanted them to win, and I was crushed when they didn't, but I realized that their winning would come at a price. It would change my way of looking at them. The Red Sox are different from the Yankees. You don't think of the Red Sox as winners. Part of their charm is in grabbing you by the heart and letting you down.

"I'm sure subliminally, psychologically, I do not think of myself as a winner, and I'm more comfortable struggling. I'm not comfortable with success. I agonize a lot over the work that I do. I'm always striving to do better, and I wasn't comfortable with the idea of their winning. That was the first thing I went into Game Six with. Another layer is that I never really expected them to win, and they kept confounding me. They went ahead of the Mets, and then there were two outs in the ninth and Bob Stanley was pitching, and Stanley was a classic Red Sox pitcher, mediocre, and this is another part of growing up: Red Sox fans never trust pitchers. For as many years as they existed, they never had the arms. In the entire time I rooted for them they never had three or four homegrown pitchers who were all winners. They would always trade for pitchers, and as soon as they did, the guy's arm would go bad. The paradigmatic example of this was when they traded for Dennis Bennett. They sent Dick Stuart for Dennis Bennett, and Dennis Bennett's arm went bad immediately. I remember reading in the paper that he couldn't throw a ball through a window. That always happens. And conversely, whenever they trade a pitcher away, he would be great. It never occurred to me that it might have been a function of Fenway. It was rather a function of fate. So you never, ever trust a pitcher. Pitchers' arms are always breaking your heart. If you're a Red Sox fan, you are constantly reminded of that. No lead is ever too big.

"I remember one year Ike Delock was 10–0. You knew that wasn't going to last. He ended up 14–8. And it was the same thing with Jim Lonborg. Lonborg was a great pitcher, and then he broke his leg skiing, the damn fool. I remember him coming back and his motion never being the same.

"And Bob Stanley was the classic break-your-heart pitcher. He was the classic .500 pitcher, the kind of person they had to keep around, and I'm still bitter about him, 'cause he's a hack, like Mike Torrez, a retread, a perfect break-your-heart kind of pitcher.

"And the sixth game in '86 was the perfect example of coming up short, having a first baseman out there who was hobbling, really hurt, and it was the equivalent of starting a pitcher with two days' rest, the troops coming up just a little bit short. It was altogether fitting and proper that they had a crippled first baseman, and all the Mets had to do was hit the ball to him. It was preordained. It's a classic Red Sox problem, that they didn't have the people.

"We all have recurring dreams, and I've often had dreams of being chased by someone and falling repeatedly as this person catches up with me and eventually overtakes me, and it's the same thing with the Red Sox. Somebody chasing after you, and you're bound to fall, and this is what happened here.

"The only way I can explain it is that a large part of my personality is wrapped up in the team. Please don't make me sound silly. I hope there will be other people who say similar things. I felt that I really started to come into my own as a person around the time that the Red Sox as a team did. I grew up in a very competitive house, and I rooted for a losing team and that was seared on my personality, and I worked hard, and I made something of myself. I was proud of myself, and I made these strides at a time when the Red Sox had also become respectable. And when the Sox lost that sixth game in '86 and then went on to lose the Series, it was as if all these layers of accomplishment had been peeled away, and some kind of subcutaneous thing was going on: I was back to my old childhood self again, and I felt like a loser again. I was very distressed, and I had trouble sleeping, because I was tied to this team. A lot of different forces came together, and I didn't sleep that night. I tossed and turned and had bad dreams.

"I was surprised by my reaction. There aren't many things that could touch me that much. And it all goes back to growing up in an era of Pumpsie Green and Eddie Bressoud and losing pitchers like Dave Morehead. Dave Morehead pitched a no-hitter! I remember the next time out he got bombed, and there was somebody who yelled, 'Atta boy, Vander Meer,' as he walked off the mound. And that typifies the way Red Sox fans think. If you pitch a no-hitter, it's a fluke. And in this case, it was.

"I had mixed feelings about the Red Sox having success in the series against the Mets. To quote Oscar Wilde, 'There are two tragedies in life. One is not getting what you want, and the other is getting what you want.' And I was very ambivalent about what would happen had they won. And in the long run I feel that something precious was maintained by their not winning. But it was very painful for me."

Cleveland Amory: "It is a terrible thing to be a Red Sox fan. There is no such thing as 'still a Red Sox fan.' Either you're a Red Sox fan, or you're not. You're a Red Sox fan from the day you're born until the day you die. And presumably after that, though I haven't heard from them and will have some criticisms to make when I get up there.

"Mothers should know about it before they even have children, to bring up their children to be any other ballteam's fans. You don't expect to win if you're a Cleveland fan, if you're a Texas Ranger fan. You don't have that awful 'almost.' The 'almost' is what hurts so bad. We know the Red Sox are not going to win in the end. When they have the lead, we are just enjoying a little momentary aberration, and we're entitled to that.

"A Red Sox fan has a built-in mechanism that doesn't allow himself to get too excited. They are twelve games ahead, and there are thirteen to play. Now he's beginning to get excited, but he knows that somehow they are not going to win. God is a Boston Episcopalian, and the Red Sox are primarily Catholic.

"The sixth game of the '86 World Series was the best example. I still can't believe it. You read the story of that game, which we will read steadily; it will become a sort of Book of Psalms for funerals. One will read a little bit of it at the funeral whenever a Red Sox fan dies. That should be read, because wherever he is going, however good he's been in this life, you know that there can be nothing worse than what he has suffered here.

"Red Sox fans have taken the vow of abstinence from ever walking into the World Series and winning, knowing it's not going to happen, that you're not going to see it, your children are not going to see it, your children's children are not going to see it. There is no possibility of anyone you know ever seeing it.

"I can only describe being a Red Sox fan as something like a lifelong disease. You don't really want to get over it, because you're so used to combating it. And it's very, very deep inside. A Red Sox fan is deep in his heart. It's like true love versus sex. And Bostonians, of course, are not allowed the latter."

Ray Goulding, late of Bob and Ray: "On my tombstone it is going to say, 'Cause of Death, Boston Red Sox.'"

CHAPTER 53

Theo-logy

Manny Ramirez' attitude had bugged Boston GM Theo Epstein all year long. Since he came in 2001, Manny had expressed unhappiness playing for the Red Sox. He was feeling underappreciated by his teammates and especially the fans. Manny even went so far as to say he wondered how he would look in Yankee pinstripes, and so on October 30, 2003, two days after the Red Sox decided to fire Grady Little, Epstein decided to teach his star slugger a lesson. Shocking everyone, he put Ramirez on irrevocable waivers. For forty-eight hours, any team that wanted him could take him for the $20,000 waiver claim price, so long as it assumed the $95 million balance of his eight-year, $160 million contract.

And if someone—the Yankees, Dodgers, or Mets—did take Ramirez, Epstein knew, he could use the money he would save to sign Nomar Garciaparra, who was in the last year of his contract, and buy a free agent starting pitcher or two.

Theo's gamble paid off, as he knew it would. No one took Manny. He remained with the Red Sox. But he never spoke about wanting to play for the Yankees ever again.

A Trade for A-Rod

Three days later, on November 1, 2003, Theo Epstein's plotting and planning intrigued Red Sox Nation when it was leaked that Epstein was attempting to trade Manny to the Texas Rangers for Alex Rodriguez, widely acknowledged as the best player in the game. As part of a grander plan, the

485

Sox would send Nomar Garciaparra to his native West Coast and acquire White Sox star outfielder Magglio Ordonez.

The denials came fast and furious.

In the same article came the first mention of the Red Sox being interested in Arizona Diamondback right-hander Curt Schilling, along with Andy Pettitte, Bartolo Colon and Kevin Millwood.

Red Sox fans, impressed with the job Epstein did in 2003, were looking forward to his moves to make the 2004 Sox stronger.

As October 2003 rolled into mid-November, the other topic of conversation among Red Sox fans was who Larry Lucchino and Epstein were going to hire as manager. The first names to surface didn't excite anyone. They were Terry Francona, bench coach of the Oakland A's; Joe Maddon, bench coach of the Anaheim Angels; Dodgers third base coach Glenn Hoffman; and Texas first base coach DeMarlo Hale, who had managed in the Red Sox farm system.

Francona was the one candidate with major league experience. He had managed the Philadelphia Phillies from 1997 through 2000. But the Philly fans had run him out of town on a rail after going 285–363. When commentators began to mention that Curt Schilling had played for Francona in Philadelphia and that the two were very close, rooting for the acquisition of Francona/Schilling began in earnest.

Epstein's third area of interest was acquiring a closer. Bill James had a theory that if a team had a decent enough pen, it would not need a closer, and in 2003 James had proved himself both right and wrong. The Sox had come within one game of going to the World Series without a closer, but the Yankees, who went, had Mariano Rivera, whose entry into a game meant almost-certain victory. In 2003 the Sox had blown a dozen games because they didn't have an established closer. That wasn't going to happen in 2004.

When the Celtics played the New York Knicks at the Fleet Center on November 24, 2003, Theo Epstein was seated next to Keith Foulke, who, while playing for the A's in 2003, had led the league with 43 saves. The Red Sox were in a battle with the Mets and the A's for Foulke's services. Neither Epstein nor Foulke had much to say, but the Hot Stove League was for dreaming, and signing Curt Schilling and Keith Foulke seemed to Red Sox fans the perfect antidote to anything George Steinbrenner had up his silk-lined sleeves.

FRANCONA AND SHILLING ARRIVE

On November 25, 2003, the Red Sox announced that Terry Francona would be the team's forty-fourth manager. He was asked whether he was tough enough to manage in Boston.

"Think about it for a second," he said. "I've been released from six teams. I've been fired as manager. I've got no hair. I've got a nose that's three sizes too big for my face, and I grew up in a major league clubhouse. My skin's pretty thick. I'll be OK."

On the heels of the announcement, Epstein got on a plane and flew to Phoenix in an attempt to sign Curt Schilling, who acknowledged that the Red Sox would have the inside track after Francona came on board.

"He's the number one attraction there for me," said Schilling, a future Hall of Fame pitcher with a low ERA and a spectacular strikeout-to-walk ratio. Only four active pitchers—Roger Clemens, Randy Johnson, Greg Maddux and Chuck Finley—had more career strikeouts. Schilling had had a 45–13 record with Arizona in 2001 and 2002. In 2003 he'd had an appendectomy and finished 8–9 with a 2.95 ERA.

Schilling, a student and fan of the history of the game, said he wanted to go to the Red Sox for another reason: the Red Sox–Yankees rivalry.

"Nothing in the world can compare to that," he said.

But Curt Schilling also was one tough negotiator. He wanted some assurance that the Red Sox management was committed to beating the Yankees, that he wouldn't be part of a rebuilding effort. He was 37, and his time was running out to pitch in a World Series.

Epstein and Schilling sparred for seventy-two hours, taking time off for Thanksgiving, and when it was over, Schilling talked about Epstein's preparation and his persuasiveness. The final issue had to do with whether Schilling, a fly-ball pitcher, was comfortable with the idea of pitching in Fenway Park. Ultimately, he decided that if Pedro Martinez could do it, so could he.

On November 28, Curt Schilling signed a two-year, $25.5 million contract extension, with a third year worth $13 million if both sides agreed. Schilling waived his no-trade clause, and Epstein traded Casey Fossum, whom he had refused to trade for Bartolo Colon a year earlier, plus Brandon Lyon and two minor leaguers no one had ever heard of to get him.

The 2004 Sox would feature a one-two punch of Pedro Martinez and Curt Schilling. Not since 1918, when the Red Sox had Herb Pennock and Babe Ruth, did the team feature two such outstanding hurlers.

"I want to be part of bringing the first World Series in modern history to Boston," said Schilling. "I guess I hate the Yankees now."

Red Sox fans all along were keeping a wary eye out for the Yankees and what their response to signing Curt Schilling might be. But on December 4, it looked as though Epstein had trumped the Yankees again, when it was announced that the Rangers were open to trading Alex Rodriguez to the Red Sox for Manny Ramirez, and that the Dodgers and Angels were interested in acquiring Nomar Garciaparra.

Two days later, Sox owner John Henry met privately with Rodriguez for six hours. The two discussed restructuring Rodriguez' contract, deferring enough money so that the Sox could afford to make the deal or declining the final three option years.

While Henry was in Texas, Nomar Garciaparra, a figure as beloved as any in Red Sox history, felt like Henry had stuck a knife in his back.

Nomar's agent, Arn Tellem, called it a "total and complete slap in the face."

Garciaparra, who was in the final year of his contract, was returning from his Hawaiian honeymoon with his wife, the soccer star Mia Hamm. He called radio talk show station WEEI to complain that the Red Sox hadn't given him the courtesy to tell him what they were doing with respect to Rodriguez. After saying he was not unhappy playing on the Red Sox, Garciaparra asked, "So why are they doing it? I'm scratching my head. . . ."

When John Henry blew up at Art Tellem, observers wondered whether Garciaparra's days were numbered in Boston. The usually mild-mannered Henry called Tellem's remarks "the height of hypocrisy" and said that Tellem had spurned his four-year, $60 million offer for Garciaparra to remain beyond 2004. The report said Nomar wanted $68 million.

"Our first choice was—and is—to sign Nomar," said Henry, "but if we can't, we need to pursue alternatives."

Then two days later the Alex Rodriguez deal appeared to blow up in the Red Sox' face. Texas owner Tom Hicks said that the Red Sox would have to sweeten the pot "considerably" before he would agree to trade A-Rod for Manny Ramirez. This from a guy who paid A-Rod $100 million more than any other owner was offering.

"The ball is in their court," said Hicks.

The excitement was building. On December 11, Andy Pettitte, the left-handed Yankees star, announced he was leaving New York to pitch for the Houston Astros. Coming on the heels of the announcement of Roger Clemens' retirement, Red Sox fans were getting pumped by the disparity between their rebuilt Sox starting rotation and the Yankees Swiss-cheese staff. Of course, they knew the Yankees would sign two expensive free agents to replace them, but they also knew that the Yankees were capable of overspending for mediocre talent. With Pedro and Schilling on board, Red Sox fans were overjoyed that their boy genius Theo was out-GMing Brian Cashman, and when it was announced on December 12 that the Sox had signed closer Keith Foulke, as unhittable a closer as Mariano Rivera, to a three-year contract worth $27 million, the Red Sox fans were really smelling pennant.

Foulke had been a hockey player, and helping to make up Foulke's mind had been Boston Bruin legend Bobby Orr, who told him, "If you win in this town, you're forever idolized here."

On December 16, 2003, the Red Sox were on the brink of getting Alex Rodriguez. The deal, as proposed by Tom Hicks two days after the end of the World Series, was to be A-Rod for Nomar, a minor league pitching prospect, and Manny minus about $25 million. Rodriguez' contract was to be reduced by $28 million, $4 million per year for the seven years left on his contract. It was all set.

After weeks of negotiation, the final deal was to be Rodriguez for Manny Ramirez, with Boston reducing A-Rod's salary by the same $28 million. Theo Epstein had also worked out a deal where he would trade Nomar Garciaparra to the White Sox for Magglio Ordonez. The announcement excited all of New England.

But Cynthia Rodriguez, A-Rod's wife, knew better.

"Gene will never go for this," she said to Theo Epstein.

On December 16, 2003, Gene Orza, the lawyer for the Major League Players Association, ruled against the reduction of Alex Rodriguez' contract, saying it violated the collective bargaining agreement. The union said it would approve a $13 million reduction at most. The ruling killed the deal and angered the Red Sox. Curt Schilling said the union was going against the wishes of its members.

Just before Christmas, a Red Sox fan e-mailed Orza, "You've ruined my summer, and it's not even winter."

The Rangers announced that Alex Rodriguez would be their new captain. The Sox were left having to smooth the ruffled feathers of Nomar and Manny.

DAMN YANKEES

Two months later, the Yankees really ruined everybody's summer when it was announced that they had traded their All-Star second baseman Alphonso Soriano for Captain A-Rod, who announced he would move to third base so that Derek Jeter could stay at short. The Yankees payroll was approaching $200 million.

"It just looks like the Yankees have no limit," said Toronto general manager J. P. Ricciari.

Quipster Dan Shaughnessy called it the "Valentine's Day Massacre of 2004."

"How pathetic does this make the Sox look?" he asked. "How are Hub kids in Boston and New York dormitories supposed to answer the taunts of those arrogant, entitled Yankee lovers?" He added, "It's like having your best girl agree to marry you, finding out you can't get married because your church won't allow it, then watching her marry the guy you hate most in the world. Hide the sharp objects and post guards at the Zakim and Tobin bridges.

"It's just one more dagger through the heart of the Nation. Damn Yankees. It just never stops with these guys."

A few days later John Henry groused about Steinbrenner's deep pockets. He said, "The Yankees are going insanely far beyond the resources of all the other teams." Steinbrenner replied tartly, "Unlike the Yankees, [Henry] chose not to go the extra distance for his fans in Boston."

Ouch.

Left to be determined was how the botched deal would affect the morale of Nomar and Manny. Manny seemed OK. Nomar didn't.

"I was definitely hurt by a lot of it," he said. He was at the end of his contract, and he vowed to fulfill it. But he said he and his agent had made a counteroffer to which the Red Sox had not responded. He was taking that to mean that an impasse had been reached.

Still, he said, "I've always said my hope was to play here in Boston and that hasn't changed."

Then on the final day of March 2004, a few days before the team was to leave Fort Myers to begin the season, it was announced that Nomar was going on the disabled list with an injured Achilles tendon in his right foot. No one was really sure how he had injured himself. He said he was struck by a batted ball during batting practice on March 5. A month later, the condition had only worsened.

He would mostly likely be out until May. It would not be easy to replace a five-time All Star, a .323 lifetime hitter. Hurting him worse, though, was the lack of a contract offer from the Red Sox.

"If they want me," he said, "then show me."

With Trot Nixon and Byung-Hyun Kim also injured, the 2004 season would start off with hurt feelings and question marks. The Sox now had Schilling and Foulke, but the Yankees now had Alex Rodriguez, the best player in the league, along with Gary Sheffield, Jeter, Posada, Giambi and the rest of their $200 million crew. Now matter what the Red Sox did, it seemed, they were no closer to beating those damn Yankees.

CHAPTER 54

Spring into Summer 2004

There may have been uncertainty surrounding the Red Sox as the 2004 regular season began, but the Red Sox Nation went into the season with an unprecedented optimism. Fueling that feeling was faith in owner John Henry, CEO Larry Lucchino, and especially GM Theo Epstein. Never before had there been an ownership team so dedicated to winning. Never before had the Red Sox management been so talented and bright. Would manager Terry Francona be able to handle the volatile personalities like Manny and Pedro and mold this group of players into a winning unit? Because Epstein had picked him, everyone naturally assumed he could.

THE SEASON SELLS OUT

The New England Patriots, winners of the Super Bowl, were popular, but the interest in football was nothing compared to the intense love of the Red Sox. Baseball ruled Boston, with 20,000 fans flocking to Fenway Park to buy season tickets. Sales were at an all-time high as almost every seat was sold for the season, including the $50 Monster seats atop the left field wall. The fans, knowledgeable and passionate, saw the acquisition of Curt Schilling and Keith Foulke as the keys to breaking the six-year string of Yankee division championships. Nothing could dissuade them of that. Nomar may have been on the DL, but the Sox had two talented fill-ins: Pokey Reese and Mark Bellhorn. And with Manny and David Ortiz hitting in the three and four slots, the fans were optimistic that the Sox would score a bushel of runs.

A pennant and World Series victory were within their grasp, the fans knew. As always, the New York Yankees, who had acquired high-priced veteran starters Kevin Brown, Javier Vasquez and Jon Lieber to replace Roger Clemens, Andy Pettitte and David Wells, and who would have Alex Rodriguez and Gary Sheffield in their star-studded lineup, stood in their way.

The Sox couldn't get through the first game of the 2004 season, a loss to Baltimore, before controversy reared its head. Pedro Martinez pitched six innings and then left the clubhouse before the end of the game without telling anyone. No biggie, except that in Boston, when the reporters get hold of a tidbit like that, it becomes a *big* story. Was Pedro disrespecting his manager? Was Francona weak because he said he didn't want to bother Pedro on his day off? Did Martinez do it because his contract was running out and he was feeling disrespected?

The next day the issue went away as Curt Schilling and Keith Foulke each contributed to a crisp 4–1 win over the Orioles. Foulke had been terrible in spring training. The whole time Terry Francona advised everyone to be patient. Foulke threw three innings of shutout ball.

In the third game Johnny Damon managed five hits in a 10–3 win over the Orioles. There had been concern over Damon's physical condition after his collision with Damian Jackson during the playoffs. He had returned and played against the Yankees, but he continued to suffer from migraine headaches for weeks. Adding to his discomfort was a sore left arm, caused when he was being jabbed with an IV needle when the ambulance in which was being taken to the hospital hit a bump. Though he played against the Yankees in the playoffs, his arm hurt so badly he could barely lift the bat. He batted .200 against the Yankees, driving in just one run and scoring once. When it was suggested that perhaps Pokey Reese should lead off and he be dropped to second in the order, Damon demurred.

He directed attention to himself by coming to camp in 2004 looking like Jesus Christ, with long hair and a bushy beard, but no one objected. Soon T-shirts would abound with WWJDD? (What would Johnny Damon Do?) It was just Johnny, the spark that fired the Red Sox run-scoring engine, being Johnny. In the same game in which he had five hits, he also made a sensational catch leaping above the centerfield wall to rob David Segui of a three-run homer.

The Tuesday after Easter, Damon attended a charity dinner hosted by Ben Affleck and *Saturday Night Live* regular Seth Meyers, who noted his Jesus-like appearance and asked him whether he could turn "clubhouse water into wine." Damon got a laugh when he replied that they were not gathered for the Last Supper.

The Sox lost their home opener 10–5 when Mike Timlin blew a lead in the eighth. The night before, Bobby Jones lost in the 13th when he walked four Orioles. The grumbling began, but just as quickly, Pedro and Schilling started, and the Sox beat Toronto in the latter game on Easter when David Ortiz hit a walk-off homer in the bottom of the 12th .

With their record at 4–4, the Red Sox hosted the Yankees. Before the first game of the series a convention of television trucks sat outside Fenway Park. Four hundred and fifty reporters attended. A life-sized statue of Ted Williams was unveiled outside Gate B.

"Reverse the Curse" T-shirts were almost as popular as the ones that said "Yankees Suck." In the first inning Alex Rodriguez grounded out to a chorus of boos, and in their half, Manny and Bill Mueller homered. The Sox won behind Tim Wakefield, 6–2. Said reporter Dan Shaughnessy with his usual sarcasm, "It's always easier beating these guys in April."

Curt Schilling then beat the Yankees 5–2 with the help of Manny's 350th home run off Mike Mussina. Rodriguez, pressing, went 0–4 for the second game in a row.

In the eighth inning Terry Francona walked out to the mound to remove Schilling, who growled at him. Francona asked for the ball as Schilling stood there stewing. It was a scene they had played out many times back in Philadelphia.

All of Boston was crowing until the Yankees ruined the mood by beating Derek Lowe 7–3. But the Sox won the series finale 5–4 against Kevin Brown in a Patriots Day thriller. The winning run was driven in by Gabe Kapler, who singled home Dave McCarty off Yankee reliever Tom Gordon. Kapler and McCarty were just two of Theo Epstein's smart grab-bag acquisitions.

Keith Foulke, who got the save, was helped by the running catch of Manny Ramirez, who grabbed a long fly by Bernie Williams as he crashed into the left field wall scoreboard.

After winning two of three games from the Blue Jays in Toronto, the Sox traveled to Yankee Stadium for three games. With Aaron Boone's ghost hovering over the stadium (along with the ghost of that fat guy wearing No. 3), the Red Sox proceeded to sweep the series. Derek Lowe won the opener against Jose Contreras, aided by an outstanding sliding catch by Johnny Damon on a Gary Sheffield line drive.

In the second game, Mark Bellhorn hit a sacrifice fly off Paul Quantrill in the 12th inning to beat the Yankees 3–2. All three runs scored on sacrifice flies. Four relievers—Scott Williamson, Alan Embree, Keith Foulke and Mike Timlin—held the Yankees hitless over the final six innings.

Then Pedro and Manny combined to beat the Yankees 2–0. It was the first series sweep against the Yankees since 1999. Pedro's four-hitter in seven innings helped propel the Sox to a 4½ game lead over New York. Manny's 20th home run off Javier Vasquez gave Pedro all he needed.

"I laugh when people say he's losing it," said Kevin Millar about Pedro. "This guy has three Cy Youngs. He knows his body. He knows how to pitch. That's why he's the best out there."

After the Red Sox took two out of three against the Devil Rays at Fenway, they completed the month of May with a 15–6 record, as the duo of Pedro and Schilling, with Foulke in the pen, did exactly what fans expected them to do. One month into the season, things were looking rosy as the Sox headed for Texas.

The opener was rained out. Breaking the era of Good Feeling, in the *Globe* that May day was a column in which Pedro Martinez said he would not negotiate his contract anymore that season. He would pitch, he said, but then he would sell his services to the highest bidder. Then he said, "I don't like people lying, trying to fake that they're signing us when they never made an effort to actually think about anything." He said he was upset the way Derek Lowe and Jason Varitek had been treated. They were the first words out of Pedro's mouth since spring training, and they took everyone by surprise. But because Pedro's record since joining the Sox was 104–29, he was immune from any front-office criticism. That left Dan Shaughnessy to express the opinion that Pedro's act was "growing old," commenting, "The Dominican Diva's diatribe is offensive on every level." Because Martinez wasn't talking to him, the evaluation would not cost him anything except a longer period before Pedro would talk to him again.

The Sox then lost five in a row: three in Texas, two in Cleveland. That was *not* supposed to happen. Pedro gave up six runs in an 8–5 loss, and then the Rangers scored three times in the seventh against Mark Malaska and Scott Williamson in a 4–3 loss. It was always a surprise when Texas won, but this team had more going for it than its predecessors, and Texas won the next night, 4–1, behind flame-throwing R. A. Dickey as the talk shifted to how much the Sox missed Nomar and Trot Nixon. The game ended with the bases loaded, two outs, and Cesar Crespo at bat. Texas closer Francisco Cordero got Crespo to fly out to end the game.

When Curt Schilling lost to Cleveland 2–1 at Jacobs Field, Johnny Damon was prompted to comment, "Any time this team loses four games in a row, there's something terribly wrong." Damon stood on third when the Sox made the final out of the game.

The next night, it got worse. After Derek Lowe gave up five unearned runs, the Indians led 7–2 going into the ninth, but then Damon hit a three-run home run, and the Sox added another to come up just short in a 7–6 loss.

After the game Terry Francona walked around the clubhouse, talking to players individually, smiling, telling everyone to stay positive. A win in the Cleveland finale settled everyone down.

GEORGE BLASTS LUCCHINO

Then on May 5, George Steinbrenner threw gasoline on the Red Sox–Yankee feud. Talking about Red Sox CEO Larry Lucchino in *Sports Illustrated*, he said, "I have nothing against him except I wouldn't want him in my foxhole." He accused Lucchino of running out on owner John Moores in San Diego. Steinbrenner said, "He ruined Eli Jacobs. He's not my kind of guy. Not a good man." Lucchino had already characterized the Yankees as "the Evil Empire." Steinbrenner, who almost always feels the need to have the last word, struck back, adding to the tension between the two teams. His remarks were also an indication that Lucchino and his boy genius Epstein were making him fearful that they would unseat his team as American League champions.

The Sox went home to Fenway to play another of the small-market, sad-sack teams, the Royals. Kansas City had a 6–2 lead, but then in the ninth the Sox caught up on Mark Bellhorn's home run. With Manny Ramirez on first after a walk, pinch hitter Jason Varitek hit a ball down into the right field corner. Manny hustled around second and third, as Juan Gonzalez threw the ball in to Desi Relaford, who threw home. Benito Santiago stood still, faking Ramirez while he waited for the ball to arrive, and at the last minute Manny slid home, safe with the game-winner.

Curt Schilling then overpowered Kansas City 9–1 in his first complete game of the year. He gave up five hits and struck out eight. The fans cheered every pitch.

Derek Lowe lost the next game when he walked the eight and nine batters, loading the bases in the sixth. Mark Malaska came in and allowed a bases-clearing double by Carlos Beltran. Lowe's ERA was over 5.00.

"Personally," said Lowe, "I'm disgusted with the way I pitched."

Byung-Hyun Kim pitched even worse against Cleveland the next night. The Sox played that game without Manny Ramirez, who had to go to Miami to be sworn in as a U.S. citizen. When he returned he kidded, "Now they can't kick me out of the country." As he took the field for the next game, Manny ran out carrying a little American flag. The Fenway PA system played "Proud to Be an American." Manny received a long standing ovation from the Boston fandom.

The Sox split games with Cleveland and Toronto, as the Yankees took over first place in the American League East on May 13. Johnny Damon, fearing the Sox would acquire center fielder Carlos Beltran from Kansas City, was feeling pressure to perform. He had put his house on the market during the winter in anticipation of his being traded. Damon figured the Red Sox would get Beltran to keep him out of the clutches of the Yankees. He envisioned a scenario where he or Beltran would shift to left, and Manny would DH, but he also pictured himself out of the picture. These were not good times for the Red Sox center fielder.

The Sox took two of three from Toronto and Tampa Bay before returning home. On May 21, Johnny Damon had his beard shaved off to launch a Gillette shaving system and to make money for ReadBoston, a literacy project for local children.

The Sox swept the Jays at Fenway, behind Bronson Arroyo, Pedro Martinez and Tim Wakefield. Johnny Damon got on base to lead off the game for the fifth game in a row. He scored twice and had two RBIs. Damon predicted that as soon as Nomar and Nixon returned, the team would catch fire.

On May 24, Nomar's name came up again. The inflamer, Dan Shaughnessy, wondered why Garciaparra was still out. Was he trying to send the Red Sox a message about his contract? Shaughnessy wrote. He also suggested that the Red Sox brass was asking the same question.

The next day third baseman Bill Mueller went on the 15-day DL to undergo arthroscopic surgery on his right knee. Kevin Youkilis, a rookie, took his place. Youkilis was coveted by Oakland A's general manager Billy Beane in the book *Moneyball* because of his high on-base percentage. Coincidentally, the A's came to town, and the Red Sox beat them 12–2 and 9–6 in the first two games. In the opener Youkilis reached base four times. Curt Schilling dominated. In the second game, Oakland rookie shortstop Bobby Crosby made an error that allowed four unearned runs. Jason Varitek broke the game open with a three-run home run. Derek Lowe pitched well enough to win.

At that point the Red Sox had a record of 28–17, and the team looked like a pennant winner. The pitching staff led the league in ERA. The team was averaging six runs a game. In the last nine games, the Sox had made just one error.

SUMMER SLUMP

Then on May 27, like the day the stock market crashed, the Sox stopped winning. The depression began with a 15–2 loss to Mark Mulder and the A's. Bronson Arroyo was hit for nine runs (six earned) in just three innings.

For the entire month of June and into July the Red Sox played sub-.500 ball (14–20) as everyone awaited the return of Nomar and Trot Nixon. The pitching was uneven after Pedro and Schilling, and the hitters were leaving too many runners on base. Taking the brunt of the criticism was manager Terry Francona. ESPN's Jeff Brantley chided Francona for leaving Derek Lowe in the game too long when the Orioles were pounding him into the dust. The Boston reporters also wanted to know why he left Bronson Arroyo in one batter too long in a game against the Angels. Also, Manny Ramirez loafed in a game, and the reporters wanted to know why Francona didn't punish him for it.

"Why are you staying so long with starters who are finished?" asked Shaughnessy. "Don't you know that He-Who-Must-Not-Be-Named [Grady Little] got fired for doing that with Pedro Martinez last October?"

To counter the Boston media pessimism, Johnny Damon, insisting the players continued to think positively, spoke up to defend his team.

"We feel we're a better team now than we were last year," he said. "We've got superstars on the shelf and yet we're battling and hanging in there. We haven't hit our stride yet. Our best baseball hasn't been played yet. That's the thing that gives us encouragement as we move on."

Nomar returned to the field of play on June 9, 2004, and in his debut at bat he acknowledged the standing ovation with a hand gesture to his heart. In his first at bat he hit a single through the shortstop hole on the second pitch. He started a double play in the second, but in the fifth made a short-hop throwing error that led to two San Diego runs. The Padres won 8–1. It wasn't what everyone was expecting.

The next evening Nomar drove in his first two runs of the season with a double high off the Monster. He helped Curt Schilling rout the Padres 9–3 in front of a full house at Fenway, which continued to cheer Nomar like a long-lost son. That Nomar was leading Derek Jeter in the All-Star balloting was proof of his popularity, despite his Achilles heel injury.

But even with Nomar in the lineup, the team didn't play any better, winning one and losing one as Tim Wakefield, Derek Lowe and Bronson Arroyo blew hot and then cold. Much of the talk radio criticism focused on Nomar, whom fans accused of dogging it out of pique after the aborted A-Rod trade. On June 17, Nomar was interviewed in the *Boston Herald*, where he complained about all the criticism headed his way.

"I can't win," Nomar said. "Twenty-one ABs [for Pawtucket] but no, 'You're faking it' and 'C'mon, what are you waiting for?' Then I come back, they are still going to say, 'See, he sucks. He's not good. You were bad last year, you're bad this year.' It's a no-win situation. They should just be glad I'm back."

To which Larry Lucchino went on WEEI and said he would have preferred it if Nomar had kept his mouth shut.

"I don't think that's what the team needs at this stage in the season," said Lucchino.

The Minnesota Twins visited Fenway toward the end of June for three games. Nomar hit a grand slam to help Curt Schilling win 9–2 in the opener, and after a 4–2 loss in a game in which Pokey Reese suffered a badly injured left thumb, the Sox lost 4–3 in ten innings—in front of the one hundredth straight sell-out at Fenway Park—on a throwing error during a difficult play by Garciaparra.

"We've played .500 ball for two months, and that's a disappointment," said Theo Epstein. "We still feel we have ways we can improve inside and outside this organization."

At this point the drama for the Red Sox was who would go and who would stay.

Johnny Damon received some good news when it was announced on June 24 that Carlos Beltran had been traded to the Houston Astros in a three-way deal. The A's got Houston closer Octavio Dotel. The A's GM Billy Beane, like Bill James, thought the A's could win without a proven closer. Like James, Beane was wrong about that. The Royals, heading down further, ended up with prospects.

The Red Sox were six full games behind the Yankees in the loss column when the Sox visited New York for three games at Yankee Stadium. In the opener Johnny Damon hit two home runs off Javier Vasquez, but Nomar made two costly errors and Derek Lowe's poor pitching allowed four stolen bases. The Red Sox lost 11–3 and fell 6½ games behind New York.

The next night brought a 4–2 loss in a game in which Nomar made yet another costly error. Dan Shaughnessy quoted basketball player Michael Ray Richardson, who once said, "The ship be sinking."

The Red Sox–Yankee finale became a contest that went down in history, in small part because Nomar Garciaparra didn't play and in a greater part because Derek Jeter, his Yankee counterpart, made one of the greatest plays in the history of the game. With the score tied in the 12th inning, Trot Nixon hit a foul pop-up into the third base stands. Jeter, running at full speed, threw himself over the railing and into the crowd as he went after the ball. After somehow catching it, he then mashed his body into the box seat railing. He returned to the field bleeding and cut. The Yankees won in the 13th, sending the Red Sox a full 8½ games behind the Yankees. In 17 games, Garciaparra was hitting .235 with nine RBIs. He committed five errors, including three against the Yankees.

Terry Francona boasted of Nomar's devotion, but on talk radio, Red Sox Nation was up in arms again. Shaughnessy called Francona "Mr. Hakuna Matata," blasting him for not making defensive substitutions in a timely manner. Then the next day Shaughnessy wrote an article saying it was ridiculous for Garciaparra to have sat on the bench against the Yankees, that Garciaparra was "damaged goods," and the Red Sox should trade him.

"One has to wonder why it always ends like this for Boston's star baseball players," Shaughnessy wrote. "Go back through time. Mo Vaughn. Roger Clemens. Mike Greenwell. Jim Rice. Bob Stanley. Wade Boggs. Bruce Hurst. Carlton Fisk. Fred Lynn. Rick Burleson. All home-grown stars who left the franchise spitting nails at the front office. Nomar Garciaparra played harder and was more popular than any of them. Ted Williams compared Nomar to Joe DiMaggio.

"Time for everybody to move on. Time for the Red Sox to trade Nomar."

But Theo Epstein had the last word, not Dan Shaughnessy, and the trading deadline would not arrive until the last day of July.

CHAPTER 55

We Say Good-bye to Nomar

The Red Sox won five of six games before the All-Star break. Johnny Damon had five hits in a game against Oakland at Fenway—a game in which Tim Wakefield gave up just three hits and no runs in seven innings in an 11–0 rout. Home runs by Mark Bellhorn and Nomar helped Pedro beat the A's 11–3 the next day. In the final game of the series, Damon came in all the way from first base a head-first slide to score the winning run on a double hit by Bill Mueller in the bottom of the ninth to sweep the A's 8–7.

"We got written off," said Damon, "but this team is much better than we've been playing, and we're going to show the world that we are."

In the very next game, Damon, out to prove he was the best lead-off hitter in the game, went five-for-six with a double and a homer against Texas in a 7–0 rout of the powerful Rangers. In four games, Damon had 14 hits. And over fourteen games, he was batting .448. Bronson Arroyo, who also had something to prove, threw a three-hit shutout.

The fifth win in the streak was a 14–6 rout of the Rangers. Derek Lowe allowed six unearned runs, but when your team scores 14, what difference does it make? Damon, Bellhorn, Garciaparra and Manny went 15-for-21 with 11 RBIs and 11 runs. Manny himself hit two long home runs in an impressive performance.

With one game to go before the All-Star Game, the Red Sox players wanted a sweep. They came close. With two outs in the ninth at Fenway, Damon on third, and the Sox trailing by a run, Mark Bellhorn struck out looking against

Rangers closer Francisco Cordero, leaving everyone disappointed going into the break as the loss dropped the Red Sox seven games behind the Yankees. Thanks to the wild card, which the Sox led over the A's by one game, no one went home unhappy.

But the game was not without controversy, the kind stirred up by the Boston press. Standing in the outfield before the game, Curt Schilling could be seen gesticulating at Manny Ramirez, who had asked out of the lineup with a sore hamstring. It was not the first time that Manny had asked out of the game before the All-Star break, and it appeared that Schilling was begging him to play. Manny pinch-hit in the ninth, popped out, and after the game hot-footed it to the All-Star Game. When Schilling refused to divulge what the conversation was about, the controversy died out.

The All-Star Game was played in Houston, and the Red Sox representatives, David Ortiz and Manny, both hit long home runs as the American League defeated the Nationals 9–4, the seventh straight American League win. The Houston Astros' Roger Clemens, the oldest starter at age forty-one, gave up six runs in the first inning, a record. Ramirez drove in the second and third runs with his homer after a hit by Ichiro Suzuki and a double by Ivan Rodriguez. Alfonso Soriano hit a three-run home run. Ortiz hit his home run off Carl Pavano.

SHAUGHNESSY STIRS THE POT

When the second half of the season began, Derek Lowe got hit hard again against the Angels in Anaheim. With a 7–9 record and a 5.67 ERA, Lowe was battered by the Angels, the Red Sox fans, and rotisserie owners all over America. After the game Dan "The Inciter" Shaughnessy questioned why Terry Francona didn't open with his best pitcher, Pedro, rather than Lowe. By not pitching Pedro, said Shaughnessy, he would not get a start against the Yankees when they visited Fenway at the end of the month. Francona disagreed, saying, "Every game is the same. We can beat the Yankees with whoever is pitching."

Pitching coach Dave Wallace volunteered that Pedro needed a rest this time of year and so he and Francona held him out an extra day. Wallace said that Shaughnessy was making too much of the Yankees series in late July.

"Our focus right now has to be putting the pitchers in the situation where we believe they can perform the best and wherever that falls, so be it," he said.

As the Red Sox were taking two out of three from the Angels, the Nomar-is-going-to-be-traded talk resurfaced with the news that the Chicago Cubs were unhappy with Alex Gonzalez and wanted Nomar badly. The Cubs said the trade would be made if the Red Sox could get Randy Johnson from Arizona in a three-way deal. Red Sox sources said that Johnson had a no-trade clause and only wanted to go to the Yankees or to a team in Los Angeles.

The final-game loss to the Mariners came after Bronson Arroyo pitched the best game of his career. He allowed three hits and struck out 12 in seven innings. The Mariners tied it in the ninth when Keith Foulke, leading 4–2, gave up a home run to Miguel Olivo and then another home run to Edgar Martinez.

The Sox' Curtis Leskanic pitched in the 11th. He gave up an infield hit, then walked Dave Hensen, who was bunting. Ichiro bunted them over, and so Francona had him walk Randy Winn intentionally. Bret Boone then drove a 0–1 pitch over the left field fence for a walk-off grand slam home run.

The next night the Red Sox won an equally gut-wrenching game, as Foulke struck out the side in the ninth, striking out Bret Boone, Edgar and the powerful rookie Bucky Jacobsen.

"My stomach was in my throat," said manager Terry Francona. "But I wouldn't trade that feeling for anything, not after a win like this."

The Red Sox headed home for three games against the Orioles before the Yankees paid a visit to Fenway. In the first game against the Birds, Pedro was hit hard, giving up eight runs in six innings, and Johnny Damon failed to catch two balls hit his way in a 10–5 shellacking. On Thursday, July 23, the two teams played a day-night doubleheader. The Sox lost the opener 8–3 in another poorly played game, but recovered in the nightcap to win 4–0 behind a superb pitching performance by Tim Wakefield. At the end of the day, Boston was nine full games behind the Yankees, who came to town and won the opener despite three home runs by Kevin Millar. After the Sox tied the game at 7, Alex Rodriguez drove in the winner with a single, moving the Yankees 9 games ahead of the Sox. In the last twelve weeks, the Sox were playing at a 37–38 clip.

Varitek Shoves A-Rod

If anyone thought the reports of bad blood between the two teams was PR, they only had to attend the game of July 24. The fireworks began in the third inning when, with two outs and the Sox trailing 3–0, Red Sox pitcher Bronson Arroyo threw a pitch that hit Alex Rodriguez in the left arm. Rodriguez, rather than trotting to first, began swearing at Arroyo, bringing out the Papa Bear instinct of catcher Jason Varitek, who advised him to shut up and go to first. A-Rod and Varitek each told the other what they could do to themselves, and then Rodriguez said the magic words: "Come on." When Varitek didn't take the bait, he said it again.

This time Varitek pushed his glove in Rodriguez's face and shoved A-Rod backward. The fight was on, and both dugouts emptied.

A lot of players gathered around A-Rod and Varitek. But near the Sox on-deck circle, the Yankees' Tanyon Sturtze grabbed the Red Sox' Gabe Kapler from behind. Kapler, one of the strongest men on either team, started punching Sturtze as first baseman David Ortiz and right fielder Trot Nixon ran over to help. Sturtze emerged bleeding near his left ear. In all, Rodriguez, Varitek, Kapler and Kenny Lofton, who tried to punch Arroyo in the back of the head, were thrown out of the game.

Aided by four Sox errors, the Yankees led 10–8 in the bottom of the ninth with Mariano Rivera on the mound in relief. Over the years Rivera had almost never blown a save, and had converted 23 save opportunities in a row. He had allowed just one home run all season. On that day, he gave up a second.

Nomar started it by doubling to left center. With one out, Kevin Millar, who had four hits on the day, scored Nomar with a single to right, making it 10–9. Bill Mueller then sent the Fenway Faithful into a state of ecstasy when he drove a long, game-winning home run into the bullpen in right center.

As Mueller crossed home plate, the entire team, including Varitek and Kapler, banished to the locker room, surrounded him to offer their congratulations. Terry Francona, who had been tossed out for arguing a play in the fifth, ran out onto the field barefoot to join the celebration.

"Twenty-four guys," said Mueller, "everybody at home. It's something you have to go through to experience."

"I hope we look back a while from now and we're saying that this brought us together," said Terry Francona. "I hope a long time from now we look back and say this did it."

A few days later, the league suspended Varitek and Rodriguez four games and fined them $2,000. Kapler, Nixon and Sturtze were suspended three games and fined $1,000. Curt Schilling, David Ortiz and Kenny Lofton got off with $500 slaps on the wrist. Ortiz had already appealed a five-game suspension for a tirade in Anaheim against the umpires.

Rodriguez said he thought the punishment too harsh. "I was on my way to first base," he said, "and I got punched in the mouth by a glove."

Terry Francona laughed at Rodriguez' account. "I'm not a lip reader, but I can read those lips," he said. "The word 'victim' wasn't coming out."

Kapler wondered why he was ejected and Sturtze wasn't.

"I saw that guy Sturtze choking the shit out of Gabe," said David Ortiz.

Francona agreed. "Gabe didn't do anything," he said.

The first game had ended 10–5 Yankees, the second 11–10 Red Sox. The rubber match was another high-scoring affair, with the Red Sox winning by the score of 9–6. A-Rod was booed every time he came to the plate by the packed Fenway crowd. The Sox led by 9–2, and the Yankees made it close when Mike Timlin gave up a grand slam home run to Hideki Matsui.

Johnny Damon, who homered, also made a big play in the first inning when he leaped high against the wall to rob Matsui of an extra-base hit. Damon went 3-for-5 with three RBIs.

"A LOT OF PEOPLE ARE GOING TO BE SAD"

After the game, Derek Lowe, who started and gave up 6 runs in the 6⅔ innings he pitched, complained that the writers had all but traded him.

"I was just trying to enjoy my last Yankees–Red Sox game as a Red Sox," Lowe said sarcastically, hoping desperately it wasn't true.

The Orioles were next, and Pedro won, but Schilling lost, as the 4:00 P.M. trade deadline neared. Derek Lowe predicted he'd be traded to Atlanta for Chipper Jones, Andruw Jones and Jaret Wright. The one trade rumor people paid attention to was the deal sending Nomar Garciaparra to the Cubs for pitcher Matt Clement and Alex Gonzalez.

In the end, Garciaparra, a Red Sox pillar for ten years, was traded to the Cubs, getting the news on the phone from Theo Epstein at 3:41 P.M. The players Theo Epstein got in return were shortstop Orlando Cabrera of the Montreal Expos and first baseman Doug Mientkiewicz from the Twins, two highly regarded players for both hitting and defense. If Boston had a weakness, it made too many errors, and this was the hole Epstein intended to remedy. Theo also got Dave Roberts, the fastest base runner in the game, from the Los Angeles Dodgers. At the time, nothing seemed to make up for the loss of Nomar.

"It was with mixed emotions that we let Nomar go," said Theo Epstein. "He's been one of the greatest Red Sox of all time."

"We just traded away Mr. Boston, a guy that meant so much to the city, and just like that, he's gone," said Johnny Damon. Manny Ramirez said that Nomar was the best hitter he had ever seen.

"They can take the shirt off my back, but they can't take away the memories I got," said Garciaparra, as he shook the hand of every newspaper reporter and headed out the door for Chicago. "They all know that every single day I went out there and I was proud to put that uniform on and what it represented."

"I think a lot of people in Boston are going to be sad," said Pedro Martinez.

Pedro was right. The editorial in the *Boston Globe* the next day blasted the deal, accusing Epstein of trading "one of the greatest players ever to put on the Red Sox uniform for a marginal upgrade." It predicted that Henry, Lucchino, and Epstein for the first time were challenging their popularity with their fan base.

But the *Globe*'s Dan Shaughnessy, whom the fans respected far more on the subject of the Red Sox than the nabobs of the editorial page, thought that Epstein had made exactly the right move.

"He had to go," he wrote. "He was more miserable than any athlete I have ever seen. In the Sox clubhouse he was as happy as Michael Moore at a Bush family reunion." Nomar, said Shaughnessy, was an angry athlete who wanted nothing to do with his teammates and nothing to do with the cause. He said that with Nomar gone, the other players could now move forward "working toward a common goal."

"The Red Sox traded a great player," he wrote. "But they have a chance to be a better team without him."

After Nomar left, Derek Lowe sat in the visitors clubhouse in Minneapolis in his street clothes, waiting for the other shoe to drop. After some time passed, and the game was about to start, Lowe was relieved that he would be a Red Sox the rest of the way.

"The fact that they ultimately decided to keep you for the stretch run," Lowe said, "is a sign of confidence that they believe in you and that you're going to help the team."

On the day of the Nomar trade, Epstein predicted that the primary beneficiary of the trade would be Derek Lowe, the ground ball pitcher with the high ERA.

He couldn't have known just how prescient he was.

CHAPTER 56

The Sox Catch Fire

The Nomar trade didn't start producing dividends immediately. For the next ten days the team played on the road, splitting two games in St. Petersburg against the improving but pitching-poor Devil Rays. Tim Wakefield won the opener 6–3, but in the second game Bronson Arroyo, leading by three runs in the seventh, gave up a grand slam home run to Rays catcher Toby Hall. The Sox still could have tied it in the ninth when Dave Roberts, running for Kevin Millar, tried to score from second with no outs. Roberts, stolen from the Dodgers by Theo Epstein, was perhaps the fastest base runner in the game. When Doug Mientkiewicz lined a single to center, Roberts seemed certain to score. But Rays center fielder Rocco Baldelli made the finest throw of his short career, gunning down Roberts at the plate on one hop. The throw reminded the loyal cadre of Devil Rays why they bothered to keep coming to games.

Mientkiewicz went to second and advanced to third on a ground out. After Gabe Kapler was hit by a pitch, Johnny Damon ended the game with a pop out to the Rays first baseman Tino Martinez.

"I feel like this loss is my responsibility," said Damon. "He gave me a good pitch to drive, and I hit it a mile up."

The Sox players could not believe they had lost to the Devil Rays.

"I thought we were going to win that game until the ball hit Martinez' glove," said Terry Francona. "I think everybody in our dugout did too."

The Red Sox had fallen 10½ games behind the Yankees when they traveled to Detroit to face another bad team. Derek Lowe lost the first game to the Tigers when he allowed a bases-loaded single by Carlos Pena. The Sox were hurt by the five-game suspension of David Ortiz, who was replaced in the lineup by Orlando Cabrera, who went 0 for 5 to drop his average to .095.

Millar Is Upset

Kevin Millar arrived in the clubhouse before the next game, looked at the lineup and threw a hissy fit when he saw his name wasn't on it. Since Doug Mientkiewicz had arrived seven games earlier, Millar hadn't played first base, his old position, once. Millar refused to accept Mientkiewicz as the everyday first baseman, not when in the last fourteen games, Millar had hit .469 with six homers and sixteen RBIs. Millar was so upset that David Ortiz couldn't stop him from venting to a small group of reporters.

"I'm not going to be lied to," Millar kept saying. "I didn't know they traded for him to be the everyday first baseman."

Then just 45 minutes before the game was to begin, Manny Ramirez announced that he had the flu and couldn't play, though he wasn't sick when he arrived for work. When Millar was inserted in Manny's place in left field, the reporters were quick to write that Manny had done it to support Millar. The players, who were aware Manny had a sore throat, weren't so certain.

The Sox had gone a desultory 43–43, and Millar was sure he knew one of the reasons why. Kevin Millar angrily blasted Terry Francona for not going with a set lineup—one with him in it.

It was time, all the Sox players knew, for them to step up. Millar got on base three times and drove in a run. Ortiz, back from suspension, hit clean up and drove in two runs. Pedro pitched beautifully, scattering five hits and allowing one run in a 7–4 victory.

The next day the charismatic Millar again played as the Sox beat Detroit, this time by 11–9. Millar apologized to Francona in a closed-door meeting. With the Sox going back to Boston for a ten-game homestand, spirits were high.

Cabrera Presses

The team, though, wasn't quite ready to jell, as Francona struggled to incorporate Cabrera, Mientkiewicz and Roberts into the mix. After a shocking series-opening loss to the Devil Rays in a game in which Tampa Bay hit three home runs and knocked Curt Schilling out in the sixth inning, the Sox fans were beginning to wonder if there was something inherently wrong with the structure of the team. One of their doubts surrounded Orlando Cabrera, a Golden Glove shortstop in the National League but a bust so far with the Sox. Had the infallible Theo Epstein made a mistake by trading Nomar for this guy? The Sox players knew better. They saw that Cabrera was pressing—that he was replacing Nomar Garciaparra was hard enough, but Cabrera was expected to play like him.

The Sox won the final three games of the Devil Rays series. Cabrera drove in a run during a five-run rally to win the first game, and then Derek Lowe and Kevin Millar combined to help win the second, 14–4. Millar, playing regularly, went 4 for 4, including a three-run home run in the first inning. In the finale Pedro pitched a shutout, walked no one and struck out 10, passing Bob Feller and Warren Spahn on the all-time strikeout list. Pedro upped his record to 13–4. He was 9–1 in his last fourteen starts.

"We're starting to jell right now," said Kevin Millar. "We're playing good baseball. And Pedro set the tone."

It was the Sox' seventh win in the last ten, prompting Dan Shaughnessy to switch from doom and gloom to dreams of glory, predicting that the Sox would be playing in late October.

The Red Sox, always unpredictable, responded by losing two ugly games to the Chicago White Sox, dropping them into a tie for the wild card with Anaheim and Texas.

The Blue Jays came to town. Going into the game, left-handed hitters had a .398 average against Jays pitcher Justin Miller, so Terry Francona inserted Doug Mientkiewicz at second base, the first time he ever played that position. The Sox won 8–4 behind Derek Lowe, who improved his record to 11–10. Five of the runs were driven in by Orlando Cabrera and Kevin Millar, right handers. So much for statistics. Keith Foulke pitched two sharp innings and earned his 20th save.

Cabrera heard the boo birds after making two errors. He continued to feel the pressure of having to replace a Boston icon, and he was having trouble making the adjustment. After the game Cabrera went to talk to David Ortiz and Pedro Martinez, who both advised him not to let the pressure get to him. Easier said than done, but the next evening Cabrera made the 35,105 fans at Fenway momentarily forget Nomar.

The Sox trailed 4–3 in the ninth against the Jays. Dave Roberts walked to lead off the inning, and he was forced at second by Johnny Damon. Cabrera stepped in against Justin Speier, the Toronto closer, and on a 1–1 pitch, he hit a walk-off home run over the Monster to win the game 5–4.

THE RED SOX EXPRESS

When Tim Wakefield beat the Jays 7–3 in the next game, helping the Sox sweep the series, the Sox were fifteen games above .500 and just one game off the pace set the year before.

The next day Theo Epstein tried to make a move that would have rocked Boston. The Astros put Roger Clemens on waivers, and Epstein claimed him. Then the Astros pulled him back. Was the Rocket trying to get back to the Yankees? We'll never know.

When the Sox hit the road, their winning ways continued with Orlando Cabrera leading the way with his brilliant infield play. After sweeping three games from the White Sox, bringing Boston within 5½ games of the Yankees, the Red Sox blew into Toronto, where they took three games out of four. They had won fifteen of their last nineteen games.

"We want to beat everybody," said Terry Francona. "At this time of year, we have to win games."

The Sox came home to Fenway and swept four from Detroit, as Bronson Arroyo, Derek Lowe and Tim Wakefield all pitched beautifully. Orlando Cabrera made spectacular plays, and Pedro, their ace, dominated. Only injuries to Manny, who fouled a ball off his knee, Bill Mueller, who suffered an injured right ankle and foot and Doug Mientkiewicz, who sprained his left shoulder, dampened the giddy mood. But Theo Epstein had traded to give the Sox depth, and their winning ways continued.

Manny, it turned out, would miss only one game. He returned for the Tiger finale and hit a two-run single to help give Wakefield his win. Maybe Manny had wanted to play in New York before, but it was clear to all that Manny was happy right where he was. And when Manny hit, the Red Sox won.

"No one may be safe," wrote Bob Hohler, "not even the Yankees."

The Anaheim Angels, the rivals for the wild-card spot, came to Fenway on August 31, and behind Curt Schilling and a three-run home run by Manny, the Sox won a slugfest, 10–7. Manny added another home run, giving him 383 for his career, as he passed Jim Rice on the all-time home run list.

"He's the baddest man in the game," said Kevin Millar about Manny.

Adding to the joy of the faithful that evening were the numbers on the hand-operated scoreboard in left field. The Yankees were playing the Cleveland Indians, and a cheer arose when a "6" was placed in the spot for the Indian total score, and another, louder cheer went up when the number grew to "9," and then after six innings the number became "16," until the end of the game when the scoreboard revealed the Indians had defeated the Yankees 22–0.

And so, on the first day of September, the Sox were only 3½ games behind the hated Yankees. In sixteen glorious days they had cut seven games from the New Yorkers' lead.

Curt Schilling's advice was to focus on the job at hand and not watch what the Yankees were doing.

The Sox beat the Angels 12–7 in the second game of the series behind the hitting of Johnny Damon, who had four hits. He ignited a four-run, first with an infield single, scoring on Mark Bellhorn's double in the left-center field gap. Damon also had a stolen base. The next day the Sox won their ninth game in a row, as Damon continued to star. He went 3 for 4, scored a run and knocked one in as the Sox won 4–3 behind a rejuvenated Derek Lowe. Orlando Cabrera and Dave Roberts contributed with spectacular defensive plays.

Texas, their other wild-card rival, came to Beantown, and the fun continued. Pedro shut out the Rangers 2–0, Boston's 10th straight win and its 80th of the season, to move them within 2½ games of the Yankees. Back in the Bronx, word filtered down that Yankee pitcher Kevin Brown had punched a wall in a loss to the Orioles and might be through for the season. There was also talk that Jason Giambi was suffering from a rare blood disorder—Red Sox fans were sure it was from steroid withdrawal—and didn't have the strength to play anymore. The Yankees seemed to be cracking under the Red Sox onslaught. The Sox win also increased their lead in the wild-card race over the Angels to 4½ games.

The Rangers ended the Sox ten-game winning streak on September 4, 2004, after Tim Wakefield reverted to early season form and allowed eight runs in seven innings. But the Yankees lost to the Orioles 7–0, and they remained only 2½ games back.

On a beautiful Sunday afternoon at Fenway Park, Curt Schilling handled the Rangers, pitching into the ninth inning with a 6–3 lead. With one out, Terry Francona walked to the mound and took him out to the boos of the faithful. Schilling tipped his cap on the way to the dugout and was cheered. Keith Foulke made it close, but helped Schilling win his 18th game, the most in the American League. After the game Schilling announced that his "splitter was back," a warning to the rest of the league. The Red Sox completed the homestand 9–1.

"I said this would be a good opportunity for us," said Francona, "and we took advantage of it."

It was on to Oakland to see if the Sox could eliminate the A's once and for all. It wasn't easy. Oakland not only was 16–4 of late, but at 45–20 had the best home record in baseball. Only the Red Sox at 34–16 had a better record than the A's since the All-Star break.

Johnny Damon, who had sprained his right pinkie, was not in the starting lineup. This was the fourth game Damon was forced to miss, and he wasn't very happy about it. Dave Roberts took his place.

Barry Zito did his best to hold off the Sox. Manny Ramirez and David Ortiz hit back-to-back home runs in the fourth, and Bronson Arroyo fought the A's to a 2–2 tie in the seventh. Then Orlando Cabrera singled and Bill Mueller and Dave Roberts doubled, and the Sox took the lead for good in an 8–3 win. David Ortiz hit a three-run double in the ninth to take the American League RBI lead with 122, tying the Orioles Miguel Tejada.

The next night Derek Lowe allowed just five hits and one run in 6⅔ innings, and Johnny Damon, back from his pinkie woes, hit a home run to lead off the game in a 7–1 win. The bullpen trio of Alan Embree, Mike Myers and Curtis Leskanic shut out the A's at the end.

Another night. Another win. Watch the Red Sox Express roar through the American League. With Pedro pitted against Tim Hudson, another of the A's Big Three, the Sox made short shrift in another lopsided win, this time by the score of 8–3. Pedro allowed just two hits in six innings to run his record to 16–5. By now the Sox were like Grantland Rice's old Notre Dame teams, a tornado wreaking havoc throughout the land. It was the Sox' 20th win in 22 games, the greatest stretch run in the entire history of the Red Sox.

"This shows we're for real," said Johnny Damon. "It shows everyone we're peaking at the right time: pitchers, defense and hitters."

CHAPTER 57

Wild-Card Winners

HAIR-RAISING

When Trot Nixon returned from the disabled list on September 8, 2004, he was sporting a Mohawk haircut. On the Yankees, he would have looked like a freak, Travis Bickle in pinstripes. On the Red Sox, he fit right in. Johnny Damon still looked like Jesus. Pedro had let his hair grow out into a jerri-curled Afro as a tribute to Dan Shaughnessy, a blond Irishman who had always worn his hair that way. Manny had also let his hair grow long. Mark Bellhorn looked like Vinny Barbarino in *Welcome Back, Kotter*. Bronson Arroyo grew blond cornrows, and Gabe Kapler and Kevin Miller were cue-ball bald. Nixon's Mohawk? Who noticed?

"That's who we are as a team," said Theo Epstein. "It's our personnel. We couldn't do it any other way. I mean, let's say we had a policy requiring haircuts and no facial hair. The benefits would be uniformity, discipline and perhaps a heightened sense of order. But we'd lose individuality, self-expression and fun. Given our personalities, our players thrive when they're allowed to be themselves and have fun."

Look no further for one of the secrets to the team's success.

Interestingly, when Curt Schilling first came to the Sox and noticed how sloppy the Red Sox players appeared as compared, say, to the Yankees, he was upset. Schilling, a rock-ribbed Republican, preferred the team polished in the image of Richard Nixon.

"The Yankees are all clean cut," said Kevin Millar. "When Schilling first came over here, he'd say, 'Look at them. They look like pros.' Over here, we're not. You see guys during BP wearing sleeveless shirts or parachute tops, no hat, game hat, red-and-blue hat. We look like sloppy, no-discipline dirtbags.

"I know Schilling didn't like it at first, but I like it. We're like a family. We don't worry about that small stuff. Johnny Damon's hair has nothing to do with how well he can hit. So who cares? We're a bunch of clowns, but when we compete, we're a team. Never mind all those rules. It's hard enough for this team just to get on the four o'clock bus."

THE IDIOTS

In 2003 "Cowboy Up" became the catchphrase. In 2004 the Sox were becoming known as "the renegades" or "the idiots," as Johnny Damon liked to call himself and the others. Whatever they were called, they were slowly becoming the best team in baseball, and everyone north of Hartford knew it. And fans everywhere else were slowly finding out.

The Sox flew to Seattle where they split a four-game series with the Mariners. They ran into two great pitching performances by rookie Bobby Madritsch and another young arm, Gil Meche, but Manny and David Ortiz hit back-to-back home runs to beat Ryan Franklin 13–2, and Bronson Arroyo shut out Seattle 9–0 to improve Boston's record to 30–9 since August 1. The win moved the Sox a full six games ahead of the disappearing Angels in the wild-card race. They continued to trail the Yankees by 2½ games.

With the lowly Orioles and Devil Rays coming to Fenway, postseason play seemed almost certain. With Pedro Martinez the starting pitcher in the first game back, the Sox were sure of victory. Opposing them was a twenty-year-old kid by the name of Scott Kazmir, the best young pitcher in the Mets organization whom the Mets had just traded to the Rays for Victor Zambrano. The Kazmir-for-Zambrano trade indicated the panic the Mets—a big-market team with no clue how to run a ball team—were in when they made the deal. Zambrano pitched once and went on the DL. On this day, the twenty-year-old Kazmir, the youngest player in the majors, gave up three harmless hits and no runs in six innings, as the Rays won 5–2.

The Red Sox made up for it the next two games as Mark Bellhorn and Kevin Millar homered in support of Tim Wakefield in a 8–6 win; and Curt Schilling won his 20th game, his seventh win in a row, in an 11–4 rout. Johnny Damon homered, and Millar hit the 100th home run of his career. Each drove in four runs.

Schilling had worried whether he would be able to pitch in Fenway Park. His 11–1 record indicated he most certainly could.

"He's done a great job making the adjustment to the American League," said Kevin Millar about Schilling. "He's been amazing."

The Yankees were up next. Here was the perfect opportunity to go into New York, sweep the three games and take the pennant against the Evil Empire, a team with a decimated pitching staff.

The series opener on Friday night, September 17, was by far the most memorable game of the 2004 season. If Theo Epstein and Larry Lucchino had written the script, they couldn't have made it more exciting and worthwhile.

The night was wet as the remnants of Hurricane Ivan swept past the five boroughs. Bronson Arroyo, slowly earning his place in the Sox rotation, faced Orlando Hernandez, who had single-handedly saved the Yankees season. Coming into the game, El Duque sported an 8–0 record. Hernandez, who left after three innings following a long rain delay, allowed one run on three hits, including a solo home run by Johnny Damon, his 17th of the season. Arroyo returned after the delay and went six innings, giving up two runs, the first on a fielder's choice, the second on John Olerud's home run leading off the fifth. The score might have been 3–1, but two pitches after Olerud's blast, Manny Ramirez made the finest catch of his career when he leaped above the left field wall to rob Miguel Cairo, a former Devil Ray, of a home run.

Tanyon Sturtze, another former Devil Ray, pitched three innings of shutout ball for the Yankees in relief.

The score remained 2–1 Yankees going into the ninth, and when Joe Torre brought in Mariano Rivera to close it, the Red Sox seemed doomed.

Trot Nixon opened the inning by drawing a walk. Dave Roberts ran for him. Roberts would turn out to be Francona's secret weapon. As Jason Varitek swung at strike three, Roberts, perhaps the fleetest Red Sox since Tris Speaker, easily stole second.

Rivera then hit Kevin Millar with a pitch. Gabe Kapler ran for Millar. Orlando Cabrera, who had twice been the Most Valuable Player of the Montreal Expos, then hit a clutch single to right field to score Roberts and tie the game. It was the second game in a row (July 24 was the other) that the Sox had solved Rivera in the ninth.

With Kapler on second and two outs, Johnny Damon was the batter. Damon hit a flare into right center to score the go-ahead run, and when Red Sox closer Keith Foulke polished off the Yankees, the Red Sox were most improbable winners.

One more win, and the Red Sox would be only half a game out in the division. They had struggled all season to get this far, and all of New England was rooting for a miracle. But in the long Red Sox tradition, they didn't get it, losing by the lopsided scores of 14–4 and 11–1 as Derek Lowe and Pedro were clobbered by the Yankees artillery, and Jon Lieber and Mike Mussina proved to everyone just how deep the Yankee pitching staff was. Two losses were all Dan Shaughnessy needed to invoke the ghost of Bobby Sprowl, one of the pitchers in the Boston Massacre of 1978.

With the Sox 4½ games out with only fourteen to play, Shaughnessy concluded, "The Red Sox' noble attempt to overtake and humiliate the Yankees in the first-place chase is just about over. The Nation will have to settle for beating these guys in the playoffs."

In the face of such negativism, Kevin Millar supplied the inspiration. "This race is nowhere near being over," he said. "This team doesn't get demoralized. This is the Sox. We keep our heads up."

CABRERA CLINCHES IT

The Sox flew home, only to absorb a third drubbing in a row, this one at the hands of the Orioles as Tim Wakefield was routed 9–6. But the Sox righted their ship and won 3–2 in a game in which Curt Schilling came within one pitch of getting his 21st win. When Javy Lopez hit a two-run homer, the O's took the lead in the ninth, but Kevin Youkilis walked, Bill Mueller doubled and Mark Bellhorn lined a two-out shot in the gap in right center to win the game.

The next night, Orlando Cabrera homered in the 12th to win it for the Sox, 7–6. Cabrera had flown home to Colombia to be with his ailing wife. She had begged him to stay an extra day, but he told her he had to go. His plane left Bogota, and when it landed at Logan Airport, he called Terry Francona and left a message that he was back and wanted to play. He took a limo to the ballpark, and he won the game.

When the winning run crossed the plate, Cabrera's teammates mobbed him. Orlando Cabrera didn't have Nomar's personality, but he sure could play. A Yankee loss narrowed the pennant gap to 3½ games.

The Sox lost the finale of the Orioles series 9–7, in a game that featured another poor outing from Derek Lowe and the bullpen. When the Yankees won, the chances for a Red Sox division title dimmed. With the Yankees coming to town for three games, only a sweep would do.

Unfortunately, the September 24 opener would be a replay of the ALCS seventh game fiasco that got manager Grady Little fired the year before. The pitcher on both occasions was Pedro Martinez, who, after throwing 101 pitches, took the mound in the eighth inning with a 4–3 lead. Johnny Damon, rewarded with a new Volvo for winning the 10th Man Award before the game, had homered off Tom Gordon to provide the Sox with the go-ahead run.

Hideki Matsui led off the eighth with a long home run to tie the game. Francona didn't take Pedro out. Bernie Williams, the next batter, doubled. Francona left him in. Ruben Sierra singled Williams home with the go-ahead run. Then Francona took him out of the game. The Sox lost 6–4.

Francona must have felt like he was back in Philadelphia when the 35,026 Sox Faithful booed him for leaving Pedro in too long—again. They were also booing him for pitching Byung-Hyun Kim, who inexplicably had lost ten miles per hour off his fastball in the ninth inning the night before.

The win lowered the Yankees magic number to 1. It would be Joe Torre's ninth time playing in the postseason in nine years of trying.

The next night, the Red Sox rewarded their fans with a 12–5 win over the Yankees that was a lot closer than the score indicated. The score was tied 5–5 in the eighth when Johnny Damon singled and Mark Bellhorn walked. Manny then drove in Damon, and Jason Varitek and Doug Mirabelli each drove in two runs. An Orlando Cabrera sacrifice fly scored a run, and Bill Mueller singled to drive in the seventh run of the inning.

Tim Wakefield, who hadn't won since August 29, started but didn't get the win.

In the series finale, the Sox again won big, knocking out Kevin Brown in an 11–4 victory. Brown pitched two-thirds of an inning, allowing six hits and four runs. The game featured some bad blood between Doug Mientkiewicz of the Red Sox and Kenny Lofton of the Yankees. They collided on a play at second, and they bad-mouthed each other for the rest of the game. Then Boston's Pedro Astacio threw a fastball behind Lofton's head, in case he wasn't angry enough. Astacio was tossed from the game. Yankee pitcher Brad Halsey was then ejected for throwing at Dave Roberts.

A resumption of the fun and games would have to wait until the playoffs.

With the regular season games against the Yankees at an end, the Red Sox flew to Tampa and then bused across the Howard Frankland Bridge to St. Petersburg to play the Devil Rays.

In the bottom of the third inning with the Rays leading 2–0, Bronson Arroyo hit Aubrey Huff with a pitch, and so in the top of the fourth Scott Kazmir, who was pitching a no-hitter, hit Manny Ramirez and Kevin Millar with pitches, causing Kazmir to get tossed from the game. With Kazmir gone, the Red Sox rolled up the score. Manny Ramirez hit his 43rd home run, a gargantuan shot high and deep over the outfield fence and three quarters of the way up the roof of the restaurant in center field. The ball traveled 458 feet.

Traveling with the team was a group of Johnny Damon fans who bore a sign reading, "What Would Johnny Do?" After the Sox defeated Tampa Bay 7–3, clinching the wild-card spot, there was only one thing for Johnny to do: celebrate with his teammates out on the field under the Tropicana Dome while the long-suffering Devil Rays fans slowly left the building.

With the cynical Boston press asking why the Sox were drinking champagne in the clubhouse when they had only clinched the wild-card berth, manager Terry Francona answered for all the players. "It's their right to do what they want," he said. "If they're excited to be in the playoffs, they have a right to be excited. That's OK. What's the big deal? They're happy to be in the wild card. What's wrong with that?"

Nothing was wrong with that, Terry. Absolutely nothing.

CHAPTER 58
The Playoffs: Hitting Bottom

THE SOX SWEEP THE ANGELS

The pairing for the first round of the American League championships pitted the Red Sox against the Anaheim Angels, and the New York Yankees against the Minnesota Twins. As far as Red Sox fans were concerned, the Angels were gnats to be swatted away. There was only one target that counted: the Yankees. If ever there was a team that could break Dan Shaughnessy's legendary Curse of the Bambino, it was this gang of rebels.

The first two games of the series were held in Anaheim, and in the opener, Curt Schilling polished off the Angels 9–3. His win lifted his career playoff record to 6–1, with a 1.74 ERA. Manny Ramirez supplied a lot of the power with a three-run home run and a first-inning double. Kevin Millar's home run was the key hit in a seven-run fourth inning.

"The guy's a horse," Millar said about Schilling. "He went out there and gave us a chance to win."

Pedro Martinez then went out against Bartolo Colon. His won-lost record pitching for the Red Sox was 117 and 34. He won 16 games in 2004 and led the league in strikeouts. But Pedro had lost his last four starts, giving up 20 runs in 23 innings, and on talk radio, the big question was whether the thirty-three-year-old Martinez still had it.

He did, pitching seven strong innings. Jason Varitek hit a two-run home run to tie the game 3–3 in the sixth, and with the score still tied in the seventh Johnny Damon hit into a fielder's choice, stole second and scored the Sox' fourth and go-ahead run on a sacrifice fly. Boston then broke the game open with four more in the ninth.

The series moved to Fenway, and it looked like Bronson Arroyo would complete the sweep with another lopsided win. He was breezing, 6–1, in the seventh when the roof caved in, and the Angels tied it up. Angels reliever Francisco Rodriguez kept the Angels in the game with 2⅔ innings of perfect relief. Keith Foulke and Derek Lowe did the same for the Sox. Lowe, the odd man out in the starting rotation, got out of the ninth with two outs and runners at the corners when he got Chone Figgins to ground to shortstop.

In the tenth, pinch runner Pokey Reese was on first with two outs and David Ortiz up. Angels manager Mike Scioscia decided to take out Rodriguez and bring in a left hander, Jarrod Washburn, who had started and had lost Game One.

In the Red Sox dugout, manager Terry Francona turned to Kevin Millar and asked, "Can he hit one here?"

The words had barely left his lips when Ortiz, a candidate for Most Valuable Player that year and the previous year, hit a slider high over the Monster to win the game and the series.

The next day the Yankees eliminated the Twins 6–5 in an eleven-inning thriller. A-Rod won it all by himself as he doubled, stole third and scored on a wild pitch by Kyle Lohse.

Three in a Row Lost

The stage was set. Red Sox against Yankees. Let the games begin. The single most burning question: can the Red Sox—finally—win the World Series? The players and fans were sick of the hats worn by New Yorkers with "1918" on them, sick of hearing about Bucky Dent and Bill Buckner and Aaron Boone, sick of having to listen to old relatives moan about wanting to see a Red Sox World Series win before they die.

Curt Schilling and Theo Epstein were promising to break The Curse. Now it was time to deliver. But before the game Schilling was being treated for a sore ankle. Could he pitch with the pain? Red Sox fans feared the worse, as history had taught them.

The opener was played at Yankee Stadium, and while Mike Mussina was pitching a perfect game into the seventh inning, Schilling allowed six runs in only three innings of work. It was the Red Sox fans' worst nightmare. When Tim Wakefield gave up two more runs, the 8–0 lead caused a lot of TV sets to be clicked off in New England.

Everyone should have kept watching. Mussina couldn't get out of the seventh. Mark Bellhorn doubled to center, and David Ortiz singled. Kevin Millar doubled to left for two runs and went to third on a passed ball. Trot Nixon singled Millar home.

Joe Torre brought in Tanyon Sturtze. Jason Varitek, who had not hit a home run in Yankee Stadium all year long, homered to make it 8–5.

Torre brought Tom Gordon in to pitch the eighth, and David Ortiz hit a two-run triple to make it 8–7. Unfortunately, that was as close as the Sox got. The Yankees scored two runs off Mike Timlin to make it 10–7, and Mariano Rivera came in to close it out. But instead of the Yankees going home with a blowout, they left knowing they had been in a war.

After the game the speculation centered on Schilling's torn ankle ligament. Was he going to need an operation immediately? Would he be able to pitch again? Would he be any good if he did pitch? Was he going to have to retire? Would his leg fall off completely? A lot of Red Sox fans thought the worst. Old timers remembered when Ted Williams was hit in the elbow right before the 1946 season ended and hit 5 for 25 with one RBI in the series against the Cardinals. They remembered that Jim Rice was hit by Vern Ruhle and couldn't play in the 1975 World Series. Anything was possible.

"It's a cruel world," said Theo Epstein. He wasn't getting an argument.

In Game Two, Jon Lieber, who was supposed to be one of the Yankees' second-tier pitchers, held the Sox to three hits in seven innings, while Pedro Martinez allowed a two-run home run by John Olerud to beat him. Pedro had jokingly referred to the Yankees as his "daddy" after a particularly painful loss, and here the Sox' best pitcher had lost to them again. The curtain was coming down on the season after a 3–1 defeat, and all of New England was beginning to prepare for the funeral.

The series moved on to Boston with the news that Curt Schilling's ankle was too sore for him to pitch as scheduled in Game Five. The big pitcher, the club said, couldn't even throw in the bullpen. What the Red Sox needed was time, and time is exactly what they got when rain postponed Game Three, a sure sign that the Sox' luck was turning in their favor.

The Red Sox faithful had barely settled in when the Yankees began pounding the home team into submission. Bronson Arroyo gave up six runs before he was lifted in the third inning. Terry Francona brought in Tim Wakefield to try to hold the score down, but the Yankees scored seven more runs for a total of 13 by the fourth inning. Four Yankee home runs, two by Hideki Matsui, and one each by Alex Rodriguez and Gary Sheffield, left the Red Sox 19–8 losers. By the time the Sox batted in the eighth, Fenway was almost half empty.

The Sox were down three games to none. No team in baseball history had ever come back from a three-game deficit. No team had ever been down by three games after losing 19–8. There was only one more humiliation to suffer: the ultimate one. A sweep.

After the game Terry Francona, always optimistic, offered some hope.

"I think we have to try and keep it simple," he said. "We'll show up tomorrow and our only goal is to win tomorrow. If you start looking ahead, it starts to look a little daunting." It was the understatement of the year.

"We'll show up and play tomorrow," he said. "We're not done yet."

Red Sox fans were sure they'd show up. The winning part was far more daunting. Had the future ever looked more bleak? Those Red Sox ghosts of seasons past—the Babe, Bucky, Buckner and Boone—were howling louder than ever.

CHAPTER 59

Miracle of
the Century

If ever the Boston fandom and media were angry, frustrated and depressed, the day after the 19–8 loss in the third game of the ALCS was it. Bob Ryan characterized the Sox as having laid "a brontosaurus egg."

"Soon it will be over," Ryan predicted, "and we will spend another dreary winter lamenting this and lamenting that. Sure, you can root for the National League team to defeat the Yankees, but just exactly how satisfying is that going to be?"

"How much more can New Englanders take?" asked Dan Shaughnessy. "For the 86th consecutive autumn, the Red Sox are not going to win the World Series. . . . Mercy."

Jeffrey Lyons: "We were visiting friends in Western Massachusetts the night the Sox lost 19–8. A Red Sox official invited me to go to Fenway. But I had really lost faith. I didn't want to drive across Massachusetts three-and-a-half hours to watch the Yankees clinch at Fenway at one o'clock in the morning in 40-degree weather.

"So I went home instead."

Despite the pessimism, the Red Sox still were alive—barely. No team in baseball history had ever come back from being down three games to none. Before Game Four at Fenway, Johnny Damon gave his teammates a talking to, telling them that there was no pressure, nothing to lose.

Terry Francona started Derek Lowe against Orlando Hernandez and the Yankee machine. In the press box, Peter Gammons noted that the first five hitters in the Yankee lineup had a lifetime batting average over .350 against Lowe.

Richard Hershenson: "At that point I thought the season mostly likely was over. I told my friend Charlie that if they could come back, it would be amazing, but I don't think I really believed it myself."

The Yankees took a 2–0 lead in the third inning on a long home run by Alex Rodriguez.

Shaun Kelly: "I have a ten-year-old boy, Max, who lives and dies with the Red Sox. After they were down 3–0 in games and were losing in the fourth game, it was time for him to go to bed because the games ran so late. I said to him, 'Sweetheart, the Red Sox are going to lose this game tonight, but they've had a great, glorious season. You should be proud of how well they did and always be loyal and support the Red Sox.'

"I said that for two reasons: it's exactly what my mother always said to me, so literally it was being passed down. Number two, we live in Greenwich, Connecticut, Yankee country, so he takes a lot of grief for wearing his Red Sox shirts and his Red Sox hat. I thought, I have to prepare this kid for a bad eventuality.

"He smiled at me and said, 'This hurts, but I will.'

"You saw on the television the expression the Sox fans had at Fenway: one of preparation for the absolute worst that could happen. We had that expression at home watching on TV. You love this team and you want to believe, but by reflex almost, you are thinking, how can they get through this? Because the odds are that no other team in the history of baseball has done it. So the odds are against them, and you have the history."

The Sox came back and took the lead with three runs in the fifth, including a two-run double by David Ortiz.

Lowe left with one out in the sixth and a 3–2 lead. The Fenway fans booed lustily when Francona brought in Mike Timlin, and they booed even louder when Timlin couldn't retire any of the five batters he faced, as the Yankees took a 4–3 lead.

Francona, as desperate as a manager could be, brought in closer Keith Foulke in the seventh, and Foulke held the Yankees scoreless. When the Sox batted in the bottom of the ninth, the Sox were still a run down with Mariano Rivera facing them on the mound.

With the end of the season three outs away, Rivera did the one thing a relief pitcher doesn't want to do: he walked leadoff batter Kevin Millar, who was replaced on first base by Dave Roberts. Even though the Yankees knew what he was going to do, Roberts managed to steal second on Rivera and catcher

Jorge Posada. When Bill Mueller singled up the middle, the score was tied, and the season extended.

Doug Mientkiewicz batted for Mark Bellhorn, and he bunted Mueller over to second. Johnny Damon hit a slow roller to first that was mishandled by Tony Clark, and the Sox had runners on the corners. Orlando Cabrera was the batter, and this time Rivera was his old self, throwing an unhittable fastball past him for strike three.

The game went into extra innings. Alan Embree and Curtis Leskanic pitched shutout ball through 12. In the bottom of the 12th, the Yankees were down to Paul Quantrill, who had pitched so many innings for Joe Torre in 2004 that almost every time he went in late in the season, he was batting practice. On this night it would be no exception.

With Manny Ramirez on first, David Ortiz got up at 1:22 in the morning and hit a laser shot into the right field stands to end the five-hour marathon and keep Red Sox hopes alive. Ortiz was mobbed by his teammates and saluted lustily by the fans at Fenway, though the bliss was modulated a little by the knowledge that the Yankees still held a three-to-one lead in games.

Jeffrey Lyons: "I watched Game Four at home with my wife. We watched it there, and it got later and later, and the karma started to kick in. Ortiz hit the home run, and at the end of the game, it was, 'Dare I hope?'"

Shaun Kelly: "After the Sox came back and won, I couldn't wait to wake Max up the next morning and tell him, 'Guess what? David Ortiz'—who happened to be Max's favorite player—'hit a home run, and we actually have another game to play.'

"In the morning I told him, and he said, 'Dad, how do you think they're going to do?'

"'You know what?' I said. 'If you take it one game at a time, if somehow we can win tonight's game—and I'm not very optimistic—but if we can get to Game Six, Curt Schilling is going to get us through it, and then you never know about Game Seven.'"

One miracle by Ortiz would not be enough, but perhaps two miracles would be. Game Two, which began on the same day Game One ended, was a game for the ages. Pedro Martinez wasn't sharp, and after Derek Jeter hit a double with the bases loaded in the sixth, the Yankees led 4–2.

The redoubtable Ortiz, who was released by the Twins after the 2001 season, hit a home run in the bottom of the eighth off Tom Gordon to close the gap to 4–3. Gordon, once the closer for the Red Sox and now the Yankees' set-up man for Mariano Rivera, walked Kevin Millar. Terry Francona, seeing an opening, sent Dave Roberts to run for him. Gordon knew Roberts was in the game to steal second, and so he kept throwing over to first, and Roberts kept diving back in. Eventually, Roberts knew, Gordon would have to throw a pitch homeward. When he finally did so, Roberts ran. Gordon was so distracted that he threw a hittable pitch to Trot Nixon, who singled to center, sending the fleet Roberts to third.

Joe Torre brought in Mariano Rivera, who had blown seven saves to the Red Sox in the regular season during his career, and one the night before in the playoffs. For the second time in two games, Rivera gave up the tying run as Jason Varitek hit a long fly ball to center that scored Roberts.

The game remained tied for five more excruciating innings. The Sox had a chance to score in the 11th. With runners on second and third, Johnny Damon came to bat against Paul Quantrill. Damon, attempting to bunt on the first pitch from Quantrill, popped the ball up for out number one. Torre brought in Esteban Loaiza to pitch to Orlando Cabrera, and Cabrera hit into an inning-ending double play.

The Yankees almost scored in the 13th, when Jason Varitek played "grab the soap" with Tim Wakefield's knuckleball. He allowed three passed balls—two that let Hideki Matsui reach second and then third, and one that allowed Gary Sheffield to reach first base after striking out. But Wakefield struck out Ruben Sierra, and Varitek held onto strike three, ending the nightmare.

The Sox' 14th began when Johnny Damon was walked with one out by Esteban Loaiza, one of the best pitchers in the American League in 2003, but a bust in 2004 for the Yankees, who got him midseason in a deal with the White Sox for Jose Contreras, another expensive bust. With two outs, Loaiza walked Manny Ramirez, moving Damon into scoring position.

David Ortiz batted next. In the five games, he had already driven in nine runs, and after working the count to 2–2, Ortiz fouled off five consecutive pitches, building the suspense and tiring Loaiza. On the next pitch, Ortiz muscled a pitch into center field, driving in Damon, who scored the winning run. For the second night in a row, an exhausted and exhilarated Beantown experienced a euphoria and joy Sox fans never could have anticipated.

"This has been so much more than I imagined it to be," said Curt Schilling, the Game Six pitcher, after the game. "I've never seen anything like this. It's never over in these games until you get the last out. It's just something special."

After the game, Red Sox fans milled outside of Fenway Park, calling out, "Papi," David Ortiz' nickname, and chanting the perennial crowd favorite, "Yankees suck!" Police in riot-control gear broke up the gathering late into the night. No one in New England got sleep. No one lost hope. "Papi" had done it twice. No team had ever come back from 3–0, but these were Johnny Damon's gang of "idiots," and with these wild and crazy guys, anything was possible.

Mark Starr: My birthday is on October 18. That was the day the Sox won two games against the Yankees in the playoffs, one at 1:00 A.M. to kick off my birthday, and one at 11:00 P.M. to close out my birthday. One in twelve innings, one in fourteen innings. That's when I began to think maybe we're talking kismet.

"The first of the two games was a great game, 12 innings, an Ortiz walkoff home run, but you sort of thought you were just playing for dignity. It was fun, exciting, kind of a relief not to be humiliated in a Yankee sweep, and it was a dramatic game that ended in a rally against Mariano Rivera.

"Only as the fifth game unfolded, the longest game in playoff history, did you begin to feel yourself being lured back in. 'If we just . . .'"

"That was a rainout game rescheduled for 4:00 P.M. I said to my brother, 'We'll eat afterwards.' That seemed reasonable for a baseball game. We'd eat at 8:30, 9:00 at the outside.

"At 11:00, I told him, 'I'm glad we decided to eat afterwards, because frankly, if I had had anything in my stomach, I would have thrown it up.'

"Game Five was the single most miserable—until the end—tense, excruciating watching experience. There were actually fans around us, real fans, not faux fans, leaving, because they said, 'I just can't take it anymore.'

"It was so tense. That game had a passed ball on a strikeout. Varitek couldn't hold onto Wakefield's knuckler. There were always runners on third for us, and for them, with less than two out. It was past fun. The tension you could feel everywhere. It was palpable in your gut. This was physically excruciating to watch."

Shaun Kelly: "During Game Five, I had to put Max to bed because it was so late. I said, 'Now listen, be prepared for a loss, but you never know.'

"'Dad,' he said, 'would you please wake me up if they win?'

"'Sure,' I said. So when Ortiz drove in the game winner, I whispered in his ear, 'The Sox won, and David Ortiz got the single to win it.'

"'Alllll riiiiiight,' he said, and he turned over and went to sleep.

"I knew it registered with him, because the next day when he came down for breakfast, he said, 'I can't believe they won. That's just tremendous.'"

Game Six featured the styling of Curt Schilling, the pitcher who was supposed to be too hurt to pitch. The problem in medical terms was that Schilling's peroneal tendons, which run across the back of the ankle, had ruptured, allowing the tendon to slip out of its groove and drift above the ankle. When Schilling pitched, it hurt like hell because the tendon snapped against the bone.

He couldn't have the recommended reconstructive surgery because the recuperation time was three months. As a stop-gap solution Red Sox medical director Bill Morgan recommended that the skin around the dislocated tendon be sutured down to the deep tendon, creating a makeshift sheath that would hold the tendon in place.

It sounded like a great idea, but there was one problem: no one, including Dr. Morgan, had ever done it before, so Morgan decided to practice first on cadavers. He didn't reveal whether any of them had been old Red Sox fans.

In a sterile back room of Fenway Park the day before the game, Dr. Morgan and three assistants secretly stitched up Schilling's ankle. The next day the

Red Sox ace went out in front of a hostile Yankee Stadium crowd and allowed just four hits in seven innings as the Sox won 4–2 to tie the series at three games apiece.

Schilling retired the first eight Yankees hitters he faced. After Jason Varitek drove in Kevin Millar with the first run, the number-nine batter, Mark Bellhorn, hit a three-run home run to left off Jon Lieber, who hadn't lost since August 20. The ball flew into the bleachers, hit a fan right in the gut, and bounced back onto the field. The umpires at first ruled the hit a ground-rule double, but Fox TV was right on it, and there was no question that it was a home run. The unofficial scorers gave the fan a big E for not catching the ball.

The Sox led 4–0 when, with one out, Bernie Williams homered in the seventh. Schilling overpowered the next two batters and retired for the night. Schilling's courage would go down in history. Red Sox fans would never forget the image of the blood on Schilling's right sock. Gabe Kapler met the big pitcher at the top dugout step and gave him a bear hug.

Bronson Arroyo pitched the eighth and allowed a quick run on a double by Miguel Cairo and a single by Derek Jeter to make the score 4–2. The next batter, Alex Rodriguez, hit a bouncer between first and the pitcher's mound. Arroyo fielded it and went up the first base line to tag Rodriguez, who deliberately slapped at the ball, sending it rolling down the right-field line. The first base umpire called Rodriguez safe, and all of Red Sox–dom began howling at the injustice. Was this how the hated Yankees were going to steal the pennant? Was this a variation on the Bill Buckner play? Would this be the cruelest blow of them all?

Terry Francona ran out to cry bloody murder, and the umpires, who had convened on Bellhorn's hit and changed it from a double to a home run, caucused again and called A-Rod out for interference. Red Sox observers would contend that Rodriguez' act of slapping the ball out of Arroyo's glove was an act of unsportsmanlike desperation, akin to George W. Bush attacking Massachusetts candidate John Kerry's war record during the 2004 elections. For most of New England, it was enough that at least one injustice was rectified.

Keith Foulke pitched the ninth, and he did his best to give New England *agita*. He walked Hideki Matsui and Ruben Sierra, and with two outs he ran the count on Tony Clark to 3–2. Then he threw him a pitch away, and Clark took it for strike three to end the game.

And so the Sox had come back from a 3–0 deficit to tie the series at three games apiece.

Jeffrey Lyons: "When we returned to the Stadium, the '1918' hats, which are now collectors' items, were everywhere. But as the Sox kept winning, they just became invincible. And it was impossible to believe."

Would this be another version of 2003, when the Sox reached the final game, only to be denied by a home run by Aaron Boone, who didn't even make it back to New York in 2004? No, Boone decided to play some basketball during the off-season, and he tore his knee up badly enough to miss the entire 2004 season—which is why the Yankees went out and acquired A-Rod. Shades of Wally Pipp, who got sick and let Lou Gehrig take his place one day—another *big* mistake.

Rich Hershenson: "What Curt Schilling did was not only great, but inspiring. Nevertheless, I couldn't help feel the old, familiar dread that the Sox would go into Game Seven and lose like they did the year before."

Mark Starr: "In football we don't really know why a player will come out of a game, but after Curt pitched in Game Six, there was such a visible mark, and it clearly redefined the meaning of a Red Sock in a certain bloody fashion. It upped the ante for all those gritty plays, and was such an antithetical to the notion of guys who sit out with a hangnail. What he did was pretty remarkable."

The Yankees made another big mistake: showing up for Game Seven, which was held at Yankee Stadium in front of a sold-out crowd of very nervous Yankees fans. All season long, critics had said the Yankees would have trouble winning the 2004 pennant after losing Roger Clemens, Andy Pettitte and David Wells. But Yankee general manager Brian Cashman, spending George Steinbrenner's money as fast as the Boss could make it, was able to sign free agents Kevin Brown and Jon Lieber, and trade for Javier Vasquez, Montreal's best pitcher. Up until Game Seven on October 20, 2004, the patched-up Yankee rotation had been solid.

Mark Starr: "Through the years, my feeling about Derek Lowe was that he always was a question mark emotionally. He was a strange combination of a jittery, jumpy guy and a guy who also had a track record as a big-game pitcher. Last year in Oakland he came into one of the toughest situations I've ever seen and threw two of the best pitches I have ever seen. Remarkable pitches! He'd already come in, in relief and won the deciding game against the A's. I can't say I felt great about him, because he never had much luck against the Yankees, but I didn't think disaster was preordained.

"One of the reasons Theo made the changes he did, including trading Nomar, was to support the infield defense behind Lowe. With Lowe, give them less outs. There were so many thoughts running through my mind about that seventh game that, when Lowe crossed it, he was one of a maze of thoughts.

"First I had to decide whether to go. History says you're going to end up at midnight in the Bronx depressed on the D train, that it will end up an unhappy ordeal. But in the end I decided to go on the chance it wasn't going to end up that way. I never would forgive myself if I missed it.

"The game was in New York, a funny town. I went with my brother. We grabbed an early dinner in midtown. We were dressed for a football game. It was pretty cold. We were in New York, and we were asked, 'Are you going to the theater?' Well, in Boston nobody would have any doubt where you were going. You might be going to theater. They have theater in Boston, too. But no one would make that as their first assumption. We rode the D train to the stadium."

ESPN's Peter Gammons called it "the biggest game the sport has ever seen." In what appeared to be an attempt by the Yankees to end the Red Sox string of victories, the Yankees brought out Bucky Dent to throw out the ceremonial first pitch.

Joe Torre started grizzled veteran Kevin Brown, who, despite his prickly personality, had led Texas, Florida, San Diego, and Los Angeles to stellar seasons. Brown had arm trouble in 2003, but still finished the season with a 14–9 record and a 2.39 ERA for the Dodgers before signing with the Yankees. Brown had remained healthy in 2004, but when he punched the wall and broke his left hand in September, he fell out of favor with Yankees management.

His performance against the Red Sox in the seventh game didn't make them like him any better. Johnny Damon opened the Sox first with a single to center, and then stole second. Manny Ramirez singled to left, and Damon flew home, only to be thrown out at the plate by Hideki Matsui. David Ortiz then hit a long home run to right field to make the score 2–0.

Derek Lowe started for the Sox. Francona had yanked him from the rotation earlier in the playoffs, but his masterful performance in Game Four got him back in the manager's good graces.

Lowe retired the side in the first, striking out Gary Sheffield to end the inning.

With one out in the Sox second, Kevin Millar singled. When Brown walked Bill Mueller and Orlando Cabrera to load the bases, Joe Torre gave Brown the quick hook, replacing him with Javier Vasquez, who had won 14 games before the All-Star break, but who was batting practice most of the time afterward.

Johnny Damon, who came into the game hitting .103 for the series, was the batter. With runners dancing off every base, Vasquez threw one pitch—a meatball—and Damon pulled it over the low wall in right field to give the Sox a 6–0 lead. The players in the Boston dugout celebrated Damon's grand slam with great glee, while the vast majority of the 55,000 fans in Yankee Stadium sat on their hands and wondered what had gone so wrong.

The pessimistic-by-nature Red Sox fans couldn't help but wonder if Lowe would give it all back in the third when Lowe hit Cairo with an errant sinkerball, let him steal second and then gave up his first hit, a single to Derek Jeter. Francona got Mike Myers and Curtis Leskanic up in the pen, but Lowe finished the inning with no further damage.

In the fourth, Damon got up again with a runner on base, and he hit his second home run off Vasquez into the upper deck in right, upping the Sox lead to 8–1. After a couple walks, Torre took Vasquez out and brought in Esteban Loaiza. As Vasquez walked dejectedly to the dugout, the Yankees fans booed loudly.

Lowe pitched six masterful innings, perhaps his best effort of the year.

"He was so special tonight," said Terry Francona after the game.

Shaun Kelly: "Game Seven was a blowout, but it ran late, and Max was exhausted, and I put him to bed before it was over.

"'They're not going to blow this one,' I said. 'They won,' and we gave each other a big high five.'

Francona brought Pedro Martinez in to pitch the seventh, and he allowed two meaningless runs.

Jeffrey Lyons: "I guess when Johnny Damon hit the grand slam in the seventh game, I really allowed myself to feel that it was in the bag. There was never a moment in that game when I thought, 'Uh oh.' But I did get nervous when Pedro came in to pitch, and he started to blow it. There was no reason for him to come in and pitch. None. Luckily, they were so many runs ahead, I began to say, 'They *can't* blow it.' Until then, if you're a Red Sox fan, you don't have faith until there are two outs in the ninth and you have an 11-run lead."

Rich Hershenson: "I was watching with friends, and it was great, but I was very restrained because there was always the chance things could turn around, especially when they brought in Pedro Martinez in relief. It just seemed like one of the stupidest moves ever to put him in. When he came in, it was like he was pitching batting practice. A bunch of us were watching, and some of the fans were half kidding: 'This is going to be the worst collapse ever.' I was very concerned. He gave up a couple of runs, and it was like a nightmare. Miraculously, he got them out, and thank goodness, after one inning Francona took him out. When Timlin came in, it was back to relatively normal."

Mark Bellhorn homered in the eighth, and Mike Timlin and Alan Embree finished off the Yankees—for good. The 10–3 Red Sox victory would go down in Sox history as its most important—ever. Though The Curse is about the Sox' inability to win the World Series, any Red Sox fan would have been content to lose the Series and beat the Yankees in such a fashion.

"How many times can you honestly say you have a chance to shock the world?" asked Kevin Millar after the game. "It might happen once in your life, or it may never happen. But we had that chance, and we did it. It's an amazing storybook."

"How can this not be one of the greatest comebacks in the history of sports?" asked John Henry.

Bob Ryan spoke for everyone when he wrote, "I am trying to digest the fact that I have just seen the greatest team in the 101-year history of postseason baseball as we know it. A team that fell behind, three games to none, has come back to win a postseason series. That team is the Boston Red Sox, and the team they have just victimized is the New York Yankees."

Mark Starr: "After the final out, the Red Sox fans stayed and celebrated in the ballpark a long time. During the seventh game at Yankee Stadium, most of the Yankee fans were very cordial and respectful. Partly because there was no controversy, no tension. It was a rout, and I think they knew they had seen something amazing, whether they liked it or not. They were very gracious. A lot of people came over to us, shook our hands, wished us well.

"When we got back to midtown Manhattan, it was late, and we were too jazzed up to sleep, so we went and had a drink. We sat at the bar of one of those bars in a deli. The woman bartender said, 'What have you guys been doing?' We told her we were at the ballgame.

"'Oh yeah?' she said, 'Who won?' I tried to think of a bartender in Boston who wouldn't have known who had won. It's a different city. It's not that they don't love the Yankees or that they're not passionate, but it doesn't consume the whole town.

"Beating the Yankees was the *whole* thing. The rest was gravy. When the World Series is over, it's over, whether you win or lose. The earlier rounds keep the fun going. You get to enjoy another whole week or two. And in the World Series, you are playing some team you have nothing against. The St. Louis Cardinals? What have they ever done to us? The fact that St. Louis beat us in '67, which I can remember, or in '46, which I know about because I've been told about it enough, doesn't quite resonate like what we've endured from the Yankees. In the playoffs, you're playing teams from your league that have performed indignities on you. The Yankees have performed more indignities on us than everyone put together. To beat the Yankees, I can tell you, obviously it was a great, fantastic moment. It was merciful it was a rout."

Shaun Kelly: "In all my years of following sports, you could say the Red Sox down three games to nothing going into the last inning against the greatest relief pitcher in the history of baseball would be about as dead in the water as any team you could imagine. Coming back to win that series was even greater than the Islanders coming back from three games to none, because in hockey you can ride a great goaltender. In baseball, there are so many more variables. In baseball, you have different pitchers going for you, and we had pitchers like Tim Wakefield, or even Curtis Leskanic, pitching inning after inning giving up no runs. When one of these guys would come in, I would have the same reaction as when the Sox brought in Steve Crawford in the American League Championship Series in 1986 to try to close out that dramatic game in Anaheim that we ended up winning. Crawford on the mound? Oh, no. And against the Yankees we had five pitchers like that in three games, and you say, 'Dear God, how are we going to get through this?'

"And after we won, you start talking to other Red Sox fans, and they recount all those little moments, 'How about that Tony Clark double that bounced into the stands?' 'How about the Dave Roberts stolen base?' 'How about 'Tek somehow holding onto Wakefield's third strike to not get the runner from third in?'

"In the ninth inning, there was a knock at my door. It was Jeff DeTeso, my next door neighbor and a close friend. Jeff is a diehard Yankee fan, though he is the son of a diehard Red Sox fan. He's a teacher. He was a catcher at Williams College, so he loves the game. He was a little upset that the Yankees were going to lose, but he said, 'You guys have been unbelievable. I know how much this means to my dad. You and he have been waiting all these years. This is tremendous and congratulations.'

"I thanked him, and that was the first thing I told Max the next day, because I wanted him to know that sportsmanship should be a part of who you are.

"'When you see Jeff,' I told Max, 'make sure you say, "Nice series."' Which Max did.

"When they beat the Yankees, my reaction basically was one of disbelief. 'My God, they have actually done it.' But so many of us were so emotionally drained, so tired, it was almost like running in a marathon, and you get to the finish line and win, and you say, 'Oh my goodness, I've won,' and you just want to sit down and catch your breath. When it finally sunk in, I said to myself, 'My God, we beat the Yankees, and how we beat them!' Over the next day or two it grew on me more and more, so that by the time the World Series came, I fully realized what we had done."

Jeffrey Lyons: "As Joe Castiglione said in his call to end the seventh game, 'Can you believe it?' I don't. I still don't believe it. I just think it was one of the great moments—it was the only open void in my life which has remained open and has not been filled. And now it's filled. If they never win another game, I won't care. Had they beaten Minnesota instead of the Yankees, or had they tied the series at two games to two and then won, that would have been nice, but this was out of a bad novel, something that has never been seen before and will never be seen again.

"I don't believe it. I *still* don't believe it.

"Do you know that the Yankees have not won in this century? Do you know that there are four-year-old kids running around who have never seen the Yankees win a World Series?

"I wish I had been a better winner. During the World Series I tormented my colleague Maurice Dubois, who has always been arrogant about the Yankees.

I would send him esoteric, unimportant statistics. 'Do you know that Trot Nixon hits .318 when he swings at the first pitch, but hits .305 when he swings at the second pitch?' As the winter went on, I began sending him catalogs of Red Sox souvenirs, with offers to buy a gold-plated set of Red Sox baseball cards or a Red Sox plate. Makes a nice gift. On the Internet I found a T-shirt. On the front it says, 'Yankees Choke.' On the back it says, 'Biggest Collapse in Sports History.' I told him, "This will make a nice stocking stuffer." The more junk I get, the more I'm going to send him. It's just been great.

"I'm ashamed of myself for not being as good a winner as I thought I should be. But no, I'm not *real* ashamed."

CHAPTER 60

The Curse
Is Broken

After defeating the Yankees, the Red Sox players sat back the next night and watched two former Red Sox pitchers, Roger Clemens of Houston and Jeff Suppan of St. Louis, battle for the 2004 National League pennant. Both pitched well, but Suppan pitched better. A run-scoring double by Albert Pujols and a long home run by Scott Rolen propelled the Cardinals into the World Series against the Red Sox.

The Cardinals knew of the Red Sox Curse, but all they could think of was that the Redbirds, winners of 105 games in 2004, hadn't been to the World Series for 17 long years, when the Cards met the Minnesota Twins in 1987. Red Sox fans not only didn't care about the St. Louis draught, as far as the players and their manic over-the-top fans were concerned, the Cardinals, which featured a hard-hitting line up with Edgar Renteria, Albert Pujols, Jim Edmonds, Reggie Sanders, Larry Walker and Scott Rolen, were there to be steamrolled.

The 2004 World Series opened in Fenway Park. Tim Wakefield, making his first start since October 1, was unable to hold leads of 4–0 and 7–2, and didn't make it through the fourth inning.

A series of Red Sox fielding miscues tied the score at 9–9 in the eighth. Kevin Millar threw one ball away, Bronson Arroyo made a bad throw, and then Manny Ramirez made two errors in a row: he overran Renteria's ground ball single, allowing a runner to score. Then Larry Walker hit a routine fly ball to Manny, who caught his spike in the grass and fell down as the ball fell behind him. The run, which never should have scored, tied the game. In the dugout the bench players were laughing hard at Manny's misadventures, despite the importance of the ballgame.

After all, Manny's two errors could have led to disaster. It was bad enough that they had caused Keith Foulke to get a blown save. With the game tied 9–9, with one on and two out in the eighth, the dangerous Jim Edmonds was up. Foulke threw a called strike three past Edmonds with the bases loaded. Arguably it was the most important pitch of the series.

In the Red Sox half of the eighth inning, a Jason Varitek hit should have been a single—it was ruled an error—that Cards shortstop Edgar Renteria couldn't handle. Then Mark Bellhorn hit a home run against the foul pole to make the score 11–9 and save Manny from becoming the goat.

"That's what teammates are for," said Ramirez. "To pick you up."

"The thing you love about this team," said Johnny Damon, "is that everybody recognizes we didn't have a good night in the field, and we went out and everyone pitched in a different way."

Shaun Kelly: "I went to Game One, and that was a real kick. It was a World Series I never expected to attend. I parked my car in Woodland, my old T stop, for good luck. It was four or five hours before the game, and the T was jam-packed. You'd have thought the game was going to start in forty-five minutes.

"There was a man standing on the train with me, bleary-eyed, and he had an overnight bag with him.

"'Where are you coming from?' I asked him, thinking he might say 'Worcester.' He said, 'Guam.'

"'Guam?' I said.

"'Ten minutes before the Red Sox beat the Yankees in the seventh game, I called my travel agent,' he said. 'I'm a bond trader in Guam, but I'm originally from Tolland, Connecticut. I had some vacation time coming, and I made reservations. I've been on a plane for 36 hours.'

"He didn't have tickets, but he wanted to stand outside Fenway Park when they played in the Series. He brought a radio for the play-by-play, and he could hear the crowd noise.

"'If they somehow win it,' he said, 'I want to be there for the parade.'

"And then I arrived at the ballpark, and I waited in the will-call line for my ticket. I had just finished teaching Doris Kearns Goodwin's *Wait Till Next Year* to my class, and who should be right behind me in line but Doris Kearns Goodwin. We had a nice talk.

"'What do you think?' I asked her.

"'You know what?' she said. 'Next year is this year.'

"'I believe so too,' I said.

"'We're going to go crazy, aren't we?' she asked.

"The game started. I began the game sitting in the new section in right field under the Budweiser sign. It was so cold though, that we moved into the minority owners' box. I ended up sitting next to George Mitchell, the former senator from Maine who helped John Henry buy the team. When Manny made that second error, Senator Mitchell reacted just like any Sox fan. He got up and started pacing very quickly up and down the back of the skybox area. When they got the last out, he had a look of relief. When Bellhorn hit the home run to win, he threw his hands up and shouted, 'Yes. Yes.'

"I said to the guy on the other side of me, 'Last year we would have lost this game because we wouldn't have been able to come back. This year it doesn't matter. The Sox come back.'"

Before his start for Game Two, Curt Schilling felt pain in his ankle caused by one of the four temporary sutures, and until he saw Dr. Bill Morgan, he didn't think he would be able to pitch. But Dr. Morgan understood the problem and undid the suture that was causing Schilling pain. Schilling felt immediate relief, and he went out in 48 degree weather and shut down the Cardinals 6–2, despite four more Red Sox fielding blunders, three by Bill Mueller. Only one team ever made more errors in a Series—the 1982 Brewers, who made eleven. But with a 2–0 lead in games, no one, not the players nor the fans, cared. This was a team of destiny, and everyone knew it.

In the eighth Keith Foulke struck out Jim Edmonds, who swung weakly at strike three. Foulke then retired the side in the ninth, the thirteenth game in a row he pitched without allowing a run.

In Game Three Jason Varitek hit a two-run triple in the first, and Mark Bellhorn, hitting ninth, hit a two-run double to the base of the wall in centerfield in the fourth. Orlando Cabrera, batting second behind Damon, drove in the other two runs in the sixth.

The only sad part about the game was that the Series was moving on to St. Louis for the next three games. The expected two Sox wins at Busch Stadium meant that was probably the final home game of the 2004 season for the Fenway faithful. The rest of the series, everyone was sure, would have to be watched on TV.

After the game the Red Sox players voted player shares, and in one of the most gracious acts, they awarded Nomar Garciaparra a three-quarter share. The generosity of the Sox players was a measure of their teamwork and sense of team. They awarded shares of the $5 million pie to just about anyone who contributed during the season.

"Anyone who spills their blood in the field out there one time helping a club win a ballgame deserves as much as anyone else in my opinion," said Trot Nixon.

Shaun Kelly: "I had been driving back from Boston to Greenwich listening to WEEI, and there was speculation Schilling wouldn't be able to go, so I was relieved just to see him on the mound. I was checking out his stuff the first couple of innings, and I thought he could go five or six, and I'm thinking,

'Who from the bullpen can come in and shut them down?' And once the Sox scored the sixth run, a fairly sizable margin, you're thinking, 'We could be up two games to nothing.' But there was also a part of me that said, 'Gee, we were up two games to nothing against the Mets in 1986, and we were coming back home then.' But then I said, 'But that team was very different from this team.' Which is true. But you can't dismiss history completely. So it did cross my mind."

Pedro Martinez started Game Three against 16-game winner Jeff Suppan. In what probably was Pedro's final start in a Red Sox uniform, he reminded everyone of his top-of-the-rotation stature by pitching seven innings of three-hit (two infield hits and a double by Edgar Renteria), shutout ball, as the Red Sox won their seventh game in a row with a 4–1 win over the Cardinals. Pedro retired the last fourteen batters he faced.

Manny Ramirez gave the Sox a 1–0 lead when he hit a line drive home run over the left field wall in the first inning with two outs. Ramirez hit safely in all 13 postseason games. Only Hank Bauer and Derek Jeter—each at 17—have done better.

The Sox caught two breaks from some horrendous base running by the Cardinals. The first came with the bases loaded in the first inning. Jim Edmonds flew out to Manny in shallow left with one out, and Larry Walker foolishly decided that Manny didn't have it in him to throw him out. Wrong. Manny made a perfect throw to end the threat and the inning.

Then, in the third with runners on second and third and nobody out, Terry Francona had the Sox play the infield back, conceding a run on a ground ball. When Larry Walker hit a grounder to second, Jeff Suppan, the runner on third, started for home and then changed his mind and stopped in no-man's-land about a third of the way down the line. Walker threw to David Ortiz at first to nip the batter, and when Ortiz saw Suppan hanging out to dry, he whipped the ball over to Bill Mueller at third. Mueller was able to tag Suppan before he was able to dive back to the bag—just more proof that pitchers should never hit or run the bases.

After that play, Pedro didn't allow another base runner. He struck out three of the last four batters he faced, including Pujols, Edmonds and Reggie Sanders. Mike Timlin pitched the eighth, and after Keith Foulke gave up a long home run to Larry Walker in the ninth, he struck out Scott Rolen looking to end it.

When the game ended, everyone surrounded Pedro and hugged him.

"My heart is with Boston," said Martinez. "I consider Boston my house. I just hope everything works out OK."

So did we, Pedro. So did we.

Shaun Kelly: "After the Suppan incident at third base, I turned to my son Max, and I said, 'Remember, Jeff Suppan came from the Red Sox farm system. It looks like he got the right kind of training from the Red Sox in terms of base running skills, because in forty-two years of following the team, what you saw is what I've seen over and over again over the years.' Max laughed.

"'But we have a different ownership now,' I said. 'A different team now.'

"I went into the final game thinking that DeLo would pitch a very good game. I thought that would be the night, though you always have a little doubt. What if they lose tonight? I did the math. 'It's not going to happen.' The Cards were starting Jason Marquis? In 1967 they had Bob Gibson. The Sox were the Little Engine That Could that year. But you had Bob Gibson in '67, and the Sox had Gary Waslewski in Game Six. Are you kidding me? It was a miracle they made it to Game Seven. But Marquis wasn't Bob Gibson. The way I looked at it, they were going to win. It was inevitable."

Was there any doubt the Sox would take Game Four and sweep? Not if you ask anyone after the fact. "I knew it all along." Yeah, right. Anytime it rains, Red Sox fans have become so used to seeing a half-empty glass that they fear a second coming of the Flood. I suspect not many would have predicted that Derek Lowe would throw a three-hit shutout for seven innings to win the fourth and final game of the 100th World Series for the Red Sox—the first World Series win for Boston since 1918, in case anyone needs to be reminded. Lowe completed one of the great performances in postseason history. To recap: he won the deciding game against Anaheim in relief; he won Game Seven against the Yankees, allowing only one run; he pitched shutout ball to win Game Four of the World Series.

Lowe was staked to a 1–0 lead on Johnny Damon's lead-off home run. Trot Nixon drove in the other two runs with a bases-loaded double in the third.

After the 3–0 win, Lowe did a perfect imitation of Red Auerbach, lighting up a cigar and smiling that I-beat-you-again smile. Lowe didn't have to remind anyone that he had been banished to the bullpen at the end of the regular season. He had pitched in relief to the Angels finale because he was odd man out in the rotation.

"That's just an incredible thing," said John Henry about Lowe's remarkable turnaround.

Relief pitchers Bronson Arroyo, Alan Embree, and Keith Foulke pitched the eighth and ninth and finished the job. For the record, Edgar Renteria hit a comebacker to Foulke, who ran toward first and underhanded the ball to first baseman Doug Mientkiewicz for the final out.

In the series, the Cardinals batted .190. Scott Rolen, the clean-up hitter, went 0 for 15.

After just three years of enlightened front office stewardship by John Henry, Larry Lucchino, and Theo Epstein, all their hard work was rewarded when the Sox defeated the Cardinals by the score of 3–0 to sweep the four-game world championship.

Mark Starr: "The World Series was anticlimactic, and it was a relief that the Series went smoothly, because I felt I didn't need any more drama or tension."

Richard Hershenson: "Each game was surprising when they won, especially how easily they did it. I'm sure other people were more delirious than I was when the Sox won the Series. I was trying to take it in stride, to be philosophical, especially since the way things went last year and having been to Game Seven of the 1986 World Series when the Red Sox got ahead 3 to 0, and my friend Charlie and I turned to each other and said in unison, 'It's not enough.' There was a certain amount of ongoing pessimism that continued even through their great victory. What's good, all those famous blunders, Pesky and Buckner, and the stupid decision in the seventh game of the Cincinnati World Series in 1975, it was nice to wipe those out."

The eight Red Sox playoff wins in a row set a record that will probably never be equaled. For two weeks the gang of "idiots" transformed New England into the sports capital of the world. In 2004 the Boston Red Sox were the world champions. Life in New England no longer would be the same. This time, they got the girl—the other guy didn't. They got the promotion—the other guy didn't. They won the lottery—the other guy didn't.

And when Red Sox fans in the future travel to stadiums around the country, the "1918" caps and the taunts of "Bucky Dent" or "Bill Buckner" will ring hollow. Bucky who? Who cares? Bill who? Doesn't matter.

"History starts today" became the battle cry. The Red Sox had done it. Red Sox fans, like Humphrey Bogart, will always have Paris.

Jeffrey Lyons: "I don't care how cold it gets this winter, I hope it never ends. I want the feeling to last a *long* time. It's the first time I ever experienced a winter like this. I didn't want the feeling to go, and it hasn't. I will never hear those taunts of '1918' or 'Bucky Dent' or 'Bill Buckner' again, and if I do, anyone who says that is stupid. And I will allow any Yankee fan to hyphenate 'world champion.' If you want, you can, as in World-Champion Boston Red Sox. Now anything is possible. Now anything is possible."

Mark Starr: "The curse of the Bambino is buried. Absolutely buried."

Shaun Kelly: "There wasn't pressure before Game Four, though I was pacing, but that was just because my team was in the World Series.

"When we got to the seventh inning, Derek Lowe was still on the mound. I have a complicated relationship with Derek Lowe. I really believe in his stuff. If he believed in his stuff as much as I did, he'd be one of the two or three top pitchers in baseball. There are stretches, especially two years ago, when no one was better, but you never knew when those stretches would come.

"You could read his body language. What I saw in Game Seven against the Yankees and Game Four against St. Louis was the great Derek Lowe.

"I thought, 'Terry, couldn't you have left him in through eight and brought in Foulke in the ninth?' But God bless, Alan Embree came in—I was nervous because with Embree and Mike Timlin, as gutsy and as much heart as they have—you never know exactly what you are going to get. But Embree was impeccable.

"So when we got to the ninth inning, and the Red Sox had the bases loaded with no outs, and we didn't score, I thought, 'Nothing is going to be easy.' But then in the bottom of the ninth, here it is, Pujols singled. I'm thinking, 'God, please don't let them come back.' Then Gabe Kapler caught a fly ball to right field that was medium deep, and I thought, 'One down.' Edmunds came up. He hadn't done a thing, and Foulke basically blew him away, and when he got strike three, I stood up. I thought, 'My God, I have to take this all in. Here it is.'

"Foulke made only two pitches to Renteria. He hit an easy one-hopper to Foulke, and as soon as Foulke caught the ball, I started jumping up and down. Max was with me, and he started jumping up and down. I must have jumped up and down for a minute.

"As I said to my wife, I haven't done anything in my life since 1962 that I've kept on doing except breathing, eating, and following the Red Sox. Everything else has changed in my life.

"I needed to let off steam, so I ran out of my house. I didn't know what to do. I was in Greenwich, Yankee country. If I had been home in Boston, plenty of people would have been outside. When I ran out the door, I was greeted by Dave Avitable, a Yankee fan, one of my best friends. He's a volunteer fireman, and he was coming back home, and he had the game on the radio, and he said, 'I have to drive over to Kelly's house and be there when they win it.' He gave me a hug and said, 'You guys did it.'

"The next day one of the reporters called the Red Sox to get a quote from one of the team officials. He called the switchboard, and the operator answered, 'Good morning, World Championship Red Sox.' And they both started to laugh. When someone said to me, 'Congratulations to the World Championship Red Sox,' I almost lost my lunch. My God. The two phrases 'World Championship' and 'Red Sox' just do not go hand in hand.

"But it has taken me very little time to get used to the title.

"This whole story was never about ghosts that never existed. It was never about Babe Ruth or Johnny Pesky or Bill Buckner. It was always about those ghosts in our own lives, who took us to our first ballgame, the baseball coach who taught us to bat like Tony C. Our aunt or grandfather who wore Red Sox hats and seemed to support them through thick and thin. A very powerful, profound string connects us to the whole game.

"And you go to that ballpark, the same ballpark where they sat and rooted for the same team with the same kind of passion, and they're all gone now, and you realize that what you were rooting for was a team that had a lot of ghosts, but none of them were ballplayers. They were all those fans who have now departed. And so going into that game we were all thinking, 'They can do it!'"

Karen Starr: "The day after the Sox won the World Series, I was sitting at the breakfast table looking for my newspaper, and I said, 'Mark, where's the paper?'

"'I'm taking it,' Mark said.

"'Where are you going with it?' I asked.

"'I'm going to the cemetery.'

"'Why are you taking the newspaper to the cemetery?'

"'I'm going to visit my father,' he said.

"And you're taking it because?...'

"'Well,' he said, 'Do you think he'd believe me if I just told him. He has to see it.'

"Coincidentally, Janet Ginns, who was a friend of Mark's father, who lives in Philadelphia, was in town, and she decided to stop at the cemetery and pay Mark's father a visit. When she got there, she said, there was that day's *Boston Globe* sitting at his grave site."

CHAPTER 61

The Ball

On the final play of the 2004 World Series, Cardinals shortstop Edgar Renteria hit a ground ball that was fielded by Red Sox reliever Keith Foulke, who trotted toward first base and tossed the ball to Doug Mientkiewicz, a late-inning replacement at first base.

After catching the ball, which he held in his fist, he raised his right index finger in triumph before joining the pile of joyous teammates. After the celebration, he looked into his glove and saw the ball. He had forgotten about it. In the locker room he gave it to his wife Jodi.

The next day in the Fenway Park offices, Major League Baseball authenticated the ball in front of Boston Red Sox president Larry Lucchino.

"I swear on my son's life—if he would have asked for it, I would have handed it to him right there," said Mientkiewicz.

On that same day the baseball that Barry Bonds hit for his 700th home run was sold at auction online for $804,129. Mientkiewicz, a back up who had come to the Red Sox on July 31 from the Twins, placed the historic relic in a safety deposit box.

In January of 2005 Lucchino complained that the ball belonged to the team, not Mientkiewicz, and he demanded that Mientkiewicz hand it over to the team.

"This is a gray area as to what players think they can take with them," said Lucchino.

Mientkiewicz refused.

Lucchino, who didn't like to be told no, responded by deriding Mientkiewicz, referring to him as a "rent-a-player." He then traded him to the New York Mets. Two years later as Mientkiewicz was being carried off the field after a collision at home plate, a fan yelled, "Quick, somebody get the ball while he's unconscious."

He would never be allowed to forget that he still had that ball.

The Red Sox, unwilling to let the issue die, sued Mientkiewicz, prompting the two sides to agree that he would donate it to the baseball Hall of Fame.

Mientkiewicz later was asked to give advice to a Chicago Cubs player if he were to catch the final out of winning the World Series, something the Cubs haven't done since 1908.

"Catch the ball, take it out of your glove, drop it on the ground and run to the pile to celebrate with your teammates," Mientkiewicz said.

"Or just tell them your dog ate it."

CHAPTER 62

Lucchino and Epstein Battle for Control

The wait for Red Sox fans to witness a World Series victory went on for eighty-six interminable years, but to listen to Sox fans, it was worth it. One pundit said it was "the best year here since the Pilgrims hit Plymouth Rock." On opening day fan Jack Leddy, who was attending his twenty-sixth consecutive opening day, said, "A holy day of obligation, but yeah, this year is heavenly." Said another joyous fan, John Faieta, discussing the comeback from 3–0 to the Yankees and the subsequent World Series sweep of the Cardinals, "People are still reveling in it."

Amy Branson: "[The Game 4 win over the Cardinals] was the pivotal moment of your life. You remember where you were when it happened. It's like the JFK assassination."

"This year it's a whole different world," said long-time fan Mike Longley.
Never again would Sox fans see themselves as lovable losers. The dreaded curse of The Bambino had been broken, never to surface again. In future seasons under the ownership of John Henry the Red Sox fans would usually go into a season with confidence—sometimes even arrogance—knowing their team would be—at least on paper—as good as any team in the division.
The slumped shoulders were a thing of the past. Replacing them would be a swagger in the step, a chest-thumping knowledge that their Red Sox were as good as anyone.
A new day in New England had dawned.

Adding to their joy was the announcement in March of 2005 that the Sox owners would refurbish Fenway Park, rather than tear it down. For years the former owners had complained that Fenway was old and run-down, that they needed a new, fancy ballpark to be competitive. In 2000 the Sox had floated a proposal to build a new park. Under the proposal the Red Sox would have ponied up $352 for construction. In addition the state of Massachusetts was to kick in $412 million for construction and infrastructure improvements, and the city of Boston was to add another $212.5 million. Boston Mayor Thomas Menino was all for it. The city council, however, voted it down, to the relief of the millions of Sox fans who cherished the history and the tradition of Fenway Park.

There had been an alternate plan: to rebuild the grandstands and build a second tier atop the Green Monster. These Monster seats would be among the best in the house. The cost would be about $180 million, and it could be done between seasons.

This was the plan adopted by John Henry and Larry Lucchino.

That summer the Red Sox owners filed an application with the National Parks Service to have Fenway Park recognized as a national landmark.

Paul Ransom: "I love Fenway. I love the fact that I'm sitting in a seat that my great grandfather could have very well have sat in to watch Babe Ruth, or my grandfather and father could have sat in to watch Ted Williams. It is a living, breathing piece of history. It *is* outdated, the seats *are* uncomfortable, there *are* bad views. I still wouldn't trade it for the most modernized park in America."

Harvey Soolman: "I could have done just fine if the Red Sox had never won a World Series championship in my lifetime. But it would have killed me had they torn down Fenway Park."

The 2005 home opener at Fenway was against the hated New York Yankees on April 11. The crowd roared as the World Series flag was raised and the Red Sox players were awarded their championship rings. After the Yankees lined up along the third base line, the PA announcer named them one by one. When Mariano Rivera's name was announced, he received a huge ovation from the Sox faithful, a reminder that the Yankee closer had blown saves in Game Four and Five in the League Championship Series. Knuckleballer Tim Wakefield then beat the Yankees 8–1, the first of his team-leading sixteen victories.

The team held first place all but one day between the end of June and the 20th of September. The Yankees then surged ahead. The Sox finished the season 95–67, the same record as the Yankees, but because the Yankees beat the Sox 10 games to 9, the Yankees won the division, and the Red Sox were wild card winners. It was the first time in American League history that two teams that tied for the division lead didn't play in a playoff game.

Despite 95 wins, the criticism aimed at Red Sox manager Terry Francona was a constant throughout the season. After a World Series victory the year before, the Red Sox fans had come to expect—no, demand—another one.

Jonathan Cole: "I never could figure out how you could break the Curse of the Bambino and be subject to criticism."

Edwin Hauryski: "We just didn't have confidence in his ability to manage the team. I still question calls he made during the course of games."

Troy Poole: "Red Sox fans love their own. Francona had no ties to Boston when he was hired."

John Dristilaris: "He was frequently criticized because he often appeared as an apologist for his players, giving the perception that he was a weak manager who let his players walk all over him. Fans in Boston, while very supportive of their team, expect accountability on all levels of organization. They know when they're getting BS'd, and they don't like it."

John Feudo: "Name one manager in Red Sox history who has never been criticized by our fans or local media. Dick Williams in '68—what have you done for me lately? Eddie Kasko—are the lights on in there? I hear you breathing but I'm not sure anyone's home. John McNamara—where to begin—and that's just because of one day. Joe Morgan—way too nice a guy. Grady Little—fuhgeddabioutit. The list goes on and on."

Leonard Levin: "Red Sox fans are hypercritical. The man won two World Series and had the team in contention most of the time, for God's sake! I can't tell you how many times I saw on a Red Sox discussion group: 'I put this loss on Francona.' Like an umpire, he was supposed to start out perfect and get better as he went along."

Never a hard-nosed leader, Francona left himself open to criticism, even from his players. In late September reliever Keith Foulke told a radio audience he couldn't wait for the season to end, he was so unhappy. Francona had made Curt Schilling a reliever after his ankle injury, and he heard criticism from Johnny Damon for doing that. Fans gave him the what-for for sticking with slumping Kevin Millar too long. They found fault with his managerial moves every time the Sox lost.

Terry Francona: "This is a hard job. The hardest thing is putting out the brush fires. It happens every day in Boston. If there isn't an issue, someone will make one.

"Don't get me wrong. These people love the Patriots. But they wake up and want to know what happened to the Red Sox. I mean, they really care. It's unbelievable. I've never seen anything like it. It's part of what's so good. But I'm right smack in the middle of it, and it gives me a headache sometimes. I know what it means to these people. I just want to do what's right for our team. I love living through this with them."

The Sox met the Chicago White Sox in the Division Series. With eight playoff wins in a row, the Sox were favored. But Matt Clement gave up eight runs in only 3 innings, and the Sox were beaten 14–2 in the series opener. In Game Two Sox second baseman Tony Graffanino made an error on what looked like a double play ball, and a 4–0 lead became a 5–4 loss. In the third and final game played at Fenway, Tim Wakefield lost 5–3, even though Manny Ramirez hit two home runs and David Ortiz one. Ortiz finished the season with 47 homers and 148 RBIs. Ramirez, who the Sox said they had tried to trade during the season for his occasional lack of hustle, finished with 45 home runs and 144 RBIs.

General Manager Theo Epstein, who was criticized for not assembling a stronger starting pitching staff, praised both Ramirez, his temperamental star, and manager Francona.

Theo Epstein: "He [Ramirez] likes to win, and he likes to play ball. Terry did an outstanding job of managing. He manages for the long haul, and he takes bullets for the team."

On October 31, 2005, revelations of a nasty fight for control of decision making on the Red Sox between Theo Epstein and president Larry Lucchino became public, when Epstein suddenly and without explanation shocked Red Sox Nation by resigning. He had turned down a three-year contract that would have paid him $1.5 million a year.

Theo Epstein: "This is a job you have to give your whole heart and soul to. In the end, after a long period of reflection about myself and the program, I decided I could no longer put my whole heart and soul into it."

In an attempt to avoid reporters, on this Halloween night Epstein wore a gorilla suit. He was seen wearing it as he drove away from Fenway Park in his Volvo.

Epstein, a graduate of Yale, had been a protégé of Lucchino when Lucchino hired him as an intern with the Baltimore Orioles. Together they moved to the San Diego Padres, and then to the Red Sox. After Lucchino made Epstein the Red Sox general manager, Epstein no longer saw himself as Lucchino's protégé. He was the GM. He wanted to make the decisions, and so the two then fought for control over personnel decisions.

Epstein, who like Oakland A's GM Billy Beane of *Moneyball* fame, believed in Sabermetrics—statistical analysis—often made moves that flew in the face of baseball orthodoxy. Among them he signed first baseman Kevin Millar, even though American teams were not supposed to sign players from the Japanese leagues; one year he went without a traditional closer, with terrible results; and in 2004 he traded the hobbled Garciaparra, the face of the franchise, a move that helped win the Red Sox the pennant and the World Series.

Lucchino, the team president whose job was to fill Fenway Park every day, wanted to keep the expensive name players. There was an irony to this because earlier he had called the Yankees "the Evil Empire," and here he was attempting to emulate their modus operandi of signing and promoting superstars.

The two men battled for control of personnel. When Lucchino, who had a reputation for ruthlessness, used sports reporter contacts to disparage Epstein in the papers in the fall of 2005, Epstein decided he had lost his trust in his mentor and quit. The tension had just become too much for Theo to bear.

With Theo gone, Lucchino, returning to the Yankees model, traded minor league phenom Hanley Ramirez to the Florida Marlins for two high-priced veterans, pitcher Josh Beckett and third baseman Mike Lowell. It's been said that this trade enabled the Sox to win the World Series in 2007. Lucchino also unloaded Edgar Renteria, who had disappointed at shortstop, to Atlanta.

Fans couldn't know it, but when on December 20 the Red Sox allowed the popular centerfielder Johnny Damon to leave for the Yankees and a $52 million, four-year paycheck, the move signaled the surprise return of Theo Epstein.

Behind the scenes John Henry brokered a truce to bring him back. Epstein was to get his way: the Sox weren't going to spend large sums on players Theo didn't think were worth the money. Theo could instead promote players from the farm system. On the evening of January 19, 2006, it was announced that Theo was returning. He, Lucchino, and principle owner John Henry told reporters they had spent the time talking over the rift. Lucchino would be less heavy handed. Theo would be in charge of personnel. Skepticism in the press abounded.

Dan Shaughnessy, the gadfly reporter for *The Boston Globe*, was certain that the strain brought about by the tug-of-war for control between Epstein and Lucchino would continue unabated despite the mutual back-slapping and glad-handing.

Dan Shaughnessy: "Nothing has changed since Theo left. No one knows how the new arrangement is going to work… There's been no discussion about who will report to whom. No one knows how this is going to work. But John Henry loves him, so he gets to come back.

"So Theo is back, and maybe he never really left. But damage has been done inside the walls of old Fenway. And if you're the GM of another big league team, who are you going to call if you want to deal with the Red Sox?"

With Theo Epstein's return harmony returned to the Red Sox front office, at least on the surface. It would be another half-dozen years before the rift in the Epstein-Lucchino relationship would metastasize, and Epstein would leave for good.

CHAPTER 63

Big Papi

The Red Sox front office in March of 2006 showered manager Terry Francona with praise and gave him a two-year contract extension that carried through the 2008 season.

Theo Epstein: "I couldn't imagine the alternative. I don't know who we'd get. He's been everything we hoped for and, you could say, more."

Despite the acquisition of pitcher Josh Beckett and third baseman Mike Lowell, the 2006 season would turn out to be a disappointment. Perhaps the biggest setback came in late May when Sox legend Roger Clemens decided to sign with his hometown Houston Astros rather than return to the Red Sox. The loss of Clemens was important because the Sox starting staff was in disarray with injuries to David Wells and lack of success from Matt Clement. Another starter, rookie Jon Lester, went to the mound in August and had to leave with what he thought was a sore back. He had been in an automobile accident the month before, and he thought that was the source of the pain. But after he saw a doctor, tests showed that he had anaplastic large cell lymphoma, a rare but treatable form of blood cancer. Lester would miss the rest of the season.

Despite these setbacks the Red Sox were able to stay in contention through August, in large part because of the efforts of rookie closer Jonathan Papelbon who had a 0.92 ERA and 35 saves in 68.1 innings of work. An injury requiring surgery to catcher Jason Varitek preceded a five-game sweep by the

Yankees in August, another Boston Massacre at Fenway Park, dooming their season as they fell six and a half games behind the hated New Yorkers.

In the fifth inning of the final Yankee game outfielder Manny Ramirez pulled himself from the game. He walked into the dugout and yelled at manager Francona, "Hamstring."

Francona, who had seen Manny loaf in some games and yank himself out of other games in the past, yelled back, "Manny, which one?"

Ramirez pointed his hands to both hamstrings.

"You pick," he said. "I'm coming out."

Francona was furious. Manny was a talented bat, but he was also a handful.

When Jonathan Papelbon suffered a season-ending injury on September 1, the Sox chances to make the playoffs were doomed.

As has always been the case, Red Sox Nation placed the blame for the team's collapse squarely on the back of manager Terry Francona. Bill Reynolds of the *Providence Journal* had a complete understanding of the dynamic.

Bill Reynolds: "You are called the ultimate enabler, as you never say a harsh word about any of your players. You routinely are trashed, your every move analyzed as if it's a protozoan under a microscope—damned if you do, damned if you don't. The Red Sox manager pays dearly for his uniform.

"Maybe this can change. Maybe you can still salvage the season, find one more push, get into the playoffs, go on a run, make the memory of August disappear like some bad dream. Maybe. Maybe. Maybe. Your kingdom for a list of maybes.

"Until then, the season goes on like some forced march in some bad war. Goes on with too many injuries, too many holes, a team in which makeup no longer hides all the warts. Until then you will continue to sit in the dugout, forever chewing on something, the tension all over your face, like you're watching some horror movie everyone knows what's going to happen, one of those where everyone dies in the end.

"You are Terry Francona, and right now you're a manager with no answers."

Reynolds turned out not to be wrong. For the first time since 2002, the Red Sox failed to make the playoffs in 2006. Despite a fine 15–7 season with a 3.97 ERA from Curt Schilling, the Sox finished 86–76.

The one bright spot for the Sox was the slugging of designated hitter David Ortiz, who in 2006 hit 54 home runs, setting a single-season mark for a Red Sox player. The record had been set by Jimmie Foxx back in 1938. Foxx hit 50 that year.

David Americo Ortiz Arias, who is from the Dominican Republic, originally signed with the Seattle Mariners, where he was known as David Arias. When he was traded to the Minnesota Twins, he decided he preferred to be called David Ortiz. He became a Red Sox because the Minnesota Twins gave him his walking papers after the 2002 season. He was a .266 hitter over six seasons and was entering free agency. The Twins organization thought they could do better than spend their money on a one-dimensional designated hitter. Another factor was a broken wrist Ortiz had suffered after a dive into home plate. He missed the last two months of the season. When the Red Sox signed him, he was one of five players including Jeremy Giambi, Shea Hillenbrand, Kevin Millar, and Bill Mueller who were expected to fill the three positions of third, first, and DH.

Six weeks into the 2003 season Ortiz played little and hit little. He called his agents and told them to get him out of Boston. Theo Epstein promised he would free up a spot for Ortiz, and he did, trading away Hillenbrand.

Once Ortiz got his opportunity, he made the best of it.

Four years later Ortiz had become a symbol of the Red Sox. If he had run for mayor, he would have won.

His bubbly presence reminded Red Sox fans of the happy demeanor of Luis Tiant, El Senor, El Tiante, the Cuban pitcher whose presence lit up the clubhouse. Like Babe Ruth, Ortiz never remembered anyone's name, and so his greeting would be, "Hey, Papi." After a while his teammates began calling him "Papi," and because of his girth "Big Papi." Today Big Papi is as beloved as Ted Williams or Carl Yaz. Maybe even more so.

One of Ortiz's trademarks is to cross home plate after hitting a home run, look up and point both index fingers to the sky. In January of 2002 his mother Angela Rosa Arias was killed in an automobile crash, and Ortiz's gesture at home plate is in tribute to his mom.

He is as emotional and genuine as he is talented.

Ortiz in 2003 hit 31 home runs and finished fifth in the American League MVP voting. The next year he helped lead the Sox with 41 home runs and 139 RBIs. In the playoffs he hit .400 with five home runs and nineteen RBIs.

In 2005 Big Papi hit 47 home runs with 148 RBIs, finishing second in the MVP voting to Alex Rodriguez of the Yankees.

In the spring of 2006 Ortiz signed a contract giving him a four-year extension worth $52 million. Ortiz could have become a free agent at the end of the season but Red Sox management didn't want to risk losing the man who had become the face of the franchise. Not only did Ortiz swing a mean bat, but his presence—his smiling face and his sharp wit—were important to the success of the team.

"I can't think of [another] player who contributes in so many ways," said Theo Epstein.

Ortiz rewarded the Sox with a career year in which he became the greatest Red Sox single-season home run hitter of all time.

On September 20 at Fenway Park Ortiz got up with two outs in the sixth inning against Twins pitcher Boof Bonser and hit a ball into the centerfield seats. It was his 50th home run of the season, tying him with the great Jimmie Foxx.

After the game Ortiz was as gracious as ever.

David Ortiz: "I guess the people in New England are going to remember me for a while. It's a great feeling being right next to a great player, a superstar just like Mr. Jimmie Foxx was. To go through history and see how many good players have been around this ball club and be right there with them is a wonderful thing."

Ortiz then praised the Red Sox fans.

David Ortiz: "It seemed like [the fans] really enjoyed what I did on the field today. Like I've said, I always tell my teammates that we have the best fans all the way around. It doesn't matter what is going on in the game. It doesn't matter if we are winning or losing. They enjoy whatever we do good in the field."

Ortiz was only the fifteenth player in major league history to hit 50 home runs in a season.

The next night Ortiz hit a home run off Johan Santana of the Twins for home run number 51 and later in the game he hit home run number 52.

Four nights later in a ceremony before the game, Ortiz presented gifts to relatives of Jimmie Foxx and Babe Ruth. That night in the third inning he hit a home run off Jason Hammel for number 54.

Shaun Kelly: "We had so many prodigious home run hitters in the past who had seminal years—from Jimmie Foxx to Yaz to Tony C. to Boomer to Dewey, but to have someone hit that many home runs was special. I remember when he hit number 50. Even Tito came out of the dugout to greet him. A very special moment."

Tom Verducci: "Every ballpark seems smaller, every room brighter, every worry lighter when you're in the company of David Americo Ortiz."

Allen Reed Nissen: "David Ortiz shattered all Red Sox records, and led the American League in home runs and RBIs. However, the team finished third and didn't make the playoffs. As spectacular a season that was for an individual, wouldn't any of the Red Sox players or fans wish they could have traded in David's season for a World Series ring? Wouldn't David have felt the same way?"

CHAPTER 64
Champions Again

On November 14, 2006, the Red Sox opened their wallets in unprecedented fashion, laying out $51.1 million dollars to the Seibu Lions of the Nippon Professional Baseball League for the privilege of negotiating with the Lions' star pitcher Daisuke Matsuzaka. They then doubled down, paying Matsuzaka $52 million for the next six years. They also shelled out $70 million for five years for the services of free agent outfielder J.D. Drew. If Theo Epstein had wanted to go the inexpensive farm system route, this sure wasn't it.

In the high school championships his junior year, Matsuzaka pitched in a game in which he lasted 17 innings and threw 250 pitches. One of the spectators watching on TV from the United Airlines Lounge at Tokyo Airport was Daniel Okimoto, a Stanford professor and former Princeton classmate of Larry Lucchino. Okimoto called Lucchino to rave about the high schooler.

"You have to fly out here and watch this kid pitch," he said.

Recruited by both the Colorado Rockies and the Arizona Diamonbacks, Matsuzaka was the first player chosen in the Japanese pro draft, and at age 18 as a rookie pitching for the Seibu Lions he led his team with 16 victories. He only lost 5. He was the starting pitcher in the All Star game.

Matsuzaka played eight years in Japan, making the All Star game seven times. In October of 2006 he signed with Scott Boras to represent him. The Red Sox bid of $51,111,111.11 was more than the bids of the New York Yankees, the New York Mets, or the Texas Rangers. The money was three times the payroll of the Seibu team.

The Red Sox had thirty days to sign him, and they did, for $52 million more. They also gave him a no-trade contract.

What followed was Dice-K mania. Christmas sales of Matsuzaka Red Sox uniforms with the number 18 on the back went through the roof. The Chamber of Commerce estimated that an extra 10,000 visitors, mostly from Asian countries, would come visit Fenway Park and its environs. The Fairmont Copley Plaza added sushi to its menu of hors d'oeuvres. All before the new arrival pitched an inning.

A hundred members of the Japanese media arrived to cover him during spring training, fifty during the regular season. The Red Sox provided him with a Japanese-speaking trainer, a Japanese-speaking media liaison, a personal interpreter, and a personal masseuse. He was also escorted by an English instructor. Pitching coach John Farrell studied Japanese with a tutor, a smart move considering that Lucchino not only signed Matsuzaka but free agent Hideki Okajima, a left-handed reliever, as well.

Two questions still remained: could Dice-K Matsuzaka adjust to pitching every five days (in Japan he was part of a six-man rotation) and could he lead the Red Sox back into the playoffs?

He not only could, but did, as the Sox won 96 games, most in the American League, then in the playoffs went on to defeat the Angels, then Cleveland, and to sweep the Colorado Rockies in the World Series.

Led by starting pitchers Josh Beckett (20–7 with a 3.27 ERA) Matsuzaka (15–12 with a 4.40 ERA), knuckleballer Tim Wakefield (17–12 with a 4.76 ERA), and Curt Schilling (9–8 with a 3.87 ERA), the 2007 Red Sox took first place on April 18 and never looked back. By May 29 the Sox had an 11½ game lead over Baltimore, and though the Sox only finished two games ahead, the division title was never in doubt.

Curt Schilling: "I'd like to think that we've started to redefine who the Boston Red Sox are. That's something I'm very proud to be associated with."

The 40-year-old Red Sox pitcher who had battled shoulder injuries all season long was also effusive in his praise of manager Terry Francona.

Curt Schilling: "It's not about being the smartest baseball man anymore. Even though [managers] are incredibly smart, it's about surrounding yourself with the right people and putting your players in the best position to succeed. Sometimes that has nothing to do with strategy; it has to do with people skills, especially when you play in these markets [Boston and New York]. You deal with things that no one else has to deal with. Fair or not, it is what it is. He does as good a job as anyone has ever done at it. He really is a highly underrated manager."

Aided by talented Rookie-of-the Year Dustin Pedroia, September call-up Jacoby Ellsbury, and Clay Buchholz, who threw a no-hitter against the

Baltimore Orioles on September 1 in only his second start, the Sox were led by veteran first baseman Kevin Youkilis, DH David Ortiz, third baseman Mike Lowell, and catcher Jason Varitek. Ortiz hit 35 homers, Lowell drove in 120 runs, and speedsters Julio Lugo (33 steals) and Coco Crisp (28 steals) were the first pair of Red Sox to steal 25 bases since Tris Speaker and Hal Janvrin in 1914.

The Red Sox clinched the division title on September 27, when they defeated the Minnesota Twins on a day when the New York Yankees lost. Fittingly, Dice-K Matsuzaka pitched eight solid innings for the victory. Jonathan Papelbon earned his 37th save of the year. It was the first division crown for the Red Sox in twelve years, ending the Yankees' long run.

Ecstatic fans in the park waited an hour for the Yankees to lose their game, and when the final score was announced, Red Sox players popped champagne in the clubhouse and out on the field the loud speaker played "Don't Stop," the Fleetwood Mac song that helped Bill Clinton become president. The Red Sox players left the clubhouse, some carrying champagne bottles, and ran out onto the field to celebrate with their fans.

John Henry: "It's as good as it gets. To win the division, that's what you want to do."

The Red Sox breezed past the Los Angeles Angels in round one of the playoffs, then faced a tough Cleveland Indians team led by pitcher C.C. Sabathia and 19-game winner Fausto Carmona.

After Josh Beckett won the opener against Cleveland, the Indians reeled off three straight wins, putting the Sox one game from elimination. In New York Joe Torre had just been fired for not meeting expectations, while in Boston the airwaves lit up with criticism of Sox manager Terry Francona. Having won the World Championship in 2004, it was becoming clear that nothing short of winning the World Series again would satisfy the Sox fandom that was berating him for starting Tim Wakefield in Game 4 instead of Josh Beckett. "A Terry-ble mistake" was how one pundit framed it. Francona explained that he wasn't just looking at one game, but was considering the entire series. Francona, for one, seemed put off by the criticism.

Terry Francona: "I mean, we're sitting at 101 wins, and people don't seem to be very happy very much of the time. That's a little perplexing, but that's the way it is."

Before Game 5 a reporter asked Red Sox outfielder Manny Ramirez whether he was feeling the pressure.

"Why should we panic?" said the often phlegmatic star. "We have a great team. If it doesn't happen, who cares? There's always next year. It's not like the end of the world or anything."

Some reporters and fans understood him.

Jeff Goldberg: "I covered the team for the [Hartford] Courant and was there when he said it. His point, which was spot on, was that they just needed to go out and play and not stress over it, which was the approach they took and led them to rally and win the series. But there was some backlash that first day that 'Manny doesn't care.' By the time J.D. Drew hit the grand slam in Game 6, no one remembered it."

Allan Reid Nissen: "Manny Ramirez was a ball player who took the game for granted and let his God-given skills carry him through his major league career. As good as he was at times, he acted just as equally as a jerk. What made me sicker wasn't Manny himself, but the media and the fans who swept his dirt under the Red Sox rug. It got to the point where people dismissed his [bad behavior] by saying, 'Manny will be Manny.' Manny would lose focus that this was a team sport, and he wasn't bigger than the game. Of course the Sox needed him to carry the team, but as soon as things went south for him in Boston, management cut him like a piece of bait."

On the TV and radio that night, Ramirez was castigated throughout Red Sox Nation for not caring whether the team won or lost.

Bruce Kenneth Macgowan: "Manny lives in his own private world, and when he says something, you often just shake your head and say to yourself, 'What was that all about?' I'll never forget going up to him when he was playing in Cleveland, and asking him a question in the clubhouse after a win over the A's in Oakland. Manny mumbled something inaudible, and I asked the question more clearly and forcefully. He looked up at me with a withering glace and hissed: 'What part of no don't you understand?'"

Roger Jackson: "I thought Manny should have stopped when he told reporters, 'Why should we panic? We have a great team.' But Manny being Manny, he didn't have much of a filter and kept going. I don't think he really meant to say he didn't give a s—t, but it was impossible to interpret his words any other way. I cringed when I watched him on TV. I thought to myself, *Well you stepped in it now.*"

Karl Cicitto: "As soon as I heard it, I dismissed it. By that time I had come to only care about what he did with his bat and glove. He was a wacky, scruffy comic character to my teenage kids. To me he was a riddle and an assassin for the good guys. His spiral out of Beantown was sad."

It was the last negative moment of the 2007 season, because the Red Sox didn't lose another game, as first Josh Beckett, then Curt Schilling, and finally Dice-K Matsuzaka swamped the Indians 7–1, 12–2, and 11–2 to reach the World Series. Before the final game reporters and fans questioned Francona's decision to start Matsuzaka because he had performed poorly in Game 3.

Matsuzaka pitched beautifully, holding a 3–2 lead until the Sox could score eight runs in the seventh and eighth innings, winning the game and advancing to the World Series.

Ray Arsenault: "The glorious 2007 season caught me unawares. A lifelong Red Sox fan, I had barely survived the near-misses of 1967 and 1975, and the heartbreak of 1986, so the World Series victory in 2004 brought me more joy than I ever expected to experience. The idea of winning a second modern-day championship was almost beyond my comprehension.

"In 2003, I had written a bittersweet article, "Beantown 1986" for a Harvard University Press book on the history of Boston sports. The article chronicled the ups and downs of that memorable year, from the Celtics NBA title to the Patriots' loss to the Bears in the Super Bowl to the tragic twist of events in the series against the Mets, with the overarching theme that the Red Sox were lovable losers who would probably never bring another World Series championship to Beantown. Of course, by the time the article was actually published in 2005, the text had to be altered to accommodate the unexpected comeback triumph of the previous year.

"Two years later, during the spring and summer of 2007, the Sox battled their way back into the playoffs, but I was preoccupied with my father's illness and didn't pay much attention to what was happening. After he died on June 1, at the age of 85, I was thankful that he had lived to see one Sox title, but neither of us ever expected to witness a second.

"Nevertheless, in mid-October I found myself in Boston in the midst of another improbable World Series run. In town to deliver a lecture, I slipped away to join two graduate school friends from the 1970s, Ted and Nancy Hammett, at the seventh game of the American League championships. The tickets cost $350 a piece, the most I had ever spent on a sporting event, but I was thrilled to be there, even though I feared that I had paid to see yet another heartbreaking near-miss. Coming back from three games to one against the Indians seemed too much to expect, but hope springs eternal in a true Red Sox fan, so there I was screaming for the Sox from a seat down the third-base line.

"The pitching match-up between Daisuke Matsuzaka and Jake Westbrook—a rematch of Game 3, which the Indians had won—didn't look very promising for the Sox. After six innings, the Sox were hanging on to a 3–2 lead. Then it happened: the baseball gods delivered eight Sox runs in two innings. After Jonathan Papelbon mopped up the ninth, it was over.

"For the third time in 22 years, the Red Sox had come back from a 3–1 deficit to win the American League pennant. I will never forget the postgame scene in Kenmore Square: the joyous crowd streaming toward the T, people hugging strangers and dancing with delight as the policemen on horseback tried in vain to keep order. And, as trite as it may sound, I could also feel my father's smiling presence looking down on me and the multitude, cheering one last time for his beloved Sox."

The red-hot Colorado Rockies, winners of 21 of their last 22 games, were next. The Rockies didn't win a game. In Game 1 Dustin Pedroia, who had struggled in April but who then become a key cog in the offense, became the first Red Sox rookie to hit a home run in the World Series since Fred Lynn in Game 6 in 1975. Josh Beckett struck out nine in a 13–1 romp.

In Game 2 Curt Schilling, Hideki Okajima, and Jonathan Papelbon combined to win 2–1. A highlight of the game came with two outs in the eighth and Matt Holliday on first. Jonathan Papelbon caught Holliday leaning the wrong way and picked him off. That was it for Colorado.

Rookies Jacoby Ellsbury and Dustin Pedroia helped Dice-K Matsuzaka, who pitched shutout ball for five innings, become the first Japanese pitcher to ever win a World Series game in a 10–5 victory in Game 3. Papelbon again came in and got the save.

To complete the sweep Jon Lester, his recovery from cancer complete, defeated Colorado in Game 4 in Colorado behind the hitting of series MVP Mike Lowell, who hit a home run and double in the 4–3 victory. Lowell, who had come to Boston from Miami as part of the Josh Beckett trade, himself had recovered from testicular cancer. Bobby Kielty, a most unlikely hero, gave the Sox a 4–1 lead with a pinch-hit home run into the left field stands on the first pitch of the eighth inning.

In the ninth inning Papelbon induced Rockies catcher Yorvit Torrealba to ground out to second. Jamey Carroll hit a bullet to left, and the crowd rose in expectation, but the ball died and it was caught at the wall by Jacoby Ellsbury. Papelbon ran the count on Seth Smith to 2–2 before throwing a fastball past the Rockies outfielder for the final out. It was the big reliever's seventh consecutive scoreless outing in the postseason. Papelbon threw his hat high in the air, did a little dance, and ran toward his catcher Jason Varitek, who jumped into his arms. The rest of the team then piled on.

It was the 2007 Red Sox second series sweep in the past four postseasons.

Tom Tully: "Colorado got swept even though they didn't commit one error…with the possible exception of playing the Red Sox in the first place."

Even though the final games were played in Denver, more than 7,000 Red Sox fans had flown in for the game. They ran behind the backstop net and chanted "Let's Go Red Sox" and "Bob-by Kiel-ty. Bob-by Kiel-ty." When Mike Lowell, who became a free agent after the final game, went onto the field to accept the World Series MVP trophy, they also chanted, "Re-sign Lowell." The celebration lasted over an hour.

In the clubhouse captain Jason Varitek put his head on manager Terry Francona's shoulders and cried like a baby. Later Francona praised his catcher for his solid leadership and play.

Terry Francona: "[Jason] had willed everybody to be so good. I think that's why I'm so calm. I know he's in charge. It's his team."

Wendy Golenbock: "The Red Sox were unstressed as the underdog, and they were having fun. The Dominican powerhouses of David, Manny, and Julio Lugo were having the time of their lives—a great recipe for success."

Sam Sears: "In my opinion the 2007 Red Sox team was the best in my lifetime, distinctly better than the 2004 team. It was a confident team with a sure-handed manager in Terry Francona, exemplified with his patience with Dustin Pedroia, whose month of April was woeful. Of course he went on to handily win the Rookie of the Year award.

"There really was no weakness in the lineup. When it came time for the playoffs, I was highly confident. The sweep of the Rockies seemed like a fitting ending to the season."

Shawn Kelly: "The Sox not only led out of the gate in 2007, they were never seriously challenged for the title. I can remember feeling, *So this is what it was like rooting for those Yankees and Cardinals teams that just swept through the seas and left a wake in their path.*

"Unlike 2004, there was very little drama. You expected them to win. While this team was my least-favorite of the three Red Sox teams that have won world championships, I will always be grateful that I got to experience such a season as a fan. Because baseball's competitive balance is so even, it really was a very different season for all of us. When Paps got the final out, I felt the same sort of pride and satisfaction that I felt when the great Celtics teams accomplished what they were supposed to do.

"It made for a very sweet winter."

CHAPTER 65
Manny Being Manny

The Red Sox managed to win 95 games in 2008, despite a long string of serious injuries. Before the season even began pitchers Curt Schilling, Mike Timlin, and Josh Beckett each landed on the disabled list. Jon Lester emerged as the ace of the staff with a 16–6 record and a 3.21 ERA. On May 19, Lester threw the eighteenth no-hitter in Red Sox history, shutting out Kansas City 7–0.

Keeping up with the Sox were the surprising Tampa Bay Rays. Hurting the Sox' chances were serious injuries to David Ortiz, who missed 45 games with an injured wrist, to third baseman Mike Lowell, who tore his labrum and missed several weeks, and to outfielder J.D. Drew whose back injury cost him most of the second half of the season.

But perhaps the most crucial loss was that of Manny Ramirez, who after eight years with the Red Sox, was showing signs he wanted to leave. All through the 2005 season Manny talked about wanting to leave Boston, and there had been trade rumors that Manny would be dealt to the New York Mets. Then Manny changed his mind and said he wanted to stay. In 2006 Manny hit his 450th home run, collected his 2,000th hit, and had a twenty-eight game hitting streak.

A free agent at the end of the 2008 season, the Sox hadn't offered him a contract extension. Angry, Ramirez spoke about not being appreciated. He did have a point. Manny was probably the greatest right handed hitter in the history of the franchise. In 2007 he hit .296 with 20 home runs and 88 RBIs despite missing two months of the season with a strained left oblique muscle. In the 2007 postseason his two home runs against the Angels gave him 23 postseason home runs, passing Bernie Williams for the most all time.

Manny would retire with a total of 555 home runs, 1,831 RBIs, and a lifetime batting average of .312. Francona later would call Ramirez the best right-handed hitter he ever saw.

On May 31, 2008, Manny hit a ball into the Camden Yard left field grandstands against the Baltimore Orioles for his 500th career home run, but less than a week later his stock began to fall when during a game against the Tampa Bay Rays he and teammate Kevin Youkilis got into a shoving match in the dugout. Ramirez was caught on camera taking a swing at Youkilis, and they had to be separated.

As Ramirez walked down the runway to the clubhouse, escorted by a coach and the trainer, Youkilis could be seen shouting at him as he ran onto the field.

Ramirez had been complaining about the way Youkilis would chronically complain about ball and strike calls by umpires, and he also was irritated at Youkilis' habit of throwing bats and helmets and other objects in the dugout after a poor at bat. This had become a constant, and Manny—and other teammates—told the third baseman to cut it out because it made him look selfish and juvenile.

Earlier in the game there had been a brawl with the Rays after James Shields hit Coco Crisp with a pitch. There was talk Youkilis was upset that Manny hadn't run out to support his teammates, arriving on the field *after* the pitchers in the bullpen. A day later everyone said the scuffle was in the past, but Ramirez was targeted for criticism for picking the fight.

Then on June 29 Ramirez got into an argument with traveling secretary Jack McCormick. The team was playing in Houston, and in the clubhouse before the game Ramirez requested sixteen tickets to the game for his family and friends. McCormick said it wouldn't be possible to fulfill it, that the request came too late. An angry Ramirez screamed at McCormick to "do your job," and shoved McCormick, who was 64 years old, to the ground. Terry Francona heard the ruckus and arrived in time to see McCormick, dazed, leaning against a table.

He grabbed Ramirez and yelled at him, "What the fuck are you doing?"

Francona was so angry that he told reporter Peter Gammons that "Manny Ramirez is the worst human being I've ever met." Later he relented saying that he had been blowing off steam and wished Gammons had never printed that. Manny was fined $10,000.

Terry Francona: "That was probably the hardest thing that happened to me with the Red Sox, and it just bothered me so much, and it ate at me so much, that year, it was hard. It was very difficult."

Manny, angry at how he was portrayed and even angrier that the Red Sox still had not extended his contract, took himself out of a Friday game on July

25 against the Yankees after Francona had already penciled his name onto the lineup card. Manny said he had a sore knee.

Dan Shaughnessy wrote in *The Boston Globe* that the Red Sox were tired of Manny's antics.

Dan Shaughnessy: "Something's got to give. The owners are mad. The manager is frustrated. The GM is frustrated. Teammates are angry."

The next day there was talk that if Manny didn't play, he'd be suspended. He played.

Manny responded by going on ESPN Desportes and saying he wouldn't block a trade if the Sox could find a trading partner. He said if the Sox weren't happy with him, all they had to do was let his contract lapse, he'd become a free agent, and he'd leave.

Manny Ramirez: "The Red Sox don't deserve a player like me. During my years here I've seen how they have mistreated other great players when they didn't want them to try to turn the fans against them." He was specifically referring to Nomar Garciaparra and Pedro Martinez, two other Hispanic players.

On July 31, 2008, the Ramirez soap opera of *As The Clubhouse Turns* ended when the Red Sox traded him to the Los Angeles Dodgers for outfielder Jason Bay. Other players were involved in a three-way deal with the Pittsburgh Pirates. Bay, a quiet presence, was batting .282 with 22 home runs and 64 RBIs for the Pirates.

Ramirez was named the National League Player of the Month in August. He hit .415 (44 for 106) with nine home runs and 21 RBIs. He finished the season with the Dodgers hitting .396, with 17 homers and 53 RBIs.

Without Manny, runs would be harder to come by for the Sox, though for a while it would be a lot quieter around Fenway Park.

At the time of the Manny Ramirez for Jason Bay trade the Red Sox trailed the pesky Tampa Bay Rays by three games in the American League East. At season's end, the Rays finished with 97 wins and the Red Sox with 95 as both teams made the playoffs. After the Sox defeated the Los Angeles Angels in four games, the Red Sox and Rays met to see who would play in the World Series.

The Rays won three of the first four games, clobbering Josh Beckett and Tim Wakefield and seemed headed for the World Series when they led the Sox 7–1 in the seventh inning of Game 5 at Fenway Park. David Ortiz broke a 1 for 17 slump with a three-run home run in the seventh off Grant Balfour. In the eighth J.D. Drew hit a two-run home run, and Mark Kotsay hit a long double over the head of Rays' centerfielder B.J. Upton. Coco Crisp tied the game at 7–7 with a single to right.

In the ninth the Red Sox had two outs when Tampa Bay third baseman Evan Longoria bounced a throw to first into the stands, enabling Kevin Youkilis to reach second. Jason Bay was walked intentionally to set up the force. Left-handed reliever J.P. Howell faced the lefty-hitting Drew, who singled over the head of right fielder Gabe Gross to score Yuke with the winning run to cap an amazing 8–7 victory.

Boston, who had come back from a three games to one deficit to win both the 2004 and 2007 World Series, threatened to do it again the next game when Josh Beckett and three relievers defeated the Rays 4–2. Jason Varitek hit a tie-breaking home run in the sixth inning to force a seventh game.

There was no magic this time. Despite a first-inning home run by Dustin Pedroia, the Rays' Matt Garza defeated Jon Lester and the Sox 3–1. Their season was over and done. For the future the low-budget Rays would prove as troublesome to the Sox as the Evil Empire Yankees.

CHAPTER 66

Spiraling Downward

The year 2009 brought 95 wins for the Sox. Four players, J.D. Drew (24), Kevin Youkilis (27), David Ortiz (28), and Jason Bay (36) led the team in home runs, but the player who made the team go was centerfielder Jacoby Ellsbury, who electrified the fandom by stealing a team record 70 bases, including a steal of home on April 26 against the Yankees.

Ortiz began the season in a terrible slump, hitting .185 with one home run during the first two months of the season. He went 149 at bats before hitting a homer. His teammates felt for him and supported him.

Tim Wakefield: "It's not fun to watch, and it's not easy to watch. But we all love David so much. He has earned the right to have a slump like this because he's been so huge for us over the last six years of clutch hitting and huge home runs. Whether he's hitting well or not hitting well, his presence in our lineup makes us good."

Everyone but manager Terry Francona wanted to bench him.

Terry Francona: "Yeah, he's just having a tough time. The only thing we'll hang our hat on, as cold as guys get, and they struggle and it looks like of ugly, when they get hot they rise to their level."

As usual, Francona was right, as Big Papi had seven homers each in June, July, and August, as Ortiz's fans got off his back and breathed a sigh of relief.

Josh Beckett led the pitching staff with a 17–6 record. Jon Lester finished 15–8, and Tim Wakefield, the knuckleballer, ended the season 11–5. Brad Penny, Clay Buchholz, and reliever Ramon Ramirez each won seven games. Dice-K Matsuzaka, who went on the disabled list after only two starts, won only four games. Jonathan Papelbon finished with 38 saves and a 1.85 ERA.

The Sox led the division at the All Star break, but slumped during the second half, going from a three-game lead over the Yankees to a 6½-game deficit in early August. The Yankees won the division with 103 wins, eight games ahead of the Sox. While the Sox were losing three-straight to the Los Angeles Angels in the opening round of the playoffs, the Yankees went on to defeat the Philadelphia Phillies in the World Series, causing great anguish to Red Sox Nation.

The year 2010 was even worse, as the Sox missed making the playoffs for the first time since 2006. Once again the Red Sox churned their roster. After running through shortstops Orlando Cabrera, Edgar Renteria, Alex Gonzalez, Julio Lugo, Alex Cora, Royce Clayton, Jed Lowrie, Chris Woodward, and Nick Green, the Sox on December 4, 2009, signed former Toronto Blue Jays shortstop Marco Scutaro. Epstein thought him a perfect fit.

Five days later the Sox signed two expensive free agents, Los Angeles Angels starter John Lackey, and star Milwaukee Brewer outfielder Mike Cameron. Lackey was handed $82.5 million for five years.

Blogger George Cain: "Theo must have been forced at gunpoint to make this signing."

Cameron signed a two-year deal worth $16 million. Boston let outfielder Jason Bay go. The New York Mets signed him for four years for $66 million. Shortly thereafter the Sox signed star Seattle Mariner third baseman Adrian Beltre.

Sox fans wondered why they had let the powerful Bay go and why Beltre, who had had a mediocre season with Seattle in 2009, was acquired. Theo Epstein said that Beltre was one of the best third basemen in the game and predicted he would become one of the leaders of the team.

In 2010 Beltre batted .321, hit 28 home runs, and drove in 120 runs, proving Epstein right, but it wasn't enough as the oft-injured Red Sox finished third in the American League East with 89 wins. The Yankees were second with 95 wins. The Tampa Bay Rays finished on top with 96 wins.

The Sox were a game and a half behind the Yankees in second place in the spring when one key player after another became injured. The list was long. Going on the DL beginning in late June were Josh Beckett (back spasms), Jacoby Ellsbury (rib fracture), Jeremy Hermida (rib fracture), Mike Lowell (right hip injury), Jed Lowrie (mono), Victor Martinez (broken left thumb), Dustin Pedroia (broken left foot), Jason Varitek (broken foot), Manny Delcarmen (forearm strain), and Junichi Tazawa (Tommy John surgery).

The sheer magnitude of all of these injuries occurring within a given season was mind-boggling. Somehow manager Terry Francona was able to hold everything together with glue and players from the minors like outfielders Daniel Nava, Darnell McDonald, Eric Patterson, and Ryan Kalish.

At least one reporter, Ernest Paicopolos of *The Boston Examiner*, nominated Francona for manager of the year.

Ernest Paicopolos: "Would the Rays and Yankees be as swaggering with that many key players sidelined? Somehow this team has managed to stay on the periphery of contention."

The year 2011 was supposed to hold so much promise for the Red Sox. Unhappy that the team missed the playoffs in 2010, management attempt to right what it saw as a listing ship, allowing veterans Victor Martinez and Adrian Beltre to leave, and then going on an unprecedented spending spree. Larry Lucchino's fingerprints were all over multi-year, mega-money deals in which the Red Sox acquired All Star first baseman Adrian Gonzalez and All Star outfielder Carl Crawford.

To get Gonzalez, the Sox sent three minor-league prospects to San Diego with Eric Patterson, and then signed the first baseman to a seven-year, $154 million contract extension. Crawford, who had starred with the Tampa Bay Rays, received a seven-year contract worth $142 million. (Epstein would later complain that he was forced by management (Lucchino) into making these deals.)

The "best team ever" was set.

Jeff Passan: "All those years Larry Lucchino had raged against the Yankees' profligate spending, calling them the Evil Empire, and here the Red Sox were imitating them. Initially I liked the Gonzalez signing. Then in retrospect, I didn't, and it wasn't because he wasn't as good as people anticipated. My opinion about signing a first baseman to a long-term contract has evolved. I now think it's just stupid to sign a first baseman for $150 million, because frankly, anyone can play first base. In reality you can take anybody from any position and stick him at first base with a moderate amount of success.

"At the time I thought the $142 million for Carl Crawford was an overpay. Left field isn't a premium position, and he didn't bring the set of skills necessary to succeed long term for that kind of salary. He's a good guy, but he didn't necessarily have the right mindset to succeed in Boston, the way he did in Tampa Bay. It takes a certain attitude to succeed in a town with so much pressure from fans and the media."

Before the season began the 2011 Red Sox were picked by most experts to win the World Series. Some declared this team to be unstoppable. As September arrived, the Red Sox held a one-and-a-half-game lead over the second-place Yankees. In the summer second baseman Dustin Pedroia went on a twenty-five game hitting tear. He had nine home runs and twenty RBIs during his streak.

Tim Wakefield, the knuckleballer, won his 200th game on September 13 at home, just a few weeks after celebrating his 45th birthday. The Boston faithful rose and gave him a standing ovation for his long years of service.

Jacoby Ellsbury, who spent most of 2010 on the disabled list, had a monster season. He hit 32 home runs, drove in 105 runs, and stole 39 bases. David Ortiz hit 29 home runs and drove in 96 runs, and Adrian Gonzalez hit 27 home runs and drove in 117 RBIs.

On August 16, the Red Sox even made a triple play. With runners on first and second, the Rays' Sean Rodriguez hit a ground ball to Jed Lowrie, who stepped on third, threw to Pedroia at second, who then threw on to Gonzalez at first for the triple killing. It was their first triple play since 1994.

By the end of August the Sox had a brilliant 83–52 record. In September it all fell apart. John Lackey (12–12 with a 6.91 ERA) had the worst season for a Red Sox starter in team history. Jon Lester couldn't win games down the stretch. Eric Bedard was acquired at the trade deadline, but the left-hander contributed little. Josh Beckett sprained his ankle and didn't do much in September.

In the final month of the 2011 season the Red Sox embarked on the biggest collapse in baseball history. (It even outdid the Philadelphia Phillies historic collapse in 1964.) The team ERA in September was 5.84—both Josh Beckett and Jon Lester had ERAs over 5.00. No one hit. The bullpen collapsed at the end of games. It was a brutal month.

The heartbreak after it was over harkened back to sharp pain felt by Red Sox fans after the Bucky Dent home run at the end of 1978. Red Sox fans may have thought that winning the World Series in 2004 and 2007 had inured them from their traditional season-ending heartbreak, but the 2011 collapse would bring back memories of Dent, Billy Buckner's ground ball, and Aaron Fucking Boone's home run as the Sox finished out the season 7–20. There seemed to be turmoil everywhere.

Jeff Passan: "On the second to last day of the season there was a situation that encapsulated the Red Sox that year. I can remember John Lackey standing by his locker, muttering obscenities under his breath as reporters were standing around, a really awkward scene. The news had come out about his getting a divorce, and here was this six-foot five-inch Texan who was threatening to beat up anyone who came within a ten-foot radius of him as Pam Ganley, the Red Sox PR director, was trying to calm him down."

Despite the poor finish, the Sox could have, and should have, made the playoffs anyway. All they needed on the final night of the season was either to gain a victory over the Baltimore Orioles or to benefit from a win by the New York Yankees over the Tampa Bay Rays. The Sox were in Baltimore, the Yankees at Tampa Bay. No one anticipated the drama that would build that night of September 28, 2011.

Jeff Passan: "It was the single greatest night of baseball that there ever has been. I cannot imagine a better night of baseball with more interesting, incredible things happening than what happened that night. I was down in Atlanta watching the collapse of the Braves. Craig Kimbrel, a great closer, gave up the lead on that last day and the Braves missed the playoffs. In the Braves clubhouse afterward, in this time of depression, of loathing, of anger, there were still players in that clubhouse watching the American League games on the TV. They were interested in what was going on because it was such an amazing night."

All night long things were looking up for Boston. The Sox were leading the Orioles 3–2 late in the game, and the Yankees seemed a lock to beat the Rays, leading 7–0 going into the bottom of the eighth inning. At that point the Rays had only made two singles.

Then came the most horrifying three minutes in Boston Red Sox history. ESPN's David Schoenfield called it "the most shocking, unbelievable, thrilling night in baseball history."

But for Red Sox fans it was anything but thrilling.

The first half of the tragic evening occurred at 12:02 in the morning at Baltimore, where the Sox were playing the last-place Orioles. After an hour and twenty minutes rain delay it was the bottom of the ninth. There were two outs. The Sox led 3–2. With a man on, there were two strikes on outfielder Nolan Reimold. He was facing Red Sox star closer Jonathan Papelbon, who was on the mound throwing heat. Reimold doubled to tie the game at 3–3. The next batter was light-hitting second baseman Robert Andino. Reimold took his lead off second.

The Red Sox were one batter away from at least tying for the wild card spot. Papelbon threw on a 1-1 count, and Andino hit a sinking line drive to left field in the direction of Carl Crawford, the ex-Ray who had suffered mightily all season long with a subpar .255 batting average, only 11 home runs, and only 18 steals for a speedster who while with the Rays stole 55, 59, 46, 58, 50, 25, 60, and 47 bases. Four times Crawford had led the league in steals, but something had happened to him in his first year in Boston. He was a shadow of his old self, and fans booed him for his lack of performance. He never felt at home. He rarely came through in the clutch.

It was not an easy catch, but one that Crawford had often made with the Rays. Crawford, who was quick to the ball, ran in and slid, his glove face up under the ball. Red Sox Nation held its breath. The ball struck Crawford's open glove—then bounced away onto the grass. Quickly Crawford grabbed it as Reimold raced around third and headed home. Crawford, who didn't have a strong arm, let fly, too late as Nolan Fucking Reimold slid in. The Orioles were 4–3 winners.

Roman Llimar: "The last play of the next tragedy in the human comedy that is Red Sox history typified this season, as Carl Crawford, newly signed left fielder, and all around (even now) Red Sox hope crusher, let a fly ball drop in to allow the winning run to score in the 9th for the Baltimore Orioles. He had dropped a ball in a similar play that cost the Sox the win on Monday night's game. If he was wearing a Tampa Bay uniform, you know the play would have been made."

Robert Dorin: "I've never liked the Red Sox Nation culture. I can make a lengthy list of Red Sox of color, including Crawford, who I believe were treated unfairly: Reggie Smith, George Scott, Tommy Harper, Jim Rice, Ellis Burks, Oil Can, etc. It takes a special kind of pro athlete to fit the Boston ("our guy") model, and it helps to be white. Guys who appear aloof or arrogant, like Josh Beckett, have problems as well. Red Sox Nation prefers the "wicked awesome" Kevin Millar types. But color has always been a tricky issue in Boston. The new ownership has done a decent job of defusing the race issue so that Crawford was not necessarily treated worse than Beckett et al. But C.C. was always an outside mercenary, at least.

"In 2011 negativity snowballed. By the time the ball bounced in front of C.C. in Baltimore, it almost seemed like an inevitable wish fulfillment of the fans and the media that these guys were chokes and didn't respect the hallowed ground they walked. They ate chicken! As for the money, the Red Sox had joined the Yankees, Dodgers, and others in playing the game. Red Sox Nation prefers its guys to be underpaid overachievers. Made it harder. I didn't feel these overpaid chokes had poisoned our Fenway sacrament, but a lot of others did."

Despite the loss the season wasn't over. If the Rays lost, the Sox would tie for the wild card spot and the season could be salvaged. All eyes in New England now turned toward St. Petersburg, Florida, where the Rays were hosting the Yankees at Tropicana Field.

Sox fans had reason to rejoice as the Yankees held their 7–0 lead going into the eighth inning, but in the eighth the Rays shocked New England when they scored six runs, the last three on a long home run by Evan Longoria.

There still was little for the Sox fans to fear. The Yankees still led 7–6. There were two outs in the ninth, and the next Rays batter, a left-handed pinch hitter, was Dan Johnson, who came to bat with a .108 batting average. Yankee pitcher Cory Wade threw two strikes past Johnson. Once again the Red Sox were a strike away from making the postseason.

Wade then threw Johnson a fastball inside, and to the horror of all of New England, Johnson, a career minor leaguer, not only did the improbable, but the unthinkable: he hit a moonshot deep into the right field stands to tie the score at 7–7.

Jeff Passan: "When I'm on Twitter I try my best to refrain from obscenities, because I don't know who's following me, but when Dan Johnson hit that home run to tie the game that night, I tweeted out three words and an exclamation point: Dan Fucking Johnson! For anyone who was watching that game it was an absolutely surreal scene, and that's why when you talk about the baseball gods being against the Red Sox—I don't personally believe in the baseball gods, but a lot of people do—and those who believe in the baseball gods saw them working their magic against the Red Sox that night."

The Sox still had a chance. The game wasn't over. It was tied.

It looked like the Yankees would win in the top of the twelfth inning when with runners on first and third and nobody out, Evan Longoria fielded a ground ball and threw home, nipping the runner at home. The Rays got out of the inning unscathed, and then at 12:05 in the morning Rays third baseman and emerging star Evan Longoria got up against Yankee reliever Scott Proctor and lined a laser shot down the left field line toward the short wall in Tropicana Field. In another horrible irony that part of the wall at that spot had been lowered several feet to give former Rays left fielder Carl Crawford the chance to make some spectacular catches. Crawford, now a Red Sox, had cost the Sox the game in Baltimore. Now he was costing them a Rays loss in Tampa Bay.

Jeff Passan: "It was a line drive, and no one knew if it had enough distance to get out, because there was a lot of topspin on the ball. We didn't know whether it would be fair or foul.

"When it went for a home run, the hysteria in Tropicana Field was incredible. I watched as a baseball fan. I had no rooting interest. I was rooting for the best story possible, and I don't think there could have been a better story than what happened that night."

Joy reigned in Tampa Bay. Shock and disbelief were the top two emotions in Boston.

The Red Sox players were subdued after the game. They too were in a state of shock. The "best team ever" had failed to make the playoffs.

Jon Lester: "It's just shocking. We should be playing a one-game playoff right now. It's just one of those things. It wasn't meant to be. It wasn't our year."

Carl Crawford: "It was very disappointing because we had high expectations. We didn't live up to them. It was definitely a heart-breaker for us. I watched (the Rays-Yankees game) as soon as I walked in, and it definitely gave us a bad feeling. It's unfortunate we didn't make it."

The fan base, looking forward to another playoff push, was far less genteel in its analysis.

Shaun Kelly: "For eight years I embraced the notion of 'In Theo and Tito We Trust.' Accordingly I was in absolute shock that the Sox lost that game and a chance for the playoffs. I never felt like some people: *Same old Red Sox.* After all, we had won two titles in seven years. We had a burgeoning farm system, an excellent core of major league players, and a superb coaching staff. I really thought they were going to replicate what the Yankees did in 2000, stumble into the playoffs and then turn on the jets. Therefore when they blew that game and then the Rays won, it was one of those nights where I slept very little.

"I was both upset and bewildered."

Sam Sears: "I have indelibly etched emotional memories of the night of September 28, 2011, memories reminiscent of the 1986 Billy Buckner ground ball through his legs game. I was sitting alone in my bedroom switching back and forth between the Sox game and the Rays game. Like most Sox fans, I had become somewhat disgusted by the Sox miserable September performance. When the evening started out on a good note, my disgust turned once again into eternal hope that all Sox fans possess. I was feeling that just maybe the Sox would get it together in the playoffs and play like it had the first five months of the season. But then the Orioles started to come back, and within a span of just five minutes, all hell broke loose.

"I was stunned and angry. As in '86, I turned off the TV and picked up a book, unable to speak. I'm good at denial, and to avoid reliving those excruciatingly painful five minutes, I did not read *The Globe* sports pages for four or five days and would not discuss that evening with anyone. After all, the Patriots were undefeated, and deserved my entire sports emotional output. Screw the Sox (at least until the next year)."

After the devastating loss some fans were content to return to the days before the 2004 World Series win, when Red Sox fans could spend their time moaning and groaning about their team.

Jay Kang: "First, we don't have to pretend to root for these assholes any more. Second, the old kick-in-the-balls feeling is back! We get to go back to our favorite pastime: complaining about this shitty team and its shitty GM and what the fuck is wrong with Crawford and did you hear what John Lackey did when he was at that bar at Back Bay? When I woke this morning I thought, *Hey, maybe this crushing defeat will kill off some of the Cowboy Uppers and the Pink-Hatters and we'll be closer to the ideal mix of Red Sox fans: old angry drunk guys in bars, young angry drunk guys in bars, old and young angry drunks guys at Fenway who heckle Harvard-y fans and/or minorities, minorities who feel weird about being Sox fans, openly hate the city of Boston, and as a result, secretly want the Sox to lose forever.*"

Even reporters gnashed teeth.

Jackie MacMullan: "Nothing can erase the ignominy of 2011, when the 'best team ever' proved to be worse than we could ever imagine."

Had the Red Sox won just one more game or had the Rays lost just one more game, none of what was to follow would have occurred. In a lot of cities a monumental collapse would have been met with a lot of hand-wringing and wailing. In Boston it was met with name-calling and nooses. The Salem Witch trials, another New England ritual, weren't that long ago. Red Sox Nation needed scapegoats, and scapegoats they would get.

A day after the final loss general manager Theo Epstein met with reporters.

Theo Epstein: "The bottom line is, we failed. And our owners deserve better, the fans deserve better, and we have to fix it. We're going to take a look in the mirror and see if we're the ones to fix it."

If by *we* Epstein meant manager Terry Francona and himself, Francona surprised Epstein and management when he announced he was no longer the man for the job.

Terry Francona: "I think [quitting] is the right thing to do for the organization and myself."

He said that one of the reasons he was leaving was a sense of entitlement by the players.

Terry Francona: "I felt frustrated with my inability to reach guys that I've been able to in the past, or affect the outcome a little bit differently and that bothers me. I wanted desperately for our guys to care about each other on the field. I wasn't seeing that as much as I wanted to. When things go bad, your true colors show, and I was bothered by what was showing. It's my responsibility."

Francona said another reason he was quitting was a perceived lack of support from ownership. Another reason, he said, was the intense scrutiny from the press and the public when you're the manager of the Red Sox.

After meeting with Francona for the last time, general manager Theo Epstein talked about what happened and expressed his support for him.

Theo Epstein: "Ultimately, he decided that there were certain things that needed to be done that he couldn't do after eight years here, and that this team would benefit from hearing a new voice. While this may be true, his next team will benefit more than it knows from hearing Tito's voice."

It quickly became apparent that Red Sox ownership wasn't going to stand by quietly and let Francona accuse them of disloyalty. In response ownership, in the person of president Larry Lucchino, orchestrated a smear campaign intended to mar Francona's reputation as he was walking out the door.

In an article written by Bob Hohler of *The Boston Globe*, Francona was accused of being unable to prevent some of the lax behavior by his players that characterized the collapse.

Bob Hohler: "Team sources said Francona, who has acknowledged losing influence with some former team leaders, appeared distracted during the season by issues related to his troubled marriage and health."

The article described how Francona had left his wife of thirty years and had moved into a hotel. It also said that Francona worried about the safety of his son and son-in-law, who were serving in Afghanistan.

This was a hatchet job of the man who had led the Red Sox to not one, but two World Series victories, after eighty six years of famine.

Francona was furious after he saw the article. He was certain Lucchino had fed the information to the reporter.

Terry Francona: "It makes me angry that people say these things because I've busted my ass to be the best manager I can be. I wasn't terribly successful this year, but I worked harder and spent more time at the ballpark this year than I ever did."

These same team sources also accused Francona of not being in top form because he was taking pain medication. Francona countered by saying he had been taking pain medication for his knees for years.

"It never became an issue," he said, "and anyone who knew what was going on knows that."

The article went on to say that trouble began to brew in late August when management proposed moving up a Sunday finale of a weekend series against Oakland so the teams could play a day-night doubleheader on Friday or Saturday. It made sense, but according to the article a number of players protested, accusing management of caring more about money than winning.

A doubleheader was played on Saturday, and the Red Sox won both games. It was the last time the team would win two games in a row.

The owners were worried that the losing in September was related to the resentment over the scheduling, so as a peace offering owner John Henry gave each player $300 headphones and invited them for a players-only gathering on his yacht on September 11.

Nothing worked.

In his article Hohler accused the players of drinking in the clubhouse, ordering take-out chicken, and playing video games during the ballgames. He accused Beckett, Lester, and Lackey of being the primary abusers, with Clay Buchholz joining in occasionally. He also accused the players, especially the pitchers, of not working out as arduously as they should have. As a result, Hohler charged, the pitchers were too fat in September, as they posted a combined 2–7 record with a 6.45 ERA, as the Sox lost eleven of their last fifteen starts.

Hohler wasn't through. He charged that Kevin Youkilis was a cancer in the clubhouse, that the third baseman criticized Jacoby Ellsbury so much the youngster became a recluse. He said that Adrian Gonzalez didn't lead, that though he was a great hitter, he provided neither energy nor passion. Hohler accused Gonzalez of being a lead grouser about the schedule.

Talk about airing dirty laundry in public.

In the article Theo Epstein received his share of criticism for the signings of Bobby Jenks and John Lackey.

What the players took from the article was just how nastily management sought to smear Francona. Former Red Sox pitcher Curt Schilling accused the team of "character assassination of the worst kind."

Curt Schilling: "[The information about Francona's pain medication] could only come from a couple of people in the organization: the trainer, the team doctor, or the executive team there. That's the distressing part. If I'm a free agent now, why would I go to that organization? At the end of the day, I think they betrayed a lot of people in Red Sox Nation.

"It starts at the top. These are some bad people. This guy (Francona) gives everything he could give. They spent nine or ten years building this into a model franchise, so to speak, and I think they destroyed it in a matter of..."

Jeff Passan: "I wasn't surprised that the Red Sox would go out of their way to trash Francona, because that's the way they operate. You see the glorious exits of stars past from Boston and recognize that when your time is up with the Red Sox, the Red Sox are going to make the first move to dirty your name, and it was unfortunate.

"Upon reflection, I'm sure it's something the Red Sox regret. Terry Francona is a good man. Considering all he gave to that city and to that franchise, he's not the type of person to be smeared like that on the way out. When someone is going through difficult times, good people stand by them. The Red Sox did the exact opposite of that, so for Terry Francona to go through that, not only was it unfortunate but completely unfair, but that's how the Red Sox operate. That's part of their business, though I'd like to think going forward things have changed and will continue to change because a good man with a peerless reputation got it taken away from him that day, and he has to rebuild it bit by bit."

Some fans were sorry to see him go.

Shaun Kelly: "When Tito was first hired, there was major criticism because he was a failed Phillies' manager. However, once he began to actually manage the team, he was the most popular and respected manager of the Red Sox in my lifetime. He was brilliant handling the press, and he seemed knowledgeable in terms of the statistical aspect of the game that Bill James and Theo Epstein were trying to integrate, Most import, he handled difficult players, like Manny, with aplomb. He outmanaged Joe Torre in the 2004

ALCS, and his World Series record as manager was 8–0. What was not to like?"

Other fans weren't as charitable.

Robert Dorin: "This is a culture of both misery and blame, and with success in 2004 and 2007, has changed to one of arrogance and entitlement. Red Sox fans take things very personally, so individuals are identified as those *who have denied me my due*. In 1946 Johnny Pesky held the ball. In 1975 Darrell Johnson made one too many pitching changes. The umpire didn't call interference on Armbrister. In 1986 it was Johnny Mac and Billy Buck. In 2003 it was Grady Little. And eventually in 2011, Terry F.

"The press has fed the paranoia, led by the curse maven, Dan Shaughnessy, who is also eager to tweak the buttons of the locals. So Shaughnessy et al. turned a few beers and a chicken snack into a cause célèbre—and Terry became *histoire*."

John Dristilaris: "He was frequently criticized because he often appeared as an apologist for his players, giving the perception that he was a weak manager who let his players walk all over him. There were several incidents that occurred in the clubhouse during his tenure—Manny throwing the traveling secretary; Ortiz barging into his press conference to complain about the official scorer; of course the infamous chicken and beer clubhouse story—that he refused to talk about or he downplayed the incident.

"Fans in Boston, while very supportive of their team, expect accountability on all levels of organization. They know when they're getting BS'd and they don't like it. Yes, he won two World Series as a manager, which should have allowed him to achieve some credibility, but when managing in Boston, one must appear that he is in charge. Francona certainly did not give that appearance, especially toward the end, and it's not how you start, it's how you finish.

"Francona's tenure ended ugly and abruptly."

Shortly after Francona announced his departure, the other shoe dropped when general manager Theo Epstein announced he was leaving the Sox to become the general manager of the Chicago Cubs. The move had been rumored for over a week, but was held up as the Cubs and Sox haggled over the compensation the Sox would receive for letting Epstein out of his contract. When Epstein told the Sox he was leaving, the public reaction was that of surprise.

Jeff Passan: "I was surprised when Theo quit, because normally in those types of power struggles, eventually there is détente. But Theo and Larry Lucchino reached a point in their relationship where it got ugly. One person said, 'It's either you or me.' It said a lot about Theo Epstein truly wanting baseball operations autonomy. And with Larry Lucchino around, you can never have that."

Curt Schilling, for one, wasn't shocked at all when Theo Epstein resigned. On the contrary, he understood exactly why Francona and Epstein were leaving.

Curt Schilling: "Why would he want to go back there? I think we all know now what Terry was saying when he said I don't feel like I had the front office's backing. I think it was very clear why. And for the ownership to follow up that interview by saying I was kind of caught off-guard by the fact that he said that was disingenuous at best."

The collapse, followed by the departures of Terry Francona and Theo Epstein, two favorites of the fans and the media, left pundits wondering whether the past successes had been something of a mirage.

Howard Bryant: "Maybe it was an illusion in the first place. Maybe nothing changed other than nicer, softer window treatments, and the winning of titles. But in the span of a disastrous September, during a bizarre and tumultuous uneven season that produced a thermonuclear aftermath that will be felt in Boston for years, the Red Sox undid it all.

"What an embarrassing way for the most successful nine years the Red Sox have had in a century to end, with a successful, likeable manager having his personal life exposed to the public; the front office appearing small and vindictive, using the old playbook of running people out of town in order to desperately get in the last word and win the public; the players failing to live up to the standards that made them idols and champions; and most of all, virtually none having the class to ruse about the anger and pettiness and ego that so often destroy the best times."

After pondering whether the gift of $300 headphones and the yacht excursion hosted by team owner John Henry made it easier for the players to undercut manager Francona, the insightful Bryant concluded that "the Red Sox are the least attractive job in baseball."

He then commented on the future of the ball club.

Howard Bryant: "Certainly, the era had to end, as they all do, but it didn't have to end like this. As Carl Crawford, Dustin Pedroia, and Adrian Gonzalez form the new core of the Red Sox, management must decide if it will support its next manager, who must establish the trust and authority Francona lost while restoring order with a renegade pitching staff that let its teammates down."

There would be a new manager in 2012. Picking the right one would be crucial to turning around the team.

CHAPTER 67
Bobby V

Red Sox management, embarrassed by reports that the players were drinking beer and eating fried chicken in the middle of ballgames, decided to crack down. There would be a return to law and order. Before choosing a new manager, management named Theo Epstein's right-hand man, Ben Cherington, as the new general manager.

Like Theo before him, Cherington was a New Englander, born and raised in Meriden, New Hampshire. He is the grandson of former Dartmouth College professor Richard Eberhart, a renowned Pulitzer Prize winning poet. Cherington went to Amherst College, then went to the University of Massachusetts at Amherst where he earned a masters in sports management. He was hired by the Red Sox in 1999 by then general manager Dan Duquette, who also was an Amherst grad. He began as a scout, went into baseball operations, was coordinator of international scouting, assistant director of player development, and then director.

When Epstein quit the team for a month and a half during the winter of 2005-2006, Cherington served as co-general manager with Jed Hoyer. When Epstein returned Cherington became the vice-president of player personnel, then senior vice-president, and then assistant general manager. He took over as general manager in 2012 when his boss left for the Chicago Cubs.

On taking over Cherington emphasized that though he and Epstein had similar philosophies, that they were different people. He said he would identify the problems of the past and move to do something about them.

Ben Cherington: "I think we have work to do this off-season to restore the culture that we expect in the clubhouse, to restore a level of accountability. I don't believe there's a silver bullet that will be the answer to that. It's multi-factorial. Certainly we have an important hire in the next manager, and he will be a big part of it. But we're all going to be a big part of it."

A month later the Red Sox announced the name of their new manager. It would be Bobby Valentine, former manager of the Texas Rangers, the New York Mets, and the Chiba Lotte Marines of Japan. At the time of his hiring Valentine was working as an analyst for ESPN. He had not managed a major league team in America in a decade.

All signs pointed to Larry Lucchino as the executive who chose Valentine. Ben Cherington's first choice was Dale Sveum, the veteran infielder who had been the Red Sox third base coach under Terry Francona in 2004 and 2005, but he was overruled by Lucchino and the other owners. The next day Sveum was signed by Theo Epstein to manage the Cubs.

Toronto Blue Jays manager John Farrell was another candidate, but Toronto refused to let him go. After passing on Torey Lovullo, Sandy Alomar Jr., and Pete Mackanin, and Red Sox pick came down to either Gene Lamont or Valentine. The laid-back Lamont, a former manager of the White Sox and Pirates, had been the Detroit Tigers third base coach since 2006.

But someone on the Red Sox, and many believed it to be Lucchino, wanted a man who would bring some law and order to the team, and that man, Lucchino felt, would be Valentine, who during his interview with owner John Henry talked about his affinity for minority owner Bill James' Sabermetrics. When Valentine was hired, he was told he couldn't choose his own coaches but would have to manage with Francona's coaches: Bob McClure, Tim Bogar, and Gary Tuck. (By the end of spring training Valentine would be at odds with all three because they were loyal not to him, but to the front office.)

Valentine was also told to crack down on the prima donna players.

One thing the Red Sox management knew about Valentine: his reign would not be without controversy. He had been fired at Texas by managing partner George W. Bush. He had been fired as manager of the Chiba Lotte Marines after a personality conflict with general manager Tatsuro Hirooka. He was fired by New York Mets general manager Steve Phillips after a stormy relationship. In 1999 Phillips fired three of his coaches, and in 2002 fired Valentine.

Perhaps his signature moment came in June of 1999 when as manager of the Mets he was tossed from a game for arguing a call. An inning later he returned to the dugout wearing Groucho Marx glasses and a fake mustache as a thinly veiled disguise. He was caught on TV, and baseball fined him $5,000 and suspended him for two games.

That season Valentine led the Mets to a 97–66 record and a wild card playoff berth. The Mets then beat Arizona before losing to the Atlanta Braves in six games. The Mets in 2000 again won a playoff berth, then defeated the St. Louis Cardinals to take them to the World Series against the Yankees. Two years later Valentine was fired, returning to Japan where he became a national hero when he led the Chiba Lotte Marines to their first Pacific League pennant in thirty-one years. The Marines won the Japan Series against the Hanshin Tigers and defeated the Korean champions.

As Valentine became more beloved and famous, the Chiba Lotte ownership became more and more envious and resentful of his fame and adoration, and after the 2009 season orchestrated a smear campaign against him. A hundred and twelve thousand Chiba Lotte fans signed a petition supporting Valentine, but ownership fired him anyway in 2009. He then took the job at ESPN as a commentator on Sunday Night Baseball.

Valentine was introduced to the public by Ben Cherington on December 2, 2011. He announced he would wear uniform number 25 in honor of Tony Conigliaro, his roommate in San Diego back in 1976. His start as the new Red Sox manager couldn't have been more congenial.

Jeff Passan, writing for Yahoo Sports, wasn't fooled. He predicted that the hiring of Bobby Valentine would turn into an unmitigated disaster.

Jeff Passan: "Bobby Valentine last managed in the major leagues in 2002, and over the last ten years the culture of baseball had changed—underwent a sea change in the way managers have to handle their players. Bobby has an exceedingly bright baseball mind, but he is an exceedingly stubborn human being, and I could see from the beginning of spring training that there would be friction. I remember the very first day of spring training, Bobby was more hands on than I had ever seen any manager. He went from station to station, manic, nit-picking the pitchers' fielding practice, which is the most benign, unnecessary crap a baseball team can do. He was giving tips and pointers. I remember thinking, *I've seen control freaks before, but this is something else.*"

It only took one week into spring training before Valentine and the Red Sox players were at loggerheads after Valentine announced a ban on beer in the clubhouse and on team flights. This was in reaction to the reports from the year before that players drank beer and ate fried chicken in the clubhouse during games.

Terry Francona, the disposed manager and ESPN commentator who had been fired by the Red Sox in part because of the accusation that he had lost control of his players, accused Valentine of doing it as a public relations stunt. The comment made Valentine seem frivolous.

Bobby Valentine (snidely): "Remember, you get paid over there for saying stuff; you get paid over here for doing stuff."

Things went south early and suddenly. The winter before All Star closer Jonathan Papelbon had fled to Philadelphia, and the anointed closer, Andrew Bailey, who the Red Sox had acquired for talented outfielder and fan favorite Josh Reddick, injured his thumb before opening day. Centerfielder Jacoby Ellsbury also got hurt in early April and went on the DL. The season began 1–5, and then on April 15 Valentine went on local television and ripped Kevin Youkilis for his lackadaisical attitude and play.

Bobby Valentine: "Youkilis is not as physically or emotionally into the game as he has been in the past for some reason."

Jeff Passan: "Youkilis is himself a hard-headed guy. And I'm not coming from the perspective that you give up control to the players. But there is an element of all the best managers where they earn the trust of their players before they turn into the Big Boss. Bobby Valentine simply didn't earn the trust of the guys, and it showed."

The players, accustomed to being stroked and supported by Terry Francona, were not used to such criticism from their manager. Francona, moreover, had been in the habit of walking over to them individually when he thought it necessary to make sure everything was all right. Valentine was much more aloof. He told the players that his office door always was often, and if they wanted something they could come see him. Few did. As injuries mounted and the losses piled up, the chasm between the manager and his players grew.

Valentine had another problem. Francona had used his coaches as go-betweens to his players. Valentine couldn't do that. His coaches—Francona's coaches—distanced themselves from him and left the manager isolated.

After Dustin Pedroia and Adrian Gonzalez defended Youkilis, Valentine then had to eat crow when general manager Ben Cherington ordered him to apologize to Youkilis. Valentine announced he was "a hundred percent behind him." Few believed him. The Sox then lost five games in a row to begin one of the most dreadful seasons in Red Sox history.

Jeff Passan: "Ten games into the season he accused veteran third baseman Kevin Youkilis of loafing. Ten games. Think about that. Valentine was the new boss who pissed off his charges, and the players felt empowered to reach out to ownership to tattle on him, in large part because they, like everyone else, knew the majority of the Red Sox front office didn't even want Valentine as manager. The emperor was naked almost from the start."

The fifth loss in a row was a disaster. The Sox led 9–0 against the Yankees, but Sox relievers Vicente Padilla, Matt Albers, Franklin Morales, Alfredo Aceves, Justin Thomas, and Junichi Tazawa allowed fourteen runs in the seventh and eighth innings. The Yankees won 15–9.

A few writers came to Valentine's defense. Mike Lupica in *The New York Daily News* reminded readers that it was Theo Epstein, not Valentine, who had lost his way, who had traded away talent such as shortstop Alex Gonzalez, who pitchers loved, who signed Carl Crawford for $140 million, who signed John Lackey "for a ridiculous amount."

Wrote Lupica, "You go ahead and make Valentine the face of this and Valentine the fall guy. But if you do, you're blaming the wrong guy in Boston."

The 2012 season wasn't two weeks old when the ascerbic Lupica was the first to ask the question: *How long do you think Bobby Valentine will last as manager of the Red Sox?*

After an 11–11 April, the Sox continued playing .500 ball in May. By late June, things weren't getting any better. On June 19 the Sox record stood at 33–33. ESPN's Buster Olney made public that whatever was plaguing the Red Sox the year before hadn't gone away.

Buster Olney: "The unhappiness that exists among Boston players and staff is multi-layered and deep."

For the Boston fans who were watching a .500 ball club with a $200 million payroll, what they were watching was frustrating and unacceptable. After three straight seasons of not making the playoffs, this would surely be the fourth unless something changed. Who was to blame? Not all fans pointed fingers at the manager.

Blogger Steve Bastek: "As much as I would love to blame Valentine, I simply can't. He came into this scenario in the worst possible circumstance.

"As fans, all we can do is sit back and keep cheering these guys on, because there are plenty of guys on the team who still want to play and win. And last but not least, we all need to pray to whatever god we may believe in that these owners sell the team after the season. Their apathy is apparent, and it's a slap in the face to every fan when these guys try to act like they actually care about any of us."

On June 24, 2012, management acted, trading Kevin Youkilis, who was hitting .233, to the Chicago White Sox for a utility player and a pitching prospect. The emergence of Will Middlebrooks at third base had made Youkilis expendable. It also removed one of the burrs in manager Valentine's side. His departure left David Ortiz as the only Red Sox player from the 2004 championship team.

The trade was announced during a game at Fenway against the Atlanta Braves. After he was pinch run for in the seventh after hitting a triple and left the game, Youkilis waved to the crowd and was given a standing ovation. He came out for a curtain call.

Cody Ross: "It brought a tear to my eye. To see him run off and tip his hat and have tears in his eyes. It was just a special time. I know how much he means to the city. Two World Series here. Played his heart and soul out every day. Just a great teammate. I'm going to miss him."

By July of 2012 a cadre of remaining the players were in the throes of a mutiny, so much did they dislike playing for Valentine. His cheap shot aimed at Youkilis in April began the rebellion. By June the Sox record was 57 and 59, 11 games behind the first-place Yankees and 5½ games out of the wild card, and Sox players were climbing the back stairs to complain to management about how much they despised him. Then on July 22 Valentine left pitcher Jon Lester in a game against the Toronto Blue Jays while he absorbed a pounding that resulted in four home runs and eleven earned runs. Adrian Gonzalez went so far as to text his displeasure about it. According to Jeff Passan of Yahoo sports, some players told management they no longer wanted to play for Valentine. Dustin Pedroia, named as one of them, posted a picture of a napping Valentine with the words: *Our manager contemplating the line up at 3:30 P.M.*

On July 26 during an off day in New York, Adrian Gonzalez, Dustin Pedroia, and other players met with Larry Lucchino and John Henry at the Palace Hotel to air their dissatisfaction with having to play for Valentine. They cited the Jon Lester shellacking, among other grievances.

Jeff Passan: "I was the one who broke the story. I got the first tip about a week after the meeting happened. I started investigating, and I called around, and I tell you, a lot of people did not want to talk about this, and so I knew it was something significant. I kept hitting dead ends, and I reached a point where I thought the story wasn't going to see the light of day."

One of his sources then came through, telling him the whole story.

Jeff Passan: "He said there had been a text message sent from Adrien Gonzalez's phone to John Henry complaining about Bobby Valentine. A team meeting was then held in which the players aired their grievances about how bad a job Valentine was doing.

"After I got two more sources to confirm the story I called Ben Cherington. I didn't know Ben very well. I read him the first four paragraphs. He asked for some time to respond, and he called me back twenty minutes later. He went on the record confirming everything that happened. My respect for Ben Cherington grew as a person that day, because he was faced with an untenable situation. He was given a manager he didn't want, and he was a good soldier, and he ate it, and he tried to make it work, and when it wasn't working, he tried to stand by him. He was as honest as possible while still trying to protect his team.

"That day, when the story came out, the writing was on the wall that there was absolutely no way that Bobby Valentine would be back the next year. When there's a full-blown mutiny against a major league manager, that's something from which you do not recover."

Publicly Ben Cherington supported Valentine, telling them he would be the manager for the rest of the year.

"We're not considering anyone else," said the GM. "He's as committed to managing the team as he ever has been, and we're committed to him and trying to do everything we can to support him and make this work."

The beloved Johnny Pesky, the Red Sox legendary second baseman after whom the right field foul pole was named, died at age 93 on August 13, 2012. Only four of the current Red Sox players, David Ortiz, Clay Buchholz, Vicente Padilla, and Jarrod Saltalamacchia attended. Red Sox fans were outraged.

Mark LeBrun: "I was absolutely appalled at the players' not showing up for Pesky's funeral. It was disgusting."

Fans were further outraged by Larry Lucchino's letter to Red Sox season ticket holders, which he issued during the All Star break. In the letter he thanked them for their support, praised the chemistry of the team citing newcomers Cody Ross, Mike Aviles, Will Middlebrooks, and Daniel Nava "mixing with our beloved Big Papi." He said he looked forward to the return of "the varsity," including injured vets Jacoby Ellsbury, Carl Crawford, Andrew Bailey, and "the ever-dirty Dustin Pedroia."

Lucchino said he was hoping the team would play in the postseason, invited fans to visit the Living Museum that is Fenway Park, and asked fans to "come over and say hello. We enjoy listening to you, and we enjoy talking to you. We're your biggest fans."

"Keep the faith," he signed out, "Larry Lucchino."

The tenor of the letter was light and cheery, but the reaction from the fans were fierce and sarcastic.

Tony Pouliot: "Tell me I am wrong, you guys. I see this letter from Lucchino, and I am stunned by the cluelessness of the front office. They cannot stop selling image, can't help themselves. I am flabbergasted. This is a joke, right? The whole sucking up to Papi, the living museum, varsity ????? Are you kidding? Boston has some of the most knowledgeable fans out there, right up there with St. Louis, and we get this pink hat pandering AGAIN!?!"

Pouliot concluded his rant: "So, everything is great in the Land of Boston. The great and powerful Oz has spoken. Good times never seem so good! New England Patriots camp opens July 26, just in case anyone is wondering."

Another fan, Matthew Bond, was similarly cheesed off.

Matthew Bond: "The letter discussed the team as if it were a little league softball roster where everyone wins a trophy. The attitude of the organization as the team deals with a frustrating season has been unacceptable, highlighted by Lucchino's absurd message to the fans.

"Lucchino is insulting the intelligence of Red Sox fans by treating his greeting as more of an assurance that all is well in the world of the Red Sox instead of being honest about the situation. It is truly remarkable that such a positively toned letter to the fans describes a vastly underperforming .500 baseball club.

"Yet by acting like everything's peachy in Red Sox Nation, Lucchino adds to the pain of those following them closely."

Having been accused by fans and the press of refusing to take drastic measures, the Red Sox front office amazed Red Sox Nation when on August 25, 2012, the Sox traded Josh Beckett, Adrian Gonzalez, and Carl Crawford, three of their most expensive players, and infielder Nick Punto to the Los Angeles Dodgers. In return the Red Sox got five players no one ever heard of. Didn't matter. The headline in *The Boston Herald*—Bums Away—seemed to sum up how the Sox fans felt about the three stars. One fan described the trade as "a Febreze-like move."

In making the deal the Sox dealt Beckett, who had struggled with a 5–11 record and a 5.23 ERA, Crawford, who hadn't done much, and Gonzalez, who had been a thorn in Bobby Valentine's paw. Shedding more than $260 million in salary would give the Red Sox huge flexibility to improve the team.

Jeff Passan: "There had been discussions earlier in the year before the July 31 trade deadline. Trades are really difficult to do after July 31 because the players have to pass through waivers, and that's not an easy thing. The player has to have a horseshit contract to pass through waivers after July 31. And that's what those contracts were.

"I remember getting a phone call from a colleague at Yahoo, Tim Brown, saying, 'Something's going on with the Red Sox and the Dodgers.' I remember thinking, *Is this really going to happen? Are the Red Sox really going to get out from under a quarter of a billion dollars worth of contract commitments that they've made? Are the Dodgers really that flush with cash that they are going to be able to take them on?*

"This trade was a bellwether for the Red Sox and their new way of thinking, and the new Dodgers, and their way of thinking—this was the first sign the Dodgers were going to turn into the spending Leviathans that they've become. And it was the first sign the Red Sox were not going to be taking on these huge, long-term contracts.

"When the trade went through, oh my God, I thought it was a great thing for the Red Sox, because it gave them flexibility. Flexibility for a big market team is an underrated thing. When you're locked into those huge contracts, ones you can't get out from under, there's nothing you can do about it. You have to sit there and eat it for a long time. And that's something I thought the Red Sox were going to have to do. Getting out from under was the best thing that could have happened to them, because it gave Ben Cherington the ability to be creative, and that's exactly what he did in the off-season."

The deal may have been cleansing, but it left Valentine with a roster of David Ortiz and a group of minor leaguers. The last months were sure to be a disaster.

A week after the big trade Valentine made headlines when he threatened to punch a radio talk-show host in the mouth over the air. The host, Glenn Ordway, probably deserved it when he commented that Valentine had arrived later than usual for the game and asked him, "Have you checked out on the season?"

Talking on the telephone Valentine replied, "What an embarrassing thing to say. If I were there right now, I'd punch you right in the mouth. Ha ha. How's that sound? Sound like I checked out? What an embarrassing thing? Why would somebody even, that's stuff that a comic strip person would write. How could someone in real life say that?"

Later Valentine told reporters, "If anyone in this room or any other room I've been in in my life wants to question my integrity, I will ask someone to referee that situation."

He was late, the manager told reporters, because he had to pick up his son at the airport, and the plane was late. Then he had to return to his hotel in San Francisco to get his game information before driving over the Golden Gate Bridge to the Oakland Coliseum.

Valentine called in his lineup at 2 and told his coaches he'd be a little late. His workday was to start at 4:30. He actually arrived at 4:02.

"For someone to say that I was late is an absolute disgrace to their integrity if they have any," he said.

During the interview he told Ordway that he was having a "miserable" season.

Bobby Valentine: "It's turned out to be not what I expected. It's been a little misery, yeah. I'm not sure it's 24/7, but I would think after a loss I'm miserable...It's been adventurous, challenging.

"It's always been personal. All year, it's been personal. That's over the line, and I'm not going to take it here in the dugout and I won't take it on the radio or TV show, thank you very much."

The 2012 season ended on October 3 with a 14–2 defeat at the hands of the hated Yankees. The final tally was 69 wins and 93 loses, the first losing season for the Red Sox since 1997 and their worst season record since 1965.

How the fans felt about the season was perfectly encapsulated by a fan who called himself Obnoxious Baseball Fan.

Obnoxious Baseball Fan: "At the end, there was no anger, no joy, no celebration, no relief, no anticipation, no rage after watching them play doormat in the Bronx, no pride, no silver lining, no satisfaction, no contentment knowing you were right all along about this manager, no more laughter, no more tears.

"Not even a hangover.

"Chicken and beer? Those were the good old days.

"As far as the 2012 Red Sox, there are no survivors to be listed in this obituary. Although Lucchino is amazingly resilient, much like that cockroach living behind your fridge after the next nuclear apocalypse."

The next day, October 4, Bobby Valentine was fired. The move was announced in a press release.

"This is not the press conference that I was expecting at the end of the season," said Valentine during an impromptu meeting with reporters.

Commented the *Boston Guardian*, it was "the end of an error."

Jeff Passan: "Much like all season, the past haunted Valentine's present. Announcing the game on TV was Terry Francona, the popular manager fired last October and replaced by Valentine. He lurked around the clubhouse, chatting up Dustin Pedroia and others, his presence a reminder of what could have been, what should have been.

"Instead, Bobby Valentine gave Boston something altogether different, a season reminiscent of so many the Red Sox of old came to know; one not just of disappointment but of top-to-bottom failure, epic in scope and metastatic in virulence.

"Finally, mercifully, the Red Sox' 2012 season is done, and so is their manager. All that's left is a call to the bugle player."

CHAPTER 68

Redemption

With the merciful end of the 2012 season the future of the Red Sox could not have been looking more grim. For two years in a row a Red Sox season had ended in a string of losses followed by the firing of the manager. Larry Lucchino's attempt to emulate the Yankee formula of buying big-name stars for big money had failed miserably. Lucchino had nixed general manager Ben Cherington's choice of John Farrell as manager and had selected Bobby Valentine instead. For whatever reason, he couldn't have made a worst choice.

This time Cherington would get his way. The Red Sox traded shortstop Mike Aviles to the Toronto Blue Jays to get Farrell and journeyman reliever David Carpenter. Farrell, who had been the Red Sox pitching coach from 2007 to 2010, signed a three-year contract. He was hired over San Diego Padres special assistant Brad Ausmus, Yankees bench coach Tony Pena, and Orioles third-base coach DeMarlo Hale, who had also been one of Terry Francona's coaches.

With Toronto Farrell led the Blue Jays to 81–81 in 2011 and 73–89 in 2012, but Cherington wasn't swayed by his record. He had wanted Farrell when Larry Lucchino chose Bobby Valentine, and this time Cherington was going to make sure he'd get his man.

Jeff Passan: "Cherington was given the job of picking the next manager, and he picked the right guy. John Farrell had the perfect temperament. John Farrell was the perfect amount of life brains and baseball brains. He brought trust back to the pitching staff, where it had eroded irrevocably. He was the guy that Boston needed."

What did please the Red Sox faithful was that their general manager, the man with the expertise, was the one who made the selection.

Jorge Aranguer Jr.: "The hiring of John Farrell, who had always been Cherington's first choice as Valentine's replacement, is an immense victory for the general manager, and it restores the decision-making in Boston to where it belongs: the front office. We have no idea how good Cherington really is as a general manager. We're about to find out.

"Boston ownership has shown so much empirical authority recently that it seems like a long time ago, in a galaxy far, far away, that Larry Lucchino labeled the Yankees as the Evil Empire for having the same qualities the Red Sox now exhibit. It's as if Boston's earlier success empowered the Fenway group to believe it could do whatever it wanted, and it would work. John Henry, Larry Lucchino, and Tom Werner are smart and successful men, but sometimes smart and successful men must also know when to back away."

With Ben Cherington calling the shots, the general manager signed a group of free agent veterans who received almost no acclaim at their signing. His first two signings, which came in November of 2012, were Atlanta Braves catcher David Ross and Oakland A's outfielder Jonny Gomes. In December he signed Shane Victorino, an outfielder for the Los Angeles Dodgers, and a relief pitcher from Texas by the name of Koji Uehara. He also received a ho hum reception from the faithful when he signed Oakland A's shortstop Stephen Drew, the brother of J.D. Drew, who the fans hadn't much cared for. Mike Napoli, a catcher/DH from Texas, was added to the mix as well. Cherington then traded with the Pittsburgh Pirates for closer Joel Hanrahan. On the last day of January 2012, he signed first baseman Lyle Overbay and three weeks later signed a first baseman by the name of Mike Carp.

Who were these guys?

Jeff Passan: "I thought the Red Sox were approaching it like there were a bunch of little holes in the dike, so let's stick our thumbs in them, when in reality there was a giant deluge coming. Frankly I thought it was the wrong way to approach it—and I was dead wrong on that, and I'm happy to admit I was dead wrong on it, because in hindsight it was a pretty brilliant approach. Ben brought in the right types of guys who fit their system well. They got almost all of them on good-money contracts. They did the right thing, and kudos to Ben Cherington and his lieutenants for seeing a plan through that a lot of the industry was shaking its head at."

Before the start of the season Passan picked the Red Sox to finish last in the division.

There were *a lot* of unanswered questions going into the 2012 season, among them: Is John Farrell the right manager for the job? Will David Ortiz, out since last July with a torn Achilles tendon, return and be productive? Will the starting pitchers, especially Jon Lester, John Lackey, and Clay Buchholz, bounce back from disastrous seasons? Can Joel Hanrahan, who pitched so well in Pittsburg, make it in Boston as the team's closer? Will Jacoby Ellsbury, who was injury prone in all of 2011, bounce back?

In the spring the curmudgeon of *The Boston Globe*, Dan Shaughnessy, began his column with the lines: "The Red Sox know you've lost that lovin' feeling. They aim to win back the hearts of disgruntled fans."

He suggested a new slogan for the team: "Please don't hate us."

Shaughnessy noted that the new players, whom he categorized as "second-tier," had been brought in not just for their baseball skills, but also for "the content of their characters."

Noting the less than fan-friendly natures of Josh Beckett, the lethargic J.D. Drew, and the aloof Adrian Gonzalez, he wrote, "The Sox are trying to assemble a likeable team."

The Red Sox "are starting at the bottom," he concluded, "working for your love."

In spring training the Sox played well, and by mid-April normalcy seemed to have returned to the Sox. John Farrell was working his magic on Jon Lester, Clay Buchholz and especially on John Lackey, as the team swept two series against the Tampa Bay Rays and the Cleveland Indians. They had an 11–4 record, first in the American League East on April 18.

Tom Verducci: "Because Lester and Buchholz look like aces, the Boston Red Sox look like serious contenders again in the American League East. That seemed very important in a town that loves its baseball. Then everything changed in an instant. Terrorism came to Patriot's Day."

The third Monday in April in the two states of Massachusetts and Maine is called Patriot's Day. It honors the patriotic spirit of America. Since 1959 the Red Sox have scheduled Patriots Day games at Fenway Park. The game was scheduled for 11:00 A.M.

On that day in 2013 the Red Sox dispatched the rival Tampa Bay Rays by the score of 3–2. The Red Sox players were dressing in their locker room, when around ten minutes to three outside could be heard the loud wail of sirens as emergency vehicles, a pack of them, screamed toward death and destruction brought on by two Chechen brothers who planted pipe bombs in two backpacks along the route of the Boston Marathon. Three spectators died, and two hundred and sixty-four others were injured, many severely, from the bomb blasts. Police wondered whether it was a terrorist attack or the work of a single deranged lunatic.

The Sox flew to Cleveland to play three games against the Indians, and when they returned they found a broken, saddened city. The bombs, police found, had been placed by a pair of brothers from Dagestan, near Chechnya in southern Russia. They were caught when their pictures were captured on surveillance photographs of them robbing a 7/11 store in Cambridge. The two then shot to death a MIT security guard and carjacked a Mercedes and drove off. They released the owner of the car unharmed a half hour later.

The car driven by the suspects was tracked to Watertown, west of Boston, where the brothers tossed explosives at the pursuing policemen. The brothers got out of the car and traded gunfire with police. An MBTA officer was wounded and Tamerlan Tsarnaev was shot and was wounded. As he lay on the ground his brother Dzhokhar ran over his body with the car, killing him. Police fired at the car, but the suspect got away, managing to escape and disappear.

While the search for the younger brother went on, the police closed down the subway line and ordered tens of thousands of residents of Watertown, Newton, Waltham, Belmont, Cambridge, Allston, and Brighton to stay in their homes. Red Sox and Bruins games were postponed.

In the last moments of daylight Friday evening, the police descended on a boat stored in a backyard in Watertown. The boat's owner had noticed the tarp on his boat had been cut, and he saw blood near the straps. He called police, who captured the wounded younger brother, much to the relief of the entire city.

The older brother has been accused of masterminding the attack. To this day no one knows the motivation behind the terrorist attack.

The first game back in Boston since the bombing was on a Saturday afternoon. The Red Sox hosted the Kansas City Royals at Fenway. The mood was like that of a second opening day. The Red Sox didn't wear the traditional uniforms that said "Red Sox" on their shirts. Instead, they said "Boston."

A ceremony began with a tribute to the Boston police on the center field Jumbotron. Police officers involved in the manhunt stood in front of each dugout as everyone stood for a moment of silence in tribute of the many victims of the tragedy. Matt Patterson, a fire fighter who saved the life of a child, and Steven Byrne, an injured spectator who shielded his friend's sisters from the blast, threw out the ceremonial first pitch.

David Ortiz, who was about to play his first game of the season after rehabbing from an Achilles heel injury, had been moved to tears by the death of an eight-year-old boy killed by the bombs while watching the Boston Marathon. The boy's sister and mother also had been hurt.

David Ortiz: "That devastated me. I put myself in the same place. It's horrible. It's horrible. It's a beautiful nation and I think our President will get to the bottom of this and make sure this country goes back to what it's always been, a safe place to be and what everybody wants it to be, a happy place like all of us know."

Ortiz was asked to speak to the sold-out throng before the game. He spoke with emotion.

David Ortiz: "This jersey we wear today, it doesn't say Red Sox. It says Boston. We want to thank you Mayor Menino, Governor Patrick, the whole police department, for the great job that they did this past week. This is our fucking city. And nobody's going to dictate our freedom.

"Stay strong."

The roar of the crowd brought goose bumps to everyone.

Jeff Passan: "You could have put Abraham Lincoln up on stage that day, and he would not have come up with a more perfect speech than what David Ortiz gave, And to see a guy who grew up in the Dominican Republic, who had a PED stain on him, who does not look like in any way, shape or form the person you'd imagine representing the city of Boston, to see him saying the defining words that brought that city together more than any, I thought was the most wonderful, beautiful thing. It really showed how much the Red Sox mean to the city of Boston and how much David Ortiz himself now means to the city of Boston.

"Every city needs its moment when tragedy strikes, and it seems like baseball is always there to provide that moment. You saw it in New York after 9/11. You saw it in Boston after the marathon bombing. Baseball is always there, and as much as the sport has lost younger viewers and has lagged behind with its growth, it always provides that jolt and the comfort that the other sports simply can't match."

The Puritans in the crowd had winced at Ortiz's profanity, but FCC chairman Julius Genachowski quickly let it be known that he approved of Big Papi's speech.

Julius Genachowski: "David Ortiz spoke from the heart at today's Red Sox game. I stand with Big Papi and the people of Boston."

In the game that afternoon Ortiz singled to drive in the tying run as Boston went on to defeat the Royals 4–3. For the remainder of the year the Ortiz-inspired saying "Boston Strong" would become the theme of what would turn out to be a surprisingly successful, historic season.

When David Ortiz returned, he brought with him a magical bat. In April he hit three home runs and drove in 15 RBIs as the Red Sox compiled an 18–8 record that month. Before the season was over Big Papi hit 30 home runs, drove in 103 runs, and hit .309. He finished in the top ten in the American

League in all three categories. On July 2 he hit his 500th career double and on September 4 collected his 2,000th hit. On July 10 he passed Harold Baines to become the all-time hit leader for a designated hitter.

He also became a legend, leading his rejuvenated team in the clubhouse as the Hall of Fame awaits.

With the veterans Ortiz, Pedroia, and Ellsbury leading the way, by the start of July the Sox compiled a 50–34 record. It was only the fourth time in Red Sox history that the team won fifty games at the half-season mark.

One of the unlikely leaders of the team was journeyman outfielder/pinch hitter Jonny Gomes, who had tee shirts printed up for his teammates after the marathon bombing with the message "Keep calm and chive on" printed on the front.

Whatever happens, said teammate Shane Victorino, another unlikely Red Sox leader, "we just say, 'All right, guys, let's get right back at it.'"

Gomes was also one of the Sox who decided he wasn't going to cut his hair. Gomes and first baseman Mike Napoli became The Bearded Bash Brothers. Dustin Pedroia by the end of the season looked like a character out of Planet of the Apes. The beards only added to the mystique of this remarkable team.

Another standout who popped up out of nowhere and became a star was 38-year old relief pitcher Koji Uehara. When Joel Hanrahan, the projected closer, became injured, and his anointed replacement Andrew Bailey, proved too inconsistent to close, and manager John Farrell's next choice, Junichi Tazawa, couldn't cut it either, Farrell called upon Uehara, who general manager Ben Cherington had signed from Texas as a free agent. Uehara proceeded to pitch lights out baseball in June, allowing but one run in fifteen appearances and posting a 1.50 ERA. In July Uehara pitched in fourteen games, pitched 15⅓ innings, garnered five saves, and had an ERA of 0.00. He allowed no earned runs the entire month.

On defense shortstop Steven Drew and second baseman Dustin Pedroia were working their magic in the infield, and kid outfielder Daniel Nava was making a name for himself with his defensive play and his bat.

Another surprise, John Lackey, the worst pitcher in the American League in 2012, was the Red Sox' best pitcher in the early going. Lackey on June 26 struck out 12 Colorado batters, only the sixth Red Sox pitcher since 1916 to strike out a dozen opponents. He didn't walk a man. Lackey was 4–1 in eight starts since May 19 with an ERA of 2.44.

Clay Buchholz, though brittle, was brilliant as he stitched together a 9–0 record with a 1.71 ERA at the All Star break. Shoulder bursitis then laid him low for a while.

If the Sox would have competition for the division title, it wasn't going to come from the New York Yankees, but rather from the Tampa Bay Rays, which ran off a 16–2 record in July and only trailed Boston by a half a game.

The Red Sox, with Jon Lester subpar and Buchholz hurt, needed another quality starter, and on July 30 Ben Cherington went out and got one when he acquired veteran starter Jake Peavy from the Chicago White Sox in a three-team trade that sent phenom shortstop Jose Iglesias to the Detroit Tigers. Peavy, a twelve-year veteran with a lifetime ERA of 3.51, was known for his control. He allowed few walks and gave up few home runs. The addition of Peavy solidified GM Ben Cherington's reputation for making smart moves.

Jeff Passan: "[Peavy] was a luxury the Red Sox could have because they had built up their farm system again and they could afford to deal a couple of players like Jose Iglesias. Jose would have looked nice at shortstop, but the Red Sox realized they had Xander Bogaerts waiting, and Xander is going to be a star. It was a luxury that they could trade Iglesias, and that's what they did."

The Sox only played .500 ball most of August and September, allowing the pesky Tampa Bay Rays to tie for the lead in the East a few times, but then the Sox got hot, and by early September they led by 7½ games after two straight nail-biting wins against the New York Yankees at Yankee Stadium in which Boston scored in the final inning to beat the Yankees.

In the first game the Yankees scored six runs in the seventh inning to take a 8–7 lead going into the ninth. The legendary Mariano Rivera, playing in his final season, came in from the bullpen. He retired the first two batters. Mike Napoli singled, and then pinch runner Quintin Berry stole second and went to third on an error by the Yankee catcher. Stephen Drew then hit a broken-bat single into right field to tie the game. It was Rivera's sixth blown save of the season.

Boston then won it in the tenth. Jacoby Ellsbury singled and stole second. With two outs and two strikes on Shane Victorino, pitcher Joba Chamberlain threw, and Victorino checked his swing. Chamberlain complained vociferously about the check-swing call and was ejected at the end of the inning after Victorino added insult to injury by hitting a broken bat single over the second baseman's head to win the game.

The next night the Sox were losing by five runs when Mike Napoli hit a game-tying grand slam home run in the seventh inning. Shane Victorino, stellar all year, hit a home run in the eighth to put the Sox ahead for good. The win put the Sox 7½ games ahead of the Tampa Bay Rays and went a long way toward eliminating the Yankees from the playoffs.

Then on September 15th at Fenway Park the Red Sox honored Rivera in a ceremony before the game and then pounded the Yankees 9–2. Clay Buchholz allowed but a single unearned run. The Sox clinched their AL East title five days later.

The Sox turnabout was nothing short of remarkable:

Jeff Passan: "I didn't see it coming. I don't know if anyone outside of Yawkey Way saw it coming. Even internally I don't think the Red Sox saw themselves ending the season as the best team in the American League."

In the first round of the playoffs the Sox had to meet the Tampa Bay Rays, and it was an ex-Ray, Jonny Gomes, who was the catalyst in the Sox' opening game 9–2 rout. The shaggy, effervescent Gomes doubled in two runs in the fourth, then scored from second on an infield single to score the go-ahead run as Steven Drew raced hard to beat the throw at first.

Johnny Gomes: "You don't get 97 wins by waiting for the three-run homer. We generate some runs any way possible. And that's just not my hustle from second. That hustle is definitely erased if Stephen Drew doesn't hustle to first. So it's double hustle and we were able to touch the plate and get a run on the board."

John Farrell: "He fits what we do so well. And the way he goes about the game rubs off on other players in the clubhouse."

Jon Lester was the winner in Game 1 and John Lackey defeated Rays ace David Price 7–4 in Game 2. The Rays beat Koji Uehara in the ninth in Game 3, but five solid innings from Jake Peavy plus some fine relief from Craig Breslow, Junichi Tazawa, and Uehara led to a 3–1 win in the finale. There were two outs in the seventh with Jacoby Ellsbury on third, when Shane Victorino hit a slow ground ball to shortstop. With Ellsbury racing home on the play, the Sox won the game when Victorino beat the throw to first.

Rays manager Joe Maddon: "They didn't make any mistakes. You could see their grit. They really promoted the character in that group."

Facing the Sox in the next round of the playoffs was the Detroit Tigers, starring their two ace pitchers, Justin Verlander and 21-game winner Max Scherzer. They would also have to face batting star Miguel Cabrera, who in 2013 finished the regular season with a .348 average, with 44 homers and 137 RBIs. Prince Fielder, the first baseman, had 25 homers and 106 RBIs.

The series went six games. Anibal Sanchez and four relievers shut out the Sox in the opener 1–0, but Boston came back to win 6–5. Before Game 3 Sox pitcher Jake Peavy complained that his buddy John Lackey was being overlooked in his match with Verlander.

"It's almost like we didn't have a starter going today," he said. "Our starter is pretty good, too."

John Lackey then went and shut out the Tigers 1–0 with relief help from Breslow, Tazawa, and Uehara to beat Verlander. A Mike Napoli home run in the seventh brought the game winner.

Jeff Passan: "[Lackey] had been bad and he had been injured, and I don't think there was any expectation that he would come back like he did, but Tommy John surgery can be a wonderful thing. It can take a pitcher who is broken and make him whole again. John got in shape. His arm was like it was during his run in 2002 with the Angels when they went to the World Series."

The Tigers beat Peavy 7–3, but then in Game 5 in Comerica Park Mike Napoli hit one over the center field fence to score three runs against Anibal Sanchez to lead the Sox to a 4–3 win. Jon Lester got the win with the help of Breslow, Tazawa, and Uehara. Starting at shortstop Xander Bogaerts, 21 years, 16 days old, became the youngest Red Sox player ever to start a postseason game.

Shane Victorino, who brought his steady play to the Red Sox all year, finished the year with a .294 batting average, 15 home runs, 64 RBIs, and 21 steals. He also brought leadership and hustle to the Red Sox team, and so it was only fitting that with the Red Sox losing 2–1 to Max Scherzer in Game 6 of the League Championship Series, Victorino went up to the plate with one out and the bases loaded in the sixth inning against reliever Jose Veras. The first two pitches were strikes, and then Veras threw him a curve ball that the Hawaiian smote over the Green Monster for a dramatic grand slam home run that gave the Sox a 5–2 victory and a trip to the World Series.

The Red Sox were looking every bit like a team of destiny.

CHAPTER 69

Champions

After what had transpired in 2011 and especially in 2012, who in their right minds could have conceived of the Red Sox making it to the World Series in 2013? At the beginning of the season the Sox had been predicted to finish last in the division in most polls. The Rays and the Yankees had been ceded playoff spots. The Sox were an afterthought. When general manager Ben Cherington signed former pitching coach John Farrell to be manager and added seven important free agents: Shane Victorino, Mike Napoli, David Ross, Ryan Dempster, Jonny Gomez, Koji Uehara, and Stephen Drew to the roster, most Sox fans yawned. Who were these guys? They certainly didn't have the star quality of Josh Beckett, Adrian Gonzalez, and Carl Crawford, three high-dollar players who had been jettisoned the year before, air mailed cross country to the Los Angeles Dodgers, where Magic Johnson spent $261 million to take the Sox problem children off their hands.

It seemed as though Sox management was churning players, just spinning its wheels.

Then came two bomb explosions by the finish line of the Boston Marathon, and everything changed. The players, led by David Ortiz, returned to the city of Boston with a renewal of purpose. Suddenly players like John Lackey and Jon Lester, who had been mediocre in 2012, found their form. Some players, like Daniel Nava and Mike Carp, came out of nowhere and contributed mightily. Moreover, the players acquired by Cherington meshed into a unit of hustling, bearded, dirt bag winners along with veterans Dustin Pedroia, David Ortiz, and Jacoby Ellsbury.

Boston Strong became the call, and Boston Strong the Red Sox became. Once again, thanks to Cherington, Farrell, and his rag tag team of overachievers, it became cool to love the Red Sox again. There would be but one more hurdle for these 2013 Sox. Could they take the talented St. Louis Cardinals and win the World Series for the third time in ten years?

The opening game of the 2013 World Series was played at Fenway Park before a vocal crowd of 38,345 fans. Mike Napoli started things off in the first inning by doubling with the bases loaded.

Mike Napoli: "I love this stage. It's in the spotlight. I really enjoy this time of the year. It's just going out there and getting the job done."

A two-run home run by David Ortiz in the seventh inning was his fourth home run of the 2013 postseason. It was his sixteenth postseason home run overall. The Sox won 8–1.

In Game 2 Ortiz hit another home run, but it wasn't enough as the Sox lost 4–2. They were only about to get four hits against Cardinal phenom Michael Wacha and two relievers. The Sox struck out 12 times. Lackey led 2–1 in the seventh and was eight outs from the win, but after Craig Breslow came in to relieve, there was mayhem, errors, and the Cardinals went on to win.

The Sox then lost Game 3 by the score of 5–4. Allen Craig scored the winning run for the Cardinals with two outs in the bottom of the ninth inning when Will Middlebrooks was called for obstruction. The Red Sox players confronted the umpires to no avail. On the play Middlebrooks dove for a low throw and was lying on the ground with both legs up in the air, when Craig tripped over him. He scrambled up and was thrown out at home, but the umpires ruled that Middlebrooks had interfered and awarded Craig home plate and the winning run.

Will Middlebrooks: "That's a terrible way to end the game."

John Farrell: "That's a tough pill to swallow."

The Sox were down two games to one, and they were losing Game 4 when David Ortiz called his teammates together for an impromptu meeting.

"If you think you're going to come to the World Series every year, you're wrong," he told them. "Take advantage of being here."

Said Jonny Gomes, "It was like twenty-four kindergarteners looking up at their teacher. He got everyone's attention."

He certainly had Gomes', who wasn't in the original lineup for Game 4 played at Busch Stadium, but when Shane Victorino's back acted up on him, manager John Farrell started Gomes, and in the sixth inning he hit a three-run home run off Cardinals' righty reliever Seth Maness to defeat St. Louis 4–2 and even the series. Gomes had been one for eighteen with no RBIs when he came to bat.

John Farrell: "His importance to this team goes above and beyond the numbers that he puts up."

Game 5 belonged to Jon Lester, who fighting a sore back pitched the Sox to a 3–1 victory over the Cardinals. He left the game with two outs in the eighth inning, scattering four hits and striking out seven Cardinal batters. In the 15½ innings he pitched against St. Louis, he allowed but one run.

David Ortiz was three for four with an RBI double. In the series he was 11–15 with six RBIs and four extra-base hits.

David Ortiz: "I was born for this."

After the game Lester voiced his appreciation for Big Papi.

Jon Lester: "I haven't played with many superstars, but this guy right here is the epitome of a superstar and a good teammate. I don't think you could ever ask for more out of an individual than what he does on and off the field. The guy's got a heart of gold. And he goes out there every single night and competes."

The Sox were returning to Fenway with two games to win the World Series. They didn't need a second chance. John Lackey, the worst pitcher in the American League in 2012, a symbol of the Red Sox' reversal of fortune, defeated Cardinals phenom Michael Wacha 6–1 before 38,447 delirious fans at Fenway Park. When Lackey walked off the mound in the seventh inning, the game well in hand, the ovation he received was thunderous. He had allowed nine hits and but one run. In winning he became the first pitcher in baseball history to win the clinching game of the World Series for two different teams. He won Game 7 for the California Angels in 2002.

Shane Victorino, who had 12 RBIs in the postseason, drove in four of the runs for the Sox.

David Ortiz, named the MVP of the Series, was walked four times, three times intentionally. Ortiz reached base nineteen times in twenty-five appearances. In the series he hit two home runs, drove in six, scored seven, batted .688 and had an incredible .760 on-base percentage.

When Ortiz was handed the MVP trophy, he looked to the crowd and proclaimed, "This is for you, Boston; you guys deserved it. For all the families that have been through the struggles, this is for you."

He then planted a World Series flag at home plate to begin a celebration that lasted into the wee hours of the morning.

Jeff Passan: "The highlight of the World Series for me was David Ortiz being on fire like very few players have ever been. It was like you couldn't get the guy out. It was incredible to watch and it was a lot of fun. He was the guy who epitomized the Red Sox, who was the bridge to the Idiots of 2004 and the '07 championship team as well. To see him front and center almost a decade later speaks to his staying power. This was a guy who a lot of people, including myself, thought was done. His swing looked slow. Guys his size who are DHs don't age well. But then he went and showed everything that David Ortiz has got something special in him."

More than anything, pundits were moved by the surprise of their winning after such a disastrous two years.

Jon Lester: "This is so incredible. All year this team has done a great job of thinking about today and not worrying about yesterday or tomorrow or next year. It brought us to this point, and as soon as spring training starts, we're going to turn the page on this one and try to win the World Series again."

Dan Shaughnessy: "The 2013 Sox truly were a gift, and managed to go six months without any controversy or bad feelings. After a season of bleep-storms, Farrell managed for almost 200 games without a single brush fire. (Bobby Valentine couldn't make it through a homestand without fanning the flames of nonsense.) This is the exception in Boston. The championship seasons of 2004 and 2007 were not always smooth. Manny was Manny, Schill was a blowhard, and Pedro a diva. Goofy stuff happened along the way to winning the World Series Cup.

"Bottom line: After the death and disruption of mid-April, the 2013 Sox made most everyone around here feel good again. The Sox were likeable, and more important, they liked one another. A franchise famous for "25 guys, 25 cabs" became a magic bus of harmony, teamwork, and camaraderie. These highly paid, professional ballplayers actually enjoyed playing baseball and ignored the white noise that is so much a part of the Boston baseball experience."

Richard Justice: "Here's the best part: No one saw it coming. Absolutely no one. Even the people in charge of the Red Sox weren't sure how competitive their team would be. Inside the industry there was nearly a consensus that the Red Sox would finish at or near the bottom of the American League East.

"They won because they were a tremendous team, a team that understood the bottom line was all that counted. To watch all these unheralded and sometimes overlooked players—Ross, Napoli, Gomes and others—win a championship was a proud day for all of Major League Baseball. There were so many lessons in how the Red Sox went about their business and how Cherington constructed this roster and all the rest. They were the appropriate finishing touch for a season that delivered on almost every level.

"So here's a farewell to 2013, a spectacular and special session. It won't be forgotten."

Notes

CHAPTER 1 **The Fans**

The Boston Public Library contains an extensive collection of baseball research material titled "Boston Tradition in Sports." The scrapbooks of Michael McGreevey are part of that collection.

"Those aren't cobblestones . . ." An undated article in the scrapbooks of Michael McGreevey.

"The other reason for the popularity . . ." *Boston Post*, August 19, 1940, by Bill Cunningham.

"Each man had his ticket . . ." A New York newspaper dated 1912 in the McGreevey scrapbooks.

"McGreevey had wanted the Rooters to have an anthem. . . . The tune was catchy and easy to sing." An article from the *Boston Post*, dated June 1, 1908.

"Tessie . . . only, only, only." From the scrapbooks of Michael McGreevey.

". . . by 1908 McGreevey was known all over the country." From a New York newspaper dated 1912 in the McGreevey scrapbooks.

". . . McGreevey had to tell him he hadn't bought a ballplayer, but a fan." From an undated newspaper article in the scrapbooks of Michael McGreevey.

He decided "he could not be sure . . . section reserved for them." From an undated newspaper article in the scrapbooks of Michael McGreevey.

"'They always have,' said the official." From an undated newspaper article in the scrapbooks of Michael McGreevey.

See also *Honey Fitz: Three Steps to the White House*, by John Henry Cutter, Indianapolis, 1962.

The Irish in America, by Carl Wittke, LSU Press, 1962.

CHAPTER 2 **The New League**

See also *Ban Johnson: Czar of Baseball*, by Eugene C. Murdock, Greenwood Press, 1982.

American Baseball, by David Voigt, University of Oklahoma Press, 1966.

Baseball: The Early Years, by Harold Seymour, Oxford University Press, 1960.

Baseball: The Golden Age, by Harold Seymour, Oxford University Press, 1971.

My Fifty Years in Baseball, by Ed Barrow and James M. Kahn, Coward, McCann 1951.

Connie Mack's Baseball Book, by Connie Mack, Alfred A. Knopf, 1950.

The Story of the World Series, by Fred Lieb, Putnam, 1949.

The Turbulent Reign of John I. Taylor

"John I. Taylor was quoted in the papers denying trouble between him and Jimmy Collins, and also between him and Ban Johnson." *The Boston Globe*, article dated December 29, 1905.

"If he refuses, he will forfeit . . ." *The Boston Globe*, article dated January 10, 1906.

"Mr. Taylor's baseball holdings represent . . ." *The Boston Globe*, article dated January 11, 1906.

"Johnson predicted that Boston 'will have a great team on the field next season with Collins in full control,'" From an undated article from *The Boston Globe's* John I. Taylor archives.

"On the way to the grounds . . . was not with him much of the time." From an undated article in the scrapbooks of Michael McGreevey.

"To think that Chick should do such a thing. . . . I cannot imagine that he had an enemy in the world." From an undated article in the scrapbooks of Michael McGreevey.

"It is odd that when a change is made . . ." Article in *The Boston Globe* dated March 28,1907.

See *The Boston Red Sox*, by Fred Lieb, Putnam, 1947.

Newspaper Story: One Hundred Years of the Boston Globe, by Louis M. Lyons, Belknap Press of Harvard University, 1971.

The Story of the World Series, by Fred Lieb, Putnam, 1949.

CHAPTER 3 Fenway Park and the Series of 1912

"Both are versed in baseball . . ." *The Boston Globe*, article dated September 16, 1911.

See also *The Boston Red Sox*, by Fred Lieb, Putnam, 1947.

1912

"The crowds packed the stands . . . almost to the baselines." A newspaper article from the Boston Public Library's Boston Tradition in Sports archive, dated September 6, 1947.

"You will never live to pitch again . . ." Undated newspaper article from the Joe Wood scrapbook in the Boston Public Library.

"I have never given out an interview. . . . I am not going to say a word." Article in the *New York World*, October 8, 1912.

"In spite of the fact that Wood beat us . . ." Undated, unidentified New York newspaper article from the Boston Public Library's Boston Tradition in Sports archive.

"There was jubilation in the two Pullman cars . . . lost one hundred dollars on the day's game." *Baseball As I Have Known It*, by Fred Lieb, Coward, McCann, 1977.

"Any high schooler . . . ball was in the air." Ibid.

"He (Mathewson) had us beaten . . . too much of a sport to blame anybody." Undated newspaper article by Edgar T. Gleason from the Boston Public Library's Boston Tradition in Sports archive.

"Mathewson moved over . . . sending Yerkes to third." *Baseball As I Have Known It*, by Fred Lieb, Coward, McCann, 1977.

"Merkle should have caught the ball. . . . the throw to the plate." Newspaper article dated August 27, 1943, by Frank Graham, from the Boston Public Library's Boston Tradition in Sports archive.

CHAPTER 4 Good-bye, Smoky Joe; Good-bye, McAleer
The Early Demise of Smoky Joe Wood

"I was in a cast. Never again." *The Glory of Their Times*, by Larry Ritter, Macmillan, 1966.

"He might easily have been . . ." Column dated 1921 from the Joe Wood scrapbook from the Boston Public Library's Boston Tradition in Sports archive.

McAleer's Departure

"Boston writers hinted at friction . . ." *The Boston Red Sox*, by Fred Lieb, Putnam, 1947.

"On April 28, he put a gun to his head . . ." *The Boston Traveller*, May 19, 1931.

CHAPTER 5 Enter the Babe; Exit Tris

"I can't live with that man Ruth . . . wants some privacy in the bathroom." *The Boston Red Sox*, by Fred Lieb, Putnam, 1947.

"Speaker, a Texan, was a member of the Ku Klux Klan. His best friend, Joe Wood, was an Orangeman." *Baseball As I Have Known It*, by Fred Lieb, Coward, McCann, 1977.

Wrote Lieb, "Gabby Street, Rogers Hornsby and Tris Speaker, fellow stars from the old Confederate states, told me they were members of the Ku Klux Klan."

Speaker and Hooper didn't speak to each other in all the years they played together. *The Golden Age of Baseball*, by Harold Seymour, Oxford University Press, 1971.

"It was a pity . . . if it had been kept together." *Boston Evening American*, September 22, 1947, by Huck Finnegan.

See also *Babe Ruth's Own Book of Baseball*, by George Herman Ruth, A.L. Burt Company, 1928.

Babe: The Legend Comes to Life, by Robert Creamer, Simon & Schuster, 1974.
The Washington Senators, by Shirley Povich, Putnam, 1954.

CHAPTER 6 **The Incomparable Ruth**
Kid and Pitcher
"My earliest recollections . . . I don't recommend it to the boys of today." *Babe Ruth's Own Book of Baseball*, by George Herman Ruth, A.L. Burt Company, 1928.
"What kind of girls . . . and some were amateurs." *Baseball As I Have Known It*, by Fred Lieb, Coward, McCann, 1977.
"There was a house in my precinct . . . They're too much fun." Ibid.

Babe Moves to the Outfield
"J.J. Lannin, who the year before . . . you're cooled off and we'll talk it over." *My Fifty Years in Baseball*, by Ed Barrow and James M. Kahn, Coward, McCann, 1951.
"When Ruth returned, Barrow refused to speak to him, prompting Ruth to quit again, until Frazee got Barrow to back down." *Babe: The Legend Comes to Life*, by Robert Creamer, Simon & Schuster, 1974.
"'Babe,' Rice said, 'I was watching your swing . . .' I'd go to my locker the next day and find my bats sawed in half." *The Tumult and the Shouting*, by Grantland Rice, Barnes, 1954.
"It's a mistake to believe that Ed . . . Ruth was always grateful to me for helping persuade Barrow to move him to the outfield." Undated newspaper article written by Burt Whitman, probably from September 23, 1947, the day after a reunion dinner for Speaker, Lewis and Hooper in Boston, from the Boston Public Library's Boston Tradition in Sports archive.
"From then on during the spring, every . . ." *Babe: The Legend Comes to Life*, by Robert Creamer, Simon & Schuster, 1974.

Triumph and Gloom
"I was living in New York . . . you'll have to announce it that way." *My Fifty Years in Baseball*, by Ed Barrow and Jean M. Kahn, Coward, McCann, 195.
"Ruth at first objected to the transfer . . . changed his mind." *Babe Ruth as I Knew Him*, by Waite Hoyt, Dell Publishing Co., 1948.
"It would be impossible . . . inconsiderate man ever to put on a baseball uniform." *Babe: The Legend Comes to Life*, by Robert Creamer, Simon & Schuster, 1974.
See also *The Boston Red Sox*, by Fred Lieb, Putnam, 1947.
"All Frazee wanted was the money . . . glad to get away from that graveyard." *The Glory of Their Times*, by Larry Ritter, Macmillan, 1966.

CHAPTER 7 **The Bob Quinn Years: "Just One of Those Things"**
A Young Ballclub
"On January 29, 1929, Jim Price . . . committed suicide by slashing his wrist with a razor blade." *The Boston Red Sox*, by Fred Lieb, Putnam, 1947.

CHAPTER 8 **Young Tom Yawkey Goes After the Vets**
See *Tom Yawkey: Gentleman, Sportsman, and Racist*, by Mark Onigman, *The Real Paper*, August 9, 1980.
Daily News Record, September 22, 1967, article titled "Yawkey Talks."
Collier's magazine, "Starch for the Red Sox," by Bill Cunningham, August 5, 1933.

"The Money Is on the Table"
"I don't believe that the Red Sox. . . . where would you go for players?" Undated newspaper article written by James Reston from the Boston Public Library's Boston Tradition in Sports archive.
"I don't want to waste my time . . . preferably a battery." *The Sporting News*, a column titled "Three and One, Looking Them Over," written by J.G. Taylor Spink and dated 1936 from the Boston Public Library's Boston Tradition in Sports archive.
"I don't know much . . . the money is on the table." Op cit., undated newspaper article by James Reston.

Lefty, Wes and Double X
"Because he had lost so much spring-training time . . . brought him burning pain." *Circling the Bases*, by Bill Werber, 1979.
"Wes always wanted to pitch . . . stopped further mayhem." Ibid.
"In the spring of 1935 . . . I was not about to tell him." Ibid.

CHAPTER 9 **Joe Cronin, the $250,000 Prize**
"When the notoriously tightfisted Griffith . . . 'They can pay you more in Boston than I can.'" *My Own Particular Screwball*, by Al Schacht, Doubleday, 1955.
"I would have fired . . . you can't find those in five minutes." *New York Times* article dated 1959, written by John Drebinger, from the Boston Public Library's Boston Tradition in Sports archive.
"Why would Yawkey . . . not from Clare to Kildare, could." Undated newspaper article written by Frank O'Neil from the Boston Public Library's Boston Tradition in Sports archive.

Fan Disillusionment
". . . leaped to the conclusion . . . peashooter for 1,000 cereal labels." *The Saturday Evening Post*, March 23, 1946, "What's Wrong with the Red Sox," by Harold Kaese.
"It was natural for them to take it out on Cronin." Ibid.
"For Christ sake Joe . . ." Ibid.
"Cronin's nerves frayed . . . prejudiced against playing managers." Ibid.

Seeds of Disharmony
See also *Sport* magazine, April 1956, "Joe Cronin: The Irishman Who Made His Own Luck," by Ed Linn.

CHAPTER 10 **Billy Evans Builds a Farm System**
The Sale of Pee Wee Reese
The account of Evans' firing comes from private notes written by Harold Kaese dated December 23, 1946. The notes are part of the Boston Public Library's Boston Tradition in Sports archive and are used with permission.

CHAPTER 11 **The Kids From San Diego**
Ted Makes a First Impression
See *My Turn at Bat*, by Ted Williams and John Underwood, Simon & Schuster, 1969.
Life magazine, September 23, 1946, Ted Williams, by John Chamberlain.
Sport magazine, April 1956, "Joe Cronin: The Irishman Who Made His Own Luck," by Ed Linn.
Ted Returns for Good
"Listen, you, I got out here by myself, and I'll get in by myself." *The New York Times Magazine*, August 4, 1946, "It's All in the Eyes and Timing," by Russell Owen.
"The day Williams doesn't put on his uniform . . ." Newspaper article dated March 10, 1942, from the Boston Public Library's Boston Tradition in Sports archive.

CHAPTER 12 **The Press and Ted: Let the Feuding Begin**
"No matter where I've played . . . I've been hitting it." *The Boston Globe*, March 22, 1939, column by Harold Kaese.
The Tommy Henrich story was from an article by Harold Kaese in the Boston Public Library's Boston Tradition in Sports archive.
"When I look at a guy all day . . . I just want a change of scenery." *The Boston American*, August 10,1940, "How Long Can Ted Williams Thumb His Nose at Baseball?" by Austin Lake.
"The second year they brought in . . . a little sour on everything and everybody." *What's Wrong with the Red Sox?* by Al Hirshberg, Dodd, Mead & Co., 1973.
"Crippled or sick kids . . ." *The Boston American*, August 10, 1940, "How Long Can Ted Williams Thumb His Nose at Baseball?" by Austin Lake.

CHAPTER 13 **Ted Hits .406**
"I don't see no blinding fastballs or exploding curveballs . . ." *Voices from Cooperstown*, Anthony J. Conner, Collier Books, New York, 1982.

"Sure, I look forward to this season . . . shows what the Red Sox thought of me." *Boston Globe*, undated column by Harold Kaese from the Boston Public Library's Boston Tradition in Sports archive. See also *My Turn at Bat*, by Ted Williams and John Underwood, Simon & Schuster, 1969.

CHAPTER 14 **The Changing of the Guard**
The War Years
"If I didn't think I was right and deserving . . ." from the Harold Kaese collection from the Boston Public Library's Boston Tradition in Sports archive.

CHAPTER 15 **Champs**
"Rival athletes gradually grew sour . . ." *The Boston American*, undated, by Austin Lake from the Boston Public Library's Boston Tradition in Sports archive.
"We felt like scullery maids . . ." *What's the Matter with the Red Sox?* by Al Hirshberg, Dodd, Mead & Co., 1973.
See also *Colliers* magazine, September 28, 1946, "Ted Williams, the Series and Me," by Kyle Crichton.
A Loss to the Cardinals
"I'd hate to be traded to the Yankees . . ." *The Boston Globe*, October 5, 1947, by Harold Kaese.
"Cronin was the man behind the trade rumors." *The Boston Globe*, October 9, 1947, by Harold Kaese.
"Cronin has decided that Williams is temperamentally unchangeable." Ibid.

CHAPTER 16 **A Plague of Injuries**
Joe McCarthy Takes Over
"Despite an enviable record . . . refuge in insolence and insulting remarks." *Colliers* magazine, April 24, 1948, "Who Will Run the Red Sox?" by Milton Gross.
For McCarthy's treatment of Pete Alexander, see *Sport* magazine, April 1950, "The Ups and Downs of Old Pete," by Jack Sher.

CHAPTER 17 **1948 and 1949**
Heartbreak Again
"Goddammit, if the old man had let me bat . . ." *What's the Matter with the Red Sox?* by Al Hirshberg, Dodd, Mead & Co., 1973.

CHAPTER 18 **The Revolving Door**
Boudreau's Folly
See the *Saturday Evening Post*, "I'll Make the Rules for the Red Sox," by Lou Boudreau as told to Al Hirshberg, dated February 23, 1952.

CHAPTER 19 **Two Kinds of War**
Crazy Jimmy
"Joe, we've got to let Piersall go." *The Boston Globe*, June 29, 1952, by Clif Keane.
"It doesn't make no sense . . . plenty of others who do." The *Atlanta Constitution*, July 8, 1952, by Furman Bisher.
"The only way I can tell how tough a catch is . . ." *Colliers* magazine, February 5, 1954, "Specialist in Armed Robbery," by Tom Meany.
"To this day, the first thing people ask . . ." *The Truth Hurts*, by Jimmy Piersall with Richard Whittingham, Contemporary Books, 1984.
See the *Saturday Evening Post*, January 29, 1955, "They Called Me Crazy—and I Was!" by Jimmy Piersall, January 29, 1955, and February 5, 1955.

CHAPTER 20 **The Death of the Golden Greek**
"Now can I let the other guys run?" *Sport* magazine, November 1950, "Boston's Golden Greek," by Al Hirshberg.
"You'll see the only 18-year-old in America who is ready to play football with the pros." *Saturday Evening Post*, October 18, 1952, "Is He College Football's Greatest Passer?" by Al Hirshberg.
See also *The Boston Globe*, June 28, 1955, column by Harold Kaese.
The Boston Globe, August 7, 1969, column by Harold Kaese.

The Boston Globe, June 28, 1955, column by Harold Kaese.

Sport magazine, December 1954, "No More All Americas," by Buff Donelli.

CHAPTER 21 **Lean Years**

"When Lou fired Bill McKechnie . . ." September 1954, "Why Boudreau Flopped as a Solo Manager," by Austin Lake.

"Lepcio was years away . . . I don't know why they're not in better shape today." The *Saturday Evening Post*, May 21, 1960, "The Sad Case of the Red Sox," by Al Hirshberg.

"Don Buddin—if nothing ill befalls him . . ." *The Boston Globe*, February 2, 1954, by Roger Birtwell.

"I think the kid has a chance of being a great ballplayer." *The Boston Traveler*, December 11, 1956, by Tom Monahan.

Malzie's Long Journey

"The Red Sox are always looking . . . you never know when one might surprise you and unexpectedly develop into a star." The *Saturday Evening Post*, May 21, 1960, "The Sad Case of the Red Sox," by Al Hirshberg.

CHAPTER 22 **Lily White**

"I have been connected with the Red Sox . . . having an equal opportunity to play for the Red Sox." *Boston Daily Record*, April 16, 1945, by Dave Egan.

"If (they) cannot make the grade . . . work their way up the ladder." Ibid.

"The decision is not up to us." *Sport* magazine, April 1956, "Joe Cronin: The Irishman Who Made His Own Luck," by Ed Linn.

"Collins feared if the Red Sox signed any of the players, it would constitute tampering with existing contracts signed by Negro League teams." *Pittsburgh Courier*, April 25, 1959.

"Cronin did not think it advisable to send black players to Louisville at that time." *The Real Paper*, Volume 9, Number 32, 1980, "Tom Yawkey: Gentleman, Sportsman, Racist," by Marc Onigman.

" the Red Sox sent Larry Woodall . . ." *What's the Matter with the Red Sox?* by Al Hirshberg, Dodd, Mead & Co., 1973.

The First, and Second

"They told me, 'We got to let you go' . . . why we had to have so much hate." Interview with Piper Davis on February 9, 1986, by David Margolick.

" He is a well-mannered colored boy . . ." *The Real Paper*, August 9, 1980, by Marc Onigman.

"There'll be no niggers on this ballclub . . ." *What's the Matter with the Red Sox?* by Al Hirshberg, Dodd, Mead & Co., 1973.

"There was no doubt in my mind about that." Interview with Earl Wilson on February 9, 1986, by David Margolick.

CHAPTER 23 **The Nadir**

Rummill's article in the *Christian Science Monitor* appeared on July 25, 1959.

"I know what's wrong with this club, but I can't do anything about it. . . ." *The Boston Globe*, May 16, 1960, by Clif Keane.

"Be ready." The *Saturday Evening Post*, May 21, 1960, "The Sad Case of the Red Sox," by Al Hirshberg.

See *Look* magazine, June 14, 1955, "Have the Red Sox Rounded the Corner?" by Tim Cohane.

CHAPTER 25 **After Ted**

Young Yaz

"If only you were still in Brooklyn." *New Times* magazine, October 30, 1978, "The Indian Summer of Carl Yastrzemski," by John Eskow.

See *Yaz*, by Carl Yastrzemski and Al Hirshberg, Viking, 1968.

The Golden Boy Retires

"If you quit I don't think you'll be proud of it later." *The Boston Red Sox*, by Tom Meany, A. S. Barnes, 1956.

"Before the game in the trainer's room. . . . the hypnotist turned away and muttered, 'Wouldn't cooperate.'" *What's the Matter with the Red Sox?* by Al Hirshberg, Dodd, Mead & Co., 1973.

The article in the *Quincy Patriot Ledger* by Lin Raymond appeared on May 1, 1961.

CHAPTER 27 **A Tale of Two Players**
Big Stu, or the Sabotaging of Johnny Pesky
"Yes, I was disappointed. . . . I don't crash into fences." *Boston Record-American*, October 31, 1963, by Larry Claflin.
"I could never understand why Pesky took it. . . . It was a pretty sad situation." *Yaz*, by Carl Yastrzemski and Al Hirshberg, Viking, 1968.

CHAPTER 28 **The Kids**
Tony C.
"It's a good thing I was so interested in sports . . ." *Seeing It Through*, by Tony Conigliaro and Jack Zanger, Macmillan, 1970.
"That's 12 for 16." *Sport* magazine, April 1965, "A Kid Who Believes in Himself," by Al Hirshberg.
Rico
"Herman had 'an almost pathological dislike' of Petrocelli." *What's the Matter with the Red Sox?* by Al Hirshberg, Dodd, Mead & Co., 1973.
"Of all the Red Sox ballplayers, the one Herman disliked most was Rico Petrocelli." *Yaz*, by Carl Yastrzemski and Al Hirshberg, Viking, 1968.
"Trade him. . . . He doesn't want to play ball." Ibid.
"I wonder how that thing would sound . . ." *Seeing It Through*, by Tony Conigliaro and Jack Zanger, Macmillan, 1970.
"Baseball is everything . . . trying to get rid of me." Ibid.
"If any of you writers . . . take Tony for two years instead of six months." *Worcester Daily Telegram*, July 20, 1965, by Phil Jackman.
"It just seemed to me . . . So should the manager." *Yaz: Baseball, the Wall and Me*, by Carl Yastrzemski and Gerald Eskanazi, Doubleday, 1990.
"Well, Billy, I hope you're having a good winter. You sure had a horseshit summer." *What's the Matter with the Red Sox?* by Al Hirshberg, Dodd, Mead & Co., 1973

CHAPTER 31 **Dick Williams Takes Charge**
"If a guy got out of bed . . ." *Yaz*, by Carl Yastrzemski and Al Hirshberg, Viking, 1968.
"If you're here next year, I don't want to be." Ibid.
The Quest
"I'm not here to make friends . . ." *Yaz*, by Carl Yastrzemski and Al Hirshberg, Viking, 1968.
"To Williams, each player was an individual . . ." Ibid.
"After six weeks in Winter Haven . . ." *No More Mr. Nice Guy*, by Dick Williams and Bill Paschke, Harcourt Brace Jovanovich, 1990.

CHAPTER 32 **Tony C. Is Beaned**
"My heart nearly stopped . . . . at this moment I actually prayed." *No More Mr. Nice Guy*, by Dick Williams and Bill Plaschke, Harcourt Brace Jovanovich, 1990.
"Funny, you never go up there . . . last thing I saw for several days." *Seeing It Through*, Tony Conigliaro and Jack Zanger, Macmillan, 1970.

The Hawk
"You know how he is—he lost his head . . ." *Hawk*, by Ken Harrelson and Al Hirshberg, Viking Press, 1969.

CHAPTER 33 **The Impossible Dream**
Yaz Is Unreal
"Yaz reminds me of John Wesley Harding . . . . then he lowers his metabolism." *New Times* magazine, October 30, 1978, "The Indian Summer of Carl Yastrzemski," by John Eskow.
"I always feel tense right before a game . . ." Ibid.
"Up until 1967, you'd see him dog it . . . other people respond to the change in him." Ibid.
"There shouldn't be any pressure. . . . Knowing that is the worst pressure of all." Ibid.

Final Stretch
"It was one of the first . . . sound of it makes me sick." *No More Mr. Nice Guy*, by Dick Williams and Bill Plaschke, Harcourt Brace Jovanovich, 1990.

"I want to congratulate you men right now. . . . Let's go get 'em." *The Impossible Dream Remembered*, by Ken Coleman and Dick Valenti, The Stephen Greene Press, 1987.

"If anyone could figure out how to pull our ass out of the sling . . . well, he could." *No More Mr. Nice Guy*, by Dick Williams and Bill Plaschke, Harcourt Brace Jovanovich, 1990.

"I've never seen a perfect player, but you were one for us. I never saw a player have a season like that." *The Impossible Dream Remembered*, by Ken Coleman and Dick Valenti, The Stephen Greene Press, 1987.

CHAPTER 34 On to the Series
"Maybe, more likely, he'd decided on another steambath buddy for the job." *No More Mr. Nice Guy*, by Dick Williams and Bill Plaschke, Harcourt Brace Jovanovich, 1990.

"His presence in our domain . . ." Ibid.

"How about that? Yawkey . . . big piece of his heart." Ibid.

"We made some mistakes" and what follows. *True* magazine, May 1968, "Red Sox Manager Dick Williams—Can He Do It Again?" by Al Hirshberg.

CHAPTER 35 The Final Days of Dick Williams
"There is no way you can like that man . . ." *Life* magazine, May 1968, "Baseball: The Great American Myth," by Leonard Shecter.

"If you had a bad game . . . he had it all the time I was there." Ibid.

"I been sold . . ." Ibid.

"Mr. Yawkey, I . . . as if to comfort him." *What's the Matter with the Red Sox?* by Al Hirshberg, Dodd, Mead & Co., 1973.

"Usually after each road trip . . . instructions to terminate me." *No More Mr. Nice Guy*, by Dick Williams and Bill Plaschke, Harcourt Brace Jovanovich, 1990.

"It wasn't just a firing . . . still makes me hurt." Ibid.

CHAPTER 37 The Yaz-Conig Feud
See *What's the Matter with the Red Sox?* by Al Hirshberg, Dodd, Mead & Co., 1973.

CHAPTER 40 On to Glory: 1975
"There were curses . . . I'd have van Gogh'ed him." *The New Yorker* magazine, November 17, 1975, by Rogel Angell.

"I suddenly remembered . . . joy a light with it." Ibid.

"The games have ended . . . for having made it happen." Ibid.

CHAPTER 41 End of an Era
See *Beyond the Sixth Game*, by Peter Gammons, Houghton, Miffiin, 1985.

The Death of Tom Yawkey

"Perhaps some people think . . . to treat human beings like human beings." *What's the Matter with the Red Sox?* by Al Hirshberg, Dodd, Mead & Co., 1973.

"Players are the most helpless . . . and he wasn't one really." *Sports Illustrated*, June 28,1965, "The Great Wall of Boston," by Jack Mann.

CHAPTER 42 The Great Collapse of '78
"I thought he meant they . . . . Sprowl never beat anybody." *The Great Rivalry*, by Ed Linn, Ticknor and Fields, 1991.

The Mike Torrez Game

"Piniella's catch was an indignity . . . . work out in the end." *Sports Illustrated*, February 26, 1979, "A Day of Light and Shadows," by Jonathan Schwartz.

"I affected bemusement. . . . It's only a game." Ibid.

"I thought: Freeze this minute . . . reach out and touch it." Ibid.

CHAPTER 43 Up and Down with the Red Sox
"They never took me seriously . . . wise to their bool cheat." *Beyond the Sixth Game*, by Peter Gammons, Houghton, Miffiin, 1985.

"When they let Luis Tiant go . . ." *Yaz: Baseball, the Wall and Me*, by Carl Yastrzemski and Gerald Eskenazi, Doubleday, 1990.

Chapter 44 **Resurgence: 1986**
One Strike Away
"When the ball went through Bill . . . Dent hit the home run." *Sports Illustrated*, November 3, 1986.
See also *One Strike Away*, by Dan Shaughnessy, Beauport Books, 1987.

Chapter 45 **Ad Infinitum**
"Is he going to apologize? . . ." *Boston Globe*, August 20, Page E1.
"I remain cynical . . ." *Boston Globe*, Dan Shaughnessy, February 25, 2000. Page C1.
"Really, wouldn't it have been easier to send flowers?" *Boston Globe*, Michael Holley, June 13, 2000. Page C1.
"He's so valuable. I don't know what the deal is." *Boston Globe*, July 23, 2000. Page D16.
"I just want [Duquette] to be accountable." *Boston Globe*, July 24, 2000. Page D5.
"Duquette must have majored in Machiavelli . . ." *Boston Globe*, Dan Shaughnessy, July 28, 2000. Page E1.
". . . a clear message that Carl Everett is in charge of the team." *Boston Globe*, Gordon Edes, September 22, 2000. Page F1.
"Maybe it's not too late to save your team." *Boston Globe*, Gordon Edes, October 4, 2000. Page D1.
"But to grow, sometimes you have to go." *Boston Globe*, Meg Vaillancourt, August 5, 2001, Magazine. Page 12.
"Just how much are the citizens of the Nation supposed to take?" *Boston Globe*, Dan Shaughnessy, December 1, 2000. Page D1.
"Dan Duquette has gone from doofus to genius . . ." *Boston Globe*, Dan Shaughnessy, December 13, 2000. Page F1.
"I feel a responsibility . . ." *Boston Globe*, December 20, 2000. Page D1.
"We expect a lot. We're just like the fans . . ." *Boston Globe*, Dan Shaughnessy, April 6, 2001. Page E1.
"Too bad he was born without a personality . . ." *Boston Globe*, Bob Ryan, April 18, 2001. Page E1.
"This is the way it's always been around Fenway . . ." *Boston Globe*, Dan Shaughnessy, June 7, 2001. Page E1.
"There's got to be an edge . . ." *Boston Globe*, Bob Hohler, July 9, 2001. Page D1.
"That Nomie. He just gets out of bed and hits . . ." *Boston Globe*, Gordon Edes, July 30, 2001. Page A1.
"Duquette should just put on a uniform . . ." *Boston Globe*, Gordon Edes, September 7, 2001. Page C12.
"It's getting fatigued and heavy." *Boston Globe*, Bob Hohler, September 5, 2001. Page C1.
Everett accused Kerrigan of being a racist and a drunk. *Boston Globe*, Gordon Edes and Bob Hohler, September 22, 2001. Page G1.
"It's like General MacArthur giving orders after he was relieved of his command in Korea." *Boston Globe*, December 10, 2001. Page C1.

Chapter 46 **The John Henry Era Begins**
"We will extinguish the curse of the Bambino." *Boston Globe*, Kevin Paul Dupont, December 22, 2001. Page G8.
"I feel the same as they do, because losing is not an option here." *Boston Globe*, Gordon Edes, March 12, 2002. Page A1.
"Buckle up . . ." *Boston Globe*, Bob Hohler, March 12, 2002. Page F1.
"This was the Big One . . ." *Boston Globe*, Bob Ryan, March 12, 2002. Page F1.
"Please come back." *Boston Globe*, Mark Blaudschun, June 9, 2002. Page D18.
"We're gonna score . . ." *Boston Globe*, Bob Ryan, June 30, 2002. Page C1.
"We're not packing, and the fans shouldn't either." *Boston Globe*, Bob Hohler, July 1, 2002. Page D1.

Chapter 47 **Good-Bye Ted, Hello Theo**
"He was like my brother. I can't believe he's gone." *Boston Globe*, Bob Hohler, July 6, 2002. Page F1.
"I wish we were undefeated." *Boston Globe*, Nick Cafardo, July 8, 2002. Page C1.

"I love when they dare me to do something." *Boston Globe*, Bob Hohler, July 20, 2002. Page E1.

"I say they should give you the Cy Young right now." *Boston Globe*, Michael Holley, July 20, 2002, Pagge E1.

"I don't know if it's just us being snakebit." *Boston Globe*, Bob Hohler, July 22, 2002. Page D1.

"I am saddened by the turmoil of the current controversy." *Boston Globe*, Gordon Edes, July 23, 2002. Page F1.

"Baseball would have never been the same if we had walked out." *Boston Globe*, Gordon Edes, August 11, 2002. Page A1.

"Ken Macha is loosening in the on-deck circle. Poor Grady . . ." *Boston Globe*, Dan Shaughnessy, September 5, 2002. Page F1.

"It's hard to remember them fondly now . . ." *Boston Globe*, Michael Holley, September 7, 2002. Page E1.

"We're going to become a championship organization . . ." *Boston Globe*, Bob Hohler, November 26, 2002 Page F1.

"The Red Sox are taking a bit of a gamble here . . ." *Boston Globe*, Dan Shaughnessy, November 27, 2002. Page F1.

CHAPTER 48 Close but No Cigar

"I made it a New Year's resolution not to respond to George's petty personal attacks . . ." *Boston Globe*, Gordon Edes, January 5, 2003. Page C2.

"Sure, and the Cross Bronx Expressway is paved in gum drops." *Boston Globe*, Bob Hohler, January 16, 2003. Page E3.

"All those gorgeous women date Donald Trump . . ." *Boston Globe*, Dan Shaughnessy, January 17, 2003. Page E1.

"It goes back to 1919 . . ." Ibid.

"Theo Epstein is not exactly on a winning streak." Ibid.

"Being back in first place in the middle of June doesn't mean anything . . ." *Boston Globe*, Bob Hohler, June 12, 2003. Page C1.

"You guys were writing my obituary, weren't you?" *Boston Globe*, Nick Cafardo, June 18, 2003. Page F1.

"That's the thing that's killing us this year . . ." *Boston Globe*, Nick Cafardo, June 22, 2003. Page C8.

"There's probably a few guys whose wives . . ." *Boston Globe*, Dan Shaughnessy, June 30, 2003. Page D6.

"He doesn't have the money to put fear in my heart." *Boston Globe*, Nick Cafardo, July 9, 2003. Page F1.

"[The past] makes zero sense to me." *Boston Globe*, Bob Hohler, August 21, 2003. Page E5.

CHAPTER 49 Cowboy Up

"This guy can give you 30 jacks and 100 RBIs . . ." *Boston Globe*, Michael Holley, October 9, 2003. Page C3.

"I think we're going to score a lot of runs." *Boston Globe*, Gordon Edes, January 23, 2003. Page E3.

"The closer-by-committee is a bust . . ." *Boston Globe*, Dan Shaughnessy, April 1, 2003. Page F1.

"We're going back to Fenway Park, where we kill the baseball . . ." *Boston Globe*, Dan Shaughnessy, October 3, 2003. Page E1.

"How could it get any better than this?" *Boston Globe*, Dan Shaughnessy, October 6, 2003. Page A1.

"Just in time." *Boston Globe*, Mark Blaudschun, October 7, 2003. Page D2.

CHAPTER 50 One Game Away

Nomar was "hurt, tired, or preoccupied with his wedding to Mia Hamm." *Boston Globe*, Gordon Edes, October 15, 2003. Page F2.

"We've been on a collision course for a hundred years . . ." *Boston Globe*, Bob Hohler, October 16, 2003. Page C1.

CHAPTER 51 **Five Outs Away**

"It might be the closest we'll ever get to the World Series . . ." *Boston Globe*, Jackie MacMullan, October 17, 2003. Page E6.

"A new generation of New Englanders has learned the risk of rooting for the Red Sox." *Boston Globe*, Dan Shaughnessy, October 17, 2003. Page A1.

CHAPTER 52 **The Psyche of the Red Sox fan**

"On my tombstone . . ." I heard him say this on the radio a short time before his death.

CHAPTER 53 **Theo-logy**

"My skin's pretty thick . . ." *Boston Globe*, Bob Hohler, December 5, 2003. Page E1.

"I guess I hate the Yankees now." *Boston Globe*, Bob Hohler, November 29, 2003. Page A1.

" A total and complete slap in the face." *Boston Globe*, Shira Springer, December 8, 2003. Page D1.

"Our first choice was—and is—to sign Nomar . . ." *Boston Globe*, Bob Hohler, December 10, 2003. Page E1.

"If you win in this town, you're forever idolized here." *Boston Globe*, Bob Hohler, December 20, 2003. Page G8.

"Gene will never go for this." *Boston Globe*, Gordon Edes, December 31, 2003. Page A1.

"You've ruined my summer, and it's not even winter." Ibid.

"It looks like the Yankees have no limit." *Boston Globe*, Gordon Edes, February 15, 2004. Page A1.

"How pathetic does this make the Sox look?" *Boston Globe*, Dan Shaughnessy, February 15, 2003. Page C1.

"If they want me, then show me." *Boston Globe*, Gordon Edes, April 1, 2004. Page C1.

CHAPTER 54 **Spring into Summer 2004**

"This guy has three Cy Youngs . . ." *Boston Globe*, Bob Hohler, April 26, 2004. Page D1.

He said he was upset with the way Derek Lowe and Jason Varitek had been treated. *Boston Globe*, Dan Shaughnessy, May 2, 2004. Page E1.

"Any time this team loses four games in a row . . ." *Boston Globe*, Bob Hohler, May 4, 2004. Page E1.

"Why are you staying so long with starters who are finished?" *Boston Globe*, Dan Shaughnessy, June 3, 2004. Page C1.

"Our best baseball hasn't been played yet . . ." *Boston Globe*, Nick Cafardo, June 5, 2004. Page E5.

"We still feel we have ways we can improve inside and outside . . ." *Boston Globe*, Nick Cafardo, June 28, 2004. Page D5.

"Time for everybody to move on. Time for the Red Sox to trade Nomar." *Boston Globe*, Dan Shaughnessy, July 3, 2004. Page G1.

CHAPTER 55 **We Say Good-Bye to Nomar**

"We got written off . . ." *Boston Globe*, Bob Hohler, July 9, 2004. Page E1.

"We can beat the Yankees with whoever is pitching." *Boston Globe*, July 16, 2004. Page E1.

"My stomach was in my throat . . ." *Boston Globe*, Gordon Edes, July 21, 2004. Page F1.

"Twenty-four guys. Everybody at home . . ." *Boston Globe*, Nick Cafardo, July 25, 2004. Page D1.

"I'm not a lip reader . . ." Ibid.

"I was just trying to enjoy my last Yankee–Red Sox game as a Red Sox." *Boston Globe*, Marc Carig, July 26, 2004. Page F6.

"It was with mixed emotions that we let Nomar go." *Boston Globe*, Bob Hohler, August 1, 2004. Page A1.

"We just traded away Mr. Boston . . ." Ibid.

"In the Sox clubhouse he was as happy as Michael Moore at a Bush family reunion." *Boston Globe*, Dan Shaughnessy, August 1, 2004. Page C1.

"The fact that they ultimately decided to keep you for the stretch run . . ." *Boston Globe*, Bob Hohler, August 1, 2004. Page C1.

CHAPTER 56 **The Sox Catch Fire**

"I'm not going to be lied to . . ." *Boston Globe*, Bob Hohler, August 8, 2004. Page C8.

"We're starting to jell right now . . ." *Boston Globe*, Dan Shaughnessy, August 13, 2004. Page F1.

"We want to beat everybody . . ." *Boston Globe*, Kevin Paul Dupont, August 26, 2004. Page C8.

"No one may be safe . . ." *Boston Globe*, Bob Hohler, August 30, 2004. Page D5.

"I said this would be a good opportunity for us . . ." *Boston Globe*, Gordon Edes, September 6, 2004. Page C1.

"This shows we're for real . . ." *Boston Globe*, Bob Hohler, September 9, 2004. Page C1.

CHAPTER 57 **Wild-Card Winners**

"That's who we are as a team . . ." *Boston Globe*, Dan Shaughnessy, September 9, 2004. Page C1.

"I know Schilling didn't like it at first . . ." Ibid.

"He's been amazing." *Boston Globe*, Ron Indrisano, September 17, 2004. Page E6.

"The race is nowhere near being over . . ." *Boston Globe*, Bob Hohler, September 20, 2004. Page D1.

"It's their right to do what they want . . ." *Boston Globe*, Gordon Edes, September 28, 2004. Page D1.

CHAPTER 58 **The Playoffs: Hitting Bottom**

"The guy's a horse . . ." *Boston Globe*, Bob Hohler, October 6, 2004. Page C1.

"Can he hit one here?" *Boston Globe*, Bob Hohler, October 9, 2004. Page E4.

"We'll show up and play tomorrow . . ." *Boston Globe*, Mark Blaudschun, October 17, 2004. Page E6.

CHAPTER 59 **Miracle of the Century**

"Soon it will be over . . ." *Boston Globe*, Bob Ryan, October 17, 2004. Page A1.

"How much more can New Englanders take?" *Boston Globe*, Dan Shaughnessy, October 17, 2004. Page A1.

"This has been so much more than I imagined it to be . . ." *Boston Globe*, Dan Shaughnessy, October 19, 2004. Page A1.

The description of Curt Schilling's medical problem. *Boston Globe*, Bob Hohler and Raja Mishra, October 21, 2004. Page C8.

"It's an amazing storybook." *Boston Globe*, Bob Hohler, October 21, 2004. Page C1.

"How can this not be one of the greatest comebacks . . ." Ibid.

"I am trying to digest the fact that I have just seen the greatest team . . ." *Boston Globe*, Bob Ryan, October 21, 2004. Page C1.

CHAPTER 60 **The Curse Is Broken**

"Everyone pitched in in a different way." *Boston Globe*, Nick Cafardo, October 24, 2004. Page C4.

"My heart is with Boston. I consider Boston my house . . ." *Boston Globe*, Gordon Edes, October 27, 2004. Page D1.

"Red Sox fans will always have Paris." For you younger fans, "We'll always have Paris," is what Humphrey Bogart said to Ingrid Bergman, the love of his life, before she went back to her freedom-fighting husband in the movie *Casablanca*.

Interviews with Shaun Kelly, Richard Hershenson, and Mark Starr, who is the national sports correspondent for *Newsweek*, and his wife Karen Starr. You can find more of Mark's reporting on the playoffs and the World Series in *Newsweek* and on the *Newsweek* website.

CHAPTER 62 **Lucchino and Epstein Battle for Control**

". . . the best year here since the Pilgrims hit Plymouth Rock . . ." *The Atlanta Journal-Constitution*, by Jack Wilkinson. Page 1C.

"This is a hard job." *USA Today*, Jon Saraceno. Page 8C.

"He likes to win . . ." *The Worcester Telegram*, Paul O'Neill. Page A1.

The Boston Globe, Dan Shaughnessy, January 20, 2006.

CHAPTER 63 **Big Papi**

"I couldn't imagine the alternative . . ." *The Providence Journal*, Sean McAdam. Page C1.

"You are called the ultimate enabler . . ." *The Providence Journal*, August 29, 2006.

"I guess the people in New England . . ." *The Boston Globe*, Amaia Benjamin, September 21, 2006.

The other players to hit 50 home runs in a single season are Barry Bonds, Sammy Sosa, Mark McGwire, Babe Ruth, Jim Thome, Albert Belle, Prince Fielder, Ralph Kiner, Johnny Mize, Luis Gonzalez, Hank Greenberg, Mickey Mantle, Roger Maris, Brady Anderson, Ken Griffey Jr., Ryan Howard, Alex Rodriguez, and Andruw Jones.

"Every ballpark seems smaller . . ." *Sports Illustrated*, June 16, 2006.

CHAPTER 64 **Champions Again**
"You have to fly out here and watch this kid pitch . . ." *The Boston Globe*, Gordon Edes, February 11, 2007.

"I'd like to think . . ." *Red Sox.com*, October 29, 2007.

"It's not about being the smartest baseball man . . ." *The Providence Journal*, Joe McDonald. Page C1.

"It's as good as it gets . . ." *ESPN* recap, September 28, 2007.

"I mean, we're sitting at 101 wins . . ." *The Washington Post*, Dave Sheinin. Page E1.

555 "Games of a huge magnitude . . ." *The Union Leader*, Alex Speier. Page D1.

CHAPTER 65 **Manny Being Manny**
"That was probably the hardest thing . . ." *WEEI.com* blog network, February 12, 2012.

CHAPTER 66 **Spiraling Downward**
"It's not fun to watch." *The Providence Journal*, Joe McDonald, May 25, 2009.

"Yeah, he's just having a tough time . . ." *Telegraph and Gazette*, Paul Jarvey, April 20, 2009. Page C2.

"It's just shocking." *AP*, September 20, 2011.

"It was very disappointing . . ." *ESPN*, Joe McDonald, September 29, 2011.

"The last play of the next tragedy . . ." *Celebrate Boston*, March 17, 2014.

"First, we don't have to pretend to root for these assholes any more . . ." *Grantland,* Jay Caspian Kang, September 29, 2011.

"Nothing can erase the ignominy. . ." *ESPN*, Jackie MacMullan, September 30, 2011.

"The bottom line . . ." *AP*, September 29, 2011.

"I think it's the right thing . . ." *The Boston Globe*, Peter Abraham, September 30, 2011.

"I felt frustrated . . ."Ibid.

"Team sources said Francona . . ." *The Boston Globe*, Inside the Collapse, Bob Hohler, October 12, 2011.

"It makes me angry that people say these things . . ." Ibid.

"It has never been an issue . . ."Ibid.

". . . could only come from a couple of people in the organization . . ." *The Boston Globe*, Gordon Edes, October 12, 2011.

"Why would he want to go back there?" Ibid.

"Maybe it was an illusion . . ." *ESPN*, Howard Bryant, October 13, 2011.

"Certainly, the era had to end . . ." Ibid.

CHAPTER 67 **Bobby V**
"I think we have work to do . . ."*MLB.com*, Ian Browne, October 25, 2011.

"Remember, you get paid over there for saying stuff . . ." *Yahoo Sports*, David Brown, February 27, 2012.

"Youkilis is not as physically or emotionally . . ." *Foxsports*, April 17, 2012.

"Ten games into the season . . ." *Yahoo Sports*, October 4, 2012.

"You go ahead and make Valentine the face of this . . ." *The New York Daily News*, Mike Lupica, April 22, 2012.

"The unhappiness that exists among Boston players . . ." *Sports of Boston*, Steve Bostek, June 20, 2012.

"As much as I would love to blame Valentine . . ." Ibid.

Some players told management they no longer wanted to play for Valentine. *Yardbarker*, Larry Brown, August 15, 2012.

"It brought a tear to my eye." *ESPN*, Tony Lee, June 25, 2012.

"We're not considering anyone else . . ." *Yahoo Sports*, Jeff Passan, August 14, 2012.

"Tell me I am wrong, you guys . . ." *Community News for Gofftown, Dunbarton, New Boston, and Ware NH*, Steve Poulist, July 14, 2012.

"I was absolutely appalled." *The New York Times*, Peter May, August 25, 2012.

"The letter discussed the team as if it were a little league . . ." *Sports of Boston*, Matthew Bond, July 14, 2012.

". . . a Febreze-like move." *The New York Times*, Peter May, August 28, 2012. Quoting Mark LeBrun.

"It turned out to be not what I expected." *CBS News*, AP, September 1, 2012.

"It's always been personal . . ." *Yahoo Sports*, Rich Blaine, September 10, 2012.

"end of an error." *The Guardian*, October 4, 2012.

"Much like all season . . ." *Yahoo Sports*, Jeff Passan, October. 4, 2012.

CHAPTER 68 **Redemption**

"The Red Sox know you've lost that lovin' feeling . . ." *The Boston Globe*, February13, 2013.

"Because Lester and Buchholz look like aces . . ." *Sports Ilustrated.com*, April 16, 2013.

"we just say, 'All right guys . . ." *The Boston Globe*, Gordon Edes, June 30, 2014.

"You don't get 97 wins . . ." *ESPN.Go*, Joe McDonald, October 4, 2013.

"He fits what we do so well . . ." Ibid.

"They didn't make any mistakes . . ." *The New York Daily News*, Roger Rubin, October 9, 2013.

"It's almost like we didn't have a starter going today . . ."*ESPN.Go, AP*, October 17, 2013.

CHAPTER 69 **Champions**

"His importance to the team . . ."*The Boston Globe*, Peter Abraham, October 28, 2013.

"I was born for this." *The Boston Globe*, Peter Abraham, October 29, 2013.

"I haven't played with many superstars . . ." Ibid.

"The 2013 Sox truly were a gift." *The Boston Globe*, Dan Shaughnessy, November 2, 2013.

"This is so incredible . . ." *The New York Times*, David Waldstein, October 31, 2013.

"Here's the best part . . ." *MLB.com*, Richard Justice, December 31, 2013.

I also want to thank all of my Facebook friends for responding to my queries, and I especially want to thank Jeff Passan of Yahoo Sports for all his help.